Also by Wyn Craig Wade

The Titanic: End of a Dream

THE
FIERY
CROSS

The Ku Klux Klan in America

Wyn Craig Wade

A TOUCHSTONE BOOK
Published by Simon & Schuster Inc.
New York London Toronto Sydney Tokyo

First Touchstone Edition, 1988

Published by Simon & Schuster Inc.
Simon & Schuster Building
Rockefeller Center
1230 Avenue of the Americas
New York, NY 10020

TOUCHSTONE and colophon are registered trademarks
of Simon & Schuster Inc.

Designed by Levavi & Levavi

Manufactured in the United States of America

10 9 8 7 6 5 4 3 2
10 9 8 7 6 5 4 3 2 1 Pbk.

Library of Congress Cataloging in Publication Data

Wade, Wyn Craig.
    The fiery cross.

    Bibliography: p.
    Includes index.
    1. Ku Klux Klan (1915–   )—History.
2. Racism—United States—History. I. Title.
HS2330.K63W33   1986   322.4′2′0973   86-26002

ISBN 0-671-41476-3

ISBN 0-671-65723-2 Pbk.

Acknowledgment is made to the *Massachusetts Review* for permission to quote from Andrew Goodman's "Corollary to a Poem by A. E. Housman," reprinted from the *Massachusetts Review*, © 1965, the Massachusetts Review, Inc.; and to *Playboy* Magazine for permission to reprint an interview that originally appeared in *Playboy* Magazine, © 1965 by *Playboy*.

In memory of my Kentucky grandmother—

Sarah Walls Dishon
1888–1986

—a fierce and steadfast Radical Republican
from the wane of Reconstruction until her
death nearly a century later

Contents

Prologue

"BEWARE THE PEOPLE WEEPING"

The Causes of Radical Reconstruction:
1865–1867

THE OLD SOUTH, THE ANTEBELLUM SOUTH, "THE SUNNY SUNNY SOUTH": Old Massa in an ivory, three-piece suit and black string tie sits on the piazza of the Big House with one hand clutching his cane and the other wrapped around a mint julep. Inside supervising the household slaves is Missy—the flower of Southern womanhood, the saintly, self-sacrificing madonna whose rose-petal fragility and marble-white purity are enough to make grown men weep, march off to war, and die for her. Suddenly Beau comes galloping up to the plantation, his golden hair tossing in ringlets around his neck. A splendid specimen of Southern virility, Beau has just returned from up North where he's been attending a Yankee college. Little Sister squeals in delight at the sight of her brother and runs out to meet him, her blue crinolines rustling and her flushed cheeks the color of peaches and cream. The ever-faithful household slaves come out onto the piazza, brush the tears from their eyes, and clasp their hands in silent devotion as Beau and Little Sister embrace and tease each other like children. And out in the sprawling fields, hundreds of happily hoeing darkies pause for a moment to watch the joyful reunion at the Big House and praise the Lord that, with whites in their haven, all's right with the world.

Such is the image of the South from the *Gone With the Wind*

9

school of literature, stamped further into American consciousness by the moonlight-and-magnolia school of history. Both schools continue to influence romantic novels and high school history textbooks. Only recently has a drastically divergent point of view been considered—that of the slaves themselves.

Take, for example, the recollections of an eighty-seven-year-old woman who was once a Tennessee slave. She recalled the time Missy got sick and she was called into the Big House to stand by her bedside and fan the flies off her face. "I would hit her all in the face," she recalled with amusement. "Sometimes I would make out I was [falling asleep] and beat her in the face." When Massa came into the room, Missy tried to tell him about the young slave's subversion, but Missy wasn't very coherent. He thought she meant the slave girl was actually falling asleep. "Then he would tell me to go out in the yard and wake up." Eventually, poor Missy died, "and all the slaves came in the house just a-hollering and crying and holding their hands over their eyes, just hollering for all they could." As soon as they had left the house, however, they grinned at each other and chuckled, "Old damn bitch! She gone on down to hell by now."

The discrepancy between black and white viewpoints of slavery and Reconstruction has led to a historical miasma that is still in the process of being dispelled. In the documents of a hundred years ago, the divergence is readily apparent as an inconsistency between white accusations and black behavior. More subtle are the inconsistencies among whites themselves. In the thirty years before the Civil War, the South had expended considerable time and effort marshaling scriptural and historical proof that slavery was inevitable. Philosophical tracts argued that slavery was a blessing to master, slave, and society alike. After all, the "inferiority" of blacks made them unfit to function outside of bondage, and their "docility" demanded the benevolent protection of whites. In spite of their belief in black docility and inferiority, however, Southern whites were plagued by the constant fear and occasional reality of slave uprisings, which they blamed on the scurrilous abolitionist literature that was perverting what they believed to be the natural order of things. The Deep South followed Maryland's lead in declaring illegal "any pamphlet, newspaper, handbill or other paper of any inflammatory character, and having a tendency to excite discontent or stir up insurrection amongst the people of color of this State." In spite of their belief that slavery benefited the slave, whites had to contend with the problem of runaways. Medical science offered a number of comforting rationalizations to the effect that blacks were susceptible to a variety of exotic psychiatric impairments: *drapetomania*, for example, accounted for the folly of blacks who ran away from the security of the plantation; *dysaethesia* explained such crazed symptoms as blacks' refusal to obey their masters' orders.

By 1860, whether Southern whites wanted it or not, slavery had become the cornerstone of Southern ideology and comfort. William Loughton Smith of South Carolina announced that slavery had become "so engrafted" on the South, that its abolition would utterly destroy Southern "happiness, tranquility, and prosperity." Slavery was the linchpin of Southern self-esteem as well. Jefferson Davis had said without compunction that "the lower race of human beings" that made up "the slave population of the South elevates every white man in our community." In 1861, the South had gone to war in defense of these beliefs. Four years later it had lost.

By 1865, the Confederacy lay a smoking ruin. Visitors to the "desolated States" were astonished to find that much of the South had been leveled to the condition of a frontier. Added to geographical devastation and economic chaos was psychological trauma. For the institution that had guaranteed Southern "happiness, tranquility, and prosperity" had been abolished. The shoes that had elevated every white Southerner above his true stature had been removed by the Thirteenth Amendment.

The first reaction of Southerners to the new status of blacks echoed the theories of slavocracy. One man told a reporter for the *Nation* that "the negro will always need the care of someone superior to him, and unless in one form or another it is extended to him, the race will first become pauper and then disappear." The Natchez *Democrat* agreed, claiming, "That child is already born who will behold the last negro in the State of Mississippi." A Texas newspaper announced the sad fact that there would "never be another crop planted in Texas," for you couldn't expect anything from a race of people who were impossible to govern "except with the whip."

"I tell you," said a Southern patrician, "the nigger is a no-account creetur. All the man are thieves, and all the women are prostitutes. It's their natur' to be that way, and they never'll be no other way. They ain't worth the land they cover. They ought to be improved off the face of the earth." An Alabama planter was more optimistic. To a Northern journalist he predicted: "The nigger is going to be made a serf, sure as you live. It won't need any law for that. Planters will have an understanding among themselves: 'You won't hire my niggers, and I won't hire yours'; then what's left for them? They're attached to the soil, and we're as much their masters as ever. I'll stake my life, this is the way it will work."

Such men were ill-prepared for what eventually happened. When Northern armies had invaded the South shortly before the end of the war, slaves fled the plantations in droves to join up with the liberating Yankees. While Southerners had expected some defections in the slave ranks, they were astonished at the mass exodus that ultimately took place. White masters were particularly embittered over the fact that their ever-faithful household slaves were the first to leave. In fact, defection to the "enemy" by household and domestic slaves was virtually complete.

Soon Northern abolitionists, educators, and members of the American Missionary Association began badgering Congress to do something for these wandering, homeless people, and on March 3, 1865, Congress created the Bureau of Freedmen, Refugees, and Abandoned Lands—better known as the Freedmen's Bureau. This unique federal program was set up for the duration of one year and combined the functions of a welfare agency, a legal aid society, a labor–management review board, and an educational endowment association. During its brief career, the Freedmen's Bureau established 3,695 schools and three universities, built more than a hundred hospitals, issued more than 21 million rations, and provided free transportation to more than thirty thousand people dislocated by war.

Without the Freedmen's Bureau, the survival of blacks would have depended on their former masters, who could have reinstituted a form of slavery along the lines predicted by the Alabama planter. Consequently, Southern whites despised the bureau. For one thing, the bureau was administered by "carpetbaggers"—a pejorative term that, given its multitude of applications, simply meant a Southern-based Northerner who didn't share the Confederacy's views on race. Southern whites also claimed the bureau "encouraged laziness, fostered the hope of getting something for nothing, and heightened the 'natural' tendency of the Negroes toward thievery, vagrancy, and vice." But the voluminous records of the bureau (preserved in the National Archives) show that far more whites benefited from outright charity than blacks.

The South particularly hated the thought that carpetbaggers were putting new ideas into the heads of their former slaves. Oliver

O. Howard, the "Christian general" who was put in charge of the bureau, informed the Secretary of War: "The people, the white race, very naturally desire to manage their own affairs, and the affairs of the freedmen also, as they formerly did. So long as the Bureau exists, it will exercise some restraint in this respect." The bureau found itself acting as legal arbiter in thousands of disputes between white planters and black contracted laborers. Planters were indignant when told by bureau agents that labor contracts should be equitable—that blacks should be paid at least as much as poor whites. Other planters were angry that the bureau supported the desires of blacks to work for people other than their former masters. And Southerners were livid over the bureau's decision that white men were legally bound to support any mulatto children they had fathered. An agent wrote from Tennessee, "The feeling of the people is very much against the Bureau, but they have a wholesome dread of the military; yet—were there no agent here—I am certain outrages and abuses would be frequent."

Of all bureau activities, perhaps the hardest for the Southern white to bear was the education of freedmen. During slavery, it had been illegal to teach a black to read and write, and the bureau's dedication to black education was considered diabolical. Many planters complained that "learning will spoil the nigger for work" and would be "the ruin of the South." Reuben Tomlinson, the bureau superintendent of education in South Carolina, noted that there was "a settled determination" among Southern whites that blacks "cannot and therefore *must not* be educated."

Under bureau auspices, some five thousand Northern teachers went south to educate blacks. A majority of these were New England members of the American Missionary Association, most of them idealistically motivated to undo the worst of slavery's legacies —the imprisonment of the black mind. Southerners looked askance at the arrival of so many prim and proper carpetbaggers into their land. At first, some of their newspapers, like the Richmond *Times*, were able to treat the invasion with humor:

White cravatted gentlemen from Andover, with a nasal twang, and pretty Yankee girls, with the smallest of hands and feet, have flocked to the South as missionary ground, and are communicating a healthy moral tone to the "colored folks," besides instructing them in chemistry, botany, and natural philosophy, teaching them to speak French, sing Italian, and walk Spanish, so that in time we are bound to have intelligent, and probably, intellectual labor.

In spite of Rebel jibes, the endeavor of "a whole race trying to go to school" (as Booker T. Washington put it) was a successful one. Mrs. Eddy, a bureau superintendent in Georgia, claimed, "The children of these schools have made in a given time more progress in the ordinary branches of education than any white schools I ever taught." A striking feature about the freedmen's schools was the enormous range of ages of the pupils—from five years to seventy-five and even older. Journalist J.T. Trowbridge visited one of these schools in Memphis. After recovering from the shock of seeing so many different shades of black (indicating the "bleaching" of the race by former masters), he noted: "There are few more affecting sights than these aged people beginning the child's task so late in life, often after their eyesight has failed."

Yankee teachers were usually warned to keep their politics out of the lesson plans, but there is plenty of evidence that the teachers failed or refused to follow this advice. After all, there was a high correlation between the New England cities the teachers had come from and depots of the underground railroad; and as Northeastern abolitionists, the Yankee teachers held some of the most radical views in the nation. Imagine local reaction to the catechism one Miss Stanley taught her black pupils in Kentucky:

> "Now children, you don't think white people are any better than you because they have straight hair and white faces?"
> "No, sir."
> "No, they are no better, but they are different, they possess great power, they formed this great government, they control this vast country. . . . Now what makes them different from you?"
> "*Money!*"
> "Yes, but what enabled them to obtain it? *How* did they get money?"
> "Got it off us, stole it off we all!"

Southern reaction to this twist was rather less than chivalrous. In time, one schoolmarm wrote home that she was habitually receiving "the polite salutation of 'damned Yankee bitch of a nigger teacher,' with the occasional admonition to take up my abode in the infernal regions."

If the South loathed the work of the Freedmen's Bureau, it would be given the opportunity to do something about it a mere three months after the bureau was launched. On April 14, 1865, Abraham Lincoln was shot at close range on the punchline of a bad joke in a second-rate play. Lincoln's murder was so shocking and bizarre that it remains an archetypal image in the American imagination. At the time, it plunged the North into weeks of mingled grief and rage. Herman Melville described it best:

> There is a sobbing of the strong,
>   And a pall upon the land;
> But the people in their weeping
>   Bare the iron hand;
> Beware the people weeping
>   When they bare the iron hand.

On April 15, Andrew Johnson was sworn in as the seventeenth U.S. president. Johnson had been an antisecession senator from Tennessee—the only senator from a Confederate state who had remained loyal to the Union—and Lincoln had wanted him on the ticket primarily to entice votes from the border states. Aside from this qualification, Johnson had little to recommend him. He was a narrow-minded, bullheaded, unlettered tailor, tortured by deepseated feelings of inferiority. During Lincoln's inauguration in 1865, Johnson had steeled himself with a bit too much whiskey and delivered a rambling vice-presidential address in which he proclaimed, "I'm a-goin' for to tell you—here today; yes, I'm a-goin' for to tell you all, that I'm a plebeian!"

In spite of his ardor as a plebeian, Johnson lacked the slightest feeling for the evils of slavery and had no compassion for the people who had suffered under it. His main objection to slavery was that it had benefited a few white men but not all of them. His main virtue, as he was wont to stress, was that he was "a self-made man" which, as Thaddeus Stevens acidly noted, "relieved God Almighty of an awesome responsibility."

On May 29, 1865, President Johnson made a proclamation of amnesty whereby former Confederates could regain U.S. citizenship and all rights thereof by seeking a presidential pardon. Then, once they had repudiated secession and the Confederate debt and ratified the Thirteenth Amendment abolishing slavery, their states could be readmitted to the Union. The presidential pardon was the crucial thing, and Johnson adored the role of pardoning the Southern aristocrats who had looked down at him all his life. He especially liked holding court for the lovely Southern belles who sought audiences with him on behalf of their wayward fathers, sons, and husbands. Eventually, fourteen thousand military and political leaders of the defeated Confederacy received Johnson's official forgiveness.

Although Johnson's naïve idea of reconstruction had the virtue of speedily restoring the Union, it was a political blunder of staggering magnitude. Congress was not in session when he began playing God, and the President's actions were diametrically opposed to its wishes. Thaddeus Stevens wrote immediately to Johnson, saying that the readmission of the South was "a very delicate question" and suggested "the propriety of suspending further 'reconstruction' until the meeting of Congress." Johnson ignored the letter. While he may have believed he could bulldoze Congress, Johnson failed to consider how loyal Unionists, North and South, would react to his lenient reconstruction policy. Blacks especially objected to Johnson's program. In the summer of 1865, a convention of Virginia blacks petitioned Congress, saying with an uncanny sense of prophecy:

> Four-fifths of our enemies are paroled or amnestied, and the other fifth are being pardoned, and the President has, in his efforts at the reconstruction of the civil government of the States, late in rebellion, left us entirely at the mercy of these subjugated but unconverted rebels in *everything* save the privilege of bringing us, our wives and little ones, to the auction block. . . . We *know* these men—know them *well*—and we assure you that, with the majority of them, loyalty is only "lip deep," and that their professions of loyalty are used as a cover to the cherished design of getting restored to their former relations with the Federal Government, and then, by all sorts of "unfriendly legislation," to render the freedom you have given us more intolerable than the slavery they intended for us.

While Johnson cared nothing for the opinions of blacks, he might have been more sensitive to the objections of Union soldiers. One of these wrote to Senator Zachariah Chandler, saying, "I fought three years and was discharged on account of wounds received in battle. I don't want to go to my grave a cripple thinking it was all in vain. Treason must be punished and loyalty looked up to, and the course Johnson is taking makes treason honorable and loyalty dishonorable." Other Union soldiers were outraged over the President's liberal pardons to Confederate military leaders. When Johnson pardoned Nathan Bedford Forrest—the Confederate general who, after his victory at Fort Pillow, had summarily executed all black Union soldiers—it was more than one survivor of that battle could stomach. He wrote to Senator Benjamin

("Bluff Ben") Wade deploring the fact that such "a foul fiend in human shape" as Forrest, well known for his "butchery and barbarity," had received a swift, unconditional pardon instead of "the punishment which his atrocious crimes so richly deserve." Other letters support the fact that, in the wake of Lincoln's assassination, Johnson's program was as impolitic as it was unjust. Soon Thad Stevens wrote to the President a second time: "I am sure you will pardon me," Stevens said, "for speaking to you with a candor to which men in high places are seldom accustomed. Among all the leading Union men of the North with whom I've had intercourse I do not find one who approves of your policy. . . . Can you not hold your hand and wait the action of Congress, and in the meantime govern [the South] by military rulers?" Again Stevens's letter went unacknowledged.

During the summer of 1865, radical Republicans exchanged animated letters condemning the policy Johnson was following. Senator Wade began referring to Johnson as "His Accidency the President." Senator Charles Sumner of Massachusetts accused Johnson of causing unforgivable "trouble, controversy and expense. *He cannot prevent the triumph of the cause.* This is certain. But he may delay it." A major problem with Johnson's pardons was the fact that, with the passing of the Thirteenth Amendment, slavery was forever abolished in the United States. In the U.S. Constitution of 1787, slaves had been counted as three-fifths of a person for purposes of Southern representation in Congress. Under the Thirteenth Amendment, they were now *whole* persons, and this meant that the South would gain some fifteen additional representatives. Radical Republicans wondered what such a freely forgiven South would do with its fifteen extra congressmen. What would prevent it from behaving exactly as it had before the war, only with more power? Congressman Ben Butler of Massachusetts wrote to Senator Wade:

> If we are to go on, as we are now tending, I certainly do not desire to take part in the Government.
> All is wrong and we are losing the first results of this four years struggle.
> The most vivid hope I have is that the rebels will behave so outrageously as to awaken the Government of the North once more out of the dream of brotherly union where brotherly love is not.

Butler wouldn't have to wait long for his "vivid hope" of Southern outrages. Soon the North was inundated with horror stories from Johnson's "reconstructed" South. Blacks who had left plantations were being murdered by henchmen of their former masters. Black preachers were being killed for preaching. Black women resisting the sexual advances of whites were being raped and shot; some were scalped and had their ears cut off. In Mississippi, a military attaché reported that many freedmen were being murdered "just out of wanton cruelty, for no reason at all that one can imagine."

Of particular interest were the widespread reports of "bushwhackers," "desperadoes and banditti," and other wandering gangs who were subjecting blacks to an increasing reign of terror. In Georgia, blacks were staggering into the offices of the Freedmen's Bureau with gunshot wounds from whites who had secretly organized "to keep the negroes where they belong." An Alabama agent complained that "organized patrols, with negro hounds, keep guard over the thoroughfares; bands of lawless robbers traverse the county, and the unfortunate [black] who attempts to escape, or he who returns for his wife or child, is waylaid or pursued with hounds and shot or hung." General Swayne reported that some of the Alabama atrocities were being committed "by men in disguise, and in the night." In Mississippi and South Carolina, squads of "regulators" were attempting to keep the freedmen "in the most abject slavery."

It is possible that these groups of wandering "banditti" were remnants of defunct slave patrols. Before the war, the "patterollers"—as the blacks poignantly called them—formed a network of surveillance over the slave community to prevent blacks from being away from their plantations without passes and to maintain vigilance over the possibility of slave insurrections. In some states, patrols were made up of professionals who hired themselves out for pay. Blacks were especially fearful of this type, claiming that most of them were "nothing but poor white trash . . . if they didn't whip some slaves, every now and then, they would lose their jobs." In other states, like Alabama, patrol duty was a conscripted service much like the military. Slave patrols were allowed to enter Negro dwellings on any plantation, by force if necessary, and administer up to thirty-nine lashes on any black caught without a pass, who was insolent, or who had broken some rule—which the patterollers had extraordinary leeway in defining.

Southerners as well as Northern Democrats scoffed at the accounts of postwar depredations by whites against blacks. If excesses were being committed, they held, it was understandable.

After all, *something* had to be done about the black wantonness and "insolence" that was being encouraged by the Freedmen's Bureau.

Since historians would later argue that black insolence helped spur the rise of the Ku-Klux Klan, it's worth looking carefully at what behaviors fell into this category. First of all, it is clear that, following the war, Southern whites expected the freedmen to behave much the same way they had under the antebellum slave codes. These codes, enacted out of fear over possible slave insurrections, had prohibited assemblies of five or more blacks. All Southern codes forbade slaves to carry guns or other weapons, or to own dogs. In Mississippi and Florida, if any black or mulatto, "bond or free," used "abusive and provoking language" to a white, the penalty was thirty-nine lashes.

After the war and their emancipation, blacks felt increasingly free to ignore the old codes. South Carolina farmers walking through the woods were therefore astonished to come across black hunting parties complete with guns and dogs. Blacks began congregating in groups of considerably more than five for prayer meetings and political discussions; in Charleston they even held parades. Traditional customs that acknowledged white supremacy, such as yielding the sidewalks to whites, were discreetly ignored by blacks after the war. The sight of armed black soldiers was anathema to Southern whites, and there were plenty of black Union soldiers still stationed in the South. These men, "like all of that class," were considered especially "conceited, whimsical, and insolent." A North Carolina planter was livid over the "insult" of a black soldier bowing and bidding him good morning as he sat on his piazza. In Georgia, another planter argued in all seriousness that one of his former slaves had shown himself "certainly unfit for freedom" because he "impudently" refused to submit to a whipping. In Union, South Carolina, a black man was murdered and his stepdaughter whipped because the latter had the insolence to "embarrass" a prominent white family by having a child by one of its members. Charges of insolence were also leveled at blacks who called whites by their first names, were overly "familiar" with the Yankee schoolmarms (who encouraged it), and who refused to complete a labor contract once they saw that their employers felt free to renege on its terms. As Louis Post, an idealistic young carpetbagger, saw it, any demonstration of "independent spirit" on the part of blacks "was regarded as 'insolence,' suggestive of an incendiary purpose and significant of such danger to the master class as to necessitate extreme measures in defense of 'self and fireside.' "

The "incendiary purpose" and danger that most worried the master class was rape. Many respectable histories of Reconstruction are full of innuendo about rape by blacks. In the documents and archival material of the period, however, the subject is conspicuous by its paucity. Even when Confederate General and Klansman John B. Gordon of Georgia spoke at length before a congressional committee about black rape and was asked if there were many incidents of it, he replied, "Oh no, sir, but one case of rape by a negro upon a white woman was enough to alarm the whole people of the state." In a study of over a hundred cases of postbellum black rape, one scholar has concluded that "the greatest majority were based on flimsy circumstantial evidence, to say the least. Women who were accosted by Negroes under the friendliest circumstances cried rape." Sometimes a black smile or the tipping of a hat were sufficient grounds for prosecution of rape. As one Southern judge put it, "I see a chicken cock drop his wings and take after a hen; my experience and observation assure me that his purpose is sexual intercourse, no other evidence is needed."

Understanding the fear of black rape after emancipation requires a special probing of the mind of the Southern white male. For, although it is true, as one patrician swore, that during this period no "respectable white woman" was willing to leave home "without some protector," it was the white male who kindled and fueled her fears. Slavery had led to a curious relationship between the sexes of the master class. In Southern white culture, the female was placed on a pedestal where she was inaccessible to blacks and a guarantee of the purity of the white race. The black race, however, was completely vulnerable to miscegenation. White men soon learned that women placed on a pedestal acted like statues in bed, and they came to prefer the female slave whom they found "uninhibited and natural." She alone could release the passion they were unable to experience with their wives. In many cases, the female slave was the first sexual partner for Southern white males. She was unable to refuse her master, his sons, and his overseers.

The more white males turned to female slaves, the more they exalted their own women, who increasingly became a mere ornament and symbol of the Southern way of life. When the Southern way of life crumbled with the hopes of the Confederacy, when the slaves were emancipated, white men realized with horror that the black "buck" was free to do to their women what they had done to his. As this concern grew into a morbid fear, every act of "insolence" by a black male was considered a prelude to rape. Every act of kindness or friendliness by a black male to a white female was considered statutory rape. The freedman was a creature to be feared—not because of his actual behavior or desires, but because of that conscience that makes cowards of us all.

In the late summer of 1865, the former leaders of the Confederacy—formally pardoned by President Johnson—convened to revise their state governments. At one level they were obliged to ratify the Thirteenth Amendment and repudiate the Confederate debt. At another level they were determined to secure and preserve the Southern way of life as much as possible. At the South Carolina convocation, Armisted L. Burt received a tremendous ovation for his speech proclaiming that America had been "discovered by the white man, settled by the white man, made illustrious by the white man, and must continue to be a white man's country." The Confederate Stars and Bars was still flown at many Southern statehouses. Much to Johnson's embarrassment, South Carolina and Mississippi refused to repudiate their debts, and the latter even refused to ratify the Thirteenth Amendment. General Thomas K. Smith reported that, in Alabama, most former Rebels were "still inspired with a hope that at some future time the 'confederacy,' as they style it, will be restored to independence." Supporting his gloomy opinion was the fact that the new Southern governments had elected to public office the former vice-president of the Confederacy and six of its cabinet members, fifty-eight Confederate congressmen, four Confederate generals, and five Confederate colonels. In other words, the very men who had urged secession upon the South had been put back in charge. Southern loyalists who had opposed secession and who were now suffering the social stigma of being called "scalawags" were especially angry over this turn of events.

The clincher came in the nature of the legislation the new Southern governments thought necessary to enact that summer. True to the prediction of the Virginia blacks, this legislation was most "unfriendly": The Johnson-supported legislatures systematically transformed the antebellum slave codes into new Black Codes denying blacks the rights of white people and returning them to a state of virtual bondage. Mississippi's Black Code denied blacks the right to rent or lease land outside the city. They were not allowed to conduct any kind of "independent business." Any black breaking a labor contract—for whatever reason—could be arrested. Unemployed blacks could be declared vagrants, arrested, and hired out to any white who paid their fines. Whites who associated with blacks "on terms of equality" could likewise be arrested and fined.

In Louisiana, if a black broke a labor contract, he was fined twice the amount of wages for the time lost or forced to work free on public projects until he agreed to return to his employer. Any black could be arrested as a vagrant on the complaint of any white man and, if unable to pay the fine, could be hired out for a year—usually to the white who brought the complaint.

Under Alabama's Black Code, "stubborn and refractory servants" could be fined $50, or in lieu of fine, be "hired out at public auction for a period of six months." In South Carolina, blacks were legally barred from pursuing any occupation other than "farmer or house servant." Black children over two years of age, whose parents were unable to teach them "habits of industry and honesty," could be "apprenticed" to white families until maturity. Under Florida's Black Code, blacks could be whipped up to thirty-nine lashes for "intruding" themselves into white assemblies or public conveyances. And in all states, penalties for crimes committed by blacks were far more severe than those for whites.

As far as the radical Republicans were concerned, the Black Codes were an obscenity. Johnson had given the South the freedom to reenter the Union on its own terms, and the South had shown unusual arrogance in defining those terms. When the thirty-ninth Congress convened on December 4, 1865, it exercised its constitutional privilege of determining the qualifications of its members and refused to seat the newly elected Southern senators and congressmen. Under Thad Stevens's leadership, it then established a joint committee of fifteen members to examine conditions in the South and to recommend a rational and just program for readmitting the former Confederacy to the Union.

The Joint Committee on Reconstruction busied itself in a lengthy, comprehensive investigation in which 145 witnesses testified to conditions in the South. Among those who appeared before the committee were Clara Barton, the Union Army nurse, and George Armstrong Custer, who had been one of the North's youngest generals during the war. Barton had recently completed a tour of the infamous Andersonville Prison and testified that Georgia blacks were being subjected to a hoax that slavery had not really been abolished and that they were still being cruelly mistreated by their former masters who were now their "employers." When asked how white Southerners generally felt toward the freedmen, Barton replied, "I think far less kindly than when they owned them themselves."

Custer reported even worse conditions in Texas. He was particularly sympathetic to the plight of the Texas Unionists—the so-called scalawags. "Union men are being murdered there to this day," he said. "There is no disguising the fact that loyalty at the South has become a byword and a reproach to those who have the courage to profess it." Custer stated that the life of the Texas freedman was precarious in the extreme. He claimed that white Texans tended to blame the freedman for losing the war, "and they do not hesitate to improve every opportunity to inflict injuries upon him in order, seemingly, to punish him for this." The bodies of dead blacks were turning up all over the state, and nothing was being done about it. He also affirmed the existence of secret bands of outlaws whose main purpose was to thwart the intentions of the federal government. "The fact that such organizations did exist," he said, "was confirmed by the statements, written and oral, of loyal men, and by the reports of officers sent there on duty." He further predicted that if the federal government didn't take a hand in the matter, the South "would inaugurate a system of oppression that would be equally as bad as slavery itself."

When the joint committee's investigation was finished, 78 percent of the witnesses agreed with Barton and Custer's assessment of the South. There was collateral support as well. Army officers and bureau agents reported increasing incidents of Southern white violence. In Murfreesboro, Tennessee, bureau agent John Seague claimed that threats on his life were getting "as thick as 'the frogs of Egypt.'" Seague eventually was beaten, had two ribs broken, and had his windows smashed and pistols fired into his home. "There has been fifteen cases of brutal treatment of blacks," Seague wrote to Senator Chandler, but local civil courts refused to prosecute the offenders. In Virginia, General Terry reported forty cases of outrages committed on blacks. In South Carolina, General Sickles forwarded thirty-six horror stories from bureau agents. Sickles claimed, "A freedman has little security for life, limb, or property in certain counties of South Carolina apart from the protection afforded by United States troops." He also noted that, in contrast to sporadic, individual acts of violence, more and more outrages were being committed by organized "bands of outlaws and marauders."

In view of the continued cruelty to the freedmen, in light of the testimony gathered by the joint committee, and especially because of the Johnson legislature's offensive Black Codes, Congress passed the Civil Rights Act of March 1866. This act was a veritable overturning of the Black Codes. It stated that blacks had the right to make contracts, to sue and give evidence, to own and dispose of property, and were entitled to *equal protection under the law*. Andrew Johnson could have accepted the Civil Rights Act without jeopardizing his lenient reconstruction policy. Instead he vetoed it as "another step, or rather stride, toward centralization and the concentration of all legislative powers in the National Government." Johnson's veto and his subsequent accusations that Congress was in the hands of "traitors" had the effect of bringing moderate Republicans into the radical camp; and a month later, Congress overrode the veto of the Civil Rights Act.

Also in April, the joint committee presented its final report with abundant documentation that Johnson's reconstruction policy was ineffective, unjust, and downright dangerous to freedman and loyal white alike. While Democrats derided this conclusion, independent confirmation came in the form of a bloody riot in Memphis on May Day, 1866. The riot began as an altercation between six Memphis policemen and a small group of blacks who had protested the arrest of two of their members. When the protesters grew loud and "boisterous," the police fired into the crowd, wounding one black. The blacks then had the temerity to fire back, wounding one policeman. Almost immediately, the entire police force gathered in the center of town with a huge crowd of white citizens. John Creighton, the Memphis city recorder, yelled to the crowd, "We are not prepared, but let us prepare to clear every negro son-of-a-bitch out of town!" The angry white mob then proceeded to "shoot, beat, and threaten every negro met within that portion of the city." When it was all over, two whites had been killed and two wounded. Forty-six blacks had been killed and eighty wounded. And scores of black churches, schools, and homes had been burned, resulting in losses of over $53,379. According to an investigation by the army, all the victims of the riot had been "helpless and unresisting negroes," a fact that stamped "lasting disgrace upon the civil authorities that permitted" such "murder, arson, rape, and robbery." Few events made uncertain Northerners more certain that the Joint Committee on Reconstruction had correctly assessed the temper of the former Confederacy.

In the aftermath of the Memphis riot, Congress attempted to

strengthen the Civil Rights Act and simultaneously place it outside the reach of the executive office and the Supreme Court by making it the core of a new amendment to the Constitution. Largely through the leadership of Thad Stevens, the Fourteenth Amendment was passed on June 13, 1866, and sent to the states for ratification. In the scope of its power and subsequent contribution to the character of American life, the Fourteenth Amendment is nearly equal to the Bill of Rights. In essence it represents a wedding of the Declaration of Independence to the U.S. Constitution; not until it was ratified was America committed *legally* to the proposition that all men are created equal. The Fourteenth Amendment defined U.S. citizenship and forbade the states to deny or to abridge the rights of U.S. citizens. Moreover, if any state denied qualified people the right to vote, its representation in Congress would be reduced proportionally. And any man having held political office requiring an oath to support the U.S. Constitution, who subsequently aided or abetted the Confederate secession from the Union, was temporarily prohibited from assuming political office.

Andrew Johnson despised the new amendment, challenged Congress's right to draft it, and—in a move that would lead to his impeachment—openly advised the former Confederate states not to ratify it. In July, Congress extended the original one-year term of the Freedmen's Bureau—clearly a necessity in light of the well-documented terrorism blacks were being subjected to in the South. In another characteristic blunder, Johnson vetoed the extension, and Congress, now more united than ever, overrode his veto. While some Americans agreed with the President's charges of congressional usurpation, Reverend Henry Bellows, in a sermon at New York's First Unitarian Church, tried to explain the motives of the thirty-ninth Congress:

> The Union has no value in itself for them, except as it covers in human rights and prospects. . . . And when they see the mere mechanical or technical integrity of the Union or the restoration of all its representative functions preferred to the establishment of the Union on its true grounds of justice and humanity, they feel as if their ruler and themselves were talking and thinking about somewhat different and incompatible things.

On July 30, another ghastly race riot took place, this time in New Orleans. From then through the remainder of the year and in early 1867, reports of outrages continued to pour in from everywhere in the South. In this period, there was a clear tendency toward tighter organization among the perpetrators of violence. In Mississippi, for example, officers complained of "roaming bands of desperadoes who make the freedmen and northern men their particular objects of murder and rapine." These bands tended to be "chiefly the debris of the rebel army, who have not devoted themselves to any industrial pursuits for their maintenance since the close of the war." In South Carolina, General R. K. Scott complained of "gangs of outlaws, styling themselves 'Regulators' . . . who committed these outrages not only on the persons of freed people but upon loyal white citizens whose houses were often burned, and they themselves driven from their homes." Scott said that "these *soi-disant* regulators offered to kill any freedmen who refused to contract with the planters for a fixed sum per head." From Georgia, General Davis Tillson wrote that "bands of men styling themselves 'Regulators,' 'Jayhawkers,' and 'Black-horse cavalry' have infested different parts of the State, committing the most fiendish and diabolical outrages on the freedmen."

The border region of Montgomery, Robertson, and Sumner counties, Tennessee, and Logan and Simpson counties, Kentucky, was a veritable hotbed of vigilante violence. A guerrilla chief named Ellis Harper was now leading a terrifying, virtually invincible band of assassins who "perpetrate outrages so numerous and revolting as to strike terror to all unorganized and unprotected citizens, whether black or white, who entertain Union sentiments." Some of the outrages attributed to Harper's men were unspeakable. For example, Hudson Perdue, a black, was shot to death while digging a grave to bury his child. His wife was driven off by the marauders, forced to abandon both her dying husband and the corpse of her child. In this same cluster of counties, placards were posted all over announcing new rules for the area:

Negro women shall be employed [only] by white persons. Negroes [meeting] in cabins to themselves shall suffer the penalty. All white men found with negroes in secret places shall be dealt with. . . . For the first offense is one-hundred lashes; the second is looking up a sapling. White man and negro, I am everywhere; I have friends in every place; do your duty and I will have but little to do.

Brevet Lieutenant Colonel Edward Leib reported that, if the troops were withdrawn from this border region, "there will be no peace or quiet for the black man. . . ."

Farther south, the army was having an even more difficult time. General Scott reported in November 1866 that the number of troops in South Carolina was "totally inadequate to meet the demands made upon it for ferreting out and arresting the perpetrators" of outrages. Congress, however, was waiting for two events: ratification of the Fourteenth Amendment and the outcome of the 1866 congressional election. During the election campaign, Johnson made a whistlestop swing through the Northern industrial cities, and many Americans had the opportunity to observe firsthand his narrow-mindedness and astounding lack of tact. His willingness to argue with hecklers was particularly undignified. In Cleveland, he ranted at one heckler: "I wish I could see you; I will bet now, if there could be a light reflected upon your face, that cowardice and treachery could be seen in it. Show yourself. Come out here where we can see you. If ever you shoot a man, you will stand in the dark and pull your trigger. I understand traitors. . . . And those men—such a one as insulted me tonight—you may say, has ceased to be a man, and in ceasing to be a man shrunk into the denomination of a reptile, and having so shrunken, as an honest man, I tread on him!" For similar harangues in Philadelphia and Indianapolis, Johnson was literally driven off the platform.

Johnson's whistlestop swing was such that the Republicans won two-thirds of both houses. Radicals briefly celebrated their resounding victory and then turned to face a sobering reality: With the exception of Tennessee, every former Confederate state had taken Johnson's advice and refused to ratify the Fourteenth Amendment. Having won a popular mandate and convinced that it was acting in the best interests of the nation, Congress then took an enormous step. Beginning in March 1867, it enacted a series of laws that would become infamous as "Radical Reconstruction."

The ten Southern states that had rejected the Fourteenth Amendment would be divided into five military districts and their Johnsonian governments annulled. Constitutional conventions were then to be held by men elected from the *entire male population*, black and white, with the exception of former Confederate leaders, who were disfranchised. This same electorate would choose new state legislatures. As soon as they ratified the Fourteenth Amendment, their states would be readmitted to the Union with full representation.

Even historians hostile to Radical Reconstruction agree that the South's refusal to ratify the Fourteenth Amendment was a mistake. The amendment disfranchised no one; it merely barred former Rebel leaders from holding office. Under Radical Reconstruction, not only were these leaders disfranchised, but their former slaves were given the vote. Only a foreign correspondent could completely appreciate the irony of the situation. Young Georges Clemenceau, later the prime minister of France, wrote from Washington to the Paris *Temps*:

> Like the Sibyl who continued to double the price of her books, in which the destinies of Rome were prophesied, as long as Tarquin refused to buy them, the North has become more and more exacting with every refusal of the concessions which it demanded. It is because they would not consent at the beginning to give civil rights to the negroes that the Southern states are now being forced to give them political rights. Years might have elapsed before the North decided to do complete justice to the black race, but the obstinacy of the slave holders forced it upon them, and the negroes now owe almost as much to the hatred of the one class as to the friendship of the other.

No longer weeping, the North had bared the iron hand.

BOOK ONE
1865-1915

"The Klux is the living dead, and it is the strength of weakness."

—EDWARD H. DIXON, 1868

"THE SHROUDED
BROTHERHOOD"

*The Birth and Expansion of the
Ku-Klux Klan, 1866–1868*

Former histories tell us that the advent of Radical Reconstruction gave rise to the Ku-Klux Klan. The radical legislation calling for "the social and political emasculation" of Southern whites and the "exaltation" of blacks was said to have spawned the Klan as a necessary self-defense movement. (As a Reconstruction Klansman put it, the "generic name of Ku-Klux was applied to all secret organizations in the South composed of the white natives and having for their object the execution of the 'first law of nature.' ") Actually, the Klan had already been born and was active in at least three Southern states before any of the state governments was radically reconstructed. It had begun in the town of Pulaski (seat of Giles County), Tennessee, sometime between Christmas 1865, and June 1866. Even the founders of the Klan could never remember exactly when.

Tennessee had been a critically divided state before and during the Civil War, harboring proslavery sentiments in its western half and—due to Appalachian influences—an equally strong abolitionist spirit in the east. Tennessee had been the only border state to fall into the Confederate camp. Shortly before Lee's surrender at Appomattox, however, political control of the state was captured by the eastern Unionists, led by the fanatical William G. Brownlow, a former circuit-riding Methodist minister. After becoming provisional governor, Brownlow disfranchised Tennessee's Rebels, allowing the eastern population of the state to ratify the Fourteenth Amendment and return Tennessee to the Union. Consequently, Tennessee escaped Radical Reconstruction even though the feelings of many of its citizens were as militantly pro-Confederate as in the deeper South.

The little town of Pulaski mirrored Tennessee as a crossroads of sorts. Located in the central portion of the state near the Alabama border, Pulaski marked the intersection of the highways from Nashville to Birmingham and from Chattanooga to Memphis. Its rural ensconcement among such well-traveled highways earned it its nickname, the Dimple of the Universe. Pulaski's citizens were proud of their town and its "many splendid plantations." They were especially proud of the purity of their Scottish ancestry, which in many cases was so revered and ran so deep that images of Rob Roy and Blind Harry were never far away.

Before the war, Giles County had been a major slave-holding region, and blacks made up nearly half the population. After the war, the freedom of so many blacks made whites extremely nervous—especially after the Memphis riot of May 1866. Reports from the Freedmen's Bureau soon described Pulaski as a scene of repeated depredations committed on freedmen and a convenient rendezvous point for "roughs" and rowdies from neighboring towns. In addition to emancipation, sporadic violence, and economic chaos, a severe cyclone in December 1865 tore through Pulaski, leveling many of its splendid plantations.

It was in these conditions of upheaval, suspicion, and desolation that six young returning soldiers found their home town after the war. They were James Crowe, Richard Reed, Calvin Jones, John Lester, Frank McCord, and John Kennedy. All six had fought bravely for the Confederate cause. Kennedy, age twenty-five, had attained the rank of captain, was wounded three times, and had been imprisoned in Camp Douglas. Crowe, age twenty-eight, had served as a major with the fourth Alabama Volunteers and had been wounded in the first battle of Manassas. The other four, also in their twenties, had served in the Tennessee Infantry. They were well educated for their day. Four of them were budding lawyers, McCord had literary aspirations and soon became editor of Pulaski's local newspaper, and John Lester would eventually be elected to the Tennessee legislature. After two weeks in Giles County, they realized that there was utterly nothing to do. Governor Brownlow was keeping Tennessee under tight military control. Jobs were nonexistent, the townspeople were sullen, and the boredom was excruciating. John Lester recalled, "The reaction which followed the excitement of army scenes and service was intense. There was nothing to relieve it."

It has been said that, if Pulaski had had an Elks Club, the Klan would never have been born. But it didn't, and the six young veterans decided to do something about their restlessness. One evening in spring 1866, they met in the law office of Cal Jones's father. John Lester suggested, "Why don't we start a club of some kind?" The others thought it was an excellent idea. A committee of three was delegated to come up with a name for the club, while the remaining three worked out a formal set of rules. About a week later, John Kennedy was asked to house-sit for Colonel Thomas Martin while the colonel and his family were away, and Kennedy couldn't wait to invite his comrades to the luxurious accommodations of the Martin mansion for the second meeting of their little club. When they reconvened, the name committee had only been able to come up with the feeble idea of calling their group "the circle." In order to give the name some class, John Kennedy proposed translating *circle* into Greek: *kuklos.*

"Call it *kuklux*," James Crowe suggested, "and no one will know what it means."

"And add *klan*," Kennedy piped, "as we are all of Scotch-Irish descent."

Kennedy's addition made more than genealogical sense to the group. To their ears, *klan* followed *kuklux* "as naturally as 'Dumpty' follows 'Humpty.'" There was something awesome, mysterious, even occult about the name Ku-Klux Klan, suggesting to John Lester the sound of "bones rattling together."

Inspired by the ghostly sound of their new name, the Pulaski Six promptly raided Mrs. Martin's linen closet, draped themselves with sheets, pulled pillow cases over their heads and went out riding and caterwauling through the town to the immense satisfaction of themselves and to the considerable curiosity of the locals. Thereafter, every stage in the development of the Klan was made to enhance or "harmonize with" the members' idea of themselves as spooks. Elaborate and menacing costumes were adopted. The Pulaski group chose long, loose-fitting white gowns, belted at the waist and decorated with meaningless occult symbols in red flannel —spangles, stars, half-moons—the less meaningful the better. Tall conical witches' hats of white cloth over cardboard completely concealed their heads; eyeholes were punched out for vision.

These headpieces exaggerated the height of the wearer, adding anywhere from eighteen inches to two feet to his stature. Imagination was encouraged in costume design, and members competed with each other to come up with the most outrageous outfit.

Developments in the Klan's formal garb influenced the Rules Committee, which came up with a hierarchy of six mystical offices, one for each of the members. The Grand Cyclops (McCord) functioned as president, the Grand Magi (Kennedy) as vice-president. Crowe became the first Grand Turk, an adjutant to the Grand Cyclops. Lester and Jones served as Night Hawks whose duty was to protect meetings of the group from outside interference, while Reed served as Lictor, charged with maintaining order within the meetings. The Rules Committee didn't see any need to have a purpose for the organization. James Crowe stated emphatically that the original Ku-Klux Klan was "purely social and for our amusement." Devoid of practical, humanitarian, or political significance, it obligated members only to "have fun, make mischief, and play pranks on the public."

The Klan's pranks were warmly welcomed by the depressed townspeople of postwar Pulaski. They enjoyed the nocturnal marches of these harmless bogymen with their "gleaming death's-heads, skeletons, and chains." Invasions by these specters provided a rollicking diversion at barbecues and outdoor evening parties. An Alabamian living near the Tennessee border remembered seeing such a Klan invasion at a moonlight picnic near Pulaski sometime in the fall of 1866. The horsemen came out of the woods wearing "rather a pretty and showy costume." They danced to the music and cavorted with the delighted guests, disguising their voices in low, mysterious tones. To this observer, the Ku-Klux was merely "a thing of amusement" and nothing more.

One of the most eagerly anticipated activities of the Klan was its initiation of new members. In fact, the initial expansion of the Klan's membership was based almost entirely on providing older members with their favorite form of entertainment. Nonmembers who had expressed curiosity or interest in the Klan were picked up unexpectedly some evening by disguised horsemen whose steeds were often draped in sheets as well. These surprised men were then blindfolded and taken out in the country to the ruins of a plantation leveled by the December cyclone. On the head of the blindfolded initiate was placed "the regal crown"—a skullcap with donkey's ears sewn on it. The candidate was then led to "the royal altar"—a large dressing mirror—and commanded to recite the popular poem by Scotsman Robert Burns:

O wad some power the giftee gie us
To see oursels as others see us.

The blindfold was then removed and, to the uproarious laughter
of the Klansmen, the initiate beheld in the mirror the ass he had
made of himself.

The expansion of the Klan was not limited to Giles County.
Interested young men in Lincoln County, Tennessee, as well as in
nearby Madison and Limestone counties, Alabama, contacted the
Pulaski Six and received permission to establish independent Klan
"dens" of their own. The idea caught on rapidly. According to
John Lester, the desire for membership in the Ku-Klux was soon
widespread, especially in the monotonous and rundown rural
areas.

Within months a significant turning point occurred in the Klan's
evolution. The novelty of hazing initiates wore thin, and Klansmen turned to the emancipated blacks as a new source of butts for
their practical jokes. According to an original Klansman, the
"impression sought to be made upon" the freedmen "was that
these white-robed night prowlers were the ghosts of the Confederate dead, who had arisen from their graves in order to wreak
vengeance on an undesirable class" of people. The Klansmen's
posture as *real* ghosts took advantage of the supposed gullibility
and superstitiousness of the freedmen, and examples of the pranks
they played on blacks grew into legends. John Lester recounted
several of them. One involved a Klansman's drawing his gown up
over his head and placing a false head on top. He would then
remove the head and hand it to a freedman, requesting that he
hold it for a while. As legend had it, the terrified black would then
run screaming into the night. A similar trick employed a skeletal
arm held in the sleeve of the Klansman's gown. An unsuspecting
black would be asked to shake hands with the false arm which, to
his horror, would be left in his grip as the Klansman rode away.

One particular gag seems to have been played by every Klan den
in the South. It required a Klansman to wear, attached to his
chest, an oilskin bag with a siphon tube running up to his mask,
through which he could pour a gallon of water. No one knows
who originated the gag, but it is likely that most Klansmen learned
it from an article in the Louisiana *Planters' Banner*:

There is much excitement among the negroes and even some of the
white folks, all over Attakapas, about the Ku-Kluxes that have lately
appeared in this country. I am not superstitious, and will not tell you

what I believe about these strange, ghostly appearances, but will give you some general items and rumors. . . .

A night traveler called at the negro quarters . . . and asked for water. After he had drunk three blue buckets full of good cistern water, at which the negro was astonished, he thanked the colored man and told him he was very thirsty, that he had travelled nearly a thousand miles in twenty-four hours, and that was the best drink of water he had had since he was killed at the battle of Shiloh. The negro dropped the bucket, tumbled over two chairs and a table, escaped through a back window, and has not since been heard from.

Southern newspapers enjoyed reporting and reprinting these kinds of stories, demonstrating that, in spite of the fate of the Confederacy, the white man's "mental superiority" still made him master.

Scholars have claimed that these "harmless" psychological techniques of playing upon the freedmen's fears represented the *first phase* of the Klan's control of blacks. (The Tennessee Freedmen's Bureau, while describing continual incidents of antiblack vigilante violence that were occurring throughout the South after the war, doesn't complain of the Klan per se until late 1867.) There is no evidence, however, that these scare tactics exerted any control over blacks whatsoever. They unquestionably terrified black children. A little girl whose father was visited by the Klan later remembered the white-robed night riders as "the awfulest boogers" she had ever seen before or since. But adult blacks were not taken in by the Klan's pretense as ghosts. In testimony later taken by a number of legislative committees, none of the black witnesses assumed that Klansmen were anything more or less than white men. James Kirkpatrick, on whom the water gag was played, told an investigating committee that the Klan called at his house, demanded water, "and made what I consider very silly remarks." Others were embarrassed at having to quote the Klan's song and dance about being the Confederate dead. "I tell it to you just like they repeated it to me," explained Joseph Gill of Huntsville, Alabama. Other blacks testified to recognizing their former masters' voices beneath the sheets or seeing the faces of their white neighbors through the eyeholes of the masks. Any fear shown by blacks in the presence of these hooded night riders was undoubtedly more inspired by what groups of disguised Rebels were known to have done, rather than what specters could possibly do. And the Klan legends of terrified "darkies" scurrying from ghosts of the Confederate dead probably say more about the aggrandizement of the white ego than about black gullibility. On the other hand, it has been suggested that blacks may have played into the Klansmen's hands, hoping that their feigned fright would avert a more violent form of intimidation. It then becomes a question of who was controlling whom.

From late 1866 to mid-1867, the Tennessee Klan began turning more and more from burlesque to night rider and "patteroller" techniques in its dealings with blacks. In November 1866, reports came from the southwestern portion of Tennessee that bands of men were making nocturnal visits to the cabins of blacks and confiscating their firearms. Other groups were breaking up black prayer meetings and social gatherings. A number of things could have prompted this change in Klan behavior. To begin with, after the Memphis and New Orleans riots, anxious whites began fearing their lives would become an unending series of "slave insurrections." Then there was the Klan's intoxication with the power it was gaining through its costumes, mummery, and public notoriety. It was inevitable that such power be applied to grander purposes than playing tricks on freedmen. Another explanation is that existing "patrols" and other groups of self-styled regulators either applied for membership in the Klan or simply adopted its accouterments and methods. Tennessee already had such night-riding vigilantes as the Yellow Jackets and Redcaps, and Tennessee bureau agents had long complained of bands of restless young men "ready for anything desperate and outrageous." And similar groups, whose violence had prompted the radical takeover of Congress, were rife throughout the South.

It was extremely easy for any white malcontent to become a Klansman. Technically, it required nothing more than permission from Pulaski to establish an independent den. More often, even that technicality was bypassed. Ryland Randolph in Alabama and countless other self-appointed Cyclopes established dens with no more connection to the Pulaski organization than knowledge of it. As more and more patterollers disguised themselves and spiced their visitations with the ghostly mumbo jumbo the Klan had made popular, the distinction between them and "legitimate" Klansmen grew blurred. The distinction was particularly irrelevant to their black victims. As freedman J. T. Tims of Arkansas recalled, "There was no difference between the patrols and the Ku-Klux that I know of. If they caught you, they all would whip you."

In April 1867, the Pulaski den called a reorganizational meeting of legitimate Klan leaders at Nashville's new posh hotel, the Maxwell House. This secret meeting coincided with a public one for the nomination of Democratic candidates for the fall election, and the overlap allowed Klansmen to keep the nature of their gathering private. The stated aims of the meeting reflected the need for stronger control over rank-and-file members:

> To reorganize the Klan on a plan corresponding to its size and present purposes; to bind the isolated Dens together; to secure unity of purpose and concert of action; to hedge the members up by such limitations and regulations as are best adapted to restrain them within proper limits; to distribute the authority among prudent men at local centers and exact from them a close supervision of those under their charge.

Obviously, the need for tighter control was prompted by the burgeoning numbers of anointed as well as self-appointed Klansmen. The fact that the meeting was convened so closely on the heels of the first Reconstruction act, however, suggests that Klan leaders wanted a tighter organization for a particular purpose—most likely that of meeting Radical Reconstruction head-on.

The brains behind this convocation belonged to George Gordon, a young, able former brigadier-general for the Confederacy and now a Pulaski resident and prominent Klansman. Gordon composed a "Prescript" or pamphlet of rules that was distributed to the leaders at the Nashville meeting.* Except for a few additional offices, the Prescript left the organization of local dens exactly as the Pulaski Six had formulated it. Above the dens, however, Gordon imposed a military hierarchy ascending from county leaders all the way to a supreme commander.

Dens within a county (Province) would be overseen by a Grand Giant and his four assisting Goblins. Counties within a congressional district (Dominion) would be headed by a Grand Titan and his six Furies. Dominions within a state (Realm) would be governed by a Grand Dragon, assisted by his eight Hydras. And in charge of all states within the Klan's "Invisible Empire" was the supreme commander, the Grand Wizard who would be assisted by ten Genii. The chain of command was clear and well worked out —at least on paper.

Although the Prescript contained a number of political aims,

---

* Gordon's complete 1867 Prescript for the Reconstruction Klan may be found in Appendix A.

such as securing the rights of the oppressed, these were deliberately left vague and innocuous. Klansmen (officially known as Ghouls) would be required to take a dire oath of secrecy. The use of secret passwords and grips was indicated, but details were not spelled out. A register of ominous code words signifying months, days, and hours were to be used for the public postings of den meetings. The Klan's revenue would be raised through the sale of Prescripts at $10 a copy and from initiation fees, fines, and taxes set by the dens; the Empire and the Grand Wizard would receive 10 percent of all revenue collected. An official flag was described as a yellow pennant five feet long and three feet wide. On the pennant was a flying dragon and a Latin motto meaning, "What always, what everywhere, what by all is held to be true." The Klan Prescript concluded with an envoy: "To the lovers of law and order, peace and justice, we send you greeting; and to the shades of the venerated dead we affectionately dedicate the * *." Nowhere in the Prescript was the name "Ku-Klux Klan" mentioned.

In Gordon's designs for a national hierarchy, heightened secrecy, and vague political aims, it is clear that he was borrowing from the traditions of other secret societies that had preceded the Klan. The Order of the Star Spangled Banner had been formed in Boston in 1849 as an anti-immigrant, anti-Catholic political party. Many of its secret codes and handclasps, arcane rituals, and signals of member identification (such as grasping the lapel of one's coat with thumb and forefinger) would eventually be adopted intact by Klansmen. With the Star Spangled Banner's evolution into the American Party or Know-Nothings in 1854, an elaborate chain of command was devised, from a National Council to state "Wigwams" and local lodges or "Clans." The Know-Nothings achieved remarkable success in the 1854 elections, largely through nocturnal skulduggery and intimidation, which became known as "dark lantern tactics." Soon after the collapse of the Know-Nothings in 1856 from sectional strife, one of its Virginia members, George W. L. Bickley, formed the Knights of the Golden Circle. The interesting name came from Bickley's fantastic scheme for a South American filibustering expedition. A great circle could be circumscribed on the globe, with Cuba as its center and with a radius of sixteen geographical degrees, that would encompass Mexico, Central America, the northern portion of South America, and the West Indies. Bickley proposed to lead private armies across the Rio Grande, conquer and annex these lands, and parcel them out as new slave states, preserving the balance of power with the North.

The constitution, rituals, secret grips and passwords of the Knights of the Golden Circle were pure Know-Nothingism. Its military organization, however, and its defense of the rights of proslavery Southern whites closely foreshadowed Gordon's ideas for the Klan. Bickley also proposed that his Knights could serve as a secret police force to identify abolitionist traitors and preserve the orderly operations of slavery.

The Golden Circle managed to establish chapters and enroll members in every Southern state, as well as in California and portions of the Midwest. Although there were two musterings and expeditions of the Knights to the Mexican border, they never managed to cross the Rio Grande. After the South seceded from the Union, Bickley turned the order into a secret instrument of Confederate support, and in several states, members of the Golden Circle formed the nucleus around which some of the first companies of the Confederate army were organized. Before Bickley was captured and imprisoned by the Union army in 1863, he had established final headquarters in Clarksville, Tennessee—a hundred miles from Pulaski. Four years later, memories of the Golden Circle were still alive in Tennessee; and its Know-Nothing flummery and avowed intention of giving the South an "organization capable of defending her rights" provided Gordon with a natural political and military framework to impose upon the young men who had become associated with the Pulaski Ku-Klux and were growing reckless from its lack of definition.

After the Nashville convocation, Klan leaders were sent home to sell the new organization to existing dens. Although Gordon had been elected Grand Dragon of the Realm of Tennessee, the office of supreme commander, the Grand Wizard, remained vacant. Within weeks, Klan leaders came up with a promising candidate for their highest office. The selection was engineered by Captain John W. Morton, who had been attending school at Pulaski and who was fast becoming an influential person in the expanded order. Morton wanted his former cavalry commander as Wizard, and with the backing of Klan officials, he rode to Memphis and offered the position to Nathan Bedford Forrest, the controversial Confederate general whose recent presidential pardon had called forth denunciations of him by Union soldiers as "a foul fiend in human shape."

Forrest had settled in Memphis in 1852 and did so well as a slave trader he acquired two plantations and $1.5 million. In June 1861, he had been authorized to recruit a regiment of cavalry for the war, which grew into the army he commanded as a lieutenant general. Forrest had been one of the Confederacy's most aggressive commanders and was probably the finest cavalry leader, North or South. Although he had gone into the war a multimillionaire, he came out of it, in his words, "A beggar. . . . When I came out of the army I was completely used up—shot all to pieces, crippled up, and found myself and my family entirely dependent." It had been a humiliating fall for a man as proud as Forrest, and he is said to have welcomed Morton's invitation to take charge of this risen phoenix of the Confederacy. As one Klansman put it, "Forrest commanded more brave men in the invisible army than he did while in the Confederate army."

Forrest was a wise choice as leader of the new invisible army. Though "shot all to pieces," he still cut a dashing figure and epitomized the ideals of manhood that the South cherished. Forty-six years old in 1867, the handsome general was described by a newspaper reporter as a man "six feet one inch and a half in height, with broad shoulders, a full chest, and symmetrical, muscular limbs; erect in carriage, and weighs one hundred and eighty-five pounds; dark-gray eyes, dark hair, mustache, and beard worn upon the chin; a set of regular white teeth, and clearly cut features." Forrest was a big man in all respects. His authority was the kind that reckless young Ghouls might respect. And in his new vocation as an insurance representative and railroad entrepreneur, Forrest had all the connections and associations necessary to fulfill one of the most important, formally ascribed duties of the Grand Wizard: the propagation of the Klan throughout the South.

After the reorganization meeting and Forrest's ascension to leadership, the Invisible Empire became more visible. A large Klan parade in Pulaski received considerable publicity, and parades became one of the most popular devices used by the Klan to call attention to itself. Using the code words supplied in the Prescript, Klan announcements of den meetings began appearing in newspapers throughout middle and western Tennessee. On March 29, 1867, the Pulaski *Citizen*, whose editor, Frank McCord, was one of the six founders of the Klan, printed what is probably the first public announcement of a Klan meeting. Then, on April 19, it described a nocturnal invasion of its editorial offices by "the Grand Turk of the Kuklux Klan. . . . Our visitor appeared to be about nine feet high, with a most hideous face, and wrapped in an elegant robe of black silk, which he kept closely folded about his person. He wore gloves the color of blood, and carried a magic wand in his hand with which he awed us into submission to any demand he might make." Editor McCord was sufficiently awed to print the notice of the den meeting, which was the only demand made by the Turk who just happened to be his crony and fellow Klansman James Crowe.

Due to their spookiness, Klan notices made interesting reading for the public. As time went on, dens tried to outdo each other in this new medium. Undoubtedly, this is one of the best:

𝕶. 𝕶. 𝕶.

We have come!   We are here!
Beware!   Take heed!

When the black cat is gliding under the shadows of darkness, and the death watch ticks at the lone hour of midnight, then we, the pale riders, are abroad.✙ ✙ ✙ ✙ Speak in whispers and we hear you.✙ ✙ ✙

Dream as you sleep in the inmost recesses of your houses, and hovering over your beds we gather your sleeping thoughts, while our daggers are at your throats.✙ ✙

Ravishers of the liberty of the people, for whom we died and yet live, begone ere it be too late.✙ ✙ ✙ ✙

Unholy blacks, cursed of God, take warning and fly.

Twice hath the sacred serpent hissed. When again his voice is heard your doom is sealed.

Beware! Take heed! Given under our hand in the den of the sacred serpent on the mystical day of the bloody moon!!

For pure rip-and-tear melodrama, however, no one bested Ryland Randolph, self-appointed Cyclops of the Tuscaloosa den:

GENERAL ORDERS NO. 3
Shrouded Brotherhood! Murdered heroes!
Fling the bloody dirt that covers you to the four winds! Erect thy Goddess on the banks of the Avernus. Mark well your foes! Strike with the redhot spear! Prepare Charon for his task!
Enemies reform! The skies shall be blackened! A single Star shall look down upon horrible deeds! The night owl shall hoot a requiem o'er Ghostly Corpses!
Beware! Beware! Beware!
The Great Cyclops is angry! Hobgoblins report! Shears and lash!
Tar and Feathers! Hell and Fury!
Revenge! Revenge! Revenge!
Bad men! white, black, yellow, repent!

The hour is at hand! Be ye ready! Life is short! J. H. S. Y. W.!
Ghosts! Ghosts! Ghosts!
Drink thy tea made of distilled hell, stirred with the lightning of
heaven, and sweetened with the gall of thine enemies!
All will be well!

Countless examples of these ghoulish tirades can be found in
Tennessee newspapers of the day, and their titillation of the public
imagination helped win popular support for the Klan. J. M. Beard,
who lived through the period, said that the average person enjoyed
the fantasy that Klansmen met "in caves in the bowels of the earth,
where they were surrounded by . . . rows of skulls, coffins and
their furniture, human skeletons, ominous pictures copied from
the darkest passages of the *Inferno* or *Paradise Lost*." All of this
may seem silly to the modern reader, but it had a primordial appeal
for nineteenth-century Tennesseans with strong ties to their Scottish ancestry. Two centuries earlier, the European witch cult was
more widespread and flourished more openly in Scotland than in
any other nation. The lonely hills and moors, the echoing glens
and glades had seemed the very places for demons to surface and
drive the country folk to band into local covens, conduct midnight
revels in graveyards, and summon the devil to bewitch King James
I, the wealthy land-owning lairds, and other less potent enemies.
Sir Walter Scott's account of the phenomenon, *Demonology and
Witchcraft*, had gone through a second edition in 1830. And in
Giles County, Tennessee, folklore still persisted about John Fian
and the North Berwick Witches, Isobel Gowdie, the Aberdeen
Witches, and the diabolical Major Thomas Weir of Edinburgh. At
the very least, the Ku-Klux played into these traditions. At most,
given the instability of the postwar South, the Klan opened up the
collective unconscious of the inhabitants where it arose and
tapped primitive, pagan sources to bear upon the frustrations of
the present.
     The Klan's increased visibility, announcements, parades, and
meetings suggest that the shrouded brotherhood was gearing itself
for a major undertaking, and this seems to be the case. Tennessee
had ratified the Fourteenth Amendment and was therefore not
subject to Radical Reconstruction. But following the example of
the Reconstruction acts, the Tennessee legislature had given
blacks the right to vote and the August 1867 elections were coming
up. In spite of its show of strength, the Klan's interference in this
election was surprisingly mild. For one thing, General Forrest

made an earnest attempt to keep Klansmen in line and, to offset suspicion of his invisible army's involvement in civil disturbances, wrote to General Thomas—the U.S. military commander of the district—warning him that the considerable animosity between blacks and "the Irish people" of Memphis might cause the latter "to offer strenuous interference to prevent the former from voting in the upper wards of the city." But the discretion of Tennessee Klansmen in the 1867 election rested more significantly on their awaiting the outcome of a Conservative bid for black votes. The Conservatives (a coalition of Democrats and old-line Whigs) had counseled blacks that their former masters were still their best friends and had their genuine interests at heart, and that these interests could best be served by voting the Conservative ticket. Tennessee blacks completely ignored this counsel, giving the Republicans a resounding victory at the polls.

Klansmen and Conservatives immediately deduced what had gone wrong. This disaster at the polls was clearly the doing of the damnable Union League, and an outcry against this particular group of carpetbaggers was heard throughout Tennessee. The Union League had been organized by Reverend Henry Bellows and Stephen Colwell in Philadelphia in 1862 to foster support for the Lincoln administration and the Union cause. After the war, it became a political arm of the radical Republicans, and its emissaries had gone South to rally support for the GOP among the newly enfranchised blacks. The Union League organizers were considered carpetbaggers of the lowest kind. They instructed blacks in the need for registering to vote and informed them about procedures at the ballot box. They also frankly urged them to vote Republican. In Tennessee, as elsewhere throughout the South, the rallies held by the League were a source of fear and loathing to native whites. Like any political rally, League meetings included a good deal of bragging and ballyhoo; and to Southern whites, such license by crowds of "free niggers" was a certain prelude to rape and rapine.

An intriguing facet of Conservative contempt for the League lay in the naïve assumption that blacks voted Republican merely because the Yankees told them to. Whites reasoned that, freed from "foreign interference," blacks would return to being the "good niggers" they had been before the war and follow the dictates of their Southern "friends." Throughout Reconstruction, committees of blacks repeatedly punctured this fantasy, but their efforts seem to have had no impact on white citizens of the time or early historians of the period. A concise explanation for blacks' endorsement of the Republicans was offered by a delegation of South Carolina blacks in an "Address to the Native Whites":

> [You] derided the idea of granting us the right to vote; when your legislature met in 1865–66, you passed that infamous Black Code. . . . Your laws provided for taking and binding-out our children and subjecting us to all manner of disabilities. We could not pursue any trade or calling in this State without written permission from some white man; we could not sell any article of barter without the consent first obtained from some magistrate. With all these facts before us, and your negro code before us . . . do you not see why we have been constrained to trust in strangers rather than to those who claim that they are our natural friends? Can you have the heart to ask colored men to vote for men who deny that they are capable of voting intelligently? Can you ask us to vote our liberties away forever? Can you ask us to sustain a party which is pledged to divest us of all the privileges in law which we now enjoy?

But native whites were unable to hear such appeals to reason. They could see no responsibility of their own for the voting behavior of blacks. To them it was entirely the doing of carpetbaggers and leaders of the Union League, "a society which teaches the negro to hate his former master." In short, black support of the GOP was the net result of a conspiracy perpetrated by outside agitators.

After the radical victory in August 1867, the Tennessee Klan spun into action. An organizational campaign was seen throughout the south–central portion of the state. Nocturnal parades of white-robed riders were more frequent. The Klan was finally mentioned for the first time by an agent of the Freedmen's Bureau. George E. Judd, agent for Pulaski, reported that the society of Klansmen "is very numerous and seems to extend all over the country. They march about the streets, nights, thoroughly disguised and in uniform." Though only minor infractions of the law were so far attributed to Klansmen, Judd greatly feared their potential for greater disturbances. The "best citizens" of Pulaski had informed him that the Klan was "merely for fun" and had no intention of interfering with anyone. "This may all be true," Judd wrote, "but I doubt it mightily. It is certainly a very extensive institution for a funny one." Judd's suspicions soon came true. In fall 1867, the Klan began a series of organized raids on black members of the Union League as well as on white teachers of black schools and other carpetbaggers. From June to October 1867, it was reported to O. O. Howard that innocent people in Tennessee had suffered twenty-five murders, thirty-five assaults with intent to kill, eighty-three assault and batteries, four rapes, and four arsons. By January 1868, agent Michael Walsh reported to General W. P. Carlin that the Klan was "an organization well matured and drilled" and had for its goal "the expulsion of loyal men, whites and blacks, from the counties of Giles and Maury."

By spring 1868, the Klan was fully launched throughout Tennessee as a vigilante army. Responsible citizens wrote to politicians and military commanders asking that action be taken against this menace. A member of the Tennessee legislature complained to General Thomas that his state was "greatly exercised by the presence in many localities of an organized body of men, who, without provocation and in violation of Law—seemingly desperate in purpose—are scouring the county by night, carrying dismay and horror to all. . . . No information is had of the number or ultimate purpose of the organization, [but] it certainly is not peaceful." General Thomas, in turn, contacted his superiors, charging the Ku-Klux with acts of a "lawless and diabolical nature." Writing to the Adjutant General, Thomas compared the Klan raids to a continuation of the Civil War. "This resistance to the law," he said, "is an outgrowth of the rebellion and means, as well, oppression and hostility to everything representing patriotism and devotion to the best interests of the country." Thomas argued correctly that since Tennessee was "a fully constructed state," responsibility for suppressing the Klan rested on local authorities—even though these men were doing nothing. "I shall be glad to receive any orders or instructions you may see fit to give," he concluded.

While the military awaited instructions on whether or not to intervene in Tennessee's civil matters, the disguised night riders continued to intimidate black and white Republicans. Democratic newspapers like the Memphis *Avalanche* welcomed the Klan and predicted that it would soon take over Tennessee for the state's own good. The Nashville *Union and Dispatch* called the Klan "the most extraordinary association that the present century has known." Republican papers promptly countered, and the Klan became the subject of a major editorial debate in the Tennessee press. By now, the newspapers of neighboring states were likewise taking a deep interest in Tennessee's shrouded brotherhood. The editor of Virginia's Richmond *Examiner*, Edward Pollard, proclaimed:

under its cap and bells [the Klan] hides a purpose as resolute, noble and heroic as that which Brutus concealed beneath the mask of well-dissembled idiocy. It is rapidly organizing wherever the insolent negro, the malignant white traitor to his race, and the infamous squatter are plotting to make the South utterly unfit for the residence of the decent white man.

The Klan itself could hardly stay out of the journalistic limelight. Province Number One sent an article to the Columbia, Tennessee, *Herald*, bragging, "There are true and tried members of this organization in each civil district of this county. Hundreds of determined and well-armed men can in two hours be rallied at every point in the county."

In preparation for the autumn 1868 elections, the Klan began, in June, what can rightfully be called a reign of terror in Tennessee. Local dens seemed hellbent on using any degree of violence necessary to "restore" the black man to his condition before the war. A. H. Eastman, the agent for the Freedmen's Bureau in Columbia, Tennessee, was afraid for his own life when he reported, "The Ku-Klux Klan appear to be on the 'war path.' Complaints of visitations by night, all over my district, of the breaking into of houses and assaults upon the inmates, are very frequent. . . . More than half the outrages perpetrated by this Klan are not reported to me. . . . I am so impressed with my own inability to fully understand the exact condition of affairs that I will be excused for not making the same comprehensible to you. This I do know—that I have been sleeping for months with a revolver under my pillow and a double-barreled shotgun, heavily charged with buck shot, at one hand and a hatchet at the other, with an inclination to sell the little piece of mortality with which I am intrusted as dearly as possible."

William Green, the agent at Winchester, claimed, "The Ku-Klux have committed so many gross outrages that it is impossible to enumerate them all. The villains seem determined to overawe the country and frighten colored people into implicit obedience to any demand they may make." Agent Brown in Bolivar said that the Klans "have compelled a more complete system of surveillance over the freedmen scarcely equalled under the old slave regime. They are completely subjugated—afraid to say their souls are their own, afraid to express their sentiments, and afraid to exercise the elective franchise conferred upon them by the laws of the State." Reverend H. O. Hoffman of Shelbyville complained that several of his associates had been cruelly treated by Klansmen. "I believe the object of the Klan," said Hoffman, "is to whip unarmed negroes, scare timid white men, break up elections, and interfere with the State government and steal and plunder the goods of the people." For Hoffman's criticism of their activities, Klansmen responded with their newest form of intimidation—a threatening note posted on his front-yard gate:

IN KU-KLUX COUNCIL, JULY 24, 1868

REV. MR. HOFFMAN: Your name is before the council. Heaven!! We will attend to you. You shall not call us "villains"—damn you.

KU-KLUX.

Other warnings, like this one sent to a teacher of a black school, were couched in the now-popular jargon of witchcraft and the *Inferno:*

HIDDEN RECESS, UNTERRIFIED'S RETREAT
Klan of Vengeance! Eternity!!

Villain away!! Ere another moon wanes, unless thou art gone from the place thy foul form desecrates, thy unhallowed soul will be revelling in the hell thy acts here hath made hot for thee! William, eat heartily, and make glad thy vile carcass, for verily, the "Pale Riders" will help on thy digestion!

You and your friends will sleep an unawakening sleep if you do! Dare you Eat!!! The sacred serpent has hissed the last time!!! Beware!!!!

K.K.K.

Eventually, the Freedmen's Bureau sent its most competent, independent inspector, Brevet Lieutenant Joseph W. Gelray, into various parts of Tennessee to investigate the Ku-Klux problem. Joseph Gelray was a highly intelligent, fair-minded, religious, and intrepid soldier whose beautifully written reports are laced with quotations from Shakespeare and Euripides. He was plainly horrified by what he found. The Klan spirit, Gelray observed, "exhibits itself in the most infernal outrages upon persons and interests that ever was heard of in any community laying the slightest claims to civilization or Christianity." For example, John Dunlap, a white teacher of a black school in Shelbyville, was stripped, whipped, and told that, unless he left Tennessee, Klansmen would return and burn him at the stake. Spencer Griffin, a fifty-four-year-old black in Sumner County, was whipped 150 lashes by Klansmen who informed him that "niggers" would soon learn "that they had to do what they were told." Black people who had gathered for a prayer meeting in Cornersville were raided by Klansmen and the leaders of the meeting taken off and beaten unmercifully. Mrs. Lewis Powell, a black woman of Hickman County, was shot to death for being active in the Union League. A white female teacher was pistol-whipped and told that "no damned Yankee bitch should live in this county." D. B. Garrett, a twenty-four-year-old black teacher from Marshall County, was driven from his home and school by Klansmen and told that, when he saw them in the future, to tip his hat and call them master. W. A. Kelley, a twenty-eight-year-old Republican and ex–Union soldier, was shot at and driven from his home by Klansmen who stayed long enough to abuse his wife, steal his money, and drive his cattle through his field, destroying his crops.

One of Lieutenant Gelray's most astute and painful observations was that "there is *no intention or desire on the part of the civil authorities or the community at large to bring the murderers to justice.* Those who could will not, and those who would are afraid. Perhaps all are more or less afraid; but the most shocking part of this whole matter is that some of those who are considered good citizens, and actual leaders of good society and moulders of public opinion, are active with both tongue and pen in defending and justifying the Ku-Klux Klan in their most horrible outrages against law and nature."

After two months of the long Tennessee summer of 1868, George E. Judd, now serving as the subassistant commissioner for the Tennessee Freedmen's Bureau, reported that blacks were leaving their farms in droves and fleeing to the towns and cities for protection. "Unless something is done immediately by the governor to protect the colored citizens of the country," he said, "the cities will be flooded by poor, helpless creatures who will have to be supported by the State or United States government." On July 27, Governor Brownlow responded by calling a special session of the Tennessee general assembly and asked for increased power to put down the Ku-Klux conspiracy. The whole body of Klansmen, said Brownlow, was nothing more than "ex–rebel soldiers" who were "violating their paroles at the time of their surrender, and violating the laws of the State, and plotting and planning mischief in every respect." Since the Klan had been particularly "violent and murderous" in middle and western Tennessee, Brownlow called for a state militia to put down the rebellion in those districts. Unfortunately, response was inadequate, probably because would-be volunteers were too frightened by the fierce determination and extensive organization of the Klan. In the meantime, the Klan operated without hindrance. Writing from Obion, Tennessee, a scalawag reported, "Some of, and I might say almost all, the Rebels are elated with the prospect of soon getting the government into their hands. . . . There has not been such a rejoicing here since the fall of Fort Pillow . . . as there is over the triumph of the Ku-Klux."

Feeling overconfident, Nathan B. Forrest on August 28 made his worst decision as Grand Wizard of the Klan—he granted an interview to a reporter from the Cincinnati *Commercial*. Although Forrest would strenuously deny the content of the interview, there's no basis for assuming that the reporter wrote anything other than what the general told him. The crux of the interview was the Ku-Klux Klan, an organization that Forrest said existed not just in Tennessee "but all over the South, and its numbers have not been exaggerated."

"What are its numbers, general?" the reporter asked.

"In Tennessee," Forrest replied, "there are over forty thousand; in all the southern States about five hundred and fifty thousand men."

"What is the character of the organization, may I inquire?"

"Yes, sir," Forrest replied. "It is a protective, political, military organization. I am willing to show any man the constitution of the society. The members are sworn to recognize the Government of the United States. . . . Its objects originally were protection against [Union] Leagues and the Grand Army of the Republic, but after it became general it was found that political matters and interests could best be promoted within it, and it was then made a political organization, giving its support, of course, to the Democratic Party."

"Is the organization connected throughout the State?"

"Yes, it is. In each voting precinct there is a captain, who, in addition to his other duties, is required to make out a list of names of men in his precinct, giving all the radicals and all the Democrats who are positively known, and showing also the doubtful on both sides and of both colors. This list of names is forwarded to the grand commander of the State who is thus enabled to know who are our friends and who are not." Forrest went on to explain that the Klan was directed not so much against blacks but against carpetbaggers and scalawags. He further asserted that, should the need arise, he could muster forty thousand Klansmen in five days.

"Are you a member of the Ku-Klux, general?" the reporter asked.

"I am not," Forrest replied, "but am in sympathy and will cooperate with them."

In Washington, members of Congress read the widely reprinted Forrest interview with interest and alarm. The general had confirmed the existence of the Ku-Klux as a counterrevolutionary army while, up to now, it had been considered, if not a wild rumor or radical fantasy, then a harmless group of silly boys who played tricks on "darkies." Secondly, Forrest had claimed that, as of August 1868, the Klan had spread from Tennessee into other Southern states. Independent evidence proved that Forrest's claim wasn't mere bravado. The general *knew* it was true because, in line with the duties ascribed to him as Grand Wizard, he had worked hard to propagate the Klan throughout the South. Dens had long existed in Alabama and Mississippi by virtue of those states' proximity to Tennessee. But between January and May 1868, Forrest used his travels as an insurance representative to visit nearly all of the Southern states and recruit leaders for his Invisible Empire. In March, he had been in Atlanta and Columbus, Georgia, just days before the first Klan notices appeared in that state; in Atlanta, he had conferred with former Confederate general John B. Gordon who became Georgia's first Grand Dragon. Later in March, he had visited North Carolina; white-robed marauders had appeared as early as January there, in Alamance County, but Forrest's visit seems to have provided a real surge in Klan activity. Two months later, in South Carolina, the Klan was active in Charleston.

There was no doubt about it—the Ku-Klux was growing and spreading. But the focal point remained in Tennessee, where the Klan's nocturnal raids were already an uninterrupted nightmare. A delegation of the Tennessee general assembly finally called on Andrew Johnson (who had just survived an impeachment trial) and begged him for federal intervention. Unless the President did something, he was told, the Klan's "contagion of rapine and bloodshed will spread over the whole state of Tennessee." Johnson was informed that attempts to prosecute the Klan in Tennessee had failed either because juries were partly composed of Klansmen or because witnesses were so frightened by threats of reprisal that they refused to testify. Johnson reluctantly agreed to order General Thomas to make his troops available to the civil authorities. One who took a keen interest in this matter was the French correspondent Georges Clemenceau. Democrats had warmly praised the President's generosity in releasing federal troops, but Clemenceau couldn't see how Johnson "could very well avoid doing his plain duty in protecting citizens against a band of assassins."

Few Americans shared Clemenceau's concern, however. The Klan was still regarded as something of a joke. How could a pack of Halloween revelers disrupt the South as much as radicals were complaining? The Southern conservative press—echoed by Northern Democratic papers—played into this sentiment: Complaints of outrages by disguised bandits were simply an attempt "to hide Radical rottenness behind a cloud of Ku-Klux." "Not Klansmen, but *Republicans* were responsible" for the outrages. A remarkable novel titled *The Masked Lady of the White House* carried this thesis to a wide reading public. Its anonymous author (with pronounced Democratic sympathies) suggested that Southern atrocities were the deliberate work of radical Republicans who planned to swell their political power through Northern indignation at a nonexistent conspiracy. Soon another book appeared. Edward H. Dixon's *The Terrible Mysteries of the Ku-Klux Klan* purported to be the confessions of a former Klansman but was nothing more than a cheap thriller in which Klansmen were portrayed as modern-day sorcerers who made pacts with the devil. The entertainment value of this portrayal didn't go unnoticed, however, and the North was soon infected with "Ku-Klux Fever."

The mysterious three Ks had an irresistible appeal to advertisers. Saloons offered Ku-Klux Kocktails. A manufacturing firm touted its Ku-Klux Knife. Even in *Harper's Weekly* readers were urged to buy only Wickes' accident-proof kerosene, because **k**ommon **k**erosene **k**ills! Musical hacks ground out Ku-Klux schottisches. In Chicago and Union Mills, Pennsylvania, bored postal workers carved *KKK* woodblocks, which they used to cancel stamps. Newspapers wrote rollicking accounts of Ku-Klux activities that seemed to one reader like "*mardi gras* comedy rather than racial tragedy." The dregs were reached when E. C. Buell—"the celebrated comedian and comic singer"—published the *Ku-Klux Songster*, which included an atrocious ballad he had popularized in the music hall:

As I went for a walk the other night,
T'other night and got tight,

When I saw a most terrible sight,
'Twas the horrible Ku-Klux Klan. . . .

With Greeley's white hat for a tub,
There was one dripping blood,
From a hole they had dug in the mud,
To bury a big black-and-tan;
While up in one end of the room,
I saw very soon
Ben Butler hung with a spoon,
By the horrible Ku-Klux Klan.

>What I saw, I'll remember forever,
>The thought of it causes a shiver,
>The dreaded three Ks, the awful three Ks
>The horrible Ku-Klux Klan.

Albion Tourgée was a broad-minded justice of the North Carolina superior court who would long remember "Ku-Klux Fever." "The nation held its sides with laughter," he recalled with bitter irony, "and the Ku-Klux took heart from these cheerful echoes and extended their borders without delay."

"WE ARE THE LAW ITSELF"

The Ku-Klux Reign of Terror: 1868–1871

On Christmas Eve in Chatham County, North Carolina, freedman Essic Harris, his wife Ann, their four children, and a nephew lay asleep in their two beds in an eighteen- by twenty-foot cabin. Harris was suddenly awakened by his wife. "Essic, Essic! There's somebody at the door." He got out of bed at the same time his door burst open, and a band of fifteen men crowded into the little room. They were dressed in grotesque costumes: long gowns that looked like women's dresses, sheepskin coverlets, and—was it paper sacks over their heads?

"'Have you ever seen the Ku-Klux before?" the leading intruder asked.

"No, sir," Harris replied.

"Well, here they are. We are the Ku-Klux."

They searched the cabin, seized Harris's gun, and asked him where he kept his shot and powder. After he gave them what they wanted, they left without saying another word.

Essic Harris was an ambitious, hard-working family man. He had experienced a satisfactory relationship with his former master, William Harris, who asked him to stay after emancipation, but Essic wanted to be with his wife and children. Ann and the kids lived with her former master, elderly Ned Finch, and his spinster sister. Mr. Ned and Miss Sally had raised Ann from a baby. She

54

was all they had and would ever have, and Ann was emotionally attached to both of them. After moving in with them on the Finch place, Harris found that the old couple were more than acceptable landlords. They allowed him to farm and do as he pleased on their land in exchange for caring for the livestock. In addition to farming, Harris found part-time work at the railroad yard. He raised good crops and earned good money. He sent his oldest two children off to school. He joined the Union League and became an active Republican. He thought well of himself and was well thought of by others. And to North Carolina Klansman, Harris was more than that. He was an insolent nigger.

He was at least insolent enough to buy another shotgun after the masked intruders had stolen his first one. About a week after the Klan's visit, a few days before New Year's, Harris sat asleep on the floor in front of the fire. He could always fall asleep in a sitting position after a hard day's work, although it irritated his wife to no end. "Essic," she said, waking him, "you'd better go to bed instead of sitting here by the fire in everybody's way." The two of them then went to bed. As was her custom, Ann took the baby to bed with them—the one Harris called his "suckling child." They had not quite fallen asleep when the dog barked. The old hound had never barked at anything except once—the night the disguised men had come for Harris's gun. Ann suddenly bolted upright in bed. "Essic!" she cried, "the Ku-Klux is coming!"

Harris bounded out of bed, went to the door, took down the bar, and looked out into the yard. The bright moonlight revealed nearly thirty masked and robed men on horseback with more riders joining them. Harris slammed the door, bolted it and threw a bucket of water, which he always kept handy, onto the fire. He dashed to the head of the bed where he kept his shotgun, but simultaneously, the barrels of two or more rifles smashed through his window and discharged. Ann screamed, clutched the baby to her bosom, and dove between the bedtick and mat (a thin quilt). Harris ducked beneath the window as gunshot rained into the cabin.

The gunfire awoke the Finches, and Mr. Ned came down in his nightshirt from the Big House and began walking among the Klansmen. "Gentlemen," he asked, "what do you want? What are you going to do? Let this nigger alone. He is a nigger that I have here to work my land. He has a family and is a hard-working nigger and doesn't bother anybody. *Please let him alone!*" Ned Finch went from Klansman to Klansman as they wildly continued to bombard the cabin with lead. They eventually became so irritated by him they threatened to "fix" him after they got through with Harris. Mr. Ned left thoroughly frightened, and Miss Sally came down to try her hand. Essic was a hard-working man, she informed them, and she knew of no one who had the least thing against him. They kept on firing, round after round.

All the while, Harris was helpless beneath the window as gunshot ricocheted throughout the cabin. The Klansmen started hammering at the door. Harris had piled bags of corn and grain in front of it so that when it finally caved in it didn't fall flat. But it was open enough at the top for the Klansmen to fire a deafening volley into the room.

"We've killed the old man!" one of the Ku-Klux exclaimed with glee. "Let's go in and fetch the others out!"

"Well, *you* go in," said a more cautious Klansman.

"Yonder he is!" said another. "I see him!" And he fired at whatever he saw.

"I saw him fall," said another. "He's dead!"

But no one was willing to venture into the cabin.

By now Harris had taken several balls and felt "shot all to pieces." Glancing around the room, he saw his children and nephew piled motionless on top of each other under the covers, looking like "a parcel of pigs." He realized they were probably dead and that Ann was shot, too. Anger suddenly steeled his fear. His arm was wounded so badly he could barely lift his gun. But he raised it high enough to aim at the Klansmen who were bludgeoning his door with rifle butts. He pulled the trigger, and the blaze of the detonation lit up the faces of two men he recognized. They were Joe Clark, the tavern keeper, and Barney Burgess, the grocer. Harris had grown up with these two men and couldn't imagine what they had against him.

Joe and Barney were seriously wounded, and the Klansmen panicked. What kind of nigger would dare shoot at the Ku-Klux? Taking advantage of their confusion, Harris shouted, "Boy! Bring me my five-shooter!" Harris had no such weapon, but it was the right time for the bluff, and it worked. Most of the Klansmen rode off, taking the two wounded men with them. The few that remained began screaming that they were going to set the cabin on fire. Harris started ramming "a dangerous load" into his shotgun, and the men outside could hear him doing it. This nigger was crazy! They quickly jumped on their horses and rode off as well.

Miss Sally immediately ran back to the cabin. "Ann! Ann!" she

cried, "are the children dead?" Miraculously, no one but Essic was
injured. Shot was embedded all over the interior walls of the cabin,
but it had been fired a few feet above the beds. Ann and the
children were safe.

The attack on Essic Harris was typical of Klan violence between
1868 and 1871. But the Harris family was among the lucky ones,
even though they—like thousands of others—would be forced to
abandon their home and move to a major city. For during this
three-year reign of Ku-Klux terrorism, no black Republican, carpetbagger, or scalawag was safe in the rural South.

Grand Wizard Forrest had taken an active step in propagating the
Invisible Empire in early 1868, but thereafter it seemed to spread
of its own accord, stimulated by newspaper stories flattering to the
Klan and feeding on Southern white fears of the new "radical"
state governments. In the border states, Klan dens appeared in the
Kentucky bluegrass region, southeastern Missouri, southeastern
West Virginia, and Tidewater Maryland. In the Deep South, the
Klan was concentrated in the Piedmont plateau and Appalachian
highlands: western North Carolina and northern South Carolina,
Georgia, Alabama and Mississippi. These regions had the smallest
numbers of blacks, and the Klan flourished where chances of reprisal were minimal. Occasionally, Klan strength was found in
regions of equal black and white populations, especially when conditions permitted the intimidation of enough Republican voters to
swing the region back into the Democratic column.

Political affiliation was the key factor to Klan membership, and
all Klansmen were sympathetic to the Democratic party. In Abbe-
ville, South Carolina, a Klansman claimed that "nearly all" the
Democrats in town were members of his den. As to other factors
in membership, it can be safely said that the expanded Invisible
Empire included men from all walks of life. A correspondent to
the Cincinnati *Gazette* claimed: "Were all the Ku-Klux arrested
and brought to trial, among them would be found sheriffs, magis-
trates, jurors and legislators, and it may be clerks and judges. In
some counties it would be found that the Ku-Klux and their
friends comprise more than half of the influential and voting population." Professional men—doctors, lawyers, and university professors—were also Klansmen. Such members, however, preferred
to operate behind the scenes in supportive roles, and often they
were active only in the beginning stage of a den's operation. Once
a den became overtly violent, the more respectable members usu-

ally found a way to dissociate themselves from it. The most extreme and long-term perpetrators of Klan violence tended to be
made up of the lower classes—small farmers and "low-downers,"
as bureau officer John DeForrest called them: men who murdered
people not so much for real or imagined grievances but who "simply kill them in the exercise of their ordinary pugnacity."

There is evidence, however, that not even all "low-downers"
entered the Klan willingly. Coercion was often used to enlist new
members. In Alamance County, North Carolina, for example,
William R. Albright was invited into the local den and told "that I
had better join it for my own protection and that of my father who
[was] a member of the Republican party." The implication was
that Albright's radical father was safe from the Klan only so long
as his son was a member of it. Another reluctant Klansman recalled being asked by the local Cyclops "if I didn't want to go in a
party for my protection and for the protection of my family and
friends." Often this "protection" wasn't so much from outsiders as
it was from Klansmen themselves, who were highly suspicious of
any Southern white unwilling to join them. A North Carolina
bureau officer reported that the object of the den he had been
observing "seemed to be to decoy as many possible into the organization by making them believe it was not a very bad thing." Once
in, there were few ways out. Klansman David Schenck claimed
that he wouldn't have criticized or abandoned his den "for any
amount of money. I believe I would have been risking my life to
do it. I say so candidly."

After the Klan had spread outward from Tennessee, there
wasn't the slightest chance of central control over it—a problem
that would characterize the Klan throughout its long career.
Prominent Southern gentlemen were later cited as state leaders of
the Invisible Empire. Alabama claimed General John T. Morgan
as Grand Dragon. Arkansas was headed by General Albert Pike,
explorer and poet. North Carolina was led by former governor
Zebulon Vance, and Georgia by General John B. Gordon, later a
U.S. senator. But the leadership of these men, originally appointed by Memphis officials, was usually in name only and nowhere lasted longer than 1869; such experienced veterans quickly
realized the impossibility of governing *in secret* such widespread
bands of young hellions and wanted no responsibility for it. Even
local Cyclopes realized that if the Ghouls under their charge
wanted to go out and terrorize someone, there was no way they
could prevent it. Klansman Randolph Shotwell later lamented that
his "so-called 'Chief'-ship was purely nominal, I having not the

least authority over the reckless young country boys who were most active in 'night-riding,' whipping, etc., all of which was outside of the intent and constitution of the Klan. . . ." In fact, the Klan empire that stretched beyond Tennessee in 1868 had virtually no communication with Imperial Headquarters in Memphis and was not beholden even to the minimal regulations established by the convocation and Prescript of 1867.

When Grand Wizard Forrest realized that his so-called "honorable and patriotic" organization had become a sprawling, intractable monster, he too wanted no further part of it. In late January 1869, he issued "General Order Number One," which was the only directive ever to come from Imperial Headquarters. In essence, it called for an official disbandment of the Ku-Klux Klan:

WHEREAS, The Order of the K.K.K. is in some localities being perverted from its original honorable and patriotic purposes;

AND WHEREAS, Such a perversion of the Order is in some instances defeating the very objects of its origin, and is becoming injurious instead of subservient to the public peace and public safety for which it was intended, and in some cases is being used to achieve personal benefit and private purposes, and to satiate private revenge by means of its masked features . . .

It is therefore ordered and decreed, that the masks and costumes of this Order be entirely abolished and destroyed. And every Grand Cyclops shall assemble the men of his Den and require them to destroy in his presence every article of his mask and costume and at the same time shall destroy his own. And every man who shall refuse to do so shall be deemed an enemy of this Order, and shall be treated accordingly. And every man who shall hereafter be seen in mask or costume, shall not be known or recognized as a member of this Order, but shall be deemed an enemy of the same. . . .

Every Cyclops will destroy this Order as soon as read to every member of their Den and Staff.

By command of
THE GRAND WIZARD

Forrest's declaration, of course, accomplished nothing. It merely dissociated Imperial Headquarters from responsibility for the behavior of rank-and-file Klansmen, which is probably all that Forrest hoped it would do. But even in the formative stages of the Ku-Klux Klan, plenty of Tennessee dens had cared nothing about orders emanating from Memphis.

Certainly few Klansmen destroyed their masks and costumes. In fact, the independence and individuality of Southern dens can immediately be seen in the wide variety of Klan uniforms that appeared throughout the South. Although the white, domestic cotton gown originated by the Pulaski den was most widespread—especially because of its notoriety—dens were free to adopt anything that struck members' fancy. Several dens chose the black robes and masks worn earlier by the patterollers; these not only capitalized on the fear blacks recalled from the past but made Klansmen less visible during nocturnal raids. Another group preferred red gowns trimmed in black. A North Carolina Cyclops wore white pants, a white hood trimmed with red around the eyes, and a red shirt with crosses sewn on the front and back. A den in Mississippi wore white gowns with the black letter O on the front. In other locales, headpieces were decorated with cloth mustaches and beards or surmounted with horns. One gown has been examined in detail, for a Union officer, Captain Albion Howe, ripped it off a Klansman and took it back home to New York as a souvenir; his descendants later donated it to the Buffalo Historical Society. The gown is a domino of dark-brown cotton with a headpiece of coarse red flannel, concealing the entire head and neck. The nosepiece and apertures for the eyes and mouth are bound in white. Dark-brown horns are sewn on top of the headpiece. It is said to be the "work of a skillful seamstress," undoubtedly the Klansman's wife.

Perhaps the majority of Klansmen never bothered to adopt an official costume at all, instead selecting the disguise of the moment. Sheets, pillowcases, handkerchiefs, blankets, sacks over the head, paper masks, blackened faces, and undershirts and drawers worn over outer clothing were all employed. A number of Klansmen used nothing more than a crude mask and one of their wife's dresses. A black female victim of the Klan was able to recognize one of her assailants because he wore a dress she herself had sewed for his wife. And lest Klansmen be thought of as less than masculine for wearing gowns and women's dresses, members at a Spartanburg, South Carolina, den padded their crotches "to make them look big—bulging out."

Unbeholden to a central governing body, Klan dens improvised protocol and initiations that varied as much as their uniforms. Oaths, when required, pledged members to little more than secrecy and loyalty, such as the one used in the Carolinas:

> I do solemnly swear that I will support and defend the Invisible Circle; that I will defend our families, our wives, our children, and brothers;

that I will assist a brother in distress; that I will never reveal the secrets of this order or anything in regard to it that may come to my knowledge, and, if I do, may I meet a traitor's doom, which is *death, death, death.* So help me God, and so punish me my brethren.

Whereas the 1867 Klan convocation had agreed upon various grips and passwords, later dens devised their own. Usually they relied on well-known traditions of the defunct Know-Nothings and Knights of the Golden Circle. There was the secret handshake with forefinger extended against the other's wrist (later adopted unwittingly by the Boy Scouts of America) and the secret gesture of recognition made by sliding one's right hand down the left lapel of his jacket. There were ritual passwords like:

Who comes here?
A friend.
A friend to what?
A friend to my country.

Or:

Say
Nothing!

Every one of these was a remnant of Know-Nothing mummery. Other Klansmen wrote secret messages to each other in a letter cipher that was simply a variation of a number cipher used by the Golden Circle.

In contrast to costumes and ritual, the operating procedure of various Klan dens was surprisingly consistent. Dens would hold regular meetings, usually once a week, in which the behavior of certain "obnoxious" individuals was discussed. Eventually a victim was agreed upon. White victims were often sent written warnings, these sometimes being enough "to alarm the victims sufficiently to induce them to reform their behavior." If the warnings were disregarded or if the victim were black, the den would then hold a "trial" and pass a sentence, which was carried out during a raid. Raids generally took place between eleven o'clock at night and two in the morning.

During a raid, all Klansmen were asked to keep silent except the elected spokesman, who was the man who could best disguise his voice. (Victims of the Klan reported voice disguises assumed by den spokesmen ranging from an unnatural bass tone to an imitation of Irish brogue.) Members were assigned numbers, so that if it became necessary to address them during a raid, names could be avoided. Signals for the movement of flanks were worked out in advance and tooted on a tin horn or a pea whistle. One final thing was often required by a den during a raid and that was whiskey—plenty of it. In fact, the hip flask became almost as necessary an accouterment for Klansmen as their costumes and firearms.

Depending upon the victim, it might be necessary to enlist the support of another den. Neighboring dens sometimes combined for a major undertaking and, occasionally in border areas, there was cooperation between dens of different states. If members of a den were unduly concerned about being recognized during a raid, they could arrange for a remote den to carry out their "sentence" and then reciprocate at a later date.

Historians would long distort the motives of the Ku-Klux Klan of 1868–1871. Perhaps no one summed up its intentions more succinctly than Ulysses S. Grant, whose election to the presidency in 1868 was one of the factors in the expansion and attenuation of Ku-Klux violence. According to Grant, the objects of the Klan were, "by force and terror, to prevent all political action not in accord with the views of the members, to deprive colored citizens of the right to bear arms and of the right of a free ballot, to suppress the schools in which colored children were taught, and to reduce the colored people to a condition closely allied to that of slavery." If this viewpoint seems biased, consider the words of Klansmen themselves. According to an Alabama Klansman, the "legitimate object" of his den was that of "punishing impudent negroes and negro-loving whites." For a North Carolina Klansman, it was that of fighting "the civil or political promotion of the colored race." And in South Carolina, it was for "killing and whipping and crowding out men from the ballot boxes . . . to advance the conservative party and put down the Republican party."

These motives sound political, and some scholars have argued an exclusively political basis for Klan activity. But Klan motives were political only insofar as the two major parties were divided on racial issues. Reconstruction Klansmen were first and foremost *white supremacists*, opposing all rights and liberties conferred upon blacks that elevated them above menial servitude. They were anticarpetbagger and antiscalawag only to the extent that these

Republicans opposed their opinion of the black man's place in the postwar South. Even white supremacy does not exhaust the reasons for Klan activity between 1868 and 1871, for bands of rowdies took oaths of secrecy, dressed in bizarre costumes, and waylaid victims for every imaginable reason—some of them unbelievably petty.

The clearest portrait of Klan motivation is afforded in an analysis of Klan victims, black and white. Carpetbaggers and scalawags comprised the Klan's white victims. Of the carpetbaggers, Klansmen did not strike transported Republican politicians as much as one would suppose. They preferred hitting those carpetbaggers more directly involved in the elevation of blacks. Foremost of these were the teachers of black schools. Free public education was a revolutionary measure for the former Confederacy. Before the war, the South's schools were only for children of the well-to-do. Radical Reconstruction brought education for all—black as well as white. Southern landowners generally resented being taxed for public schools, especially "schools for niggers," whom they didn't want educated in the first place. By 1868, teachers were being threatened, flogged, run out of town, or murdered, and their schoolhouses burned to the ground by the Klan. Even a historian sympathetic to the Klan has said that "the worst work the Ku Klux ever did was its opposition to negro schools. . . ."

Although a Klansman bragged that the "carpetbaggers lived in constant dread of a [Klan] visit and were in great measure controlled through their fears," overt violence was frequently used on male schoolteachers. John Dunlap of Shelbyville, Tennessee, was shot at and his body badly lacerated from a whipping. Another Tennessee teacher, L. S. Frost, was beaten and his body coated with a mixture of turpentine, tar, and lampblack. In Cross Plains, Alabama, schoolmaster William C. Luke and his four black teaching assistants were arrested and jailed on trivial charges; Klansmen then took them by force from the jail and murdered them. Many other white schoolmasters barely escaped similar fates. In Madison County, Alabama, E. Mulligan was taken from his home by Klansmen who told him, "We do not intend that any school shall be organized or allow any school teacher to stay or live in this portion of the country." After whipping Mulligan's two black assistants, they said to him, "Come up here, you God-damned schoolteacher, it is your turn next." Mulligan sprang and ran from them as fast as he could, barely ducking two shots fired at his head. The same thing happened to a twenty-three-year-old Irish immigrant

Cornelius McBride, who taught a black school in Chickasaw County, Mississippi.

As a rule, women schoolteachers were safer than men from Ku-Klux violence. The Klan preferred to scare female teachers into leaving through written warnings, such as this one:

> Ere the next quarter be gone! Unholy teacher of the blacks, begone ere it is too late. Punishment awaits you, and such horrors as no man ever underwent and lived. . . . Fool! Adulterer and Cursed Hypocrite! The far-piercing eye of the grand Cyclops is upon you. Fly the wrath to come.

Other schoolmarms were subjected to obscene pictures and narratives that Klansmen sent through the mail. Some were whipped. And many had to stand and watch helplessly as Klansmen set fire to their schoolhouses. Sarah Allen from Geneseo, Illinois, who was teaching in Mississippi, said of the Klansmen who visited her, "They treated me gentlemanly and quietly, but when they went away I concluded that they were savages—demons!" The Ku-Klux had a different opinion of themselves. To one teacher, they wrote, "We can inform you that we are the law itself and that an order from these Headquarters is supreme above all others."

Of other carpetbaggers targeted by the Klan, the next most frequent victims were local officials such as Republican sheriffs, election managers, and revenue officers. Revenue officers were especially given a hard time. Klansmen despised being taxed for any portion of the Reconstruction governments; and "moonshiners" resented having their illegal activities interfered with by the federal agents then stationed in the South. R. J. Donaldson, a revenue officer in North Carolina's seventh district, was finally compelled to write to the U.S. Office of Internal Revenue. "I am no alarmist," Donaldson wrote, "nor am I easily convinced of danger, and although for a year past I have been frequently warned of danger to my self and family, I have carefully avoided mentioning or even acknowledging the existence of any party or organization here antagonistic to myself or to the Government. Now the time has come when my duty to the General Government and to the loyal citizens of this District demands my immediate action. . . . I know that throughout this district there exists a well organized society whose object is to control social and political action. . . . In every county they are destroying representative men, friends of the Government, both white and colored." From

North Carolina, another agent reported, "The spirit of defiance of the laws . . . is so violent that no officer dare undertake to enforce the law without running the risk of being bushwhacked or 'Ku-Kluxed,' and the people . . . boast that they will let no revenue officers come in here."

Of all "carpetbagging" revenue officers, collectors of school taxes were the most hated. Allen P. Huggins offers a representative case study. Huggins was a native of Michigan. He had served in the Union army, rising from private to lieutenant colonel by the end of the war. In 1865 he, like many Union soldiers, moved south. In Monroe County, Mississippi, Huggins rented a large tract of land and planted for two years; although he was successful at it, he realized the life of a farmer didn't suit him. He also didn't fit in very well with the locals. When he attempted to join the Baptist Church in Aberdeen, the pastor informed him that, as a Union soldier, he "had done wrong to the South" and "must repent of it" before he could be accepted into the congregation. Huggins icily refused. It bothered him that in Mississippi he was "not recognized as a Christian at all," and at this point his Republican principles began assuming something of a moral fervor. He joined the Freedmen's Bureau and served eighteen months as an officer. He came away from the bureau deeply impressed with the need to provide continuing support to Southern blacks. He didn't shrink from publicly expressing his belief that blacks were equal to whites in every respect and, according to local Klansmen, he encouraged blacks to assert themselves in obtaining their full measure of rights under the law. This behavior was obnoxious enough to native Mississippians, but after returning to Monroe County from his stint in the bureau, Huggins had the audacity to become superintendent of schools as well as assistant assessor of internal revenue.

Huggins did a good deal of traveling throughout his district, and it was his practice to pay various residents, black and white, to put him up overnight. On March 9, 1871, he was staying with a white man, Mr. George Ross. Earlier that day, he had been warned by a concerned black that the Ku-Klux was on his trail, that they had visited the house where he had spent the night previously, and that he should leave the county for his own safety. Huggins lightly dismissed the man's warning, telling him that no band of ruffians was going to attack a United States officer.

That evening, both he and Mr. Ross were awakened by a loud call outside for "the man who is in the house." Looking through the window, Huggins saw that the grounds were completely filled with white-robed horsemen whose steeds were also draped in white. He recalled:

I opened the door myself and stood where I could see them. I asked them if it was me they wanted and what they wanted of me. They answered that their business was with me altogether, that they were Ku-Klux or the law-makers of that county, and that they wanted to talk with me. They told me that at a regular meeting of their camp my case had been under consideration, and that they had certain warnings which it was necessary for them to give me. They said that, as I was in their power, like all other men I must obey and come out. I told them that I did not recognize their power over me and that under no circumstances would I venture out. . . . I told them, then, that if I could do anything to hasten their departure—to get them away from the house—I would do so, as the family was scared; that if they had any warnings to give me I would hear them and then do just as I chose about obeying them. They answered that it was against the rules of their camp to give their warnings in the presence of women and children. I told them that that being the case, it was useless to argue any further, that I would not go out. I then stepped inside and shut my door.

Huggins was dealing with one of the most disciplined Klan dens in the South, consisting of ex-Confederate soldiers, law students, and sons of good families—most of them in their twenties. The goal of this den was "to make it as disagreeable as possible" for agents of Reconstruction to live in Mississippi. And they believed that through Major Huggins's dealings with local blacks, he was making them "restless and intractable."

After Huggins refused to come out, the Klansmen lit a torch, rode up to the house and threatened to burn it down. By then, the entire Ross household was panicstricken. Huggins therefore went back to the door and asked the Klansmen what pledge they would make for his personal safety should he come out and talk with them. Their spokesman replied, "Not a hair of your head shall be injured. We are now as anxious as you are to get through this business and let the fears on the part of the family cease."

Huggins left the house, walked down to the gate, and the spokesman for the Klansmen rode forward. Huggins carefully observed that the Klansmen wore two-piece white costumes with pearl buttons sewed up the front—obviously the handiwork of their womenfolk. The Klan chief proceeded to read a decree that

Huggins must leave the county within ten days and that they should be relieved of all taxes within that time. According to Huggins, the decree was pronounced "in a very pompous manner and said it was given at a certain place and registered in hell." Unruffled by their decree, Huggins informed them that he could not possibly be held responsible for any tax except the school tax and that the state and county taxes amounted to over three times that amount. This information irked the Klansmen. One of them came forward and charged that Huggins was collecting "obnoxious taxes from southern gentlemen to keep damned old radicals in office." Another said that they were "opposed to the free school system entirely; that the whites could do as they had always done before; that they could educate their *own* children; that so far as the negroes were concerned, they did not need educating, only work."

"Well, sir," said the chief to Huggins, "what do you say to our warning? Will you leave?"

Huggins replied that he would leave Monroe County at his own pleasure and not until he was damned good and ready.

He was suddenly surrounded by twenty of the Klansmen and disarmed of his pistol. They then took him a quarter mile down the road into the woods, halted, and asked him if he still refused to leave the state. Huggins again refused. "You *must* leave the state," the Klan chief said. Undaunted, Huggins warned them to consider their actions carefully; if they left him alive he would do what he could to them, that he was a United States officer and would suffer no abuse from them. They then ordered him to remove his coat, and when he refused, they took it off by force. They asked him if he was *now* ready to leave the state. He wasn't.

They then showed me a rope with a noose and said that was for such as myself who were stubborn; that if I did not consent to leave, I should die—that dead men told no tales. At this time, I saw a man coming. . . . He had a stirrup-strap some inch and a quarter in width and at least an eighth of an inch thick.

The Klansmen proceeded to beat Huggins, the chief calling out the number of strokes and the strap being passed from man to man. This sharing in the torture was a common practice among Klan dens. It was done not so much to assure every member a part in the entertainment as to make each a *"particeps criminis"*: if one Klansman was caught, all would be liable and therefore likely to aid their captive brother.

After fifty lashes, Huggins was asked if he was now prepared to leave the county. He again refused, for, as one of the Klansmen himself acknowledged, Huggins "was pretty gritty" and had been taking his beating "like a little man."

Things now seemed serious to the Klansmen. It looked as if they would have to kill Huggins, "for, of course, the incident could not end there." But one of the den's big "six footers" walked up and asked for the strap. "He deliberately turned the buckle end, and with a terrific swing, he brought it down across the shoulders of Huggins." This burly Klansman gave the victim an additional twenty-five wallops, and Huggins passed out. When he regained consciousness, he saw the Klansmen still standing around him.

"He's not dead yet," one of them said. "He's a live man, and dead men tell no tales."

They pointed their pistols at him and said that if he were not gone in ten days they would kill him, "either privately or publicly." The disguised horsemen then trotted away as if they had been doing nothing more that evening than "stealing sheep." They later sent a rollicking account of the encounter to the Aberdeen *Tri-Weekly Examiner:*

> We gave him twenty-five lashes gently, then asked him if he would leave this part of the "moral vineyard." He replied very independently that he could not make any such promise. . . . Count Bismarck then took charge of the ribbon, and went up among the stars with it and came down on him, and if there is any truth in him he belched it out. We gave him ten days. . . . We hope he will fulfill his promise, for if we have to call on him any more, Ulysses will have to appoint an internal revenue officer to fill his place. We understand that [Huggins] and others have gone down to Jackson to see about organizing the militia; if so, when they return please tell them to notify us through your paper. We want them to move their command up on Splunge and Sipsey. We want them all up there to fertilize and enrich the soil.

Huggins was far more "gritty" than the Klansmen imagined. Not only did he refuse to leave Monroe County but he prosecuted two of the Klansmen he recognized, and from their confessions, twenty-six more of the den members were arrested and jailed. Huggins would also go to Washington, D.C., and effectively lobby for anti-Klan legislation.

If anything, Klansmen treated scalawags worse than they did carpetbaggers. They saw carpetbaggers as "foreigners" who "did not understand the negroes and were both incompetent and unwilling to control them," but there was no excuse for the scalawag, the native-born Southern white who happened to be a Republican. Scalawags were traitors who had turned knives in their brothers' backs, and their so-called crimes covered a broad spectrum. In Georgia, Joseph Addison was shot at and the lives of his family threatened just for voting Republican. John L. Coley was whipped for selling a pistol to a black. James Nance was "kluxed" for reporting to a magistrate the murder of a black by one of his white neighbors. In South Carolina, fifty-two-year-old Anthony Foster, who suffered from bad health, was forced to dance at gunpoint by Klansmen for voting Republican. John Neason was whipped for letting blacks hold meetings on his land. In Louisiana, a gentleman planter was threatened with the burning of his property for "renting niggers land." And in North Carolina, Republican state senator John Stephens, who also worked for the Freedman's Bureau, was decoyed into the Yanceyville courthouse and murdered by a large company of Klansmen containing some of the most respectable citizens of Caswell County.

Klan attacks on scalawags often involved some kind of sexual abuse. It was as if the behavior of scalawags represented a form of infidelity to the South, and Klansmen gladly assumed the role of vengeful spouses. For example, Mrs. Skates, a native of York County, South Carolina, hid three blacks who were running from the Klan in her home. After finding these men and beating them, Klansmen took Mrs. Skates outdoors, tore her clothing off, and poured tar into her vagina.

An infamous sexual outrage was committed on William "Buster" Champion in Spartanburg County, South Carolina. Champion was a scalawag in every respect. He had been a Union man before the war. An injured leg had kept him from serving in the Confederate army, so he was able to remain a loyal Unionist throughout the war. After the war, Champion served as a trial justice, and his impartiality whether dealing with blacks or whites made him an object of suspicion among his white neighbors. These suspicions deepened when Champion became a Republican and joined the Union League in his township. He also allowed a black school to be built on his land. Champion's neighbors eventually accused him of "affiliating" with the blacks and preaching black–white equality, which he denied. "I was a Republican," he explained, "and it drew the negroes to a person. I showed friendship to the negroes." As far as black–white social equality was concerned,

Champion didn't preach it because he knew his generation would never accept it. But he expected fellow whites, like himself, "to neighbor with" the freedman and "be friendly to him."

Two additional factors marked Champion as a target for the Klan. A Republican, he was appointed election manager in his predominantly Democratic township. And he took a public stand against the Klan, arguing that "no Christian-hearted or civilized man" could possibly join such an organization.

One October evening at eleven o'clock, a detachment of nearly fifty disguised Klansmen broke down Champion's door and began firing their pistols. "Get up, you damned radical son of a bitch!" they shouted. A friend staying with Champion was shot in the shoulder. The Klansmen grabbed him and Champion, tied their hands behind their backs, and booted them out the door. The two men were then marched several miles up the road, the Klansmen lightly informing Champion that he was going to be drowned in the Broad River.

In the meantime, an independent den of Klansmen (including a professor from Limestone College using his academic gown as a robe), had broken into the cabin of Mr. and Mrs. Clem Bowden, sixty-year-old blacks. Bowden was pursuing a successful career as a carpenter. He had managed to put away enough money to buy some land and, like Champion, had been appointed an election manager. The Bowdens were pulled from their bed and an ox yoke put around Mr. Bowden's neck. The two were then roughly led down the same road being traveled by the Champion party. At a clearing, the men with the Bowdens stripped them, tore switches off a tree, and whipped them.

Eventually, the men with Champion arrived at the same clearing. Neither den knew of the other's activities, for the Klansmen with the Bowdens proceeded to scatter and form battle lines. When they realized they were all brothers of the shroud, they rejoiced and consulted each other over how to make the most of the event.

Champion was blindfolded, stripped naked, and told to get on his knees and pray, since he only had moments to live. He was then beaten with sticks, switches, whips, pistol and rifle butts while Klansmen shouted, "Take that, you radical son of a bitch!" Champion suffered wounds on every part of his body. Two of his teeth were knocked out. A Klansman gave the frightened and injured Clem Bowden a switch and ordered him to join them in whipping Champion. Bowden managed to give Champion five feeble licks before the angry Klansman pushed him away and knocked him in the head for being such a timid torturer.

Next, Bowden was ordered to lie face down on the ground with his legs spread, and the nearly unconscious Champion was thrown onto Bowden's naked body. Two Klansmen spread Bowden's buttocks and forced William Champion to kiss his anus.

"Is he doing it? Is he doing it?" someone yelled excitedly.

"How do you like *that* for nigger equality!" crowed another.

Champion was then shoved against the terrified Mrs. Bowden and ordered to have sexual intercourse with her. He told them that in his condition it was impossible, and the Klansmen were satisfied with his kissing her genitalia.

Glutted by the evening's entertainment, the Klansmen ordered Champion and the Bowdens never again to vote the Republican ticket and led them back to their respective homes. A few days later, after Champion reported the outrage to the local magistrate, he received a letter in the mail:

HEADQUARTERS KU-KLUX CLAN, Algood, S.C.

BUSTER CHAMPION: We have been told that our visit to you was not a sufficient hint. We now notify you to leave the country within thirty days from the reception of this notice, or abide the consequences.

K.K.K.

One Klan visit was enough for these people. Both Champion and Mr. and Mrs. Bowden took the advice and moved to the city of Spartanburg, Champion abandoning his land and mill and the Bowdens their twelve acres of corn and cotton.

No group suffered more from Klan violence than blacks. The number of outrages committed upon them between 1868 and 1871 still defies reasonable estimation. The multitude that were murdered left no accounts. And most who survived were too frightened to report attacks on them to the law. The realness of their fear can be sensed in a postscript to a description of a Klan raid, hastily scrawled on a scrap of paper by a poor black farmer and sent to a local bureau officer.

I write this to you in confidence that you will not reveal my name. I have been call[ed] all the hard things that any poor man ever did bear, and [have] been nearly murder[ed] by a crowd holding me and cutting me with their [k]nives. I would have come to [see] you before now but I would be in danger of my life if it was [k]nown.

Even the few blacks who dared to prosecute their assailants invariably lost their cases, for members of Klan dens were notorious for providing alibis for each other. And after unsuccessful prosecutions, it was common for victorious Klansmen to retaliate and to sue their black accusers for defamation of character or to charge them with perjury.

The vast majority of black victims of Klan violence were voting Republicans. Sometimes being a Republican was sufficient to warrant a visit and whipping by the Klan. This was particularly true in such areas as the South Carolina upcountry, where the suppression of enough GOP votes could ensure a Democratic victory. In these regions, such people as Jackson Surratt and Alfred Richardson could be whipped for nothing more than "voting the radical ticket." Elsewhere, it took a Republican vote combined with some "misdemeanor" to warrant a Klan visit. Willis Johnson in Newberry County, South Carolina, for example, was "kluxed" not only for voting Republican but for distributing Republican ballots to his friends. Seventy-year-old Wallace Fowler was murdered not just for being a Republican but for catching the son of a Klansman stealing his watermelons. Klan raids on black communities often increased right before an election. Tom Rosboro would long remember the visit paid on his father by Klansmen who said they "would take notice of him on election day," and there's no question that Klansmen and their informers closely watched the polls. Scipio Eager of Georgia was whipped and his brother killed for voting Republican after Klansmen told them not to. Once under Klan surveillance, a black had little recourse for his personal safety other than publishing a statement in the local paper that he had renounced the Republican party:

Anthony Thurster, the negro preacher who was so severely whipped by a party of disguised men near Maxley's lately, asks that we announce to his white friends that from this time forward he will prove himself a better man; *will never again make a political speech, deliver a sermon, or vote a Republican ticket:* from henceforth he is an unswerving Democrat. We are glad that Anthony's eyes are at last opened to a proper course for him to pursue, but sorry that such stringent measures had to be adopted ere he would, as it were, be "born again."

The upshot for the Southern black Republican was, tragically, as Essic Harris claimed: "They way things are, we cannot vote. That's just the way it is. It's not worthwhile for a man to vote and run the risk of his life."

A black Republican increasingly risked his life to the degree he was willing to assume the political and educational leadership of his people. Black schoolteachers suffered twice as many homicides as their white colleagues. Some Klansmen had orders to shoot black leaders of the Union League on sight. Thus in Madison County, Alabama, a League organizer named Campbell, whose wife was seven months pregnant, was shot in his bed by a Klan den and then taken outside and shot another six times until he died. Abraham Wamble, a Mississippi minister and speaker at black political rallies, was shot through the head seven times by Klansmen. Charles Hendricks, an election manager of Gwinnett County, Georgia, survived being shot in the intestines by Klansmen, but his injuries prevented him from further political activity.

A black politician literally carried his life in his hands. Among political murder victims of the Klan were State Representative James Martin and Senator B. F. Randolph of South Carolina; and Representatives Benjamin Inge and Richard Burke of Alabama. Representative Thomas M. Allen escaped being murdered because Klansmen mistakenly killed his brother-in-law. Other black politicians who were "kluxed" and survived included Representatives George W. Houston, Romulus Moore, and Abram Colby. Colby had been offered $2,500 to turn Democrat and refused.

One of the most remarkable black political leaders to survive a Klan assault was Elias Hill of York County, South Carolina. Hill had contracted muscular dystrophy at age seven, and the disease took an insidious course. His legs never grew larger than a man's wrists and he was unable to walk, crawl, or even move about in bed without the use of a "pry stick." Over the years, his arms withered, his jaw became affected, and he could eat and speak only with great difficulty. He was more or less in constant pain. While Hill was still a small child, his father had managed to buy his freedom from his master and, after working a while, returned to buy his wife. Not wanting to care for a hopeless cripple, the master threw Elias in free with his mother. Elias Hill therefore grew up before the war as a free man in an intact family. Unable to walk or function, he became something of a pet to white schoolchildren who taught him to read and write—after all, what was the harm of teaching forbidden knowledge to such a helpless individual?

Due to superior intelligence, however, and the courage necessary to overcome the limitations of a profound handicap, Hill became an influential and charismatic leader among his people. The little gnomelike man was carried on a platform to a number of schools where he taught and lectured. He studied and obtained a license as a Baptist minister, and his sermons on overcoming one's limitations were especially stirring. He became president of his local Union League. His political opinions were highly valued, and his little cabin became a regular meeting place for discussions of religious and political matters. In all, Elias Hill embodied the triumph of the black will—a fact that irritated York County Klansmen to no end.

In 1871, Hill was fifty years old. One evening in May, he was awakened by the sound of dogs barking and horses tramping into the yard. Hill's brother and his wife lived on the same tract of land with him, and the Klansmen went first to their cabin. Hill could hear the men slapping his sister-in-law.

"Where's Elias?" they demanded.

She finally broke down. "Yon is his house."

Two of the men broke down Hill's door and looked all over the cabin before spying the little body curled on the mat.

"Here he is! Here he is! We've found him!"

The two men took hold of each of Hill's puny arms and dragged him out into the yard. The Klansmen then accused him of inciting the blacks to burn barns and ravish white women, which he denied. Unhappy with that answer, they beat him in the head with their fists. Then they said they knew he had been corresponding with Congressman A. S. Wallace. What had he been writing?

"Only tidings," Hill weakly replied.

"Damned good tidings!" said one of the Klansmen. "Haven't you been preaching and praying against the Ku-Klux?"

Hill told them that copies of the letters were in his cabin. If they allowed him, he would get them so they could read them. Two Klansmen went into the cabin and ransacked it. Hill heard them smash his prized clock.

"Don't break any private property, gentlemen," said the Klan spokesman outside. "We got him that we came for and that's all we want."

The cabin was too dark for the letters to be found. The Klansmen outside dragged Hill to the middle of the yard, knowing that he couldn't move from the spot, and all six went into the cabin to search for the letters. Finding what they wanted, they came back outside. One of them picked up Hill by his crippled legs, which had severely contracted over the years. He screamed out in pain.

"God damn it, hush!" the Klansman snapped. He told Hill to pull up his shirt and proceeded to beat him with a horsewhip until he was senseless.

The Klansmen then informed Hill that they were going to take him and throw him in the river. When they saw that Hill was prepared to meet this fate, they consulted with each other. They then asked him if he would put a notice in the local paper renouncing Republicanism. Would he cancel his subscription to the weekly Republican paper he was receiving from Charleston? Would he stop preaching? After Hill agreed to their demands, they dragged him over to his brother's house and dumped him on the stoop. Before riding off, one of them said, "Don't you pray against the Ku-Klux. . . . Don't pray against us. Pray that God may bless and save us."

One attack like this was enough for Elias Hill. Through Congressman Wallace and the American Colonization Society, Hill arranged to emigrate to Liberia along with nearly seventy black families. Before leaving the United States, Hill told a Congressional committee: "We do not believe it is possible, from the past history and present aspect of affairs, for our people to live in this country peaceably and educate and elevate their children to any degree which they desire. They do not believe it possible. Neither do I."

Aside from Republican politics and leadership, other blacks were "kluxed" for legal and labor squabbles. Aleck Stewart of Monroe County, Mississippi, was whipped by Klansmen for having the gall to sue his white employer for back wages. Jake Dannons, a successful blacksmith in Walton County, Georgia, was shot dead by Klansmen after refusing to do any more work for a white man who never paid him. Daniel Lane of Georgia was raided and whipped with hickory sticks by Klansmen after hiring a black woman to hoe his land who had earlier refused to work for a white farmer. In South Carolina, Harriet Hernandes and her child were whipped when she refused to break her labor contract with one white man to work for another. Columbus Jeter was raided after declining to buy a horse from a Klansman who wanted 20 percent interest. Samuel Simmons carried out his landlady's request and traded her horse to a white man for a mule; later wanting his mule back, the disgruntled trader had Simmons "kluxed" after he refused to renege on the deal.

Issues relating to land rights and use caused countless incidents of Klan violence upon blacks. William Coleman, an industrious black who purchased eighty acres of choice land in Winston County, Mississippi, was brutally whipped by a Klan den and left to die. Caroline Benson, her daughter, and her son-in-law were all whipped for buying a small tract of land from a widow who had previously refused to sell it to a white. The practice of sharecropping caused endless altercations between blacks and whites. All through the South, white landowners soon learned that share-cropping contracts could be drawn up, blacks could work the land, and Klan raids could be used to drive the blacks from the land as soon as their portion of the crops came due. Major cities became refugee centers for blacks run off by the Klan at harvest time. A black spokesman for the people exiled in Atlanta said, "As soon as their crops are made they are driven off and not allowed to gather them. They are here suffering through the winter because they are not allowed to remain in the country."

The exaggerated charges of black rape during Reconstruction have been discussed earlier, but the incidents of rape committed on black women by Klansmen have received less coverage. It appears, however, that the desire for group intercourse was sometimes sufficient reason for a den to go out on a raid. In Broomtown, Alabama, the family of Mrs. Reaner Berry was visited by a den of Klansmen who broke down her door before she could open it. Inside the cabin were Mrs. Berry's son George, his wife, and a neighbor girl who was staying with them. The Klansmen informed the women that they "wanted to bed with them." When they refused, the Klansmen gave George thirty lashes and raped Mrs. Berry and the neighbor girl; George's wife escaped rape only through her plea that she had recently miscarried and was still bleeding. Near Raleigh, North Carolina, the nineteen-year-old daughter of Mrs. Gilmore was repeatedly raped and beaten by Klansmen who later set fire to her pubic hair, leaving it "singed to the flesh." Sometimes during a political raid, Klansmen would rape the female members of the household as a matter of course. It was inevitable for the excitement of "kluxing" helpless victims to carry over into sexual forms of expression. Caroline Benson reported that the Klansmen who stripped her and her daughter prior to beating them "laughed and made great sport. Some of them just squealed the same as if they were stable horses just brought out."

While Klansmen sometimes violated black women simply for being women, they occasionally assaulted black men simply for being prosperous. Although the economic independence of the ex-slave was one of the primary goals of the Freedmen's Bureau, it was anathema to the white South. When O. O. Howard learned that the Klan was crushing one of the bureau's major hopes, he was beside himself. Writing to the Secretary of War, he claimed that prosperous blacks were being driven from their farms and businesses by the Klan: "Other good industrious freedmen are about to leave; [they] say that the old slaveholders cannot bear that they 'should be getting up and doing well.' Their intelligence and prosperity *exile* them." Seventy-seven-year-old Andrew Cathcart of South Carolina had the skill and prudence to save enough money to buy a ninety-eight-acre plantation; he was whipped by a den of Klansmen who stole his money and valuables and then burned down the schoolhouse he had built on his property for his daughter. Alfred Richardson was a successful businessman who owned three separate tracts of land and co-owned a grocery store with his brother. Nervous whites had warned him, "They say you are making too much money [and] they do not allow any nigger to rise that way." During a Klan raid, Richardson took nearly twenty shots into his hip and legs before escaping. Anderson Ferrel of Georgia was another independent black, and a den of Klansmen whipped him, as they said, "to teach you the difference between a white man and a nigger."

Unfortunately the fate suffered by Henry Lowther at the hands of Klansmen was not unique. Lowther was a forty-one-year-old freedman from Wilkinson County, Georgia. In addition to being an active Republican, he was a prosperous shopkeeper as well. "I worked for my money and carried on a shop," Lowther said. Some of the white citizens "got broke and did not pay me, and I sued them. They have been working at me ever since I've been free. I had too much money."

The first time the Klan visited him, Lowther managed to escape through the back door and hide in the brush. Before leaving, the frustrated Klansmen told Mrs. Lowther that her husband had five days to leave town. The next day, taking them at their word, Lowther gathered up his money in preparation for leaving, but his friend Bose Lavender talked him out of it. Lavender suggested getting up a company of men and standing guard at Lowther's house to repel the Ku-Klux when they returned. By a curious coincidence, on this same day, a white woman who lived near Lowther and whose land he occasionally tended propositioned him to have sex with her. Unfortunately, Lowther complied. The woman was considered a "low-down tramp" in town and was known to sleep regularly with black as well as white men. But the fact that she had propositioned Lowther the day after the Klan's visit suggests that the Klan may have put her up to it, possibly even paying her for the setup.

In any case, Bose Lavender's band of men guarded Lowther's house for the next three nights. A few days later, Lowther was arrested for "maintaining an armed camp" and put in jail. Lowther was terrified of being in jail. Matt Deason, the Republican sheriff, had just been murdered; and the bailiff and deputies now in charge of the jail were known to be active members of the local Klan den. Lowther's fears were quickly justified. At two o'clock in the morning, a disguised Klansman entered the jail and took Lowther out into the street. Looking around, he saw to his horror that the streets were filled with shrouded Ku-Klux—perhaps over one hundred of them.

They took him off to a swamp, some two miles from town. Within a hundred yards of the swamp, one of the Klansmen brought out a rope, and thinking he was going to be hanged, Lowther fell to his knees and begged for his life. There was some conversation among the Klansmen, and they marched him further on. Well into the dark swamp, the party again halted and there was more conversation. Suddenly, every Klansman cocked his gun and pointed it at Lowther. Lowther was certain he was going to be shot to death and, as he recalled, "I didn't care much then."

To his surprise, the Klan leader came up to him and asked whether he preferred to be murdered or "altered." After choosing the latter, Henry Lowther was pushed to the ground and castrated.

"Now," said a Klansman after the crude surgery had been performed, "as soon as you can get to a doctor, go to one. You know the doctors in this county. And as soon as you are able to leave, do it—or we'll kill you next time." Lowther asked how long it would take for him to get well and was told five to six weeks. The Klansmen then rode off.

Nearly naked and profusely bleeding, Lowther walked two and a quarter miles before coming to the first house. It was the jailer's house, and lights were on. Lowther called out for help, but the jailer refused. "You must!" Lowther cried. "I am naked and nearly froze to death!" It was obvious he would get no help from the jailer, so he walked on into town and stopped at the first store that had a light. It was filled with men. Lowther begged them for help, but they too refused to come out. He continued walking, clutching the sides of buildings, until he came to the local doctor's house. He cried out for the doctor, but the doctor wasn't at home.

At this point, Lowther fell to the ground unconscious. He woke up several hours later and barely managed to get to a black woman's house who ran to Lowther's son who, finally, got his father a doctor. The next day, the black community reported that Henry Lowther's blood was spread all over the downtown area. The white community agreed that Lowther's punishment had been severe, but what did he expect after ravishing a white woman? After five weeks of recuperation, Lowther abandoned his home and business and moved to Atlanta.

"Great is chivalry!" mocked the Memphis *Daily Post*. "Do scenes like this indicate progress in civilization or in barbarism?" There were arguments for both sides. In the North, people were starting to become concerned about the Klan; Republican papers and journals, such as Greeley's influential New York *Tribune*, had kept the atrocities committed by the Klan in the forefront of the news. Democratic papers, however, rationalized Ku-Klux violence as a necessity aimed at quelling disturbances caused by insolent and incendiary blacks.

One thing is certain: By 1871, the Klan had rendered Southern Republicans, law officers, and military commanders equally helpless. In Texas, General John Reynolds reported that murders of blacks were "so common as to render it impossible to keep an accurate record of them." In Mississippi, the Klan was driving nearly every teacher of a black school out of the state. In Georgia and South Carolina, unsolved murders were being committed at the rate of nearly two a month. All over the South, hundreds of blacks were sleeping in the woods for fear of Klan visits to their cabins. Some, like a group led by Charles Snyder in North Carolina, decided to call it quits and emigrate to Liberia, claiming, "There is nothing in this country for a black man that has common sense but cruelty, starvation and bloodshed." The rest, like a black schoolteacher in Alabama, stuck to their course and hoped for the best: "Bands of Ku-Klux prowl like wolves through the country for prey," he wrote to his superintendent, "and every week brings us tidings of some fresh work of midnight villainy. . . . This place is threatened, and you may yet have to write my obituary. God only knows. I am now living by the moment."

"LET US HAVE PEACE"

*Congress, the Klan,
and the End of Reconstruction:
1870–1877*

*I*n 1868, "Let us have peace" was a campaign slogan that had appealed to everyone, and no candidate could have espoused it more sincerely than Ulysses S. Grant. The squat, bearded general who had won the war seemed destined to be the President who could win the peace. Already he had won the hearts of the people. To Northerners, he was a military genius and hero; to Southerners, he seemed a gentleman because of his kindness toward Lee at Appomattox. In an era of self-importance, Grant's humility was endearing. No one seems to have better typified the average American of his day. "Let us have peace" were words that would launch Grant's political career and provide the inscription over the portals of his tomb. He was a man whose beginnings often foreshadowed their ends. Consider, for example, his first inauguration.

On March 4, 1869, the President-elect was greeted at the Capitol by a large cheering crowd. While "Smiling" Schuyler Colfax was sworn in as vice-president in the senate chamber, Grant sat wonderfully "calm and self possessed," looking dapper in a black suit and ruining an expensive pair of straw-colored kid gloves with his ubiquitous cigar. Escorted out onto the portico, Grant waited impatiently for the cessation of a twenty-two gun salute, followed by the screaming of sirens, brass bands, and cheers of his countrymen. After being sworn in as the eighteenth president, he began his inaugural address. There was "no sign of embarrassment" as he spoke. "His words were firm, his delivery was clear," and for all anyone knew it might have been a great speech, if only they could have heard it. As it was, his softspoken words were inaudible "at a distance of more than thirty feet all around him."

The inaugural ball was held in the brand-new Treasury Building next to the White House. Only two matters had disturbed the planning committee: Should Andrew Johnson be invited, and what should be done about any "colored people" who might want to come? The committee decided against inviting the ex-president, and the other problem was mercifully solved "by the colored people themselves, who declined to attend in any event." At least that was the way the newspapers explained it.

From the moment the doors of the Treasury Building were opened until eleven in the evening, the "stream of living beings pouring into the reception rooms was continuous. By nine o'clock the rooms were crowded, by ten o'clock it was a jam." No one had bothered to anticipate how many people would come to celebrate the happiest occasion in Washington since the ending of the war. Soon, the atmosphere laden with respiration and perspiration began stifling not only the guests but the gaslights, which faded to "a hazy twilight." President Grant appeared at 10:35 P.M. Taking one look at the sea of eager faces, he hurriedly squeezed through and disappeared for the rest of the evening. The crowd of celebrants then grew so congested, that the police had to be called out to cut a swath through them. Dancing was virtually impossible. Although the orchestra bubbled with polkas and quadrilles, the chock-a-block couples could barely move. Whenever dancers snapped at each other "on account of the reckless treading on corns or the careless trespassing on ladies' trains," some wit would say, "Let us have peace," and composure was restored in the laughter that followed. But not for long. Plenty of food had been provided, but no one could get through to the banquet table. "Seven-eighths of the crowd went home hungry without obtaining even a sight of the table."

At 2:00 A.M., the New York Times correspondent wired a post-script to his first story: "The scene at the ball now baffles all description. The crowd has degenerated into a perfect crush. The confusion in the cloak room is beyond conception. Hundreds of gentlemen are leaving the building without coats or hats; and ladies, faint with exhaustion, are in vain waiting or making fruitless search for their outer wrappings." Starving guests had finally been driven to break down the doors of the kitchen but were repulsed by a terrified cook who threw nasty wet towels at them. In the meantime, there was "bedlam among the hackmen" in Fifteenth Street, and guests who had been successful in finding their coats went outside to discover that their cabs had abandoned them. Tired, hungry and irritable, many were forced to walk home. "Everything today has been a great success," the *Times* correspondent concluded. "But the inaugural ball tonight is too much of a success to be really a good thing."

In its first four years, this is how the new administration would deal with the problem of the Klan: Grant's determination to secure the safety of Southern Republicans by fighting the Ku-Klux would be compromised by poor planning and meager appropriations; more Klansmen would be arrested and indicted than could be accommodated by the Justice Department; courts would be left starving for funds and personnel; and hopes for peace would end in confusion and disappointment.

Ever since the passage of the Reconstruction acts, the South had taunted the North with the injustice of enfranchising Southern blacks when they were still denied the ballot in a majority of states above the Mason–Dixon line. Although it could be argued that only in the South was the ballot necessary to prevent the reenslavement of blacks, the accusations were nevertheless true. It became embarrassingly true when liberal organs such as the *Independent* scolded Republicans for the fact that black equality was "sooner achieved in Mississippi than in Illinois—sooner on the plantation of Jefferson Davis than around the grave of Abraham Lincoln." Congress eventually came through with the Fifteenth Amendment, which forbade denying suffrage anywhere in the United States on the basis of race. Grant threw his enthusiastic support to the amendment and, in his finest hour as president, hailed its ratification on March 30, 1870, as "the most important event that has occurred since the nation came into life." In Washington, D.C., cannons boomed to announce "this greater revolution than that of 1776."

With the paradox characteristic of Reconstruction lawmaking, the Fifteenth Amendment served both the interests of democracy and the Republican Party. It was likely to boost Republican strength in the North and arm the party, at last, with a means of fighting the Klan in the South. General Howard and others intimate with Klan terrorism had long argued that "unless Congress interferes in some way," the Klan would devastate Republican strength in the South; but GOP lawmakers had bickered over how they could interfere in a way that was both effective and constitutional. The Fifteenth Amendment now permitted the federal government to take any action necessary to enforce its provisions, and in spring 1870, Republicans began working on a bill aimed at curbing the Klan.

Democrats thought it unnecessary to legislate against a "myth." After all, the Klan was "poppycock" to the New York *World*. The Columbia, South Carolina, *Daily Phoenix* compared it with "ghosts, hobgoblins, jack-o'-the-lanterns" and other humbugs of "the witches of New England, whose larvae, having long lain dormant . . . in the carpetbags of some pious political priests, germinated in the too credulous minds" of Southern blacks and radicals. Republicans responded to the jibes by reading long, sickening accounts of Ku-Klux violence into the *Congressional Globe*. These recitals infuriated Democrats who condemned them as transparent attempts at manufacturing an emotional issue for the 1870 campaigns. "The Republican leaders need new material for inflaming the public mind," said the New York *World*. Alluding to a passage in Gibbon's *Decline and Fall of the Roman Empire*, the *World* predicted that Southern outrages would provide Republicans with "a 'bloody shirt' to be borne aloft in their electioneering processions." Over the next several years, accusing Republicans of "waving the bloody shirt" for political reasons would become an effective gimmick for Democrats to dismiss the reality of Klan violence.

Given their majority, Republicans passed the first act to enforce the Fifteenth Amendment on May 31, 1870. The new statute banned the use of force, bribery, or intimidation to interfere with voting. Election officers would be held accountable for justice at the polls. Troops of the U.S. Army would supervise elections and make arrests if necessary.

In spite of or because of the Enforcement Act, the 1870 elections witnessed an unprecedented wave of Klan violence in portions of the South. The fact that the enforcement machinery depended so much upon local authority was at the heart of the problem. In Madison County, Alabama, Probate Judge Lewis M. Douglas wrote to General Crawford, claiming, "The civil authorities are insufficient to check the outrages upon its citizens, and I most respectfully request you to send troops. . . ." Even when troops were sent they were hamstrung by having to remain subordinate to ambivalent local officials. From Alabama, a frustrated Lieutenant Charles Harkins reported: "The civil officers are paralyzed with fear and make no effort to discharge their duties. Public sentiment is suppressed. Men are afraid to denounce or expose criminals. . . ." This deplorable situation, said Harkins, was "the work of a strong, well-organized secret society and not the acts of a few individuals as supposed by some of the citizens." Even when a Klansman was arrested, he was soon free on bail. Major Charles Morgan reported from North Carolina that "the commissioner's office is made the scene of merrymaking and levity during the making out of bail bonds."

Elsewhere in the South, the Enforcement Act had little effect. Essentially a voters' rights bill, it could hardly stop the Klan from burning down schools in Mississippi. It was useless in Tennessee, where Klan intimidation of Republican voters had already swung the state to the conservatives; a Tennessee Republican complained, "We are driven to the wall, and can't go any further. . . . Not one Ku-Klux has ever been punished, not one even arrested." And Ku-Klux terrorists had virtually taken over the South Carolina upcountry; in two of these northern counties, Governor Scott reported that "few Republicans dare sleep in their houses at night."

Only in North Carolina, however, did an intrastate war break out between the Republican state government and the Ku-Klux Klan. In his third annual message of 1870, Governor William Holden presented a grim analysis of the Invisible Empire in North Carolina. Holden found it impossible to say how many people had fallen victim to the Klan, but their number included state legislators, sheriffs, schoolteachers, and countless black voters. "Some of these victims were shot," he said, "some were whipped, some of them were hanged, some of them were drowned, some of them were tortured, some had their mouths lacerated with gags; one of them had his ears cropped; and others, of both sexes, were subjected to indignities which were disgraceful not merely to civilization but to humanity itself." Holden claimed that nearly forty thousand Klansmen were active in the state of North Carolina alone—all of them united by an infernal bond of loyalty. "Consequently," he continued, "grand juries in many counties frequently refused to find bills against the members of this Klan for the gravest and most flagrant violations of law."

Governor Holden was eventually forced to call out the militia to put down the Klan in North Carolina, but the plan backfired miserably. Due to the blunders of the militia under the inept command of Colonel George Kirk and the outraged response to it by the Democratic press (as well as continued Klan intimidations of black voters), the conservatives won the 1870 elections in North Carolina. At this point, Governor Holden panicked. Writing to President Grant, he said, "This organized conspiracy is in existence in every county of the State. And its aim is to obtain the control of the government. It is believed that its leaders now direct the movements of the present Legislature." The governor was right. Within weeks, the new legislature began proceedings to impeach Holden who was ultimately forced to resign. The Klan had "redeemed" the Tarheel State, which was back in the Democratic fold.

When the lame-duck Congress convened after the 1870 elections, it was obvious to every Republican that far more had to be done to secure the rights of citizens under the Fifteenth Amendment. Moving so swiftly that Democrats were dumbfounded, the GOP passed a second enforcement act providing for more direct federal supervision of congressional elections. This act unnerved many in the North as well as the South, who feared that the government was becoming "centralized." And it is true that this point in American history—not the New Deal—marks the first major peacetime absorption by the federal government of powers and protective functions formerly allotted to the states. Even so, the "centralized" government was too new and uncertain to deal effectively with the harassment of individual citizens by such an elusive, guerrilla-like organization as the Klan.

Senate Republicans therefore called for a complete investigation of the outrage to civil rights that had occurred in North Carolina, and ruffled Democrats just as promptly asked "What outrage?" Senator Eugene Casserly of California exclaimed that he was sick and tired of this "exaggerated outcry of outrages in the South." Senator Allen Thurman of Ohio chided Republicans for their obsession with a "mysterious or mythical Ku-Klux Klan." At this point, Justin Morrill, the hoary abolitionist senator from Vermont, rose to speak. "Is there a senator from one of these 'restored' states who does *not* avow and does *not* bear testimony to the frequency of these outrages and murders?" he asked. "Why, Mr. President, there can be no one so blind, I think, as to dispute the general fact of these murders throughout the South. . . . And it is a matter of lamentation to us all, or *should* be."

Senate Democrats were forced to go along with the appointment of a select committee headed by John Scott (Republican, Pennsylvania) to investigate the situation in North Carolina. From January to February 1871, the Scott Committee examined fifty-two witnesses, including Klan victims, frustrated law-enforcement personnel, and six flesh-and-blood Klansmen. Of the latter, the most dramatic witness was James E. Boyd—former Confederate soldier, devout Southerner, and ex-Klansman whose growing revulsion toward the Invisible Empire compelled him finally to renounce it. The Civil War might formally be over, Boyd said, but through the Klan the "Lost Cause" had simply gone underground. The Confederate veterans who made up the bulk of Klan membership were encouraged to whip, maim, and murder—to do anything they had been required to do as Rebel soldiers to achieve their goals, which were now aimed at the overthrow of Reconstruction and the complete disfranchisement of blacks. Boyd's testimony made chills run down the spines of the Republican investigators. The idea of the Klan as the "ghost" of the Confederacy had long been laughable, but it now took on new meaning. Boyd was asked whether the Klan was composed of disconnected bands of night riders or if it was organized. "The organization is very complete," he replied, "from the commander-in-chief down to the lieutenants in the camps."

After completing its investigation, the Scott Committee would report that the Ku-Klux Klan was anything but a myth: Its numbers were large and its organization strong; its goals were those of the "defeated" Confederacy; it used any degree of violence necessary to achieve its illegal ends and was impervious to existing forms of law enforcement. While Capitol Hill calmly awaited this balanced conclusion, the zeal and impatience of a singular congressman made him draft a third and formidable enforcement bill with long-reaching effects. The man was former General, now Congressman Benjamin Franklin Butler of Massachusetts.

During the war, the New York Times determined that Butler was the object of more "public interest and attention" than any other military man. The North had applauded his controversial and highly creative decision of 1861 proclaiming slaves a "contraband of war." After capturing New Orleans, Butler had ruled the city justly but with complete intolerance for the slightest brooking of his authority or expression of Confederate spirit. He hanged a New Orleans man simply for tearing down the Stars and Stripes. And when the city's genteel ladies persisted in verbally abusing and spitting on Union soldiers, he issued a general order that hence-forth any such woman was to be treated as a prostitute "plying her avocation." This gross insult to Southern womanhood so infuriated the Confederacy that its newspapers reviled Butler as "the Beast." Jefferson Davis responded with an order that if Butler were captured he could be summarily executed without formal hearing, and Butler delighted in the fact that no other Union general received such an honor.

As a radical Republican, Congressman Butler took the unswerving position that the rebellious South had been thoroughly trounced in the war; and as a vanquished foe, Dixie could either toe the line or receive a Yankee boot up her collective behind. Consequently, during an 1870 tour through the former Confederacy, Englishman David Macrae noted that "Butler is detested in the South more perhaps than any man that lives." He was a controversial figure in the North as well. To many, he was simply a cross-eyed, bald-headed son of a bitch. To others, he was the most outspoken champion of civil rights since the death of Thaddeus Stevens in 1868. If Democrats detested his libertarian views, they could be thankful that he was only a congressman and not president of the United States. As a turncoat Democrat, Butler had been Lincoln's first choice for vice president in 1864; when offered the slot, however, he sent the President a jocular refusal, saying he would consider running for vice president only if Lincoln could assure him he would die in office within three months of the inauguration.

Butler now had considerable influence with President Grant. Nearly nine months before the Scott Committee's investigation, Butler and his son-in-law Adelbert Ames (a carpetbag senator from Mississippi) had counseled and cajoled the President to get rid of his mossback attorney general, Ebenezer Rockwood Hoar, and appoint in his place a Southerner with a strong commitment to civil rights. When Butler pointed out the benefits that could accrue to the President beyond that of strengthening Reconstruction policy, Grant acquiesced. The "virtuous Hoar," as he was sometimes called, was fired and replaced by Amos T. Akerman, who became the most influential attorney general of the Reconstruction period. Akerman was a complex man—New Hampshire born and Georgia raised, a veteran of the Confederate Army and a champion of civil rights. As a U.S. district attorney for Georgia, Akerman's devotion to justice and contempt for the Klan brought him to the attention of prominent Republicans. Butler knew that, with a man like Akerman heading the newly created Department of Justice, the time was right for a really radical approach to fighting the Ku-Klux Klan.

On February 13, before the Scott Committee had submitted its report, Butler presented to the House of Representatives a new enforcement bill of such stringency and revolutionary import that it stunned members of his own party and sent Democrats reeling into paroxysms of rage. For the next sixty years, historians would denounce the "Ku-Klux Act," as it was called, as the most loathsome, despotic piece of legislation since the Alien and Sedition Acts. Despite his best endeavor, Butler was unable to get his bill passed in its original form. Republicans seemed genuinely frightened of it and preferred to buy time with less controversial measures, such as a resolution calling for a complete investigation of the Klan throughout the South. This joint investigation by members of the House and Senate would again be chaired by John Scott and would hopefully offer insights as to the best way to legislate against the Klan. And there matters sat.

Miraculously, a number of events were reported from the South that turned things completely around. First of all, Governor Scott reached the end of his rope in South Carolina and asked President Grant for troops to suppress the Ku-Klux nightmare in the up-country of his state. Grant immediately complied. Mississippi then captured the news. In Meridian, a riot broke out during a court-house trial with results that left congressmen speechless: The judge and seven of eight black witnesses were shot to death right in the courtroom; when the eighth witness was found to be still alive, he was thrown from a second-story window; the mayor of Meridian was then thrust on board a train by an armed band and told not to get off till he reached the North; and State Representative J. Aaron Moore, a black, was hunted through the Mississippi woods like an animal, barely escaping with his life. Unable to find Moore, the outlaws burned down his house. Writing to Senator Ames, Moore said: "I am driven from home, and have no house that I can put my family in. What shall I do? I thank my God that I am yet alive. There will never be any peace at Meridian until it is put under martial law. . . ."

Close on the heels of the Meridian riot came news of the Klan's assault on Major Allen P. Huggins, the Mississippi revenue officer and school superintendent who had refused to leave the state in spite of his brutal beating by Klansmen. Major Huggins was now in Washington giving an account of his experience to the Treasury Department. His story received wide attention in the press.

Next, from Kentucky of all places—a state that had remained in the Union during the war—came a petition from a delegation of Frankfort blacks, begging for protection from the Klan. "We believe you are not familiar," they told Congress, with the number of Klansmen "riding nightly over the country . . . spreading terror wherever they go by robbing, whipping, ravishing and killing our people without provocation." The Kentucky legislature had recently adjourned, they said, refusing to enact any form of legislation to curb the Klan's violence. "We would state," they continued, "that we have been law-abiding citizens, pay our tax, and in many parts of the state our people have been driven from the polls, refused the right to vote. Many have been slaughtered while attempting to vote; we ask how long is this state of things to last? We appeal to you as law-abiding citizens to *enact some laws that will protect us.*"

Finally, on March 23, Grant himself went to the Capitol to find out why Republicans were divided on the Butler bill and to hear what they intended to do about the Ku-Klux problem. When he was given reports of the recent outrages in the South and shown samples of the North Carolina testimony collected by the Scott Committee, Grant sat down and drafted an extemporaneous message to Congress:

A condition of affairs now exists in some of the States of the Union rendering life and property insecure and the carrying of the mails and the collection of revenue dangerous. The proof that such a condition of affairs exists in some localities is now before the Senate. That the power to correct these evils is beyond the control of the State authorities I do not doubt; that the power of the Executive of the United States, acting within the limits of existing laws, is sufficient for present emergencies is not clear.

Therefore I urgently recommend such legislation as in the judgment of Congress shall effectually secure life, liberty, and property and the enforcement of law in all parts of the United States. . . .

There is no other subject upon which I would recommend legislation during the present session.

"The message of the President clears away the fog and indicates with precision the duty of Congress," said the *New York Times.* The Davenport (Iowa) *Daily Gazette* called the message "significant" and said it would be regarded "with feelings of real satisfaction by the people of the whole country." On the other hand, the Richmond *Dispatch* imagined the worst, saying, "He proposes to subvert the civil law and establish martial law in its stead."

The President's message galvanized the House of Representatives into action. Republicans caucused around the clock, salvaging sections of the Butler bill they could swallow and haggling over the rest of it. Democrats girded themselves for the stormy debate that was sure to follow. The work was especially painful for such moderate Republicans as Representative James A. Garfield (ten years away from realizing his life's chief distinction as the second president to be assassinated). Garfield was spiritually torn between the moral and legal aspects of the new bill. On March 30, he wrote hasty letters to two different friends, saying to the first: "We are trying to legislate to put down the Ku-Klux of the South, and it hardly seems possible to add anything to the stringent laws already on our Statute Books without going clear across the state boundaries and assuming the control of local affairs." To his second friend, Garfield complained, "I have never suffered more perplexity of mind on any matter of legislation than on that we are now attempting concerning the Ku-Klux. We are working on the very verge of the Constitution. . . ."

The Ku-Klux bill was finished in record time and laid before the House on March 29, 1871. Though watered down from Butler's original version, it was nevertheless formidable in scope and severity. Its first section permitted any U.S. citizen to sue *in a federal court* those persons who had deprived him of "rights, privileges, or immunities" guaranteed by the U.S. Constitution. Its controversial second section created a new crime: conspiracy to deprive one of his civil rights. It would now be illegal for "two or more persons" to "conspire together, or *go in disguise upon the public highway or upon the premises of another*" with the intent of depriving anyone of the right to vote or testify in court, or to deny anyone twenty other rights secured by the U.S. Constitution. Sections three and four allowed the President to use the military to put down any civil disturbances that deprived citizens of their constitutional rights and, for a limited time, to suspend the writ of habeas corpus "when in his judgment the public safety shall require it. . . ." Sections five and six compelled jurors to take an oath that they were not in any way beholden to the Klan and made citizens with foreknowledge of Klan violence liable for any suffering to victims they could have prevented.

Reaction to the Ku-Klux bill was sharply divided. The *American Missionary* reviewed the extent of Klan violence in the South and rejoiced "that the nation is beginning to be aroused to the subject." The New York *Standard* argued that if it was necessary to arm the

President "with unusual powers" to put down the Klan, then congressmen "had not only the right to do so, but they are right in doing it." But other newspapers opined that allowing the President to suspend habeas corpus in peacetime was a dangerous move. The *Journal of Commerce* was alarmed that the bill gave the President the same freedom to "use the army and navy against one section of the country that Mr. Lincoln had at the height of the rebellion." The once-Republican New York *Evening Post* declared that "we have gone as far toward centralization as we dare to go" and branded supporters of the bill as "the enemies of the Union, the haters of liberty, and the secret plotters of our ruin as a free people." The South more than agreed, though many of its newspapers took the more interesting point of view that it was federal intervention that created violence and not the other way around. The new bill, said the Savannah *Republican*, "will make twenty Ku-Klux where there is now one." "It is such villainous contrivances as this [bill] that produce Ku-Klux organizations," argued the Jackson *Clarion*.

The House launched a highly theatrical debate on the Ku-Klux bill that went on for over a week. Democrats denounced it as unnecessary and unconstitutional. Even if Klansmen did exist in the numbers claimed by Republicans, the Invisible Empire was infinitely preferable to the obscenity of letting crazed radicals trample on the U.S. Constitution. Some Democrats conjured horrifying visions of how a soldierly simpleton like U. S. Grant would use the extraordinary powers conferred on him by the fourth section of the bill. Representative Philadelph Van Trump, a race-baiting former Know-Nothing from Ohio, castigated Grant as "a mere military chieftain, unlearned in the civil policy of the Government" and "indifferent to the great interests of the country." Nothing could be worse, Van Trump argued, than to increase the executive powers of "this man on horseback." Besides, the federal government had already spent too much time and money protecting an "ignorant" and "barbarian" electorate in the South.

It was poetic and fitting that the Republican Party entrusted its difficult defense of the Ku-Klux Bill on constitutional grounds to Congressman Robert B. Elliott of South Carolina, a member of the race that Democrats had derided as "ignorant" and "barbarian." Elliott's background is still obscure. In 1868, the *New York Times* described him as "very black, very well spoken, and bitter as gall"—which says much for his intelligence and self-respect. There's little question about his intelligence. A graduate of En-

gland's Eton College, he could speak four languages; and his ora-
tory, according to the New York *Tribune,* "had a finish and
elegance not often heard in Congress."

On April 1, Elliott stood before the House. Only twenty-nine
years old, this "full-blooded black of medium height, close cropped
hair and neatly trimmed mustache" was probably the youngest
legislator in Washington. He began his speech with a tightly reasoned rebuttal of an earlier argument by Congressman Kerr of
Indiana that the Ku-Klux bill was unconstitutional. On the contrary, said Elliott, the lawfulness of the bill was grounded in Section 4, Article 4 of the Constitution, which obliges the President
and Congress to guarantee "a republican form of government" in
all states and protect them from domestic violence. Further support for the constitutionality of the Ku-Klux bill came from the
Fourteenth Amendment, which Congress had the right to enforce
by appropriate legislation. "Is not this bill 'appropriate legislation'?"
Elliott asked. "I apprehend, Mr. Speaker, that it is obnoxious to
the Democratic Party chiefly because it *is* appropriate and strikes
at the homicidal proclivities which have become chronic" in the
South.

After reviewing examples of Ku-Klux violence in his home state
of South Carolina, Elliott observed that most of the Klan's victims
were black: "And here I say that every Southern gentleman should
blush with shame at this pitiless and cowardly persecution of the
negro."

So far, House Democrats had been guffawing and talking loudly
throughout Elliott's speech, but they now began leaving the chamber en masse. Undaunted, the junior congressman continued.

"It is the custom, sir, of Democratic journals to stigmatize the
negroes of the South as being in a semi-barbarous condition. But
pray tell me, who is the barbarian here—the murderer or his victim? . . . I trust, sir, that this bill will pass quickly and be quickly
enforced. . . . Murder unabashed stalks abroad in many of the
southern states. If you cannot now protect the loyal men of the
South, then have the loyal people of this great Republic done and
suffered much in vain. And your 'free' Constitution is a mockery
and a snare."

Three days later, the absurd argument that the Klan wasn't
really a serious problem was spectacularly debunked by the origi-
nator of the Ku-Klux bill—cross-eyed "Beast" Butler. A prepared
address by Butler was always a special event, and by noon, April 4,
the galleries of the House were packed with newsmen. It seemed

to one correspondent that General Butler had "been gotten up for the occasion." For an afternoon speech, he appeared in full evening dress, complete with boutonniere, and "his head exhibited signs of careful tonsorial manipulation."

After biting into a lemon (lest he "fail in acerbity of expression"), Butler informed the House that an American was safe in every country but his own. "Does that proposition need more argument than the statement of it?" he asked in his high rasping voice. Whereupon he launched into an hour-long, state-by-state recital of Ku-Klux atrocities. The cases Butler selected for review were appalling, and Democrats couldn't leave the chamber quickly enough. Especially heartrending was the case of William Luke, a member of the American Missionary Association, who had been murdered by the Alabama Klan. Before hanging him, the Klansmen had allowed Luke to scribble a final note to his wife which Butler quoted in full:

> MY DEAR WIFE: I die tonight. It has been so determined by those who think I deserve it. God knows I feel myself innocent. I have only sought to educate the negro.
>
> I little thought when leaving you so far away that we should then part forever.
>
> God's will be done! He will be to you a better husband than I have been, and a father to our six little ones.
>
> There is in the company's hands about two-hundred dollars of my money; also my trunk and clothes are here. You can send for them or let Henry come for them as you think best.
>
> God of mercy bless and keep you, my dear, dear wife and children.

"Let each member of the House read that letter," Butler intoned, "and ponder on the circumstances of his death . . . then let him vote against a bill to repress such outrages, if he dare, and then reckon with the people of his country and afterward with his God."

Seldom had the "bloody shirt" been waved with greater effect.

The Ku-Klux bill sailed through the House, was passed by the Senate with a few alterations, and signed by President Grant on April 20, 1871. Now all the government had to do was enforce it.

Out on the rugged western plains, the Seventh United States Cavalry Regiment was busy fighting Arapaho, Cheyenne, Sioux, and Comanche Indians. Under the command of Lieutenant Colonel George Armstrong Custer, the Seventh Cavalry had received much favorable publicity as a colorful, high-spirited, and well-disciplined regiment of soldiers who charged Indian camps to the tune of an Irish jig, "Garry Owen," played by their band. On March 8, 1871, twelve troops of the Seventh were transferred from the Department of the Missouri to the Department of the South based in Louisville. From Louisville, six troops were joined by a regiment of the Eighteenth Infantry and proceeded by rail to the South Carolina upcountry. President Grant had sent the troops in answer to Governor Scott's request for help in fighting the Ku-Klux Klan.

Prior to the arrival of the troops in the Palmetto State, Grant issued a proclamation demanding that South Carolina Klansmen "disperse and retire peaceably" within twenty days. The Detroit *Free Press* found this order to the "imaginary Ku-Klux" absurd; "Don Quixote's attack upon the windmills is mildness itself in comparison," it said. The "Garry Owens" of the Seventh more than agreed. Most of them couldn't imagine why they were being moved from the real menace of Indians out west to the "imaginary" menace of Ku-Klux in the defeated Confederacy. Major Lewis Merrill, for example, had heard so many "enormous exaggerations" about the Klan that, in Louisville, he asked department commander General Alfred Terry if the matter really warranted troops at all. "When you get to South Carolina," Terry replied, "you will find that the half has not been told you." Major Merrill would soon appreciate Terry's cryptic remark. In time, he would learn more about the internal operations of the Invisible Empire than any outsider in America. And no single person would be more responsible than Merrill for bringing a Klan Realm to its knees under the Ku-Klux Act.

Lewis W. Merrill was born in New Berlin, Pennsylvania, in 1834. His father had studied law in Thaddeus Stevens's offices and, like his mentor, became an attorney and an early champion of civil rights; he also seems to have had a lasting influence on his son. Lewis went to West Point at age sixteen, graduated in 1855, and was immediately sent for duty suppressing the riots between abolitionist and proslavery forces in bloody Kansas. In the Union Army, Merrill was breveted major in 1862 for "gallant and meritorious service" in the Missouri campaign and was wounded in the battle of Little Rock. After the war, he resumed the rank of captain in the Second Cavalry, serving first as inspector general, then as acting judge advocate. In the latter position, he achieved the reputation of an "efficient and conscientious officer" with a formidable understanding of the law and "an excruciating precision." Merrill was promoted to major when he joined the Seventh Cavalry in April 1869. He was then thirty-four years old. Tall and robust, with extravagant chin whiskers and wire-rimmed glasses, Merrill was described by a reporter as having "the head, face, and spectacles of a German professor, and the frame of an athlete." The dichotomy of his physique was perfectly matched by his talents; for, in addition to being a competent soldier, Merrill was considered the intellectual superior "not only of the other field officers, but also of most of his own contemporaries" in the Seventh Cavalry.

The combination of intellect, legal acumen, capacity for reasoned action, and unyielding contempt for injustice made Major Merrill ideally suited for his duty at York County, South Carolina, where he arrived with K Troop on March 27, 1871. For the first couple days, the little Piedmont village of Yorkville was the picture of rustic calm. The weather was extremely pleasant and, given their "easy access to whiskey-shops," the men of K Troop began enjoying their new assignment immensely. Even the major relaxed in the thought that the Ku-Klux Klan was probably an isolated pack of hooligans who could be nailed down in a few weeks. As he gathered information, however, Merrill grew increasingly concerned that the Ku-Klux organization was "not only a very large one and exceedingly well organized, but a very dangerous one" as well. Four months later, he would say, "I never conceived of such a state of social disorganization being possible in any civilized community as exists in this county now."

As it turned out, nearly two-thirds of the white citizens of York County were involved to some degree with the Klan. And the crimes committed by them—such as the assault on Reverend Elias Hill—were among the worst in the nation. As elsewhere in the South, the powers of the military to intervene were limited. Merrill could provide protection and shelter to victims of the Klan, but responsibility for instituting arrests lay in the inert hands of local authorities. By the middle of May, Merrill was so frustrated that he called a meeting of leading citizens in the hope of spurring them to take a strong stand against the Klan. He opened the meeting by going through a long list of local outrages which, according to the local newspaper, dramatically revealed to those present that the major was unusually well informed "as to the operations of disguised persons in this county." Merrill then informed the group that he knew the names of several Klansmen who had committed various crimes; that the civil officers had been miserably derelict in failing to arrest these men; and that, consequently, victims of the Klan—mostly blacks—were no longer willing to make charges against members of the order. He then warned that unless law-abiding citizens did something to rectify this inexcusable situation, the President might very well invoke the new Ku-Klux Act and suspend the writ of habeas corpus in York County. The choice was theirs.

The Yorkville *Enquirer* took Merrill at his word:

> The Ku-Klux Act comprehends all persons found in disguise, or in unlawful assemblies on the highways, or on the premises of another. This act will be enforced and rigidly enforced; and unless our people at once determine that there must be no further acts of violence in the county, we will soon have occasion to observe the practical oper- ations of the law in its utmost severity, and with all its unpleasant consequences.

A few days later, a public petition condemning Klan violence was circulated and signed by several hundred York County residents —including two Klan leaders and five members, whose signatures conveyed to fellow Klansmen that they were on top of things, should the army major try anything serious.

Merrill had already begun collecting a dossier on the York County Klan. His best informants were local blacks who liked and trusted him enough to tell him everything they knew about the Klan's activities, its members, and interconnections between the Invisible Empire and the respectable white community. Even dis- gruntled Klansmen eventually confided in Merrill, and these he sent back to their dens as spies. Over the next few months, Mer- rill's files would burgeon with case studies of Ku-Klux violence and arcane Klan secrets.

On June 9, 1871, Merrill sent a lengthy report to General Terry in Louisville. Though hastily written in Merrill's sprawling, often illegible penmanship, it was the most detailed and complete report on the Ku-Klux Klan that had ever been compiled. In South Caro- lina, he reported, a Grand Cyclops was in charge of several "chiefs," each of whom commanded squads of ten to eighteen men. He described how citizens could be duped into joining a squad. When a promising initiate was identified, Klan members would casually talk to him and check out his opinions about the Ku-Klux. Afterward, they would visit him as a disguised group:

"He is told that it is undertood among the K.K. that he has been inquiring into their secrets and has become possessed of information which is considered unsafe for him to have. That he is watched and runs many chances of being injured in his person or property, and that in self-defense he had better join the order. His assent obtained, a ceremony of initiation is gone through with, intended to be terrible but in reality ludicrous. . . . The new brother is then tested in some minor act of lawlessness until he is fully committed and is, according to his zeal and unscrupulousness, confided with graver and graver crimes to be committed. If he holds back too much, he is not allowed to know anything of the more serious operations or to participate in them."

Merrill reviewed the Klan's entire grimoire of secret signs, codes, and passwords, including its distress cry, which was "Avalanche!" He even wrote out the Klan's whistle signal in two bars of musical notation. "This signal has been in constant use among them on their night rides," he remarked, "and is described by every negro who has heard" it.

Toward the end of his narrative, Merrill offered an opinion of the Klan's motives: "Beyond doubt the object of the organization in this vicinity is to terrify the negroes into obeying the whites in voting or to compel them to stay away from the polls. The more active and intelligent of the negroes who have influence with their own color and who advise them are to be driven away or killed, and such white men as affiliate with the negroes politically are to be handled the same way. . . . Out of some six-hundred white men in this county who voted with the negro majority at the last election, there are not more than thirty or forty who have not openly renounced their party under threats or acts of violence. . . ."

Merrill concluded by observing that the local sheriff was probably a Klansman. In later reports, he would state that the "Intendant" or mayor of Yorkville, several physicians and attorneys, and one of the county's trial justices were Klansmen—"and I have good reason for suspecting that several of the state officers of justice in this and the neighboring county (Chester) are either members of the order or so closely affiliated with them as to practically amount to the same thing."

General Terry was deeply impressed with Merrill's success in penetrating the mysterious KKK and forwarded his reports to the War Department, commenting that Merrill was "an officer of great intelligence, and I think that the utmost confidence may be placed in his representations." Terry also remarked that the Klan was so diffused throughout the South that it could never be broken in all states simultaneously. If the Klan was given a decisive blow in one state, however, it might have a demoralizing effect on the Klan elsewhere. On the basis of Major Merrill's grasp of the situation, Terry recommended South Carolina as the exemplary state to hit. Secretary of War William Belknap, in turn, forwarded this information to the new joint select committee of the House and Senate that was investigating the Klan through hearings conducted in Washington. Convinced that much headway could be gained by a direct involvement in the South Carolina situation, Chairman John Scott delegated himself and Representatives Job Stevenson (Republican, Ohio) and Philadelph Van Trump (Democrat, Ohio) as a special subcommittee to go to South Carolina and conduct local hearings. Throughout July, this uneasy threesome collected testimony from Klan victims and other pertinent witnesses in the counties of Spartanburg, Chester, Union, and finally York.

Writing to General Terry, Merrill remarked with some amusement that the subcommittee's prospective visit to Yorkville had so "frightened the order here that I anticipate little trouble for some time. If the present demoralization of the Ku-Klux could be summarily followed up by the arrest and punishment of some of the worst of them . . . I would hope for the almost [quick?] cessation of acts of outrage." Unfortunately, these arrests couldn't be made as "summarily" as the major hoped, but when the subcommittee arrived in Yorkville, he reviewed with them six cases of murder, five schoolhouse burnings, and sixty-eight floggings committed by York County Klansmen. The two Republican members were naturally impressed, but Democrat Philadelph Van Trump tried to impugn Merrill's evidence with questions about his political loyalties.

"I am an officer in the Army," Merrill told the congressman, "bred up in a school which taught me that officers of the Army were not proper persons to mix in politics."

"Are you not known here as a pronounced Republican?" Van Trump asked.

"If I am, I do not know it."

"Are you not a Republican?"

"Perhaps in the main my political opinions coincide more nearly with the Republican than with any other party on questions relating to public affairs . . ." Merrill replied, "but I do not take an active part in politics and am not decided in expressing political opinions, except it be in social or domestic conversation."

Van Trump then suggested that the information Merrill had received from blacks was unreliable, since they would "take considerable vainglory" in concocting stories for a sympathetic officer of the army. Merrill disagreed. Blacks were trustworthy informants, he said. They wished only "that justice may be done them, and they may be secured in quiet lives. . . ."

"Is not the negro a vainglorious animal if entrusted with any authority?" Van Trump persisted in asking.

With tense precision, Merrill replied, "I do not think that that is so generally true that I would say it was a fact."

After the subcommittee left South Carolina, Senator Scott stayed in touch with Merrill, who kept him updated on crimes committed by the Klan in York County. On August 31, Scott made a digest of these outrages and incorporated it in a long letter to President Grant. These facts, said Scott, justified bringing the full force of the Ku-Klux Act down on the South Carolina Klansmen. The next day, Grant met with his cabinet and discussed the wisdom of suspending habeas corpus. The President was quite willing to go through with the measure but wanted to be absolutely certain that it was justified. He therefore dispatched Attorney General Akerman to the Carolinas to verify the urgency of the situation.

In the meantime, the court of sessions met in York County, and Major Merrill anxiously awaited its indictments of Klansmen whose cases he had submitted. To his horror, he learned that not only would the court refuse to indict but that it intended to discredit Merrill's evidence to both Senator Scott and Secretary Belknap. On September 19, at his request, Merrill held a meeting with Judge W. M. Thomas with whom he shared his private files on the Klan. "The conversation which followed," Merrill recounted, "convinced me that he did not honor the obligations of his office. It is with reluctance that I speak with such apparent indelicacy of a high judicial officer, but . . . milder expression is not consistent with the truth." The grand jury met for ten days, six of which were spent belittling Merrill's arguments for indictments. Merrill later learned that a third of the members of the grand jury were Klansmen, two of whom had been accessories to murder.

When the farce of the court of sessions concluded, an angry Merrill went straight to Columbia to complain to District Attorney D. T. Corbin. There, to his relief, he learned that Attorney General Akerman was on his way. Merrill met Akerman at the train station and escorted him back to Yorkville, where the attorney general spent several days examining Merrill's records. Nothing could have pleased Akerman more than the meticulousness with which Merrill had gathered and organized his evidence. On October 12, Akerman wired the White House that the government had a solid case in South Carolina. To comply fully with the terms of the Ku-Klux Act, it was necessary for the President to issue another warning to South Carolina Klansmen, which Grant dispatched the same day.

On October 16, as a matter of form, Akerman sent the President written justification for implementing the Ku-Klux Act in nine South Carolina counties, where Klansmen were

> organized and armed. They effect their objects by personal violence, often extending to murder. They terrify witnesses. They control juries in the State courts and sometimes in the courts of the United States. Systematic perjury is one of the means by which prosecutions of the members are defeated. . . . I am justified in affirming that the instances of criminal violence perpetrated by these combinations within the last twelve months in the above named counties would be reckoned by the thousands.

The next day, October 17, 1871, Grant suspended the writ of habeas corpus in the South Carolina upcountry—the first occasion for a president to do so in peacetime.

The U.S. Army now superseded local authority. Troops D and L of the Seventh Cavalry joined K Troop in Yorkville. The immediate effect was that fifty of the Klan's Cyclopes and squad chiefs quickly fled the state, "leaving their poorer followers and ignorant dupes to stand sponsors for the crimes of which they had been the chief authors and instigators. . . ." Captains Thomas Weir and Owen Hale and Lieutenants Nowlan, Godfrey, and Braden began routing the countryside, bagging Klansmen by the score. "The troops were so disposed," Merrill happily recounted, "that a large number of arrests were effected simultaneously over the county. . . ." Hapless Klansmen soon filled the county jail and overflowed into an old sugar house that Merrill converted into temporary cells. The cavalrymen observed commendable discipline, and only occasionally did indiscretions occur. For example, once when Captain Hale used a local resident to lead him to the hideaway of a Klan chief, the wily guide led him instead on a fifteen-mile, overnight wild goose chase. In his own words, Hale felt "trimmed to the Queen's taste" and angrily threw the guide in the slammer in place of the elusive Klansman.

From Major Merrill's point of view, the effect of the Ku-Klux Act was wondrous: Rank-and-file members "were bewildered and demoralized. Looking about for their chiefs and counselors, and finding that to get orders or advice they must go to them in jail or follow their flight, they recognized the fact that the game was up, that the organization was broken, and all over the county they betook themselves to flight or came in and surrendered." In some instances, entire squads, headed by their chiefs, came to headquarters and surrendered en masse. Given the limited jail space, Merrill was forced to release a majority of self-confessed Klansmen on their own recognizances, but Klansmen captured in flight and those guilty of serious crimes were kept locked up under twenty-four-hour guard.

In jail, these Klansmen quickly learned that none of the usual ploys could secure their release, and one by one they began to confess—or, in the colorful word of the day, to "puke." At first, only the small fry puked, but as they felt the weight of time in their dreary surroundings, men higher up in the order gave in, and "confessions became quite the fashion." From Columbia, District Attorney Corbin sent Merrill a twenty-one-year-old New Jersey stenographer, Louis Post, who worked day and night "shorthand-ing" the Klansmen's confessions (the experience would indelibly affect Post's life).

Local newspapers in the nine South Carolina counties bitterly denounced the suppression of their liberty under the Ku-Klux Act; and although it must be admitted that martial law is never pleasant, the effects of military occupation in South Carolina were far less dreadful than the picture anti-Reconstruction historians would popularize. For example, Louis Post, who greatly admired Major Merrill, recounted the evening when a messenger came to the major's office bearing a note from a prisoner. Merrill read it with a glow of exultation, telling the messenger, "Bring him here at once!" To Post, the major said, "At last, one of the big ones wants to puke!" The Klansman was brought into the office, but to Merrill's surprise, he said, "Major, my little boy is sick; he is dying; my wife sends me word; I want to see him; may I go home on parole? I give you my honor to come back."

Merrill was speechless with shock. Finally, he asked the prisoner, "How old is your boy?"

"Fourteen."

"How ill is he?"

"My wife don't think he'll live till morning."

Merrill glumly pondered the request. After getting the prisoner's solemn promise to return in the morning, he told him, "You may go." Merrill risked a court-martial for this decision, but fortunately the Klansman was true to his word—the novel situation in South Carolina hardly allowed him to do otherwise.

Only two months after Grant's suspension of habeas corpus, nearly eight hundred South Carolina Klansmen had fled the state, were arrested and paroled, or were jailed. The trials of the latter began in November in U.S. District Court at Columbia. They were well covered by the press and had a deleterious effect on the Klan nationally. Many native white Carolinians admitted disgust over the facts that came out of the trials. At one point, Judge Hugh Bond lost his temper with the defendants and denounced them for recounting the details of a brutal murder with "as little apparent horror" as one would "relate the incidents of a picnic." Even the defense attorney Reverdy Johnson, who had come to South Carolina expecting a red herring, confided to the jury, "I have listened with unmixed horror to some of the testimony which has been brought before you. The outrages proved are shocking to humanity. They admit of neither excuse nor justification. They violate every obligation which law and nature impose upon men."

By the end of 1871, the action taken by the Grant administration in South Carolina had effectively dissolved the Klan in that state. Lighter Ku-Klux prosecutions were successfully pursued in Mississippi. But as General Terry had anticipated, the heavy blow dealt to the South Carolina Realm rebounded to the Ku-Klux Klan everywhere. Conservative Southerners began to regard the Klan as a liability. In fact, the possibility of federal soldiers, armed with guns and bayonets, charging into the South and establishing martial law frightened every middle-class Southern white. Newspapers that had formerly defended the Klan now condemned it and, like the Augusta *Constitutionalist*, exhorted their readers "to rise up" and "show that they are capable of protecting the lives of their own citizens" and "bring to punishment those who defy the laws of the State." If they didn't, they would hardly be in a position to "raise a clamor against the unconstitutional" intervention of the federal government.

Despite the immediate success of implementing the Ku-Klux Act in South Carolina, it was, in the long run, too much of a success to be really a good thing. The number of Klansmen arrested in South Carolina virtually swamped a primitive, outmoded system of federal courts that was barely capable of handling existing business, much less accommodating the enormous burden imposed on it by the recent, sweeping acts of Congress. And despite their willingness to "centralize" the government and swell the size of the federal judiciary on paper, Republicans were reluctant to back up their decisions through increased appropriations. The pittance allocated to the Justice Department (nearly $2 million) was ridiculous in view of the manifold responsibilities it was asked to assume under the Ku-Klux Act. The *Nation* remarked, "If it be true that black men are kept from the polls by intimidation, we ought to see that going to the polls is made as safe as going to church; but to pass bills providing for this, without voting the men or the money to execute them is a wretched mockery. . . ."

At first, Attorney General Akerman was optimistic about the problem, advising his personnel that "we must do the best we can with such means as we have." When the Columbia court was able to hear only five out of five hundred cases, however, Akerman warned Congress in his annual report that without additional funds, present efforts at prosecuting the South Carolina Klansmen would fail: "If it takes a court over one month to try five offenders, how long will it take to try four hundred, already indicted, and many hundreds more who deserve to be indicted?" But the money didn't come. Akerman was eventually forced to recommend compromises to the officers of justice dealing with arrested Klansmen. He suggested that Klan leaders—those whose acts revealed "deep criminality" or who had contributed "intelligence and social influence" to the organization—should be indicted, tried, and severely punished if found guilty. Those whose guilt was marginal were to be released on "light bail" and their cases pressed only if time allowed. Those whose connection with the Klan had been "compulsory and reluctant" should sign a confession and then their cases could be dropped. At the end of the Columbia session, the 5 Klansmen who were tried were found guilty and sentenced to prison, along with 52 others who confessed in open court. But 161 Klansmen who had been indicted were never tried; and 281 others were never indicted.

In February 1872, District Attorney Corbin complained to the attorney general's office that the next term of the circuit court, to be held in Charleston, would last just four to six weeks and could handle only "a fraction" of the cases ready and waiting for trial. The present federal court system was "utterly inadequate," Corbin said, and if Congress didn't provide "speedy and effective" relief, "most of the prosecutions" of Klansmen in South Carolina would fail. But federal court costs had already tripled in South Carolina, and by midyear the Justice Department exhausted its annual budget. Corbin was told that the expense of prosecuting Klansmen "cannot be allowed to continue," and the district attorney had no choice but to drop most of the cases.

"In view of the large number of indictments found in the several courts . . . we recommend such an increase of the judiciary of the United States by districts and circuits . . . as, in the judgment of Congress, will secure speedy and certain justice . . . and leave no hope of impunity to criminals by the law's delay." This important though unheeded recommendation was offered by majority members of the joint select committee of Congress, which wrapped up its investigation of the Ku-Klux Klan on February 19, 1872, at the same time the Justice Department was becoming swamped by cases. In less than eight months, this committee had conducted the most elaborate and extensive investigation in the history of Congress. After the three-man subcommittee's visit to South Carolina, additional subcommittees had been dispatched to Tennessee, Alabama, Mississippi, Georgia, North Carolina, and Florida. Newspapers avidly followed the investigation's progress. The Republican press called the committee "well intentioned." Democrats compared it to the Spanish Inquisition. The testimony collected by the committee ultimately filled twelve large, closely printed volumes, containing vital information on the Klan (which has been indispensable to the present study) and significant details on society, government, and race relations in the Reconstruction period.

The investigation had been conducted in an intensely partisan manner, with the thirteen Republican members usually outmaneuvering the eight Democrats. The two sides produced separate, diametrically opposed reports which filled a thirteenth volume. The Republicans' majority report—largely the work of John Scott —was a complex, poorly organized document that was defensive in tone but which nevertheless addressed the facts in a restrained and logical way. It methodically debunked the various explanations for the rise of the Klan that were then being played up by the Democratic press. For example, it emphasized that the Reconstruction acts did not *cause* the Klan; the Klan was active in name and certainly in deed well before the South was radically reconstructed. The disfranchisement of Confederate veterans did not cause the Klan: "No man under [disfranchisement] has avowed himself as either committing or encouraging outrages for that reason, and no member of the organization has justified their acts upon that ground." The so-called danger from impudent blacks was a ridiculous explanation for Klan terrorism; the evidence was overwhelming that blacks were victims, not perpetrators of violence. Bad government didn't cause the Klan either. Corruption was truly present in some of the Southern governments, but the evidence clearly showed that graft was a bipartisan temptation to which Democrats succumbed equally with Republicans.

The real cause of the Ku-Klux Klan, according to the majority, was the need to express in the shadows "that tyranny and lawlessness which was, before the war, open and unrestrained. . . . We should remember how common it was to scourge colored men, and how perilous for northern citizens or southern emancipationists to be found in the Gulf States." In short, the Klan had been caused by a continuation of Southern Civil War passions, carried on by the most violent diehards of the former Confederacy who denied that blacks were entitled to anything more than a servile role in society. In time, the Klan had become "a political organization" whose purpose was to overwhelm blacks, preserve the South inviolate from Northern and federal influence, and to guarantee white Democratic supremacy. In so doing, the Klan had harmed the South and had made Southern blacks devoutly Republican by methods that were as manifestly stupid as they were cruel:

> Having the rights of a citizen and voter, neither of those rights can be abrogated by whipping [the freedman]. If his political opinions are erroneous he will not take kindly to the opposite creed when its apostles come to inflict the scourge upon himself and outrage upon his wife and children. If he is ignorant, he will not be educated by burning his schoolhouses and exiling his teachers; if he is wicked, he will not be made better by banishing to Liberia his religious teachers. If the resuscitation of the State is desired by his labor, neither will be secured by a persecution which depopulates townships and prevents the introduction of new labor and of capital.

In addition to increased appropriations to the Justice Department for the prosecution of Klansmen, the majority recommended that federal troops remain at their present posts in the South. Even though Ku-Klux terrorism had drastically declined, it was no reason to assume "that communities would be safe if protection measures were withdrawn." Finally, it recommended that the President's right to suspend habeas corpus (which the Ku-Klux Act allowed only temporarily) be extended until the end of the next session of Congress.

In contrast to the majority report, the document offered by the Democratic minority was a concise, straightforward, and highly volatile polemic. It was predominately the work of Philadelph Van Trump whose previous experience as an Ohio newspaper editor gave his writing readability and high drama. He could be rapier sharp, especially when he tore apart the witnesses whose testimony figured importantly in the majority report. According to Van Trump, Democratic members of the committee had given the most weight to testimony from respectable, intelligent, Southern aristocrats, including such Klansmen as Edmund W. Pettus, John B. Gordon, and retired Grand Wizard Nathan B. Forrest (who later told friends that he had "lied like a gentleman" before the committee). In contrast, the majority had willingly listened to former slaves "of the most forbidding personal appearance" and of "the very lowest grade of intelligence belonging to human beings." Little would be lost, Van Trump said, if the whole body of black testimony (167 witnesses) was thrown out of the record; partisan newspaper accounts should have "far greater force and weight than a large portion of the negro evidence taken before the committee."

The evidence of "venal" carpetbaggers and "malicious" scalawags was hardly better. "In one form or other," Van Trump recounted, "these swift witnesses hung round and obtruded themselves upon the committee, notebook in hand, when they could write, ready to tell all they had been able to gather from all sources in a busy search for months—often for years—for slanderous reports; rolling every bit of scandal as a sweet morsel under their tongue, doubtless expecting the important information they gave would entitle them to a collectorship at least, if not a foreign mission."

After discrediting the opposition, Van Trump offered a moving and fascinating account of Reconstruction in which the white South was portrayed as a defenseless damsel who had been mercilessly crushed under the heels of a vindictive Congress and wanton blacks. After the war, he said, the South had been "goaded to desperation by the insolence of the negroes." And how did Congress respond? By enfranchising them! It was apparent to every thinking man that black suffrage was an "egregious political blunder," for the "dumb mule" on whose back the freedman "vaingloriously rides to the polls might just as well vote as his rider." With such an "ignorant and degraded" electorate to exploit, "carpetbaggers rushed down to the South, fierce and rapacious as hungry wolves, marshaled the negroes through the midnight discipline of the Loyal Leagues, marched them up to the ballot-box like herds of senseless cattle, and inaugurated a system of plunder and corruption through negro legislation, so startling and gigantic as to stagger the common belief." According to Van Trump, most of the blame for the pitiful condition of the white South belonged to the carpetbagger, who was a "demon of discord and anarchy; his infernal schemes and intrigues with the negroes have thrown a whole people into utter and hopeless despair." (Elsewhere, Van Trump makes pointed reference to a "Jew carpetbagger.")

In "hopeless despair," the white South turned to the Ku-Klux Klan to save itself from ruin. Outrages attributed to the Klan were gross exaggerations, usually resulting from personal or local feuds or from "the pilfering, often to the plundering disposition of the negro race. . . ." There could be no doubt that the Klan was exclusively an organization of self-defense. In his most striking argument, Van Trump said:

> It is an axiomatic truth that bad government will produce bad men among the best people on earth; and that has clearly been the cause of Ku-Kluxism. . . . In this we are only "repeating history." It has been so in all ages of the world. It produced the *Carbonari* in Italy; it gave rise to the *Free Companions* in France, in the bad reign of Louis XI; and it filled all England with *Moss Troopers* under the iron rule of the Normans, and who reappeared in Scotland against the tyranny of the English Crown prior to the Union. Even *Robin Hood* and his burly followers, whether mythical or real, whether their exploits were matters of mere romance or of veritable history, serve to "point a moral" in the philosophy of government; for they stand both as the representatives and the exemplars of the indisputable fact that good as well as bad men will band themselves together in resisting the aggression of tyrants wielding political power.

Van Trump's comparison of Klansmen to Robin Hood and his ilk was clever, provocative, and ultimately tragic. It was tragic because the Democrats' slick minority report became the key document upon which histories of the Klan would be based for the next sixty years.

Ulysses S. Grant's second inauguration took place on March 4, 1873. The temperature had begun falling the night before, nearly reaching zero by morning, and icy winds began blowing "in a perfect gale" from the southwest. Flags and other decorations were ripped off public buildings, and the banners that remained sagged from the weight of icicles. As people huddled along Pennsylvania Avenue, the universal exclamation was, "Isn't it cold!"

The procession from the White House was led by troops of West Point cadets and midshipmen from Annapolis. It wasn't long before many of the boys had to break ranks on account of frostbite. (A number of them would be left behind in Washington hospitals, several succumbing fatally to pneumonia.) The band was next to go. Condensation from the breath of the brass musicians froze the valves of their instruments, causing the music to peter out halfway to the Capitol. Shivering well-wishers were too numb to give the President anything more than a half-hearted cheer. At the Capitol, the wind nearly whipped the manuscript of Grant's speech out of his hands. Fortunately, his address was short.

The inaugural ball had been painstakingly planned to avoid the mishaps of four years previously. This time, the ball would be held in a huge temporary structure built specially for the purpose on Judiciary Square. It was said that the "magnificently decorated" and spacious ballroom would constitute "the most princely feature" of the entire inauguration. An enormous banquet had been prepared so that, this time, no one would go home hungry. The menu included 10,000 fried oysters, 8,000 scalloped oysters, and 8,000 pickled oysters; 140 turkeys, 150 capons stuffed with truffles, 350 boiled chickens, 100 roast chickens, 400 partridge, and 200 dozen quail; 40 sides of beef; 200 Virginia hams; 15 saddles of mutton; 25 stuffed boars' heads; 2,000 pounds of cold lobster; 8,000 assorted sandwiches; 150 fancy cakes, 400 small cakes, 25 barrels of Malaga grapes, hundreds of cases of oranges, apples and other fruit, and mountains of exquisitely decorated ice cream.

Only one thing had been overlooked by the planning committee: the "magnificently decorated" temporary building had not been supplied with a single source of heat.

With a bow to the Fifteenth Amendment, the committee had opened the ball to everyone "without distinction of race, color or previous condition," and newsmen remarked with varying degrees of disdain on the presence of well-dressed black couples. Even *The Nation* was a bit taken aback at the sight of the Annapolis boys dancing spiritedly with "the wives of colored congressmen." Certainly the dancing began with enthusiasm, but fierce winds wracked the flimsy building, and soon everyone was chilled to the bone. At her husband's side, Julia Grant sat gamely shivering in a white silk dress, but the other ladies were forced to put on their fur coats, and the gentlemen their overcoats and hats, "as they endeavored to keep warm by vigorous dancing." Hundreds of canaries had been provided to the ballroom in the hope that their chirping would provide a pleasant accompaniment to the evening's festivities. As the mercury dropped, however, so did the little warblers; they were soon a mass of frozen yellow corpses. A well-dressed lady was then "seized with a congestive chill" and herself dropped dead on the ballroom floor. At this point, tragedy and temperature overcame "the ardor of even the most enthusiastic lover of Terpsichore. . . ."

The magnificent feast had by now congealed into a frigid, unappetizing mess. It didn't seem to matter, because all anyone wanted was coffee and hot chocolate—"the only things warm in the building." Eventually even the coffee chilled to the consistency of a frappé, and the ball had to be aborted. As an eyewitness observed, "The guests, each one of whom had paid $20 for a ticket, were frozen out before midnight."

Over the next four years, the Republican ardor for civil rights would cool, Reconstruction itself would be "frozen out," and prospects for racial justice would be put on ice for nearly a century.

The end was signaled in 1873 by the general collapse of the federal government's enforcement policy. In late 1871, Grant had made one of his worst mistakes by dismissing Attorney General Akerman, who had offended wealthy GOP backers by unfavorable rulings on their railroads. His replacement, George Williams, was far less dedicated to civil rights than Akerman and more squeamish about bringing criminals to book in the South. More and more prosecutions were dropped. When Congress failed to vote increased funds for the Justice Department, Williams acted on the naïve hope that, by showing Southerners a conciliatory attitude, they would in turn respect the rights of blacks. "My intention," he announced in June 1873, "is to suspend these prosecutions except in some of the worst cases, with a hope that the effect will be to produce obedience to the law and quiet and peace among the people." By 1874, the enforcement acts were virtually dead letters.

For many, the lapse of the enforcement acts was justified since their reason for being—the Ku-Klux Klan—had been effectively smashed as a result of the dramatic showdown in South Carolina. But violence continued routinely in the South, fomented in broad daylight by groups of whites without costumes or regalia. Sometimes whites banded together in paramilitary units such as Louisiana's White League and South Carolina's Red Shirts and Rifle Clubs. These groups intimidated blacks at the registration booths and polls mostly through a show of force but didn't hesitate to bully or murder them whenever they could get away with it. These techniques were cruelly effective in separating blacks from the ballot. Georgia went Democratic in 1871. Texas followed in 1873, Alabama and Arkansas in 1874, and Mississippi in 1875.

Grant continued to send federal troops to quell election-day disturbances, but vacillation and inconsistency weakened his use of the military. He felt a genuine concern for the plight of Southern blacks and was personally invested in preserving the fruits of the Union victory. But he was edgy over the lack of precedent for frequent military intervention by executive order and sensitive to charges of being a "military dictator" that had been leveled at him by the Democrats. Grant was also overly dependent on a number of Cabinet members who urged cooperation with native-born Southern whites. Some historians have dealt harshly with him for his lack of nerve in using troops to maintain civil rights, but history also shows that Grant intervened more than any president before him, and no later president would equal him in this regard until John F. Kennedy. A real problem lay in the fact that there weren't enough soldiers to place in the South, and, when sent, they couldn't stay in one place long enough to have a lasting effect. More and more soldiers were being mustered out of the service, and those remaining were needed out west. (With the exception of Major Merrill, the men of the Seventh Cavalry, who had contributed so much to breaking the Klan in South Carolina, were returned to frontier duty, and on the hot afternoon of June 25, 1876, they were massacred with Custer at Little Big Horn.)

Knowing that something was desperately needed if Reconstruction was to survive, Republicans passed a second Civil Rights Act in 1875, which promised "the full and equal enjoyment of the accommodations" of inns, public conveyances, and the like to all persons regardless of race or color. With the recovery of the Democratic Party in the South through the intimidation of black voters, however, Republican strength was severely on the wane. After the Democrats had captured the House of Representatives in 1874 (the first Democratic victory in a national election since the war), it was all but guaranteed that the Act would never be enforced. Three years later, Radical Reconstruction itself ground to a halt.

In retrospect, the Ku-Klux Klan and its kindred organizations didn't weaken Radical Reconstruction nearly as much as they nurtured it. So long as an organized, secret conspiracy swore oaths and used cloak-and-dagger methods in the South, Congress was willing to legislate against it—legislation that would provide vital safeguards for the cause of racial equality in the future. Not until the Klan was beaten and the former Confederacy turned to more open methods of preserving the Southern way of life did Reconstruction and its Northern support decline. After the controversial compromise between Democrats and Republicans that elevated Rutherford B. Hayes to the presidency in 1877, hopes began evaporating for fulfilling the dream of racial justice that Reconstruction had heralded. The North may have won the war, but the South had now won the peace. It was a peace in which Southern blacks found themselves noncitizens, unable to vote, consigned to inadequate housing and menial employment and their children to inferior schools. This was the peace that marked the end of both the Ku-Klux and Reconstruction.

"But this is not true peace. True peace is not merely the absence of tension; it is the presence of justice." The man who spoke these words was a minister named Martin Luther King, Jr., and he wouldn't come on the scene for nearly a century.

POSTSCRIPT
1877–1915

The decades between the fall of Reconstruction and the dawn of the twentieth century were marked by an abandonment of Southern blacks by the Republican Party, the legalization of segregation, and a national swing from the idealism that had forged Radical Reconstruction to a selfish nativism and bigoted intolerance.

By the late 1870s, Northerners regarded the erosion of civil liberties in the South with detachment and then apathy. The liberty-loving passion of the 1860s (as it had a century before and would a century later) seemed to burn out completely, and many believed that the revolution in civil rights had run its course. Northerners especially grew weary of the constant need for intervention in the South and were frustrated by the insolvability of "the negro problem." Their own racism was brought to the surface when Congress passed the ill-fated Civil Rights Act of 1875.

The flagging idealism of the North went hand in hand with the waning conscience of the Republican Party, triggered by the loss of its most powerful and egalitarian leaders. Thad Stevens had died in 1868, Charles Sumner in 1874; and the national Democratic victory in 1874 swept from office some of the Party's best spokesmen for civil rights, including "Beast" Butler. The post-Reconstruction breed of Republicans was motivated more by self-interest and concerned less with a free South than a prosperous North.

112

This was a marked change for the onetime abolitionists. The New York *Evening Post* observed, "The moment any party identifies itself with its office-holders, and not with the great political inspirations which gave it birth, it has reached its climax, and its hours are numbered." The pursuit of wealth, however, provided the party with a new direction. A handful of Republicans continued to agitate regularly on behalf of Southern blacks but, by 1890, their efforts ceased altogether. Republicans now bowed to the wishes of party bigwigs and businessmen who insisted that cooperation with Southern whites was vital to Northern economic interests. Besides, the party had made significant inroads in the states of the Old Northwest, and Southern support wasn't as vital as it had been during Reconstruction.

The Republicans' abandonment of Southern blacks was strongly abetted by the U.S. Supreme Court. In crucial decisions made between 1876 and 1898, it steadily eliminated the human protections of the Fourteenth Amendment while it expanded its meaning in terms of property. By 1883, the court had struck down the most stringent clauses of the Enforcement and Ku-Klux acts; although it left significant scraps that would be useful a century later, its declaration that the enforcement acts protected only federal, not states', rights effectively curtailed the enforcement program. In the same year, the court declared the Civil Rights Act unconstitutional and wiped it from the books completely. Finally, in the *Plessy* v. *Ferguson* case of 1896, the court legitimized racial segregation. Only Justice John Marshall Harlan dissented in this historic decision, saying that "the judgment this day rendered will, in time, prove to be quite as pernicious as the decision made by this tribunal in the Dred Scott case."

Southern Democrats took heart from the court's rulings and, beginning in 1890, passed measures to eliminate black voting altogether. At Mississippi's new constitutional convention, nearly 123,000 blacks were "wiped off voter rolls almost overnight." State after state legally disfranchised blacks through voting tests ("How many windows in the White House?"), poll taxes, the ability to understand state constitutions, property qualifications, and "grandfather clauses." After the *Plessy* v. *Ferguson* decision, the South began enacting segregation laws, barring blacks from white public vehicles, train depots, restaurants, circuses, pool halls, drinking fountains, bathrooms, beaches, parks, pools, and recreation centers.

The North justified the South's actions with books and tracts on black inferiority. Some of these works posed as scientific anthropology. Others, such as the anonymously written *The Negro A Beast*, argued that blacks were animals, not human beings. The main thrust of Northern bigotry, however, was leveled at immigrants and Catholics. In the late nineteenth century, Northerners saw the arrival of huge ocean liners filled with immigrants from every part of the globe; they watched a second generation of American Catholics gain a foothold in industry, commerce, and education. Convinced that the "native American" was becoming extinct, attorney Henry F. Bowers and six friends formed, in March 1887, the American Protective Association—an antiforeigner, anti-Catholic secret society similar to the Know-Nothings. The goals of the APA included restricting immigration, knowing English as a prerequisite to American citizenship, removing Catholic teachers from public schools, and banning Catholics from public office. In the main, their methods were nonviolent. They circulated bogus documents and phony quotes proving the Pope's intention of "making America Catholic." They arranged lecture tours by fraudulent "ex-priests" and "escaped nuns" who recounted the titillating sexual horrors of convent life. In other ways, the APA could be quite cruel. Members antagonized Catholic candidates for office, and their seventy national periodicals urged the firing of Catholic servants and immigrant laborers. Reverend John Haynes Holmes of New York likened the APA to a Northern Ku-Klux, saying, "The Ku-Klux Klan agitation of the last few years was kindergarten play compared to that furious scourge that swept the hearts of men." Most APA members were Republicans. At high tide in 1894, the movement boasted 500,000 members and elected twenty of its sympathizers to Congress. By splitting completely from the Republican Party in 1896, the APA ruptured its own unity, and by 1900, it had completely wasted away.

The Whitecap movement of the same period was much more reminiscent of the Ku-Klux. The sheeted vigilantes known as Whitecaps first appeared by name in Indiana's Crawford and Harrison counties in 1888, where Tennesseans had migrated from the Klan's birthplace. Disconnected bands of Whitecaps soon sprang up throughout the Midwest, South, and Northeast. Their goals were entirely local. In Georgia, they drove away witnesses and government agents from illicit whiskey stills; in Mississippi they were identified with agrarian violence; in north Texas they were anti-black and in New Mexico anti-Republican. In Indiana, Ohio, and elsewhere in the Midwest, Whitecaps took an initial stance as law-

and-order "regulators" but soon degenerated into night-riding bullies and thugs. Their despicable qualities were brought to national attention in Booth Tarkington's best seller, *The Gentleman from Indiana*. The movement seems to have died out shortly after the turn of the century.

Coalescence between the anti-Catholicism of the APA and the brutish vigilante tactics of the Whitecaps would provide the grass-roots support for a revival of the Klan. But before the revival, a crucial role was played by the scholarly historians of Reconstruction. Heavily influenced by the 1872 joint committee minority report, these historians, from 1893 to 1907, systematically distorted the motives of radical Republicans, falsified the behavior of Southern blacks, and glorified the Ku-Klux Klansmen as heroes. Their influence on subsequent histories, both academic and popular, was enormous. The most important of their works were Woodrow Wilson's *A History of the American People*, John Ford Rhodes's *History of the United States* (volume 6), John S. Reynolds's *Reconstruction in South Carolina*, William A. Dunning's *Reconstruction, Political and Economic*, and the numerous Reconstruction monographs by Columbia University historian Walter Lynwood Fleming.

A composite sketch of Reconstruction and the Ku-Klux Klan from these five sources reads like this:

Radical Reconstruction was initiated by the "despotic" Thaddeus Stevens, who wanted to crush the defeated South out of pure "vindictiveness." Under Stevens's leadership, the Republican Congress plotted "to put the white South under the heel of the black South." To achieve this, it passed laws "enfranchising ignorance and disfranchising intelligence. It provided that the most degraded negro could vote, while Robert E. Lee [and other Confederate leaders] could not." Greedy carpetbaggers "swarmed out of the North to cozen, beguile, and use" the new black electorate; these miscreants, "who brought nothing with them, and had nothing to bring, but a change of clothing and their wits, became the new masters of the blacks." Southern loyalists, called scalawags, "vied in rascality with the bad carpetbaggers." With the aid of these two groups, "the ignorant Congo negro" attained political office—"men who could not so much as write their names and who knew none of the uses of authority except its insolence."

Blacks began flaunting their new freedom "to the disgust of the white citizens and the terror of their wives and children." Black "insolence" was rampant. "Murders were frequent, and outrages upon women were beginning to be heard of." Naturally, the "white men of the South were aroused by the mere instinct of self-preservation to rid themselves, by fair means or foul, of the intolerable burden of governments sustained by the votes of ignorant negroes and conducted in the interests of adventurers." Out of their concern was born the Ku-Klux Klan.

At first, the Klan directed its energies "against local incidents of radical misrule." Later, it began to "silence or drive from the country, the principal mischief-makers of the Reconstruction regime. . . ." The Klan "accomplished much good in reducing to order the social chaos." It "kept the negroes quiet and freed them to some extent from the baleful influence of alien leaders . . . property was more secure; people slept safely at night; women and children were again somewhat safe when walking abroad—they had faith in the honor and protection of the Klan."

This is what Americans would be taught about Reconstruction and the Ku-Klux Klan for the first sixty years of the twentieth century. More importantly, the distortion of history would be a critical factor in reviving the Klan. In the course of that endeavor, the impact of the historians would be magnified a hundredfold by a misguided genius who made the Reconstruction Ku-Klux the subject of the first motion-picture box-office smash.

BOOK TWO
1915-1930

"Your whole 'Invisible Empire' is a cancer in the body politic! It is like some foul and loathsome thing that grows and flourishes in the dark, away from the sight of honest men and women."

—HENRY FRY TO JOSEPH SIMMONS, 1921

"WRITING HISTORY WITH LIGHTNING"

D. W. Griffith and The Birth of a Nation: *1915*

On January 8, 1915, a major motion picture premiered at Clune's Auditorium in Los Angeles. Based on Thomas Dixon's novel *The Clansman*, it had been conceived and directed by rising young film maker D. W. Griffith who, along with his cast and crew, was on hand for this first showing. The entertainment world was buzzing with rumors about the film: It was supposedly the longest movie ever made. Its investors had lost faith in the project midway and believed Griffith insane. And Griffith had nearly gone bankrupt finishing the picture.

Ticket sales had been excellent, however. By early evening, a long line of people stood outside Clune's hoping to get in from last-minute cancellations. Inside, the house was packed, and the audience babbled and pointed at the symphony orchestra that was tuning up. An organist sat at a huge console with semicircular rows of gaudily colored stops. In an unusual move, Griffith had commissioned a complete orchestra score to accompany his new film. Its composer, Joseph Carl Breil, eventually strode to the podium and nodded at the audience while the house lights dimmed.

Breil raised his baton at the forty musicians and the house quieted. A projector started whirring at the back of the auditorium. And the title, *The Clansman*, came on apparently too soon, for the curtain hadn't been raised and the lettering was barely visible

119

on its dark fabric. It wasn't an accident. In silence, the big curtain rose all the way to reveal the title full and clear on the screen. Breil's baton swept downward and an immense chord exploded from the orchestra, underscored by the throbbing drone of the Mighty Wurlitzer. The spectators were visibly lifted out of their seats.

Three hours later, they came out of the theater—some misty-eyed, some talking animatedly, and others in a mute state of shock. The film was more than a success: It represented a new era in motion-picture history! A few weeks later, a grateful Tom Dixon told Griffith that *The Clansman* was "too tame" a title for the film version of his book. Such a revolutionary work of art should be called *The Birth of a Nation*. Griffith approved and the title was soon changed. Reporters began writing stories calling Griffith "a twentieth-century Homer" and predicting that his new art would catapult him to the forefront of the industry. A flock of newsmen surrounded Griffith and excitedly asked him to explain what makes a man great in his profession. What makes him stand head and shoulders above the competition? Griffith stared absentmindedly for a few seconds and twisted the ring on his finger.

"I dunno," he finally said. "How should *I* know?"

There were a lot of things Griffith didn't know that night. He didn't know that he had created the first motion-picture blockbuster—one that would gross well over $60 million, establish movies as a major American industry, and enshrine Hollywood, the dull, parched countryside where the film had been shot, as *The Motion-Picture Capital of the World*. He didn't know that what had been shown that evening would soon envelop the nation in a bitter controversy, trigger race riots, and embarrass the President of the United States. And the last thing he could have possibly imagined was that *The Birth of a Nation* would revive the Ku-Klux Klan of Reconstruction, giving it a new lease on life in the twentieth century.

David Wark Griffith was born in Oldham County, Kentucky, in 1875—just a few months before the first Kentucky Derby. His father was a former Confederate colonel known as Roaring Jake, and from him Griffith first learned to appreciate the romance of the Old South and the heroic tragedy of the Lost Cause. Roaring Jake died when his son was only ten years old, and Griffith was forced to seek work in Louisville. After a series of disappointing and insignificant jobs, he wound up touring with various fly-by-night theatrical companies that specialized in blood-and-thunder melodramas. After selling a play he had written for $1,000, Griffith fancied himself a professional playwright and moved to New York City, where his dramatic talents were grossly unappreciated. By chance, he wandered into the infant film industry, whose little one-reel "photoplays" were then flickering in the sleaziest dives in the nation.

By 1908, Griffith was directing for Biograph Studios and, in collaboration with his favorite cameraman Billy Bitzer, was experimenting with startling innovations in lighting and camera setups. By 1910, Griffith had developed the long shot, midshot, and close-up in an artistic combination that remains today the basic grammar of motion pictures. Griffith's films got good reviews and, for the most part, Biograph's producers tolerated Griffith's unusual ideas. But they objected to the expense of his methods and could never understand why he liked to cut back and forth between two entirely different situations. The ultimate impasse was reached over the length of his films. Griffith went from one to two reels in *Enoch Arden* in 1911. Two years later he made the first American four-reel film, *Judith of Bethulia,* which Biograph refused to distribute.

Griffith paced his ace cameraman's workshop. "We are just grinding out sausages, Billy," he complained, "and will continue to do so as long as we remain here." He spoke of an opportunity offered by Harry Aitken, president of the new Mutual Film Company. Aitken had promised Griffith a free hand and the chance to make any picture he wanted. "I want you on camera, if you'll only come," Griffith told Bitzer. "We have a chance to make it big. We will bury ourselves in hard work out at the coast for five years, and make the greatest pictures ever made, make a million dollars, and retire; and then you can have all the time you want to fool around with your camera gadgets, et cetera, and I shall settle down to write."

On October 1, 1913, Griffith resigned from Biograph after contributing five of the most significant years of motion picture evolution. As a measure of his co-workers' faith in him, Griffith succeeded in taking Bitzer and nearly every one of the Biograph players, including Lillian Gish, with him. His new contract with Aitken called for a large salary, a stock participation in the profits, and the right to make two independent pictures of his own choosing each year. From December 1913 to March 1914, they made a couple of five-reel films and a few potboilers. Then, in April, Griffith announced to his company that they were finally going to make the *big* picture.

The new film had come about through a deal Griffith had made for the rights to Thomas Dixon's *The Clansman*, a novel about the Civil War, Reconstruction, and the defeated South's "redemption from shame" by the secret brotherhood of the Ku-Klux Klan. The book had been enormously popular, and an attempt had already been made to film it. The Kinemacolor Company had spent $25,000 on the venture before going bust. Frank Woods had worked on the Kinemacolor project and told Griffith about it shortly after it had collapsed. Griffith was immediately interested and asked Woods to approach Tom Dixon about the rights. Griffith had once acted during his salad days in one of Dixon's small theatrical ventures and was worried that Dixon would think he wasn't a big enough man for the job. Before sending Woods off, Griffith cautioned him, "Now remember, don't mention I'm the actor that once worked for him, for he wouldn't have confidence in me."

Frank Woods arranged a meeting with the author of *The Clansman* over lunch, which for Dixon consisted of crackers, nuts, and milk. Woods assured Dixon that this time the film project couldn't fail. "We are going to sell Wall Street," Woods bubbled, "and get the biggest man in the business!"

"Who?" asked Dixon, munching placidly.

"D. W. Griffith!"

"Oh yes," Dixon nodded. "I've heard a lot about him—he used to work for me."

Thomas Dixon was born in 1864 to an old, respectable North Carolina family. He studied law and history at Johns Hopkins and was elected to the North Carolina legislature even before he was old enough to vote. Politics didn't suit him, however, and he entered the Baptist ministry and held pulpits in North Carolina, Boston, and finally New York. Dixon was undoubtedly the first in a string of twentieth-century, Southern-born, fire-breathing evangelists who greatly appealed to Yankees. After nine years as minister of New York's Twenty-third Street Baptist Church, he was reportedly attracting larger congregations than any other Protestant preacher in the country. A fiesty, acid-mouthed racist, Dixon electrified his flocks with forebodings of "creeping negroidism" and the gospel of white Christian supremacy. He was once indicted for slander from the pulpit but beat the charge handily. One of his admirers, John D. Rockefeller, offered to pay half the expense of building Dixon his own cathedral in downtown Manhattan. But Dixon declined, for he had already decided to try to reach a much larger audience. Without radio or television, it would have to be through the written word, and Dixon chose popular fiction. The sales of his book, *The Leopard's Spots* were very respectable in 1902. Three years later, *The Clansman* was a best seller.

Dixon's novels were essentially "racist sermons in the guise of fiction," of which *The Clansman* is prototypical. His race baiting was not unusual in turn-of-the-century America. Pseudoscientific works on the inferiority of blacks had already found wide audiences. But Dixon was unique. The degree to which he saw the difference between good and evil determined entirely by race was unrivaled until *Mein Kampf*; and his delusions and fears would have fit comfortably among the case studies in *Psychopathia Sexualis.*

The Clansman is filled with painful descriptions of black mobs with "onion-laden breath, mixed with perspiring African odour." Its author is obsessed with the theme of rape—the literal rape of whites by blacks as well as the symbolic rape of the South by the North in its program of "negro rule" during Reconstruction:

> "For a Russian to rule a Pole," he went on, "a Turk to rule a Greek, or an Austrian to dominate an Italian is hard enough, but for a thick-lipped, flat-nosed, spindle-shanked negro, exuding his nauseating animal odour, to shout in derision over the hearths and homes of white men and women is an atrocity too monstrous for belief. Our people are yet dazed by its horror. . . . The issue, sir, is Civilization! Not whether a negro shall be protected, but whether Society is worth saving from barbarism."

At the end of his book, Dixon's South is saved from "barbarism" by the Ku-Klux Klan, whose likes "the world had not seen since the Knights of the Middle Ages rode on their Holy Crusades."

There were a number of reasons for a book like *The Clansman* to become a best seller at this time. With the North's increasing fears over Negro migration; with Woodrow Wilson's federal segregation policy and his cutbacks of blacks from the Civil Service; and with the renewed talk about Negro deportation and colonization, Dixon's book on the alleged bestiality of blacks during the freedom of Reconstruction confirmed, in the past, what many whites were fearing about the present.

Dixon sold Griffith the screen rights to *The Clansman* for $2,500 and one quarter of the profits—a handsome contract for its day. The deal was closed on April 15, 1914, and a number of Griffith's employees thought the boss had gone mad. Many of them were aware that a dramatized version of *The Clansman*, written by Dixon, had already proved a failure. The play had had miserably short runs in New York and Washington, D.C. Even Southerners had been bored. The Atlanta *Journal* had called it "mediocre" and the Columbia *State* had belittled it as "a fairy tale." Apparently Dixon's gospel fared well as fiction but proved unbelievable when brought to life on the stage. Billy Bitzer was painfully aware of this problem. "I was from Yankee country," Bitzer recalled, "and to me the K.K.K. was sillier than the Mack Sennett comedy chases. A group of horsemen in white sheets? Preposterous." Bitzer's assistant, Karl Brown, was even more discouraged. Reading *The Clansman*, Brown found it "as bitter a hymn of hate as I had ever encountered. It was an old-fashioned hellfire sermon, filled with lies, distortions, and above all, the rankest kind of superstition."

But Griffith had never been more enthusiastic. To hell with *The Clansman!* Dixon's excesses could be balanced with historical scholarship. The important thing was the story—a saga of the Old South, its downfall in the Civil War, and its humiliation and redemption during Reconstruction. It was a story Griffith had absorbed at his father's knee and one ideally suited to his new art. In late June 1914, Griffith and his company set out for California. He rehearsed the cast for six weeks but began shooting on the Fourth of July. He soon lost sight of practical considerations and started acting more and more impulsively. He eventually threw away the shooting script and never again looked at the notes he had made from the book. By midsummer he had run out of money. After nine weeks of shooting, he had spent $78,000, exceeding his budget nearly twice over. A telegram from the Mutual Film Company was final: WE WILL SEND NO MORE MONEY. FINISH PICTURE IMMEDIATELY. Griffith had already exhausted his personal savings in the project and his faithful cast members were working without pay. Bitzer, too, had emptied his life savings of $7,000 into the film, and Griffith had come up with another $9,000 from an anonymous woman. But the picture wasn't finished.

Griffith finally went to Bill Clune, who owned Clune's Auditorium, one of the largest theaters in Los Angeles. He invited Clune to the lot to view some of the more spectacular shots of the battles and the heroic ride he had filmed of the Klansmen. He also hired some cheap musicians to accompany the footage. The two men watched the rushes while the makeshift band ground out a painful rendition of "Dixie."

"That's a pretty bad band," Clune observed.

"But think how that tune would sound if your orchestra played it," Griffith suggested.

Clune brightened. "I've got the best orchestra west of the Mississippi. That tune would sound great played by *my* orchestra in *my* theater."

For the right to an exclusive, premiere run of the new movie in his theater, Bill Clune invested $15,000 in the project, and Griffith finished shooting the picture. Another two months was spent editing the film, and *The Clansman* was finally completed in twelve reels at a record cost of $110,000.

The huge success of the Los Angeles premiere was a relief to everyone, and Griffith quickly made plans for a New York showing of the film, now titled *The Birth of a Nation*. Then the trouble began. Four days after the premiere, the Los Angeles branch of the National Association for the Advancement of Colored People informed its parent organization in New York that the Dixon–Griffith photoplay was in town and that "every resource of a magnificent new art" had been used "to picture Negroes in the worst possible light." The newly formed NAACP was becoming an increasingly effective voice for black Americans. Created to challenge the conservatism of Booker T. Washington, it owed much of its effectiveness to the brilliant leadership of W. E. B. DuBois, who was both editor of *The Crisis* and director of the NAACP's publicity and research. With DuBois there could be real problems ahead, but Tom Dixon had already anticipated it. Several years earlier there had been criticism of the dramatized version of *The Clansman*, and Dixon knew that *The Birth of a Nation* was ten times more powerful. He was well prepared.

On January 27, Dixon had written to an old Johns Hopkins chum who now happened to be President of the United States. Arrangements had been made for a private meeting between Dixon and Woodrow Wilson on February 3 at the White House. At this meeting, Dixon had explained that he had a favor to ask of the President, "not as the Chief Magistrate of the Republic but as a former scholar and student of history and sociology." Wilson was suspicious, fearing that Dixon was yet another old friend seeking a job in Washington. But Dixon surprised him. He wanted the President to see a motion picture, not because his old classmate had written the story but because it represented "the birth of a

new art—the launching of the mightiest engine for moulding public opinion in the history of the world."

Wilson was visibly relieved that Dixon's only request was that
he see a motion picture. The President liked movies but told Dixon
that he couldn't possibly go to the theater since he was still in
mourning over his wife's recent death. (He was two months from
courting the charming lady who would become the second Mrs.
Wilson.) The President suggested instead that the film be brought
to the White House and shown privately. It was more than Dixon
had bargained for, and a date was set for two weeks later.

On February 18, the film was projected in the East Room for
the President, his daughters, and members of his cabinet and their
families. Both Dixon and Griffith were present at this unique
showing, Griffith quite nervous. The President was much absorbed by the film and afterward shook hands with the young
projection crew and with the film's creators. "It is like writing
history with lightning," he told them, "and my only regret is that
it is all so terribly true."

The next day, Dixon was in a triumphant mood and, as long as
they were in Washington, he wanted the endorsement of another
individual—the Chief Justice of the Supreme Court. Justice Edward D. White, like Dixon, was a Southerner; and Dixon asked an
old friend and fellow Carolinian Josephus Daniels, who now was
Secretary of the Navy, for an introduction to the Chief Justice.
Daniels phoned White and, within minutes, Dixon arrived at
White's home and was escorted into the library.

The seventy-year-old crotchety judge, whose chief contribution
on the bench had been the weakening of antitrust legislation, sat
at his desk examining some papers. Refusing to look up at Dixon,
he grumbled, "Well, well, sir, what can I do for you?" When Dixon
explained that he wanted the Chief Justice to view a moving picture, White looked up in shock. "Moving picture! It's absurd, sir.
I never saw one in my life and I haven't the slightest curiosity to
see one. I'm very busy. I'll have to ask you to excuse me."

It looked as if Dixon had botched it, but in a clever parting shot,
he appealed to the judge's Southern roots, telling him that the
movie told the true story of Reconstruction and the redemption of
the South by the Ku-Klux Klan.

At once a change came over the Chief Justice's face. He slowly
removed his glasses and pushed his work aside. Leaning toward
Dixon, he murmured, "I was a member of the Klan, sir. . . .
Through many a dark night, I walked my sentinel's beat through

the ugliest streets of New Orleans with a rifle on my shoulder. . . .
I'll be there!"

With complete faith in Dixon's connections, Griffith was meanwhile busy renting and setting up the ballroom of Washington's
Raleigh Hotel for this second, special showing. That evening, the
ballroom was filled to capacity with a fashionable crowd. Near the
screen, the Chief Justice sat with his wife and invited guests. Behind them sat numerous members of the House and Senate, a
"sprinkling" of members of the State Department, and "scores of
high officials." Many newsmen were also present. Their reaction
to the film was as enthusiastic as it had been in Los Angeles.

The next day, an elated Griffith and Dixon transported the film
to New York City for a formal review by the National Board of
Censorship. With endorsements by the President and the cream
of Washington society, how could the board possibly go against
them? In fact, the board passed it fifteen to eight, the vote of its
chairman, Frederic C. Howe among the dissenters. Huge advertisements (the largest ever for *any* theatrical production) appeared
in all the papers for the New York premiere, set for March 3 at the
Liberty Theater. Whereas admission to nickelodeons had only
been a nickel, the cost of seeing *The Birth of a Nation* was an
unprecedented $2 a head. Twenty-four-sheet billboards appeared
along Broadway proclaiming the film "The Dawn of a New Epoch
in the Theatres of the World." Prospective viewers were promised
"A Red-blooded tale of the true American Spirit . . . A composition of National figures with the Universe as its background."
Huge painted figures of Klansmen bearing fiery crosses and
mounted on rearing horses were raised high over Times Square.

The NAACP snapped into action. Appearing at the office of the
National Board of Censorship, they requested the names of the
board members who had approved *The Birth of a Nation*, the
names and addresses of the full board, and a list of the cities where
the film was scheduled to be shown, and an opportunity for a
committee of its own members to preview the film before its New
York premiere. They were flatly denied every request. They then
appealed to the board's chairman, Frederic Howe, who was one of
the few to have cast a negative vote against the film; Howe gave
them the names of the full board and arranged a private showing
of the film for March 1, two days before the premiere. In the
meantime, the NAACP sent letters of protest to every member of
the full board.

On March 1, out of the twelve tickets promised to the NAACP

by Howe, the full board allowed only two; and these were specified for use *by whites only*. For the two white members who saw the preview, *The Birth of a Nation* more than confirmed their suspicions. The film had indeed used a breathtaking new art to depict blacks in the worst possible way; it depicted them as *dangerous* and was guaranteed to swell the worst fears of white America.

In a last-ditch effort on the morning of the premiere, the NAACP had the film's producer and director, Aitken and Griffith, summoned to the New York Police Court on the ground that they were "maintaining a public nuisance and endangering the public peace." Aitken's expensive attorneys argued effectively, concluding with a casual mention that the film had been shown in the White House and that President Wilson hadn't reacted as if the film were a "nuisance." Incredulous, the NAACP called the White House, reaching the President's daughter Margaret. Oh yes, Margaret confirmed, the film had been shown to her father and his guests—and, she thought, the Supreme Court and members of Congress had seen it as well. The chief magistrate quickly ruled that it was beyond his jurisdiction to stop the New York performance unless it led to an *actual* breach of the peace.

That evening, March 3, Broadway's Liberty Theater was jammed with a sell-out first-night crowd. Befitting the theme of the film, ladies dressed in antebellum crinolines escorted patrons into the theater, and ushers in Union and Confederate uniforms escorted them to their seats. Complimentary programs explained the technical as well as the historical aspects of the spectacle they were about to view. The orchestra tuned up, the curtain raised, and the New York premiere of *The Birth of a Nation* began rolling. Entranced, the audience watched a fascinating prologue on the abduction of slaves from Africa to Boston, when "the first seed of dis-Union" was planted in America. The story then shifted to a tale of two families, one on each side of the Mason–Dixon line.

The Northern family is headed by Congressman Austin Stoneman, an obvious caricature of Thaddeus Stevens complete with pinched face, ill-fitting wig, clubfoot, and a mulatto "mistress." Stoneman has two sons and a charming daughter Elsie, played by lovely Lillian Gish. In South Carolina, where life runs in "a quaintly quiet way," we find the Cameron household: Dr. Cameron and his saintly wife, his two sons and daughters, and his dogs and faithful "darkies." A visit between the two households results in mutual love interests. Phil Stoneman falls in love with the elder Cameron daughter, Margaret; Ben Cameron, dashingly played by handsome Henry Walthall, falls for the delectable Elsie Stoneman. As love blossoms, the orchestra swells into Carl Breil's only original piece for the score, "The Perfect Song" (later to become famous as the theme to "Amos and Andy"). But romance is suddenly interrupted by the Civil War. Lincoln signs the bill calling for volunteers. Rebel troops march off to the tune of "Dixie," while animated crowds of women, children, and black slaves cheer and wave handkerchiefs.

Orchestrated to the "Light Cavalry Overture," the Civil War scenes are thrilling. With its limited range of hues, Griffith's orthochromatic film has the unpolished texture of older photography, and the battle scenes are virtually Brady photographs come to life. In the battle of Petersburg, close-ups of savage fighting—including one of a bayonet plunging into a soldier's chest—are interspersed with panoramic long shots of heavy artillery and smoke-drenched charges staged four miles distant from the camera. At the end, stills of trenches piled high with dead soldiers poignantly illustrate "war's peace."

A barely open iris shows Elsie Stoneman and her brother Phil. The iris opens fully to reveal them taking seats in Ford's Theater on the night of April 14, 1865. Lincoln arrives at his box, and the ensuing shots tensely capitalize on one's knowledge of what will happen. Gauzed close-ups reveal John Wilkes Booth and his derringer. Booth creeps up behind Lincoln and fires. A narrow spotlight (Bitzer used sunlight reflected from a mirror) follows Booth as he leaps from the box to the stage. *"Sic semper tyrannis!"*

The film broke for an intermission, which the breathless audience very much needed. During the eight-minute break, Tom Dixon appeared on the stage and announced that he "would have allowed none but the son of a Confederate soldier to direct the film version" of his novel. To a standing ovation, Griffith came on stage looking quite uncomfortable. The director made some nervous, barely audible remarks about "freeing motion pictures from the curb of censorship." After more applause, the audience settled down for part two.

After Lincoln's assassination, Congressman Stoneman has become "the greatest power in America" and launches Radical Reconstruction —"an era of cruel chicanery and political upheaval." Stoneman's policies are to be carried out upon a prostrate South by his mulatto protégé, Silas Lynch, played by George Siegmann with a combination of obsequious charm and subtle lechery. Soon "the newfound freedom" of the former slaves "turns to rude insolence." Black militiamen take over South Carolina's streets in a reign of terror. Flashes are shown of helpless white virgins being whisked indoors by lusty black bucks. At a carpetbaggers' rally, wildly animated blacks carry placards proclaiming EQUAL RIGHTS, EQUAL POLITICS, EQUAL MARRIAGE. At the subsequent election, whites are disfranchised while grossly stupid blacks vote—some of them more than once. Silas Lynch is easily elected lieutenant governor of the state and begins lusting after Elsie Stoneman, the daughter of his benefactor.

The overtaking of the state by the blacks grows more vicious, tragic, and obscene. A session of the "black-and-tan" legislature at Columbia, South Carolina, is on the order of a minstrel show, with black delegates swigging whiskey, eating chicken, and propping their bare feet upon their desks. Bills are introduced compelling all whites to salute black officers and sanctioning interracial marriage; both are passed with uproarious enthusiasm.

"In agony of soul over the degradation and ruin of his people," young Ben Cameron conceives the idea of the Ku-Klux Klan. Disguised in white sheets, the new vigilantes take advantage of the superstitiousness of blacks and begin frightening them into law and order.

A caption forewarns that Congressman Stoneman's "insistence on full racial equality brings grim tragedy." Gus, a free Northern black "renegade," takes a fancy to the youngest Cameron daughter, winsomely played by Mae Marsh. The girl goes to the woods to gather spring water and is secretly followed by Gus. "Little Sister's" innocence is emphasized in crosscuts between her and a cute squirrel, which she watches in delight. The black "renegade" skulks up behind and grabs her. "I'se a captain now," he tells her, "and I wants to git married." She throws her bucket at him in horror and runs away.

Shots of the terrified girl are intercut with those of Gus in hot pursuit. He runs low to the ground with his shoulders thrown back like an ape. He froths at the mouth (Griffith had the actor swill hydrogen peroxide), and his profusely dripping sputum suggests the ejaculation of semen. The segments of Little Sister in flight and Gus in pursuit become shorter and shorter, creating unbearable suspense. The orchestra plays hootchy-kootchy music wth driving tomtom beats, suggesting to one listener the image of "a black penis pushing into the vagina of a white virgin." Gus chases the now-hysterical girl to the edge of a cliff, where the two are seen in sudden close-up— then long shot. "Stay away or I'll jump!" she implores. Gus staggers forward. The audience screams as a long shot shows Little Sister falling from the cliff. A midshot brings her body rolling to a stop in a glen, her mouth dripping blood and her hair blowing lightly in the wind. Her brother Ben finds her and caresses her broken body, his face wrenched in fury and resolve.

Ben summons the white-hooded Klansmen who capture Gus for "a fair trial." A cowering Gus is shown in their clutches; a wooden cross burns in the background. An image of Little Sister in a coffin flashes.

"Guilty!" the Klansmen decree. Gus's corpse with a *KKK* note pinned to the chest is thrown on Silas Lynch's front porch. In retaliation, Lynch orders the elderly Dr. Cameron arrested. Cameron is carried away by the obnoxious black militia but is rescued by his faithful servants, his surviving daughter Margaret, and her beloved Phil Stoneman. They escape to a little cabin in the woods, owned by two Union soldiers.

In the meantime, Lynch gets drunk "on wine and power." Elsie Stoneman goes to him to plead for Dr. Cameron's life and Lynch can no longer restrain his passion. He barricades her in his house and orders his henchmen to prepare for a forced marriage. Outside, the streets run riot with crazed blacks. Lynch calls Elsie's attention to them. "See," he tells her, "my people fill the streets. With them I will build an empire and you shall be its queen!"

But her true love Ben Cameron has summoned the Klan. Hooded riders and their white-draped mounts are seen riding in small groups, combining into larger and larger ones. Soon the entire screen is filled with an army of Klansmen. Ben Cameron rears up in his stirrups, holding aloft a flaming cross. The orchestra and the Mighty Wurlitzer burst into "The Ride of the Valkyries" and they're off to the rescue! The Klansmen dash over hills, across meadows and streams. They pour over the screen like "an Anglo-Saxon Niagara" and the audience goes wild, clapping, cheering and jumping out of their seats.

The Klansmen overcome the black militia in the streets, rescue Elsie from Lynch, and dash off to save Dr. Cameron and his party who are trapped in the cabin of the Union men, now under siege by blacks. Inside the cabin, "the former enemies of North and South" unite "in defense of their Aryan birthright." Blacks break in the windows and doors, but cutbacks show the Klansmen close at hand. As the blacks enter the cabin, Dr. Cameron is ready to dash his daughter's brains out with the butt of his pistol to save her from a fate worse than death. But the Klansmen suddenly arrive and everyone is saved.

The finale shows a "parade of the liberators." The triumphant Klansmen ride gloriously into town with Ben and Elsie, Phil and Margaret in the lead. Southern families watch them joyfully, relieved that law and order are secure in the hands of these wondrous white knights.

For the rest of his life, Griffith would swear that *The Birth of a Nation* was "based upon truth in every vital detail" and would be indignant over criticism suggesting otherwise. In response to an exceptionally harsh magazine article written shortly before his death, Griffith replied: "I will take this occasion of Lincoln's birthday to request that you permit me to say just this. I am not now and never have been 'anti-Negro' or 'anti' any other race. . . . In filming *The Birth of a Nation*, I gave to my best knowledge the proven facts, and presented the known truth, about the Reconstruction period in the American South. These facts are based on an overwhelming compilation of authentic evidence and testimony." In support of his argument, Griffith cited the history books of Woodrow Wilson, John Ford Rhodes, William A. Dunning and the others. If Griffith's defense is investigated, one finds that he was essentially correct. He may have simplified the textbooks in his film, but he had not exaggerated the distortions of the scholars. *The Birth of a Nation* must not be confused with truth, but whether written with lightning or not, it was indeed history. It was a faithful composite of the "proven facts" and "authentic evidence" contained in the most reputable history books of 1915. The unfortunate thing was that *The Birth of a Nation* would bring these distortions powerfully to the masses, indelibly affecting the way white America regarded Reconstruction for the next forty-five years.

The day after the New York premiere, the newspapers bubbled over with lavish descriptions and rave reviews. Griffith's epic was "beyond question the most extraordinary picture" that had ever been made. "If there is to be a greater picture than *The Birth of a Nation*, may we live to see it." The production was "stupendous in scope and gorgeously prodigal in detail." It was bound to capture "everyone who cares for novelty, spectacular drama and thrills piled upon thrills." Griffith's art was "an impressive new illustration of the scope of the motion-picture camera" and was far more important than the script. "If anything can justify Mr. Dixon's story of racial hatreds, that thing is Mr. Griffith's pictorial representation of it."

Of special interest were the articles that sustained the film's version of Reconstruction history. In a widely reprinted review, columnist Dorothy Dix claimed, "What followed in the days of Reconstruction is the blackest page in American history, a story so horrible that it has never been adequately told until in these pictures." The New York *American* pointed out that the important thing about the thrills of the film was that "they are made out of historic facts, not fancies." In another widely reprinted feature, Reverend Thomas B. Gregory swore that the value of the film lay in its truthfulness: "That the story as told by the picture is true, I am ready to swear on the Bible, the Koran, the Zend and all the other 'Holy Scriptures' put together. I know it is true, because I lived through the actual realities themselves."

Griffith's film aroused considerable interest in Reconstruction. The Chicago *Daily News* printed a serialized version of the pertinent passages from President Wilson's A *History of the American People.* Elderly Klansmen began coming out of the woodwork. For forty-four years they had remained silent, but *The Birth of a Nation* was telling the country their story, and public curiosity compelled them at last to speak. Their eyewitness confirmation of incidents in the movie appeared in numerous newspapers.

An ecstatic Tom Dixon wrote to Woodrow Wilson, telling him that "the big picture" had swept New Yorkers "off their feet. . . . I shall never cease to be grateful to you and your lovely daughters for our beautiful reception." Dixon sent clippings of all the reviews to the President, with one exception: "The New York *Evening Post* is the only one I have not sent you—it's a rag I never allow in my house or touch without a pair of tongs. Oswald Villard, a noted negro-lover, owns it—you may have heard of him!"

Certainly Wilson had heard of him. Oswald Garrison Villard was William Lloyd Garrison's grandson and a founder of the NAACP. A Wilson supporter in 1912, he was now one of the most outspoken opponents of Wilson's segregation policy in Washington, D.C. Villard condemned *The Birth of a Nation* as "a direct incitement to crime. It is a deliberate effort to arouse racial prejudice and to injure a large class of our citizens." In language akin to his grandfather's, Villard wrote to Mayor John P. Mitchell, demanding that he put a stop to the showing of this "improper, immoral, and unjust" film. On March 10, more members of the NAACP went to the show. After listening to their impressions and objections, the NAACP board filed criminal proceedings against Aitken and Griffith.

Amid this flurry of litigation, the National Board of Censorship decided to view *The Birth of a Nation* again; this time they thought that perhaps a few cuts were in order. The cuts made, however, weren't enough for Chairman Howe who promptly went public with his objections. "The ground of my protest," he told the press, "is that the play affects 10 million citizens who are degraded by this production." The next day, March 13, the much-admired Jane Addams challenged the historical accuracy of the film in an article in Villard's *Evening Post.* The second half of the film, she said, was "a pernicious caricature of the Negro Race." She deplored the fact that the Ku-Klux Klan was "made to appeal to the enthusiasm of the spectator as the heroic defender" of victimized whites. "None of the outrageous, vicious, misguided outrages which [the

Klan] certainly committed are shown. . . . The production is the most subtle form of untruth—a half truth." The film drew additional criticism from high circles. Dr. Jacques Loeb of the Rockefeller Institute called it "a glorification of homicidal mania," while novelist Upton Sinclair thought it "the most poisonous play" he had ever seen. A few scholars, including Drs. Samuel Crothers and Albert B. Hart, disparaged the historical basis of the film. Dr. Hart claimed that *The Birth of a Nation* was an "absolutely unfounded series of pictures intended to leave upon the mind the conviction that in Reconstruction times Negro soldiers freely plundered and abused the white people of the South, and were encouraged to do so by their white officers. No such thing ever occurred in the whole history of Reconstruction." Others pointed out that Reconstruction came about in the first place to protect blacks from the tyranny of whites.

Tom Dixon promptly came back with a peppery defense of his interpretation, published in the New York *Sun*. He pooh-poohed any suggestion that the Reconstruction laws were enacted to protect blacks from whites. That, he said, "is a silly campaign falsehood of 1868. . . . The reconstruction laws were passed for one reason only, to give the radical majority of Congress an indefinite lease of power through negro votes. That these laws were a disgrace to the nation is proved today by the fact that the Supreme Court of the United States has declared them null and void." He repeated his main point that Southern belles were in great danger from black males during Reconstruction and referred anyone who thought otherwise "to the sworn testimony of the ten enormous volumes [actually, there are twelve] of the Government reports on the Ku-Klux Klan Conspiracy." Dixon offered $5,000 to anyone who could disprove his version of Reconstruction or the Klan, and no one took him up on it.

The pace of the controversy suddenly quickened. On March 15, the NAACP was informed that *The Birth of a Nation* had now been officially approved by the Board of Censorship, although Chairman Howe forbade his name from appearing on the seal of approval. The NAACP viewed the "revised" version of the film and was disappointed; only very slight cuts of the objectionable scenes had been made. After repeated hounding of City Hall by Villard, DuBois, and Harriet Stanton Blatch (representing New York's suffragettes), the film's detractors were granted a March 30 hearing with Mayor Mitchell.

On that day, the mayor told an overflowing delegation that he had seen the film and agreed with the adverse criticism of it. He shared the belief that the film might incite breaches of the peace and had so advised the manager of the Liberty Theater and the producers of the film. The latter had agreed to cut an obnoxious epilogue depicting blacks being deported to Africa and other disagreeable scenes, and the photoplay would be produced in this new form that evening. The NAACP viewed this second revision of the film and was still unhappy. Racism was an integral feature of the second half of the film and deletions here and there could not diminish its overall effect.

A few weeks later, the first "breach of the peace" occurred. A young man threw two eggs at the screen that fell short of their mark and landed on the musicians in the pit. He was dragged out of the theater by Pinkerton detectives specially hired by Dixon. The incident, fairly innocuous by today's standards, was recounted in newspapers coast to coast. Never had a motion picture aroused such feeling and generated such national interest. The film was now bringing in $13,000 a week at the Liberty Theater, and New York's NAACP let its opposition slide. DuBois conceded that Griffith was an ill used but "mighty genius" and that further protests would only add to the profits being realized by Dixon and the film's producers.

The controversy was far from over, however, for in April the film opened in Boston—home of such liberal organs as William Monroe Trotter's *Guardian* and the Boston *Post.* Alarmed by New York's failure, Boston mustered a massive attack on the film. Mayor James Curley offered immediate public hearings on April 7, which Griffith attended. Tempers were short. Blacks hissed mention of the President's and Justice White's endorsement of the film and disputed Griffith's claim that he had based the film on scholarly historical sources. Moorfield Storey, who had been an aid to Senator Charles Sumner during Reconstruction, asked Griffith if it was historically accurate that a colored lieutenant governor of South Carolina had locked up a white girl in preparation for a forced marriage. Griffith merely smiled and said, "Come and see the play." He extended his hand to Storey who drew back, saying, "No sir!" Mayor Curley ultimately agreed to more deletions in the film than New York had made but said that his agreement to the cuts was more a concession than an act of conscience.

In the meantime, Rolfe Cobleigh, editor of *The Congregationalist and Christian World* at Beacon Street, made contact with Tom Dixon. Dixon sent the editor the rave reviews of the film, adding that the "only objection to it so far is a Negro Society which advises its members to arm themselves to fight the whites." Later, Dixon would embellish his delusions of the NAACP by calling it a "Negro Intermarriage Society." On the morning of April 9, Dixon called in person at Cobleigh's office. In answer to the question of what his real purpose was behind the play, Dixon answered that he "wanted to teach the people of the United States, especially the children, that the true history of the Reconstruction period was as it was represented in *The Birth of a Nation.*" Emphasizing the alleged passion of black males for white females, Dixon added that it was also his intention "to create a feeling of abhorrence in white people, especially white women, against colored men."

On April 17, violence finally erupted when a group of blacks were refused tickets to see the film at Boston's Tremont Theater. In a few minutes, a crowd of black demonstrators appeared. A few of them managed to get inside and pelt the screen with eggs. Two hundred policemen were called out and dragged them from the theater. Monroe Trotter was the leader of the group, and he and eleven other blacks were arrested. The mayor closed the theater the following Sunday. On Monday, Governor David Walsh attempted to push a bill through the Massachusetts legislature that would allow for the suppression of racially inflammatory films. The bill sailed through the house but was declared unconstitutional by the senate judiciary committee. Having failed at the state level, the opposition turned to Washington.

Justice White rued the day he had agreed to see *The Birth of a Nation.* His willingness to preview and approve a film glorifying the Ku-Klux Klan turned out to be as indiscreet and unprofessional as he had originally thought. After continuous pressure, he finally wrote to the film's producers, saying that he was "so situated" that if the "rumors" about his sanctioning the show were continued, he would be "under the obligation of denying them publicly"—even to the point of saying that he *did not like* the film. "Therefore," wrote the judge, "if the owners were wise they would stop the rumors." It was a good bluff, but the judge's readiness to lie showed how worried he was.

Not so the President, who regarded the matter a nuisance. He studiously ignored the controversy over the film and the use of his name to promote it, until it was pointed out that his continuing to do so might lose Democratic votes. The New York Headquarters of the National Colored Democratic League wrote him, asking for an explicit answer on whether or not he had endorsed the film.

Letters asking the same question came from various congressmen. When clippings of the Boston riot and Monroe Trotter's arrest reached the White House, Wilson's chief of staff, Joseph Tumulty, suggested that the President write "some sort of letter showing that he did not approve" the film. Wilson responded in a memo:

> Dear Tumulty,
>   I would like to do this if there were some way in which I could do it without seeming to be trying to meet the agitation which in the case referred to in this clipping [of the Boston riot] was stirred up by that unspeakable fellow Tucker.

(The President of course meant "Trotter," but recollections of painful past confrontations with this black leader of the National Equal Rights League undoubtedly prompted the slip.) When an emotional letter arrived from Massachusetts Congressman Thomas Thatcher, Wilson was finally moved to write a disclaimer:

> Dear Tumulty,
>   I would suggest as an answer to this letter the following:
>   "It is true that *The Birth of a Nation* was produced before the President and his family at the White House, but the President was entirely unaware of the character of the play before it was presented and has at no time expressed his approbation of it. Its exhibition at the White House was a courtesy extended to an old acquaintance."

Wilson's disclaimer went out under Tumulty's signature on April 30 and dampened opposition to the film considerably. Some liberals continued the fight in Boston, but the show went on and the Tremont Theater was daily filled to capacity. The film's would-be censors finally accepted the enormity of their failure when Cambridge Unitarians, overwhelmed by the movie's magic, succumbed to its message and began praising the Ku-Klux Klan. Reverend Lyman Rutledge, pastor of the Harvard Street Unitarian church, sermonized: "There is no possibility of ever effacing the vivid memory of those night riders, and their memory is to be forever associated with a thrill of joy. They stand here for that divine spirit which is above law, which in defiance of inadequate law rises to defend its honor in the face of tyranny."

Gloating over the fact that "the silly legal opposition" to the movie was simply putting more money in his pockets, Tom Dixon wrote to Joseph Tumulty at the White House:

I had a good laugh over the soft answer with which you turned away the wrath of our African friends. . . . Of course I didn't dare allow the President to know the *real big purpose back of my film—which was to revolutionize northern sentiment by a presentation of history that would transform every man in my audience into a good Democrat!* And make no mistake about it—we are doing just that. . . . Every man who comes out of one of our theaters is a Southern partisan for life—except the members of Villard's Inter-Marriage Society [the NAACP] who go there to knock.

Dixon later felt confident enough to repeat his belief to the President: "This play is transforming the entire population of the North and West into Sympathetic Southern voters. There will never be an issue of your segregation policy."

Dixon's megalomania aside, his assertions were partially true. The film was indeed reaching millions of people. Twenty-four prints were being worn out in the major cities of the nation. Special trains brought the rural masses to the cities to see it; and for probably half of the 25 million original viewers, it was the first motion picture they had ever seen. In the North, protests over the film's showing occurred in Atlantic City, Pittsburgh, Chicago, Milwaukee, Spokane, and Portland, but overwhelming enthusiasm easily quashed any criticism. And many diehard Yankees were deeply affected by the film. As one said after leaving the theater, "It makes me want to go out and kill the first Negro I see." Others wondered aloud whether their ancestors had fought on the wrong side during the Civil War. A "Ku-Klux fever," similar to that of Reconstruction, was revived in the North, and manufacturers responded with the production of Ku-Klux hats (patterned after the eighteen-inch hoods in the film) and Ku-Klux Kitchen aprons. New York society matrons held Ku-Klux balls. And on Halloween, students at the University of Chicago threw a party where two thousand young people cavorted in improvised Klan costumes.

If the North's response to *The Birth of a Nation* was festive, the South's response was profound. The Chester *Semi-Weekly News* pronounced the film "a sacred epic," and for many people below the Mason–Dixon line, *The Birth of a Nation* was a near-religious experience. Southern audiences "wept, yelled, whooped, cheered" and on one occasion shot up the screen in an attempt to save Little Sister from Gus the rapist. In the Piedmont region of South Carolina—where, thirty-four years earlier, President Grant had suspended habeas corpus to fight the Klan—people were especially enthusiastic. Interestingly, Dixon's dramatized version of *The*

Clansman had failed in this region, but Griffith's film was another matter. Droves of Yorkville citizens piled into trains bound for Charlotte, North Carolina, where the film was being shown, and didn't return home—thrilled and drained—until four in the morning. At the film's premiere in Spartanburg, audiences were "almost hysterical."

In an astonishing few months, Griffith's masterpiece had united white Americans in a vast national drama, convincing them of a past that had never been. The film's impact was especially strong on American collectives. The *Chicago Examiner* declared it impossible to convey the effect of *The Birth of a Nation* upon "social groups and societies of every description—fraternities, sororities, 'brotherhoods,' secret orders, clubs, regional organizations, houseparties, week-end parties, theatre parties, commemorative gatherings and the like." Many of these groups thought it would be a good idea to revive the Ku-Klux Klan. And it wouldn't take long before the notion was acted upon.

5

"HERE YESTERDAY, HERE TODAY, HERE FOREVER"

The Klan Revival: 1915–1921

Clarence Darrow observed during the 1920s that "the number of people on the borderline of insanity in a big country is simply appalling, and these seem especially addicted to believing themselves saviors and prophets." Darrow's remark is particularly apt of the alcoholic preacher who took the steps necessary for a full-scale revival of the Klan.

William Joseph Simmons was born in Harpersville, Alabama, in 1880. College records fail to support his claim that he studied medicine at Johns Hopkins University. After a stint in the Spanish–American War, "Joe" was converted to a born-again Christian at a revival meeting. After a brief term at Southern University, he was licensed as a Methodist minister and began riding circuits in Alabama and Florida. Although the job of Methodist circuit rider in the rural South was adventurous, it was abysmally unremunerative. Joe rarely netted more than $300 a year and was compelled to give public lectures on moral topics, such as "Women, Weddings and Wives." Though "equally at home in pulpit or platform," Simmons much preferred the platform. Public speaking came naturally to him. He was reasonably well read, adept at homespun homilies, and people found him "as full of sentiment as a plum is of juice."

He was also a lonely man, and his most constant evening companion was a bottle of bourbon. One summer night, sitting drunk at the window and staring at the moon, he saw a vision of ghost-riders in the sky. Swiftly they raced through the clouds and across the heavens, while the moon's surface became a relief map of the United States. Joe fell to his knees, beseeching God for an explanation. None came, but he would later proclaim this vision a divine augury of his true calling.

People often referred to Simmons as "a dreamer" which was a polite way of saying he didn't have a practical bone in his head. Wedded to his zeal for saving souls was complete incompetence when it came to handling the administrative duties of the cloth. At the 1912 Methodist Bishop's Conference, he fully expected to be awarded a "big-city pulpit" in Mobile or Montgomery, but was instead upbraided before the committee, charged with ineffi-ciency, and suspended for a year. Though Simmons reported shock at this action, his superiors had long been accustomed to the fact that he held a "much higher estimate of his abilities" than was warranted. Finally confronted with reality, Joe sank into a two-year depression which he spent in a Birmingham boarding-house run by relatives.

He wandered from one job to another, selling garters and "teaching history." Then he hit on the chance of becoming a promoter for Woodmen of the World. At this time in America, new fraternal orders were springing up every week—Woodmen, Redmen, Icemen, Moose. The fraternal boom coincided with America's concentration in the cities, as Charles Merz explained in the *New Republic*:

> Once we had a neighborhood. People lived next door to friends. There was no talk of "community spirit." Communities had it without trying. That is less true nowadays. Friends in cities live a mile apart. Even in the villages, factory, radio, motor car and moving pictures are pushing sections of the old communities apart, sandwiching new interests in between. What are lodges, anyway—for all their Joves and Neptunes, their rituals and their myths of gay dogs who have left their wives at home—but homesick tribesmen hunting their lost clans?

Joe liked clannishness and he loved being with the boys. A mem-ber of two different churches, he also joined the Masons, Knights Templars, Knights of Pythias, the Odd Fellows, and eight other lodges. He was a good promoter for the Woodmen. His success at the new job and his budding fraternal memberships seemed to buoy his self-esteem. His $10,000 a year in commissions didn't hurt either.

In 1914, he was made district manager for the Woodmen and moved to Atlanta, where he made a concerted effort at becoming well known. His physical appearance helped considerably. He stood six-feet, two-inches tall and had flaming red hair. A gold-framed pince-nez hung from a short chain clipped to the lobe of his right ear. He liked old-fashioned cutaway frock coats and striped trousers. He walked the streets covered with his lodge pins: "Their weight was well distributed on lapel, vest, fingers, and hung pendant-fashion from the heavy gold watch chain, which was the hallmark of the salesman, or confidence man, of the times." He was gallant and charming to the ladies, most of whom were fooled by the mints and cloves he habitually chewed to cover his bourbon. He introduced himself as Colonel Simmons, after his honorary rank in the Woodmen. Others called him Doc after his reputed medical study. Some considered him a "pious, prissy-walking big man." But his close associates spoke of him with the "half-condemning, half-affectionate, sometimes profane phrases reserved for the amiably fraudulent who managed to be equally at home leading prayer, preaching, taking a dram, or making a fourth at poker."

Early in 1915, while Simmons was standing on an Atlanta street-corner, a touring car skidded around a corner and rammed him in the back. Confined to bed for three months, he slipped into the most sustained period of monomania of his life. He began having dreams of the ultimate fraternity. He remembered the vision he had experienced while staring pie-eyed at the moon. And he pondered the fact that Tom Dixon's novel about the Klan had just been made into a smash moving picture. Soon he began drawing figure after figure of Klansmen on horseback and on foot. He obtained a copy of the 1867 Reconstruction Klan Prescript and worked out an expanded ritual and hierarchy of offices, staying as close to the Prescript's terminology as possible. He became utterly obsessed with the use of the letters *KL* to begin the name of every Klan office and function. The Klan constitution became the *Kloran*. When two Klansmen wished to talk secretly to each other, they held a *klonversation*. "It was rather difficult, sometimes, to make the two letters fit in," he recalled later, "but I did it some-how." He also made up catchy little passwords. *AYAK?* meant "Are you a Klansman?" *AKIA* meant "A Klansman I am." He used every bit of his knowledge of fraternal lodges to round out his prospectus for a new Klan. By the time he was done, he was convinced he had created a masterpiece: "Its ritualism is vastly different from anything in the whole universe of fraternal ritualism," he claimed. "It is altogether original, weird, mystical, and of a high class. . . . It unfolds a spiritual philosophy that has to do with the very fundamentals of life and living, here and hereafter."

After three months of plotting and paperwork, Simmons asked Atlanta city clerk Walter Taylor what he thought of the idea of reviving the Ku-Klux Klan as a locker club. (At this time, Georgia had already passed Prohibition, but gentlemen could keep "any kind or quantity" of liquor in their own lockers at their own clubs; this loophole resulted in a herd of Atlanta locker clubs, variously called the Badgers, the Panthers, and the Buffaloes.) "What do you think of it, Walter?" Simmons asked. "The name I mean. For a locker club. Will they join?"

"Naw," Walter retorted, "they all want to be animals."

And there matters rested until Colonel Joe "Doc" Simmons's hopes for a revived Ku-Klux Klan were realized jointly by the Atlanta premiere of *The Birth of a Nation* and the Frank murder case.

On April 27, 1915, Mary Phagan, a fourteen-year-old employee of a Marietta, Georgia, pencil company, was found raped and murdered in the basement of the building where she worked. Her employer, Leo M. Frank, a Jew originally from New York, was arrested, tried, and convicted of the murder. The evidence against Frank was biased and inconsistent. (Not until 1982 would Frank's complete innocence come to light as the result of a witness's deathbed statement.) After various civil liberties groups denounced the injustice of Frank's death sentence, the governor of Georgia commuted it to life imprisonment. Georgians' fury over their governor's apparent capitulation to outside pressure was kindled to a white heat by venerable Atlanta citizen and former U.S. Representative Thomas E. Watson.

Watson's was a populism gone sour. An agrarian Rebel and champion of the common man in the 1890s, Watson by 1915 had hardened into a genuine paranoid. "When mobs are no longer possible," he proclaimed, "liberty will be dead." His racism was unabashedly expressed in two magazines he owned and edited, *Watson's Magazine* and the *Weekly Jeffersonian*. For Watson, blacks represented a "hideous, ominous national menace," and his depiction of the stomach-churning lust of black men for white women eclipsed even Dixon's. He didn't like Catholics any better.

He referred to the Pope as "Jimmy Cheezy" and wrote sensational stories about "Jimmy's" worldwide hordes of "libidinous priests." But Jews were probably the most dangerous. When Frank was found guilty of the Phagan murder, Watson wrote, "Our Little Girl—ours by the Eternal God—has been pursued to a hideous death and bloody grave by this filthy perverted Jew of New York." When Frank's sentence was commuted, Watson swiftly decided that the action had been effected by an international Jewish conspiracy. After all, like niggers, Jews had "a ravenous appetite for the forbidden fruit." Furthermore, Frank belonged to the "Jewish aristocracy," and it was easy for the Jews of the world to arrange that "no aristocrat of their race should die for the death of a working-class Gentile." He ended with a boldfaced exhortation: "RISE! PEOPLE OF GEORGIA!"

One hundred men answered his call. Gathering at midnight on Mary Phagan's grave, they selected a team of twenty-five, including a Methodist minister, to avenge the little girl's death. A month later, August 16, 1915, Frank was abducted from a Georgia prison farm and hanged by the first lynching party in America to use automobiles. The members of the party christened themselves the Knights of Mary Phagan, and exactly two months after the lynching, they climbed Stone Mountain (a 1,780-foot-high chunk of granite eighteen miles from Atlanta) and burned a gigantic cross that was "visible throughout the city." Many Georgians approved of the lynching and applauded the cross burning. Watson certainly did. He was fifteen years old when the old Ku-Klux had ridden, and in the September 2 issue of the *Jeffersonian*, he suggested that "another Ku Klux Klan" be organized "to restore HOME RULE."

Public response to the Frank lynching galvanized Doc Simmons into action. A revived Ku-Klux Klan could certainly be more than just another lodge or locker club. He gathered together thirty-four fellow fraternalists, including members of the Knights of Mary Phagan and two former Reconstruction Klansmen; and on October 26, 1915, they signed an application to the State of Georgia to charter the Knights of the Ku Klux Klan as a "purely benevolent and eleemosynary" fraternal order. Simmons designated himself Imperial Wizard. One month later, he was determined to repeat the burning of a cross on Stone Mountain, where he intended to swear in the charter members. On Thanksgiving morning, he drove out to the mountain, stopped at a lumberyard, and carried a sixteen-foot cross on his back to the top of the mountain—an experience he never forgot and rejoiced in retelling. On Thanksgiving evening, he convened his Klansmen at the Piedmont Hotel. When he told them they were going to revive "the ancient glories" of the Klan atop Stone Mountain, city clerk Walter Clark protested. "Jesus, Doc," he said, "I can't climb Stone Mountain in the daytime. Can't you revive the ancient glories in the flatlands?" But capitalizing on the infamy of the Frank lynching was important, as was the staging of the ceremony on Thanksgiving. *The Birth of a Nation* had already been shown to ecstatic audiences in over a dozen Southern cities, and its well-publicized Atlanta premiere was scheduled for the following week. Simmons knew that Griffith's film would give "a tremendous popular boost" to a Klan that had already been revived.

Anticipating protests such as Walter Clark's, Simmons had rented a sightseeing bus for $25, which was waiting outside the hotel. Only fifteen of the thirty-four charter members agreed to go with him to Stone Mountain. The actual ceremony is best recounted in Simmons's own words:

> It was pitch dark, and we had to use flashlights. Down at the bottom of the mountain there's a spring of sparkling cold water. I stopped at the spring and took some of the water in my old army canteen and stopped to make a few remarks on purity and honor. Then we struggled to the top. . . . Each pilgrim, when nearing the crest, gathered a granite boulder, and on the summit of Stone Mountain the sixteen boulders were built into an altar. . . . They builded in their crude altar greater than they knew. . . . I put the canteen of water on the stones with a few remarks. My father had once given me an old American flag, which had been carried in the Mexican War, I had brought with me. I laid it across the altar, with some more remarks. Next I placed a Bible on the altar, explaining my reasons for doing. . . . Suddenly I struck a match and lighted the cross. Everyone was amazed. And while it burned I administered the oath and talked. . . . And thus on the mountain top that night at the midnight hour while men braved the surging blasts of wild wintry mountain winds and endured a temperature far below freezing, bathed in the sacred glow of the fiery cross, the Invisible Empire was called from its slumber of half a century to take up a new task and fulfill a new mission for humanity's good. . . .

Several years later, a reporter consulted the National Weather Bureau and discovered that the lowest temperature at Stone Mountain that evening was only forty-five degrees—well above freezing. But the fiery cross had a power facts couldn't diminish. Throughout his Imperial Wizardship, Simmons often pointed out that the Knights of the Ku Klux Klan were directly descended from the Reconstruction Ku-Klux. He wisely included two former Reconstruction Klansmen among his charter members; he kept the names of offices, the organizational structure, and the Klan's "mystic" language as close as possible to the 1867 Prescript; he made the date of the Reconstruction Klan's reputed birth, May 6, a national holiday for Klansmen; and his literature and public utterances continually emphasized the spiritual unity between the old and new organizations—"the same soul in a new body."

What Simmons feared most was that *The Birth of a Nation* would foster rival Ku-Klux fraternities, and in at least one case, his fears were justified. Shortly after the world premiere of the film in Los Angeles, a San Francisco group formed the American Order of Clansmen—"a nation-wide, patriotic, social and benevolent secret society" for the purpose of "uniting all loyal, white American citizens." It is more than likely that similar lodges sprang up and just as quickly withered as Griffith's film toured across America. Actively linking a "revived" Klan to the original one was essential to its survival, and this achievement was probably Simmons's most significant contribution to the reincarnation of the Klan in the twentieth century.

The cross-burning ceremony, however, was a new wrinkle on the sheets. Burning crosses had *never* been part of the Reconstruction Ku-Klux. They had come from the exotic imagination of Thomas Dixon, whose fictional Klansmen had felt so much tangible pride in their Scottish ancestry, they revived the use of burning crosses as signal fires from one clan to another. The ritual of the burning cross figures dramatically in Sir Walter Scott's *The Lady of the Lake*.

Simmons received a preliminary Georgia charter for the Klan on December 4—two days before the Atlanta premiere of *The Birth of a Nation*. On that day, readers of Atlanta newspapers saw two ads side by side—one for Griffith's film and another for Simmons's Klan. The new Imperial Wizard's ad featured a robed Klansman rearing on horseback, an image he had plagiarized from *The Birth of a Nation* posters. "*Knights of the Ku Klux Klan*," it proclaimed, "*The World's Greatest Secret, Social, Patriotic, Fraternal, Beneficiary Order . . . Col. W.J. Simmons, Founder and Imperial Wizard, 85 West Peachtree Place, Atlanta, Ga.*" Right before the film began, Simmons picked a group of his new fraternity, decked them out in bedsheets, and ordered them to ride on horse-back down Peachtree Street and fire rifle salutes in front of the lines of patrons waiting to get into the Atlanta Theatre. It was an enormously effective stunt, and Simmons would repeat it at other premieres, making *The Birth of a Nation* a hapless gimmick in Klan publicity. Response to the Atlanta premiere was as Simmons expected. Reviewing the film in the *Constitution*, Ned McIntosh claimed, "Never before, perhaps, has an Atlanta audience so freely given vent to its emotions and appreciation. . . . Cheer after cheer burst forth from the audience. . . . It makes you forget decorum and forces a cry into your throat. . . . It makes you actually live through the greatest period of suffering and trial that this country has ever known."

In two weeks, Simmons initiated ninety-two members into his Invisible Empire. After that he hired a local company to make regular hooded white uniforms. Aside from stunts attached to *The Birth of a Nation*, however, his early promotion of the Klan was crude. Ads soliciting membership called it "A Classy Order of the Highest Class . . . No 'Rough Necks,' 'Rowdies,' nor 'Yellow Streaks' admitted." This lack of sophistication betrays a lack of program, and it's true that in spite of his religious reverence for its predecessor and his passion for fraternalism, Simmons hadn't the slightest idea of what a revived Ku Klux Klan should *do*. For new members there was always the elaborate initiation ceremony he devised, which, between its Sunday-school puerility and comic exchanges between "Kludd" and "Klexter," was almost out of the funny papers.* But aside from that, though nationalistic in its pitch, the Knights of the Ku Klux Klan at this point was hardly different from any other fraternal lodge. A change seems to have been soon effected by charter member Jonathan Frost who, influenced by Watson, edited an Atlanta magazine that emphasized racial distinctions. Gradually the Klan's publications became increasingly nativistic: "Only native born American citizens who believe in the tenets of the Christian religion and owe no allegiance of any degree or nature to any foreign Government, nation, political institution, sect, people, or person are eligible. . . . We avow the distinction between races of mankind as same has been decreed by the Creator, and we shall ever be true to the faithful

---

* The initiation ceremony as well as other Knights of the Ku Klux Klan documents may be found in Appendix B.

maintenance of White Supremacy and will strenuously oppose any compromise thereof in any and all things."

At the same time, rising nativism was part of the national scene. From 1900 to 1920, 14.5 million immigrants arrived at American shores, averaging two thousand per day. Unlike the old-stock immigrants, this new migration was largely from southern and eastern Europe, and Americans bristled at the unfamiliar languages, customs, and religions of these Cheskies, Hunkies, Ities, Ruskies, Polacks and Yids. In 1916, Madison Grant published a best seller, *The Passing of the Great Race*, that warned that America risked polluting her Anglo-Saxon heritage by admitting these inferior but sensual aliens. "If the Melting Pot is allowed to boil without control," said Grant, "and we continue to follow our national motto and deliberately blind ourselves to all 'distinctions of race, creed or color,' the type of native American of Colonial descent will become as extinct as the Athenian of the age of Pericles, and the Viking of the days of Rollo." A few years later, William McDougall, a talented psychologist whose work on motivation is still respected today, recommended that the government establish a Bureau of Eugenics where prospective brides and grooms could look up each other's ancestry before taking what could be a fatal step. Dr. Prescot F. Hall offered further proof that behavioral scientists have no business in politics when he suggested that our "fatuous belief in universal suffrage" and "lust for equality" were symptoms of paranoia.

By the time of America's entry in World War I, Polish-Americans, Italian-Americans and other "hyphenated" Americans had become objects of national suspicion. Many hyphenated Americans opposed America's involvement in the war. German-Americans were reluctant to fight soldiers who might be their relatives; Irish-Americans were reluctant to fight anyone at war with the British. And President Wilson feared the effect of an Unmelted Pot upon a united front, saying that "any man who carries a hyphen about with him carries a dagger that he is ready to plunge into the vitals of this Republic whenever he gets ready." When the Russian Revolution broke out on the heels of America's entry in the war, the U.S. government's fears skyrocketed. A number of Americans, native as well as hyphenated, openly supported the Bolshevik revolution; these included eastern immigrants, labor unionists (especially the I.W.W.'s or "Wobblies"), teachers, liberal intellectuals, and socialists such as Indiana's Eugene Debs and Oregon's John Reed.

In order to check any chance of revolutionary stirring while America was at war, worried citizens formed the National Security League and the American Defense Society to boost "one-hundred percent Americanism" and keep a watchful eye on the doings and sayings of nonnative Americans. In 1917, Congress passed a literacy test, curbing immigration, and an Espionage Act directed at broadly defined treason. The next year, Congress passed a Sedition Act that, in flagrant violation of the first amendment, prohibited uttering or publishing anything "disloyal, profane, scurrilous or abusive" about the government of the United States; another statute empowered the federal government to deport those immigrants who failed to comply. These had an immediate effect: German music—especially Wagner—was banned from public concerts. Sauerkraut was renamed "liberty cabbage." Schmidts changed their name to Smith. Americans began carefully weighing the patriotism of their neighbors. Buying bonds, supporting the Red Cross, uttering ritual expressions of loyalty and contempt— like "Down with the Kaiser!"—became measures of one's patriotism. Wilson's Justice Department created the American Protective League, which organized twelve thousand local units to spy on American citizens. These units combed their towns for Bolsheviks, draft dodgers, and would-be violators of the Sedition Act. In the *New Republic*, Frank Cobb suggested that Wilson's administration had "conscripted public opinion as they conscripted men and money and materials. Having conscripted it, they dealt with it as they dealt with other raw recruits. They mobilized it. They put it in charge of drill sergeants. They goose-stepped it. They taught it to stand at attention and salute."

Imperial Wizard Simmons firmly allied the Ku Klux Klan to Wilson's domestic war effort. Working in loose conjunction with an Atlanta member of the American Protective League, Simmons turned his Klansmen into junior G-men who promptly began harassing prostitutes around military bases, threatening people who seemed insufficiently fired by wartime zeal, and bullying laborers "infested with the I.W.W. spirit." One of the earliest twentieth-century Klan parades took place in Montgomery, Alabama, in 1918 when nearly a hundred robed and hooded Klansmen marched through the streets, warning spies to get out of town and yelling at the others to buy bonds.

Now that Klansmen were G-men, secrecy became a Klan obsession. From 1915 to 1917, membership in the Klan had been a relaxed matter but, as Simmons recalled, "I issued a decree during the war submerging membership in the Klan. Our secret service work made this imperative. I ordered members to keep their membership in the Klan a secret from everybody, except each other. I told them not to admit publicly that they belonged to the Klan. Membership in the Klan was *always* a secret thereafter." Whereas potential Klansmen had previously been solicited in the newspapers, they now had to be proposed individually by initiated Klansmen. To those recommended, Simmons sent an anonymous form letter:

> Your best friends state you are a "Native Born" American citizen, having the best interest of your community, city, state and nation at heart, . . . and believe in—
>
> The Tenets of the Christian Religion
> White Supremacy
> Protection of our Pure American Womanhood
> Preventing unwarranted strikes by Foreign Labor Agitators
> Upholding the Constitution of the United States of America
> The Sovereignty of our State Rights
> Promotion of Pure Americanism. . . .
>
> REAL MEN whose oaths are inviolate are needed. Upon these beliefs and the recommendations of your friends, you are given an opportunity to become a member of the most powerful, secret, non-political organization in existence, one that has the Most Sublime Lineage in History, one that was "Here Yesterday," "Here Today," "Here Forever."
> Discuss this with no one. If you wish to learn more, address
>
> "TI-BO-TIM"
> P.O. Box 782, Atlanta, Georgia

The Klan's newfound secrecy greatly enhanced its appeal. Soon it attained nearly three thousand members, stretching beyond Atlanta into Birmingham and Mobile with about fifteen Klan chapters. Simmons sent Jonathan Frost to Alabama to organize the Klan in that state and to get him off his back. Frost had been complaining that the Klan had a greater potential than Simmons was realizing. Accordingly, Frost made an immediate attempt to take over the Klan in Alabama, and before Simmons caught up with him he absconded with several thousand dollars. By the war's end, the Klan was in serious financial difficulty. "There were times," Simmons recalled, "when I walked the streets with my shoes worn through because I had no money." In desperation, the Imperial Wizard succumbed to one of Frost's original ideas—turning the Klan over to a professional advertising agency. Miraculously, Simmons could not have done so at a more favorable time. If the war had brought a boost to the Klan, the country's emotional climate at the war's end brought a windfall.

Armistice had come on November 11, 1918, and, with it, the labor boom came to a sudden drastic end, putting thousands out of work. During the boom, over 750,000 blacks had been encouraged to come north and were now regarded as dangerous and loathsome competition by Northern whites who were just beginning to discover the depths of their racism. From June to December 1919, twenty-six race riots erupted in American cities, the worst occurring in Washington, D.C., Knoxville, Chicago and Omaha. The black soldier who had been treated as a human being and hero in France came home ready to resist attempts at restoring his past servility. W.E.B. DuBois said that blacks had been right to enlist in the war: "Under similar circumstances, we would fight again. But by the God of heaven, we are cowards and jackasses if now that the war is over, we do not marshal every ounce of our brain and brawn to fight a sterner, longer, more unbending battle against the forces of hell in our own land." Such a viewpoint was anathema to whites, especially in the South. In 1919 seventy-four blacks were lynched—the largest number in a decade—including black veterans still in uniform.

Wartime Prohibition had been turned into a constitutional amendment, and the Volstead Act of October 28, 1919, offered muscle to complete the transformation of a temperance movement into the legislation of national morality. Prohibition further divided the natives, who were dry by conviction, from the hyphens, who were wet by tradition. And there were gnawing doubts that Prohibition could even be enforced. Liquor companies openly advertised, "Before Prohibition Is Effective, Your Home Should be Supplied with BACARDI." A new wave of "lawlessness" was predicted in the land.

That lawlessness was already manifest in labor strikes. Nearly three thousand six hundred strikes took place in 1919, none of which were resolved to labor's satisfaction. Capitalizing on wartime hysteria over the Bolshevik revolution, management argued that labor had fallen into the hands of "Reds" who were using strikes to overthrow the U.S. government. A good number of

American unionists were avowedly Communist, and some used bombs and firearms to subvert management and to defend themselves against armed strikebreakers and police, but emotion played an enormous role in amplifying their potential threat to American institutions. Teachers and professors who suggested anything positive about the Russian revolution were fired. Editors, writers, and humanitarians, from Oswald Garrison Villard to Jane Addams, were denounced as "Red" for any kind of criticism of United States policy. A Tennessee senator suggested using Guam as a concentration camp for disloyal Americans.

Taking advantage of Woodrow Wilson's illness and seclusion in the White House, America's "fighting Quaker," Attorney General A. Mitchell Palmer, launched a strategic attack on the Red Menace. He created within the Justice Department a General Intelligence Division (GID, later the FBI) and put twenty-four-year-old J. Edgar Hoover in charge of it. Hoover's legal talents were unremarkable, but as a former employee of the Library of Congress he brought to the GID a striking innovation—a card catalogue. In a few months, Hoover assembled a file of over 200,000 cards that identified American Reds, pinks, and suspected pinks, classifying them by state, city, and local organization. The GID quickly became the "nerve center" of the Justice Department, and on December 21, 1919, Palmer secured the deportation of 249 radical nonnatives, including Emma Goldman, who announced before her ship departed, "I consider it an honor to be chosen as the first political agitator to be deported from the United States."

The following month, Palmer's network staged a phenomenal raid, rounding up four thousand Reds in twenty-three states. When it came to their deportation, however, it was discovered that although the warrants for the deportation of Reds could come from the Justice Department, the Department of Labor was responsible for shipping them out. Like Wilson, the secretary of labor was ill, and ironically, the job fell to his assistant, Louis F. Post. Post had been Major Merrill's stenographer and assistant during the great South Carolina Ku-Klux roundup, later "shorthanding" the 1871 trials of Klansmen in Columbia. In forty-nine years, he had lost none of the idealism that had sent him to South Carolina during Reconstruction. Before accepting Wilson's appointment as assistant secretary of labor, he had edited The Public, a progressive journal published in Chicago, and had been a charter member of the NAACP. As a twenty-two-year-old he had been a firsthand witness to a fledgling Department of Justice's failure at prosecuting the Ku-Klux; as a seventy-one-year-old he was now the final arbiter in a strong Department of Justice's attempt to deprive innocent people of their liberty.

From January to April 1920, Post carefully reviewed the files of those Palmer had recommended for deportation and promptly threw out over half of them. A majority of those arrested had been detained and confined without counsel. Besides, Post said, not all radicals were necessarily dangerous. Press and Congress went wild, screaming for Post's hide. With electric parliamentarianism, the House of Representatives voted articles of impeachment against the assistant secretary of labor, and Post was called before a Congressional committee. While confused congressmen scratched their heads and listened open-mouthed, Post explained to them the important ideological differences among followers of Marx, Lenin, Trotsky and Proudhon. He reviewed the flagrant violations of law that the Palmer raids had incurred. "He completely confounded his accusers." Not only were impeachment proceedings dropped, but Post's dismissal of the deportation warrants was upheld. The newspapers' plans for Post's tar and feathering were quickly aborted. Said the *Christian Science Monitor*, "In the light of what is now known, it seems clear that what appeared to be an excess of radicalism on the one hand was certainly met with something like an excess of suppression." In short, America was in no danger from a Bolshevik revolution. A former librarian's card catalogue and a "fighting Quaker's" terrible swift sword had largely by themselves created America's first Red Scare.

Though the press was satisfied, the average American was not. Post had deprived the nation of a most promising enemy. The Kaiser was now gone, huddled somewhere in Holland, but a tangible enemy was still needed by an America tumescent with the passion of a war that had ended too soon. "We had imagined ourselves in the act of intercourse with the Whore of the World," said a survivor of the era. "Then suddenly the war was over and the Whore vanished for a time and we were in a condition of coitus interruptus." Into this vague but pressing need, the Ku Klux Klan would plunge headlong.

In Atlanta, Edward Young Clarke was president of the Southern Publicity Association. A short, intense, long-faced man with bushy black hair and black-rimmed spectacles, Clarke had learned his public relations skills from journalism, and his brother was managing editor of the Atlanta *Constitution.* Clarke had handled publicity and subscriptions for the Anti-Saloon League, the Armenian Relief Fund, and the Theodore Roosevelt Memorial Association. (The last group had been unhappy with his work, suing him for over $1,000 it claimed he'd embezzled and another $4,000 he'd been unable to account for.) Clarke's sole business partner was Mrs. Elizabeth Tyler, a gutsy woman in her mid-thirties who had been married at fourteen and widowed at fifteen with a daughter. Chunky, buxom and blowzy, she was an unusually independent woman for the South of the 1920s. Even a man who detested her was forced to call her "an extraordinary woman. She was untaught, but endowed with unusual mentality." Tyler first met Clarke when each was involved with the great Harvest Festival in Atlanta. Shortly afterward, the two had formed the Southern Publicity Association—a shoestring ad agency that had stayed afloat by running "booster campaigns" for such low-paying clients as the Salvation Army, the Red Cross, and the YMCA. Although Clarke was a married man, he and Mrs. Tyler were once arrested in their nightclothes for drunk and disorderly behavior at an Atlanta bawdyhouse, so there's little reason to assume their relationship was purely platonic.

Tyler recalled that she and Clarke "came into contact with Colonel Simmons and the Ku Klux Klan through the fact that my son-in-law joined it. We found Colonel Simmons was having a hard time [getting] along. He couldn't pay his rent. The receipts were not sufficient to take care of his personal needs. He was a minister and a clean living and thinking man, and he was heart and soul for the success of his Ku Klux Klan. After we had investigated it from every angle, we decided to go into it with Colonel Simmons and give it the impetus that it could best get from publicity."

To the keen-minded Clarke, the national temper suggested a market hungry for a hardboiled nativist movement, and he wanted to go after it in a big way. "Mr. Simmons," he said, "it's going to cost a large sum of money to create an organizational force. We have no machinery of that nature, and I've got to find men. We'll have to spend a lot of time finding men, and this machinery must be constructed, and it'll cost something." Clarke then convinced Simmons to make the Southern Publicity Association the independent "Propagation Department" of the Klan, which would keep 80 percent of all fees collected from new Klansmen. Out of this 80 percent, the Propagation Department would pay all its expenses, including the wages and commissions of employees and fieldmen.

Simmons agreed, a contract was signed on June 7, 1920, and Clarke became the Klan's first Imperial Kleagle.

Clarke's most pressing need was for ready cash. He allegedly put $7,000 of his own money into a general fund and then sold, in Atlanta, $26,000 worth of bonds, notes, and similar obligations on the Invisible Empire, Knights of the Ku Klux Klan, Inc. His methods were entirely legal and thoroughly businesslike. He moved Klan headquarters from Simmons's "chaotic and slipshod" office in the Silvey Building to a more pleasant and spacious suite in the Haynes Building. Along the lines of the 1867 Klan Prescript, Simmons had already divided the nation into nine domains, but Clarke now made them effective. He put nine Grand Goblins in charge of the domains, basing them in Boston, New York, Philadelphia, Washington, Chicago, Atlanta, St. Louis, Houston, and Los Angeles. He then hired a King Kleagle for each state to oversee a corps of local Kleagles. Operating like insurance or Fuller Brush salesmen, Kleagles sold memberships in the Klan at $10 apiece, keeping $4 for themselves. (It was important to Clarke that a Kleagle be able to make a decent living from full-time kleagling.) The remaining $6 were sent to the King Kleagle, who pocketed $1 of it and sent the remaining $5 to his boss the Goblin. The Goblin pocketed fifty cents, sending $4.50 to Clarke and Tyler, who kept $2.50 for themselves and deposited the remaining $2 in the Imperial Treasury.

In less than a year, Clarke had an active eleven hundred Kleagles in the field, making things "hum all over America." Every week, Kleagles were required to turn in a report to Clarke, stating the number of prospective initiates canvassed, the total amount collected, the towns they had worked that week, and where they expected to work the following week. In large cities, Kleagles invariably haunted showings of *The Birth of a Nation*, and this paid off well in Dallas, Richmond, Portland, New York, and Chicago. Kleagles also hung around other fraternal lodges and were especially successful at wooing the Masons. Many Kleagles were Masons themselves. (In fact, the King Kleagle of Wisconsin put an ad in the August 26, 1921, edition of the Madison *State Journal*, reading: "Wanted: Fraternal organizers, men of ability between the ages of 25 and 40. Must be 100% Americans. Masons preferred.") Most importantly, however, Kleagles were told to sell the Klan in a way that most appealed to the community. If a town was afraid of labor unions, then Kleagles pushed the Klan's position against alien-inspired strikers. If the Kleagle was working a dry commu-

FORM K-115

APPLICATION FOR CITIZENSHIP
IN THE
INVISIBLE EMPIRE

Knights of the Ku Klux Klan
(INCORPORATED)

To His Majesty the Imperial Wizard, Emperor of the Invisible Empire, Knights of the Ku Klux Klan:

I, the undersigned, a native born, true and loyal citizen of the United States of America, being a white male Gentile pers
of temperate habits, sound in mind and a believer in the tenets of the Christian religion, the maintenance of White Supremacy an
the principles of a "pure Americanism," do most respectfully apply for membership in the Knights of the Ku Klux Klan throug

Klan No. ...., Realm of ....

I guarantee on my honor to conform strictly to all rules and requirements regulating my "naturalization" and the continuance
of my membership, and at all times a strict and loyal obedience to your constitutional authority and the constitution and laws of th
fraternity, not in conflict with the constitution and constitutional laws of the United States of America and the states thereof. If
prove untrue as a Klansman I will willingly accept as my portion whatever penalty your authority may impose.

The required "klectokon" accompanies this application.

Signed.. Applicant

Endorsed by   Residence Address ....

Kl...   Business Address ....

Kl...   Date ...., 192....

The person securing this application must sign on top line above. NOTICE—Check the address to which mail may be sent.

NOTICE

The sum of this donation MUST accompany application, if possible. Upon payment of same by applicant this certificate is made out and signed by person securing application, then detached and given to applicant, who will keep same and bring it with him when he is called, and then turn it in on demand in lieu of the cash.

DO NOT detach if donation is not paid in advance.

OFFICIAL CERTIFICATE OF DONATION

*This certifies that*_____

has donated the sum of TEN DOLLARS to the propagating fund of the

Knights of the Ku Klux Klan (Inc.)

and same is accepted as such and as full sum of "KLECTOKON" entitling him to be received, on the acceptance of his application, under the laws, regulations and requirements of the Order, duly naturalized and to have and to hold all the rights, titles, honors and protection as a citizen of the Invisible Empire. He enters through the portal of

Klan No. ...., Realm of ....

Date...................................., 192....

Received in trust for the
KNIGHTS OF THE KU KLUX KLAN, (INC.)

By Kl...

Membership Application for the Klan and Attached Receipt (circa 1921)

nity, he promised that the Klan and the Klan alone had the guts to deal with deadheads and bootleggers. If a city was being swollen by immigrants, Kleagles proclaimed that the Klan stood for 100 percent Americanism and would never allow the country to be taken over by a pack of radical hyphens. And when neighborhoods expressed fears over the postwar "New Negro," they were quietly reminded that the Ku Klux Klan had always known how to handle niggers. In short, Kleagles pandered to every regional prejudice and fear, offering a scapegoat for every local tension. "Never before had a single society gathered up so many hatreds or given vent to an inwardness so thoroughgoing." It was very much a twentieth-century success story.

Clarke took charge of the Klan's literature, bending it toward a highly elastic nativism. "The Declaration of Independence is the foundation of our patriotic ideals," an early Klan flyer proclaimed. "If you are a Native Born, White, Gentile, Protestant, American citizen, eventually you will be a Klansman and proud of that title." He perfected the machinery by which unorganized Klan initiates would formally enter the Invisible Empire. The organizing Kleagle would remain in charge of his initiates until the particular community had been thoroughly milked for potential members. (One quarter of the potential number was usually sufficient.) These initiates could then apply for a charter and be granted the status of a Klan or "Klavern," which could elect an "Exalted Cyclops" to head it. After a Klavern was chartered, the fees of additional members would be divided equally between it and Imperial Headquarters. The King Kleagle was in charge of the various Klaverns in his state; but after the necessary number of Klaverns had been chartered, the state could apply for a charter and be granted the status of a "Realm," over which the Imperial Wizard would appoint a "Grand Dragon" to preside.

The impact of Clarke's program was quickly and strongly felt in the Southwest—Texas, Louisiana, Oklahoma and Arkansas. It then fluttered about the Southeast and, in the Northwest, surprisingly, captured Oregon. By the summer of 1921, it had crossed the Ohio River into the Midwest, the Potomac into the Northeast, and was creeping up the Atlantic Seaboard. In less than fifteen months, Klan membership mushroomed from 3,000 to nearly 100,000, and initiates spent over $1,500,000 in "klectokens" (the $10 fees *donated* for membership), white robes, literature, and paraphernalia.

It is difficult to determine how much Clarke and Tyler earned during these fifteen months, but it may have been in excess of $212,000. Wizard Simmons received $170,000 in "commissions" for doing almost nothing. He was basically a figurehead, a living successor to the legendary Nathan B. Forrest. And he began acting the part. While Clarke and Tyler commanded their Kleagles, Simmons had himself photographed in his purple silk Wizard's robes decorated with seven-pointed stars and spangles. In Philadelphia, he fell to his knees at the Liberty Bell while photographers clicked away. He was a rousing speaker at Klan gatherings, once exhorting a crowd for three hours at the Decatur, Georgia, courthouse. Eventually the Klan caught the attention of the New York dailies, and several reporters were dispatched to Atlanta to find out more about the Klan and especially about the Wizard. According to the New York *Herald*:

KLAN CHAIN OF COMMAND

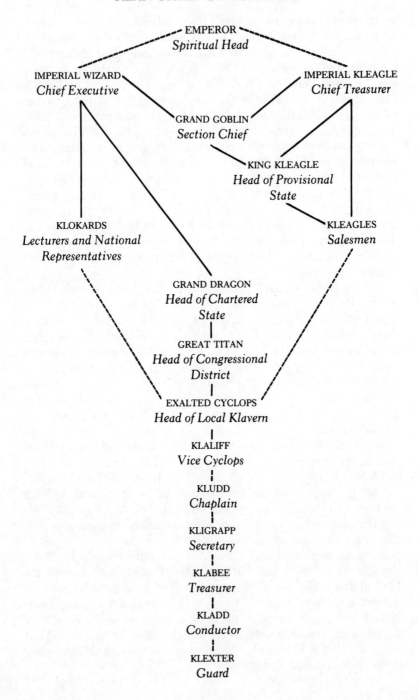

The Klan is organized along military lines and the leader is surrounded by his chief of staff and staff officers. The executive offices occupy the third floor of a downtown office building and spread over into half a dozen rooms in another building. As you approach the offices there appear in black letters on the door "Ku Klux Klan," and below the name "Col. William J. Simmons, Imperial Wizard." Inside is a big force of clerks, stenographers, and assistants. Colonel Simmons sits at a desk in an inner room with a large American flag draped at his back.

The Imperial Wizard is a powerful man, something over forty years of age, smooth-shaven, clear-eyed, deep-voiced, more than six feet tall. When he grasps your hand you feel that he has to hold himself back to keep from crushing it. He was for many years a circuit-rider of the Methodist-Episcopal Church.

With the help of such flattering stories, the Klan continued to prosper. Imperial Headquarters were moved from the Haynes Building into a $65,000 Imperial Palace—a large, white-pillared Georgian mansion on Peachtree Street. A local company was purchased that could make the Klan's cheap robes even cheaper. On May 6, 1921, the Klan presented Simmons with birthday presents of a $40,000 house, which he named Klan Krest, and a sedan. On August 1, his income was set at a fixed $1,000 per month; in addition, back pay of $25,000 was awarded him for his lonely first five years as the Klan's director.

"There was so much money in sight that we could lay almost any sort of plans," Simmons recalled. But the ordeal of making plans was unbearable for him. And now that the Klan had vastly expanded, the Wizard was even more uncertain about what the Klan should do. In summer 1921, he told his Invisible Empire, "The Ku Klux Klan has not yet started to work and may not do so for a year. We are merely organizing at the present time and we do not intend to start any definite activity until we have sufficiently organized to make sure success." Although as chief executive of the national organization, Simmons may not have known what a Klan should do, local Klansmen who had seen *The Birth of a Nation* certainly did. General Forrest's grandson, Nathan Bedford Forrest III, had been asked to serve as Cyclops of Atlanta's Klavern Number One and confided that people were "continually calling" him with requests for the Klan to redress petty grievances with threats or floggings. Women had even asked him to arrange lynchings for them. Forrest complained that calls and letters like that averaged twenty a week.

From late 1920 through 1921, local Klaverns' violence and vigilante tactics began hitting the newspapers. On the eve of the 1920 election, when Harding won the presidency, large numbers of Klansmen paraded through Southwestern towns, warning blacks to stay away from the polls. The smaller encounters were worse. In Houston a properous black dentist was "irreparably mutilated" by a gang of disguised Klansmen who claimed he had been consorting with a white woman. In Bolton, Texas, a black youth who had been jailed for "insulting a white woman" was kidnapped from jail and severely beaten; a placard attached to his back said, *Whipped by the K.K.K.* In Miami, an archdeacon of the Episcopal church was stripped and whipped by eight Klansmen who condemned him for preaching "racial equality." In Birmingham, the white proprietor of a butcher shop was flogged for his "friendly relations" with blacks. In Pensacola, Florida, a Klansman drove up to a Greek restaurateur and handed him a note reading, "You are an undesirable citizen. You violate the Federal Prohibition Laws and laws of decency and are a running sore on society. Several trains are leaving Pensacola daily. Take your choice, but do not take too much time. Sincerely in earnest, K.K.K."

For several months, the Pulitzer-owned New York *World* had conducted a careful investigation of the acts of violence and intimidation associated with the Klan, and on September 6, 1921, it launched a sensational exposé of the Invisible Empire. For two weeks, its pages were filled with the most revolting information possible on the hooded order. It belittled Klansmen as "nightie Knights." It revealed the Kleagles' techniques of selling hate and speculated on the fortune Klan leaders were reaping. On September 19, it published a detailed account of 152 Klan outrages, including four murders, forty-one floggings, and twenty-seven tar-and-featherings. "It would be impossible to imagine an attitude more essentially lawless," said Rowland Thomas, the editor in charge of the exposé. "Ku Kluxism as conceived, incorporated, propagated, and practiced has become a menace to the peace and security of every section of the United States. Its evil and vicious possibilities are boundless." At the same time, the *World* handsomely patted itself on the back for its exposé. One-third of its front-page coverage was devoted to self-congratulation and the congratulations of others, from poet Louis Untermeyer to the Bishop of Cleveland.

Since the *World*'s exposé was syndicated in eighteen other major newspapers, the Ku Klux Klan became the talk of the nation—for many people it was the first time they had ever heard of it. Kansas journalist William Allen White praised the exposé, saying, "The picayunish cowardice of a man who would substitute clan rule and mob law for what our American fathers have died to establish and maintain should prove what a cheap screw outfit the Klan is." Baltimore savant H. L. Mencken—who considered the average American of the 1920s "a goose-stepping ignoramus and poltroon" —managed at the same time to be sanguine and outrageous:

> The former Methodist exhorter who seems to be at the head of the revived Ku Klux Klan does not differ in any essential from the suave fellows who run the other tin-pot orders. He is simply more efficient than the rest of them, a better student of boob psychology. . . . Meanwhile, the Ku Klux Klan serves a good purpose by showing what ideas move it and what means it favors for propagating them. In particular it shows clearly the intimate relationship between this running amuck of the mob and the aims and principles of a certain ecclesiastical organization [the Methodist church], long a public nuisance.

Don Marquis in his popular "Sun Dial" column for the New York *Sun* turned commentary over to his little friend archy the cockroach, who could type only in lower case:

i dropped into
a clam chowder the
other evening
for a warm bath and
a bite to eat
and I heard a couple of
clams talking
it seems that they
are sore on the
oyster family and
have formed an
organization to
do away with them
they call it the
ku klux klam

yours for the frequent stew
ARCHY

As the *World* ranted and exposed, it also demanded a complete investigation of the Klan by the U.S. government. On September

21, Congressmen Peter F. Tague of Massachusetts and T.J. Ryan of New York introduced a resolution for a congressional investigation of the Invisible Empire.

At the Imperial Palace in Atlanta, the mood was one of intense ambivalence. On the one hand, the *World* exposé was doing wonders for Klan membership. Tyler happily announced, "The publicity given us has caused thousands of inquiries from every section of the nation to flood our office, and I now have under my personal supervision in Atlanta three secretaries constantly employed answering these inquiries." On the other hand, Imperial Kleagle Clarke was upset by the *World*'s digging up his indiscreet shackup with Tyler, and he was terrified of the possibility of a congressional investigation. He nervously tendered his resignation to Wizard Simmons, giving the excuse that Tyler's honor had been besmirched. Tyler was furious. She told the Atlanta press that Clarke was "weak-kneed and won't stand by his guns. I am not thankful to him for making my situation the basis of his actions. . . . Mr. Clarke has done me a gross injustice by not first consulting me before he took such a step." Simmons refused to accept Clarke's resignation, and the next month marked his finest hour as Imperial Wizard.

On September 30, Simmons spent over $2,000 in telegrams to every member of the House asking for an affirmative vote on the bill proposing an investigation of the Klan:

> We demur to the wording of the bill in so far as charges against the Klan are concerned, but we unreservedly agree with the purpose of the bill or any other resolution that will provide for and assure a congressional investigation of the Knights of the Ku Klux Klan.
>
> We know that such an investigation will be impartial, and when completed the Klan will be fully exonerated from all charges, and slanders made against it. . . .
>
> From our knowledge of the Klan, its membership and activities, we know that the investigation will officially reveal that the Klan was founded only on the principles of democracy, does not countenance religious or racial prejudice, and seeks only to bind together men for mutual service, and is inspired by love of justice, respect for the law, and a deep faith in the glorious future of the American people.

Congress turned the resolution over to the Committee on Rules, which began preliminary hearings in October.

Simmons arrived by train in Washington on October 10 and was immediately corraled by reporters. He was friendly and jocular with them, and when photographers asked for pictures, he "seated himself, turned profile or looked forward, tilted his chin, and became a perfectly tractable subject." Because many politicians and a horde of spectators wanted to attend, the hearings were held in the great caucus room of the House of Representatives. On the twelfth, Simmons was called to the stand. He looked debonair in his maroon Prince Albert coat and tight white collar. As he approached the stand with royal dignity, an elderly lady in the audience inched her chair closer, murmuring, "They say he dwells in a marble castle. Oh, isn't it just too perfectly grand for anything!" Her unimpressed neighbor muttered, "And when we get through with him, madam, he may be dwelling in a steel cell, so don't get sentimental."

In a "clear and markedly sonorous voice" reminiscent of a "southern camp meeting," Simmons announced to the committee, "I am a sick man. . . . I have suffered with an attack of tonsillitis combined with laryngitis which developed into bronchitis with threatened pneumonia. So it looks like I've had all the 'itises.' . . . I will state to you frankly that at any time, under the strain of talking, I'm liable to have a coughing spell that may result in a vomiting spell, which has been with me now for over ten days. So if I get in one of those conditions, I very respectfully request that y'all have a short adjournment until I can get through these paroxysms and get back on the job."

And with that caveat, Simmons slid into a monologue that lasted the rest of the afternoon.

He recounted the history of the new Klan from his moonlit vision to the present. He fully explained his business relationship with Clarke and Tyler. He answered questions about the Klan's finances to the best of his ability and submitted accounts of Klan receipts and expenditures, which, though lacking in detail, showed no obvious signs of malfeasance. As to the Klan's alleged cabalism and "hideous oaths," Simmons provided the committee with copies of the Kloran and other Klan documents which, after all, had been copyrighted and were readily available in the Library of Congress.

The Wizard indignantly denied charges that the Klan was a racist organization. The Klan was a Christian order and excluded Jews because they didn't believe in Christianity. It excluded Catholics, "but neither does the Knights of Columbus permit Protestants to become members of that order." And *every* fraternal order discriminated against blacks. The Klan's position on "white supremacy," however, was not a matter of "race hatred" but of "race pride." "I was born among, reared among, and associated with Negroes all my life," Simmons told the committee. "I have played with them in the yard of the old home. I have gone fishing with them in the old mountain streams. I have hunted with them. . . . My mind goes back to my fourteenth and fifteenth years. Every Sunday morning I had my class of Negro children and many old Negro men; I taught them their ABC's and taught them how to write. . . . I have always been the friend of the Negro. And this committee, in its most searching investigation, can go back to the old town of Harpersville, Shelby County, Alabama, and ask those old Negroes something about Joe Simmons. *They'll* tell you."

Confronted with various atrocities allegedly committed by Klansmen, Simmons claimed they were the work of impostors who weren't Klansmen at all. Klansmen were not in the vigilante business, he said. Of course they frequently dressed up and gallivanted about in hooded gowns, but so did paraders at Mardi Gras.

"That is a frolic!" interrupted Chairman Philip Campbell of Kansas.

"That's true," Simmons agreed, and so were the activities of the Klan. "Our mask and robe, I say before God, are as innocent as the breath of an angel."

After two days of intense questioning, a now perspiring Simmons grew hoarse and ended his testimony with a deathbed speech: "Again I want to express to you, Mr. Chairman, my deep gratitude and thanks for the courtesies you have extended to me." Turning to face the audience, he continued, "I want to say to all those men and women who have given assurance—with your permission—of their belief in me that they have my thanks. And I want to say to my persecutors and the persecutors of this organization, in all honesty and sincerity, . . . that you do not know what you're doing. You are ignorant of our principles as were those who were ignorant of the character and work of the Christ. I cannot better express myself than by saying to you who are persecutors of the Klan and myself, 'Father, forgive you, for you know not what you do.' Mr. Chairman, I am done."

And with that, the sick and maligned Wizard slipped from his chair to the floor in a state of unconsciousness. He just "tumbled into a heap."

Several comrades rushed to his broken body with stimulants while the audience roundly applauded. As Chairman Campbell banged his gavel and called for order, another member of the committee muttered, "For cheap theatrical effect, *damn* such a faker!"

But to the general public, the Ku Klux Klan and its founder had been exonerated. In truth, Simmons's performance before the Committee on Rules had been far more successful than General Forrest's appearance before a similar body in 1871. Two months later, the pastor of the East Side Christian Church in Portland, Oregon, told a large gathering that Simmons had been "exalted to a position of honor and glory where he will be recognized and proclaimed by our children and our children's children as an American too big to be brought down, or even injured by the most powerful guns that America's most powerful foes could assemble against him." Congress, in fact, was unable to find grounds to warrant further investigation, and its failure to do so was like a government stamp of approval on the Invisible Empire. H. L. Mencken was much amused:

Not a single solitary sound reason has yet been advanced for putting the Ku Klux Klan out of business. If the Klan is against the Jews, so are half of the good hotels of the Republic and three-quarters of the good clubs. If the Klan is against the foreign-born or the hyphenated citizen, so is the National Institute of Arts and Letters. If the Klan is against the Negro, so are all of the States south of the Mason–Dixon line. If the Klan is for damnation and persecution, so is the Methodist Church. . . . If the Klan uses the mails for shaking down suckers, so does the Red Cross. If the Klan constitutes itself a censor of private morals, so does the Congress of the United States. If the Klan lynches a Moor for raping someone's daughter, so would you or I.

Simmons's ultimate vindication came when President Warren G. Harding agreed to be sworn in as a member of the Ku Klux Klan. A five-man "Imperial induction team," headed by Simmons, conducted the ceremony in the Green Room of the White House. Members of the team were so nervous that they forgot their Bible in the car, so Harding had to send for the White House Bible. In consideration of his status, Harding was permitted to rest his elbow on the desk, as he knelt on the floor during the long oath taking. Afterward, the President appreciatively gave members of the team War Department license tags that allowed them to run red lights all across the nation.

Immediately after the congressional investigation, Klan membership jumped 20 percent. Some people sent their $10 directly to Atlanta on the facsimile application blanks the *World* and its syndicates had reprinted. Less than three months later, Clarke proudly announced that membership requests were being received in excess of a thousand a day. More than two hundred new Klaverns were chartered. And in less than a year, the Invisible Empire had leaped from a hundred thousand to over a million members. Fondly recalling this time, Simmons remarked, "It wasn't until newspapers began to attack the Klan that it really grew. Certain newspapers also aided us by inducing Congress to investigate us. The result was that Congress gave us the best advertising we ever got. Congress *made* us."

6

"I FOUND CHRIST THROUGH THE KU KLUX KLAN"

The Klan and Fundamentalism: 1922–1925

*I*n the spring of 1922, Harry Emerson Fosdick, the leading spokesman for Protestant liberalism in America, delivered a provocative sermon titled, "Shall the Fundamentalists Win?" Preaching at New York's First Presbyterian Church, Fosdick charged fundamentalists with being so intolerant that they were driving away "multitudes of reverent Christians" from the faith of Jesus Christ. Angry fundamentalists spent months refuting Fosdick's sermon and condemning him as "a scoundrel, a hypocrite," and "a seducer of the young." Fundamentalism by name was not yet two years old, but it had been a long time coming and was now in its days of glory.

In the late nineteenth century, the Social Gospel had dominated the Protestant religion in America. The Social Gospel was a liberal optimistic creed—a Christian alliance with progressive politics. Briefly stated, it held that God's true wishes had been clarified by the new social and physical sciences. Evolution, for example, explained the method God used to create mankind; advancements in the physical sciences had made humans healthier and had even prolonged the lifespan. The Social Gospel therefore argued that Christianity should dedicate itself to the further progress of civilization—to reform, to good works, to advancing knowledge and technology—and ultimately the Kingdom of Heaven could be realized on earth.

The Social Gospel's naïve faith in material and technological progress was dramatically shattered by the sinking of the R.M.S. *Titanic* in 1912. Here was the epitome of man's technology, a "practically unsinkable" marvel of engineering and the largest moving object in the world, which sank on her very first voyage with a loss of over fifteen hundred lives. On the Sunday after the disaster, ministers had searched their souls and harangued their congregations on the folly of trusting mankind more than God. It wasn't long before the Old Testament began outstripping the New in Protestant thought; and as the Social Gospel declined a militant evangelism took its place.

Evangelism had always been around, but shortly after the *Titanic* disaster, a twelve-volume series called *The Fundamentals* reached a receptive audience of American theologians. Financed by a Southern California oil tycoon, *The Fundamentals* attacked science and the Social Gospel on one hand and, on the other, defended a literal interpretation of the Bible, the infallibility of Scripture, the reality of miracles, and the second coming of Christ. *The Fundamentals* were widely read and debated. During World War I, their supporters used Germany's "higher criticism" of the Bible and acceptance of evolution as a general explanation of her wickedness. They began equating Christianity with Americanism. The popular evangelist Billy Sunday argued in 1917 that "Christianity and Patriotism are synonymous terms, and hell and traitors are synonymous." After the war, the Red Scare and the changes in American society wrought by immigration convinced many believers in *The Fundamentals* that the United States was in a serious state of moral decay. A World's Christian Fundamentals Association was organized in the convulsive year 1919; and in early 1920 the term "fundamentalist" was coined to describe those "willing to do battle for the Fundamentals."

Fundamentalists wanted the Protestant Bible restored to its pre-Civil War place in American public schools. They denounced evolution and free interpretations of Scripture. They rejected social concerns and human progress as irrelevant to salvation ("The soul of reform is the reform of the soul"). And they rejected all forms of religious "modernism." Applying fundamentalist doctrine to an analysis of American social ills, David S. Kennedy wrote in 1920:

It must be remembered that America was born of moral progenitors and founded on an eternally moral foundation. Her ancestors were

Christians of a high order, purified by fire, and washed in blood. Her foundation is the Bible, the infallible Word of God. . . . There has been some weakening of this moral standard in the thought and life of America. . . . There is but one remedy: the nation must *return* to her standard of the Word of God. She must believe, love and live her Bible. This will require the counteraction of the German destructive criticism [of literalism] which has found its way into the religious and moral thought of our people. . . . The Bible and the God of the Bible is our only hope.

Kennedy's interesting distortion of American history was essential to the fundamentalist argument that the United States had fallen away from something and was suffering accordingly. A "return" to principles our "progenitors" had supposedly held became a fundamentalist panacea for postwar America's growing pains.

President Harding was undoubtedly right that America wanted "not nostrums but normalcy," and the simplistic remedy fundamentalism offered had an immediate popular appeal. By 1922, it had become the loudest, most written about, and most widespread religious doctrine in America. "Heave an egg out of a Pullman window," said H. L. Mencken, "and you will hit a Fundamentalist almost everywhere in the United States." Fundamentalism was especially successful in its appeal to the emotions. It was basically a nontheological faith that anyone could understand. The average American Protestant agreed with Billy Sunday when he said, "I don't know any more about theology than a jack-rabbit knows about ping-pong, but I'm on my way to glory!"

While fundamentalism would make a controversial, often divisive contribution to religion in twentieth-century America, its most critical impact on our social and political history was that, without it, the Ku Klux Klan could never have enrolled the fantastic numbers nor have gained the remarkable power it wielded between 1922 and 1925.

Imperial Wizard Simmons was a former preacher himself and a deep believer in the Klan's "mystic" spirituality. He had always wanted the Klan to "stimulate a renewed interest in religion and the Church." Simmons's Kloran, Klan oaths, and other ceremonies were essentially religious rites, complete with prayers and hymns. In a sociological analysis of the Klan in 1924, John Mecklin observed that the "orthodox tenets of Evangelicalism from the Blood Atonement to Verbal Inspiration are all [in the Kloran], by implication at least. A Fundamentalist would certainly find himself thoroughly at home in the atmosphere of the Klan ceremonies."

But it fell again to Imperial Kleagle Clarke to make the most of Simmons's ragged inspiration. From the beginning Clarke had realized the Klan's potential appeal to evangelical ministers. Before his careers in journalism and publicity, Clarke had studied for the Southern Presbyterian ministry and, during his youth, was active in evangelical work for the church. Like Simmons, he also shared the Calvinist conviction that his career had been "foreordained by Almighty God." From his booster work with the Anti-Saloon League, Clarke knew that many fundamentalists wanted to organize in order to enforce a rigid Protestant ethic on American society. And he realized that Klansmen and fundamentalists shared several important characteristics: an intolerance for ways of life different from their own, a frustration with postwar change, and a passionate commitment to restoring things as they used to be.

In the summer of 1921, Clarke instructed his army of Kleagles to approach fundamentalist ministers in local communities and to enlist their support for the Klan. Soon ministers were the first target Kleagles hit in their districts. They shared with these pastors their concerns over bootlegging, crime, and vice and, of course, presented the Klan as the only force equipped to deal with these problems. The Kleagles' pitch exploited three basic vulnerabilities in these ministers: their genuine concern about changes in society they regarded as evil, their need for the increased church attendance that Kleagles promised, and their susceptibility to flattery. As a rule, clergymen were given free membership in the Klan as a token of how much their services were needed.

When the first tremors of fundamentalist support were noted, Clarke increased the Klan's appeal to this market at a national level. Imperial books, tracts, magazines, pamphlets, flyers, and placards overflowed with the Christian message, wedding the goals of fundamentalism to those of the Klan. A flyer titled "The Klansman's Creed" proclaimed:

> I believe in God and in the tenets of the Christian religion and that a godless nation cannot long prosper.
> I believe that a church that is not grounded on the principles of morality and justice is a mockery to God and to man.

In numerous tracts Klansmen avowed:

> We magnify the Bible—as the basis of our Constitution, the foundation of our government, the source of our laws, the sheet-anchor of

our liberties, the most practical guide of right living, and the source
of all true wisdom.
We teach the worship of God. . . .
We honor the Christ as the Klansman's *Only Criterion of Character.*
And we seek at His hands that cleansing from sin and impurity which
only He can give.
We believe that the highest expression of life is in service and in
sacrifice for that which is right; that selfishness can have no place in a
true Klansman's life and character; but that he must be moved by
unselfish motives, such as characterized our Lord the Christ and
moved Him to the highest service and the supreme sacrifice for that
which was right.

All this sounded splendid to fundamentalists. In Indianapolis,
even a Catholic priest admitted, "If they had brought their pledge
to me in the early days of the Klan, I declare that I would have
signed it. It proclaimed what I have always held as an American
citizen." It was the Protestant ministers, however, who jumped on
the Klan bandwagon. Possibly as many as forty thousand fundamentalist ministers joined the Klan. Many of them became the
first Exalted Cyclopes of their local communities. In Pennsylvania,
Texas, North Dakota, and Colorado, they became Grand Dragons
of their entire states. Others preached pro-Klan sermons from
their pulpits, turned their churches over to Klan meetings, spoke
at Klan rallies, or became national lecturers for Imperial Headquarters. (Of the thirty-nine Klokards or national lecturers employed by the Klan, twenty-six of them were fundamentalist
ministers.) In Missouri, Iowa, Indiana, Ohio, North Carolina,
New Jersey, Rhode Island, and Maine, the support of the clergy
was indispensable to Klan growth.
In their sermons and published articles, pro-Klan ministers
often revealed the motives that had attracted them to the Invisible
Empire. The most prevalent was the feeling that they had suffered
a postwar loss of power and status in the communities they served.
After the war, there was more frankness in discussing the taboo of
sex and an increased freedom of expression for both men and
women. The mass production of the Model T, which ministers
denounced as a "bawdyhouse on wheels," permitted earlier sexual
experimentation by young people. Movies and radio brought
worldly ideas and attitudes to rural communities that otherwise
would have remained unthreatened. The drive of youngsters to
savor the new age resisted traditional restraints, and concerned
citizens despaired over the "disappearance of strict parental disci-

pline." Clergymen found their influence undermined and their authority increasingly contested. In a published sermon titled *Christ and Other Klansmen*, Reverend E. F. Stanton of Kansas City complained:

> Fifty years ago, practically every adult and most children were Christians. Now the reverse is true. The old-fashioned shouting camp meetings and other spiritual feasts have passed away. The masses do not attend church at all unless some evangelist excites them. Sinners no longer cry for mercy. . . . Society is no longer sobriety. . . . Women who once dressed decently now wear clothes high and low. High at the bottom and low at the top. Girls have lost their timidity and are more brazen than boys. . . . Men do not love their wives as Christ loves the church, and women blaspheme God by disclaiming their husbands.

The Klan would enormously reinforce the power of ministers like Stanton. In Spokane, the Klan was heralded as "the return of the Puritans in this corrupt and jazz-mad age."

The tracts of pro-Klan ministers often emphasized the theme of "militance" and "virility." The theme had risen before in fundamentalist rhetoric—whenever Billy Sunday imitated the "modernist" ministers he minced about the platform squeaking in a falsetto—but in the Ku Klux clergy it became fully erect. The pastor of the Mattoon, Illinois, First Christian Church called the Klan "the masculine part" of Protestantism. Reverend I. M. Hargett of Racine, Wisconsin, said, "I believe the future of American Democracy hangs on the virility of the Protestant Church," and his study of the Klan convinced him that "it is about the most American institution I know of." Writing in the Klan magazine *Kourier*, an anonymous minister observed, "The Klan, which is awakened Protestantism, realizes the church must be both militant and Spiritual, or it will fail." In the same journal, another said, "As a Protestant minister of the Gospel, I joined the Knights of the Ku Klux Klan because: I believed in Jesus Christ and His church; I believed in a militant Christianity; I believed in the Cross—a symbol of service and sacrifice for the right. . . . If there isn't enough in that to challenge a real red-blooded, virile minister to a sense of duty, he has lost his vision."

The Klan's appeal to the power motives of fundamentalist ministers can be appreciated in the fact that, typically, those most attracted to the Klan were at the lower levels of their denominations. William E. Wilson wrote tellingly of the plight of the rural Midwestern preacher before the Klan came to his rescue:

> A few years before, he would have forsaken his calling if there had been anything else to which his limited talents could have been applied. The tiny spark of revelation had long since flickered out in him, and he knew it was only a matter of months until his thumbed and oft-repeated sermons would no longer suffice to hold his pulpit. His wife wore the discarded dresses of his deacons' womenfolk. His children were underfed. The church itself was falling into disrepair.

Certainly the "limited talents" of a Maryland Klan preacher are evident in his enthusiastic claim that the "pilgrim fathers arrived at Plymouth Rock with a Bible in one hand and the Stars and Stripes in the other."

Still, Klan ministers were genuinely irritated by restraints they felt from higher church authorities in doing battle for the Lord. At executive levels in the church, the Klan was condemned by deacons, bishops, and almost universally in the journals published by every Protestant sect. But condemnation from the top of the diocese had little effect on rank-and-file ministers. Even the authoritarian Church of the Latter Day Saints couldn't prevent Mormon ministers from joining the Utah Klan. And the Klan's secretiveness undoubtedly helped ministers disobey orders from their superiors. Klan membership was an inviolate secret and Klan rallies were invariably celebrated under the hood and mask. Not surprisingly, pro-Klan ministers found scriptural support for "Klandestineness." In Portland, Maine, Reverend C. H. Marvin sermonized:

> Secret associations are no modern invention. . . . The early church was, to some extent at least, a secret organization. . . . The pilgrims of the Faith, since the coming of Christ, were enabled by their secret tokens to reveal themselves to the faithful. But for their secluded retreats and secret signs which served as a protection and enabled them to work unitedly in behalf of a common cause without attracting the attention of their enemies, neither the Sacred Scriptures nor the Church itself could have survived the persecutions of the early and middle ages.

Occasionally, church administrators got into heated battles with their hooded clergymen. In St. Louis, Methodist minister Charles D. McGhee was upbraided by Bishop W. B. McMurray for his

Klan activities. "If he wants to parade at night in a mask," said the bishop, "that's his business, but I don't believe it will help his work as a disciple of Christ." But Reverend McGhee resisted. "If it comes to a choice between the Methodist Church and the Klan," he said, "then I shall choose the Klan." McGhee clung to his sheets and Bishop McMurray was forced to remove him from his pulpit. The irate McGhee retorted, "The Klan has your number, Bishop! We have had it for months. We know just where to find you and will attend to your case!" Certainly H. L. Mencken was right when he noted that Klan ministers "felt the might of an army behind them." And that army frightened many church authorities away from exercising a healthy restraint over their subordinates.

Aside from their attraction to the Klan's power, fundamentalist clergymen were also drawn to the Klan out of anger over the helplessness of governmental and local law-enforcement agencies in dealing with postwar turmoil and crime—especially the crime that was created by the passage of Prohibition. In Phoenix, Baptist minister C. M. Rock argued that local law enforcement was unable to do anything about bootleggers and that the Klan was "our only hope." In Brooklyn, Episcopal Canon William Sheafe Chase praised the Klan because it was "organized to resist the corruption of politics and the lawlessness of our times." In Indianapolis, Methodist-Episcopal Dr. William Forney Harris said that he was generally opposed to mob rule, "But when judges and other officials fail to demand redress for wrong through orderly process, then I welcome the Ku Klux Klan or any other clan which will startle justice into action." And in Youngstown, Ohio, Reverend W. O. Hawkins suggested that, since the church itself lacked law-enforcement powers, "It must teach men the principles of the Klan."

"Fighting Bob" Shuler was a minister who couldn't sit still, as long as there was vice and corruption about. Born in a log cabin in the Blue Ridge Mountains, Shuler was the pastor of Los Angeles' Trinity Methodist Church, whose membership he would increase fivefold in less than three years. Fighting local corruption was an obsession with Shuler. He got into fistfights with saloonkeepers. He made front-page headlines with a sermon denouncing Valley girls for having their pictures taken in the nude. When he won a ham on the Wheel of Fortune at a Shriners' charity bazaar, he had the proprietor arrested for running a "gambling ring." He once waited all night to catch the Los Angeles County sheriff coming out of a brothel, and his sermons on the matter ruined the sheriff's career. He hired private detectives to uncover vice all over Los Angeles. And the Ku Klux Klan was "Fighting Bob's" kind of an organization. "Good men everywhere," he said, "are coming to understand that the Klan is dangerous only to the lawless and un-American elements within [our] midst."

Shuler's chief rival in Los Angeles was the glamorous evangelist Aimee Semple McPherson. (In a book he wrote that reveals the degree of her threat to him, Shuler condemned McPherson's "unholy vileness practiced in the name of religion.") And Shuler used the Klan and its support to offset her popularity. In the most influential published defense of the Klan by a prominent clergyman, Shuler wrote that the Klan stood "for the maintenance of virtue among American women, sobriety and honor among American men, and for the eradication of all agencies and influences that would threaten the character of our children." In truth, "Fighting Bob" could "love the Klan for the enemies she has made."

When Clarke saw that the Klan had struck a mother lode in fundamentalism, he increased its religious appeal even more. At the crest of its power, the Klan owned or held the affections of over 150 periodicals. (A subscription to the national organ, the *Imperial Night-Hawk*, was offered free to any Protestant minister who requested it.) Soon the Klan press abounded with articles pleasing to fundamentalists; especially fulsome was its campaign to restore the Bible to its "rightful place" in the American public school. Klan periodicals regularly rang out with catch phrases: "Go to church every Sunday; give your support and encouragement to your ministers." "One of the foremost duties of a Klansman is to worship God." "*Klansmen! Do your boys and girls attend Sunday school?*" Ohio's weekly *Kluxer* effused:

> The Ku Klux Klan is sweeping this great nation like a forest fire. No organization of its kind or otherwise—nothing of its kind ever has swept America like this wonderful movement for Christianity. . . . Under the ritualistic work of the Klavern of the Ku Klux Klan, we are bringing new timber into the Church—and who never would join any church, had they not taken up with this great movement.

Ministers saw with their own eyes that the Klan dramatically increased church attendance, and they could hardly argue with success.

Exalted Cyclopes put further pressure on local Klansmen to

attend church and to engage in conspicuous Christian activities. At the state level, Grand Dragons sent decrees to local Klaverns on special occasions. At Christmas, for example, Grand Dragon G. E. Carr sent a proclamation to all Michigan Klaverns asking them to "evidence their devotion to our Lord through their activities in making this great day a bright one for all they can consistently reach." After the Christmas holidays, the Klan press teemed with news of Klansmen's kindness in giving clothing to the needy and baskets of food to the hungry—even to blacks.

But without a doubt, the cleverest gimmick conceived by the Klan to manipulate the clergy was the "church visitation." A group of gowned and hooded Klansmen would go unannounced into a local church, march solemnly down the aisle, and interrupt the sermon to present the pastor with a substantial donation of money. "Visitations" usually took place in the middle of the sermon when people were dozing off, and the interruption could be electrifying. Sometimes the Klansmen would make a short speech or hand the minister a note. In Phoenix, for example, Reverend Jerry Jeeter accepted a donation of $100 and read the note handed him to his congregation:

> Dear Mr. Jeeter: The Unseen, All Seeing Eye has looked upon you and the noble work you are doing and found it good. We know that you stand for Law, Order, Decency and Christianity. . . . We, like you, fear none but God, whose work you are doing.

In Indianapolis, robed Klansmen interrupted Reverend Dr. E. J. Bulgin's sermon at Cadle Tabernacle and gave him $600. As they quietly marched out of the church, Reverend Bulgin observed, "In the early days of Christianity, the children of God had to hide their faces too," and the entire congregation rose to its feet and applauded.

Such highly effective bits of showmanship were acted out all over the country. Whether sympathetic to the Klan or not, most ministers could hardly refuse their offerings, and Klan leaders took smug satisfaction in the fact that men of God could be bought. Occasionally there was an exception, as in Pittsburgh, when an angry pastor ordered his ushers to throw the hooded intruders out of the church. But these rare individuals were denounced as "modernists" in the Klan press, and their limited influence was more than offset by such charismatic and popular evangelists as Billy Sunday and Bob Jones, Sr., who, though not Klansmen themselves, endorsed Klan principles and certainly accepted their gifts of love. After an excruciating three-week revival in Andalusia, Alabama, Bob Jones happily accepted a donation of $1,568 from Klansmen. And at a revival in Dallas, Reverend Jones looked the other way while Klansmen distributed this remarkable flyer, curiously reminiscent of the Reconstruction Ku-Klux:

> I am a Searchlight on a high tower.
> I run my relentless eye to and fro throughout the land; my piercing glance penetrates the brooding places of Iniquity. I plant my eyes and ears in the whispering Corridors of Crime.
> Whenever men gather furtively together, there am I, an austere and invisible Presence. I am the Recording Angel's Proxy.
> When I invade the fetid dens of Infamy there is a sudden scampering and squeaking as of rats forsaking a doomed ship.
> I am the haunting dread of the depraved and the hated Nemesis of the vicious.
> The foe of Vice, the friend of Innocence, the rod and staff of Law,
> I am—
>
> THE KU KLUX KLAN.

The tacit support of underpaid pastors and the open support of such popular men as Shuler, Sunday, and Jones were very helpful to the Klan, for they brought clergy and laity alike who were inclined to straddle the fence on the Klan issue into the white-robed fold. This utterly disgusted such elected officials as Governor Henry Allen of Kansas, who complained that Klansmen could provoke all kinds of local agitation, then deny it "and give $50 to a loose-mouthed preacher who would thank God for the Klan." Aside from Mencken, only a few deplored the Klan's seduction of fundamentalism. Writing in the *Atlantic Monthly*, Leroy Percy was disturbed that "good men, Christian men, pastors of churches, have enrolled themselves as members, feeling that in some way through this mysterious order they would be able to combat the forces of evil. . . . They fail to realize that our government has been established by free American people, who will handle it without interference by, or dictation from, church or clan;

that it is to be governed by neither priest nor wizard, knights nor klansmen." In *Century* magazine, Glenn Frank accused the Klan of "putting Christianity to a use that is utterly alien to its spirit and purpose." But the Klan held the trump card; Imperial Headquarters asked, "Would hundreds of Protestant ministers retain their membership in an organization that is such a menace to Protestantism as is claimed?"

As fundamentalists flocked to the Invisible Empire, it was eventually recognized that, in addition to increasing church attendance, the Klan was becoming a unifying force for disparate Protestant sects. American Protestants had always been divided by sectarianism, often of a petty nature. Thomas Jefferson and James Madison had approved of this divisiveness, believing that it would keep any one sect from attempting to establish itself as a national religion. But the Klan was now joining together diverse sects of fundamentalist Christians in a spirit of egoism and intolerance. The Klan was proclaimed "a Clearing House for the cause of Protestantism" that would soon "overcome all sectionalism." Imperial Headquarters sent out flyers saying: "Denominational lines have been broken down, so far as Christian co-operation is concerned, so that the Protestant denominations are working together on religious activities as never before. . . ." In St. Louis, Presbyterian minister James Hardin Smith extolled the Klan as "an effort on the part of the Protestant laymen to get together, just as the Catholics have gotten together in the Knights of Columbus, and the Jews have gotten together in the B'nai B'rith." (Smith further avered that if Jesus was still walking the earth, He'd be a Klansman.)

Reverend Smith's remarks held an onimous portent. Throughout the centuries, whenever Christians have wielded theocratic power or united in great numbers, they have frequently persecuted those they regarded as sinners. In the Middle Ages, the various Peoples' Crusades murdered hundreds of Jews on their way to the Holy Land; and the Church burned thousands of people accused of heresy. Before the formation of the United States, the Puritans of New England executed both Quakers and "witches" without remorse. With their twentieth-century unity in the Invisible Empire, fundamentalist Christians found a new nest of wickedness in the form of Catholics and Jews.

The Klan's position on Jews can be quickly gleaned from the titles of articles in its press: "The Mightiest Weapons for the Jews Are Dollars and Cents" and "Jewish Rabbi Gets Rabid." Klansmen considered Jews "insoluble and indigestible" in a Protestant America. Jews were criticized for keeping their shops open on Sunday. Their "codes of business ethics" didn't harmonize with "Christian ideals or Christian principles." They were frequently condemned for taking the Bible out of the public school: Once the Bible was out of the classroom, "it becomes easy for the Jew then to strike a deathblow at Christianity." But Jews were not as evenly distributed throughout the United States in the 1920s as were Catholics. So Catholics became the major thrust of the Klan's bigotry in the 1920s.

The United States had already suffered two major bouts of anti-Catholicism, from the Know-Nothing Party before the Civil War and from the APA after it. And it was strangely anachronistic— almost astounding—that the Klan was able to turn otherwise sensible Americans into rabid anti-Catholics for the third time. This was due not just to the fact that the numbers of Catholics and Catholic churches had increased because of immigration; nor that Protestants were being displaced from the job market by "Romanists." Catholics did seem exclusive in a democracy, insisting on their own schools and Bibles and not allowing intermarriage or doctrinal mingling with non-Catholics. But a careful analysis of the Klan press, pro-Klan sermons, and attitudes of rank-and-file Klansmen suggests that their anti-Catholicism flourished primarily from an emotional need for a concrete, foreign-based enemy who could somehow be held accountable for the problems at home. And the Klan found that enemy in the Pope.

To Klansmen, the Pope seemed just as dangerous as Kaiser Bill. In some ways he was worse, for he had "foreign emissaries" (priests) operating within America's own borders. Reverend C. E. Jefferson explained the problem. Catholicism, he said, was "Christianity in an Italian dress." All Catholics "have sworn obedience to the Pope, and the Pope is a Foreigner. The Pope is an Italian. You must grasp *that* in order to understand why many men are opposed to the Catholic Church." Other Klan spokesmen explained it in verse:

DO YOU KNOW
> That the Pope is a political autocrat?
> That a secret treaty made by him started the war? . . .

and:

> I would rather be a Klansman
> in a robe of snowy white,

Than to be a Catholic Priest
   in a robe as black as night;
For a Klansman is an American
   and America is his home,
But the Priest owes his allegiance
   to a Dago Pope in Rome.

Eventually Klansmen envisioned a plot whereby the Pope planned on taking over the country and "making America Catholic." The logic of Klansmen on this subject often approached the surreal:

> Patriots, view the hellish countenances of hundreds of thousands of Knights of Columbus and millions of members of the Roman Catholic Church. The latter despise real Americanism, hate our government, hate you patriots. They class your mothers, sisters and daughters as harlots, while the former is the monstrous iron wheel on which the Roman Catholic Church hopes to crush America, American government, American institutions and purity of our women for the sake of the Dago on the Tiber. . . .

Klansmen went to great lengths to support this idea. They circulated a phony Knights of Columbus oath that suggested Catholic treachery and lechery. They also circulated photographs of the Episcopal Cathedral, then under construction on Mount Alban in Washington, D.C., and claimed it was the new Vatican under construction in the nation's capital. They arranged lecture tours by the elegant fraud Helen Jackson, who claimed to be an "escaped nun" but had actually escaped only from a Catholic reformatory in Detroit and was eager for revenge. "Sister" Helen's book *Convent Cruelties* sold quite well, and her lectures were popular in the rural areas. Her lectures were usually segregated by sex. She told the women about the Pope's plans to take over the minds of their children, and she showed men the little leather bags in which the newborns of priests and nuns had been conveyed to the convent furnaces.

In the course of feeding the fears of its members, the Klan supplied spurious but inspired statistics on the growing Catholic menace in America:

> Five states now have Catholic administrations;
> 20,000 public schools have one-half Catholic teachers;

Roman Catholics are in the majority of the councils of 15,000 cities and towns of the United States;
Seven out of ten convicted criminals in America are Roman Catholics.

The Ku Klux clergy added to this roster. In Sacramento, Reverend W. A. Redburn, a Methodist, claimed that "nearly all the bawdy-houses, bootleg joints, and other dives are owned or controlled by Romanists." Reverend Newell Hillis of Brooklyn fervently urged, "The Klan should be defended by every white American who is not under the domination of the Church of Rome."

Bishop Alma Bridwell White was the most successful minister to combine a defense of the Klan with attacks on Catholics. Born in Kentucky and raised in Montana, White had been a wildcat evangelist in Denver until pressure from her husband, as well as from local ministers, forced her to divorce Mr. White and to found her own church, the Pillar of Fire, with headquarters in Zarephath, New Jersey. The *New York Times* called White "the only woman bishop in the world." She was also probably the most active and prolific fundamentalist minister of the 1920s. Her Pillar of Fire Church eventually established forty-nine branches. In her lifetime, she founded three colleges and two radio stations; edited six magazines; and wrote over thirty-five books, two hundred hymns, and two morality plays. Incredibly, her alliance with the Ku Klux Klan arose from her feminism. "Women have always been the greater sufferers under the violation of law," she wrote in 1922, "and those who stand for law enforcement are the espousers of woman's cause." Her value to the Klan, however, came from her viciously anti-Catholic magazine, the *Good Citizen*, and her easily readable theological tracts that simultaneously found scriptural support for the Invisible Empire and excoriation for the Catholic Church. To Bishop White, Catholics were "toe kissers" and "wafer worshipers." Her books abounded with conspiracy themes: "We hail the K.K.K. in the great movement that is now on foot, as the army divinely appointed to set the forces in operation to rescue Americanism and save our Protestant institutions from the designs of the 'Scarlet Mother.' " "Were it not that the press is throttled by Rome and her Hebrew allies, astounding revelations would be made, showing the public the necessity for the rising of the Heroes of the Fiery Cross." Arguing that Catholic pressure had removed the Bible from public schools, White warned that unless America fought Rome, "we shall be swept into paganism."

As long as Protestant fears were kept high, the Klan thrived. And Klansmen and their wives began to thank God for the invisible army that would deliver them from the clutches of the Pope. An us-versus-them tone pervaded the Klan press, and a naïve reader could get the impression that Protestants were the minority in America instead of Catholics. The pages of official Klan organs shrieked at Catholic atrocities: "Gideons Attribute Mutilation of Bibles in Hotels to Romanists!" for example. From the dust of four centuries, Klansmen dug up Martin Luther's bone-rattling harangues against the Catholic Church: "All who have the spirit of Christ know well that they can bring no higher or more acceptable praise offering to God than all they can say or write against this bloodthirsty, unclean, blasphemic whore of the devil."

Sometimes the Klan's anti-Catholicism could take fantastic turns. In *Dawn* magazine, published by the Chicago Klan, Augusta Stetson wrote a diatribe against the movement toward making "The Star-Spangled Banner" the national anthem. As she explained it, it was a song inspired by the War of 1812 and directed against England—"a Protestant Anglo-Saxon nation." How could Americans endorse an anti-Protestant song? "I prophesy," she wrote in 1923, "that this anthem will never be accepted, nor sung by genuine Americans, and the refusal to sing this song will be the test of the true American." Elsewhere, Klan scholars spent much time proving that Leif Ericson, a Protestant, had discovered America—not Columbus, a Catholic. The Klan also denounced the Boy Scouts of America as un-American because it extended membership to Catholics as well as Jews.

In one instance, the Klan's anti-Catholic propaganda was both interesting and effective. *Harold the Klansman*, published by the Western Baptist Publishing Company, is an engrossing pro-Klan novel. Its villainous priests have human dimensions as well as fiendishly clever plans for keeping Protestants divided and weak. "We must put out propaganda to discredit the [Klan]," says one priest. "The press of the country for the most part is very helpful. . . ."

After a Catholic plot has been put down by Harold and his white-robed knights, Harold and Ruth watch a fiery cross blazing on a hill. "Isn't the cross beautiful and inspiring?" Ruth asks. "Yes," replies Harold, "and it represents a wonderful movement. A movement that will mean better citizenship."

The ultimate result of the Klan's virile Christianity, its alliance with the fundamentalist clergy, its anti-Catholicism and uniting of diverse white Protestants under the twin banners of fear and prejudice was that, by 1924, the Klan had essentially become its own church. From 1921 to 1924, Klan membership grew to 4 million, and available evidence suggests that most of these people were led into the Invisible Empire primarily by spiritual needs. They believed Klan exhorters who told them their membership was "coveted by angels." "Klansmen believe implicitly that God Almighty has raised this great white army," said a Los Angeles Cyclops. At a national convention, a Pennsylvania Cyclops remarked, "I've attended a lot of church gatherings and conventions, but I never attended one where the revival spirit was as pronounced as it was at the Klan Klonvokation." Occasionally the Klan's status as a church suppressed outside criticism of it. When an anti-Klan petition was put before the Memphis City Club in late 1923, it was turned down because the Klan was a Protestant faith, "and religion is not a topic of discussion before the Club."

Klansmen often referred to their unique faith as "Klankraft," and in examining Klankraft, consider first the Klansman's costume:

> a white robe of lightweight cotton cloth, made with cape of same material, and of proper length, with white girdle around waist, and insignia of this Order worn on the left breast. [The insignia was a yin-yang circle within a square over a Prussian cross enclosed within a greater circle.] The cowl or helmet shall be made of same material as the robe, and with whatever material necessary to give it the proper stiffness, and so made that it will be collapsible, and when worn shall be of a cone shape. There shall be one red tassel attached to the peak of same. There shall be an apron of the same material in both the front and rear, so as to completely conceal the identity of the wearer. The front apron shall have two holes of the proper size and location to facilitate the vision of the wearer.

The very act of donning this costume was often recounted as "a holy experience" by Klansmen and their wives, who were allowed to join the Klan as early as 1922. Interestingly, with the exception of the identity-concealing apron or visor, the Klansman's robe was most akin to that of his worst enemy—the Catholic priest. In a number of other ways, Klankraft was strangely similar to Catholicism. The unity, secrecy and exclusiveness of Klansmen rivaled that of the "Romanists" they detested. While denouncing Catholics as "crossbacks" and "idol worshipers," every Klansman who could afford to spend $10 bought a miniature "fiery cross" either of mahogany studded with "artificial rubies" or of metal with red lightbulbs that lit up. These were reverently displayed on an "altar" in the home. Although the Pope was condemned by the Klan as an "autocrat," the Imperial Wizard's proclamations were law and he could "excommunicate" any Klansman and dissolve any local charter at will. This very autocracy was part of the Klan's mystique. As a woman from Muncie put it, "I am a member of the Klan, because I believe before Almighty God that it is His appointed instrument. This country needs a Moses to lead this great people of ours. That leadership we have in the Klan." Klansmen liked the tight order that could be imposed by imperious leaders. And though they condemned it in Catholics, they never felt closer to God than when they massed in huge outdoor rallies and lost their individual identities in a great white-robed collective.

Klankraft could bring families closer together. Like other households, the three members of the Frank A. Rowe family of Glenn's Ferry, Idaho, were photographed in sheets and hoods for the *Fellowship Forum* magazine. "This is a one-hundred percent American family," said the *Forum*, "which has made it a point to attend all of the Klan demonstrations and parades in that section of the state. Frank A. Jr., who is not quite four years old, has given recitations before thousands of Klansmen on several occasions."

Klankraft could unite man and woman in the bonds of holy matrimony, and many young couples had Klan weddings. Sometimes the minister, like the couples, performed the ceremony in his Klan robe. At one such sacrament in Penns Grove, New Jersey, the shrouded bride approached the fiery electric cross at the altar and was met by the shrouded groom, who extended his left arm outward to her in the official Klan salute. At what was touted as the first Klan wedding of the West, reporters described a Reno ceremony as "a tableau of some ancient rite." While the white-robed bride marched up to her groom at the fiery electric cross, Klansmen lined up on either side "in formation resembling a phalanx."

Klankraft could be combined with theater. In the summer of 1924, an immense crowd filled Trinity Auditorium in Los Angeles where two huge American flags hung from the flies of the stage. As the flags were borne aloft, a large white cross was revealed: "a beautiful young woman, with flowing blond hair reaching to her waist, was seen clinging to the cross in an attitude of supplication." The orchestra suddenly struck up "Rock of Ages," and that was only the beginning. The day after this rally, a woman went to a Baptist minister saying, "I want to join the church. Last night I visited Trinity Auditorium and heard a lecture upon the Ku Klux Klan. There in the presence of hundreds of Klansmen, a speaker upon the platform, talking for the Klan, turned me back to God. If you want to know why I am joining the church, I want to tell you. It's because I found Christ through the Ku Klux Klan."

Klankraft could offer the pinnacle of religious ecstasy at outdoor rallies on high places where an enormous, burlap-wrapped and kerosene-soaked wooden cross was set on fire. So controversial were cross-burning ceremonies that Klan officials had to conduct them with utmost care. Foes of the Klan denounced them as public nuisances and fire hazards. Among the papers of an Ohio Klavern is this memo:

> No person or persons shall burn a cross or crosses without first securing permission of the Exalted Cyclops, and then only will permission be granted by the Exalted Cyclops when he is satisfied that the burning of a cross or crosses is not in violation of any city ordinance. After a city permit is obtained for the burning of same, where required, and the cross is to be burned on private property, the permission of the owner must first be secured in writing.

Though similar to the pagan fire festivals of central Europe during the middle ages, the Klan's cross burnings in the 1920s were invariably constrained by a strict Christian ritual. The ceremony opened with a prayer by the "Kludd," or Klavern minister. The multitude then sang "Onward Christian Soldiers." After the hymn, the cross was lit, and the explosion of the kerosene and the rush of flames over the timbers was thrilling, to say the least. (In the mining districts of Pennsylvania, Klansmen augmented the effect by simultaneously detonating charges of dynamite.) Children sometimes wet their pants.

Bathed in warmth, left arms outstretched toward the blazing icon and voices raised in "The Old Rugged Cross," Klansmen felt as in one body. These were moments they would always remember. To outside foes who witnessed them, cross burnings were something they would never forget. They were grotesque rituals to be enacted on American soil. They were spectacles no one had ever seen before. And their likes wouldn't be seen again until Berlin of the 1930s.

"PRACTICAL PATRIOTISM"

The Klan and Politics: 1922–1925

F or those at Imperial Headquarters, the Klan's apotheosis as a Christian crusade was too good to be true. In the particular case of Imperial Wizard Simmons, it was too good to last. As the Klan accumulated members in a militant Protestant direction, more and more of them wanted the Klan to get involved in the political process. And the most spirited Klansmen became dissatisfied with the Simmons–Clarke regime. Aside from spouting high-flown rhetoric and raking in the cash, the Imperial Wizard and Imperial Kleagle evinced little interest in the leadership needs of Klansmen-at-large. Clarke was obsessed with the money-making end of the organization. He had already begun investing the Klan's undeclared profits in real estate. In addition to the Imperial Palace and Simmons's Klan Krest, he bought a printing plant and regalia factory at Buckhead, Georgia, ten acres of the Peachtree Creek Civil War battlefield; the apartment building in which he lived; and a small Atlanta college, Lanier University, which went bankrupt barely a year after the Klan bought it.

Eventually one of Clarke's most valuable employees in the Propagation Department, Z. R. Upchurch, quit the organization in disgust, charging Clarke with keeping Simmons in a perpetual state of drunkenness so he could fleece the Imperial Treasury. A number of Kleagles also quit, claiming that the Klan was little more than a get-rich scheme for its leaders. And state and local officers objected to Imperial Headquarters' tendency to delay the delivery of a charter as long as possible, so that fees didn't have to be shared with Klaverns and Realms.

Not long after this, a small group of insurgents began thinking about removing Simmons from office. Heading the insurgents was Dr. Hiram Wesley Evans of Dallas. Like Simmons, Evans was born in Alabama but had moved to Texas before the war and opened up a dentist office. Evans's dentistry credentials were a bit shady—some said he had obtained his degree from a correspondence school, others said he was a veterinarian dentist—but his Dallas practice was successful enough. Shortly after the Klan's drive for members in 1920, he became head of the Dallas Klavern. His followers liked him for his frankness and practicality, as well as for his rousing speeches before the public. (One who knew Evans well said he could convince the average Klansman "that Jesus wasn't a Jew.") Evans was more interested in the Klan as a political rather than a religious movement; and he considered Simmons's ineptitude in politics as his principal failing.

After a short term as Great Titan of Province #2 in Texas, Evans was brought to the Imperial Palace by Clarke and Tyler, who talked Simmons into making him national secretary or Imperial Kligrapp. Evans was probably given the position as a sop to his fellow Texas Klansmen who wanted more direct representation in Atlanta. As Kligrapp, Evans was in charge of the thirteen states that had already been chartered. In addition to a salary of $7,500, he received a cut from all fees coming in from the states under his supervision. Evans traveled extensively through these states, cultivating relationships with the Klan's key state and local officers. One he quickly saw eye-to-eye with was David Curtis Stephenson of Indiana. Stephenson, or "Steve," was only thirty-one years old and had lost his first bid for public office, running in Indiana's Democratic primary for the first congressional district. But he was quickly becoming the dominant force in the Indiana Klan. Even more than Evans, Steve realized the Klan's political potential and knew how important it could be for his own public career. As Evans and Steve grew closer, they decided to remove Simmons from the Wizardship and to divvy up the Klan between themselves.

Evans had already secured Clarke's unthinking agreement to pressure Simmons into taking a vacation, and Doc was only too happy to comply because he hadn't been feeling well lately. In the interim, Clarke was made Wizard pro tem, and Evans consolidated his plans for ousting Simmons after he returned. A national Klan convention, or Klonvokation, was scheduled for Thanksgiving week, 1922, in commemoration of the revived Klan's seventh anniversary. The Klonvokation was to be held in a large auditorium erected on the Confederate battlefield now partially owned by the Klan. Entire floors in Atlanta hotels were taken up by Klansmen who swarmed to the convention. With Steve's help, Evans planned to manipulate the delegates into making him Wizard at the general election scheduled for the second day.

Simmons threw them a curve on the first day, however, with a dramatically successful appeal to the emotions of the crowd. At the opening session, he asked them to get down on their knees with him while he led them in prayer. (According to Simmons, six Klansmen "were converted right then and there.") With tears in his eyes, he then led them in "Onward Christian Soldiers." In a speech that followed, he said, "Doubtless the angels themselves, as they peer over the battlements of the eternal city, hold a kind of envy of you, in your position and of the work you have to do." It was just what crowds of Klansmen liked to hear.

That night, Evans and Steve evaluated the best way to counter Simmons's successful appeal to the delegates. A scheme was finally hatched with the help of Fred Savage, a sleazy New York strikebreaker whom Simmons had brought to the Palace to head, of all things, the Klan's Department of Investigation. Steve and Savage called on every delegate, saying, "Tomorrow morning comes the election of Imperial Wizard. Emperor Simmons has so much work to do that he has asked us to select a Wizard as an assistant for him. Simmons holds two offices—Emperor and Imperial Wizard." It was true that, since Simmons had invented these top offices, he held them; but the office of Emperor was more spiritual than political. Steve's idea was to "kick Simmons upstairs" to the office of Emperor while the more powerful role of Wizard would be taken over by Evans. "We think," they told the delegates, "it will be best to elect Hiram Wesley Evans to be Imperial Wizard, and leave the *greater* powers of Emperor to Colonel Simmons." After securing the votes of a majority of delegates, Steve and Savage drove out to Klan Krest and woke Simmons at four in the morning.

At first they told the drowsy Wizard that, unable to sleep with all the convention excitement, they had been out for an early morning drive. Then they got to the point. Steve asked Simmons what he was going to do about the general election the next day. Since Simmons assumed the delegates would unanimously reconfirm him as Wizard, he told them he hadn't planned on doing anything.

"Well, Colonel," Savage began, "we both just dropped around to tell you that, whatever happens on the convention floor tomorrow, there will be armed men stationed round on the floor to protect your honor."

"Protect my honor!" Simmons exclaimed. "What do you mean?"

Steve and Savage then told Simmons that if he sought reelection, a large group of insurgents planned to denounce him from the floor, but they assured Simmons that he need not worry. "The first man who insults your name will be killed by a sharpshooter right on the spot as he speaks," said Steve. "There'll be enough of us with firearms to take care of the whole convention, if necessary." Of course, if Simmons wanted to avert bloodshed, he might do something like recommend Evans for the office of Wizard and retain and develop for himself the office of Emperor.

As Simmons recalled, he nearly collapsed at the vision of "a bloody shambles" among a thousand Klansmen: "Well, I didn't sleep any more that night." At a private prayer meeting for Klan executives the next morning, Simmons hoarsely announced his willingness to let Evans be nominated. The signal immediately went out to the delegates and Evans was elected Imperial Wizard by acclamation.

Soon after the Klonvokation, Simmons went to the Imperial Palace and was startled to find Evans sitting at his desk. "Colonel Simmons," the new Wizard said, "I'm going to put you on a great white throne in this palace. I am planning to make a throne room for you where you can meet all visitors." But the throne never materialized. Simmons watched the "cheery" atmosphere of the Palace turn cold and commercial as Evans implemented plans for politicizing the Klan. The Peachtree Creek battlefield was sold and the profits put back in the treasury. A few weeks later, copies of the Klan's new constitution arrived from the printers. Even the few political powers Evans had promised Simmons as Emperor had been deleted. There was some major additions as well, including:

> Article I, Section 2: The government of this Order shall ever be military in character, especially in its executive management and control.

Evans had even more ideas. He demanded Mrs. Tyler's half interest in the profits earned by the Klan's Propagation Department, and when Clarke refused, he canceled the Klan's contract with the Southern Publicity Association. Members of Atlanta's Klavern Number One had enjoyed the Imperial Palace as a "loafing place," and Evans threw them out, telling them they had no more right to the Palace than any other Klavern.

All this greatly upset Simmons. In early 1923, he set out on a speaking tour in an attempt to tell Klansmen what was happening to their Christian crusade, but Evans met him at every turn with injunctions that prevented his speaking. In Ohio, Steve hired a drunken derelict to impersonate Simmons at an outdoor Klonklave, seriously tarnishing the former Wizard's reputation among temperate Midwesterners. Simmons finally had enough. While Evans was out of town, he obtained a court injunction on April 2, 1923, giving him temporary authority over the Klan and its treasury and barring Evans from the Palace. The next day, hundreds of Klansmen loyal to either Simmons or Evans flocked to Atlanta to join the civil war. By April 8, Evans won a court decision that allowed him back in the Palace though it didn't give him executive control. After more legal skirmishes, with alternating victories for each side, the courts put the Invisible Empire, Knights of the Ku Klux Klan, Inc., in the hands of a three-man commission, headed by the marshal of the municipal court of Atlanta—an arrangement that neither Simmons nor Evans wanted.

The commission allowed an out-of-court settlement determined by an Imperial Kloncilium of fifteen members, five of whom Simmons chose, five Evans chose, and five Klansmen-at-large. Since the five at-large were loyal to Evans, he held the edge in the Kloncilium. Steve, in fact, was appointed to chair the Kloncilium and did so with elegant parliamentarianism. The fifteen members concluded that Evans was the legal and rightful Wizard and commended his "fearless and generous" behavior throughout the litigation. But Simmons had the last word: The Klan's rituals, charter, regalia, and titles had all been copyrighted in his name. In exchange for transferring these copyrights to the Knights of the Ku Klux Klan, Inc., Simmons demanded and obtained a salary of $1,000 per month as well as the office of Emperor for as long as he lived.

It was a hopeless truce. When Simmons launched an independent women's auxiliary of the Klan, Evans blocked it. (The Women's Klan would soon become a reality, however.) Simmons ranted publicly at Evans and Evans sued for libel. Evans published a pamphlet that convincingly portrayed Simmons's attempts to "destroy the Klan." At a gathering of Klansmen in Steve's hometown of Evansville, he called Simmons and his followers "a bunch of soreheads." Then, in the most bizarre turn in the entire battle, a minor official at the Imperial Palace shot and killed Simmons's attorney, Captain William S. Coburn. Simmons was shocked and frightened. "This murder was too much for me," he recalled. "I didn't want to fight men who could kill that way." Evans wasn't happy about it either and claimed he knew nothing about it. In the wake of publicity on the murder, he moved the Klan's Imperial Headquarters to Washington, D.C., leaving the Palace in the hands of secretaries to answer routine correspondence.

On January 11, 1924, a meeting of Grand Dragons at Washington voted to banish both Simmons and Clarke from the Invisible Empire. (Seeing the inevitable, Mrs. Tyler had already left the Klan to marry a prominent Atlanta businessman.) Clarke belittled the banishment, saying it was effected "because Evans and his associates are desperate and realize it is only for a short time they will be able to hold the reins of the organization and trample in the dust all the founding principles and ideals of the Knights of the Ku Klux Klan." Clarke had been fighting harder than Simmons by this time. In a letter to President Calvin Coolidge, Clarke had charged Evans with attempting to turn the Klan into "a cheap political machine." The Klan was never meant to be political, he had told the President. Instead "it was to be an organization designed to up-build and develop spiritually, morally and physically the Protestant white man of America." When Evans realized that this could go on forever, he offered Simmons a cash settlement to sever himself permanently from the Klan. Simmons was now pliant. "Like General Lee at Appomattox," he said later, "I had neither the men nor the munitions to carry on." On February 12, 1924, Simmons agreed to a $145,000 cash settlement, in lieu of his copyrights and his lifetime office of Emperor. Evans told newsmen, "The settlement means the complete elimination of Colonel Simmons's connection with the Klan."

The press had a field day with the Klan's internal squabble. The *New York Times* remarked, "In no other society claiming to have benevolent objects is it even imaginable that a change of administration could be brought about in this way. Shrewd schemers buy and sell [Klansmen] as if they were sheep or cows." The Syracuse *Herald* said, "The country is now getting a new view of the Ku

Klux Klan, this time as a sort of a public-utility corporation, with considerable tangible and intangible assets, barring, of course, good-will, of which it has none." With sadness, Simmons explained to his followers, "The reason I resigned as Emperor of the Klan and as a member of same was because of the constant and continuous turmoil and friction prevailing in the organization. I have resorted to every honorable means to correct the same, and find my efforts to be fruitless."

Evans didn't know it at the time of the settlement, but Simmons already had plans to create a new rival fraternity. In fact, only days after receiving $90,000 of the settlement (which was all he would ever get), he invested most of it in his second-born brainchild. Chartered in Florida, the "Knights of the Flaming Sword" was intended to rescue the romantic ideals and religiosity that Evans had allegedly undermined in the Klan. Simmons spent the latter part of 1924 promoting the new order. On the evening of February 21, 1925, he was returning to Atlanta from Florida when he lost control of his car and skidded over an embankment. His traveling companion was instantly killed. Simmons wound up in a hospital with four broken ribs and a punctured lung. Complicated by his hypochondria, Simmons's recovery was slow and painful, and the Knights of the Flaming Sword petered out during his convalescence. Simmons spent several more years in Atlanta and then returned to his native Alabama. In the city of Luverne, the forgotten and frequently tipsy Wizard haunted the lobbies of second-rate hotels until his death in 1945.

In spite of the nastiness of the Simmons–Evans schism and the unfavorable coverage it received in the press, the Klan continued to grow and, in fact, reached the peak of its membership under Evans. Undaunted by his battles with Simmons, Evans succeeded in bringing a marked increase of leadership to the Klan at a national level. As soon as he became Wizard he began publishing a spate of pamphlets for the use of local Klaverns. Some of these, such as "Articles on the Klan and Elementary Klankraft," attempted to coordinate the various approaches Klansmen used to proselytize the public. The pamphlet "Klan Building" was meant to help unify the operations of various Klaverns around the country. The Exalted Cyclops was urged to "make the Klan the civic asset of his community." Klaverns were advised to hold meetings around a central topic: "Never attempt to hold a Klonklave without a definite program." If Klansmen were at a loss for a program, Evans recommended such topics as the History of Protestantism, Immigration, American Public Schools, and White Supremacy.

In nearly every case, Evans downplayed the religious angle of the Klan, supplanting it with hyperpatriotism, militant nativism, and political activism. "The Klan is an organization to promote practical patriotism," he told an interviewer. "Its ideal is to restore and then to preserve and develop the old, fundamental ideas on which the Nation was founded and which have made it great; to provide for the uncontaminated growth of Anglo-Saxon civilization. . . . ." Though he permitted and even encouraged the anti-Catholicism, anti-Semitism, and white supremacy that had by now become dogma to Klansmen, Evans simultaneously encouraged Klansmen's social relationships and obligations to each other. During the Evans regime, the Klan press began teaching "klannishness" as a virtue: "Every true Klansman should practice klannishness. Do you strive to aid your brother by patronizing his business?" Klan merchants advertised in the Klan press, and readers learned that Liberty Bell Coffee was a "100% American brew." On the other hand, the products of merchants hostile to the Klan were earmarked for boycotts. When Alfred Fuller, president of the Fuller Brush Company, denounced Klansmen as "fools and radicals," Klansmen boycotted his products until he recanted a month later. Klansmen also worried about the fleurs-de-lis that decorated (and still adorn) Campbell soup cans. Imperial Headquarters conducted a searching investigation into whether the fleur-de-lis was a Catholic symbol and determined that it was French, not Catholic, and that "every single officer" of the Campbell Soup Company was a Protestant. The group cohesion of Klansmen was promoted through Ku-Klux *Kultur*. Klansmen could purchase clothing, jewelry, knives, watches, and rings with the clever tri-K logo—⟁—and phonograph record and player-piano roll companies offered selections, from "Onward Valiant Klansmen" to "Daddy Swiped the Last Clean Sheet."

Even though the Klan was on an up-swing, Evans called an important convention of Grand Dragons in July 1923, at Asheville, North Carolina, where he announced his hopes of more than doubling Klan membership to 10 million. He wanted to see more coordination among Klaverns. He wanted Klaverns to increase their visibility by publishing monthly newsletters and bulletins and holding public events as often as possible. Klansmen should take an increased interest in the civic affairs of their communities and the political leadership of their states. Moreover, when Klansmen broke the law, rather than support them, Klaverns should do everything possible to see that the violator was brought to justice.

Evans realized that the problem of Klan violence was a major deterrent to Klan membership. Acts of violence invariably received prompt attention by newsmen. In Mer Rouge, Louisiana, Klansmen committed one of the most grisly unsolved crimes of all time when they murdered two whites who had been loudly opposed to them. The badly decomposed bodies of the victims eventually surfaced in Lake Lafourche. According to forensic pathologists, the two men had been brutally beaten and then repeatedly run over by heavy machinery before their bodies were dumped in the lake.

Another well-publicized incident was a riot in the sleepy town of Lorena, Texas. When fully robed Waco Klansmen began a parade through the streets of Lorena, Sheriff Bob Buchanan told them that parading by masked men was against the law in the Lone Star State. Aided only by a single deputy, Buchanan did his best to stop the parade peaceably—he hadn't the forces to do otherwise. But egged on by the spectators lining the street, the Klansmen got rowdy. Suddenly a Klansman took his fiery electric cross and bashed the sheriff over the head with it. Gunfire rang out and bullets ricocheted off cars parked at the curb. In the aftermath, one man was dead from a knife wound and ten lay injured from bullets. Sheriff Buchanan survived two gunshot wounds, only to suffer a stinging rebuke from the McLennan County grand jury. The townspeople agreed that the sheriff had no right "interfering with something that wasn't his business." Leon Jaworski, one of Waco's younger residents, disagreed with his friends and neighbors. The grand jury that had censured the sheriff had been dominated by Klansmen and would always serve as a model to Leon Jaworski of what justice was not.*

Things were hardly more genteel in the North. At Beaver, Pennsylvania, Klansmen abducted and hanged a black. Cutting the rope before he died, they then proceeded to kick and beat him to a state of unconsciousness. In Denver, Klansmen abducted a member of the Knights of Columbus, drove him to a spot near a cemetery and clubbed him with the butts of their revolvers; three months later they did the same thing to a Jewish attorney, using blackjacks this time. Obnoxious night riding by Klan "black squads" was as frequent in Oregon as it was in Oklahoma.

Instead of denying Klan violence as had Simmons, Evans made

---

* Texas attorney Leon Jaworski eventually became special prosecutor in the Watergate constitutional crisis in the mid-1970s, which resulted in the resignation of President Richard Nixon on August 9, 1974.

a decided effort at curbing it. He didn't think Klan violence was evil but rather that it was impolitic. He believed that most acts of hooded violence were perpetrated by small groups, often just pairs of Klansmen, and so he ordered local leaders: "Robes and helmets must not be permitted to be retained by Klansmen personally." Instead, regalia should be kept in the Klavern under the custody of a responsible officer. Most of the time, Evans urged indirect rather than direct action. For instance, if there was lawlessness in the community, the best thing to do was put pressure on local police:

> In some instances officers of the law are averse to the enforcement of certain laws [especially Prohibition] because their enforcement in that community would be unpopular. . . . This, however, under no circumstances relieves the Klansmen of that community of their responsibility to the law and its enforcement *through legal channels.* By the crystallization of public sentiment in favor of law enforcement, an aroused public conscience will, by its weight, force the officers of the law to fulfill their duty to the commonwealth.

Similarly, Evans said it was foolish and impractical to harass local hyphens. Klansmen could be much more productive by barraging their congressmen and senators with letters demanding immigration restriction. (The Klan would later take a large share of the credit for passage of the restrictive 1924 Johnson Immigration Act.)

The new Wizard also tried to clean up the rhetoric of local Klaverns. "It is a good policy," he told Klan officers, "not to permit discussion on the floor of the Klavern on any subject which, if published, would reflect discredit upon our great movement." Some local groups agreed with him. In a memo called "Suggestions for Klan Speakers," an Ohio Klavern recommended:

- DON'T RANT . . .
- DON'T LIE OR EXAGGERATE . . .
- DON'T ABUSE THE "ENEMY." Nothing is to be gained by raving hysterically about Catholics, Jews, Negroes, Bootleggers, Foreigners, and the like. A scientific, sympathetic, sportsmanlike presentation of facts will win more people and leave you under the necessity of making no apologies to anybody. . . .

These suggestions were largely for the sake of appearances. An Indiana Cyclops revealed that "open meetings always stressed the need of an organization like the Klan to unite the Protestants . . . in closed meetings the danger from Catholic and Jew was stressed." Like forty-five thousand fellow Missourians, haberdasher Harry S. Truman joined the Klan in Kansas City. But after the first meeting, where he listened to a violently anti-Catholic diatribe, he angrily demanded and received his $10 back.

To some degree, Evans's efforts at turning the attentions of Klansmen toward politics were successful. Klan violence diminished noticeably during the Evans regime, especially in the Southwest, where Klan vigilantism had been a recurrent problem. And, the Invisible Empire as an important voting bloc was a major topic of discussion among political pundits between 1923 and 1925. It is nearly impossible, however, to characterize generally the Klan's politics. Since Klaverns were organized on the basis of local needs, the goals and campaigns of Klansmen varied widely from one locale to the next. Some Klaverns attempted to win discriminatory legislation against minorities in their communities. Others, such as the Orange County, California, Klavern, supported measures reflecting positive civic mindedness. When it came to electing men for public office, the Klan revealed its worst weakness as a political coalition. Local concerns could be strangely forgotten when Klansmen's decisions to endorse a candidate invariably depended more on what he said about the Klan than on where he stood politically. Sometimes Klansmen would even endorse a quiet Catholic if his Protestant opponent was loudly anti-Klan. Wily politicians learned to manipulate the votes of Klansmen by staying discreet on the subject of the Klan until they attained office. Conversely, perennial losers and candidates about to be defeated for reelection jumped enthusiastically on the Klan bandwagon, draining support from another candidate who could more effectively realize Klan aims. Ultimately, Klan politicking was little more than an amateurish show of strength that only rarely achieved Klan goals and never achieved Klan unity.

Klansmen did win elections, however. In cities from Portland, Oregon, to Portland, Maine, and from Denver to Dallas, the number of mayors, sheriffs, and councilmen Klansmen put in office has yet to be fully counted. The Klan also helped elect sixteen men to the U.S. Senate (nine Republicans and seven Democrats), eleven governors (six Republicans, five Democrats), and an unknown number of congressmen. As the Know-Nothings had done before the Civil War, Klansmen usually allied themselves with the party in power—the Republican in the North and Democratic in the South. Only five of the sixteen senators were actually Klansmen, including Hugo Black of Alabama, who later repented and became a noteworthy U. S. Supreme Court justice; and only four of the eleven governors. The others were endorsed because their opponents offended the Klan or because they took stands on issues that were congenial to Klansmen—such as Prohibition in the North and states' rights in the South—and would probably have won without Klan support. Above the municipal level, the only state dominated by the Klan was Indiana.

Klan-backed legislators rarely conceded to Klan pressure on major issues, aside from the 1924 Immigration Act. Despite the Klan's opposition to the move toward ratifying the World Court in 1926, it was able to sway the votes of only two of its senators. Only two state legislatures made Klan-supported bills law: the one in Indiana was completely innocuous; an Oregon law forcing children to spend their elementary years in a public, as opposed to parochial, school was overturned by the Supreme Court.

The Klan's greatest show of political strength came in the election year 1924 and especially at the Democratic Convention, where its influence was entirely destructive. Two weeks before the Democratic Convention in New York, Klansmen had successfully pressured the Republicans into refraining from criticizing the Klan in their platform. For his role in the achievement, Evans made the cover of *Time* magazine. Immediately afterward, Evans and an entourage of Imperial officers moved into New York's Hotel McAlpin. The Democrats, meeting at Madison Square Garden, were expected to offer stronger resistance to the Klan's efforts at keeping the Party from denouncing it. Klansmen had already blighted the hopes of anti-Klan senator Oscar Underwood to win the Democratic nomination. During the campaign, Underwood had said that the Klan was "a national menace. . . . It is either the Ku Klux Klan or the United States of America. Both cannot survive. Between the two, I choose my country." For this and similar remarks, the Klan had slandered the Alabama senator most effectively in the critical Southern primaries, denouncing him as the "Jew, jug, and Jesuit candidate." The two remaining candidates were William Gibbs McAdoo and Al Smith. Klansmen considered Smith a "crossback" Catholic from "Jew York," which left McAdoo as their candidate. McAdoo didn't fully agree with the Klan's principles but accepted its support because he lacked it elsewhere.

Trouble broke out on the second day, when a nominating speaker for Underwood condemned "the hooded and secret organization known as the Ku Klux Klan." For over an hour, delegates cheered or hooted; fistfights broke out in the Colorado and Missouri delegations. The moment of truth came on the fifth day, when a minority plank to the platform condemned the Klan by name. The demonstration that followed is reported to have been the ugliest brawl ever to occur inside a national convention hall. After two hours of pandemonium, delegates got down to a roll-call vote, and the hair-splitting of votes showed the Klan's divisive powers. Humorist Will Rogers, who covered the convention for the *New York Times*, reported:

> When North Carolina announced to the Chairman that three and eighty-five one-hundredths of a delegate were in favor of the Klan amendment, and that twenty and fifteen one-hundredths of a delegate were against it, why, there was a round of laughter that broke-up what was the most tense moment ever witnessed in a convention hall.
>
> I left the press stand on a run. I wanted to see what manner of architectural anatomy a man or woman must have to be only fifteen one-hundredths percent of a delegate. . . . [The] Chairman could not do anything until they had called in some surgeons from Bellevue, because this was evidently a case of compound fractures, assisted by assorted sizes of operations in surgery.
>
> Fourteen thousand people in the hall and 14,000,000 radios had to stand at attention while the doctors held a clinic over the North Carolina delegation.

In the end, the anti-Klan plank was defeated by 543 $\frac{3}{20}$ to 542 $\frac{7}{20}$ —or four-fifths of a single vote.

The acrimonious struggle over the Klan hopelessly divided the convention into two bitter factions and spelled disaster for the Democrats. One commentator remarked, "The deadlock that developed might as well have been a political contest between the Pope and the Imperial Wizard of the Klan, so solidly did the Catholic delegates support Smith and the Klansmen support McAdoo." By the time of the seventieth ballot, several delegations had begun running out of money. The chairman of the Massachusetts delegation told his group, "Gentlemen, we are faced with a choice— either we move to a more modest hotel or to a more liberal candidate." When McAdoo threw in the towel after the ninetieth ballot, the race was left between the anti-Klan Underwood and the Catholic Smith. The Klan maintained its unyielding resistance to both candidates, forcing the Democrats to nominate an entirely color-less compromise candidate, John Davis, on the 103rd ballot.

Summarizing the convention, H. L. Mencken remarked, "The battle that went on between the Kukluxers and their enemies was certainly no sham battle. There were deep and implacable hatreds in it. Each side was resolutely determined to butcher the other. In the end, both were butchered—and a discreet bystander made off with the prize." It can hardly be said that the Klan was "butch-ered," however. Since a majority of Klansmen intended to vote for Coolidge anyway, the nomination of Davis was of little signifi-cance. But Mencken was right about the sad consequences for the Democrats. With the smell of the Teapot Dome scandal still in the air for the Republicans, 1924 had seemed like a Democratic year. It wouldn't be with a soporific unknown like Davis. Will Rogers returned to Hollywood, assuring his readers that his employers at the *New York Times* had nothing to do with bringing such a fiasco of a convention to New York City, and thanking Gotham's boot-leggers for their "hearty cooperation in keeping the price within the reach of all."

Inevitably, the nonissue of whether or not to condemn the Klan continued throughout the presidential campaign. The matter was especially important to the blacks who could vote in 1924. Al-though the Klan was far more hostile to Catholics and immigrants than to blacks during the 1920s, blacks were acutely aware of the Klan's historic and present potential for racial violence; and they thought only a candidate who condemned the Invisible Empire was worthy of their support. There was one important exception. Marcus Garvey, a militant black nationalist and leader of the Uni-versal Negro Improvement Association, advised blacks that liberty was impossible for them in America, and that their only hopes lay in emigrating to Africa. Garvey used the Klan to prove his point, and his flirtations with leaders of the Invisible Empire mark one of the more curious political alliances in American history. W.E.B. DuBois, who strongly opposed Garvey, gave a terse synopsis of it:

> Garvey's motives were clear. The triumph of the Klan would drive Negroes to his program in despair. . . . Garvey openly advertised the Klan's program as showing the impossibility of the Negro's remaining in America, and the Klan sent out circulars defending Garvey and declaring the opposition to him was from the Catholic Church!

One of the major battles between moderate blacks and Garvey was fought in the White House mailroom. Moderate blacks sent scores of letters to Coolidge asking him to denounce the Klan publicly. A petition from Boston's blacks said: "We ask you to tell us whether the Party of Lincoln the Emancipator is seeking the support of the Imperial Wizard and his hooded bands." On the other side, Garvey's supporters and Garvey himself told the President that he had "the full sympathy of 4 million of our organization in his refusal to be drawn into the Ku Klux Klan controversy."

Coolidge's refusal to say anything about the Klan rose more from his penchant for avoiding controversy than from outside pressure. Plenty of Republican leaders supported his silence. And his Klan adviser, Edwin Banta, a New Jersey journalist and part-time Klansman, told him, "May I advise, without offending, that a soft-pedal be used in the K.K.K. and let the Democrats reap the whirlwind they have sowed." In the aftermath of the "whirlwind," Davis had little to lose when he finally came out against the Klan. Speaking at Sea Girt, New Jersey, on August 23, Davis claimed that the Klan "does violence to the spirit of American institutions and must be condemned by all those who believe, as I do, in American ideals." But Davis's statement came too late for the liberals, and it cost him the votes of many Northern Democratic Klansmen as well as the support of his own state of West Virginia. In November, "Silent Cal" Coolidge won handsomely.

Nineteen-twenty-four was a lucky year for the Klan. A mere infant in politics, it had scored some surprising upsets and had gotten the nation talking about it. But as a political bloc it had a lot to learn. In spite of Evans's effort at sophisticating Klansmen, at polls they continued to hand out cards with such low-level clap-trap as

> When cotton grows on the fig tree
>   And alfalfa hangs on the rose
> When the aliens run the United States
>   And the Jews grow a straight nose
> When the Pope is praised by every one
>   In the land of Uncle Sam
> And a Greek is elected President
>   THEN—the Ku Klux won't be worth a damn.

Klan leaders nevertheless took pride in having "awakened the public mind" to practical patriotism and for bringing about "more respect for the franchise and a freer exercise of it." In support of the last claim, the Klan pointed out that since it had gone into politics, 25 percent more eligible voters were exercising their franchise.

This was a strange way of taking credit for a backlash it had provoked in the first place. What is more significant is that the Klan's move into politics had prompted those opposed to it to band together to defeat it. Probably the first formal anti-Klan group was the Dallas County Citizens League, organized April 4, 1922. "Who can teach Americanism," asked the league, "tried patriots or the Night Prowlers?" In 1923, at least seven anti-Klan coalitions were founded, including New York's Knights of Liberty, organized by a reformed and penitent Grand Goblin; Oklahoma's Anti-Klan Association; and San Francisco's Minute Men of the West. Some anti-Klan groups copied their enemy's organizational structure and flummery, such as Pennsylvania's Knights of the Blazing Ring. The *New York Times* called the Knights of the Flaming Circle, based also in Pennsylvania, "just about as ridiculous as the Klan itself." The Order of Anti-Poke Noses in Searcy County, Arkansas, was "opposed to any organization that attends to everyone's business but its own" and expressed confidence in elected officials who "do not need to be eternally prodded by the Ku Klux Klan." Some anti-Klan groups fought fire with fire, especially the Loyal Legion of Lincoln which occasionally burned fiery Ls.

The most effective anti-Klan organization was the National Vigilance Association, incorporated in Washington, D.C. The Vigilance Association worked for the passage of laws by the legislatures of every state making it illegal to wear masks and a federal statute outlawing mob violence. The second goal was controversial in the 1920s because it added to the powers of the federal government, but several states passed strong antimask laws which held that intent to intimidate was not necessary for conviction. Such statutes became effective in 1923 in the weak Klan states of Minnesota, New Mexico, and North Dakota and in the strong Klan state of Oklahoma; the next year, Louisiana, also a strong Klan state, joined the other four. Other states considered bills against wearing masks in public if an intent to intimidate could be proved. These softer bills became law in 1923 in Arizona and Illinois and a year later in Iowa—all of which were states with moderate Klan strength.

A number of fraternal organizations and unions took a stand against the Klan. The American Federation of Labor particularly hated the Invisible Empire. The Ancient Order of Hibernians asked President Coolidge to follow "the honored example of Pres-

ident Grant" and to "suppress with the strong arm of the Federal
Government 'The Invisible Empire of the Ku Klux Klan,' which
has no right or title to exist in a free Republic." The American
Legion's criticism of the Klan tied it to the left wing: "By their
example, the hooded Peeping Toms give license to every 'Red' and
I.W.W. to continue [their] underhanded operations. . . ."

Several newspapers waged anti-Klan crusades as zealous in spirit
as the Klan itself and won Pulitzer prizes for doing so. Among
these were the Indianapolis *Times*, which carried the details of the
Klan's incredible debacle in Indiana to the entire nation; also the
Memphis *Commercial Appeal*, which poked so much fun at the
"nightie knights" that no one could take them seriously. The most
intrepid anti-Klan editor to win the Pulitzer was Julian Harris of
the *Enquirer-Sun*, based in the Klan's backyard of Columbus,
Georgia. The son of Joel Chandler Harris, author of the Uncle
Remus stories, Julian Harris assailed Klansmen as "grafters, black-
mailers, spy-chiefs," and "cluck-clucks":

> When intolerance becomes active, it is known as fanaticism, and fa-
> naticism is the thing that murders Socrates, burns heretics, arrays
> class against class, tramples fundamental law in the mud in order to
> gain its bigoted ends, makes possible a cowardly masked gang like the
> Ku Klux Klan, and fetters that finest attribute of the human mind, the
> spirit of honest inquiry.

Harris's had been the only Georgia paper to carry the complete
1921 exposé by the New York *World*. With little regard for his own
safety, Harris revealed that the governor, the attorney general, the
commissioner of agriculture, the commissioner of fish and game,
the state superintendent of public instruction, and the chief justice
of the state supreme court were Georgia Klansmen. He lambasted
any politician who courted the Klan for votes. His editorials were
reprinted by newspapers across the country. There were many
anonymous threats on his and his wife's life. Parades of hooded
Klansmen in front of the *Empire-Sun* Building failed to faze him.
Even when a Klan plot to bomb his home—supported in part by
the Columbus Police Department—was uncovered, he continued
in his opposition to the Invisible Empire. When the Pulitzer committee awarded Harris its prize in 1925, H. L. Mencken said, "It is
the most intelligent award the committee has yet made."

The most articulate critic of the Klan, however, was not an
American. Nguyen Sinh Cung was a young Indochinese who had

moved to Paris as a youth, where he became an apprentice in the great kitchens of *haute cuisine*. In London's Carlton Hotel, he briefly worked under the famous chef Escoffier, who liked his work and promoted him to pastry cook. Wanting to travel, Cung took a job in the galley aboard the French liner *Latouche-Tréville*, which brought him to America several times. Though he felt the Statue of Liberty was a bit too French, he was impressed with the United States and was genuinely inspired by the story of the American Revolution. As a foreigner and an Oriental, he tolerated American prejudice toward himself but was incredulous at America's treatment of her own citizens, the blacks.

After the nationwide lynchings of blacks in 1919, Cung had become an expert on the subject. He accumulated statistics and collected clippings on American lynching:

> from the New Orleans *States:* TODAY A NEGRO WILL BE BURNED BY 3,000 CITIZENS . . .
>
> from the Jackson *Daily News:* NEGRO J.H. TO BE BURNT BY THE CROWD AT ELLISTOWN THIS AFTERNOON AT 5 P.M. . . .

In an article written in French for a 1924 edition of the *Correspondance Internationale*, Cung told readers:

> Imagine a furious horde. Fists clenched, eyes bloodshot, mouths foaming, yells, insults, curses. . . . This horde is transported with the wild delight of a crime to be committed without risk. . . .
>
> Imagine in this human sea a flotsam of black flesh pushed about, beaten, trampled underfoot, torn, slashed, insulted, tossed hither and thither, bloodstained. . . .
>
> In a wave of hatred and bestiality, the lynchers drag the Black to a woods or public place. They tie him to a tree, pour kerosene over him, cover him with inflammable material. While waiting for the fire to be kindled, they smash his teeth, one by one. . . .
>
> The Black is cooked, browned, burned. But he deserves to die twice instead of once. He is therefore hanged, or more exactly, what is left of his corpse is hanged. . . .
>
> When everybody has had enough, the corpse is brought down. The rope is cut into small pieces which will be sold for three or five dollars each. Souvenirs and lucky charms are quarreled over by the ladies. . . .
>
> While on the ground, stinking of fat and smoke, a black head,

mutilated, roasted, deformed, grins horribly and seems to ask the setting sun, "Is this civilization?"

Not even so vigorous a foe of lynching as W.E.B. DuBois had portrayed the practice so graphically.

Nguyen Sinh Cung took a scholarly interest in the Ku Klux Klan that led him all the way back to 1866. His 1924 account for French readers is one of the earliest revisionist studies of the Reconstruction Klan. And Cung announced categorically that the revived Klan was "doomed to disappear." He predicted that at some time in America, blacks would attain sufficient strength to fight the organization without fear. He predicted that, after enough gross excesses, those who had earlier joined the Klan would renounce it. He pointed out that opposed to the Klan were "20 million American Catholics, 3 million Jews, 20 million foreigners, 12 million Negroes [and] all decent Americans. . . ." Finally he said:

> the Ku Klux Klan has all the defects of clandestine and reactionary organizations without their strengths. It has the mysticism of Freemasonry, the mummeries of Catholicism, the brutality of fascism, the illegality of its 568 various [Klaverns], *but it has neither doctrine, nor program, nor vitality, nor discipline.*

Cung was remarkably accurate in his assessment and predictions, but no American heard him in 1924. Ten years later, Cung returned to Indochina and changed his name to Ho Chi Minh.

A Ku-Klux attack on a black cabin during Reconstruction, similar to that made upon the Essic Harris family.

Northern outrage at increasing Ku-Klux attacks is reflected in this 1874 political cartoon by Thomas Nast for Harper's Weekly.

A still from D. W. Griffith's 1915 masterpiece The Birth of a Nation, *showing "Gus" in the hands of Klansmen—a portrayal of the Klan that would help revive it in the twentieth century.*

Klan strength is mustered at this mass initiation at Williamson, West Virginia, in 1924.

The professed religious ideals of the Klan are displayed at this Klan baptism of an eight-week-old child in 1924.

Grand Dragon D. C. Stephenson made the Indiana Klan the largest Realm in the Empire. Stephenson is caught here in a rare photograph by reporters at his arraignment for the murder of Madge Oberholtzer.

Fiery Summons

By virtue of the power vested in
me as Exalted Cyclops of this Klan,
I hereby summon you to attend a
Klonklave of our Klan on February
21
$\overline{\text{22}}$, in the Year of our Lord Nineteen
Hundred and Twenty-Eight. This is
the Klonklave about which our Imperial Wizard and Grand Dragon have
written you. Klansman, be there.

                                 Exalted Cyclops.

A Klansman must be in good standing to sit in this
meeting.

Imperial Wizard Hiram W. Evans (center), flanked by Imperial officers, smiles at well-wishers during the 1925 March on Washington—a ceremony that marked the last gasp of the phenomenal 1920s Klan.

An announcement sent to Michigan Klansmen in 1928. The postscript at the bottom ("A Klansman must be in good standing to sit in this meeting") indicates that many disgruntled Klansmen were no longer paying their dues.

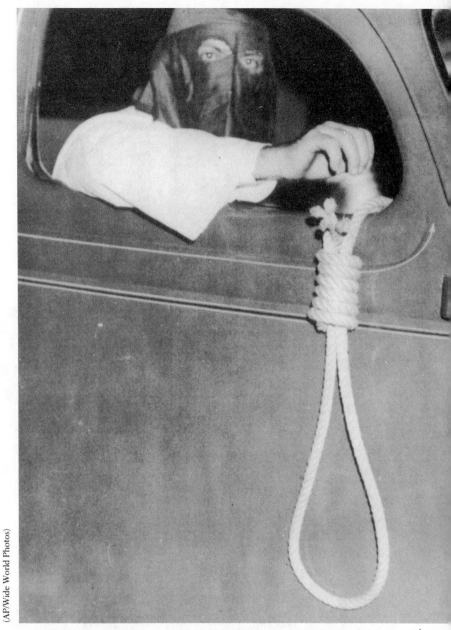

In the wake of nationwide outrage that attended the murder of union leader Joseph Shoemaker in Tampa, Florida, a Miami Klansman warns blacks to stay away from the polls during the 1939 municipal primary election.

Grand Dragon Arthur Bell addresses a joint rally of Klansmen and members of the German Bund near Andover, New Jersey, August 18, 1940. A proposed merger between the two extremist groups moved Congress to investigate the Klan and suppress the Bund.

Dr. Samuel Green, Grand Dragon of the Association of Georgia Klans, opposes President Truman's civil rights program during a 1948 demonstration in Wrightsville, Georgia.

(UPI/Bettmann Newsphotos)

(AP/Wide World Photos)

A young girl is caught in Klan regalia by reporters during an initiation of 300 Klansmen, including 150 women, at the City Auditorium in Macon, Georgia, December 10, 1948.

Writer Stetson Kennedy unmasks for reporters after his dangerous undercover investigation of Doc Green's Atlanta Klavern #1. Kennedy would spend the next two years writing articles and giving lectures on the extent of Klan violence.

(AP/Wide World Photos)

(Stetson Kennedy)

211

The imperturbable Robert Shelton, Imperial Wizard of the United Klans of America and the dominant force behind the militant 1960s Klan.

David Duke, Imperial Wizard and reviver of the Klan in the 1970s, listens to CB reports during his highly publicized watch over the Mexican border in 1977.

(AP/Wide World Photos)

Bill Wilkinson, the Imperial Wizard and leader of the 1980s Klan, presides in full regalia at the dedication of a KKK headquarters in Bogalusa, Louisiana.

Louis Beam (in plaid trousers) inspects his paramilitary squad during the Klan's dispute with Vietnamese fishermen along the Texas Gulf in 1981.

Klansmen protest gay rights during a march in Houston, January 1985. Gays claimed the march helped their cause.

8

"AIN'T GOD GOOD TO INDIANA?"

*The Klan's Triumph and Debacle in
the Hoosier State: 1922–1925*

*I*n no other state would the Klan have the impact it had on Indiana. Political analysts who closely followed the progress of the Invisible Empire declared that, in the Hoosier State, kluxdom spread "like a prairie fire." It was the only state where Klaverns were chartered in every one of its ninety-two counties. It was the only state where the Klan elected the governor and both U.S. senators. Here the Klan reached the zenith of its power. And here it would eventually collapse in so sordid a scandal that the national Klan was dragged down with it and injured beyond recovery.

The largest, most famous outdoor gathering of Klansmen in history took place in Kokomo, Indiana, on the Fourth of July, 1923. The "Klonklave in Kokomo" would formally celebrate Indiana's transition from provisional status to a Realm chartered by Imperial Headquarters. After all the publicity the Indiana Klan had received in the papers, Wizard Evans decided to be there in person for the ceremonies. Plans had been under way for months. Every Hoosier Klansman was urged to attend, and Klansmen from neighboring states, as well as reporters, were invited too. A number of trains and interurbans had been reserved. The planning committee saw to it that no one would go hungry. Six thousand pounds of beef, eight thousand pounds of ham, fifty-five thousand buns, twenty-five hundred pies, and truckloads of other delicacies had been secured, and celebrants were asked to bring even more food with them. Kokomo had been chosen as the site primarily for its two Ks, and with a population of only thirty thousand, city fathers rightly worried about the town being swamped. Farmers were persuaded to loan their cornfields as parking space, and the honking of cars entering the little town at Wildcat Creek were heard all through the night of July 3. Some people can still remember the ordeal of getting there, because the county roads were packed bumper-to-bumper "just like a big-city traffic jam."

The next morning, a crowd of 200,000 white-robed Klansmen and their wives and children filled the 185 acres of Melfalfa Park, which the Kokomo Klavern owned as a tax shelter. Automobiles were crammed in every available space. Many of the cars were colorfully arrayed in patriotic bunting and with signs proclaiming AMERICA FOR AMERICANS and other slogans. The ceremonies began at nine-thirty in the morning, with prayers offered by two local Methodist ministers. After that the Imperial Wizard addressed the crowd. "Klankraft in Indiana," said Evans, "is now completely organized and the red-blooded citizens of this Realm . . . constitute an unconquerable power for the right, which will forge ahead brooking no interference from malingering disloyalists."

After Evans's speech it was time for lunch, and Klansmen and their kin enjoyed a monumental feast. Indiana was the most militantly antiliquor state in the union. Hoosiers prided themselves on their temperance, and as Clarence Darrow observed, temperate people made pigs of themselves at social outings:

> Only when it became "impossible to swallow another mouthful," were they allowed to stop stuffing themselves with chicken, pork-and-beans, apple dumplings, cottage cheese, sausage and buckwheat cakes, corn muffins, noodles, cider and grapejuice, onions, waffles and honey, catsup, fried fish, sauerkraut, headcheese, hot bread, jellies, soda biscuits, pigs' feet, sardines, coffee and doughnuts, crumpets, rich gravies, rice, and cream "that you could cut with a knife" and preserves and pickles and cucumber "delight" and homemade pepper-sauce and banana fritters and horseradish and maple syrup, and root beer and cocoa and lemonade, and milk, and cold meats on the side, and salmon, and smoked raw ham and things like that . . . until none of them could down another crumb that day.

Then it was time for some music. Hoosier high-school bands blared out patriotic tunes, and glee clubs and church choirs offered devotional selections.

Starting at two-thirty, everyone moved to a large, raised clearing near the center of Melfalfa Park, where the "Old Man" would be arriving. High-ranking Klansmen circulated through the crowd, whispering, "The 'Old Man' will be late today. . . . The President summoned him last night to devise a means of repelling a Papal invasion." The Old Man had been up all night saving the country, but he promised he'd get to Kokomo and would be there soon.

Expectant eyes shaded by white visors began watching the skies, because the Old Man would be descending from the heavens. A flake of the sun flashed from behind a cloud. A keen-eyed Klansman flung a hand toward the sky and exclaimed, "He's coming! He's coming!" A distant drone was heard overhead as all eyes strained upward. Then it came into view—a sleek airplane with beautifully gilded wings and the huge letters *KKK* painted underneath. The waiting crowd exploded in cheers.

As the pilot of the craft recalled, "We'd circle around over their heads . . . and they'd be looking up at us as if we came from another world." The plane kept circling, descending in a spiral to the clearing where it landed. When the squat but agile figure clad in a silk robe and eighteen-inch pointed helmet leaped from the plane, there was tumultuous applause and reports of several women fainting. The Old Man shook hands with several officials while armed escorts cleared a path for him to the dais. After bowing stiffly right and left, he ascended the platform and waited for complete silence. He then thrust his left hand forward in the Klan salute and simultaneously threw back the visor on his helmet exposing his cherubic rosy face. The crowd returned his salute as a single body.

"My worthy subjects," he began, "citizens of the Invisible Empire, Klansmen all, greetings. It grieves me to be late. The President of the United States kept me unduly long counseling upon vital matters of state. Only my plea that this is the time and place of my coronation obtained for me surcease from his prayers for guidance." He showed them a rolled-up paper. "Here in this uplifted hand, where all can see, I bear an official document addressed to the Grand Dragon, Hydras, Great Titans, Furies, Giants, Kleagles, King Kleagles, Exalted Cyclops, Terrors, and all Citizens of the Invisible Empire of the Realm of Indiana. . . . It continues me officially in my exalted capacity as Grand Dragon of the Invisible Empire for the Realm of Indiana. It so proclaims me by Virtue of God's Unchanging Grace. So be it."

The anointed Grand Dragon then launched into his prepared speech titled "Back to the Constitution." Few could hear the speech, which only added to its appeal. At its conclusion, someone tossed a coin onto the platform, and it started a demonstration. More coins, then rings, stickpins, and watch fobs were showered upon the Grand Dragon who stood fast, beaming, until the tribute subsided. His cohorts moved in to gather the loot and the Dragon retired with Wizard Evans and fellow officers to discuss the future of the Ku Klux Klan in Indiana and the nation.

The Klonklave ended in the evening with a noisy parade through town. No Klansmen liked to parade as much as the Hoosiers. Bystanders were held spellbound by the ghostly spectacle of long trains of Klansmen marching four abreast—"white-robed figures with heads and faces covered with pointed hoods, bodies completely draped in loose flowing cassocks. . . ." The most popular marching song among Indiana Klansmen was "Onward Christian Soldiers"—

Marching as to war,
With the cross of JE-sus
Going on before. . . .

Another marching song loved by Hoosier Klansmen was "Give Me That Old Time Religion"—

It was GOOD e-NOUGH for JE-sus
And it's GOOD e-NOUGH for ME.

After the parade through Kokomo's streets came Fourth of July fireworks, followed by the burning of probably the largest cross in Klan history. Its materials, including the lumber, cloth, and kerosene, were said to have cost over $2,000.

Five months after the Klonklave in Kokoma, Indiana would boast of having nearly 350,000 Klansmen—more than any state in the nation. The East Coast was fascinated. The number of Klansmen in Indiana represented 10 percent of its population. How could a Northern, landlocked state like Indiana—uninvaded by immigrants, unpolluted by Reds, undivided by racial strife, and with Catholics and Jews combined accounting for only a small minority—fall so completely into the hands of the "cluck-clucks"? Nearly every Hoosier writer working for a New York magazine was sent back to the homeland for a story, and what they found didn't please them. When Duncan Aikman, working for *Harpers*, asked the folks in his home town about the Klan, they replied, "My God, you're not going to write anything about this, are you?" Aikman concluded that "Hoosiers no longer cherish individuality with the old-time zest." Robert Hull wrote in *America*, "There was not the same Hoosier candor nor the same spirit of hospitality of yore." Writing for the *Atlantic Monthly*, Lowell Mellett was upset by the connection he saw between the Klan and religion in Indiana and warned his beloved state that it was in for its "share of bitter regrets unless some means is found to clear the air before the storm descends." Novelist Meredith Nicholson was so inundated by requests for explanations, he claimed to have postcards printed blaming the "foul, strange, unnatural" phenomenon of the Indiana Klan on "the malevolent activity of sun spots." But a more likely explanation was offered by Indiana's past.

In the late eighteenth century, Yankee pioneers traveling through the northern part of Indiana Territory had been repulsed by its dismal swamps and unimpressed with its dull, lifeless prairies. If that wasn't detraction enough, the Indians objected to the white man's usurpation of their land and frequently made pioneer life in the northern section of the state downright dangerous. Yankee pioneers therefore left Indiana alone, remaining in Ohio or pushing westward to Illinois and beyond or northward to Michigan. Consequently, Indiana was settled from the bottom up by homesteaders from Kentucky, Tennessee, and the Carolinas. The effect of its settlement by Southerners would show in Indiana's dialect, in its antipathy toward state-supported schools, and in its politics. Moreover, as one always becomes much like his enemy, early Hoosiers adopted many aspects of Indian dress and homemaking. These details set Indiana apart from the Eastern frippery of the adjacent states, and as Elmer Davis noted, Indiana became "a more salient and individual commonwealth than most of its middle-western neighbors." In fact, its neighbors often poked fun at Indiana's ideas of fashion, its clannishness and backwardness, and the word *Hoosier* came to mean a displaced, uneducated Southern rustic. Growing more insulated, proud, and belligerent, Hoosiers gloried in the description.

By the time of the Civil War, Indiana's large population of Southerners made it a microcosm of the divided nation. Even after 74 percent of its male population capable of bearing arms enlisted in the Union cause, Indiana remained a mare's nest of Copperhead sentiment. The Knights of the Golden Circle found more support in Indiana than any Northern state, and Lincoln used severe measures to suppress rebellion in the state where he had

spent his adolescence. After the War, there was considerable support for the Reconstruction Klan in Indiana—certainly Democratic minority leader Thomas Hendricks was one of the Klan's
best friends in the U.S. Senate. And following Reconstruction,
the Whitecap vigilante movement was born in the southern counties of Indiana. Its ornery breed of independence made Indiana
one of the most politically unpredictable states in the union, so
politicians literally swarmed into Indiana during national elections, flattering Hoosiers with descriptions of Indiana as the most
representative state in the nation—which Hoosiers already knew
—and praising it as the repository of America's heart and soul,
which Hoosiers had long suspected. The amorous courtship of
Indiana by oily politicians inflated Hoosiers' opinions of themselves and helped make Indiana the politically active state it has
remained to this day.

From 1880 to World War I, Indiana celebrated its Golden Age,
a curious combination of Greek revival and galloping capitalism.
It was a period of money making and urban growth, which allowed
Indiana to triple its industry and yet retain its agricultural base and
its glorification of rustic simplicity and pioneer Protestantism. The
American Protective Association with its anti-Catholic and anti-
immigrant sentiment made considerable headway in Indiana during this time, but so did such spokesmen for tolerance as Booth
Tarkington, whose best-selling novel *Gentleman from Indiana*
condemned vigilante activity. As a matter of fact, the national
success of the Hoosier writer was one of Indiana's proudest claims
during this period.

At the height of its Golden Age, Indiana cherished its simplicity,
its steady but stable growth, the national acclaim of its writers, its
political awareness, and its national image as "America's Crossroads"—the heart and soul of America. All of these qualities were
praised in the popular doggerel of James Whitcomb Riley's chief
imitator, William Herschel:

> Folks, a feller never knows
> Just how close he is to Eden
> Till, sometime, he ups an' goes
> Seekin' fairer, greener pastures
> Than he has right here at home
> Where there's sunshine in th' clover
> An' there's honey in th' comb:
> Where th' ripples on th' river

Kind o' chuckles as they flow;
Ain't God good to Indiana?
Ain't He, fellers? Ain't He, though?

By 1920, the word *Hoosier* implied a practical simplicity that quickly got to the heart of things; at its worst it implied a narrow-minded arrogance that neither saw nor heard. It was the weakness that the Ku Klux Klan would exploit to the hilt. And the exploitation was almost exclusively the work of a single individual—the most talented psychopath ever to tread the banks of the Wabash.

The Old Man, as he liked to be called, was David Curtis Stephenson, whom most people called Steve. After Steve's important role in snatching the Imperial Wizardship from Simmons and handing it to Evans during the 1922 Klonvokation, his career in kluxdom rose meteorically. Before that time, his background is obscure, which was the way he wanted it. "It's no one's business where I was born or who my folks were," he once told a reporter. He was probably born in Houston, Texas, in 1891. He quit school in the elementary years and began drifting through Texas and Oklahoma, often working as a printer in newspaper offices. When the paper he worked for in Hugo, Oklahoma, ran a contest to find the prettiest girl in the state, Steve married the winner. He flirted with socialism in this period and also with other women. Soon tiring of his wife, he abandoned her and moved to Iowa when she became pregnant.

At the age of twenty-six, Steve enlisted in the National Guard. During World War I, he showed a talent for military life. Thirteen days after his enlistment he was made a corporal and was sent to Officers' Training School at Fort Snelling. In February 1919, he was honorably discharged as a Second Lieutenant at Camp Devans, Massachusetts. He started drifting again and settled in Akron, Ohio, where he found a job as a salesman for a linotype company. He married again in January 1920 and again left town, leaving his second wife behind. He eventually wound up in Evansville, Indiana, in the southernmost extreme of the state. In Evansville, he sold stocks in a coal corporation and began organizing the veterans of the outfit he had served during the war. Although he lost his bid for the Democratic nomination to congressman, the citizens of Evansville were nevertheless impressed with him.

Steve was short in stature, overweight, but always impeccably dressed. His heavy-jowled face wore a friendly smile. His blond hair and thin-plucked eyebrows gave him a boyish appearance.

His penetrating, steel-gray eyes seemed "like they could look into your soul." A more discerning observer noticed that Steve's eyes didn't sparkle—"They observe, study, impress one with expediency. . . ." He was a good buddy to the guys, charming and polite to the ladies, and especially winning with children, who were enormously fond of him. Rumor had it that he was a wealthy Texas oilman—a rumor he probably started himself.

Evansville's Klavern was the first one organized north of the Ohio River. After noting Steve's organizational talents and growing respect in the community, Evansville Klansmen invited Steve to join in 1921, and he accepted. The local group was already having financial disagreements with Imperial Headquarters in Atlanta, and Steve was delegated their representative to iron out the difficulties. Not only did Steve succeed in the mission, but Edward Young Clarke was so impressed with his business sense that he made him King Kleagle for Indiana. In six months, Steve enrolled five thousand Hoosiers in the Invisible Empire.

It was in his role of King Kleagle that Steve had met Imperial Kligrapp Evans, and the two had experienced instant rapport. In return for his considerable aid in making him Imperial Wizard at the Thanksgiving Klonvocation, Evans had made a number of concessions to Steve. First of all, he had appointed Steve Imperial Klaliff, a minor national position that would nevertheless make Steve Wizard if Evans died in office. Secondly, Steve had been given authority to oversee the development of the Klan in twenty-three Northern states. Finally and most importantly, Steve had demanded and had received absolute control over the Klan in Indiana. Soon after the Klonvocation, Steve took a suite of offices in Indianapolis and, as a full-time Klansman, began in earnest the task of what he called "kluxing Indiana."

Steve's program for selling the Klan revealed a keen understanding of salesmanship and the vulnerability of Hoosiers. He knew from the outset that selling the Klan in the North would require something quite different from the haphazard, vulgar, and occasionally violent methods that prevailed among what he ruefully called "that southern crowd." He knew from his own experience that selling anything well took skill, so he hired Kleagles with demonstrated sales ability, even importing real-estate supersalesmen from the Florida land boom. He maintained tight control over his Kleagles, reviewing their sales, offering suggestions, and ruthlessly eliminating those who couldn't bring in members. He sent his top Kleagles to trouble spots. Sometimes he removed incompetent officers from Klaverns, replacing them with his own appointees and thereby centralizing his program. He believed that every Klavern should have its own identity, and to nurture that identity, he urged Kleagles to "divide the community" into pro-Klan and anti-Klan factions. The more Klaverns felt outside hostility, the greater would be their solidarity.

The *World's* 1921 exposé had thrown a cloud of suspicion over the Klan, and Steve's most important goal was that of making the Hoosier Klan respectable. He would proudly claim, "I did not sell the Klan in Indiana on hatreds—that is not my way. I sold the Klan on Americanism, on reform." To achieve this, he used a five-pronged approach.

First of all, Steve was a model to the national Klan in his successful appeals to the fundamentalist clergy. He ordered Kleagles to send him lists of such ministers in their communities, and he made every one of them an honorary member of the Klan. When ministers were reluctant or suspicious, Steve advised his Kleagles to tell them: "Now we're going to sign up a lot of people in this neighborhood, and whenever we get a new member of the Klan who doesn't go to church we make him or her join some congregation. We can turn them your way if you'll agree to join." Steve carefully reinforced agreeable pastors. Those who gave pro-Klan sermons from their pulpits were rewarded by a "church visitation" and a substantial donation. Those who made pro-Klan speeches or gave benedictions at public rallies were generously compensated. (Eventually, nine out of ten Klan lecturers in Indiana were introduced as "Reverend.") Additional monetary inducement was offered to ministers to become Klavern officers. In South Bend, for example, Reverends Jack Horton and George Titus picked up an extra $75 per week as Kligrapp and Cyclops, respectively. Hoosiers deeply trusted their ministers, and political observers later concluded that nearly every fundamentalist or "Campbellite" (a fundamentalist sect) minister in Indiana helped spread the Klan.

Another technique Steve used to sell the Klan took advantage of the Hoosier penchant for joining clubs. It has often been remarked that Hoosiers are, by nature and habit, joiners. John Gunther observed that, in Indiana, "You do not meet with three neighbors to play bridge; you organize the Upper Tenth Avenue Bridge Club, with a membership of four, and choose your president and secretary-treasurer." By 1920, Hoosiers belonged to the largest number of fraternal orders of any state. They were members of the Masons and Odd Fellows, the Redmen, the Knights of

Pythias, the Royal Arcanum, the Knights and Ladies of Honor, the Elks, the Lions, the Woodmen, the Harugari, the Tribe of Ben Hur, the Ancient Order of Druids, and more. Steve had his Kleagles infiltrate all these groups and praise the benefits of also joining the Klan.

He exploited the Hoosier's love of all-day outings. Klansponsored outdoor bashes in Indiana were legion. Steve would arrange and finance these celebrations, signing up new members in the process, and then pass the collection plate at the end of the day and turn a profit. These gatherings could be small, like the one held in Winchester in October 1924, featuring a band and glee-club concert, a few speeches, and a lunch. Or they could be monster rallies like the one held at the Valparaiso Fair Grounds in May 1923. The Valpo celebration featured an actual jousting tournament with "gaily caparisoned horses, flying banners, martial music, marching ranks of robed and hooded Knights, and thousands of spectators, gaily bedecked, and forming a part of the inspiring spectacle." Also included was the once-in-a-lifetime chance of seeing a fully robed and hooded tightrope walker three hundred feet above the ground, with a cross in one hand and the Stars and Stripes in the other. These large rallies, including the one at Valpo, usually climaxed with Steve's dramatic arrival in his gilded KKK airplane. Steve often wore a little paper tablet on his wrist like a watch. After landing, he would jot a message on the tablet, hand it to a waiting official, and then fly off again. According to Steve's pilot, "The official would read the message of greeting to the crowd, and the folks who were taking the whole thing seriously would open their mouths and act as if they had received a message from Heaven." This put the Klansmen in the right mood for the cross-burning ceremony when, arm in arm, they would sing "The Old Rugged Cross." At some of these Klonklaves Steve would sign up as many as fifteen hundred new members.

Steve's fourth tactic in the kluxing of Indiana appealed to all lovers of law and order and to every Hoosier male who liked playing cops and robbers. Back in 1852, the Indiana legislature had passed a law authorizing a volunteer constabulary for the apprehension of "horse thieves and other felons." Any group of men could band together and, after obtaining the permission of their county commissioner, act as bona-fide policemen. Originally the statute had been an expedient for curbing horse thieves in the thinly populated northern counties. It was still on the books in 1922 but was no longer used because there were so few horses.

Steve had the brilliant idea of dusting off the statute and reviving the Horsethief Detective Association as a completely legal adjunct of the Klan aimed at the enforcement of Prohibition and the breaking up of immoral, roadside "petting parties." Although the Horsethief Detectives were nominally independent of the Klan, the overlap was substantial. All detectives were made honorary Klansmen with a waiver of the $10 klectoken. Local units of the association made their reports at weekly Klavern meetings. The association was subsidized by Klan funds, and Klansmen were encouraged to report violations of the law to their affiliated detectives.

The Horsethief Detectives were highly obnoxious when enforcing Prohibition and were helped immeasurably by the stringent antiliquor laws passed by Hoosier legislators. Most notorious was Indiana's "Smell Law," whereby anyone caught with an empty bottle that faintly smelled of liquor could be arrested for possession. Anyone who drove while intoxicated could go to jail for thirty days to six months. Anyone who transported a spoonful of liquor could be locked up for one to two years. And if any fluid was poured out while one's premises were being searched—no matter what fluid, "even if Grandma emptied her chamber pot"—it was prima facie evidence of destroying illegal hootch.

The Horsethief Detectives made the most of these provisions. They indiscriminately stopped motor cars, subjecting men and women to searches, and in time caused Indiana to be blacklisted by numerous travel associations, including the Chicago Motor Club. But the Klan could honestly claim that from June 1922 to October 1923, more than three thousand prohibition cases were prosecuted in Indiana courts through the help of the Invisible Empire. It was eventually revealed that much of the liquor confiscated during these raids was imbibed by Klansmen later in the evening. Nevertheless, Klansmen had put teeth into their claim of upholding law and order, and Hoosiers admired them for it.

Steve's final tactic was possibly his best. Well before the Imperial Headquarters organized a woman's adjunct to the Klan, Steve created the Queens of the Golden Mask. Not only did women flock to the Indiana Klan, but by 1923, officials reported that "women are proving the best supporters of the organization, and many Klansmen credit their wives with having suggested their joining."

From February 17 to July 14, 1923, Steve remitted $641,475 in klectokens to Imperial Headquarters, reporting the total cost of his operation at only $159,786. Evans was ecstatic and in a letter commended Steve's "magnificent record." At the end of 1923, after a single year of recruiting, the Realm of Indiana was the strongest Klan state in the nation. With bewilderment, the *New York Times* remarked, "Out in Indiana, *everyone* seems to belong." Klan rallies were a weekly affair in every county. As one journalist noted, the candle lights were still gleaming through the sycamores, but their flame was being dimmed more and more by the glare of fiery crosses. Klansmen were in Indiana police departments and city councils. The mayor of Portland complained to the governor that in his city the Klan had completely taken over the National Guard. Hoosier shopkeepers who joined the Klan received placards for their windows with the letters *TWK* ("Trade with Klansmen") and began boosting business at the expense of their non-Klan competitors. Newspapers hostile to the Klan, including the South Bend *Tribune*, Indianapolis *News* and *Times*, and the Vincennes *Sun-Times*, were boycotted and lost thousands of subscribers. Steve's Indianapolis-based magazine *The Fiery Cross* became an organ of considerable influence, and mayors who spoke out against the Klan could expect to read articles in *The Fiery Cross* documenting the extent of prostitution, vice, and crime in their cities. Eventually, *The Fiery Cross* and the Indiana Klan found a common enemy—the Catholic Church.

Few states became as virulently anti-Catholic as Indiana. Hoosier Protestants had always distrusted Catholics. And in a state 90 percent white and Christian, Catholics were the most visible minority. Many "undesirable immigrants" were Catholic. And to Hoosiers of the 1920s, Catholic sacraments, rules, and the funny clothes worn by their leaders seemed unnatural if not "downright un-American."

Remarkable stories were circulated. It was said that, in Indiana, every time a male child was born to a Catholic family, the local Knights of Columbus donated a rifle to the Catholic church; and that the reason steeples on Catholic churches were so high was so they could rain gunfire down on helpless citizens when the Pope declared war against the Protestants. And the sewer system of Notre Dame University was actually a gigantic arsenal filled with explosives and heavy artillery. In Muncie, a Klanswoman showed Helen Lynd (who was co-researching the book *Middletown*) a photograph of a girl with missing fingers, saying, "See, all those fingers gone—just stumps left! She was in a convent where it was considered sinful to wear jewelry, and the Sisters, when they found her wearing some rings, just burned them off her fingers!"

The most frightening story concerned the Pope's desire and firm intention of moving the Vatican to Indiana. Warnings were issued that Indiana was in danger of becoming a papal satrapy—or "saptrappy," as Hoosiers called it. In New York, Hoosier journalist Elmer Davis attempted with embarrassment to explain the delusion:

> Just why, out of all the Protestant communities on this planet, the Pope should select Indiana as the object of his wicked desires, is not apparent to the foreigner; but to the Hoosier it is clear enough. Indiana is the most desirable spot on earth, and any potentate might reasonably [covet] it. . . . At any rate this theory seems to be widely held in the rural districts, and the Protestants are all on guard.

So on guard were they that the little community of North Manchester experienced a rare episode of mass hysteria. An overzealous Klan lecturer had been telling them that the Pope would be arriving any day. "He may even be on the northbound train tomorrow! He may! . . . *Watch the trains!* The next day, nearly fifteen hundred North Manchester residents boarded the northbound *Monon* in an attempt to ambush the Pope. The only passenger on board was a quiet little man who saw the mob was in a lynching mood. In desperation, he explained to them that he was only a corset salesman. They didn't believe him. He got out a valise crammed with his wares, and after a while, they let him and the train go, figuring that not even the Pope would carry that many corsets.

But it wasn't funny to Indiana Catholics who suffered boycotts of their shops and were dismissed from school and hospital boards. For the Hoosier Catholic there was a growing suspicion that his Protestant neighbor was a Klansman "ready, at the behest of concealed superiors, to betray his confidence." Most Indiana Catholics kept a low profile; in fact their priests urged them to avoid engaging in controversy. But some fought back. In Huntington, the little Catholic weekly *Our Sunday Visitor* was a militant voice of common sense. In Mishawaka, where there were strict city ordinances on cross burning, Belgian Catholic teenagers lit crosses all over town and let the Klan take the blame. The boldest Catholic Klan fighter was "Mad" Pat O'Donnell, whose Chicago-based organization was called the Unity League. In the league's magazine *Tolerance*, O'Donnell regularly published Klan membership lists, which he sometimes obtained illegally. *Tolerance* infuriated Klansmen with its lists of names published under the arch caption: "Is Your Neighbor a Kluxer?"

A South Bend branch of the Unity League opened on January 29, 1923. When it mistakenly published the names of six men it alleged were Klansmen, those accused promptly sued. The South Bend Chamber of Commerce held a meeting on the problem, where local Protestant ministers raved at the league and denounced *Tolerance* as a "rotten rag." Father John W. Cavanaugh, president emeritus of Notre Dame, listened to the angry ministers until it was his turn to speak. "Reverend clergy," he began, "you are six months too late. For six months, that libelous and cowardly magazine of the Klan, *The Fiery Cross*, has circulated among you without let or hindrance. For six months, this sheet has been before your eyes and before the eyes of your congregations. And not once have you said anything to prevent the spread of that spirit of hatred of Catholics which fills the pages of *The Fiery Cross*."

It was true. When not actively fanning the flames of anti-Catholicism, Indiana ministers kept their mouths discreetly shut. And it was true that *The Fiery Cross* was filled with invective against "crossbacks" and "mackerel snappers." Steve also shared Cavanaugh's regret over the Hoosier Klan's anti-Catholicism. He disliked narrowly defined scapegoats. He much preferred broad categories—like un-Americanism—in which anyone could fit when you needed to ruin him. Steve was no bigot, but anti-Catholicism was selling well in Indiana and he couldn't argue with success.

Steve was quite a success himself by this time. In addition to his iron rule in Indiana, his opinions and public appearances were much sought after by Klan officials in Ohio, Illinois, and Michigan. And in his role of Imperial Klaliff, he wielded influence as far west as California and as far east as Pennsylvania. His share of Hoosier klectokens and the profits on cheap robes and paraphernalia had netted him more than $2 million. He owned a fleet of expensive automobiles and a yacht on Lake Erie. In addition to a suite of rooms he held in an Indianapolis hotel, Steve bought a luxurious mansion in nearby Irvington. "The Imperial Palace of the Klan of the North" had bodyguards stationed inside and fourteen police dogs ran loose on the grounds. In spite of the Klan's loud stand on Prohibition, liquor "flowed as freely as water" at Steve's palatial home. Many parties were held there with "wild women" in attendance, and Steve's was the most talked-about residence in the neighborhood. The Old Man ran rather well on alcohol. Moderately soused, he was at his best, working fourteen hours a day for weeks at a time. He jeered at those who couldn't drink "without becoming maudlin." He would sometimes drink too much, however, and became abusive and grandiose. On these occasions he would ramble about the nation being on the brink of a great revolution—and that a "Civic Messiah" would soon "be born in the Manger of the Hoosier Ballot Box."

Steve's private offices were located on the third floor of the Kresge Building, on the southwest corner of Washington and Pennsylvania avenues in downtown Indianapolis. Over the door of Steve's personal office was a sign saying, "All bearers of evil tidings shall be slain." Inside was his library of psychology texts. He maintained that he was the "foremost mass psychologist" of his day—a claim that hardly seems exaggerated. He kept a bronze bust of Napoleon in his office and told friends that he was the reincarnation of Napoleon, born again to complete an interrupted destiny. His flair for the dramatic led him to install a battery of eight telephones on his burnished rolltop desk, including a fake "hotline." His private secretary recalled:

> He would talk over one of these dummy telephones in such a way that you would think he was giving orders to the greatest officials in the land. . . . "No, certainly I won't do that! You tell [Senator] Jim Watson that I don't want [Senator] Harry New to do that!"

Whenever a conference grew especially unsatisfactory, Steve pressed a concealed button making his hotline ring and talked over it in a strangely subdued fashion. Right before hanging up, he'd say, "Thank you sir; and please give my regards to Mrs. Coolidge as well." It was a wonderful trick that could cow the most obstinate officeholder into submission.

At his best, Steve emanated strong charisma. Out-of-state journalists wrote of his "powerful personality and great magnetism." His movements were described as "decisive and energetic, his speech brisk and incisive." He easily endeared himself to Hoosiers. He could get down on the floor and crawl around with a baby at a downstate farmhouse. He gave away fistfuls of ten-cent dance tickets at a lakeside resort and stood smiling on the sidelines while the young folks danced. He threw rabbit shoots and fishing trips for "the boys." In summer, he would drive his Cadillac into small Indiana towns and park it slantwise at the curb; and Klansmen and non-Klansmen alike came over and chatted with him about taxes and crops while resting a foot on the Caddy's running board. His friends claimed he had deep "flashes of spiritual beauty." Like

Santa Claus, the Old Man seemed to belong to another world and inspired a childlike devotion.

He was also a power to be reckoned with in the state of Indiana. As early as 1922, he had mustered enough strength to help defeat the anti-Klan progressive Albert Beveridge in his race for the U.S. Senate. By mid-1923, the extent of Steve's influence was revealed when Lawrence Lyons resigned as state chairman of the Republican Party. Shortly after Lyons's resignation, the Unity League intercepted a telegram Steve had sent to Secretary of State Ed Jackson, saying: "Permit no selection to be made and permit no one to be named until I have had an opportunity to confer with you." Who was this man who could dictate to the secretary of state? He was, above everything, a competent salesman with a genius for organization, who had already laid the groundwork for an unequaled American political machine.

The Stephenson Machine (or "G-1 System," as Steve called it) was a network of carefully selected Indiana Klansmen obedient to Steve's every command. Its core was an espionage system made up of two informers from every Klavern in the state. (The informers were often affiliated with the Horsethief Detectives.) Through this system, Steve could gather evidence of corruption in every congressional district and use it against politicians who opposed the Klan. The same system gave him reports on anyone in the state within two or three hours, and he demonstrated this on a number of occasions. Through the Queens of the Golden Mask, Steve created a rumor mill that he fondly called his "poison squad." This vicious little organization consisted of Klanswomen using the telephone to spread rumors—usually defamations of character—across the state. It was said that their "poison" could begin in Evansville and reach Gary within twenty-four hours. The pages of *The Fiery Cross* allowed Steve to confirm and to amplify these rumors. It was not without justification, then, that Steve could say, "God help the man who issues a proclamation of war against the Klan."

With his spies and "poison squad" working at maximum efficiency, Steve moved the Indiana Klan thoroughly into the Hoosier's favorite sport—politics. The crux of his plan was contained in field instructions sent to every Indiana Klavern on May 6, 1923. The instructions carried the following warning:

Failure on the part of those responsible for the achievement of the purposes set forth, and the establishment and functioning of the machinery necessary to produce satisfactory and efficient results within a reasonable period of time, will be sufficient cause for dismissal from office and the election of successors, or, in case of insubordination or indifference, a suspension or complete withdrawal of [Klavern] charter.

Steve herewith ordered all Klaverns to establish a weekly program in which something would be proposed for the betterment of their community and a written report sent to Realm Headquarters outlining these programs. They were also ordered to procure the names, addresses, and vocations of every individual of voting age in their district who fell into such "undesirable" categories as foreigners, "Bolshevists, Reds or Agitators"; bootleggers, owners or "inmates" of whorehouses, Jews, blacks, and Roman Catholics; they were also to include reports of any organized activity by these groups. Finally, Klaverns were ordered to secure the names, addresses, nationalities, and political affiliations of every county officeholder, district court judge, and all members of school boards, police and fire departments, including information on the schools their children attended, their religious denominations, and where they stood on the Ku Klux Klan.

Steve enjoined his Klaverns to comply enthusiastically with the orders. "It was the enthusiastic sincerity of Napoleon," he told them, "that conquered Europe and it was the burning torch of enthusiastic devotion which emblazoned in letters of fire the teachings of the Master; and it will be enthusiasm which will keep aglow the torch of patriotic devotion so deep set in the Spirit of the Klan."

All evidence suggests that the Klaverns went along with the plan dutifully and that the effects were far reaching. Under Steve's orders to do a good deed every week, Klaverns earned increased respect in their communities. Even more people joined the Klan, and those who didn't at least grew more sympathetic to it. The greatest effect came from Steve's uses of the voluminous data forwarded to him by individual Klaverns. From his lists of statewide "undesirables," he was able to identify every one of them who ran for public office. And he promptly injured their chances with innuendo and slander, thus keeping people likely to be antagonistic to the Klan out of power. With his data on existent officeholders, Steve was able to make monetary gifts to their churches and to donate milk and American flags to the schools their children attended, turning these folks toward approval of the Klan.

By early 1924, Steve was using Klavern-supplied data to select slates of candidates acceptable to the Klan for the forthcoming primaries in every county in Indiana; Steve himself chose the candidates for the state race. Sample ballots, called "information sheets," were printed and sent to each Klavern. Every Klavern was responsible to get the candidates on these sample ballots elected, and they worked hard at it. They praised Klan candidates and condemned non-Klan candidates in every Hoosier club, at every bridge game, at every ice-cream social, and at the latest private basement sampling of someone's home brew. In his determination that Klansmen and women ignore party ties and vote the Klan ticket, Steve sent out 250,000 letters saying, "It matters not whether we are Republicans and Democrats, in the final analysis we all have the same common heart throb of sympathetic devotion to our state." And that devotion could best be expressed by voting for Klan-endorsed candidates. On the day of the primaries, Klaverns offered the innovation of providing babysitters and car service to any Protestant housewife, cooped up at home, who wanted to vote. At the polling places, Klansmen distributed little, glossy cards with rounded corners that said:

REMEMBER

Every criminal, every gambler, every thug, every libertine, every girl ruiner, every home wrecker, every wife beater, every dope peddler, every moonshiner, every crooked politician, every pagan papist priest, every shyster lawyer, every K. of C., every white slaver, every brothel madam, every Rome-controlled newspaper, every black spider is fighting the Klan.

Think it over.

WHICH SIDE ARE YOU ON?

No one came even close to predicting the overwhelming success the Klan achieved in the 1924 primary. Ed Jackson, the bumbling Klan candidate for governor, hadn't been given the slightest hope before the primary and yet won the Republican nomination with a handsome majority. By their own admission, political experts were "flabbergasted." Journalist Stanley Frost made some acute observations:

In Indiana, [the Klan] has shown better leadership, greater stability, more power to take care of internal quarrels, and a stronger unity than had been expected by any but its own leaders—far above the average of political organizations. It plays politics with a crusading spirit which is willing to make greater sacrifices and work harder than any organization has done in recent times. Its evangelistic enthusiasm wins many converts who are not members, so that it casts considerably more than its own vote. It also makes its members desert their usual party affiliations, split tickets, and put the Klan ahead of any other consideration. . . . Its organization is not only permanent but self-sustaining, so that it has no need of spoils and the quarrels they bring. I am convinced that it is—while it lasts—*the most effective political organization the country has ever seen, not excepting Tammany.*

Steve was jubilant over the Klan's triumph at the polls and was now ready to take a step he had been sitting on for months: He was going to split the Indiana Klan from the national organization. He had been wanting to do this as early as the 1923 Klonklave in Kokomo. Shortly after the Klonklave, Steve had had the opportunity to purchase Valparaiso University, a small college that was deeply in debt. The deal had been all set and Steve was waiting for backup funds from Atlanta. Newspapers had reported it as a *fait accompli*. Valpo U was a fine little school that allowed students to get an excellent education at very low prices. It was called "the Harvard of the West" by literary magazines whose editors gagged at the thought of its purchase by the Klan. They wondered what kind of football uniforms would be worn at the new Ku Klux U. The Philadelphia *Ledger* assumed the college cheer would assume tones of "unprecedented savagery." The New York *Call* wondered if the "kurrikulum" would offer courses in "horsewhipping" and "tarring and feathering." They needn't have wondered, because the backup funds failed to come through from Atlanta.

Steve had been furious and blamed Evans. He argued that the Imperial Wizard was willing to spend plenty of national dues on Southern projects—including a proposal by sculptor Gutson Borglum to carve Stone Mountain into a Confederate forerunner of Mount Rushmore—but not on Northern ones. Evans had personal reasons for withholding the funds. He was becoming worried over Steve's phenomenal success and knew Steve could offer formidable challenges to his own authority. It was no secret that Steve intended to run for Indiana's U.S. Senate seat in 1926 and that he would likely win; and from the Senate he hoped to gain enough strength to salt the Republican National Convention with enough Klan delegates to win the GOP presidential nomination in

1928. With Steve in the White House, Evans's authority over Klansmen would be virtually nullified.

On September 27, 1923, Steve had resigned his state and national offices in the Knights of the Ku Klux Klan,

> because I cannot with any element of decency or self-respect continue to be a party to such small bickering. . . . I am endeavoring to defend the good name of the organization in this section of the country by ridding it of political mountebanks and shysters. . . . [The Klan is being] prostituted and cheated in a manner which to a fourth-grade school boy would seem either dishonest or silly and incompetent.

Steve's words allude to the fact that the national Klan's activities were a growing source of embarrassment to the Hoosier Klan. He was upset by the press coverage of the Evans–Simmons court battles, which he thought Evans was handling incompetently. He felt Evans's leadership of the Klan in politics was inconsistent and shoddy. And the South Bend *Tribune* and Indianapolis *Times* made it a practice to give front-page coverage to every act of violence associated with the Klan in the nation. The sensational Mer Rouge murders in Louisiana made a mockery of every ideal the Hoosier Klan professed. The final straw had come when various Imperial representatives from Atlanta visited Indiana Klaverns and suggested that "a few beatings and some tar and feathering" could do much to "arouse interest and increase the membership." Steve felt this was stupid and wouldn't stand for it.

For the next eight months, Steve's resignation meant nothing. Evans appointed an unknown lackey to take Steve's place as Grand Dragon, but the Indiana Klan remained entirely under Steve's control. Evans had struck a deal with Steve whereby no friction would surface between the two men until after the primary. Evans, as much as Steve, wanted to see the Klan win big in Indiana.

Almost immediately after the primary, on May 13, 1924, Steve summoned his state leaders to Indianapolis and told them their "great victory" at the polls warranted a complete independence from Imperial Headquarters. He made the schism one between North and South and even dragged out "the bloody shirt" of the Civil War. Imperial Headquarters, he told them, "donated $100,000 to erect a monument to the memory of the rebels who once tried to destroy America, yet they refused to give a single dollar for Valparaiso University to help educate the patriots of the

North who saved the Union to posterity, unsullied from the contamination of Southern traitors." He said he would no longer tolerate the dictates of "yellow-livered Southerners who hate everything that is pure throughout the State of Indiana." And no longer would he be nice to the Imperial Wizard. Evans, he told the gathering, was "an ignorant, uneducated uncouth individual who picks his nose at the table and eats his peas with a knife. He has neither courage nor culture. He can not talk intelligently, and he can not keep a coherent conversation going on any subject for five minutes. . . . The only thing he was ever known to do was to launch attacks upon the character and integrity of men eminent in talent and virtue."

The assembled delegates unanimously reinstated the man eminent in talent and virtue, David Curtis Stephenson, as Indiana's Grand Dragon. The Hoosier Klan had bolted. As the crowd cheered the decision, Steve shouted, "We're going to klux Indiana as she's never been kluxed before!"

Steve was concerned over a persistent weak spot in the kluxing of Indiana—a pocket where the Klan had had much difficulty. The area was South Bend, the state's second largest city. The publisher of the South Bend *Tribune*, Frederick Miller, was stridently anti-Klan. The city had a thriving chapter of the Unity League and a sizable population of immigrants and Catholics. But the biggest problem was that "mackerel-snapping" Notre Dame University. The legendary Knute Rockne was in charge of its famous football team, and recently, the celebrated George "the Gipper" Gipp had converted to Catholicism on his deathbed. Notre Dame was quickly becoming the state's most popular instrument of nationwide publicity, and the St. Joseph Valley Klavern was at a loss over what to do about it. One of its members volunteered to fly over the university in a helium baloon and dynamite it from the air. That idea had been shelved, and instead, a flimsy whispering campaign was launched to spread the fact that, since most members of the Notre Dame football squad were Protestants, under Rockne the "Fighting Irish" could be more properly regarded as "Fighting Scandinavians." But this didn't help Klan recruiting in South Bend, and frustrated Kleagles had actually been forced to try to sell the Klan to Catholics. The story is told of the Kleagle who addressed the South Bend Celtic Club, telling the gathering, "The Klan has no quarrel with you Irish Catholics—it's those *Roman* Catholics we're against!"

But South Bend remained a canker on the Hoosier Klan, and

Steve decided that a Klonklave in the city might improve the prospects of Klan candidates there in the November election.

On May 17, 1924, just four days after the Hoosier Klan had left the national Klan, Klansmen began arriving in South Bend by train and car and treated many local residents to their first glimpse of Klansmen in full regalia. Robed and hooded knights stood on streetcorners, directing their brethren to Island Park, where a rally was scheduled. Within an hour, cars packed with Notre Dame students pulled into the city. The students jumped out and proceeded to tear the robes off Klansmen, some of whom were left in such a complete state of undress, they were forced to seek refuge in nearby filling stations. The students then cheerfully took on the task of welcoming Klansmen to the city. "Are you from the Klan?" they would ask. "Have you come for the parade? This way, please." Up they went into an alley, down a side street, through a dark entrance, and the Klansman later emerged with his robe stripped or stolen and a black eye to boot. Like Notre Dame's Four Horsemen, the students formed a flying wedge and began bulldozing white-clad figures all over town.

By noon, every Klansman was off the street, having taken refuge in Klan headquarters downtown. When headquarters lowered from its windows a fiery electric cross, a hundred students stormed the building. They were held back at revolver point by Exalted Kligrapp Reverend Jack Horton, pastor of South Bend's Calvary Baptist Church. A truce was reached whereby Klansmen promised not to conceal their faces under their hoods and the students agreed not to beat or strip them. Meanwhile, two thousand Klansmen had found their way to Island Park. Steve had arrived in his Cadillac flanked by two squads of siren-screaming motorcycles. In view of the trouble, he called off the parade, but swore that, sometime in the future, the Klan would march in South Bend—even if it had to call on "the United States Army for protection." Later in the day, a thunderstorm completely ruined the speeches and scheduled festivities; and grumbling Klansmen began leaving the city.

Others stayed, however. And two days later, when downtown headquarters again lowered the cross of fiery lightbulbs, Notre Dame students stormed the building again. This time the Klansmen were ready for them. They came out of headquarters hurling rocks and bottles, and a full-scale riot ensued. The news spread through the city, and the students were soon joined by Catholics from the West Side's Polish and Hungarian neighborhoods. The

South Bend Police were called out, and as the Klan would later report, the police sided flagrantly with the anti-Klan faction. Patrolman Jones went so far as to distribute Irish potatoes to the West Side crowd to heave at the white knights. By the end of the evening, there were a few arrests and a few minor injuries, but nothing of consequence. It was nevertheless the most violent incident associated with the Ku Klux Klan in Indiana; and the violence had clearly been instigated by the other side.

Returning to Indianapolis, Steve put his Klan machinery into high gear for the November general election. It would be a vigorous campaign, and the pages of *The Fiery Cross* were filled with diatribes against every non-Klan candidate in the state. All the successful methods of the primary were repeated, with the addition of a few novelties. For example, Klan sample ballots of preferred candidates were rolled up tightly and jammed into the tines of clothespins; these were thrown from automobiles onto nearly every front porch in Indiana. The moral superiority of Klan-backed candidates was loudly proclaimed, and the religious angle grew more pronounced as the campaign developed. Steve sent requests to all of the Protestant ministers in the state, asking them to preach sermons from a select group of topics on the two Sundays before election day; the topics included: "The Need for a Revival of Pure Protestantism," "Moral and Civic Forces Seen and Unseen," and "The Duty of a Protestant Citizen." Each Klansman was to see that his minister followed through with this request. On the Sunday before election day, several Klaverns intercepted the Protestant Sunday School papers and slipped a Klan "information sheet" into each one before distributing them to the churches.

On November 4, 1924, the Klan was again the winner. Ed Jackson became the new governor. Steve's candidates for the mayor and Indianapolis city council and other offices in Marion County won handsomely. All across the state, the Klan enjoyed a considerable victory, electing state senators and representatives, mayors, sheriffs, and complete school boards. There would be an interesting complication when the legislature convened, however. Although the executive branch, senate, and state Republican Party chiefs would be loyal to Steve, the Indiana house would include many Klansmen who had retained ties to Imperial Wizard Evans and the national organization. As it turned out, this division would render nugatory most of the Klan-sponsored legislation in the seventy-fourth session of the state legislature, even though the Invisible Empire as a whole represented a substantial bloc.

Two days before the Indiana General Assembly met, the Klan called a meeting of all pro-Klan legislators. In this meeting, the Evans–Stephenson factions discussed their differences and came to an agreement on how they would proceed. Consequently, the first order of business at the General Assembly was some old-fashioned gerrymandering, whereby Lawrence County would be made safe for the Republican Party. Fifteen angry Democratic senators promptly destroyed the quorum by walking out, driving to Dayton, Ohio (from where it was impossible to extradite them), and getting roaring drunk. The gerrymandering was reluctantly terminated, and the senators came home.

Thereafter, the activities of the Klan-dominated legislature ran the gamut between dogfighting and Gilbert-and-Sullivan opera. Petitions from Indiana Klaverns to ban the teaching of evolution in public schools couldn't even get out of committee. Compulsory reading of the Bible in public schools failed in the Indiana house. The house eventually passed a bill permitting "the reading of the American Revised Version of the Holy Bible . . . without comment" in public schools, but Steve had it killed in the state senate —it was more important for him to undermine the Evans-controlled house than to pass legislation favorable to Klansmen-at-large. The "Religious Garb Bill," which would have effectively banned Catholic nuns from teaching in public schools, also passed the house and was killed in the senate at Steve's orders. The same fate befell a bill that would have compelled parochial schools to use the same textbooks used in public schools. One by one, the Klan's hopes and fears were tediously turned into legislative English, fought over, and then destroyed. The only piece of the Klan's platform that became law in Indiana was a totally innocuous requirement that Hoosier high school students study the United States Constitution.

But Steve loved every minute of it. He didn't give a damn if the Klan failed completely in its legislative program; as a Klansman, Steve was utterly without creed. But he adored the game of political bargaining and the role of power broker. He would sometimes allow the introduction of completely insane bills, harmful to various interest groups, and then have them killed for the groups at a price. His aid invariably entailed a fee and was regarded by many as essential to the passing of responsible legislation as well.

After only three months of the new legislative session, David Curtis Stephenson—just thirty-four years old—was riding the crest of his success. Then, suddenly, this modern reincarnation of

Napoleon met his Waterloo. It came not at the hands of a cunning, invincible Wellington. The Old Man's downfall came instead at the hands of a gentle but determined young woman.

Her name was Madge Oberholtzer. She lived with her parents, the George Oberholtzers, at 5802 University Avenue, Irvington, just a few blocks from Steve's mansion. Madge was twenty-eight years old and wore her chestnut hair swept back in a twist. She was attractive in a soft, clean, wholesome way, and she was very intelligent. She had graduated with honors from Butler College, taught public school at Hagerstown, Indiana, and was currently employed as manager of the Young People's Reading Club, a project run by the office of the State Superintendent of Public Instruction.

She had been introduced to Steve at the inaugural banquet held for Governor Jackson, and the Grand Dragon had taken an immediate interest in her. She was brighter and more sophisticated than the women who usually appealed to Steve, and unlike his usual bevy of female admirers, Madge refused his initial requests for a date. She finally acquiesced to a dinner with him at an Indianapolis hotel. When Steve learned that Madge's job might be terminated as a result of a bill being debated in the house, he had it killed in committee. Flattered, Madge accepted another dinner with him and eventually attended a party at his home, which he apparently cleaned up for her benefit, because—unlike Steve's usual parties—there were only "ladies and gentlemen" present.

On Sunday, March 15, 1925, just three months after they had met, Madge came home around 9:30 P.M. and was told by her mother that Mr. Stephenson had been telephoning all evening for her. Madge returned the call, and Steve told her he had to see her at once on a matter of the greatest importance. He would be sending Earl Gentry, one of his bodyguards, for her. Gentry was a big, cigar-smoking ex-cop. He soon arrived at the Oberholtzer residence and walked Madge over to Steve's.

Madge didn't come home that night. Her father had been in bed ill, and her mother, who didn't want to disturb him, was worried half out of her mind. When Madge didn't return the next morning, she woke her husband, and the two of them went to the police. That afternoon a telegram arrived from Hammond, Indiana. It was from Madge and read: DRIVING THROUGH TO CHICAGO. BE HOME ON NIGHT TRAIN. That evening, Mr. Oberholtzer waited all evening at the station but Madge never arrived.

Mrs. Eunice Schultz roomed with the Oberholtzers, and early in the afternoon of the next day, May 17, Mrs. Schultz was fixing lunch for her son when she heard the front door open and the sounds of terrible groaning. She ran into the living room and saw Madge being carried in by a strange man.

"Is Madge hurt?" she asked.

"Yes," the man replied, "she was hurt in an auto accident."

"Badly?" Mrs. Schultz asked.

"I don't think any bones are broken," he replied.

Mrs. Schultz immediately called the family physician, while the man took Madge upstairs, placed her on her bed, and quickly departed. Mrs. Schultz went upstairs to check on the girl. Madge looked frightful. Her body was a mass of black-and-blue marks and her lips were ghastly pale. She began throwing up. "Oh, Mrs. Schultz," she moaned, "I'm dying."

In less than an hour, Dr. John Kingsbury arrived and found Madge in a state of shock; her body was cold and her pulse rapid. Informed of the auto accident, Kingsbury began checking for broken bones. There weren't any, but he discovered bruises and minor avulsions all over Madge's body. The skin on her right cheek and left breast was torn open. On her left hip and buttock were contusions the size of a dinner plate. Tissue on her genitals had been torn off. Kingsbury began coaxing Madge to tell him what had happened. Slowly, painfully, the story came out.

When Madge had arrived at the Stephenson residence two days earlier, she had found Steve and another bodyguard, Earl Klinck, in the kitchen. They were both drinking, and Steve was obviously drunk. No one else was in the house and Madge suddenly became alarmed. Steve invited her to drink with them, but she refused and went to the phone. Steve forcibly took the phone out of her hand. He and Klinck then moved in on her and insisted that she drink with them. She was now afraid and took three, small drinks. She wasn't used to liquor and soon became ill.

"I want you to go to Chicago with me," Steve said to her.

Madge said she wouldn't. She wanted to go home.

Steve pointed out her condition and told her she couldn't possibly go home now. "You're going to Chicago with me," he said. He looked at her intently. "I love you more than any woman I've ever known."

Gentry went to the phone and arranged for a drawing-room car on the midnight *Monon* to Chicago. Then they all went up to Steve's bedroom to pick up the grips which had already been packed. Steve opened a large dresser drawer filled with guns, and each man selected a revolver. Steve chose one with pearl handles. The four of them got into Steve's car, stopped off at the Washington Hotel to pick up the train tickets, and Klinck dropped the three of them off at Union Station.

In the drawing-room car, Gentry climbed into the upper berth. When he had disappeared from view, Steve suddenly grabbed the bottom of Madge's dress and peeled it over her head. She tried to protest, flailing at him, but was unsteady from the liquor and panic-stricken by what was happening to her. Steve took off all her clothes and shoved her into the lower berth. After the train started up, Steve undressed and got in with her. He pinned her so she couldn't move. Madge screamed.

Throughout his life, D. C. Stephenson had consumed anything of value to him—power, objects, people's favors and loyalties. He now began to consume Madge.

> He chewed me all over my body, bit my neck and face, chewed my tongue, chewed my breasts until they bled, my back, my legs, my ankles, and mutilated me all over my body.

Steve had gone into an alcoholic frenzy, and Madge mercifully passed out.

She woke up the next morning at 6:15 A.M. The train had stopped in Hammond, Indiana. Steve was already awake and was sitting up in the berth, playing with his pearl-handled revolver. Madge gazed over at him and asked him to shoot her. He menacingly stuck the pistol into her ribs. She didn't flinch. Steve finally put the gun away in his grip and told her they were getting off at Hammond. In view of what had happened, he had decided not to transport Madge across the Illinois state line. The three of them walked the block from the depot to the Indiana Hotel, where Steve checked in Madge and himself as "Mr. and Mrs. W. B. Morgan." They were given Room 416 and Gentry was given 417, next door.

Once in the room, Steve made a phone call to his chauffeur in Indianapolis and then ordered breakfast. Madge asked if she could send a telegram to her mother. Steve dictated it while Madge wrote and signed it. Steve had it sent out and then lay down for a nap. While Steve slept, Madge dug out his revolver and aimed it at his head. She couldn't bring herself to pull the trigger. She then thought of killing herself. She walked to the mirror, pointed the gun at her temple, and stared at the reflection.

Just then, Gentry walked in, took one look at Madge, and grabbed the pistol from her. He told her to lie down. After she complied, Gentry left the room and returned shortly with hot towels and witch hazel and began swabbing her wounds. The witch hazel stung, and Madge cried out, waking Steve.

Steve was probably unaware of the degree of injuries he had inflicted on Madge and watched as Gentry tried to ease her suffering. "I'm sorry," he finally said to her. "I'm three degrees less than a brute."

"You are worse than that," Madge replied.

After breakfast, which Madge was unable to eat, Steve's chauffeur arrived, having driven all the way up from Indianapolis. Madge told Steve that she wanted to buy a hat—anything to get out of the room—and Steve told Shorty, the chauffeur, to give her $15. Shorty then drove Madge to a downtown store, where she purchased a small, black silk hat for $12.50. On the way back, she asked Shorty to stop at a drugstore near the hotel so she could buy some rouge. Alone in the store, Madge hurriedly bought a box of mercuric chloride tablets.

When Madge and Shorty got back to Room 416, Steve was drunk again. (The chambermaid who cleaned the room would later testify that the place had reeked of liquor.) Genuinely afraid of the combination of Steve and alcohol, Madge asked if she could go to 417 and lie down.

"Oh no," Steve replied, "you're going to lie right down here by me." Madge obeyed and waited until Steve was sound asleep. She then rose, went into 417, and laid out all eighteen of the mercuric chloride tablets. She swallowed six of them and would have taken more if they hadn't burned her throat so badly. She lay down, got violently ill, and began vomiting blood.

Shorty came in and asked her if anything was wrong. Madge asked if he could keep a secret. When Shorty said he could, Madge straight out told him that she had poisoned herself. Shorty suddenly turned pale and fled the room. Steve and Gentry immediately came in.

"What have you done?" Steve asked her.

Madge told him.

"I don't believe it," he said.

"If you don't believe it," Madge said, "there's evidence on the floor and in the cuspidor."

Steve looked into the cuspidor; it was half full of clotted blood. Steve ordered a quart of milk and insisted that Madge drink all of it. She did, and promptly threw it up. Steve conferred with Shorty and Gentry and then came over to Madge.

"We'll take you to a hospital and you can register as my wife," he explained to her. "Your stomach will have to be pumped out. You can tell the hospital that you took mercury tablets by mistake instead of aspirin."

This, of course, is what Madge had hoped would happen. Once in the hospital she would be free of Steve. But she hadn't counted on being registered as Steve's wife, and on that point she utterly refused. If it came to that she would prefer remaining in the hotel room.

Steve again conferred with the two other men. "We'll take you home," he then told her, adding that they would first stop off at Crown Point where he and Madge could get legally married.

"What would I want to marry you for?" Madge asked.

"You can use my name," Steve offered.

This didn't appeal to Madge in the least, and she said so.

Steve snapped his fingers at Shorty and barked, "Pack the grips!"

They got into Steve's car and started out for Indianapolis. After a few miles, Steve had the car pulled over and ordered Shorty to remove the license plates. If they were stopped, Steve explained, they would say that they had been parked in the last town and the plates had been stolen.

Madge began to experience intense pain and started crying. She begged Steve to stop at the next town and let her see a doctor. At the next town, Steve had the car slowed down and asked if Madge was ready to marry him. She wasn't. Steve ordered the car moved on. "Drive fast," he told Shorty, "but don't get pinched."

In the back seat, Madge had begun vomiting again. Shorty glanced over his shoulder at her and mentioned that things looked pretty bad. Steve agreed, but commented, "I've been in worse messes than this before and got out of it." Steve was hitting the bottle again. Madge's pain was now excruciating. She asked, since they weren't going to get her a doctor, would they please just dump her alongside the road. Steve refused.

"I'll have the law on you," Madge sobbed.

"I am the law in Indiana," Steve replied.

Late that evening, they pulled up in front of the Oberholtzer home, but Madge's mother was on the porch and Steve didn't want to be seen, so they drove on to his house. They carried Madge to a bedroom loft above the garage, where Steve sometimes slept whenever he was afraid of an attack being made on his house.

Madge was placed on the bed and Steve told her, "You will stay right here until you marry me." The last thing Madge remembered was Steve saying to her, "You must forget this, Madge. What is done is done."

The next morning, she was awakened by Earl Klinck, who told her that she must go home. Madge asked where Steve was. Klinck said he didn't know and repeated that she had to go home. He transported her to her residence, carried her inside, and took her upstairs to her bedroom.

Dr. Kingsbury soon realized that Madge had gone too long without medical attention. The mercuric chloride was completely dispersed through her system and causing acute nephritis; there was little hope for recovery. Less than two weeks after Madge returned home, Kingsbury told her that she was probably not going to live.

"That's all right, doctor," Madge replied. "I'm ready to die." Again it was explained to her. "I understand you, doctor. I believe you and I'm ready to die." Madge was asked to dictate a formal account of the ordeal she'd been through, and she complied on March 28 before Dr. Kingsbury, two attorneys, and her best friend. Madge's deposition would singlehandedly bring the Klan to its knees in Indiana.

On April 8, Madge's kidneys stopped. "The waste content of her blood is more than six times that of normal," a specialist told her parents. "She will not live." Six days later, April 14, 1925, Madge Oberholtzer died. Steve had already been arrested on assault and abduction charges and was out on $25,000 bail. The charge was now changed to second-degree murder and Steve was jailed. He optimistically told reporters, "I've been framed before and this is another frame-up."

The bizarre story of Steve and Madge appalled the nation. The behavior of Indiana's Grand Dragon made a rank obscenity of everything the Klan had stood for. What had Steve said about the Klan's enemies—that they were criminals, thugs, libertines, girl ruiners, and moonshiners? The Klan's championship of Christian morality was now ironic, to say the least. As one journalist gleefully described it, "There's Mud on Indiana's White Robes!" Angry Hoosier Klansmen burned their paraphernalia and began disavowing membership in the Invisible Empire. (Now and then a box of carefully stashed away Klan materials from the 1920s still surfaces in some Hoosier grandmother's attic.) Women's groups, which had previously found Steve such a charming defender of the faith, now asked for swift justice in convicting him. Protestant ministers swore they had never fully trusted the Klan. In Gary, the Methodist Hospital returned a Klan gift of $500.

Steve's trial dominated the newspapers of Indiana and the nation for over a month. Throughout the trial, Steve was confident of acquittal. According to Steve's airplane pilot, Klan officials told him that "the jury was fixed and that no matter what anyone testified, the jury would bring in a verdict of not guilty." If the worst happened and he was convicted, Steve would undoubtedly be pardoned by the incompetent he had put in the statehouse, Governor Ed Jackson. Perhaps for these reasons, Steve's defense was less careful than it could have been. The defendant never took the stand. His attorneys argued that Madge had poisoned herself and died a suicide, pure and simple. The prosecution contended that Madge had poisoned herself as a last resort to escape from a dangerous man who did "strike, beat, bite and grievously wound" her before "ravishing and carnally" knowing her. The prosecution argued that Steve had known Madge was dying from the effects of the mercuric chloride and that he had nevertheless denied her adequate medical treatment. Capitalizing on a belated sense of shame in Hoosiers, the prosecution identified Steve with Indiana's Ku Klux Klan: To convict Steve would therefore be equivalent to condemning the Klan. The chief prosecutor told the jury: "I am asking you to write your verdict with a view of stopping this sort of thing that is going on. Write so . . . the one who said 'I am the law in Indiana' can say so no more."

The jury of ten farmers, a truck driver, and a manager of a utility company convicted Steve of second-degree murder. Reporters claimed he "almost fainted" when the verdict was read. "They can't! They can't," he muttered. Steve was given the maximum sentence: life imprisonment in the Indiana state prison in Michigan City.

Within a year after the trial, the Hoosier Klan had shrunk from its peak of 350,000 members to a mere 15,000. Then came the climax. Steve grew tired of waiting in prison for a pardon. Governor Jackson had been too fearful of associating himself with the rapist Dragon, and it was obvious he would never pardon him. Steve threatened Indiana politicians with exposure unless something was done for him. Finally, he revealed to the press that he had several "little black boxes" of incriminating evidence on Hoosier officeholders, and the courts allowed him to leave prison to retrieve the information. Among the juicier items in the "boxes" were political IOUs signed by such people as John Duvall, mayor of Indianapolis. Mayor Duvall had signed a pledge saying:

> In return for the political support of D. C. Stephenson, in the event that I am elected Mayor of Indianapolis, Indiana, I promise not to appoint any person as a member of the board of public works without they first have the endorsement of D. C. Stephenson.
> I fully agree and promise to appoint Claude Worley as Chief of Police and Earl Klinck as a captain.

The disclosures provided some of the most fascinating reading Hoosiers had ever been treated to in their newspapers. Eventually, evidence of unreported campaign funds given by the Klan to Governor Jackson came to light. The Vincennes *Commercial* and the Indianapolis *Times* began independent investigations, revealing the astonishing extent to which the Ku Klux Klan had dominated politics in Indiana. The United States Senate undertook a special investigation of corrupt tactics and unreported funding of Klan-backed Hoosier statesmen. These senate hearings painted an ugly picture of the Klan at a national as well as state level. Finally, Indiana Attorney General Arthur Gilliom launched an independent and exhaustive investigation of the Hoosier Klan in an attempt to revoke its charter and to throw it out of the state completely.

As a result, the mayor of Indianapolis and the chairman of the Indiana State Republican Party were sent to prison for violating the Corrupt Practices Act. Governor Jackson was indicted for failing to report Klan campaign contributions; though he pleaded the statute of limitations by the time of his trial and got off, his political career was finished. The entire Indianapolis city council paid fines on bribery charges and resigned as a body. Judge Clarence W. Dearth of Muncie was impeached. And the careers of hundreds of officeholders were ruined throughout the state

> Where there's sunshine in th' clover
> An' there's honey in th' comb . . .
> Ain't God good to Indiana?
> Ain't He, fellers? Ain't He, though?

In a sober analysis of the debacle, novelist Meredith Nicholson said that Indiana had been wrecked "by as cheap a lot of adventurers as ever scuttled a ship of state." But he didn't allow individual

Klansmen to escape responsibility. Reflecting on Indiana's loss of national prestige, he remarked, "This is a high price to pay for the privilege of hating one's neighbor and wearing a sheet."

Later Hoosier writers such as Jeannette Nolan said, "We will redeem ourselves and the honor of the state. And as to what has just happened—the less said about that, the better." Dale Burgess agreed. Offering a scant two paragraphs about the Klan in his book on Indiana history, he suggested, "Let's change the subject." Hoosiers still don't like to talk about the Klan in Indiana during the 1920s, but they haven't forgotten about it. What they remember most is Steve's sadistic orality: "He just chewed that poor girl all to pieces!" "That sonofabitch acted like a goddamn *cannibal* with that girl!" In Indiana Steve remains a fitting metaphor for the Ku Klux Klan, which consumed all that was good in the state.

It is also interesting that the Klan in the twenties began and ended with the death of an innocent young girl. The Mary Phagan–Leo Frank case had been the spark that ignited the Klan. And the Oberholtzer–Stephenson case had put out the fire. Thereafter, Klansmen who tried to praise the Klan's Christian principles and its fight for law and order were asked if those ideals were properly reflected in the death of Madge Oberholtzer. No longer could ministers like "Fighting Bob" Shuler offer the Klan as a bulwark "for the maintenance of virtue among American women, sobriety and honor among American men." Madge's death finished the Protestant Ku Klux Klan crusade of the 1920s more than any single factor.

POSTSCRIPT
1925–1930

The Klan's decline after the Stephenson case was hastened by a simultaneous disaster that befell its principal bedfellows, the fundamentalists. The Scopes trial of 1925 over the teaching of evolution in schools proved to be the collapse of the fundamentalist juggernaut. This media event in rural Dayton, Tennessee, was covered by both press and radio, and Americans were enthralled by the fascinating debate between Clarence Darrow and William Jennings Bryan on the literal interpretation of the Bible. Bryan had gone to Dayton trumpeting that he alone would save the faith from the "modernist" heathens. After making a pitiable spectacle of himself and suffering the mockery of American journalists, he died shortly after the trial.

The outcome of the Scopes trial was a technical victory for religious pluralism in America. Certainly the shakiness of many fundamentalist tenets was never more laughably revealed. Klansmen were naturally upset. "We will take up the torch as it fell from the hand of William Jennings Bryan," said the Grand Dragon of Ohio, for "America cannot remain half Christian and half agnostic." At a meeting of Grand Dragons in late summer, 1925, Klan leaders discussed how they could best preserve the old-time religion in public schools. After the debacle in Dayton, they agreed that banning the teaching of evolution wasn't practical. The

Dragons finally decided that Klansmen should lobby for the teaching of the Biblical doctrine of Creation alongside evolution in American classrooms. Typically, their "solution" came to nothing. It was the first of several instances in the last half of the decade when the Klan tried to take on more than its waning popularity could sustain.

Another example was the Klan's 1925 march on Washington, which proved to be its most spectacular last gasp. The proposed march was a costly and elaborate affair, but Imperial Wizard Evans was determined to go through with it to scotch rumors that the Klan was dying. On August 7, Klansmen began arriving in the capital by cars, trains, and buses, most of them coated with dust and worn out from long journeys in the ninety-degree heat. Twenty-three acres in the northeast section of the city had been reserved for the expected sixty thousand Klansmen, who began setting up pup tents and makeshift dwellings. The *Washington Post* observed, "Among the visiting Klansmen themselves, a good-natured spirit prevailed. . . . Outwardly they are here for a good time, the same as the Shriners or the Elks might have." August 8 was the day of the parade, but only half of the sixty thousand expected showed up. They included a great many people under twenty-five—as many women as men. There were also older couples with families. All wore the familiar white robes, but under strict orders from Evans, their visors were raised and faces exposed. Many carried placards honoring their home states. Others carried banners with mottoes and slogans, such as:

DO YOU WANT TO KNOW WHAT GOD
THINKS OF US?

Read Revelation 7: 9–17

And of course the usual handbills were distributed, condemning Jews for what they controlled in America, Greeks for what they controlled, Italians, *etc.*

As the thirty thousand marchers stood poised and alert on Pennsylvania Avenue, they were warned through loudspeakers: "Regardless of what happens, what is said to you from the sidewalk, keep your eyes directly on the man in front of you. Never falter!" Various amateur bands began bleating, and the hooded troops started marching, sixteen to twenty abreast, with their arms folded across their chests. Rev. H. E. Woolever was nearly overcome with emotion: "There was not an individual among its white-robed tens of thousands who was not a Protestant, nor one who had not declared his faith in Christ!" Hiram Evans was in the middle of the parade, dressed in his purple and gold robe of office and flanked by his platoons of Dragons and Kludds. One observer saw few experienced marchers in the ranks: "At times their lines, extending the full width of the Avenue, swayed hopelessly back and forth." And for many the intense heat proved too much. Nearly a hundred Klansmen and -women collapsed in the street and wound up in Washington hospitals.

As the columns veered left to the Washington Monument, where speeches were scheduled, thunder clouds rolled ominously overhead. L. A. Mueller, the Grand Kleagle for Washington, D.C., shouted through loudspeakers, "It will not rain. We shall pray. Never yet has God poured rain on a Klan assembly." Within minutes the heavens opened, and Klansmen were deluged. Thousands of them broke rank and scurried for cover, in spite of Kleagle Mueller's shouts for them to remain. Struck by a sense of purpose, a clergyman who was scheduled to speak, Rev. Dr. A. H. Gulledge of Columbus, Ohio, got down on his knees on the rostrum. "Oh God," he intoned, "I pray that the remainder of this service will be conducted without rain." Whereupon it rained even harder— "a damp, penetrating rain that soaked the Klansmen to the skin."

Although the success of the march on Washington was as much as any Klansman could have expected, the national gathering of thirty thousand was less than what Steve could have mustered in Indiana alone during the Klan's heyday. Careful observers noticed a quiet desperation in the Klan's march on the capital. And the expense the march incurred was hardly worth it, given the troubled times the Invisible Empire was now facing.

On January 1, 1926, many Americans heard the Liberty Bell ring both figuratively and literally. On New Year's Day, the wife of the mayor of Philadelphia gingerly tapped out 1–9–2–6 on the cracked icon of American freedom (which hadn't been rung since the 1835 funeral of Chief Justice John Marshall), and her music was broadcast nationally over radio. Although Klan editors remarked on the contrived event with appropriate awe, they failed to see any inconsistency between a celebration of human liberty and an organization as undemocratic as the one they espoused. The Klan's conflict with democracy had been clearly on record in the 1924 *Klansman's Manual:*

The military form of government must and will be preserved for the sake of true, patriotic Americanism, because it is the only form of government that gives any guarantee of success. Both experience and history demonstrate the fallacy and futility of a so-called democratic form of government for any such movement as the Knights of the Ku Klux Klan. We must avoid the fate of the other organizations that have split on the rock of democracy.

If Klan leaders could not see this chink in their patriotic armor, thousands of rank-and-file Klansmen began to see it, for 1926 witnessed a landmark in defections from the Klan.

In the North, Klansmen read the sordid details of the Stephenson–Oberholtzer case, watched the protracted humiliation of their Indiana brethren, and simply refused to pay the 1926 dues that would continue their membership. From his jail cell in Michigan City, Steve cooperated with authorities in sinking the Klan even further at a national level. He supplied damaging information to a U.S. Senate committee investigating campaign fraud by candidates who had been backed by the Klan. In the case of a civil suit between two rival Klan factions in Pennsylvania, he supplied a deposition that revealed how willingly Klan leaders bamboozled the rank and file. For example, in the matter of the Imperial Klonvokation held biennially for Realm delegates, Steve wrote that it was "nothing but a gesture designed to deceive the membership and for the purpose of creating the appearance that the membership acting through authorized delegates and representatives, are in a deliberative body to pass upon the acts of the officials . . . and shape their policies. [The] national convention has not now and never had any such function during my knowledge of the Ku Klux Klan." After revelations such as this, six hundred Klansmen in New Haven, Connecticut, resigned in a body and sent a resolution to Imperial Headquarters saying it was impossible to belong to the Klan and keep one's self-respect:

> [The Klan] has become a travesty on patriotism and a blasphemous caricature professing Protestantism. . . . Real Americans must be awakened and made to use every effort to stamp out this slimy serpent that threatens the very life of our Nation.

In the South, the Association of Southern Newspaper Publishers had already condemned the Klan by unanimous vote, and the attorney general of Alabama would soon renounce his membership in the Invisible Empire and publicly vow to bring Klan law-breakers to justice. Things were hardly more congenial in the Klan's home state of Georgia. Julian Harris, editor of the Columbus *Enquirer-Sun*, had long mocked his state's motto "It's great to be a Georgian." How could it be great, Harris asked, when night-shirted "cluck-clucks" could dominate the state's politics and public institutions? Georgian Klansmen looked forward to victory in the 1926 primary, but after it was over and the votes counted, every single candidate backed by the Klan had lost. "It's great to be a Georgian," Harris then wrote, "for Georgians have purged their state of political rottenness."

It is worth noting that Klan defections began with the prominent, the educated, and well-to-do, and proceeded down through the middle class. Klan leaders must have taken stock of what remained of their membership, because starting in 1926, Klan rhetoric became aimed more and more at the less-than-average American. "We are a movement of the plain people," Evans wrote in 1926, "very weak in the matter of culture, intellectual support, and trained leadership. . . . This is undoubtedly a weakness. It lays us open to the charge of being 'hicks' and 'rubes' and 'drivers of second-hand Fords.' We admit it." In the January 1926 issue of the *Kourier*, Rev. Dr. Frank Crane mused:

I am Bourgeois. Hopelessly, natural born, and can't help it, Bourgeois.
I thought I didn't belong to any class, but I discover that I do.
I am Bourgeois. . . .
I don't belong to the Vere de Veres, and my ancestors probably came over steerage.
I guess I'm hopeless. I even go to church.

Although Klan leaders hoped this tack would consolidate their remaining membership and recruit more of its kind, the plan backfired miserably. Few Americans cared to be part of a dying order that glorified impotence and homely virtues.

Evans realized that something drastic had to be done to save his crumbling Empire. Early in 1926 he arranged a national speaking tour. Typical of Evans's receptions during the tour was the way he was welcomed in Kansas by William Allen White:

Doctor Hiram Evans, the Imperial Wizard of the Kluxes, is bringing his consecrated shirt tail to Kansas this spring, and from gloomy klaverns will make five Kansas speeches. We welcome him. Enter the Wizard—Sound the bullroarers, and the hewgags. Beat the tom-toms.

He will see what was once a thriving and profitable hate factory and bigotorium now laughed into a busted community; where the cock-eyed he-dragon wails for its first-born, and the nightshirts of a once salubrious pageantry sag in the spring breezes and bag at the wobbly knees.

Things grew even worse for the Klan in 1927. When Klansmen joined a Memorial Day Parade in the Borough of Queens, New York City, the result was a near riot. The Boy Scouts and Knights of Columbus dropped out of the parade as soon as they learned that Klansmen would be marching. In the course of the parade, angry spectators began throwing rocks at the Klansmen. "Women fought women and spectators fought the policemen and the Klansmen as their desire dictated. Combatants were knocked down. Klan banners were shredded." The Klansmen bore the brunt of it. Motorists actually tried to run them down in the streets. And an expensive wreath they placed at a war memorial monument was promptly stolen and destroyed.

In 1928, the Klan wasted even more of its energy and depleted what remained of its treasury in an all-out effort to defeat Al Smith, the Catholic candidate for President. Klansmen made hundreds of speeches warning that Smith would make the presidency "the tail to the Roman Catholic kite." They published thousands of pamphlets and leaflets smearing Smith and his religion. One leaflet depicted Smith kneeling at the feet of a cartoon pope with exaggerated Italian features: "The Ku Klux Klan holds that any man who kneels before his fellow man kissing hand or ring will do the bidding of that fellow man." In a new low even for the Klan, another leaflet pretended to be a letter to Al from the Pope; in this "epistle," the pontiff declared he was saving his toenail clippings for Al's use as sacred relics. They needn't have bothered, because Smith handily lost regardless of the Klan's influence. A tired and ailing Klan nevertheless took credit for Smith's defeat.

At its peak in 1924, the Ku Klux Klan had boasted more than four million members. By 1930, that number had withered to about forty-five thousand. "Once the world's most high powered 'racket,' today a crumbling shell," said the *Washington Post*, in what it believed was an obituary. No other American movement has ever risen so high and fallen so low in such a short period of time. In retrospect, the revived Klan of the 1920s had been a child of its age, overreacting to fears unique to its epoch—postwar fears of change and the anxieties of a society rapidly evolving into the twentieth century. The revived Klan had benefited immensely from a friendly fundamentalist clergy. It also had benefited from the myths about its predecessor. If historians had portrayed the Reconstruction Klan with any measure of accuracy (or if Griffith had filmed it differently), the revived Klan would have had a much harder time generating the public interest and sympathy necessary for its growth. The 1920s Klan achieved some victories—notably the Immigration Restriction Act of 1924, which did much to incur Japanese enmity toward the American nation—and, as in the case of many issue-oriented political movements, success is often reason enough to abandon it.

It is surprising how little damage the Klan's many enemies did to it. Journalists were the Klan's most aggressive opponents, but as in the case of the New York *World* and others, newspaper crusades sometimes made the Klan stronger. What weakened the Klan more than anything was its own hypocrisy and negativism. It upheld Prohibition, while many of its members not only enjoyed liquor but made and sold it. It championed morality and the sanctity of womanhood, while its most successful Grand Dragon was convicted of the most sordid rape–murder of the decade. It revered the teachings of Jesus, while its hopes and endeavors may be called the least Christian and certainly the least charitable of any American popular movement. Lies have a way of being found out, and the Klan's lies were exposed in the natural course of Klansmen being Klansmen.

The revived Klan of the 1920s had been a thoroughly negative movement that clung to the corpse of an age that had fallen in World War I. An astute sociologist who lived through the period, John M. Mecklin, believed the Klan flourished by "creating false issues, by magnifying hates and prejudices. . . . It can not point to a single great constructive movement which it has set on foot. Men do not gather grapes of thorns nor figs of thistles." In the end, thorns and thistles couldn't hold members' interest very long.

By 1930, the Klan's little strength was concentrated in the South. Over the next half-century the Klan would gradually lose its Northern members, regressing more and more closely toward its Reconstruction ancestor until, by the 1960s, it would stand as a near-perfect replica.

BOOK THREE
1930-1987

"I've found the Klan more than just another secret society. . . . It resembles a shadow government, making its own laws, manipulating local politics, burrowing into some of our local law-enforcement agencies. . . . When a pitiable misfit puts on his $15 sheet, society can no longer ignore him."

—RICHMOND FLOWERS
ATTORNEY GENERAL OF ALABAMA, 1966

9

"THE KLAN IS AN AMERICAN INSTITUTION"

The Invisible Empire and the New Deal: 1930–1944

*I*n summer 1930, the corporate owners of *The Birth of a Nation* decided to reissue a shortened version of Griffith's masterpiece with a music track and sound effects added. The revised *Birth of a Nation* opened on Broadway on December 22 at the George M. Cohan Theatre. The *New York Times* reported that audiences laughed at Griffith's outdated sentiment but were engrossed by his action scenes. The *Times* also took the precaution of warning readers, "It is not necessary to accept this interpretation of the South in Reconstruction as the product of meticulous research." The *Outlook's* harsh review of the film was limited to aesthetic considerations, but between the lines, one senses a condemnation of the film for spawning the Klan revival: "Today it carries but little of its old punch. Its photography is jerky, erratic, and ruinous to the eyes. The acting, even that of the lovely Lillian Gish, is of the off-and-on variety."

Ticket sales for the film's revival were not good, and the Kleagles who haunted the theaters in search of new recruits found few people willing to join the Klan after they had seen the picture. After all, the Great Depression was on, and as the Memphis *Commercial-Appeal* observed, "Not many persons have $10 to throw away on an oversized nightshirt."

The Ku Klux Klan was one of many organizations struggling to stay alive during the Depression, but it suffered with the additional hardship of having to find a new program. Its old hatreds seemed hollow in the face of nationwide poverty and hunger. "We have reached the end of one political era in this country and have not yet started upon the next," said the *Kourier*, in explanation for the Klan's apparent paralysis. But the Southern wing of the Klan suddenly found something to combat when Communism came to Dixie. In the first few years of the decade, representatives of the American Communist Party had established headquarters in Atlanta, Birmingham, and several other industrial Southern cities. Their two goals were to organize labor and to organize blacks, and often the goals converged. The party's labor organizers insisted on rigidly integrated meetings; they dined and lodged with blacks and tolerated no antiblack prejudice within their ranks. The ACP's pamphlets—*The Communist Position on the Negro Question* and *Self Determination for the Black Belt*—were the most egalitarian statements on race made by white Americans since Reconstruction. It is hardly surprising that a number of blacks were attracted to the party. These were a minority of intellectuals, however, for the vast majority of Southern blacks found Communism antithetical to their religious beliefs.

By December 1930, Georgian Klansmen were investigating charges that Communists were circulating "propaganda and reading material" among Atlanta's blacks. In March 1931, fourteen armed Klansmen abducted and whipped two Communist organizers in Dallas for speaking out on behalf of black equality and against lynching. The next year, flocks of leaflets fluttered down from a building in downtown Birmingham, saying: "Negroes of Birmingham, the Klan is watching you. Tell the Communists to get out of town. They mean only trouble for you. . . . Report Communist activities to the Ku Klux Klan, Box 661, Birmingham."

In Communism, Klansmen believed they were faced with a new and virulent form of carpetbaggery (organizers were invariably from out of state), and their fears of its effects on local blacks often had tragic consequences. Dennis Hubert was the son of a respected black minister and a sophomore at Morehouse College. In an Atlanta park close to where he lived, Hubert observed three white women drinking together and getting quite tight. When one of them staggered and fell to the ground, Hubert remarked to the other two, "You better take the drunk lady home." The next day, a white youth shot and killed Dennis Hubert for insulting a white woman. He was acquitted by an Atlanta jury. Commenting on the incident, the *Kourier* regretted the murder but remarked that, since Communist-inspired blacks were demanding "social rights," then "extreme measures might be necessary." For years afterward, Southern Klansmen would claim—and rightly so—that they had been the first to recognize the evil of Communism and run the party out of town. What they omitted was that the evil they objected to was the party's radical position on race.

Southern Klansmen hadn't suspected they would be raising similar objections to the presidency of Franklin D. Roosevelt. In 1932, they welcomed FDR's campaign, and many of them were active in Roosevelt clubs. Toward the end of the campaign, however, they sensed that they had been hoodwinked. FDR freely accepted the support of Catholics, Jews, blacks, and radical union organizers. Shortly before the election, the Klan had a complete change of mind and warned its members:

> Don't be fooled. Farley is ROOSEVELT; Tammany Hall, Catholic controlled, is ROOSEVELT. . . . EVERY PROMINENT ROMAN CATHOLIC YOU CAN FIND IS FOR ROOSEVELT. . . . The Underworld is a unit for Roosevelt. The gangsters of Chicago, St. Louis . . . and New York are for Roosevelt. . . . Roosevelt, their subservient tool, will turn our country over to Tammany and thus we will have CATHOLIC CONTROL OF AMERICAN GOVERNMENT AND LIFE, if he is elected. . . . BEWARE OF THE 8th OF NOVEMBER!

After the election, Roosevelt seemed even worse than the Klan feared. The President handed out cabinet posts to all sorts of undesirables—like "the Jew Morgenthau," "the Jew Ickes." By 1934, Klansmen had joined conservative Republicans in denouncing the New Deal as a danger to the very fiber of American life. Hiram Evans actually called a "crusade" against the New Deal. "Public-spirited people," said Evans, "Klansmen and non-members alike, realize that this nation is in great danger. Because of its record of heroic achievement, the Klan has been called upon by them to mobilize and co-ordinate those who are interested in preserving our Constitutional Government set up by our forefathers." At last the Klan had a new program.

How Klansmen interpreted Evans's vaguely worded message depended on the locale, but in the South, where the Klan was strongest, the program took the form of harassing organized labor—especially in the textile mills of the Carolina Piedmont and the citrus and cigar industries of Florida. As had the Communists before them, organizers for the American Federation of Labor (AFL) threatened to upset the Southern way of life by demanding equal pay for equal work—for blacks as well as whites. AFL organizers varied in the degree of their personal commitment to blacks, but all agreed that the practice of paying unequal wages to blacks and whites was the main method used by Southern factory owners to justify menial wages for all. "You may not be making a lot," mill owners told white employees, "but you're still making more than the niggers." For many Southern laborers—especially Klansmen—this distinction was one of the few sources of self-esteem they had; and they feared losing it through unionization more than they valued the prospects of a higher income.

Southern Klansmen waged a militant antiunion campaign. They paraded through mill towns, they harassed organizers, and they burned crosses in sight of union gatherings. They were especially hostile to the International Labor Defense committee, a national organization that offered free legal counsel to union advocates. In Atlanta and Birmingham, ILD offices were "raided and wrecked" by Klansmen, usually with the cooperation of the local police. Alabama Klansmen pushed for legislation that would prohibit ILD lawyers from defending clients in their state—they wanted a law that would keep "outsiders" from "embarrassing our courts." In April 1934, Frank Norman, an organizer of citrus workers and ILD member in Lakeland, Florida, was abducted by Klansmen and never heard from again. A less ambiguous outrage would make headlines the following year.

The cigar moguls of Tampa, Florida, were extremely irritated by organizers' efforts at unionizing their laborers. They were especially upset with Joseph Shoemaker, a young organizer from Bennington, Vermont, who had been expelled from the Vermont Socialist Party because of his support of Roosevelt and the New Deal. In Tampa, Shoemaker had founded the Modern Democrats, a group that called for public ownership of utilities, a thirty-hour work week, and unemployment insurance. On the evening of November 30, 1935, Tampa police broke up a formal meeting of the Modern Democrats at a private home on East Palm Avenue. Arrested were Shoemaker as well as Eugene Poulnot, head of the Florida Workers' Alliance, his friend Dr. Samuel Rogers, and three other men, including a local fireman, who happened to be a spy. At the station, the police grilled the men on their "Communist activities," which they denied. They pointed out that the Modern Democrats regularly sang "America" and read from the U.S. Constitution at their meetings. After the questioning, the police told the six they were free to go, but escorted Shoemaker, Poulnot, and Rogers outside and told them that officers would drive them home. Shoemaker at once suspected the worst and began shouting for help to passersby. The police shoved the trio into a squad car and explained to curious onlookers that they were taking some crazy men to the mental hospital.

The police instead dropped off Shoemaker and the other two at a warehouse at the Tampa docks where they were surrounded by forty-two men and two women wearing official Klan robes. Using a dozen cars, the Klansmen drove with their captives to Brandon Woods, fourteen miles from Tampa, where Shoemaker and the other two were stripped, whipped, beaten unconscious, and tarred and feathered. Shoemaker bore the brunt of it. After beating him unmercifully, the Klansmen mutilated his genitals with a hot iron poker. They shoved his leg into a bucket of boiling tar. After the marauders abandoned them, Poulnot and Rogers regained consciousness but were too weak to carry Shoemaker, who lay bleeding and half dead. The next day, Shoemaker's nearly frozen body was found and taken to a hospital. Doctors tried to save his life by amputating his charred leg six inches below the knee but were unsuccessful. After nine days of agony, Shoemaker died, and the nation's newspapers responded to the obscene tragedy with appropriate horror and disgust.

Local investigations were quickly launched. In New York, Socialist leader Norman Thomas denounced the murder as "an act of complete and utter sadistic depravity." He was convinced that Tampa authorities would not seek the justice that the case demanded. (Following the murder, the Southern Lumber and Supply Company had put on their billboard: TAR TODAY—WHITEWASH TOMORROW—TAMPA: THE YEAR ROUND CITY.) Thomas therefore organized the National Committee for the Defense of Civil Rights in Tampa. The ACLU offered a reward of $1,000 for information leading to the arrest and conviction of Shoemaker's murderers. The crime was denounced nationally and Tampa was subjected to a steady influx of outside agitators who demanded justice in the case. (The Southern Lumber Company soon changed its billboard: THE BOYS AT THE OLD TOWN HALL ARE NOT SO K-K-KLANNISH THESE DAYS.) A thorough investigation revealed that the murder resulted from a collaboration between Tampa Chief of Police R. G. Tittsworth and local Klan Kleagle Fred M. Bass. When Tittsworth, Bass, and six policemen were indicted, their bail in the amount of $100,000 was put up by local cigar manufacturers. After two trials, Tittsworth and Bass were acquitted. Five of the other policemen were convicted and sentenced to four years in prison. It seemed like a small but solid victory for civil liberty, but a year later the convictions were overturned by the Florida Supreme Court. In the end, no one was punished for Shoemaker's murder.

Hollywood provided its own kind of justice the next year with a film called *The Black Legion*. Starring Humphrey Bogart, the movie portrayed a robed and hooded Klan-like organization that was largely involved in labor issues. When a hard-working Slav, Dombrowski, is given the factory promotion Bogart was hoping for, he allows himself to be inducted into the Black Legion, which takes place in the back room of the local pharmacy. He and his brethren then raid Dombrowski's home, burn his house down, and force him to quit his job. In one of his best moments, a power-crazed Bogie crows, "We ain't afraid o' nuttin' or nobody!" Bogie gets Dombrowski's job at the plant and is pulled deeper into the nefarious activities of the legion, becoming alienated from his wife and best friend. When Legionnaires murder the latter, Bogie surrenders to the police and testifies against his brothers-of-the-cloth —a message the film's producers hoped real live Klansmen would take to heart. Despite its improbable ending, *The Black Legion* realistically showed how a frustrated, average American could be lured into the Klan; and how difficult it was to get out once he was in. The Knights of the Ku Klux Klan disliked the movie enough to sue Warner Brothers for using copyrighted Klan insignia on the Legionnaires' robes.

Ignoring the criticism of the Klan that the Shoemaker case had generated, Imperial Wizard Evans pushed forward with his program to make Klansmen the guardians of the nation, who would keep it free from Communists, union organizers, and Communist union organizers. "We shall fight horror with horror!" he proclaimed. By 1937, Evans had targeted the Congress of Industrial Organizations (CIO), the more militant offspring of the AFL. "The CIO is infested with Communists," Evans charged. "The Klan will not sit idly by and allow the CIO to destroy our social order, nor shall the CIO flout law and promote social disorder without swift punishment." In the South, the Klan's campaign against the CIO's Textile Workers' Organizing Committee and the Steel Workers' Organizing Committee resulted in its largest gain in membership in fifteen years. Crosses were burned on the lawns of CIO organizers in Tennessee and Georgia. Klansmen posted hundred of intimidating antiunion posters around the textile mills of South Carolina. An Atlantan was captured by Klansmen and whipped for being "too busy in the CIO." Pierce Toney, another Atlantan active in CIO organizing at the Scottdale Mill (owned by the Georgia Savings Bank and Trust Company), was kidnapped by Klansmen, severely beaten, and told, "Now, I guess you'll let that damned union alone. We're going to break up all these damned unions." CIO workers strongly suspected that Klansmen were being paid by mill executives to carry out this wave of terrorism. In Porterdale, Georgia, a town virtually "owned" by the antiunion Bibb Manufacturing Company, the mayor, a city councilman, the chairman of the school board, and at least six policemen were Klansmen. Whenever CIO organizers came to Porterdale they were beaten. Delegates to the 1939 convention of the Textile Workers Union of America were told that the main reason for the failure of full and complete unionization of Southern mills was "the vicious hostility of a revived Klan." Certainly the Klan's fight against Southern unionism was its major dubious achievement during the 1930s. But Stetson Kennedy, the CIO's new, young Southeastern editorial director, saw the problem on a larger scale: "In a very real sense, the conflict between progress and reaction on the Southern front is the struggle of the CIO vs. the KKK, for these two organizations spearhead the opposing forces: democracy versus white supremacy."

In addition to antiunion terrorism, an Atlanta Klavern launched a wave of ridiculously motivated but violent floggings between 1939 and 1940. On the evening of February 5, 1939, forty to fifty robed Klansmen used ten cars to kidnap six people off the Atlanta streets between eight-thirty and ten. One man who struggled and resisted was told, "We want you for inciting niggers against the whites." When horrified onlookers appealed to Patrolman Roy Eddleman, he yelled back, "This is none of your damn business! If you don't watch out, they'll get you, too!" The next month, the dead bodies of Sarah Rawls and Benton Ford were found in a car parked in a local Atlanta lovers' lane. Apparently their fate was a victory for the Klan's ideal of prenuptial purity. Five days later, Ike Gaston, a thirty-six-year-old black barber, was stripped naked and savagely whipped with a four-foot braided strap attached to a baseball bat. Abandoned by his attackers, Gaston eventually died of shock and exposure.

Prodded by Ralph McGill, the intrepid editor of the Atlanta

Constitution, a grand jury investigation revealed that some fifty floggings had taken place in the Atlanta vicinity. W. L. Allen, a tenant farmer, had been beaten by Klansmen for his friendship with "an old black man we had living on our place." Rev. Grady Kent was beaten because he and his Ben Hill congregation were "making too much noise." J. L. Matthews, the white proprietor of a movie house for blacks, was beaten because Klansmen objected to the nature of his business and because Matthews refused to fire a black employee Klansmen didn't like.

Most of these acts of cruelty turned out to be the work of Atlanta's East Point Klavern in collaboration with deputy sheriffs Herb Eidson, Edwin Burdette, and W. W. Scarborough (who, it was revealed, served the East Point group as Exalted Cyclops). Deputy Scarborough admitted that it was customary for him to muster the Klansmen "whenever someone wasn't doin' like he ought to." Eight Klansmen, including the three deputies, were eventually sentenced to prison, but were soon pardoned by Eugene Talmadge, Georgia's corn pone governor ("I can carry any county that don't got streetcars") and father of Herman Talmadge. So breathtaking was the governor's logic in pardoning the rowdies that *Life* magazine did a feature story on it: Talmadge claimed he had pardoned the floggers because, after all, Saint Paul had been a flogger once, too. "That proves to me that good people can be misguided and do bad things."

In the midst of the Atlanta floggings and murders, a weary Hiram Evans announced that he was serving his last term as Imperial Wizard. In 1936, due to the Depression, Evans had liquidated most of the Klan's real estate, including the Imperial Palace, which was sold to an insurance company. When the insurance company later sold the property to the Roman Catholic Church, Klansmen wondered if they had been foully duped:

PROTESTANTS! WHY DID THE CATHOLICS BUY OUR OLD NATIONAL HEADQUARTERS AND TURN IT INTO A CATHOLIC CHURCH? DID THEY WANT THAT PARTICULAR PROPERTY BECAUSE OF ITS FITNESS FOR A CHURCH, OR JUST TO SHOW YOU UP?

In 1939 Bishop Gerald O'Hara of the Savannah–Atlanta diocese invited Evans to the dedication ceremonies of the new Cathedral of Christ the King on the grounds of the former national center of Klandom. To everyone's amazement, the Imperial Wizard accepted. "I frankly confess I was surprised to receive the invitation," Evans remarked. "I accepted it with pleasure."

Meeting with priests in the new rectory—once the Imperial Wizard's private office—Evans bubbled with good humor. "I've been in here often," he quipped. "In fact, it seems a little bit like home." The dedication service was conducted in Latin; and Evans, the lifelong enemy of the "Roman octopus," remarked, "It was the most ornate ceremony and one of the most beautiful services I ever saw. It had everything a religious ceremony should have." When Ralph McGill heckled the Wizard for his hypocrisy, Evans sent him a note: "You were hard on me, but not for publication, I will tell you, I was not a fool. I wanted out. This was a good exit." And a good exit it was, but it wasn't the last to be heard of this man who had dominated Klan affairs for seventeen years.

In the mid-1930s, when the Imperial Treasury had dried up, Evans had taken a position with a Georgia construction company. In return for his help in Governor E. D. Rivers's 1936 campaign, he was allowed to sell asphalt and paving material to the Georgia Highway Board without having to compete with other bids. In May 1940, Evans and the former state highway purchasing agent were charged with fixing asphalt prices and violating the Sherman Anti-Trust Act. Ruthlessly pursued by Georgia's urbane attorney general, Ellis Gibbs Arnall, Evans was eventually forced to repay the state $15,000.

On June 10, 1939, the Imperial Wizardship of the Ku Klux Klan went to James A. Colescott, a forty-two-year-old ex-veterinarian from Terre Haute, Indiana. Jimmy Colescott was a "flushed and porky," balding, round-faced, sixteen-year veteran of Klandom. He had received his training under Stephenson, serving as a lieutenant in the "Old Man's" Indiana political machine. From there he had become Grand Dragon of Ohio, later serving as Midwest representative to Imperial Headquarters. In 1936, he was brought to Atlanta as one of Evans's chief staff members. Colescott took pride in the fact that he was the first Imperial Wizard to attain the office by coming up through the ranks. The Wizardship had been given to General Forrest. Colonel Simmons had given it to himself. Evans had stolen it from Simmons. But Colescott, as he often proudly remarked, had earned it. Colescott told reporters that he was interested in "mopping up the cesspools of Communism in the United States" and that the Klan would continue to look out for the interests of "native-born, white, Protestant, Gentile" America. As the first Northern-born Imperial Wizard, Colescott went on record against violence. "I am against floggings, lynchings and intimidations," he said. "Anyone who flogs, lynches or intimidates ought to be in the penitentiary." Consistent with this, and in response to the Atlanta floggers, Colescott forbade Klansmen from using the face-concealing visors of their robes.

The new Wizard was very busy during his first six months in office. Sensitive to the effects of the Depression on the working class, he reduced the Klan's initiation fee from $10 to $6. He cut the cost of the white robe from $6.50 to $3.50. Using membership lists from the 1920s, he tried to lure ex-Klansmen back into the fold. "The fiery cross will again blaze on the hilltops of America," he promised them. Colescott was especially concerned over the Klan's pitiful rosters in the once powerful North and trained new Kleagles, Stephenson-style, to recruit members above the Mason–Dixon line. Indeed, strange things were happening in the Klan's tattered remains in the North.

The strongest nondomestic concern of Americans during the 1930s was Adolf Hitler and Nazi Germany. To sensitive observers, comparisons between the Nazi movement and the Ku Klux Klan were inescapable. The first to comment on the similarity was Will Rogers in 1933. "Papers all state Hitler is trying to copy Mussolini," Rogers noted. "Looks to me like it's the Ku Klux that he is copying. He don't want to be emperor, he wants to be kleagle." A few months later, Mark Sullivan remarked in the New York *Herald Tribune* that "the ideas and methods of the Nazis and the Klan are significantly similar."

This was hardly news to Klansmen who had maintained a mutual admiration with the leaders of German fascism for at least ten years. In fact, a Klan Klavern had been introduced in Germany by Rev. Otto Strohschein, a naturalized American and Klansman. (Klaverns in communities with high immigrant populations would sometimes take naturalized Americans as members, so long as they were respectable and Protestant; and Rev. Strohschein was a Protestant minister.) In late 1923, Rev. Strohschein returned with his son to Berlin and formed the German Order of the Fiery Cross. Strohschein made a number of modifications in the German Klan —the Exalted Cyclops became an Exalted Wotan, candidates knelt before a cross flanked by the German and American flags— but it was all still very much Klankraft. The goals of the organization included winning freedom for Germany and "ridding the country of undesirables by fighting the Jews."

The German Order of the Fiery Cross boasted nearly three hundred members, one of whom was later a defendant in a political murder trial, but it was just one of many secret fascist societies in Germany in the 1920s, and the Vienna *Neue Freie Presse* made light of it:

> Germany is full of such groups of ill-balanced and romantic youths. All these "werewolf" and other unions with their nocturnal drills, their little secret hoard of arms, their aping of military methods, inevitably exhibit phases of more or less criminal folly from time to time. The "German Order of the Fiery Cross" is the most recent symptom of this disease.

It was Hitler who eventually wiped out the German Order of the Fiery Cross and its kindred organizations. Hitler hated secret societies. His reasons are interesting, because they were entirely practical. "The aim of secret organizations can only be illegal," he wrote in *Mein Kampf*. "In this way the scope of such an organization is automatically limited." He argued that members of secret societies could never be brought "to the silence that is necessary for them to be useful." "Only very small societies might succeed in disciplining their members," Hitler said, but then, "the very smallness of such organizations would remove their value. . . . All these are considerations which caused me again and again to forbid participation in secret organizations and to preserve the SA itself from the character of such organizations."

Although Hitler wanted nothing to do with Klan-like organizations, many of his followers were more sympathetic. Shortly after the Second Klonvokation, Leipzig's *Hammer Magazine* paid a glowing compliment to America's Ku Klux Klan:

> May these American reports tend to encourage many German minds; may they be valuable as evidence that the Nordic people in all parts of the world are arousing themselves, and consider themselves on a holy mission: to be a guardian of the spirit of truth and the highest human ideals. If the Klan fulfills its task, it will necessarily reach out its hand over the borderlands with a similar endeavor, to a realization of mutual aims. Then as the cunning enemy of people is united internationally, we will also need a world-wide confederacy of the Nordic races in order to shatter the bonds in which the Jewish offender has smitten all honorable nations.
>
> Thus, then, we greet the gallant men of the Ku Klux Klan with our warmest sympathies and cherish the hope to find such cordial expres-

sions of feeling with them in the accomplishment of our mutual aims, as are necessary to victory over the powerful enemy.

Not only did the Klan proudly accept the compliment, but ten years later, in *Kourier* magazine, it took credit for inspiring the Nazi movement:

> While the Ku Klux Klan has been waging its valiant fight to save America for Americans, we wonder if it has not done a more effective job (or so it seems at the moment) of keeping Germany safe for Germans. . . . The spark that fired Hitler and other German nationalists to build a new Germany may easily have been ignited by the example of the American Ku Klux Klan. . . . Frankly, we are not so concerned with German problems as we are with the affairs of our own country, and it is indeed high time that those of true American stock follow the banner of the Ku Klux Klan to preserve our own ship of state with the same zeal that patriots of foreign nations display in following the Klan's example.

Throughout the 1930s, Klansmen especially in the North praised the Nazis and readily came to Hitler's defense. At a Klan rally in Westchester County, New York, an unidentified, masked speaker told his audience, "Hitler has appreciated the evil influences of the Jews and has realized that most of them are Communists. He has not been portrayed properly in this country." Klansmen in the bedroom communities of the Detroit area thought Hitler could help them a great deal with their "Jewish problem." In Miami, a member of a local Klavern confided, "When Hitler has killed all the Jews in Europe, he's going to help us drive all the Jews on Miami Beach into the sea!" It was natural for Klansmen and Nazis to move closer toward each other during the 1930s, and by the end of the decade, they would meet in a brief but embarrassing embrace. The form it would take would be a rally sponsored jointly by the New Jersey Klan and the German-American Bund.

Shortly after Hitler came to power, German-Americans established a number of small sympathy groups, including the Swastika League, Teutonia, and Friends of Hitler. In 1936 these groups were amalgamated into the *Amerika-Deutscher Volksbund* by Fritz Julius Kuhn. Kuhn was born in Munich in 1895. He studied chemistry in college, joined the German army in 1914, and was wounded three times. A devoted follower of Hitler, Kuhn participated in the Munich beerhall *putsch* and afterward emigrated to the United States. From 1928 to 1934 he was employed as a chemist at the Ford Hospital in Detroit. The Michigan Klan and Henry Ford's anti-Semitic essays published in the Dearborn *Independent* gave him much to hope for in the future of the United States. In 1934, Kuhn became an American citizen.

As Kuhn conceived it, the Bund would build within the United States a solid core of support for Nazi Germany (a mission Hitler cared little about) and would instill in German-Americans a respect for their cultural heritage. Kuhn, who now called himself the American *Bundsführer*, was remarkably successful in the second half of his mission. He was especially sensitive to the fact that German-American youths were alienated from their parents and their heritage. As post–World War I children they had suffered from anti-Hun prejudice and had all but disowned the part of themselves that was German. Kuhn therefore made the Bund very youth and family oriented. At rallies, families could dance, sing, and see movies about the fatherland. At the Bund's large private camps, families could stroll through the little streets named after Nazi heroes, swim, enjoy authentic German food prepared in a clean restaurant, play baseball, and stay overnight in neat little cottages with swastikas embedded in the masonry. In special youth programs, children were tutored in the German language, taught how to salute the swastika, learned to sing the "Horst Wessel Song," and listened to Hitler's speeches over shortwave radio. If they wanted to, they could correspond with German pen pals. Prizes were given for essays written on anti-Semitic topics, with an emphasis placed on how the "Jewish problem" in America resembled that in Germany.

The Bund was a target of persistent criticism. Congressman Samuel Dickstein of New York, himself a Jew, filled the *Congressional Record* with pages of invective against the Bund, claiming that 95 percent of its literature was printed in Germany and that its camps were "secret Nazi centers" where foreign agents were training U.S. citizens "to overthrow the American government." After an FBI probe in 1937, however, J. Edgar Hoover reported that the Bund had violated no federal law and warranted no legal intervention. Kuhn nevertheless realized that he was walking on dangerous ground and that the Bund needed something to insulate it from outside criticism. As a token gesture, he changed the "*Sieg Heil!*" salute to "Free America!" His next project was that of merging the Bund with some native American organization that would shield it from charges of being a "foreign" agency. Kuhn's fondest hope was to form an alliance between the Bund and the American Indian. He correctly reasoned that you couldn't get a more native American than the Indian; he also decided that they were "a type of true Aryan."

The Bund distributed reams of literature to Indian reservations, and Indians were always honored guests at Bund rallies. At Camp Nordland in New Jersey, Chief New Moon, who called himself "a full-fledged Nazi," was a very popular speaker; and if it can be believed, he often spoke on the urgent need for a Nazi–Indian "entente against Communism." Equally popular was Chief Red Cloud, leader of the Siletz tribe, who appeared in full, authentic Indian costume—except his fringe had been replaced with hundreds of shiny little swastikas. Red Cloud toured the entire northwestern United States and Canada in search of Indians willing to join the Bund. And he held audiences spellbound with stories that the Jews represented the *chuck-na-gin* of his people, or "the children of the devil."

When Kuhn's dream of a Nazi–Indian entente failed because of profound indifference on the Indians' part, he flirted with numerous American right-wing groups, including William Dudley Pelly's Silver Shirts (a short-lived fascist movement even more bizarre than the Klan). Why he didn't come to the Klan sooner than he did can only be explained by the persistence of his mania for the Indian. In a postwar interview, Kuhn revealed that during the 1930s he spent three years talking to Klan leaders about a merger. "The Southern Klans did not want to be known in it," he said. "So the negotiations were between representatives of Klans in New Jersey and Michigan, but it was understood the Southerners were in. We all approved of what Hitler was doing. Had Roosevelt not brought us into the war we would have got together against the Jews and Negroes."

Kuhn's negotiations with the Klan were cut short in 1939 by his arrest for embezzling over $14,000 from the Bund treasury. He was sentenced to two-and-a-half years in Sing Sing and, after the war, was deported to his beloved fatherland. Negotiations for a Klan–Bund merger did not stop with Kuhn's arrest, however, but were carried on by G. William Kunze, a native-born American who took over the office of *Bundsführer*, and by Deputy Führer August Klapprott. Eventually a joint rally was agreed upon by Klapprott, Arthur H. Bell (Grand Dragon of New Jersey), and E. J. Smythe, director of the Protestant War Veterans Association and a close friend of both the Bund and Klan.

The joint rally was held at the Bund's two-hundred-acre Camp Nordland near Andover, New Jersey. On August 18, 1940, nearly two hundred Klansmen and several hundred of their friends and relations were met at the camp by some eight hundred Bundsmen. The robed Klansmen were graciously escorted around the grounds by storm troopers dressed in black trousers, white shirts, and black ties. After dinner in the camp's German restaurant, both groups took turns speaking. The Bundsmen may have been taken aback by the Klan speakers' condemnation of "Romanism" and "dumb ring kissers," but they were certainly in agreement when Klansmen praised their courage in the face of the "persecution" they had suffered for their loyalty to Nazi principles. During New Jersey Dragon Arthur Bell's speech, he announced that the Klan was not anti-Semitic but nevertheless voiced his firm conviction that American Jews were "attempting to get this country into war." Bell also condemned Irving Berlin's "God Bless America" as a Semitic dirge unfit for singing by patriotic Americans. E. J. Smythe told the gathering, "Fritz Kuhn and I have tried for three long years to bring about a meeting like this, but it never worked out till this year." Smythe expressed sympathy for Kuhn's political imprisonment. "His only crime was in trying to bring friendship between the United States and the German Dominion."

Finally Deputy Führer Klapprott spoke: "When Arthur Bell, your Grand Giant [sic], and Mr. Smythe asked us about using Camp Nordland for this patriotic meeting, we decided to let them have it because of the common bond between us. The principles of the Bund and the principles of the Klan are the same." Whereupon the Dragon and Deputy Führer shook hands to resounding applause. Bell read a letter from Imperial Wizard James Colescott, and the participants moved to an open field where two sweethearts were married in full Klan regalia beneath a blazing cross. Curiosity seekers soon gathered along the camp's fence, shouting "Put Hitler on the cross!" and singing the national anthem. It was the only discord in an otherwise harmonious day.

The next morning, however, the editors of the nation's newspapers were furious. The New York Times demanded that both the Klan and Bund be put "under close and constant surveillance," given the strong possibility of war with Germany. An embarrassed Colescott immediately removed Bell as Grand Dragon of New Jersey, saying he had failed "to adhere to the principles and ideals of the Klan." "There can be no sympathy on the part of the Bund and the Klan," he added. Brimming with indignation, Bell countered by saying that Colescott had known and approved of the joint rally from the beginning. That's why he had sent a letter to be read at the ceremony.

The uproar in Congress was worse than in the newspapers. Congressman Dickstein claimed that collusion between the Nazis and the Klan could destroy the nation. The problem was turned over to the Dies Committee, which, after being made a permanent standing committee in 1946, would become known as the House Un-American Activities Committee, or HUAC.

The creation of the Dies Committee had been urged and supported by liberals and Nazi haters who wanted it used as a congressional forum against fascism. But in the hands of chairman Martin Dies of Texas, an arch-segregationist, and his reactionary colleagues, including J. Parnell Thomas and Joe Starnes, the committee instead had become an anachronistic pack of witch hunters who harassed labor leaders, demanded the impeachment of Secretary of Labor Frances Perkins, and discovered "Communists" in every imaginable shape and place. The committee had already made some strong enemies in Congress and among newspapers, like the St. Louis *Post-Dispatch* who found its inquisitorial methods "in the best KKK tradition." Many in Congress doubted the committee's ability to probe into the Klan problem, since it shared so many of the Klan's antiunion, anti-New Deal sentiments.

In spite of these doubts, the committee began its investigation of the Bund–Klan merger in the first week of October 1940. The investigation was short but sufficiently thorough. The members gave the Bundsmen a much rougher grilling than the Klansmen. Führer Kunze declared that the Bund was a completely legitimate organization with the sole goal of protecting German-Americans from discrimination. Deputy Führer Klapprott explained that the Klan had paid no rent for the use of Camp Nordland but had promised to patronize the camp's restaurant and to pay parking fees. He denied any agreements or plans for the future between the Klan and the Bund. Ex-Dragon Arthur Bell more or less echoed Klapprott's testimony. When asked what he thought about a Klan–Nazi merger, Bell said that he had thought it a good idea at the time, "but I don't now."

The intervention by the Dies Committee squelched further cooperation between the Klan and the Bund. On May 30, 1941, New Jersey Attorney General David T. Wilnetz decreed Camp Nordland "a Nazi agency" and shut it down. America's entry in World War II would finish what was left of the Bund.

After Pearl Harbor, Imperial Wizard Colescott announced that, in the interest of national unity, he was withdrawing from circulation all Klan literature "of a controversial nature," but he apparently overlooked one particular item. In what was a truly reckless and stupid move, Klan editors had assembled ninety-six of Henry Ford's anti-Semitic essays from the Dearborn *Independent* and bound them in a volume they entitled *The International Jew*. The book subsequently was reprinted in Germany by the Nazi World Service. On January 12, 1942, an embarrassed Henry Ford wrote Colescott saying that he did "not subscribe or support, directly or indirectly, any agitation which would promote antagonism against my Jewish fellow citizens." Ford claimed that he had long ago recanted his misguided venture into anti-Semitism and threatened the Klan with legal action unless it ceased publication and circulation of his misbegotten essays. Congress immediately was stirred by the incident, and once again, the Dies Committee became involved with the Ku Klux Klan.

For months liberals had been complaining that the Dies Committee had been picking on American left-wing organizations while leaving right-wing groups alone. When the Ford–Klan issue arose, Martin Dies was in the process of mustering congressional support for extending the life of his committee another year. He decided to throw a crumb to the liberals by announcing a complete, a *really complete* investigation of the Ku Klux Klan.

Prior to the proposed investigation, the committee summoned Imperial Wizard Colescott to Washington on January 22, 1942. Colescott was an extremely friendly witness—in fact, he admired the Dies Committee a great deal. He revealed the embarrassing fact that there were only ten thousand paid-up members of the Klan and discussed the decaying condition of the Realms, state by state. Florida was the strongest Klan state, he said. The Wizard promised to send the committee complete financial statements as well as other Klan documents. In the pontifical role he assumed so well, Chairman Dies scolded Colescott for the Klan's anti-Catholicism and demanded to know why the Klan was so hard on the Catholic Church when it had proved itself a valiant foe of Communism. He admonished the Wizard to lead his followers "back to the original objectives of the Klan," and Colescott enthusiastically agreed that it was a good idea. The other members of the committee were even friendlier to Colescott, especially Noah Mason and Joe Starnes. Starnes of Alabama remarked that "the Klan was just as American as the Baptist or Methodist Church, as the Lions Club or the Rotary Club."

Before leaving Washington, Colescott telephoned his Atlanta office and dictated a message to be sent to every Grand Dragon:

ESTEEMED KLANSMEN: The Dies Committee, investigating un-American activities for the past few years, has accomplished great results. Congress now has under consideration the extension of the life of the committee for twelve months. . . . The committee has rendered a great service to our country. I therefore urge you as State head of your realm to immediately contact your congressmen, urging that they support the continuation with ample finance of the Dies Committee.

The letter was soon reprinted in the *Kourier* for the instruction of all other Klansmen.

During the debate over extension, the committee promised a complete investigation of the Klan, but liberals were highly suspicious. Certainly the Klan needed investigating. But was it worth extending the life of the committee? With Colescott's sugary support of Dies & Company, could the committee objectively probe an organization as friendly to it as the Klan? The editors of *The Nation* suggested that it would be "just as logical and just as fruitful for the Klan to investigate the committee." Congressman Thomas Eliot of Massachusetts (grandson of Harvard president Charles W. Eliot) was afraid that the investigation would result in the committee's sanctioning the Klan. "The Klan is a dangerous organization," Eliot told fellow representatives. "It should be investigated and exposed. But we should not appropriate a penny to investigate the Klan only for the purpose of whitewashing it." In the end, the committee won its extension. And it did nothing further about the Klan. Dies's successor, Congressman John E. Rankin of Mississippi, explained why: "After all, the Ku Klux Klan is an American institution. Our job is to investigate foreign 'isms' and alien organizations."

After congressional failure to do anything about the Klan, the option passed to the executive branch. The nation was now in the midst of World War II—a conflict that was becoming more and more identified as a struggle between the forces of democracy and fascism. It was inconsistent, if not humiliating, to have an organization like the Ku Klux Klan operating in the United States of America, and FDR began viewing it as a genuine threat to national unity and security. He had a private reason for doing something about the Klan. Southern Kluxers were turning Southern Democrats from the party. FDR was preparing to run for a fourth term, and the Klan had responded by distributing cartoons of him saying to his wife Eleanor:

You kiss the niggers, and I'll kiss the Jews,
And we'll stay in the White House as long as we choose.

In spring 1944, Imperial Wizard Colescott was paid a surprise visit by Marion Allen, Internal Revenue agent at Atlanta, who presented him with a bill for $685,000. "I was sitting there in my office in the Imperial Palace in Atlanta one day, just as pretty as you please," Colescott recalled, "when the Revenuers knocked on my door and said they had come to collect three-quarters of a million dollars the Government had just figgered out the Klan owed in taxes on profits earned during the 1920s! We had to sell all our assets and hand over the proceeds to the Government and go out of business." To avoid liability for what remained of the bill, Colescott called a special Klonvokation on April 23, 1944, and members voted to revoke the charters of all established Klaverns, disband all provisional Klaverns, and suspend the constitutional laws of the Knights of the Ku Klux Klan, Inc. To inquiring reporters, the Wizard announced, "The Klan is dead—the whole thing is washed up. After Reconstruction when the Klan disbanded the Klansmen continued to function in clubs and on their own, and it will likely be that way from now on." In another press conference, he said, "I am still Imperial Wizard. The other officials still retain their titles, although of course the functions of us all are suspended." Pressed for the reason for disbanding, Colescott replied, "I do not consider it as a subject for discussion outside the Klan." Privately, Colescott was much more candid: "It was that nigger-lover Roosevelt and that Jew Morgenthau who was his Secretary of the Treasury who did it!"

For the first time since the Civil War, America would be without a Klan or a Klan-like organization. From 1944 to 1945, Americans had the luxury of perceiving their shadow as an alien and external thing—a monstrous evil borne by Hitler and other outsiders.

10

"DIVISIBLE INVISIBLE EMPIRE"

Revival and Transition after
World War II: 1945–1960

At the annual meeting of the National Committee for Mental Health in 1944, a University of Wisconsin anthropologist announced, "There is a real possibility in the postwar years of a revival in full force of the Ku Klux Klan." Professor Mekeel observed that fighting Hitler had made Americans liberty conscious, but scattered fascist groups like the Klan still existed and could fulminate at the war's close. "Let us all work to stem the tide of hate before the most susceptible among us are swept into the stream," he urged. Barely two months after V-J Day, Georgia's Stone Mountain lit up with an eerie glow that could be seen for nearly sixty miles. Klansmen had put hundreds of barrels of fuel oil mixed with sand in niches on the face of the mountain to form a cross three hundred feet long. According to one of the men who worked on this extravagant light show, the cross was "just to let the niggers know the war is over and that the Klan is back on the market."

In spite of Colescott's formal order of disbandment, a number of Klaverns in Atlanta and vicinity had continued meeting secretly during the war. After the spectacle on Stone Mountain they proclaimed themselves the Association of Georgia Klans (AGK) and Dr. Samuel Green their leader. In spring 1946, advertisements in Atlanta papers announced a big, formal celebration of the Klan's revival, again to be held on the mountain, and nearly a thousand spectators turned out for the show. Three hundred new Klansmen were initiated at this ceremony—most of them unskilled or semi-skilled tradesmen, or farmers with a sprinkling of white-collar and professional men. It was apparent from the striped blue trouser legs beneath the sheets that a good many of the initiates were officers of the law. After the formalities of oath taking and cross burning, Green unctuously announced, "We are revived."

"Some folks play golf; I Ku Klux," said Doc Green, a fifty-four-year-old Atlanta physician specializing in female complaints. Green was a "little pouter-pigeon of a man" with a wispy, tooth-brush mustache. He gazed through watery blue eyes, spoke in a high-pitched voice, and dealt with people in an imperious manner. A twenty-five-year veteran of the Klan, he had held every office in the organization but Imperial Wizard and, at the time of the Klan's disbandment, had been Grand Dragon of Georgia. He still was, for Green contended that the "Klan has never been dead and the Klan is never going to die"—at least not in its birthplace.

When the Klan was a national organization, its Wizards and Dragons had been obliged by Atlanta headquarters to exercise a certain amount of discretion in their public utterances. Now that it was a local affair, Green was free to say what he pleased. When *The Nation* sent a black reporter to interview Green, the Dragon was completely candid. "There ain't a nigger that's the equal of a white man," he told Roi Ottley, the author of *Black Odyssey*. "If God wanted us all equal, He would have made all people white men." Ottley tried to share with Green scientific data and changing perspectives on race in the United States and abroad, but the doctor wanted none of it. "I'm still livin' in Georgia, no matter what the world and science thinks," he said. Ottley dismissed Green as "a museum piece . . . a primitive fanatic, without the slightest knowledge of affairs beyond his neighborhood. . . ." But Green did have a neighborhood, and considerable influence within it. In addition to building a strong alliance between his Klaverns and the Atlanta Police Department, he also courted the city's taxicab drivers. "The time may soon come when we might need every cab in Atlanta to do some quick work," he explained. He appreciated and encouraged the postwar fear of blacks among the white citizens of Atlanta. "If anyone wants to eat with niggers that's their business," he said, but the AGK would resist such abominations. Green agreed with his good friend Eugene Talmadge, forgiver of floggers, who announced that if blacks wanted whites to continue holding them in "the historic esteem" that was a Southern tradition, they would have to "stay in the definite place we have provided for them." "No CIO or AFL carpetbagging organizers or any other damned Yankees are going to come into the South and tell Southerners how to run either their businesses or their niggers," Green said.

Green's bluster was prompted not just by postwar white anxiety over blacks but by steps that were being taken by the federal government. On December 5, 1946, President Harry S. Truman created an executive commission on human rights with the express purpose of preventing a postwar revival of the Klan. "This country could easily be faced with a situation similar to the one with which it was faced in 1922," he warned the commission. Truman's concern was augmented by the fact that the United States was now a member of the United Nations and had subscribed to its Declaration of Human Rights. It would be difficult for the U.S. to assume a role of leadership in the United Nations—or in the world, for that matter—if its championship of civil rights at home fell below UN standards. (He would persistently refer to this fact in messages to Congress and in his vetoes of discriminatory legislation.) Truman believed that the country was making progress in civil rights —there was the wartime Fair Employment Practices Committee, which he was trying to extend into peacetime; and his conscientious attorney general, Tom Clark, was looking into cases of racial discrimination that violated federal statutes—"but we are not making progress fast enough," he told the commission. Truman asked the members of the group to review current practices of discrimination, examine existing laws, and then recommend a comprehensive package of civil rights reforms he could submit to Congress.

The Association of Georgia Klans detested what the federal government wanted to do and what it had already done. They were highly suspicious of the UN. They hated the Fair Employment Practices Committee, which had elevated many Southern black laborers to higher positions than they had ever achieved during prewar conditions of near-peonage. They loathed the fact that some Southern blacks had registered to vote during the war. To the facts they added rumors. They alleged that at the army's Lawson Hospital, white nurses were massaging the bodies of black soldiers and black doctors were delivering white women's babies.

By harping incessantly on these issues, the AGK soon spread from its Atlanta environs, where five Klaverns met regularly, into the rest of Georgia. Georgia would remain the stronghold of Klux-dom during the 1940s, (by 1949 there would be a Klavern in each of the state's 159 counties), but Doc recruited Klansmen and chartered Klaverns in neighboring states as well. The first one outside Georgia was in Birmingham, Alabama, where on March 29, 1946, eight crosses blazed through the night proclaiming the Klan's return. One elderly white gentleman was ecstatic about it. "This will teach niggers to stay put in their place," he exulted. "If they don't we'll stack 'em up like cordwood." When a reporter quoted these words to a young, black NAACP worker, he merely shrugged and asked, "Where can I buy a bulletproof vest?" The AGK also found welcome receptions in Miami and Key West, in Chattanooga and Knoxville, and in both Carolinas. Like the NAACP worker in Birmingham, however, blacks took the Klan revival in stride, showing little of the fear Klansmen had hoped for. The editor of a little black weekly, the Carolina Times, wrote: "We welcome the Ku Klux Klan to North Carolina, because if it is active it will focus the attention of decent citizens on how asinine, vicious and low in the scale of human depravity some people can descend. . . . It will bring about a choosing of sides between that element of white people who believe in giving the Negro full rights of citizenship and those who do not."

Soon Doc Green was boasting that the AGK had assumed the proportions of the mammoth movement of the 1920s, that it had crossed the Mason–Dixon line and was flourishing in "California, Ohio, Indiana, even in New York and New Jersey." Asked why no one had heard anything about the Klan in the North, Green confided, "There's such an enormous foreign population there, they have to stay under cover." There were definite rustlings of Klandom in other parts of the country at this time. A large cross was burned in the outskirts of Los Angeles, and another in front of a Jewish fraternity house on the campus of the University of Southern California. (The fiery cross had now become more an instrument of intimidation than a religious icon.) But several Northern states moved swiftly to prevent the Klan from getting a foothold. One by one, California, New York, New Jersey, and Wisconsin legally barred the Klan from operating within their borders, and similar legislation was under way in Indiana and Illinois. The New York law was so stringent that anyone attempting to organize a Klavern in the Empire State faced a fine of $10,000 and six months in prison.

Closely watching this trend in the North was Ellis Gibbs Arnall, former prosecutor of Hiram Evans's shady asphalt deals and now governor of Georgia. Arnall instructed his feisty assistant attorney general, Daniel Duke, to look into the possibility of revoking the Klan's charter. A young man who was deeply invested in this matter was a thirty-year-old writer named Stetson Kennedy, who had first written and proposed to Governor Arnall that the charter be revoked. In an article in the *New Republic*, Kennedy argued that Simmons's original charter had been given for a "purely benevolent" fraternal order. Green's AGK was still operating under this charter—the disbanded Knights of the KKK and the AGK were "*de jure* and *de facto* one and the same." Far from being a "benevolent" fraternity, Kennedy charged that Green's group was nothing but a pack of petty terrorists, so there should be no problem revoking the charter. He also offered sound advice for fighting the Klan. It was futile to inveigh against the Klan and investigate it as a body. Instead, people should investigate "specific violations of specific civil liberties of specific persons by specific Klansmen." Kennedy spoke with compelling authority, for good reason. He had infiltrated the Klan over a year before and was still engaged in undercover work in Green's headquarters Klavern.

A biographer of folksinger Woody Guthrie (who was a close friend of Stetson Kennedy) has called Kennedy "a quietly outrageous character," which is as good an introduction as any to this remarkable man. William Stetson Kennedy was born in Jacksonville, Florida, in 1916, with the kind of pedigree that many Klansmen bragged about having, whether they did or not. Two of his ancestors had signed the Declaration of Independence. The Stetson side of the family was descended from the famous hat manufacturer. His grandfather had been a lieutenant in the Confederate Army, and his uncle had been an active Klansman in the 1920s. Instead of sliding easily from this heritage into a life of comfortable Southern gentility, Kennedy became one of the most militant and persistent opponents of injustice of his generation—a stance that refused to soften in later years.

Little in Kennedy's background could have predicted his career. "My family was typically white Southern in racial attitudes," he said, "which we acquired with the very air we breathed." Stetson did have "a skinny childhood," however, which "may have been conducive to a dislike for bullies." But Kennedy preferred to think that he had a "congenital hankering after justice of all descriptions, and a dislike for the obverse." He also had a talent for writing, which came out in junior high and high school. He continued writing during his student days at the University of Florida, and rejection slips from *Esquire* marked "not quite" kept him going. In college he became politically active and joined the League against War and Fascism, the American Student Union, and the North American Committee to Aid Spanish Democracy. After college, he discovered the WPA's Writers' Project, which paid people to write state travel guides and to collect the oral histories of senior citizens. The Writers' Project seemed made to order for Kennedy's talents, and his work in a team assigned to write the Florida Guide so impressed author Erskine Caldwell that he invited Kennedy to write the Florida volume in his American Folkways Series. The result was Kennedy's first book, *Palmetto Country*, written when he was twenty-six. The unusually enlightened attitude toward unionism and race in *Palmetto Country* brought its author to the attention of the CIO, and Kennedy was made Southeastern editorial director for the CIO's Political Action Committee. From there, he went to work for the Anti-Defamation League, becoming its Southeastern research director.

Stetson Kennedy's concern with the Ku Klux Klan ("the ugliest skeleton in our closet") began in his Writers' Project days, when he had recorded a number of narratives about unprosecuted Klan violence during the 1920s. His CIO work made him aware of the Klan's antiunion activities during the 1930s. And in *Palmetto Country*, he had researched the Reconstruction Klan with a remarkably objective eye. Kennedy had been inspired by FDR's Four Freedoms—the freedoms of speech, of religion, from want, and from fear—and, like many other Americans, had viewed World War II as an antifascist endeavor. Although he had been ineligible for military service, there was nothing to prevent him from waging a private war against the Klan and other "homegrown fascist groups" in America's own back yard. Since his ADL work would be taking him to Atlanta, Kennedy decided to infiltrate Doc Green's home base.

In Atlanta, the slim, prematurely balding young writer assumed the identity of "John S. Perkins," an itinerant peddler of *Southern Outlook*, a Klan-styled hate sheet. He began hanging out at a local pool hall "whose habitués had the frustrated, cruel look of the Klan about them" and, as he expected, was approached by a Kleagle. It wasn't long before Kennedy was initiated in full flapping regalia atop Stone Mountain. In later years, other men would replicate Kennedy's feat. While FBI informers would have the ready backup of the bureau, however, Kennedy would have to survive by his own wits; and unlike later publicity-minded journalists who joined skimpy Klaverns of wimps, Kennedy had become a member of Nathan Bedford Forrest Klavern Number One, the most powerful and dangerous Klavern in the South.

During his undercover years, Kennedy survived on payments from the ADL, whose officers were especially interested in getting the goods on a Hitlerian brown-shirt sect known as the Columbians—the first important neo-Nazi organization in the United States. The Columbians had specialized in dynamiting the homes of blacks who had moved into white Atlanta neighborhoods. Kennedy was also paid a nominal sum (amounting to expenses) by the Georgia attorney general's office, which he began to supply with the documents necessary to take away the AGK's charter. The rest of his income came from freelance work for *The Nation, PM, Common Ground*, and other periodicals and newspapers—articles that are now critically important sources of Klan history during its postwar reemergence.

Although Kennedy may have been unprepared for how really dangerous the Klan was, any misperceptions were quickly corrected once he began attending weekly Klavern meetings. At these secret gatherings, lists of people who needed "kluxing" were reviewed and methods of mayhem debated. Time could be given for special commendations to such men as "Itchy-Trigger-Finger Nash," an Atlanta policeman. "Itchy" stood up and proudly accepted the applause of his brethren "for killing his thirteenth nigger in the line of duty." Kennedy was a keen observer of personality and left valuable accounts of such high-ranking Klansmen as Jimmy Colescott; and Doc Green who told him, "Medicine is the way I earn my living; the Klan gives me my pleasure." Perhaps more interesting, however, are his portraits of the Klan's rank and file, the simple men drawn to the hooded order out of frustration and feelings of inadequacy. For example, there was the young war veteran: "I had to be drafted into the war against Hitler, but when the war of the races comes I'll be one of the first to volunteer"; and the backwoods preacher: "In God's sight it's no sin to kill a nigger, for a nigger is no more than a dog."

The Atlanta meetings sometimes were visited by traveling Klansmen, men who would eventually make sinister contributions to the Klan's unbroken record of violence. One of these was a pimply-faced, razor-witted Tennessee Kleagle named Jesse B. Stoner, who was only twenty-two at the time. During the war, Stoner had written to the U.S. Congress, asking it to pass a resolution recog-

nizing that "Jews are the children of the Devil." Apparently geno-
cide in Germany hadn't tempered his views. In his visit to the
Atlanta Klavern, "J.B." gave a wild, incoherent speech, saying:

> We ought to get all Jews out of our country, and I don't mean send
> them to some other country! I'll never be satisfied as long as there are
> any Jews here or anywhere. I think we ought to kill all Jews just to
> save their unborn generations from having to go to Hell!

"I sat up on the edge of my chair," Kennedy recalled. "This guy
must be stark, raving crazy, I thought to myself."

In addition to preserving the speeches of lunatics for posterity,
Kennedy became interested in the Klan's penetration into politics
and law enforcement. At a private birthday party for Doc Green
at the Atlanta Municipal Auditorium, the guest speaker was Herman ("Hummon") Talmadge who, with the Klan's solid backing,
would be elected governor of Georgia in 1948. At the birthday
party, "Hummon" said he was happy to speak before Klansmen,
who were the kind of folk "that will save America for Americans";
and that Georgia was fortunate to have Klansmen "ready to fight
for the preservation of our American traditions against the Communists, foreign agitators, Negroes, Catholics and Jews."

In the area of law enforcement, Kennedy delighted in getting
Atlanta policemen to return the Klan's secret signs of recognition
and reported the men to Assistant Attorney General Dan Duke.
Once when he was stopped for running a red light, Kennedy fum-
bled through his wallet for his driver's license until his Klan membership card popped up. "Why didn't you make yourself known to
start with?" asked the arresting officer, who promptly tore up the
ticket he was writing. On another occasion, Kennedy reported to
Duke that at an initiation of eighty-two Klansmen, thirty-six were
Atlanta policemen. When Klansmen murdered a black taxicab
driver, the police members of Klavern Number One went over the
impounded vehicle to remove all fingerprints. And the Klan's subversion of the law didn't end with the police. Kennedy learned that
Judge Luke Arnold was a popular lecturer at Klavern meetings;
and that "Brother Judge" Caleb Callaway had been sent a letter of
commendation for rendering judgments "conforming with the
principles of Klannishness."

While he continued gathering the evidence Duke would need
to revoke the Klan's charter and file indictments, Kennedy began
sending dispatches to Drew Pearson, the no-nonsense radio com-

mentator and columnist of "Washington Merry-Go-Round." Every week Pearson broadcast Kennedy's information as "Minutes of the Klan's Last Meeting" and named the names Kennedy had sent him. Shortly after Pearson identified Cliff Vittur as the "Chief Ass-Tearer" of Klavern Number One, some of the trucks in Vittur's Atlanta trucking firm were set on fire. An angry Doc Green complained that he might as well phone Pearson himself and collect the fees. Green grew to hate Kennedy, whom he assumed was a damned Yankee, and publicly offered a reward of $1,000 per pound of "the traitor's ass, FOB Atlanta."

Kennedy didn't stop there. In one of his most creative moves, he contacted the scriptwriters of radio's *Superman* show and offered to supply them with his Klavern's current agenda and its latest passwords. The writers jumped on the idea, and Superman, the ultimate antifascist—played by Bud Collyer—began trouncing the Klan over the airwaves, a battle replete with obviously authentic detail. During the first broadcast, Doc Green was called by the Atlanta AP bureau chief:

> "Superman's really on your trail. . . . Sounds to me like Superman's got a pipeline into your klaverns somehow. You'd better watch your step."
> "I smell a rat!" the Dragon said bitterly. "Just wait till I get my hands on him!"
> "You'd better make it snappy—Superman just flew over your Imperial Palace to case the joint!"
> "Nuts!" the Doctor said, and hung up.

The fact that the Invisible Empire had been penetrated by a spy—probably a "Communist spy"—put Klansmen into a lather. Nothing could have made them feel so vulnerable. One reporter noted that they were "so bitter in their denunciation" of the traitor "that their exact words cannot be quoted verbatim." They were especially embittered when their own children began playacting Superman's fight with cowardly Klansmen, even to the extent of rattling off the secret passwords that had just been given out the previous week.

Doc Green tried a number of ploys to find the spy. Periodically he would order the Kladds to bar the doors of the Klavern and announce that "the rat" had been identified, hoping the infiltrator would make a run for the door. Once the gimmick came dangerously close to being successful. During one of these door-barring melodramas, Green announced, "The bald-headed bastard is sitting right here tonight." Kennedy looked hurriedly around and saw to his relief that there were six other balding men at the meeting. No one bolted. The task of ferreting out the "rat" was eventually turned over to the Klavalier Klub, the Klan's special hit team. With characteristic bravado, "John Perkins" inquired about joining the Klavaliers. "Do you like blood?" he was asked. When he said he did, "Perkins" was admitted and made a fellow "ass-tearer." Stetson Kennedy had become a member of the special force assigned to exterminate Stetson Kennedy. "I had found Kluxers to be an ugly lot," he said, "but this handpicked gang of strong-arm Klansmen was the meanest I had ever seen under one roof. Frustration, cruelty and alcoholism showed on every face." Although the Klavaliers had no idea on how to go about identifying their spy, they were obsessed with plans for what they would do when they found him: "Let's take him out in the woods, fasten him to a log with a staple around his testicles, set fire to the log, give him a knife, and tell him to 'Cut or burn!' "

Why did Kennedy take such personal risks? Did he enjoy living on the edge of disaster? Kennedy claims he did not, that he was "always painfully aware of risks." But as fast as "Perkins" could gather evidence, Kennedy exposed it, making every effort to avoid linkage in the Klan's mind. He was also gifted with an imperturbable face that betrayed little signs of anxiety. But undercover work wasn't Kennedy's idea of fun: "I don't think I ever enjoyed it. Worse still was having to associate with such scum, and the necessity for occasionally aping them." An added burden for him was having to share Klansmen's tastes: "I felt that if I had to listen to Georgia jookbox country corn much longer, I would blow my brains out."

Kennedy was determined to do as much damage to the Klan as one man possibly could. When he was finally able to break cover, his vengeance was relentless. His book *Southern Exposure*, a brilliantly documented exposé of "the anti-democratic forces in the deep South," revealed the worst he knew about Klansmen and their friends in high places. Next, he had accumulated plenty of data proving that the AGK was using all the old money-making properties of the Knights of the KKK, Inc., including its name, copyrighted *Kloran* rituals, patented insignia, and numerous paper forms. It was enough for Georgia to begin legal proceedings to revoke the old Klan's charter, under which Green was operating. In its brief of quo warranto, which Kennedy helped prepare, the state charged that the AGK had substituted trial by ordeal for trial by jury, made false arrests of citizens, invaded homes, and committed acts of violence and terrorism. As Dan Duke put it, "The Klan contains the germs of an American Gestapo." In 1947, Doc Green bitterly surrendered the charter, and shortly afterward, U.S. Attorney General Tom Clark put the Ku Klux Klan on the subversive list.

Next came legal prosecution of individuals, which Kennedy anticipated with relish: "By that time I was as mad as they were and was determined to get off my chest some of the things I had been wanting to say to the rats ever since the day I 'joined.' " Accompanied by burly union friends as bodyguards, Kennedy's testimony in Georgia courts resulted in a satisfying sentence for the ringleader of the Columbians and lesser sentences for others. He had hoped for many more prosecutions, but "Hummon" Talmadge soon became governor and was a friend of the Klan—at least as long as it wielded any vote power.

Kennedy's next endeavor was his most creative. Since the Klan's national charter had now been revoked, Kennedy attempted to recharter it outside Georgia with himself as Imperial Wizard. Assuming all control of the Klan's name, uniform, and paraphernalia, Kennedy's "mock" Klan would be in a position to enjoin any racist group from calling itself the Ku Klux Klan or using its accouterments:

> As soon as an understanding secretary of state grants us a corporate charter, we will proceed to appoint registered agents in each state. Then when hate-mongering Kluxers stick their necks out, we will seek an injunction if necessary to stop them. . . .

His first steps toward this were taken in Chicago, where he was lecturing on the Klan. In his application for an Illinois charter, he listed among the "mock" Klan's purposes: "To combat organized and unorganized racial and religious prejudice, bigotry, intolerance, hatred, segregation, and discrimination in every aspect of life—social, economic, political" and "to work toward a democracy in which total equality shall be guaranteed by organic law." For the six charter members, Kennedy chose a Baptist (himself), a Catholic, a Jew, a black, a Cherokee Indian, and a Japanese-American. In Atlanta, Doc Green was nearly speechless with rage when he heard of Kennedy's plan. "Only a pervert could come up with such a foul idea as that," he said.

Illinois secretary of state Edward J. Barrett denied the application. Writing to Kennedy, he said that "in view of the activities of organizations with similar names in other states, I do not believe the name is acceptable under the statutes of this State." Barrett personally felt that Kennedy's motives were "commendable," but he had "definitely concluded that neither this nor any similar name will be granted to any corporation for any purpose in this State. . . ."

Having failed to interest state officials in his anti-Klan crusade, Kennedy turned to the federal government. HUAC had continued its official neglect in the matter of the KKK, but—with the added zeal of its newest member Richard Nixon, and the support of Joseph McCarthy's Senate subcommittee—it was now going after Communists on a grand scale. HUAC's new chairman J. Parnell Thomas (soon to be jailed for defrauding the government by payroll padding) refused Kennedy's offers to come to Washington at his own expense and turn over to the committee "trunkloads of documentary evidence of the Klan's un-American activities." Kennedy finally decided to dramatize the committee's hypocrisy and neglect. He did go to Washington at his own expense, and during the taxi ride to the House Office Building, he put on his Klan robe and mask. At the HUAC reception room, the sight of the white-robed Kluxer threw the secretarial pool into a panic, and Kennedy was collared by the Capitol police and hauled away. The next day, HUAC's chief investigator Robert Stripling offered Kennedy a perfunctory interview but refused a briefcase full of documented Klan violence that Kennedy offered him. The committee was interested in "Communism—a foreign 'ism,' " not the Klan, which Congressman Rankin had recently pronounced "as American as illegal whiskey selling." Kennedy's only satisfaction came from his proof that HUAC rejected KKK data even when offered "on a silver platter."

Kennedy then directed his anti-Klan crusade at that other American secret society, the Federal Bureau of Investigation. Doc Green often bragged that the FBI called him from time to time to seek the Klan's cooperation in obtaining certain information on dealing with various problems. That may have been stretching the truth, but it was no exaggeration that J. Edgar Hoover detested civil rights cases. The director had just recently written to Attorney General Clark, asking to be excused entirely from further civil rights matters. Hoover argued that the bureau was "expending a considerable amount of manpower" investigating crimes in the South "in which there cannot conceivably be any violation of a

Federal statute." After investigating these civil rights cases, he said, the bureau became saddled "in the public mind and in the press with the responsibility" for solving them. Hoover said he didn't "condone the type of activities" involved in these cases, but he strongly believed they should be left to "the State Courts."

The attorney general didn't share Hoover's feelings. In an extremely tactful letter, Clark informed Hoover that "in each case the complaint made is indicative of a violation, and if we do not investigate we are placed in the position of having received the complaint of a violation and of having failed to satisfy ourselves that it is or is not such a violation. I know of no way to avoid at least a preliminary inquiry into the facts of a complaint which alleges a civil rights offense. I am sure you agree that we should not be in the position of avoiding such actions."

Hoover didn't agree at all. From the testimony of agents who worked for the FBI during the 1940s and 1950s, the U.S. Civil Rights Commission later learned that Hoover routinely dismissed civil rights cases as "burdensome." He "distributed a monthly bulletin to police departments all over the country and [made] no secret therein of the sort of information in which the FBI is interested, *i.e.*, kidnapping, bank robberies, but never civil rights." Hoover's agents claimed the boss said that "civil rights cases shouldn't even be in there."

Stetson Kennedy was fully aware of the mare's nest he was entering by prodding the FBI on civil rights violations by the Ku Klux Klan, but he pushed all the same. When agents repeatedly refused his evidence in the interest of "the tranquility of the South," Kennedy arranged to be interviewed about the FBI's official neglect on a national television program, *We the People*, sponsored by Gulf Oil. Finally the bureau took action. Agents contacted Gulf Oil and pressured their executives into canceling Kennedy's appearance on the show. Kennedy, they said, was a "possible psychopathic case" who had participated in "various Communist-inspired programs." (In Kennedy's confidential FBI file, however, persistent agents could ultimately find "no reason to question his basic loyalty to the U.S.")

Kennedy's mission had now been rejected at both the state and federal levels of his country. "I had bowed out of the Klan feeling certain I had accumulated more than enough evidence for the authorities to crush it," he said. "But the repeated refusal of public officials on every level to act on the evidence gave the Klan a new lease on life." At least it did in the South. Nevertheless, the protracted efforts of "the nation's number-one Klanbuster," as Drew Pearson called Kennedy—his prolific writing, exposés, radio and television appearances, university lectures, and persistent hounding of authorities—were the single most important factor in preventing a postwar revival of the Ku Klux Klan in the North.

In the South, severing the AGK from the old Klan's charter had little effect on embittered Georgia Klansmen who remained as obnoxious and aggressive as ever. This was especially true in the 1948 gubernatorial campaign, when they became determined to put " 'Hummon' Talmadge in the saddle." Doc Green told Klansmen that electing Talmadge governor was the "number one job in '48," and that they should "appeal even to Catholics and Jews on the basis of white supremacy, but don't let them know you're a Klansman, because they know we are sworn against them." A systematic program was implemented to frighten blacks from the polls. The Klan held a series of noisy motorcades through the black community in Milledgeville. It burned crosses and paraded in Wrightsville. It dropped leaflets from an airplane all over the state. Miniature coffins labeled *KKK* were left on the porches of black activists; and on election eve, registered blacks found scorched bits of paper in their mail boxes saying, *U beter stay at work tomorro—kkk*. The campaign—strongly redolent of Reconstruction Klan tactics—was successful, and the Kluxers' friend "Hummon" wound up in the statehouse.

A more far-reaching effect of the charter loss was that Green could no longer claim to be ruler of the one-and-only Ku Klux Klan. His loss of authority spurred dissident factions of Klansmen to pull out from under him whenever disagreements arose; and in a few years, brand new Klans were sprouting overnight, free to appropriate whatever they wanted of the old Klan's rituals and regalia. In an article titled "Divisible Invisible Empire," *Newsweek* took stock of at least a dozen different Klans operating autonomously in the South by 1949. "They're Bolshevik Klans," Green sneered, "which pulled out because they couldn't run things themselves." Green hated these new rivals and blasted their leaders as men who simply wanted "to make a potful of money."

One of the first "Bolshevik Klans" was the Federated Ku Klux Klan launched in Birmingham under the dragonship of Dr. E. P. Pruitt. "The Klan don't hate nobody!" Pruitt exclaimed. "In fact, the Klan is the good nigger's best friend. . . . I've delivered many a nigger baby without charging a cent for it. My nigger maid even washes my Klan robe for me." In June 1949, several of Pruitt's sheeted followers broke into the home of Mrs. Hugh McDanal and accused her of renting rooms to unmarried couples, selling whiskey, and "dancing nude on her front porch." Then they dragged her outside and forced her to watch them burn a cross on her lawn. ("It sure was pretty," a neighbor woman testified.) An angry Mrs. McDanal tore off one of the Klansmen's hoods and recognized Brownie Lollar, whom she prosecuted. Unfortunately for Mrs. McDanal, Brownie and his friends were let off by the jury after the defense presented a photograph of one of her nocturnal ballets.

A notorious breakaway from Green's Association was Thomas Hamilton's Association of Carolina Klans. Hamilton was a beefy, bug-eyed, cigar-smoking, former wholesale grocer who was religiously committed to Klandom. His public rallies were very much like old-time revival meetings. At a September 1951 rally in Columbus County, North Carolina, Hamilton proclaimed his Klan would "band white Protestant Gentiles together" in opposition to the National Council of Churches, which he claimed was trying to tell folks that "Jesus was a bastard child." "Do you want some burr-headed nigra to come up on your porch and ask for the hand of your daughter in marriage?"

"Not that!" the crowd responded. "Uh-uh!"

"But the nigra has put his foot in the door in this country," said Hamilton, alluding to the fact that a few blacks had enrolled at the University of North Carolina. "If I had a daughter in that place, I would never let her darken its doors again." In sad, pulpit tones that rose in pitch at the end of each phrase, Hamilton sighed, "I have been in the Klan for twenty-six years, and if I live I'll be in it for twenty-six more. . . . When I cross the great divide it don't make any difference what happens to my body because God has promised me a new body, holy and incorruptible."

In a less holy and more easily corruptible body, Hamilton and his henchmen were arrested the next year for abducting two lovers and beating them with a machine belt nailed to a pick handle. Between blows, the white-robed reformers made the victims "pray and listen to sermons and hymns." Two little weeklies, the Tabor City *Tribune* and the Whiteville *News Reporter*, raised such a stink over the incident and over Hamilton in general that they attracted national attention and won Pulitzer prizes. Fortunately for the abducted lovers, Hamilton had transported them across the state line, and the Klansmen were tried in a federal court for kidnapping under the Lindbergh law. Hamilton was sentenced to four years in prison. Fifteen of his men were sent up for an average of three years each, and forty-nine others were fined a total of $18,250. The surprising verdict was roundly applauded by journalists and clergymen across the country.

One of the most absurd of the independent Klans was the Alabama-based Knights of the Ku Klux Klan of America who declared a "war on bureaucracy," which they denounced as "the graveyard in which the mutilated and crucified bodies of American liberty and freedom are being buried." Without a doubt, the Knights of America was headed by the most colorful and eccentric fraud since the days of Colonel Simmons. Assuming the redundant title of Imperial Emperor, Dr. Lycurgus Spinks claimed he had been born on a farm near Thomasville, Alabama, where he was "raised by a Negro mammy and ate pot licker out of the same bowl with the pickaninnies." At age sixty-five, Dr. Spinks wore his shoulder-length white hair under a broad-brimmed Texas hat. His doctorate was self-awarded. "No college ever give me that title, son," he told a reporter. "I've just been known as 'Doctor' Spinks nearly ever since I could remember." Like Simmons, Spinks had given a number of platform lectures on sex education topics, modestly segregated "for men only" and "for women only." But he was especially fond of giving patriotic lectures dressed up like George Washington.

Through a sense of humor or perversity, Lawrence E. Spivak, editor of the *American Mercury*, arranged with Albert Warner of the Mutual Broadcasting System to invite Dr. Spinks to a nationally broadcast hour of *Meet the Press*. Faced with such elite antagonists as Spivak, Warner, Drew Pearson, May Craig of the Portland *Press-Herald*, and Edward T. Folliard of the *Washington Post*, Spinks was a veritable lion in a den of Daniels.

SPINKS: I'd just like to say this—that I'm fully conscious of the fact that every newsman that I'm facing tonight is an arch-enemy of the organization that I represent. I naturally presume that you hate me because I'm a Klansman. And now, as soon as I say hello to the finest grandbaby on earth, I'll be ready to start battling it out with you. Hello, little son! Stay in there and pitch for your granddaddy! I'm going to make him a Klansman at ten years old.

CRAIG: May I say first, Doctor, that newspaper people don't hate anybody. We just try to find out what makes them tick. Can you tell me how many subjects you've got in your Invisible Empire?

SPINKS: I wouldn't tell you that if I knew.

CRAIG: Why? Is it a secret?

SPINKS: Yes, ma'am.

CRAIG: Why a secret in a democratic country?

SPINKS: Because it's expedient to have secrecy in a democratic country.

CRAIG: A secret organization in a democratic country? Do you think you're above the law?

SPINKS: Have you any privacy in your home, or in any organization of which you're a member?

CRAIG: Well, sir, I'm to ask you the questions. I'm sorry.

SPINKS: I thought we'd finally get over to that. . . .

CRAIG: Isn't the purpose of your organization to control and keep down the Negroes? Isn't that your prime purpose?

SPINKS: No sir. One of the purposes of our organization is to see that the Negroes in the United States get a square deal at the hands of white people and everybody else that has to do with the laws of this country.

CRAIG: Then why are all Negroes and all Negro organizations against you?

SPINKS: They are not against us.

FOLLIARD: Name one that is for you.

SPINKS: All the niggers down South know that the best friend they've got on earth is the Knights of the Ku Klux Klan!

When the round of questions passed to Drew Pearson, Spinks became noticeably agitated. Pearson was still being supplied with inside information from Stetson Kennedy at this time and was more knowledgeable about the Klan than any other man in the media.

PEARSON: Emperor, do you represent the Georgia Klans?

SPINKS: I represent the Knights of the Ku Klux Klans of America, all of them.

PEARSON: Do you represent the Federated Klans?

SPINKS: Every Klansman in America.

PEARSON: They claim you don't.

SPINKS: I'm here to speak for them and defend them in any attack that you make. And I'd like for you to start making them, old man! Every criticism that you ever made of the Knights of the Ku Klux Klan on your program has been—not—not one single word of truth in it!

PEARSON: And now, Emperor—

SPINKS: And this spy that you've got down in—in one of our Klans in Atlanta is a moral degenerate! A leper! And every time you quote him over the radio you are aiding and assisting a man who has repudiated one of the most sacred oaths that a man ever took! . . .

PEARSON: You once posed as the reincarnation of George Washington.

SPINKS: I did.

PEARSON: Which did you find, the—

SPINKS: And I made a good job of it!

PEARSON: Which did you find the more lucrative, posing as George Washington or running the Ku Klux Klan?

SPINKS: Well, I haven't tried running the Klan long enough to give you that answer.

Lawrence Spivak pointed out that an organization of Southern Baptists had denounced the Klan as un-Christian.

SPIVAK: They say the cross must be borne, not burned. . . . Do you as a Baptist minister believe that the cross should be burned or borne?

SPINKS: Both. How you going to "borne" a cross? Who ever heard of such a fool thing?

SPIVAK: That's what Jesus said.

SPINKS: Jesus never said any such thing!

And in this, at least, Dr. Spinks was right.

When Edward Folliard remarked on the fact that some thirty Alabama and Georgia Klansmen had been indicted for acts of violence, Spinks became defensive.

SPINKS: Where do you get your information?

FOLLIARD: In a very reputable newspaper, the *New York Times*.

SPINKS: Well, they don't know what they're talking about. . . . One of [the indicted Klansmen] talked to me about it and told me that he was in Florida on his vacation when the flogging that they accused him of took place, and he could prove it by a hundred witnesses. I begged the courts in Birmingham to try these men they indicted six or eight weeks ago, begged them like a dog to try them. They've got more judges in Birmingham than they have fiddlers in Hell but you can't get them to try them. . . . You know why? They're *scared* to do it! They're afraid the whole thing'll wash out—what—what I got here?

WARNER: You're too close to the microphone.

SPINKS: Well, all right.

WARNER: You don't need a microphone.

SPINKS: I *told* you I didn't need this thing. Come on, let's go, brother, let's go!

It was certainly a rollicking performance, but not the kind to win the Klan any new friends. Within a year after Spinks met the press, his Klan following—whatever there was to begin with—evaporated, and the old curmudgeon himself passed into obscurity.

In spite of the comic relief Dr. Spinks briefly lent the Klan, an increasing problem associated with Klan splintering was violence. As in Reconstruction, the more autonomy a Klavern possessed, the more aggressive it became. In Atlanta, Doc Green died in 1949 and his lieutenant Sam Roper took his place. Roper was a twenty-five-year veteran of the Atlanta police force, and in exchange for Klan support in 1948, Governor Herman Talmadge made Roper the chief of the Georgia Bureau of Investigation. As Grand Dragon of Georgia, Roper claimed that he was involved nearly full time in suppressing Klan violence. "Every damn tomtit in the country calls on the Klan for help," he told a reporter. "Here's a letter from a woman wants me to get a Tennessee Klan to go out and whip a couple of her neighbors because they go out at night and leave their children alone. Sometimes you find a dumb Klansman who has got no better sense than to get mixed up in something like that."

Florida Klansmen were especially willing to get mixed up in private vendettas. There were three active Klan factions in the state: The Knights of the Ku Klux Klan of Florida, the Association of Florida Klans, and the Southern Knights of the Ku Klux Klan. Florida Klansmen had two specialties: anti-Semitism and dynamite. Their anti-Semitism reflected a migration of Jewish retirees to the Sunshine State. In Inverness, sixty miles north of Tampa, a Klan lecturer drew cheers of approval from a crowd by saying, "God stamped ugliness on the face of the Jew for the same reason he put rattlers on the snake." The dynamite problem reflected the fact that, with the amount of offshore drilling, dynamite was easily obtainable. There were also many veterans in the state who had been trained in demolitions during wartime stints in the navy and marines. In 1951, eighteen bombs exploded in Miami, demolishing black homes, Jewish synagogues, and Catholic churches. This series of explosions culminated on Christmas Day, when a blast killed Mr. and Mrs. Harry T. Moore in their home near Mims, Florida. The murder of the Moores was one of the most sadistic and, until recently, mysterious Klan assassinations of all time.

Professor Moore was a superintendent of public instruction who also headed the Florida NAACP and was executive secretary of the Progressive Voters' League. A softspoken but determined man, he had spent the previous seventeen years traveling the entire state urging black voter registration and fighting discrimination in teachers' salaries. He was a persistent critic of the overlap between Klansmen and law-enforcement personnel and had become involved in the case of Lake County Sheriff Willis V. McCall, who was under investigation for murdering one and wounding another black defendant in his custody.

Shortly before Christmas, a Wauchula policeman approached one Raymond Henry, a twenty-two-year-old marine who was spending a holiday furlough at Fort Pierce, and told him that Klansmen would pay him $2,000 for building a bomb and helping them plant it at the Moore residence. Sheriff McCall promised to furnish the automobiles necessary and to pick up the bar tab for a victory celebration after the deed was done. The job was carried out by Henry, six Klansmen, and a policeman, all of whom were under the age of twenty-three. Arriving at Moore's residence on Christmas Day, 1951, they sent a confederate to the door who asked for Moore's help in locating a relative. Mrs. Moore was already away visiting friends. Moore left with the confederate, and the Klansmen gained entry by picking a lock. They located the master bedroom and fastened the bomb to the bedsprings of the Moores' bed. Not only was it Christmas but it was the Moores' silver wedding anniversary. Ten minutes after the couple put out the lights, the Klansmen detonated the bomb.

Moore died shortly after arriving at the hospital (he had to be transported by his brother-in-law because Florida ambulances refused to carry blacks at this time). Mrs. Moore lived another week. When asked to comment on the tragedy, Bill Hendrix, a forty-one-year-old plumbing contractor and Grand Dragon of Florida's Southern Knights, said, "Moore was a good fellow who wanted for the good of his race, but he just found out that he was going about it the wrong way."*

Another act of cooperative violence between Klansmen and lawmen ended less tragically. Mamie Clay, a resourceful black landowner in Georgia's Dade County, had been repeatedly pressured by whites to sell her property. When she refused, she was raided by three sheriff's deputies, who accused her of "running a disorderly house." She was later subjected to a series of crossburnings on her front lawn. Mrs. Clay became frightened, and a group of blacks began spending nights at her house to protect her. Soon afterward, Sheriff John Lynch and three deputies appeared and took Mrs. Clay's friends into custody, accusing them of being drunk and disorderly. The seven blacks were turned over to a squad of seventy, fully robed Klansmen who took them to a nearby schoolhouse and brutally flogged them. When Mrs. Clay's efforts at seeking justice at local and state levels failed, she turned in desperation to the federal government.

Attorney General Tom Clark had been waiting for a case like this. It was perfect to test something that very much interested him. The Reconstruction Enforcement Acts of 1870–1871 were still on the books, though they had been considerably watered down by many Supreme Court reversals and had atrophied under the neglect of thirteen presidents. Nevertheless, two remnants were still in the U.S. Code. Title 18, Section 241 proscribed "two or more persons" from conspiring "to injure, oppress, threaten or intimidate" any citizen in the free exercise of his constitutional rights; it also prohibited "two or more persons" from "going in disguise on the highway, or on the premises of another" with the same intentions. Title 18, Section 242 prohibited anyone from the same offenses while acting "under color of law." Clark decided that Section 242 fit the Clay case, since Sheriff Lynch had acted "under color of law" in arresting Mrs. Clay's bodyguards and turning them over to the Klan.

---

* The case remained a mystery for twenty-seven years. In 1978, Raymond Henry confessed his role in the murder to a Florida civil rights leader. The FBI was brought in and taped Henry's confession. The FBI refused to act, for the statute of limitations on civil rights violations in 1951 had expired. Local lawmen refused to hold Henry, although there is no statute of limitations on murder. Stetson Kennedy had long been involved in the case (Moore was a friend and had supported Kennedy in his 1950 run for the Senate). In 1982 Kennedy filed a request under the Freedom of Information Act for Henry's FBI confession. It was denied, and Kennedy and the NAACP appealed it in 1983; they were joined by ABC's 20/20 news program. As of the present writing, no action has resulted.

The Justice Department moved swiftly and prosecuted Sheriff Lynch and his deputies under the eighty-year-old Ku-Klux statutes in a federal court. Lynch and one of his deputies were convicted, fined $1,000 each, and sentenced to the maximum of one year in prison.

Clark's use of the Reconstruction statutes was a striking novelty. It was the first time in the twentieth century that they had been used in the context for which they had been created. President Truman encouraged Clark to continue using them—especially in view of the fact that Congress had flatly refused to act on the ten-point civil rights legislation he had recommended, and Southern Democrats were bolting the party over the issue. But a crushing setback came from the Supreme Court in 1951. In the case of *United States* v. *Williams*, the court ruled that use of the Klan statutes was limited to violations of federal rights—and of very few federal rights at that. For the next fourteen years, the Justice Department turned to the statutes only rarely, and when it did, no convictions were won.

The nation itself had grown weary of Klan violence, however. A number of Southern states enacted their own laws against the Klan. After much agitation, pro and con, antimask laws were finally adopted in Alabama, Florida, and Georgia. In 1953, North Carolina passed a law making it illegal for members of "a secret society" to engage in activities "hindering or aiding the success of any candidate for public office." Between 1952 and 1954, it looked as if the Klan were withering away. Incidents of Klan activity virtually disappeared from the newspapers. All this changed after May 17, 1954—what many Southern whites would call "Black Monday." On that day, in a landmark decision that reversed seventy years of its own thinking, the U.S. Supreme Court ruled that "the philosophy that all men are created equal" is "the American creed" and that henceforth it is unlawful to maintain schools segregated by race.

> "They've gone in," a man roared. "Oh, God, the niggers are in the school."
> A woman screamed, "Did they get in? Did you see them go in?"
> "They're in now," some other men yelled.
> "Oh, my God," the woman screamed. She burst into tears and tore at her hair. Hysteria swept the crowd. Other women began weeping and screaming.

Such was the scene described in Relman Morin's Pulitzer prize–winning, eyewitness account of the attempted integration of Little

Rock Central High School on September 23, 1957. Two weeks earlier, Harry Ashmore, editor of the Arkansas *Gazette*, had warned his readers, "Somehow, some time, every Arkansan is going to have to be counted. We are going to have to decide what kind of people we are—whether we obey the law only when we approve of it, or whether we obey it no matter how distasteful we may find it." Ashmore would lose more than fifteen thousand subscribers for his editorials, and his newsboys were daily threatened on their routes. After the near-riot described above, which resulted in the black children's immediate withdrawal from school, Ashmore wrote, "We can hope that we yet escape the tragic consequences of federal soldiers deployed on the streets of Little Rock for the first time since the post–Civil War period of Reconstruction."

While the edition containing this editorial was being delivered, Little Rock's Mayor Woodrow Wilson Mann was telling President Eisenhower, "I am pleading with you as President of the United States in the interest of humanity, law and order, and because of democracy worldwide to provide the necessary federal troops within several hours." Ike was highly annoyed by the whole mess. The President's chief black adviser, E. Frederick Morrow, recalled, "Civil rights in the Eisenhower administration was handled like a bad dream, or like something that's not very nice, and you shield yourself from it as long as you possibly can, because it just shouldn't be." Overriding Ike's annoyance, however, was his fury at Arkansas governor Orval Faubus, who had repeatedly promised he would handle the Little Rock desegregation crisis and who had repeatedly failed to do so. (With every delay, Faubus had also encouraged the active resistance of his white constituents.) Nor could the President ignore any longer the desperate entreaties of Mayor Mann. If Ike's sense of racial justice left a lot to be desired, his military strategy did not. He quickly dispatched five hundred men from the 101st Airborne Division, another five hundred miscellaneous paratroopers, and he federalized ten thousand men in the Arkansas National Guard. When the troops began rolling into Little Rock, Ike further directed that only paratroopers with bayonets were to take charge of the school, with the Arkansas guardsmen acting as backup. In that way, "brother-to-brother" conflicts could be held to a minimum.

Eisenhower's action sent shockwaves through Dixie and horrified Southern whites to the depths of their souls. As historian C. Vann Woodward noted, the spectacle of troops imposing the will of the federal government on a prostrate Southern city was "a flesh-and-blood materialization of ancestral nightmares that had troubled their sleep since childhood." It was Radical Reconstruction all over again. After the President's late evening television appearance explaining the reasons for his action, station WLBT in Jackson cut the national anthem that followed on the network and went directly to a spot ad from the Mississippi Citizens' Council: "Don't let this happen in Mississippi. Join the Citizens' Council today!"

The Southern White Citizens' Councils of the 1950s represented a confused attempt to defy the Supreme Court's ruling and at the same time to prevent a buildup of the Ku Klux Klan. With such extreme motives, the effort was doomed from the start. In Mississippi, a councilman announced, "We want the people assured that there is responsible leadership organized which will and can handle local segregation problems. If that is recognized, there will be no need for any 'hot-headed' bunch to start a Ku Klux Klan." Another councilman warned that white Southerners must "keep and pitch our battle on a high plane . . . keep our ranks free from the demagogue, the renegade, the lawless and the violent. . . ." What is reflected here is the fact that, over the years, untold millions of dollars had come into the South, expanding business and industry. Violence was bad for business, and most of the council leaders were businessmen. The councils were therefore determined to operate within the law and, in fact, took pride in being peopled by decent, respectful, middle-class white folks.

On the other hand, the official handbook of the councils was *Black Monday*, written by Thomas P. Brady, judge of the circuit court of the fourteenth district of Mississippi and later an associate justice of the State supreme court. Brady's handbook was as trashy a piece of negrophobia as ever put out by the Klan: "The Negro proposes to breed up his inferior intellect and whiten his skin and 'blow out the light' in the white man's brain and muddy his skin" —though exactly how the Negro would accomplish such wondrous alchemy Brady declined to say. In other council publications, Southerners were alerted to the fact that blacks were breeding grounds for syphilis, and "little white girls" would be "highly susceptible" to contracting syphilis from integrated "drinking fountains, books, towels, and gym clothes."

Since the councils practiced boycotts and cruelly intimidated free-thinking blacks, their much-paraded respectability was open to question. For example, when fifty-three blacks signed an integration petition in a Mississippi town, the council took out a full-page ad in the paper and printed their names and addresses; the blacks were subsequently fired from jobs, refused service in local stores, and a number were forced to leave town. Probably a majority of Southern whites disapproved of such practices, but most of them were afraid to speak out. Less hesitant were such gritty journalists as Montgomery's Grover Hall, Atlanta's Ralph McGill, and Greenville's Hodding Carter. "The manicured Kluxism of these White Citizens' Councils is rash, indecent, and vicious," wrote Hall. "The night-riding and lash of the 1920s have become an abomination in the eyes of public opinion. So the bigots have resorted to a more decorous, tidy, and less conspicuous method— economic thuggery." McGill and Carter likewise railed at the councils' hypocrisy and charged that they were simply "a scrubbed up cousin of the Klan," "a hoodless Klan," "an uptown Klan," "a button-down Klan," and "a country club Klan."

Certainly the councils represented the elite faction of militant segregationists, and an important effect of their organization was not so much eliminating the Klan but leaving it nothing but the violence-prone dregs of Southern white society. In the mid-1950s, sociologists began remarking on the fact that the Klan had become a collection of uneducated misfits, composed mostly of unskilled and semiskilled workers in the textile, construction, automotive, aircraft, coal, and steel industries. Robbed of effective leadership and public approval by the councils, such Klansmen had little recourse but to engage in violent acts. Between 1955 and 1959, the Southern Regional Council * reported 530 cases of suspected Klan violence in eleven Southern states. In 1959 alone there were twenty-seven bombings. "We feel an obligation to call attention to the dangers posed by the record-dangers," the Regional Council reported, "for which all of us, through silence or inaction, must share the responsibility."

A far more important effect of the White Citizens' Councils was the response they elicited in the black community. When blacks saw that even middle-class "respectable" whites had organized to deprive them of rights secured by the Supreme Court, they began to organize, too. A notable group was led by Robert Williams in

---

* The Southern Regional Council is an Atlanta-based civil rights agency. Formed in 1918 by a group of Southern whites, it has encouraged voter registration, published significant documents on racism, helped desegregate schools, and offered seminars and workshops on race relations.

Monroe, North Carolina. Williams was an ex-marine and war veteran who didn't scare easily. With a number of other black veterans, he formed a particularly strong chapter of the NAACP. Undaunted by the local council, Williams successfully integrated the Monroe Public Library and geared up to end discrimination in housing, employment, and public facilities. After his group began a "stand-in" at an all-white swimming pool, Klansmen began a very visible drive for members in Monroe and started riding in motorcades through the black community, honking their horns and firing pistols and shotguns. At one point they stopped a black woman on a streetcorner and forced her to dance at gunpoint.

When Williams's protests to local and state officials and even to President Eisenhower went unheard, he applied to the National Rifle Association and received a charter. Sixty members of his association began arming themselves, and Williams provided the training. When Klansmen learned of this, they nearly went berserk. In the summer of 1957, an armed motorcade of Klansmen drove into Williams's neighborhood, and Williams and his men shot it out with them, until the undisciplined Klansmen were forced to flee for their lives.

In total contrast was the response of the Montgomery Improvement Association,* organized by black clergymen to sustain a boycot against discriminatory practices on city buses. A suave and erudite twenty-seven-year-old minister, Martin Luther King, Jr., soon emerged as the leader of the movement. In one of his earliest addresses to the boycotters, King explained that they were going to use Gandhian methods of nonviolence, which he contrasted with those of the Klan:

> There comes a time that people get tired. We are here this evening to say to those who have mistreated us so long that we are tired—tired of being segregated and humiliated. But in our protest there will be no cross burnings. No white person will be taken from his home by a hooded Negro mob and brutally murdered. There will be no threats and no intimidation.

After a year-long, trouble-filled boycott, Montgomery blacks achieved a resounding victory. So successful were they that the

---

* Under Martin Luther King's direction, the Montgomery Improvement Association evolved into the Southern Christian Leadership Conference (SCLC), which spearheaded the black civil rights movement of the 1960s.

local Citizens' Council was all but destroyed. As one white put it, "A lot of people figured there wasn't much sense in sending their contributions and paying their dues to the Citizens Council after it spent all that time and effort in fighting the boycott and couldn't win. Some of them just quit, and some of them joined the Klan instead."

The failure of the councils in Little Rock, Montgomery, and other Southern cities did indeed turn more and more people to the Klan, and the buildup was visible by 1957. A year later, the Klan reached a peak of nearly forty thousand members, distributed in at least twenty-seven warring factions. The number of different Klans confused Klansmen themselves. William J. Griffin, Dragon of the Associated Florida Klans, claimed, "The old countersigns and passwords won't work because all Klansmen are strangers to each other." (As columnist Heywood Broun once remarked on the divisible empire, "Too many cooks spoil the witches' brew.") Florida Dragon Bill Hendrix called Klandom in the late 1950s "a conglomeration of different organizations breaking up, going together, and not getting along." Individual Klans were constantly involved in either splitting off from parent bodies or stealing members from each other. In a few instances they even took each other to court. As in the Klan of Reconstruction, there was considerable variation from one group to the next. Some Klans were quietly ineffective, some were violent, and some were borderline psychotic.

In January 1957, immediately after the success of the Montgomery bus boycott, the Klan bombed four black churches and a number of black residences in the city. A year later, a bomb nearly destroyed the Bethel Baptist Church. An elderly black man shook his head and said, "When they bomb the house of the Lord, we are dealing with crazy people." In fact, they were dealing with a "stark, raving crazy" person—as Stetson Kennedy had diagnosed J. B. Stoner twelve years earlier. Stoner was responsible for the Bethel bombing.* He had led a checkered career as a Klansman. He had been thrown out of a number of Klaverns because his rabid public addresses calling for the extermination of the Jews were too much even for the Klan. In 1952 Stoner formed the

---

* After nearly twenty years, Stoner was finally indicted for the Bethel bombing in 1977. He was convicted in 1980. He disappeared for several months and then resurfaced and began serving a ten-year sentence in 1983. At the present writing he is still in prison.

Christian Anti-Jewish Party. In 1959, he renamed the organization the Christian Knights of the Ku Klux Klan and appointed himself Imperial Wizard. Any Klansman was also welcome to affiliate with Stoner's freewheeling organization, and J.B. himself was something of a Klansman-at-large, quick to smell a potential for violence in an area and quick to get there and exploit it.

Slightly more crazy than Stoner's organization was Asa "Ace" Carter's Alabama-based Original Ku Klux Klan of the Confederacy, which resembled a cell of Nazi storm troopers. Regular members wore Confederate-gray robes instead of white, while "Ace"— once an acid-mouthed radio announcer who had been expelled from a White Citizens' Council for his extremism—called himself "Grand Marshal" and enjoyed strutting about in khakis and paratrooper boots. Initiations in Carter's Klan included a ritual slashing of wrists and documents signed in blood. A tragic consequence of these blood rites occurred on Labor Day, 1957, when a Klavern of Original Ku Klux abducted Edward Aaron, a thirty-four-year-old black handyman, near Birmingham; castrated him with razor blades; and then tortured him by pouring kerosene and turpentine over his wounds. According to the testimony of the Klansman who turned state's evidence (he had vomited and nearly passed out when Aaron's testicles were passed around in a paper cup),the mutilation had been committed simply as a test of one of the members' mettle before being elected "captain of the lair." The four men responsible for the atrocity were sentenced to twenty years each but were paroled shortly after George Wallace became governor in 1963. Soon after the mutilation, "Ace" Carter himself whipped out a revolver and plugged two of his own Klansmen for probing too deeply into how Klan dues were being spent. Carter got off without conviction and later became a top-ranking aide to Governor Wallace.

If Carter's Klan was the most demonic of the late 1950s groups, then the North Carolina Knights of the Ku Klux Klan was the most ludicrous. James "Catfish" Cole was the driving force behind the Carolina Knights, and Cole had been convicted numerous times for reckless driving, drunken driving, and driving without a license. Once a carnival huckster and circus pitchman, Cole now fancied himself a Baptist minister. "I'm a minister of the Gospel," he informed a gathering, "and I'm here to tell you God's side: He never meant for niggers and whites to mix." If Catfish had stuck to such profound sermons, he might have been better off. Instead he decided to launch a crusade against the Lumbee Indians of Robeson County.

The proud and independent Lumbees, who had never had a tribal organization, had lived peaceably and prosperously as farmers in Robeson County for over two hundred years. Members of the county upheld a formal three-way segregation for blacks, whites, and Indians, but Cole charged that "Indian women and white men" were "running around together." His group burned crosses in front of the home of a Lumbee woman who was supposedly guilty of relations with a white man, as well as on the lawns of Lumbees who had moved into a white neighborhood. Catfish decided to hold a mass rally against the Lumbees on January 18, 1958. Although he announced that five hundred Klansmen would turn out for the rally, only forty showed up. When the little group got to the deserted field where the rally was to take place, they found to their horror that the road was lined up and down with nearly a thousand Indians. Reporters and photographers soon arrived. Although the Klansmen refused to have anything to do with the press corps, the Lumbees happily posed for photographers. Some of them laughed, gave whoops, and one performed a war dance in the middle of the road. When Cole realized that no more Klansmen were coming, he tried to begin the evening's festivities. Without warning, the Lumbees began whooping, rushed the Klansmen, smashed their floodlight, and demolished their electrical generator and public address system. After gleefully running off with the large *KKK* banner, several of them paused to fire shotguns at the dust-churning tires of Klansmen who couldn't escape from the scene fast enough. Journalists had a field day: "Look who's biting the dust! Palefaces!" *Life* magazine concluded that, like Custer, "the Klan had just taken on too many Indians." For his misguided part in the fiasco, Catfish Cole was indicted for inciting a riot and was sentenced to eighteen to twenty-four months in prison.

The strongest and best organized Klan was the only one able to maintain satellites outside of its home state. In 1953, Eldon Lee Edwards, a paint sprayer at the Fisher body plant in Atlanta, had gathered up the remnants of the Association of Georgia Klans and renamed the organization U.S. Klans, Knights of the Ku Klux Klan. He then revised Colonel Simmons's original rituals and had them recopyrighted. With the help of his attorney Sam Green, Jr. (son of Doc), Edwards obtained a new Georgia charter for the U.S. Klans in 1955. In effect, he had refurbished a direct link between his organization and the Klan of the 1920s. With some justification, then, Edwards could dismiss all other Klans as "outlaws and counterfeiters." By 1959, he had established a thriving parent organization in Georgia, with strong chapters in South Carolina, Alabama, Louisiana, and lesser ones in five other Southern states. Edwards was determined to exert strong central leadership over these satellites, and for the most part, he succeeded by talking big and acting discreetly. Newsmen claimed the new Imperial Wizard was possessed of "a certain force of personality and an almost benign expression on his nicely mustached face." In any event, Edwards made "a better appearance in Klan regalia than most of his rivals."

On Stone Mountain in late September 1956, Edwards hosted the best-attended ritual cross burning since the end of World War II. Nearly fifteen hundred more people came than had participated in Doc Green's revival ten years earlier, and the new Wizard proclaimed the Invisible Empire "as solid as Stone Mountain." The next year, a CBS television special on the Klan gave Edwards the spotlight. Northern viewers learned that Southern Klansmen pronounced the name of the organization "Cue Klux Klan." In the course of the telecast, Edwards said that the Klan's purpose was "maintaining segregated schools at any and all cost." He also said the Klan was composed of "decent, respectful, law-abiding, and level-headed people" concerned for the Southern way of life. "We have been accused for over ninety years as cutthroats and those who take the law into their own hands," Edwards blared. "If the Supreme Court can't maintain our Southern way of life then we *are* going to do something about it." By 1959, Edwards's domain extended over fifteen thousand multistate Klansmen—the largest Klan of the 1950s and one that would survive into the next decade.

In spring 1960, journalists reported a dynamic change in the Klan. On the first of March, Klansmen announced plans for a whirlwind drive to recruit 10 million members in thirty states. On Saturday evening, March 26, crosses were set on fire shortly after ten o'clock all over Dixie. An official of the Anti-Defamation League said that "the wave of cross-burnings indicates a coordinated effort to unify all the Klans." In Monroeville, Alabama, one-third of the city's population attended a rally and cross burning. Klan signs were posted alongside those of service clubs welcoming motorists to major Southern cities.

There were at least three reasons for this sudden mobilization in the spring of 1960. First of all, it had become obvious that the

Citizens' Councils had completely failed by "respectable" means to stay the tide of school desegregation. *U.S. News & World Report* correctly observed that "if legal barriers to integration continue to crumble, more people will turn to the Klan for the last stand." Secondly, a new generation of blacks was becoming more demonstrative in demanding civil rights. In February, McNeil Joseph, a seventeen-year-old freshman at Greensboro's North Carolina Agricultural and Technical College, had taken three friends to a segregated lunch counter at Woolworth's and staged what he called a "sit-in." The tactic soon spread to Atlanta and, within two months, was being used in sixty-eight Southern cities. Members of the Congress of Racial Equality (CORE) and the Student Nonviolent Coordinating Committee (SNCC) enlisted volunteers for the sit-ins and coordinated their activities. The involvement of outsiders was especially galling to Southern whites. In Montgomery, Safety Commissioner L. B. Sullivan declared, "Not since Reconstruction have our customs been in such jeopardy. . . . We can, will and must resist outside forces hellbent on our destruction." Around this time, author John Steinbeck was completing a cross-country tour of America with a dyspeptic poodle named Charley. "I knew I was not wanted in the South," Steinbeck observed. "When people are engaged in something they are not proud of, they do not welcome witnesses. In fact, they come to believe the witness causes the trouble."

Finally, 1960 was an election year—the first presidential contest since the practical meaning of the 1954 Supreme Court ruling had been fully grasped. The leading Democratic contender had automatically raised the hackles of Klansmen because he was a Catholic. Even worse, he favored mandatory integration and had blithely approved the sit-ins. "It is the American tradition to stand up for one's rights," said John F. Kennedy, "even if the new way to stand up for one's rights is to sit down."

11

"THE ROARING SIXTIES"

JFK, the Klan,
and the Second Reconstruction:
1960–1964

During the presidential campaign of 1960, the two candidates met in a unique series of televised debates. It was the first time that most of the American people were able to hear and see both major party candidates argue issues face-to-face, and the novelty of it had schoolteachers and news analysts recounting the Lincoln–Douglas debates a century earlier. During the first debate, Republican Richard Nixon assumed Eisenhower's posture and cautiously sidestepped the issue of civil rights. In contrast, his Democratic opponent John F. Kennedy launched into a moving description of the plight of American blacks, supporting it with detailed statistics that would soon become one of his trademarks. Kennedy said that a black baby in 1960 had "about one-half as much chance of completing high school as a white baby born in the same place on the same day, one-third as much chance of completing college, one-third as much chance of becoming a professional, twice as much chance of becoming unemployed . . . a life expectancy which is seven years shorter, and the prospects of earning only half as much." Certain Southerners realized there was something objectionable about Kennedy, but like certain Northerners their first objection was to his religion. A number of Southern Protestant leaders joined Norman Vincent Peale and the Citizens for Religious Freedom in decrying Kennedy's Catholicism. Alabama Methodists expressed fear of the "political machinations of a determined, power-hungry Romanist hierarchy," and the president of the Southern Baptist Convention raised doubts about any candidate "under control of the Roman Catholic Church."

This was old-time Klan rhetoric, and Klansmen were hardly willing to be outdone by outsiders on their own bugaboos. South Carolina Kligrapp Robert E. Hodges told a gathering: "You cannot afford to support or vote for anyone or group that represents the Roman Catholic Church. . . . Heaven help your soul if you vote away your religious liberty." Other Klansmen realized that Kennedy's religion was far less dangerous than his civil rights platform, on which he had said he could run "with enthusiasm and conviction." As in 1928 and 1948, Klansmen again tried to turn Southern Democrats away from the Democratic Party. "Anybody that'll vote the Democratic ticket," said a Klan speaker at a rally, "will become a traitor to the Southland and to the Constitution of the United States." Alabama governor John Patterson had won his office with the help of Klansmen who had drummed up votes for him and had torn down his opponent's campaign posters. After endorsing JFK for President, however, Patterson was visited by a delegation of thirty-two Klansmen headed by the Imperial Kladd who asked, "Did it ever occur to you that you are being used as a guinea pig by the Communist-Jewish integrators to sample the political sentiments of the South for . . . John Kennedy?" When Patterson confirmed his support of Kennedy, Alabama Klansmen included him in their attacks on the Democratic candidate. Kennedy, they said, "has got Negroes all over the South working; in fact, he stated that he would integrate Negroes everywhere possible in his campaign for the presidency. Now how can our governor come out and support an integrationist, an outright integrationist?" Florida Grand Dragon William J. Griffin announced flatly that, in spite of ancient ties to the Democratic Party, he and his white-robed flock would vote for Richard Nixon.

As a Catholic, Kennedy was more knowledgeable about the Klan than any candidate since Al Smith, and he delighted in Florida Klansmen's endorsement of his opponent. After Harlem congressman Adam Clayton Powell complained that "the Ku Klux Klan is riding again in this campaign," Kennedy was asked to comment during the third televised debate. "Well," he said, "Mr. Griffin, I believe, who is the head of the Klan, who lives in Tampa, Florida, indicated in a statement, I think two or three weeks ago, that he was not going to vote for me and that he was going to vote for Mr. Nixon. I do not suggest in any way—nor have I ever— that that indicates that Mr. Nixon has the slightest sympathy . . . in regard to the Ku Klux Klan."

Nixon wholeheartedly agreed: "I obviously repudiate the Klan."

In response, Florida Klansmen reaffirmed their support of Nixon and spent an evening burning crosses. Said the Palatka (Florida) *News:* "Every time human beings make a public spectacle of burning a cross we can't help but wonder if Christ remains nailed on it."

If the Klan contributed little to the outcome of the 1960 election, the Kennedy campaign contributed significantly to the growth of the Klan. In March 1960, Klan membership was estimated at around ten thousand. Ten months later, when JFK took office, that number had more than doubled. In the brief course of the Kennedy presidency and that of his successor, Lyndon Johnson, the Klan and its sympathizers fought what they perceived to be a second Reconstruction. They felt that, once again, a federal government was trying to pass "fanatic" legislation that would overturn the South's "cherished way of life." Hordes of federal agents and marshals and swarms of Northern carpetbaggers would descend upon Dixie to "destroy our time-honored customs." Scalawags sympathetic to civil rights would be intimidated by anonymous letters, obscene phone calls, and worse. "Uppity" blacks would be flogged, maimed, shot, and blown up. And the Ku Klux Klan would take its most violent stand since 1871.

Historian C. Vann Woodward had seen it coming for several years. "*It is a real Constitutional crisis that we are facing,*" he warned, "*not a sham parade in ancestral costume.*" Woodward's worst fear was that the second Reconstruction would be doomed in the end to repeat the frustration and failure of the first. He nevertheless saw four reasons for hope. The old Reconstruction had driven the border states into sympathy with the former Confederacy; this was less likely to be repeated now. A century earlier, Southern resistance had been galvanized by mass appeals to prejudice; Woodward saw a new generation in the South and an overall attitude nationally that would resist such appeals. Thirdly, although Reconstruction had split the Protestant churches at the Mason–Dixon line, "virtually all major national churches, supported by their Southern branches, have in some degree come out against the segregation system." Finally and most importantly, "Blacks were infinitely better equipped to defend themselves and advance their cause than were their newly emancipated grandfathers and great-grandfathers."

There were at least two more reasons for optimism. A new electronic media would keep a watchful eye on daily happenings, revealing them starkly to the American public and preventing distortions by future historians. And the second Reconstruction benefited from the talents of two men who were masters of the electronic media: an inspired black minister, Martin Luther King, and a pragmatic white politician, JFK, who would work in an uneasy but highly productive tandem.

The Supreme Court had ruled against segregated bus stations in 1958, and in the first months of the Kennedy administration James Farmer of CORE decided to dramatize how little the ruling was being respected in the South. Two buses carrying a total of six white and seven black "freedom riders" set out on May 4 to challenge segregation in stations and snack bars from Washington, D.C., to New Orleans. Down to Atlanta, things went reasonably well, but trouble was waiting in Alabama. When the first bus reached the Anniston station, it was overturned and torched by a crowd of angry whites "Let's roast 'em!" someone yelled. Riders were barely able to evacuate the bus before it exploded in cascading flames before the cameras of horrified newsmen. The second bus was boarded by eight young hoodlums who beat the riders with clubs. "Goddamn niggers!" they screamed. "Why don't you white Communists stay up North?" The shaken riders tried to clean and bandage themselves while the bus rolled on to Birmingham.

At the Birmingham station, a group of twenty-five plainclothes Klansmen from the Eastview Klavern was already waiting, and their planned assault was fully backed by the Birmingham police. A detective on the force had told them they had exactly fifteen minutes "to beat them, bomb them, burn them, shoot them, do anything [they] wanted to with absolutely no intervention whatsoever by the police." Among the Klansmen was an FBI informer who had reported the planned attack, as well as the collusion of the police, to his bureau contact three weeks earlier. According to the informer, his contact said, "We have to, by law, instruct you that you're not to participate in any violence." But the bureau was not going to interrupt or otherwise try to stop the attack. The important thing, the informer was told, was "to get information."

Among the freedom riders were James Peck of New York and

Walter Bergman, a sixty-two-year-old retired director of the Detroit public school system. Peck recounted: "As we entered the white waiting room and approached the lunch counter, we were grabbed bodily and pushed toward the alleyway leading to the loading platform. As soon as we were out of sight of onlookers in the waiting room, six of them started swinging at me with fists and pipes."

"You're a shame to the white race!" shouted one.

"Get him!" said another. "Get him! Jesus, get him good!"

After fifteen minutes of unrestrained brutality, the police finally arrived, and the officer in charge was surprised and then furious that the boys had exceeded their allotted time. "Goddammit!" he roared at the Klan leader. "Goddammit, your fifteen minutes is up! Get 'em out of here." When outraged reporters asked Police Chief "Bull" Connor why his men hadn't been at the station when the bus arrived, Bull explained that it was Mother's Day. A lot of officers were with their mothers and the force was undermanned. The fact that the FBI had been tipped off and did nothing wasn't even revealed until fourteen years later.*

The most seriously injured riders took a plane to New Orleans, and their places were filled by student veterans of the sit-ins and black and white members of SNCC and the Southern Christian Leadership Conference (SCLC). The Kennedy administration provided them with a new bus which they boarded, now bound for Montgomery. There they were again met by a Klan-led mob who greeted them with swinging clubs and pipes. Governor Patterson had previously assured Attorney General Robert F. Kennedy that he would provide protection for the riders in Montgomery, but it was apparent to the attorney general that the governor had either lied or was unable to do so. John Doar from the Justice Department phoned Bobby Kennedy from Montgomery, saying the viciousness of the mob was "the most horrible thing I've ever seen. It's terrible, terrible."

The attorney general immediately asked for federal injunctions against the leader of the Alabama Klansmen and another against the Montgomery police. He also dispatched more than five hundred deputy federal marshals to Montgomery. Governor John

---

* In spring 1983, after a long series of legal volleys, Bergman and Peck sued the FBI for the permanent injuries they sustained from its failure to prevent the Klan's attack. In February 1984, Bergman was awarded $50,000 by a federal court in Kalamazoo and Peck $25,000 by one in New York.

Patterson was aghast at the use of marshals and phoned the attorney general to carp and criticize. Those in Kennedy's office heard him say to the governor, "John, John, what do you mean you're being invaded? Who's invading you, John? You know better than that."

Few Americans were sympathetic toward the freedom riders. The general feeling was they had pretty much gotten what they had asked for. Newscaster Howard K. Smith was fired by CBS News for his vivid but accurate account of the Klan beatings. Apparently, said Smith, CBS's "southern affiliates were complaining rather bitterly." The President, however, believed that the right to move freely in interstate commerce was as legitimate as freedom of the press. "Whether we agree with the purpose for which they travel," he said in a press conference, "those rights stand—providing they are exercised in a peaceful way." Consequently, the Kennedys asked the Interstate Commerce Commission to order the desegregation of all facilities and terminals used in interstate bus travel. The ICC obeyed on September 22. When a few cities pleaded local ordinances as an excuse for noncompliance, the Justice Department brought suit and, at the same time, took action against segregated airports and railroad stations. It was a small victory but a dramatic one. "Bless God!" exclaimed an amazed black Alabama woman. "We now have a President who's going to make sure we can go anywhere we want like the white folks in this country."

The invasion of the South by Greyhounds filled with courageous carpetbaggers—not to mention the five hundred marshals—provided a critical rallying point for splintered Klandom. Important changes were already occurring within the Invisible Empire. Eldon Lee Edwards, Imperial Wizard of the dominant U.S. Klans, had died in August 1960. His successor "Wild Bill" Davidson was unacceptable to Edwards's widow, so "Wild Bill" and his second-in-command, Calvin Craig, the Grand Dragon of Georgia, not only defected but took with them 97 percent of the U.S. Klans' membership. Davidson and Craig then formed the Invisible Empire, United Klans, Knights of the Ku Klux Klan of America, Inc., that was given a charter in Fulton County, Georgia, on February 21, 1961. Soon afterward, Klansmen became irritated with "Wild Bill" when he objected to their anti-integration demonstrations at the University of Georgia, and Davidson resigned in April. Negotiations were then opened between Calvin Craig and the dynamic leader of the independent Alabama Knights, Robert Marvin

"Bobby" Shelton, who had the distinction of being recently served with an injunction from the U.S. attorney general for the role his men had played in beating the freedom riders.

In the wake of the "invasion" of Alabama, five hundred Klansmen from Craig's and Shelton's organizations, as well as from splinter Klans in seven Southern states, held a meeting on July 8 at Indian Springs, Georgia. In the course of the meeting, interstate squabbles were resolved, and the splinter groups merged with the Georgia and Alabama units into a new organization that would be called the United Klans of America (UKA). The UKA would continue to use the Fulton County charter. The undeniable star of the conference was Bobby Shelton, who came attended by an eight-man military guard dressed in white shirts, red ties, khaki paratrooper pants, black boots, and marine helmets, with bayonets hooked to the left side of their white belts. The swaggering militance of Shelton and his followers was just what was needed in future showdowns with the Kennedys, civil rights activists, and all others who dared dispute the Southern way of life. At the end of the conference, Shelton won the office of Imperial Wizard by acclamation. Imperial Headquarters of the UKA would now be transferred from Atlanta to Shelton's home in Tuscaloosa, Alabama.

In one respect, Imperial Wizard Shelton was like the new President he detested: Each was the youngest man ever elected to his respective office. In 1961, Shelton was only thirty-two years old. He had joined the Klan after experiencing integration in the Air Force. Returning to Tuscaloosa, he had taken charge of the Alabama realm of the U.S. Klans and worked for the B. F. Goodrich Company, first in the tire plant and then as a salesman. After throwing Klan support to the election of John Patterson, Shelton secured Goodrich a $1.6 million contract with the state. While Grand Dragon of Alabama, Shelton had been twice removed and once reinstated by Imperial Wizard Edwards for failing to turn in Klan dues. According to Shelton, he and Edwards had "had some differences in opinion about policies and procedures." When Edwards's "dictatorial powers" grew too much for Shelton, he took the Alabama realm and bolted. Now as full-time Wizard of the UKA, the largest multistate Klan, Shelton became the leading figure of the Invisible Empire during the 1960s.

A lean, long-faced, emotionless man, Shelton impressed reporters with his bright blue eyes. He carried himself with conscious pride and was seldom seen to smile. Suspicious of interviewers and reporters, the new Wizard nevertheless liked to talk. He felt no need to downplay his beliefs, which were often interesting for their shock value alone. His softly flowing, self-assured speech was all the more engaging for its malapropisms and mispronunciations— like "confisicate" for "confiscate" and "sway-doe" for "pseudo." Most of Shelton's early statements concerned race, and his information sometimes seemed to have come from an occult grimoire. For example, he learned to expect "a spontaneous rise" in black activity "when the moon comes full. My research shows that the full moon brings out the animal instincts, increases their excitement, and they become violent, restless, inclined to get in trouble and brawls." Blacks were also a dangerous source of contamination. "Tell anyone you know that is hiring a nigger," he warned, that "it is very dangerous to hire them, especially as a baby sitter. All they have to do is cut their finger, drop a drop of blood in the baby's food and it will be dead within a year from sickle cell anemia."

In other matters, Shelton hated foreign-made products as much as labor unions. He was an early proponent of the belief that the fluoridation of water led to mind control. "What's a better way to take over this country than to give an overdose of fluoridation?" Consistently enough, he opposed the National Mental Health Association as a Communist plot, bent on brainwashing the South into accepting integration. A devoted family man and devout Methodist, Shelton believed in a strong Christian foundation for the Klan, coupled with an equally strong anti-Semitism: "I don't hate niggers, but I hate the Jews. The nigger's a child, but the Jews are dangerous people. . . . All they want is control and domination of the Gentiles through a conspiracy with the niggers." Shelton believed that all Jews—even Albert Einstein—were by nature "communistic."

Shelton commanded a strong trio of lieutenants. Calvin Craig was the UKA's Grand Dragon in Georgia. Craig had been led into the Klan by his mother, and what he liked about the organization was its power. "I can take five Klansmen into any small city in the U.S.," he told *Life* magazine, "and it's just like an army. They're feared and they're respected." Robert Scoggin was Grand Dragon of South Carolina and worked diligently to arouse Klan interest in that state where there had been little interest since Reconstruction. Scoggin also worked hard for himself, managing one year to deposit $15,690 in personal accounts while reporting an annual income of only $574.

Shelton's most effective lieutenant was hefty James R. "Bob" Jones, a lightning-rod salesman and Grand Dragon of North Carolina. The son of two Klan parents, Jones was seemingly indestructible. As a construction worker he survived having a steel beam smash into his face, requiring 119 stitches and leaving him permanently scarred; a car wreck left him with a limp. His friends called him The Horse. He spent eighteen hours a day on Klan work, driving 100,000 miles a year across North Carolina, surviving daily on twenty cups of coffee, four to five packs of cigarettes, and countless cheese crackers. Jones was a bit more tolerant than the average Dragon. "The trouble is not the colored people," he would say. "Trouble is the radicals and the niggers." A devoted family man whose wife shared his enthusiasm for the Klan, he tried to exert a father's authority over his intractable "children":

It has been brought to my attention that some towns and counties while putting out posters and circulars, put these in mail boxes. This as you know and have been told is illegal. The postmaster general says I am going to have to pay for each poster and circular and in turn, each county and town responsible is also going to pay. From now on please do not mess with anything belonging to the federal government.

There has been a lot of unnecessary talking and confusion behind the ropes at rallys. This distracts the speakers and the audience, so please refrain from this as much as possible. . . .

. . . any man in leadership capacity of United Klans of America found under the influence of alcohol will be replaced without fear or favor. . . . not drinking in public is a small price to pay for the freedom of our country.

By 1966, the North Carolina realm of the UKA was the largest of its empire, boasting 192 Klaverns, nearly seventy-five hundred members, and furnishing at least one-third of the Imperial Treasury. The North Carolina Klan was relatively nonviolent—a surprising fact attributable to its visible strength, which it tried to channel politically, and to the paternal control of Bob Jones.

In addition to the UKA, at least a dozen other independent Klans operated during the 1960s. Efforts by the UKA to bring these groups into the fold were usually resisted out of desires for local autonomy and because independent Klansmen didn't want to send part of their dues to the Imperial Treasury in Tuscaloosa. As a measure of self-preservation, some of these Klans formed a loose federation which they called the National Association of Ku Klux Klans. They selected as their chairman James R. Venable, an Atlanta attorney.

Venable was something of a paterfamilias of Kluxdom. He was a forty-year veteran of the Invisible Empire who had remained active in one Klan or another since 1924. Much of his law practice was devoted to the defense of Klan lawbreakers. His family owned part of Stone Mountain. His philosophy reeked of the ideas of Thomas Watson and Thomas Dixon. "I can't see how any white man can think the nigger is equal," said this professional lawyer. "In Africa, the richest land in the world, he's never been able to build a skyscraper. Without the Klan we all would have been spotted, or some other color." Venable longed for the good old days when the Klan was a real power in Georgia. When it became obvious that such a loose-knit group as the National Association couldn't rekindle that power, he formed his own organization in November 1963, called it the National Knights of the Ku Klux Klan, and appointed himself Imperial Wizard. Venable's National Knights was largely a paper-and-pencil, mail-order outfit with hardly any following outside Georgia. Anyone could join it by simply writing and mailing in the $15 fee. This practice led to Venable's national embarrassment in 1965 when he admitted Paul L. Bellesen from Nampa, Idaho. Not only was Bellesen black, but Venable appointed him Grand Titan of Idaho and told him to set up a Klavern in his local community.

In 1962, James Meredith, a twenty-nine-year-old black Air Force veteran, attempted to enroll in the all-white University of Mississippi in Oxford. In the short run, Meredith's enrollment would lead to another crisis for the Kennedy administration; in the long run it would provide the impetus for spawning a new Klan—the most fanatic and violent Klan of the 1960s. President Kennedy spent hours on the phone talking to Governor Ross Barnett about Meredith and taped a number of the conversations. What is striking about these conversations is how far Kennedy went toward accommodating the anxiety of Mississippi whites; and how hard he tried to get the governor to share responsibility for Meredith's safe enrollment.

"Here's my problem, Governor," he said. "I don't know Mr. Meredith, and I didn't put him in there. But under the Constitution, I have to carry out the law. I want your help in doing it. . . .

What we are concerned about is whether you will maintain law and order—prevent the gathering of a mob and action taken by a mob. . . . As I understand it, you will do everything you can to maintain order. Next, Governor, *can* you maintain order?"

Governor Barnett couldn't and wouldn't, and received plenty of support for his position. Typical of the response of Mississippi's newspapers was Tom Ethridge's acid editorial in the Jackson *Clarion-Ledger*: "Little brother [RFK] has evidently concluded that the South must be forced to abandon its customs and traditions in deference to 'world opinion'—especially that of Asiatic cow-worshippers and African semi-savages not far removed from cannibalism." Klansmen in Anniston, Alabama, wired Barnett, assuring him that hundreds of white knights were "on a stand-by alert waiting for your call to protect the state sovereignty of Mississippi."

On October 1, 1962, when federal marshals attempted to escort James Meredith onto the campus of Ole Miss, the result was an all-night blitzkrieg by white students and out-of-state demonstrators—some of them Klansmen—who fired guns, hurled abuse, and threw rocks and molotov cocktails. While the President went on national television asking students to "uphold the honor" of "Ole Miss," Robert Kennedy stayed glued to the phone, listening to the mounting riot. The attorney general asked his representative Edwin Guthman how it was going.

"Pretty rough," Guthman replied. "This place is sort of like the Alamo."

"Well," Bobby said hopefully, "you know what happened to *those* guys."

Only after JFK sent three thousand armed troops and National Guardsmen into Oxford was Meredith allowed on campus. The insurrection had proved costly, not just in terms of dollars. Two people had been killed, including a French correspondent; and in a press conference, the President announced that American prestige abroad had suffered. He further stated that his actions in Oxford were fully justified: "This country, of course, cannot survive if the United States Government and the executive branch do not carry out the decisions of the Court. It might be a decision, in this case, which some people may not agree with. The next time it might be another matter, and this government would unravel very fast." Privately, JFK was angry over the fact that he had given Mississippi every possible chance to avert bloodshed and it had refused. He had been critical of Eisenhower's abrupt and overwhelming response in Little Rock and, in contrast, had used a series of small, intermediate steps, naïvely trusting the good will of the white South. (*Time* magazine commented, "President Kennedy could have learned one lesson from Eisenhower's performance . . . if forced to intervene, then intervene with sufficient force.") Kennedy's reluctance to use greater force sprang from his own misconceptions about the first Reconstruction. Not only was the President misinformed, but he himself had helped perpetuate some of Reconstruction's worst myths. In *Profiles in Courage,* Kennedy had written about how the radical Republicans attempted to "crush their despised foe" and wreak "vengeance" on poor Andrew Johnson; he had called Benjamin Franklin Butler a "demogogic Congressman" and Thaddeus Stevens "the crippled, fanatical personification" of extremism. All these factors, Kennedy had said, "helped make the Reconstruction period a black nightmare the South would never forget." As President, Kennedy certainly wanted to avoid reviving that nightmare a century later.

The President began to revise his thoughts on the South's past and present. He was shocked and disgusted by a report prepared by the Mississippi legislature that laid the entire blame for the riot on the federal government and the U.S. marshals. Kennedy's special counsel Theodore Sorensen recalled: "These and other similar incidents convinced the President that historians who rely on local documents may not be getting a true history, and he specifically wondered aloud whether all that he had been taught and all that he had believed about the evils of Reconstruction were really true."

Over the next few days, Kennedy devoured C. Vann Woodward's books on Reconstruction and told his brother, "If southern whites could behave this way now, they must have behaved the same way a hundred years ago." When an assassin murdered Medgar Evers, the Mississippi NAACP leader who had counseled James Meredith during his ordeal at Ole Miss, Kennedy was utterly sickened. "I'm coming to believe Thaddeus Stevens was right," he told Arthur Schlesinger. "I had always been taught to regard him as a man of vicious bias. But when I see this sort of thing, I begin to wonder how else you can treat them." Henceforth, the President would be less hesitant in handling civil rights matters. A month after Ole Miss, he issued an executive order forbidding segregation in federally owned or insured housing. He asked his cabinet to start thinking about a civil rights bill. Alluding to Ole Miss, he asked the attorney general if there were "any more like this one coming up soon." Bobby replied that there was another lawsuit in progress and wryly suggested that his brother be prepared to lose the electoral votes of Alabama in 1964, just as he had undoubtedly lost those of Mississippi.

The President didn't react to the joke. "Let's be ready," he said grimly.

The civil rights bill Kennedy sent to Congress in February 1963 soon died in committee. "There wasn't any interest in it," explained the attorney general. "There was no public demand for it. There was no demand by the newspapers or radio or television." In this centennial year of the Emancipation Proclamation, Martin Luther King decided to give prospective civil rights legislation the publicity it needed. For the site he selected Birmingham, Alabama, where 40 percent of the residents were blacks living under conditions of blatant segregation and humiliation.

On April 3, 1963, King issued a "Birmingham Manifesto" that called for the end of segregation in public facilities and the establishment of a local biracial committee for racial fairness in other aspects of the community. When local whites flatly rejected King's terms, the SCLC began sit-ins and marches. When the city served injunctions to prevent these demonstrations, King ignored them and was locked in solitary confinement in the local jail. Thus far, the Kennedys could do little, but the attorney general called the Birmingham police, demanding that King be released from solitary and allowed to call his wife on the phone. When Coretta King explained what Robert Kennedy had done, her husband remarked with surprise, "So that's why everybody is suddenly being so polite." In the middle of April, King composed a moving and eloquent "Letter from Birmingham Jail," now regarded a classic of American protest literature. In response to his continued confinement, hundreds of high-school-age and younger black students began nonviolent marches, and television viewers across the nation watched as they were hauled off to jail in Birmingham paddy wagons and school buses.

On May 2, when the children as well as adults resumed the marches, Chief "Bull" Connor unleashed his worst. Fire trucks rolled in, and demonstrators were hosed down by thrashing torrents of water that ripped their clothes and battered them against buildings and the pavement. Connor then set loose specially trained "nigger dogs," who lunged, snarled, and bit the protesters. Cameras whirred and clicked, capturing one of the ugliest spectacles ever seen in the nation. "God bless America," said one reporter as he walked away in disgust. On the CBS evening news, political commentator Eric Sevareid proclaimed, "A snarling police dog set upon a human being is recorded in the permanent photoelectric file of every human being's brain." Certainly some whites were sympathetic to the protesters, but many others, Northerners as well as Southerners, felt the Birmingham police had simply been pushed past their limit by radical blacks willing to risk the lives of their children in such demonstrations of futility. When asked to comment on which was worse, the use of children by the protesters or the use of fire hoses by the police, JFK declined and instead remarked on how the situation was damaging the reputation of both Birmingham and the United States. "And it seems to me," he added, "that the best way to prevent that kind of damage, which is very serious, is to in time take steps to provide equal treatment to all of our citizens."

It was the profit-drained white businessmen of Birmingham who ultimately forced a settlement to the conflict. Robert Kennedy's Justice Department adroitly stepped in at this point, and Burke Marshall, the much-respected head of the Civil Rights Division, helped negotiate an agreement between the white and black communities. By May 10, a settlement was reached promising desegregation and equality for all. King was entirely satisfied with the arrangement and left for Atlanta.

On the next day, Saturday, the UKA held a large and noisy rally outside Birmingham. A reporter from WRVR, a small radio station operated by New York's Riverside Church, managed to work his way to the front of the rally and secretly tape-record it. In contrast to the written record, what emerges from the tape is the degree of fear Klansmen and women were feeling at this time—a fear that their very world was crumbling around them. Grand Dragons from Mississippi, Tennessee, Georgia, and South Carolina came and promised undying support for the decent white folks of Birmingham who had been ravaged by "that nigger" and his "nigger-loving friends in the White House." It is clear that the UKA's support helped buoy the confidence of the white community and turn it into defiance.

The meeting began with a "Brother Kleagle" announcing that Birmingham was suffering "the greatest darkness this nation has ever faced." Then Calvin Craig voiced his conviction that "Martin Luther King and the Attorney General has done more to create unrest in this country than Castro has in Cuba."

"Right!" "That's right!" the crowd shouted.

"We need to go back to the old-time religion," said Craig, "and to the old-time *Klan* religion."

"Amen!"

"Twenty years ago, Martin Luther King couldn't have got across this state alive preachin' inter-gration."

Cheers and applause.

The Grand Dragon of Tennessee then spoke. "We are all in sympathy with you people here in Alabama," he said. "We're the 'Volunteers' in Tennessee. Just call us. We'll help ya."

The Grand Dragon of South Carolina assured the Alabamans, "We'll live and die for you." He also remarked that it "cuts deep to know the federal government urged this Communistic tie" with blacks.

The Kleagle concluded the ceremonies with a sales pitch: "Let's make it the Roaring Sixties! Be a white man—a *real* man. Join the Klan!" The meeting then closed with a prayer from the Reverend Kludd: "Heavenly Father, we're grateful we're white. . . ."

In the early hours of the next morning, Birmingham was rocked by a series of loud explosions. Two bombs had demolished the home of A.D. King, Martin's brother, and more blasts had damaged the Gaston Hotel from which Martin and other SCLC leaders had just departed. It was probably the work of Klansmen who had attended the rally of the previous evening. Making bombs was one of the specialties of the UKA Klansmen. As early as October 1961, the UKA had sponsored training seminars, led by a former Navy frogman, who had showed them how to rig dynamite, select the proper fuse, and attend to all the various details of proper bombmaking. Fortunately no one was killed from the Birmingham blasts, but outraged blacks began a riot that was eased only by the strategic intervention of Burke Marshall and by Dr. King's return to the city. When Alabama state police threatened to stop the riot by massive force, JFK flew three thousand troops to an air base near Birmingham and kept them there until a peace was reached by diplomatic means.

The next month, the integration of the University of Alabama at Tuscaloosa was scheduled. The state had a new governor, George Wallace, who in his inaugural address had paraphrased a very well-known Klan motto: "In the name of the greatest people that have ever trod this earth, I draw the line in the dust and toss the gauntlet before the feet of tyranny. And I say, Segregation now! Segregation tomorrow! Segregation forever!" Klansmen adored Wallace, and he didn't reject their friendship. He employed the notorious "Ace" Carter—former head of the Original Ku Klux Klan of the Confederacy—on his personal staff; and he appointed Al Lingo, who was on very good terms with Klansmen, to head the

Alabama State Police. In retrospect, however, no one used and manipulated the Klansmen more than Wallace. He gave them very few rewards for their efforts on his behalf; often his approval was enough. And in spite of his fiery cant and cries of "Never!" that so thrilled Klansmen, Wallace was a former judge who well understood the law—especially how far he could bend it.

On the morning of June 13, "the little judge from Barbour County" (as Klansmen affectionately called Wallace), stood on the steps of the administration building at the Tuscaloosa campus and refused entrance to two blacks who were accompanied by a few marshals. The President immediately federalized the Alabama National Guard. Robert Kennedy learned from Grover Hall, editor of the Montgomery *Advertiser*, that Wallace would "use his own influence with the Klan" to prevent violence. In fact, Sheriff Lingo informed Robert Shelton that "any known Klansmen seen in the Tuscaloosa area during the coming confrontation would be arrested on sight."

In at least one case, this actually happened. About fifty Klansmen, traveling in cars equipped with arsenals of weapons, were stopped by Lingo's troopers and thrown in jail. "Bobby Shelton came down and arranged the release for approximately thirty-five of us," one of them recalled. The next day, an Alabama judge quietly told the others, "I had to put you boys in jail last night. If I didn't, the troops would probably come into Alabama, and I don't want that." The guns and other weapons were then returned. "Take your weapons and use them well," said the judge. Elsewhere, it seemed as if Shelton had Klansmen under control. Rallies held before and after the campus showdown were unusually subdued. Shelton was very pleasant to newsmen, advising them where to place their cameras for the best shots, and even offering them free sandwiches.

Meanwhile, National Guardsmen were filtering into the crowds on campus. When the marshals asked for the black students to be admitted in the afternoon, Wallace quietly stepped aside. Instead of being recognized, at best, as a practical politician or, at worst, a pompous coward, Wallace was instead hailed by Klansmen as a dauntless hero. That same evening, the President of the United States went on national television to announce that he was asking Congress for a new civil rights bill. The fact "that race has no place in American life or law," said Kennedy, was "a moral issue"—"as old as the scriptures and . . . as clear as the American Constitution." The final bill would become the most comprehensive civil rights legislation drafted since the ill-fated Civil Rights Act of 1875.

On the surface, the Klan seemed to be fighting a losing battle. In midsummer 1963, while civil rights leaders were working on plans for a massive and memorable rally in Washington, Klansmen held their own cross-lit gatherings in the cow pastures of Dixie. Something new and weird was happening in the UKA. "Let's be nonviolent," Calvin Craig announced. "We've got to start fighting just like the niggers." North Carolina knights began an uncomfortable campaign against integrated restaurants, and Greensboro student Bill Fishburne looked in with amazement and growing delight at a row of robed Klansmen sitting at a counter. "It's a sit-in," he crowed to a companion. "They're *learning* from us. It's a sit-in!" Robert Shelton now seemed to be working on the Klan's image. He wanted Klansmen to be as cool as he was. "We don't want people of an emotional crowd feeling or leaders to satisfy that excited emotional feeling, that can stomp and talk at meetings and then they'll go out and beat or kill a nigger." No, said Shelton, "We wish to provide satisfaction to people in a more constructive manner."

The Klan's public rhetoric concealed a carefully laid plan. In private conferences in Atlanta, Klan leaders said that "until Klan membership could be increased, and until it could enlist the help and aid of large segments of officialdom," it would be best to deemphasize hostility to the Jewish race and to Catholics and the foreign born. They reasoned that by not antagonizing these groups, Klansmen might well enlist their support in a program of forceful resistance to integration. Exalted Cyclopes were asked to appoint a special committee within each Klavern to carry this plan forward.

In his public utterances, Shelton began to downplay antiblack sentiment and instead emphasized the Communist basis of the civil rights movement. "Many well-meaning nigras," he claimed "know their own people are being used by Communists." What Shelton was doing was throwing UKA support to a plan led by Wallace and other Southern governors to terminate federal intervention in the South and to defeat the civil rights bill by accusing civil rights leaders of being Communist-inspired, Communist-organized, and Communist-funded. This argument was gaining popular support. Many nonfanatics, as well as J. Edgar Hoover, were convinced of the Communist basis of black protests. The President, however, steadfastly denied it. When the matter arose in a press conference, he responded, somewhat peeved, "I think it is a convenient scapegoat to suggest that all the [civil rights] difficulties are Communist, and if the Communist movement would only disappear that we would end this. . . . The way to make the problem go away, in my opinion, is to provide for a redress of grievances."

Shelton's efforts at cleaning up the Klan's image through Redbaiting were largely unsuccessful. Why would anyone want to be a Klansman if he couldn't talk and act like a Klansman? At a large Savannah rally that summer, an elderly man in the audience grew impatient with the Wizard's new rhetoric. "I didn't come out here to hear him talk about all this Communist stuff," he said. "Why doesn't he talk about the niggers?" Shelton nevertheless believed in the new direction he was taking the Klan and planned to stage a counterdemonstration during the March on Washington, scheduled for August 28, 1963. Two days before the march, he took off in a private plane filled with Klan leaflets. While en route to pick up Grand Dragon Scoggin of South Carolina, however, the single-engine Cessna crashed into some trees near Greenville. Shelton's 350-pound pilot was killed, and it was barely short of a miracle that the Imperial Wizard walked away with only a broken arm.

The same good fortune didn't extend two weeks later to four young black girls who were killed instantly by a bomb exploding in Birmingham's Sixteenth Street Baptist Church. (Blacks were now bitterly calling their section of town "Dynamite Hill" and the city "Bombingham.") The job looked very much like the work of Klansmen. On September 29, Robert E. Chambliss and two other members of the Eastview Klavern were arrested for possessing dynamite. They argued that their Great Titan wanted the explosives to clear some ground for building a new Klavern headquarters. There was no evidence connecting them with the church bombing, however (not much effort at looking for evidence either), and at a subsequent trial all charges were dismissed.

The most nefarious aspect of the Sixteenth Street bombing is that three eyewitnesses had told Birmingham FBI agents that they had seen Chambliss and other Klansmen at the church eight hours before the explosion. When the agents notified Washington, however, J. Edgar Hoover told them to forget it. As he had argued since the 1940s, Hoover reiterated that the "chance of successful prosecution is very remote." Five months later, the Birmingham agents believed they had collected enough information for an airtight case against Chambliss and again contacted Washington for permission to relay their information to the attorney general. Hoover was adamant in his refusal. Under no circumstances were Robert Kennedy and the Justice Department to be informed. "We must not give a 'blow-by-blow' account to the Justice Department, Hoover said, "because it will appear in the [Washington] *Star* or the *Saturday Evening Post*." Hoover's words make his position clear: If the Klan's role in the bombing was made public, it would only fuel the civil rights movement. And Hoover wanted to avoid that at all costs.*

More than a few unconvicted bombers were walking the streets. J.B. Stoner was still Imperial Wizard of his Christian Knights in Atlanta but was now also affiliated with the neo-Nazi National States' Rights Party which he served as general counsel. Stoner was also a professional hatemonger for any Klan faction that could stomach him. He was guest speaker at a number of Birmingham rallies in the summer and fall of 1963, exhorting audiences to exterminate the Jews and teaching them how to make homemade bombs. He was definitely in the city on September 15 when the Sixteenth Street Baptist was bombed, although to date no evidence has surfaced implicating him.

Shortly after the Birmingham bombing, Stoner visited a number of towns in Florida and wound up in St. Augustine. There, in the nation's oldest city, a black dentist and NAACP leader, Dr. Robert Hayling, was actively involved in seeking racial justice. Handbills were being distributed throughout St. Augustine inviting "all white people" to a United Florida Klan rally in a clearing at the edge of a woods, a half-mile off U.S. Highway 1. Besides Stoner, a special attraction of the St. Augustine rally was his old friend and companion Reverend Charles Conley Lynch.

"Connie" Lynch was a fifty-year-old curly-haired native of Clarksville, Texas. He advertised himself as a "war hero" and "Jap killer," but as a journalist noted, "if he single-handedly wiped out any enemy battalions, it was by voodoo," for Lynch's army experiences were confined to the mess hall where he had served as a cook. Before the war, he had been ordained a minister in the General Assembly of Jesus Christ, a California sect. After the war, he was reordained in the Church of Jesus Christ Christian, a fanatic, right-wing, militaristic cult based in St. Petersburg, Florida, which by 1985 would evolve into the Aryan Nations. In 1962, Connie Lynch also became affiliated, along with Stoner, in the Na-

---

* Fourteen years later, in November 1977, Alabama state authorities tried and convicted Chambliss on first-degree murder charges for the Sixteenth Street bombing. Hoover's role in suppressing the evidence wasn't uncovered until 1980.

tional States' Rights Party. But his income was derived exclusively from his gigs as a professional race baiter. Anyone could hire him to drive audiences into orgies of racial hatred. "Wherever I speak," said Lynch, "I put teeth into the white people. I stiffen their resistance."

As was his custom, Lynch arrived late for the St. Augustine rally in his coral-colored Cadillac. With sweating brow and string tie, with flailing hands and jutting jaw, Lynch began speaking to the eager crowd of white-robed men and women. As his invective rose in speed and pitch, he not only pulled out all the stops but slammed down the swell and crescendo pedals.

"For the last thiry years, the Klan has not been strong, has not been militant. But the Klan is on the move again, and it is not going to let the niggers and the Jews take over our country.

"Now, some of you say: 'But Jesus was a Jew.' That just goes to show you how these cotton-pickin' half-witted preachers have fooled you. Jesus wasn't no Jew, he was a white man. . . . I've been through a lot of battles in my time, and I am still battling for what I know is right. I'm speaking for God, and *you'd better hear what I say!*"

Alluding to the murders at the Sixteenth Street Baptist, Lynch said, "I'll tell you people here tonight, if they can find these fellows [responsible for the bombing], they ought to pin medals on them. Someone said, 'Ain't it a shame that them little children was killed?' In the first place, they ain't little. They're fourteen or fifteen years old—old enough to have venereal diseases, and I'll be surprised if all of 'em didn't have one or more. In the second place, they weren't children. Children are little people, little human beings, and that means white people.

"There's little dogs and cats and apes and baboons and skunks and there's also little niggers. But they ain't children. They're just little niggers.

"And in the third place, it wasn't no shame they was killed. Why? Because, when I go out to kill rattlesnakes, I don't make no difference between little rattlesnakes and big rattlesnakes, because I know it is the nature of all rattlesnakes to be my enemies and to poison me if they can. So I kill 'em all, and if there's four less niggers tonight, then I say, 'Good for whoever planted the bomb!' We're all better off. . . . I believe in violence, all the violence it takes either to scare the niggers out of the country or to have 'em all six feet under!"

"Tell us about King," a Klansman shouted over the applause.

"Oh," grinned Lynch, "you mean Martin Lucifer *Coon!* That's the biggest enemy we've ever had. He's crooked as a snake. He ought to have been killed a long time ago. I heard him on TV the other night saying, 'the *Neee*-gro is not satisfied.' Well, he never will be, because before they are satisfied they all will be six feet under the ground!"

Lynch's speech lasted an hour and fifteen minutes, and its conclusion was met with screaming, Rebel yells, stomping feet and applause. But then came cries from the bushes near the speaker's platform: "Niggers! *Niggers!*"

Four black men, including Dr. Hayling, had been caught spying on the rally. Lynch jumped from the podium, jerked a pistol out of his Cadillac, and handed it to another man. Pistols, clubs, and brass knuckles quickly appeared throughout the crowd. The Klansmen weren't quite sure what to do. Rhetoric was one thing, but the chance to put it into practice was something else. The women, on the other hand, were itching for blood. At once a cackling female chorus arose of "Castrate the bastards!" "Knock their heads off!" "Kill them! Kill them!" "They had to trespass to get here, they've got no right to live!" "Come on, do something!" "String 'em up."

"Go get the head chopper," a white-robed lady told her husband, "and get the rope, and for God's sake, take off your robe and leave it in the car. You don't want to mess it up."

Men and women began beating Dr. Hayling and the three other blacks with fists, clubs, and gun butts. Fortunately there was another trespasser at the rally, a white man, Irvin Cheney, who was associate director of the Florida Council on Human Relations. He had attended the rally out of mere curiosity and could scarcely believe how vicious the mob had become. Afraid for his own life as well as those of the encircled blacks, Cheney slipped to the rear of the crowd and casually sauntered to his car, "kicking aimlessly in the sand as I walked along." Once in his car, his heart began pounding as he drove to the nearest pay phone and called the local sheriff. Worried that the sheriff wouldn't care, Cheney phoned the Florida adjutant general's office and then the FBI in Jacksonville. By the time the lawmen arrived, the Klansmen were getting ready to douse the blacks with kerosene. One of them exclaimed, "Did you ever smell a nigger burn? It's a mighty sweet smell."

Although the blacks survived, what they suffered afterward was nearly as brutal, as far as justice is concerned. A local jury dismissed all charges against the Klansmen and women but tried and convicted one of the black victims for assaulting members of the rally. Writing shortly after the event, historian David M. Chalmers ironically suggested, "In a right-thinking community like this, a useful organization such as the Klan might have a real future."

With bombs exploding in Birmingham, murder in Mississippi, and mob violence in St. Augustine, it was shocking but not inconsistent when the President of the United States was assassinated in Dallas on November 22, 1963. Moderate segregationist Hale Boggs of Louisiana had been saying for some time that, while Martin Luther King was hated and racial activists were much disliked, he had never seen anything to compare to the "virulence and violent feelings" that many Southern whites held for JFK. While the nation and many parts of the world were plunged into profound mourning, Klansmen regarded Kennedy's murder as the first good news of the decade. UKA leaders suggested that Kennedy had reaped the consequences of his own misguided policies. At a Georgia rally, a Grand Dragon of James R. Venable's National Knights, Charlie Maddox, said, "We need to do a lot to stop these national politicians. A boy down in Texas did a lot already. . . ."

It was typical of their mentality for Klansmen to believe that violence and more violence—even the murder of the nation's chief executive—could halt the civil rights movement. Hadn't the tactic worked for Reconstruction Klansmen exactly a century ago? What they didn't count on was that in Lyndon Johnson's first message to Congress four days after Dallas, he urged the passage of the civil rights bill as a memorial to the late John F. Kennedy, who had foremost envisioned "the dream of equal rights for all Americans, whatever their race or color." In the first Dixie drawl heard from a president since James Polk, Johnson announced, "We have talked long enough in this country about equal rights. We have talked for a hundred years or more. It is time now to write the next chapter . . . in books of law."

Until its passage, the civil rights bill was a coiled spring that kept Klansmen wound up and thrashing. They saw the bill as much a "Communist plot" as their forerunners had seen the Reconstruction acts as "radical rottenness." The UKA went on an all-out crusade for new members. Catholics were now welcome to join the Klan—the Communist conspiracy more than made up for the Klan's former anti-Catholic fears of Americans loyal to a foreign power. Violent and intimidating acts were reported on a weekly basis. In December, gunfire and a thrown grenade damaged the home of a black voter-registration worker in Dawson, Georgia. In

January, more than 150 crosses were burned near black homes and churches throughout the state of Louisiana. In February, a bomb shattered the Jacksonville, Florida, home of the Godfrey family, whose six-year-old son was the first black to attend a local school. After an FBI investigation, Sterling Rosecrans (a Klan-obsessed Hoosier) and five Florida Klansmen were arrested. Rosecrans pleaded guilty and was sentenced to seven years. The other five maintained their innocence and were acquitted.

In May, St. Augustine was again in the headlines and on televi-sion screens. Dr. Hayling had gone to see Martin Luther King. He complained of abuse by the local sheriff, L.O. Davis, whose dep-uties included many Klansmen. Whenever the NAACP tried to hold civil-rights marches, Hayling told King, lawmen would beat and jail the peaceful demonstrators but drag their heels when Klansmen shot up or bombed their homes. King was also dis-tressed to learn that St. Augustine had secured $350,000 from the federal government for the celebration of its quadricentennial in 1965. Like Birmingham, King decided that St. Augustine could expose combined Klan and constabulary hatred to the nation. He pledged full support to Dr. Hayling and promptly sent to St. Au-gustine an SCLC team that included its executive vice-president, Andrew Young.

The black community of St. Augustine had been properly pre-pared for a major civil rights confrontation, and some of their preparation was due to Stetson Kennedy. In 1952, the "number-one Klanbuster" had gone to Geneva, Switzerland, to testify be-fore the United Nations Committee on Forced Labor and had spent the next eight years in Europe, always managing to be around whenever and wherever " 'all hell' was breaking loose." In Rome, he had been arrested for tearing down posters of Italian political candidates funded by the CIA. He had walked into East Berlin while the fires of the 1953 revolt were still burning. In Bu-dapest, while bringing up the rear of a funeral procession for a victim of the revolt of 1956, he was almost crushed against a wall by an escort for a Soviet tank. Kennedy had kept up an active writing career, publishing articles in Jean Paul Sartre's *Les Temps Modernes* and other periodicals. He also had written two more books—an account of his undercover work in the Klan and *Jim Crow Guide to the USA*, a searing indictment of segregation and racial oppression in America.

After he returned to the USA in 1960, Kennedy became the Southern correspondent for the Pittsburgh *Courier*, a black newspaper, and served as the director of development of St. Augustine's Florida Memorial College, a small black Baptist college that had been built in 1879. One of the projects Kennedy had sponsored for the city was bringing Ivy League college students from the North during the summer to tutor black public school students. The Ivy Leaguers not only offered instruction in English and math but in black history, civics, and the constitutional rights of black Americans. As Kennedy recalled, "Thus, when the time for marching downtown came, the local youth were well prepared."

Indeed, many of the St. Augustine blacks answering the SCLC's call to march were in their early teens—"They trooped out of schools as though embarked upon some children's crusade." When Andrew Young tried to lead a march to the Old Slave Market, however, Klansmen and their sympathizers poured out of the market and beat the demonstrators with clubs and bicycle chains, while newsmen frantically tried to capture the scene on film and policemen stood idly by. Andrew Young remarked, "When you have one man, wearing civilian clothes, beating you while another, wearing a badge, stands waiting to arrest you when the first one gets tired, well, that makes you think."

Not only did St. Augustine Klansmen have a close relationship with the police, but on many occasions they acted and were treated by whites as a special paramilitary squad. They traveled in four-wheel drives equipped with short-wave radio, long before CBs became popular. Using their radios, they were able to converge, armed with ax handles and baseball bats, whenever a march began or when blacks attempted to integrate a public facility. They maintained a special alert during the lunch hour, when blacks were likely to attempt the integration of an all-white restaurant. At a popular restaurant specializing in Southern-fried chicken, Klansmen maintained an all-day vigil, hiding in a vacant gas station next door. When a group of blacks seated themselves at the restaurant, the men would charge in, swinging their ax handles and bursting forth with Rebel yells. According to Stetson Kennedy, "The management cooperated fully with the Klux, giving them a call whenever blacks showed up at unexpected hours."

After repeated harassment from the Klan and police, Martin Luther King asked Washington for federal marshals, but the President and the attorney general declined. The Senate was about to vote on cloture for the civil rights bill, the failure of which would allow a destructive filibuster by Southern Democrats. Cloture depended heavily on the support of Senate Minority Leader Everett

Dirksen ("the Wizard of Ooze"), who had voiced concern over the bill's expansion of federal powers. If Johnson sent marshals into the South at this critical moment, he risked fueling the fire of Southern opposition and losing Dirksen's vital support. The hoary Illinois senator with a wrinkled relief map of a face was being treated with kid gloves by pro-administration Democrats. One of them told a confidante, "We are carving out that statesman's niche and bathing it with blue lights and hoping that Dirksen will find it irresistible to step into it." Johnson therefore asked, for the time being, that King and the SCLC turn to federal authorities within the state of Florida.

While Jacksonville's U.S. District Judge Bryan Simpson, a native Southerner, studied a list of complaints from the SCLC, King arrived in St. Augustine and at the Shiloh Church addressed black demonstrators who had been injured during the Slave Market fracas. "I know what you faced," he told them, "and I understand that as you marched silently and with a deep commitment to nonviolence, you confronted the brutality of the Klan. But amid all of this you stood up." After his address, King learned that a committee of local whites had categorically rejected his demands for desegregated public accommodations, qualified blacks on the police force, and equally reasonable measures.

Soon word came that Judge Simpson had overruled the local ordinance against civil rights marches and had harshly criticized Sheriff Davis for "cruel and unusual punishment" of black prisoners. The stage was set for more demonstrations and violent counterdemonstrations. This brought the peripatetic bomber J. B. Stoner and his friend Connie Lynch, who now wore a Confederate-flag vest. Speaking in the Slave Market on June 9, Lynch and his infernal incantations once again whipped a white crowd into a froth. "Martin Lucifer Coon!" he screeched. "That nigger says it's gonna be a hot summer. If he thinks the niggers can make it a hot summer, I will tell him that one-hundred-forty-million white people know how to make it a hotter summer! . . . Now I grant you some niggers are gonna get killed in the process, but when war's on that's what happens." After the speech, a screaming white mob descended upon four hundred blacks and attacked them as they quietly marched through the city's plaza. When state policemen dispersed the whites with tear gas, one of them complained, "Niggers have more freedom than we do!" An appalled Dr. King called St. Augustine "the most lawless city I've ever seen."

The publicity helped. The next day Everett Dirksen threw his support to the civil rights bill as "an idea whose time has come," and cloture was won. After this major step toward passage of the bill, Klansmen poured into St. Augustine from Jacksonville and other parts of the Southeast. Escorted by sympathetic lawmen, they led a raucous march of their own through a black neighborhood, carrying Confederate flags and signs saying KILL THE CIVIL RIGHTS BILL. Klansmen also made hit-and-run assaults on blacks attempting to desegregate the city's whites-only beaches. One evening they danced and frolicked in their robes on the beach for photographers of *Life* magazine, little knowing how damaging the photo would be to their cause.

Soon civic leaders grew worried about the effects of the distasteful publicity on the future of St. Augustine's vital tourist trade— especially with the quadricentennial coming up. A bank executive lamented, "I just don't see how we're going to find our way back to sanity." Under steady pressure from Judge Simpson, Governor Farris Bryant finally established an emergency biracial committee to reach a settlement between local black and white leaders, and King curtailed SCLC activities in St. Augustine on June 30. A week before, however, the attention of the nation had shifted westward to Mississippi. Three civil rights workers had disappeared near Philadelphia, Mississippi, and their disappearance had all the earmarks of Klan involvement.

12

"HIS HOT AND AWFUL LIGHT"

*Violence, Retribution, and the End
of the Second Reconstruction: 1964–1974*

During World War II, a group of black soldiers were asked what should be done with Hitler if he were captured alive. "Paint him black and sentence him to life in Mississippi," they suggested. Twenty years later, Mississippi was still "the closed society." Its public facilities were the most segregated of any state, and only 6 percent of its sizeable adult black population was able to vote. The White Citizens' Councils had been born in Mississippi, and because of their effectiveness in preventing integration, there was little need for the Klan in the Magnolia State. The councils' power was deflated overnight, however, when Ole Miss was forcibly integrated by the Kennedy administration. Shortly after "the Battle of Ole Miss," an independent Klan called the Original Knights of Louisiana crossed the Mississippi River and established a Klavern in Natchez. In February 1964, the Mississippi chapter split from its parent and announced its independence as the White Knights of the Ku Klux Klan of Mississippi. In April it elected Samuel Holloway Bowers, a forty-year-old businessman, as Imperial Wizard. The popular description of Bowers as "an unasylumed lunatic" does little justice to his intelligence, charisma, and organizational skills, but there's little doubt that Bowers was the most mysterious and dangerous leader in the entire history of the Klan. In his five-year reign as

Wizard of Mississippi, Bowers is suspected of "masterminding" at least nine murders; nearly seventy-five bombings of black churches; and three hundred assaults, bombings, and beatings.

The child of a broken home whose father later disowned him, Bowers was a loner deeply attached to his mother. He took pride in the fact that one of his Louisiana grandfathers had been a wealthy planter and the other a four-term U.S. congressman. After serving in the navy during the war, Bowers attended Tulane University and then transferred to the University of Southern California, where he majored in engineering. At USC he met Robert Larson. The two of them dropped out of school, and Bowers brought his new friend to Laurel, his father's hometown in southeastern Mississippi. By then his childhood fascination with erector sets and gadgets had evolved to pinball games. Together Bowers and Larson formed the Sambo Amusement Company, leasors of pinball and vending machines.

Slim, clean-cut, and six feet tall, Bowers had an intelligent face with high cheekbones. He frequently hid behind dark sunglasses. His private life was shrouded in mystery, and some of his habits were quite strange. To entertain visitors, he would sometimes put on a swastika armband and bark "Heil Hitler!" to his dog, which had been trained to snap to attention. A confirmed bachelor, Sam had no use whatever for the company of women. He was known to get into arguments with Larson, his roommate as well as business partner, and not speak to him for months. Some Klansmen wondered if their Wizard was a homosexual, which is quite unlikely. Bowers seems to have completely sublimated his sexuality in upper-case paranoid political tracts, religious fanaticism, and obsessively elaborate schemes for Klan violence.

"The typical Mississippi red-neck," he would say, "doesn't have sense enough to know what he is doing. I have to use him for my own cause and direct his every action to fit my plan." Indeed, given his college education, Bowers ranked as an intellectual among Klansmen, who regarded him with respectful awe. What made his leadership dangerous, however, was his conviction that the White Knights had been called into being to express God's own wishes. Although Christian ideology had been steadily eroding from Klan rhetoric since the 1920s, Bowers resurrected it with a fanatic's zeal and restored to the hackneyed word *crusade* its thirteenth century purpose of murdering infidels. "As Christians," he wrote in an early statement of purpose, "we are disposed to kindness, generosity, affection and humility in our dealings with others. As militants we are disposed to the use of physical force against our enemies." Bowers exhorted his followers to be prepared to kill for Christ. But whenever an "elimination" became necessary, he added, "it should be done in silence, without malice, in the manner of a Christian act." By 1965, the White Knights of Mississippi would reach an impressive membership of over five thousand men.

A challenge to Mississippi's "closed society" finally came in 1964 from the Council of Federated Organizations (COFO), which had been organized shortly after the freedom rides. COFO was made up of members of CORE, SNCC, SCLC, the NAACP, and the National Council of Churches. In January 1964, COFO announced a "Mississippi Summer," during which trained volunteers would be transported to Mississippi to educate blacks and help them register to vote.

One of the first applicants to be accepted by COFO was Michael Schwerner. Mickey, as his friends called him, was an Ohio native and a graduate of Cornell. He and his wife Rita were employed as social workers in New York and were active in civil rights. COFO sent them to southeast Mississippi to set up a headquarters before the other volunteers arrived. In Meridian, the Schwerners secured five dingy rooms—formerly doctors' offices—on the second floor above the town's only black drugstore. They cleaned up the place, built bookcases, made blue curtains for the windows, and helped local black youths build a Ping-Pong table. They stocked their shelves with ten thousand books on black history and civil rights, including W.E.B. DuBois's classic volumes that previously had been unavailable to Mississippi blacks. Mickey seemed older than his twenty-four years, more self-assured and politically sophisticated. Since he sported a wispy, chin beard, local whites snidely called him "Goatee" and "Jew-boy." He reacted with good humor to obscene phone calls and to his conviction that local police had wiretapped the office. "If you're lucky," he joked, "you can hear the police calls going back and forth." The police were a constant problem. Almost weekly, they picked him up, hauled him to the station, and questioned him about his activities; but Mickey was surprised that local reaction to him and Rita wasn't worse than it was. "We're actually pretty lucky here," he told a friend. "I think they're going to let us alone."

The Schwerners believed that the COFO operation in Mississippi was a good idea. "The people who say it's foolhardy to work in Mississippi are missing the point," Mickey argued. "You can cut years off the fight throughout the South by concentrating on Mississippi and showing how there can be progress even in the toughest state." (The same logic had led President Grant and General Terry to concentrate their Klan fight in South Carolina a century earlier.) The Schwerners moved cautiously in gaining the confidence of the local black community and were helped immeasurably by twenty-one-year-old James Chaney, a native of Meridian who eventually became a full-ranking member of their staff. Chaney represented a new generation of Mississippi blacks. He came from a large family who had long survived by keeping a low profile. His mother worried constantly over her son's activities with COFO, but Jim told her, "That's the trouble, Mama, too many people afraid." With Chaney's help, the Schwerners made effective inroads in the black community. Mickey dearly loved tutoring the youngsters and fell easily into a black patois with them. He asked all adults who visited the center if they were registered to vote, telling them, "Nothing is more important than that." Blacks learned to trust COFO and its young Yankee administrator. One woman said, "They made us aware we could get equal rights and how to do it. These Negroes around here never did know that before."

On June 14, all COFO volunteers attended an orientation meeting sponsored by the National Council of Churches at the Western College for Women in Oxford, Ohio. There they were given crash courses in Mississippi survival. Idealistic students from Howard and Antioch universities, as well as the universities of Chicago, Michigan, and Wisconsin and a dozen other centers of learning were instructed on how to fall to the ground and cover their faces when policemen beat them with clubs. They were taught never to travel alone, "especially in a car." "Always draw the shades at night." "Never sleep by an open window." A naïve white girl asked how she should handle interracial dating in Mississippi, and black instructors reeled. "*Don't!*" they told her. To get the point indelibly across, SNCC's James Forman told the students outright that there was a strong chance that some of them would be killed. After that, a tearful group of students met in a dorm room. "What is there in Mississippi that I'm willing to die for?" a distressed girl asked herself.

One of the most quiet but alert and committed volunteers at the orientation was Andrew Goodman of New York City. Like the Schwerners, Andy was Jewish. A twenty-year-old anthropology major at Queens College, he had recently joined SNCC. Andy was the exemplary young, white civil-rights idealist of his generation. So photogenic were his dark features that *Life* photographers and CBS cameramen at the orientation instinctively homed in on him. Andy was also sensitive and intelligent. For a creative writing course at Queens, he had written a disturbing poem on the pain of social awareness:

See how heaven shows dismay
As her stars are scared away;
As the sun ascends with might
With his hot and awful light

He shows us babies crying
We see the black boy dying
We close our eyes and choke our sighs
And look into the dreadful skies.

The Schwerners and Jim Chaney also attended the orientation —Chaney was especially excited by it—and all three were pleased that Andy Goodman was assigned to the Meridian operation. Andy's intellect and dedication were exactly what Mickey wanted in a volunteer. Leaving Rita at the conference to join them later, the three young men and some other volunteers set out on June 20 for Meridian.

Meanwhile, white Mississippians prepared themselves for the rape of their sovereign state by "carpetbaggers," "Communist students," and "tennis-shoed beatniks." A correspondent to the *New York Times* reported, "The average citizen has been led to believe that this will be an 'invasion' to make Mississippi the battleground for Federal intervention in behalf of Negro rights." *U.S. News & World Report* said, "Signs point toward Mississippi as a major battleground in this summer's campaign. White students from the North are moving in to help Negroes—and white Mississippians are preparing their defenses." The Neshoba (Mississippi) *Democrat* was more blunt: "Outsiders who come in here and try to stir up trouble should be dealt with in a manner they won't forget."

Imperial Wizard Bowers promptly issued an Imperial Executive Order that was to be "read . . . and understood by every member" of the White Knights:

It is absolutely necessary that each and every member of this organization stand fast and remain calm at this time; while he is working deliberately to prepare himself and his unit for effective combat against the enemy.

The military and political situation as regards the enemy has now reached the crisis stage. Our best students of enemy strategy and technique are in almost complete agreement that the events which will occur in Mississippi this summer may well determine the fate of Christian Civilization for centuries to come. . . .

This is indeed an awesome and critically responsible position in which we now find ourselves. Every member must Soberly and PRAYERFULLY face this Responsibility, and draw his strength from the Spiritual Source which tells us, deep in our hearts, that our Cause is truly Just. . . .

This summer, within a very few days, the enemy will launch his final push for victory here in Mississippi. This offensive will consist of two basic salients, which have been designed to [envelop] and destroy our small forces in a pincer movement of Agitation, Force by Federal Troops, and Communist Propaganda. *

Bowers predicted that COFO would try to engage the Klan in open warfare, which would bring federal troops into Mississippi just as they had been brought in during Reconstruction. Klansmen should not fall into the trap of open violence. Violence should be cautious, secretive. And instead of hitting the "mass enemy," the Klan should target the "individual enemy." In the middle of May, Klansmen selected the individual enemy: the "Jew-boy with the beard at Meridian." Mickey Schwerner was now formally marked for "elimination."

At a joint meeting of Klansmen from Meridian and nearby Philadelphia on June 16, the main topic was exactly how they were going to kill Mickey. Another meeting was going on that evening at Mt. Zion Methodist, a black church. Since COFO had formed a relationship with Mt. Zion's congregation, the Klansmen figured that "Goatee" was there. "This is as good a time as any to go and get him," said a Klansman. Upon arriving at the backwoods church, however, the Klansmen discovered that Mickey was still in Ohio. They therefore contented themselves with beating two black men close to death and burning Mt. Zion Methodist to the ground. The incident wasn't even reported in the local papers.

Three days later, on the evening of June 20, Schwerner, Chaney, and Goodman arrived in Meridian after a hot, all-day drive

---

* The complete text of this order, as well as other White Knights documents, may be found in Appendix C.

from Ohio. They arose early Sunday and drove out to inspect the charred remains of Mt. Zion. Schwerner interviewed the beating victims and asked them if they would be willing to sign affidavits. The three climbed back into their Ford station wagon to visit other blacks but were stopped on Highway 19, three miles east of Philadelphia, by Deputy Sheriff Cecil Price. Price arrested Chaney for "speeding" and locked up all three in the Neshoba County jail.

Barely twenty-four hours after arriving in Mississippi, Andy Goodman must have realized how real were the warnings of his COFO orientation leaders. Segregated in black and white cells, the three men were given dinner by the prison matron. At 10:30 P.M. Deputy Price told Mickey that he and his companions could go if they paid a $20 fine for speeding. Mickey had been detained without reason by Mississippi police before. Relieved that this was the end of their ordeal, he handed Price a $20 bill. Accepting the fine, Price said, "You came here to stir up trouble. These folks were getting along all right before you got here and they can do without your help now."

Without saying a word, the three men left the jail, climbed into their blue station wagon, and drove off. They would never be heard from again.

Since Mickey had taken the precaution of telling the new recruits at COFO headquarters to expect them back late in the afternoon, COFO notified authorities that they were missing. Local whites treated the disappearance as a hoax. When COFO's concerns reached the state level, Governor Paul Johnson ("Stand Tall with Paul") offered the opinion that the boys had most likely run off to Cuba. Eventually COFO's appeals reached the federal government. Robert Kennedy immediately ordered J. Edgar Hoover to treat the disappearance as a kidnapping (which would legitimize federal intervention) and to "spare no effort in this matter."

If Neshoba County had regarded the COFO project as an invasion, residents were scarcely prepared for the breadth of the invasion that now took place. Within two weeks, Hoover had 153 agents combing the countryside. Agents were joined by four hundred sailors from a nearby naval base, and nearly as many reporters and journalists, including two from London and one each from West Berlin and Paris. The FBI launched the most intense manhunt it had ever undertaken in a civil rights case. Agents combed kudzu-tangled lowlands and groves of scrub pine. They dragged snake-infested bayous and swamps. The locals continued to regard their efforts as a wild goose chase. One man remarked to a reporter that finding a dead body in a swamp meant nothing. "We throw two or three niggers in every year to feed the fish," he chuckled.

In an open letter from the Klan to the community, Imperial Wizard Bowers expressed outrage over Mississippi's "crucifixion" by outsiders:

> We are now in the midst of the "long, hot summer" of agitation which was promised to the Innocent People of Mississippi by the savage blacks and their Communist masters. . . . We were NOT involved, and there was NO DISAPPEARANCE. . . . We refuse to be concerned or upset about this fraud. What we are concerned about is the welfare of the citizens of the State of Mississippi. . . .
>
> We are going to serve notice that we are not going to recognize the authority of any bi-racial group, NOR THE AUTHORITY OF ANY PUBLIC OFFICIAL WHO ENTERS INTO ANY AGREEMENT WITH ANY SUCH SOVIET ORGANIZATION. We Knights are working day and night to preserve Law and Order here in Mississippi, in the only way that it can be preserved: by strict segregation of the races, and the control of the social structure in the hands of the Christian, Anglo-Saxon White men, the only race on earth that can build and maintain just and stable governments. We are deadly serious about this business. . . . Take heed, atheists and mongrels, we will not travel your path to a Leninist Hell, but we will buy YOU a ticket to the Eternal if you insist. Take your choice, SEGREGATION, TRANQUILITY AND JUSTICE, or, BI-RACISM, CHAOS AND DEATH.

The FBI was unmoved by the threats. Agents seemed to be everywhere and were easily recognized by their dark pants, white shirts, and their practice of always traveling by pairs in cars equipped with long antennae. (One of the White Knights' most enthusiastic projects was gathering poisonous snakes to throw into FBI cars.) The Mississippi Bar Association informed residents of the Magnolia State that they were under no obligation to cooperate with FBI agents, especially in civil rights matters. The Meridian *Star* offered nine suggestions for dealing with the FBI, including:

> The FBI agents are given special training in regard to the silent subject who refuses to answer questions. They will try to make you angry, in order that your tongue may be loosened. They will play upon your sympathy. ("I don't like this assignment, Mr. ***, I'm a Southerner

too—but I have been ordered by my Kennedy-appointed superior to question you.") and they will try flattery as well. The best way to defeat such training is to apply the following three rules: (1) silence, (2) more silence, (3) still more silence.

The FBI nevertheless succeeded in getting a thousand white Mississippians as well as 488 White Knights to talk.

The FBI's diligence in investigating the Klan in Mississippi was remarkable, considering Hoover's deep-seated reluctance and repeated failure to involve the bureau in civil rights cases. Hoover had recently told the *Washington Post* that he frankly objected to "wet nursing" those "who go down to reform the South," and his main preoccupation up to this time had been electronic eavesdropping on Martin Luther King's sex life in order to discredit the civil rights movement. Three things seem responsible for the change. First, Hoover was anxious to disprove charges made in 1961 by the Civil Rights Commission that the FBI was negligent in civil rights cases. Secondly, the special agent put in charge of the Mississippi investigation was six-foot-two, square-jawed Joseph Sullivan, whose father had fought the Klan in Bolton, Massachusetts, during the 1920s. Sullivan still had disturbing memories of the anti-Catholic Klan of his childhood and plunged into the Mississippi project with vigor. The third factor was the influence of Robert Kennedy. In addition to ordering the FBI into Mississippi, Kennedy also sent a private team from the Justice Department—a crack team he had called the "Get-Hoffa squad," headed by crusty Walter Sheridan. (Now that Teamster boss Jimmy Hoffa had been "got," the squad was free for new assignments.) There was considerable friction between Sheridan's squad and Sullivan's agents, and the competition caused the FBI to outstrip the Justice Department in thoroughness and eventual expertise in dealing with the White Knights. Once it was clear that the FBI had taken firm hold of the situation, Kennedy allowed the "Get-Hoffa squad" to withdraw.

The FBI soon learned that White Knights could be bought. Two key Klansmen were hired as informers: a Meridian police sergeant and Kleagle, and a Southern Methodist minister and Kludd who was also a highly trusted lieutenant to the Imperial Wizard. With the undercover information of these men and the confessions of two other panicky Klansmen, the case was broken a little over six weeks after the three COFO workers had disappeared. On August 4, the FBI began tearing apart a dam site where the decomposing bodies of Schwerner, Chaney, and Goodman were unearthed. Mickey and Andy had been shot once through the heart. Jim, the black member of the trio, had been beaten before being shot three times. The FBI named twenty-one Klansmen responsible for the crime, including Sheriff Lawrence Rainey and Deputy Cecil Price. The murder of the three COFO workers—like that of Joseph Shoemaker in 1935 and countless others before—was a classic case of Southern lawmen releasing prisoners directly into the clutches of the Ku Klux Klan.

The collusion of the police galled the nation. Prior to the workers' disappearance, a Harris Poll revealed that 57 percent of Americans disapproved of COFO's Mississippi project. That disapproval quickly evaporated. *Life* magazine published a chilling and now-famous photograph of a grinning Deputy Price and a smirking Sheriff Rainey (stuffing Red Man tobacco into his jowls) as the two sat in a Meridian courtroom during an arraignment for conspiracy before a U.S. commissioner who would dismiss all charges against them. For the *Saturday Evening Post*, William Bradford Huie wrote, "What makes this lynching a high crime against humanity is the role of the police. The three young men were not criminals. They were unarmed. They were well-intentioned. They were peaceful and peace-loving. Mississippi requires no visa for an American citizen to visit it." Even Walter Cronkite was unable to conceal his disgust. After referring to "bloody Neshoba County" on the evening news, Cronkite was assailed by Mississippians who put so much pressure on CBS he was forced to apologize the next night. Mississippi's ruffled feelings were explained by one of its attorneys: "We were invaded by whores and Jews who tried to tell us how to run things. Good people are killed every day in Mississippi, but the FBI only comes in on it when worthless Jews and nigger-lovers are killed."

With the exception of Kennedy's assassination, no incident of the 1960s was more responsible for the sudden liberalization of thousands of complacent white college students in the North. Typical was the reaction of a previously apathetic psych major, a junior at the University of Michigan, who wrote to an even more conservative friend: "Despite what you may think about Negroes and Civil Rights, the notion boils down to this. We're guaranteed the right of protest in the Bill of Rights. Negroes are guaranteed freedoms in the 13–15 Amendments. . . . And yet these 'individual kingdoms' exist in the U.S. which can proclaim everything by the federal government null and void. Don't these bastards below the Mason Dixon line realize that they lost the Civil War?" Such non-radical students as these, awakened to the ugliness of Klan violence, would join en masse the Vietnam War protests two years away.

Northern blacks were also affected. After Birmingham, the brutal murders in Mississippi seemed indisputable proof that a nonviolent civil rights movement was doomed to failure. And the plight of their Southern brothers and sisters under obvious conditions of injustice added to Northern blacks' frustration with the more subtle and possibly more pernicious racism above the Mason–Dixon line. On July 18, black rage erupted in a riot in Harlem, followed by others in Jersey City, North Philadelphia, and four other cities.

Mississippi authorities were unwilling to act upon the evidence uncovered by the FBI—the confessions of the two Klansmen were dismissed as "hearsay." Accordingly, the Justice Department asked for federal indictments against the Klansmen under the Reconstruction Ku-Klux statutes. In the face of these indictments, the White Knights' arrogant optimism was scarcely believable. Shortly after the three bodies had been exhumed, the Klan Air Force (a single plane) flew over Neshoba County and dropped leaflets saying, "Schwerner, Chaney, and Goodman were not civil rights workers [but] Communist Revolutionaries, actively working to undermine and destroy Christian Civilization." The literary talent of Sam Bowers was unmistakable, and the Imperial Wizard was quite busy during this period. He organized a boycott of local "scalawag" businessmen who showed the slightest sympathy toward the fate of the three victims. He continued to engineer acts of Klan violence. During the next four years, Mississippi's Knights bombed a synagogue in Jackson. They burned another twenty-six churches (SNCC called Mississippi "the church-burning capital of the world," and it may be recalled that Mississippi's Reconstruction Klan had specialized in burning black schools). There is court testimony that Bowers specially ordered the firebomb murder of Vernon Dahmer, a respected NAACP leader who helped blacks to register; and that he is said to have approved the murder of two other blacks as well as numerous hit-and-run shotgun attacks on black homes. The FBI kept careful tabs on Bowers, and his apparent involvement in the Dahmer murder allowed agents to add his name to the list of indicted Klansmen. In a raid on Bowers's private residence, police found a cache of eight different firearms, including a submachine gun, several revolvers, six canisters of .30 caliber

ammunition, and a case and several bandoliers of other ammunition. They also found a detailed memo calling for the "elimination" of Robert Kennedy.

The Justice Department suffered a setback in the spring of 1965
when Federal District Judge William A. Cox decided that the Ku-
Klux statutes were not applicable to the Klansmen accused of the
COFO murders. Said Judge Cox: "The right of every person not
to be deprived of his life and liberty without due process of law is
a right that existed *prior* to the Federal Constitution. It is a right
which is protected by *State laws* and is merely *guaranteed* by the
Constitution of the United States." In short, murder was a state,
not a federal matter, and the U.S. government had little if any
jurisdiction in the case. Since Judge Cox was a well-known segregationist, many assumed he had allowed bigotry to override a sense
of fairness. Actually Cox had interpreted the case in light of the
1951 Williams decision, which had seriously restricted the range of
crimes indictable under the Ku-Klux statutes. Any other conservative jurist, North or South, would have likely reached the same
decision. The Justice Department decided to appeal Cox's ruling
to the Supreme Court. It was a very good time to do so, for a
similar Klan murder had just occurred in Georgia.

The college town of Athens, Georgia, had been tense ever since
the university had been integrated in January 1961. In spring 1964,
black students began picketing a restaurant that served only
whites. Klansmen from the Clarke County Klavern of the UKA—
dominated by Howard Sims and Cecil Myers—had counterpick-
eted in full Klan regalia. The team of Sims and Myers was an
unsavory one. They liked traveling in cars filled with sawed-off
shotguns, pistols, and rounds of ammunition. Sims was a hotrod
buff whose police record included beating a black demonstrator
over the head with a pistol, flogging and intimidating blacks, and
firing a shotgun into the windows of a black apartment complex.
He suffered from migraine headaches and temper tantrums. His
debt to society would include additional time served for shooting
his wife in the face.

On July 11, 1964, three black army reserve officers were returning home to Washington, D.C., after serving two weeks of reserve duty at Georgia's Fort Benning. At five in the morning
they stopped their car near Athens and Lieutenant Lemuel A.
Penn took over driving. Penn was a forty-nine-year-old educa-
tor who had taught in the Washington, D. C. school systems for
twenty years and was in the process of completing a doctorate

in education. He had seen combat in the South Pacific during World War II and afterward remained active in the army reserve. For the previous two years, he had been an assistant superintendent of schools in charge of vocational and adult education; he was also a highly respected leader in the Boy Scouts. A quiet, achievement-oriented man, Penn belonged to no civil rights organizations and was inclined to avoid all forms of racial confrontation.

Near the Broad River Bridge on Highway 172, the Penn car was sighted by Klansmen Sims and Myers, who were riding in a station wagon driven by James Lackey. Remarking on Penn's D.C. license plates, Sims said, "That must be some of President Johnson's boys." He ordered Lackey to pull alongside the vehicle.

"What are you going to do?" Lackey asked.

"I'm going to kill me a nigger," Sims replied.

When the station wagon was directly alongside, both Sims and Myers fired their shotguns. The left side of Lemuel Penn's head was blown away and he died instantly. The other two occupants struggled to control the car, which eventually veered off the road and overturned in a ditch. Three days later, Penn's body was conveyed with full honors on a military caisson to Arlington National Cemetery. The caisson was the same one that had been used for the funeral of John F. Kennedy. A year later, Penn's forty-nine-year-old wife, a home economics teacher and mother of three, died of a rare form of arthritis, seriously complicated by the stress she had suffered from her husband's murder.

J. Edgar Hoover had been enmeshed in the Mississippi Klan problem and was returning to Washington aboard a plane when he was informed of the Penn case. The bureau chief quickly smelled the Klan. To his aide and confidante Clyde Tolson, Hoover muttered, "If they get away with this, they'll think they can get away with anything. Ask Atlanta how many extra agents they need. I want them all to report there today." After an exhaustive month-long investigation by seventy-eight agents, the FBI broke the case, and Sims and Myers were tried for murder by the state of Georgia. Unfortunately the key witness, Lackey, recanted his confession at the last minute, and the two Klansmen went free. The next evening, James Venable's National Knights held a rally on Stone Mountain. Venable was jubilant. "You'll never by able to convict a white man that kills a nigger what encroaches on the Southern way of life," he cackled.

As in the COFO case, the Justice Department attempted to indict Sims and Myers under the Ku-Klux statutes. As in that case, a federal district judge, William A. Bootle, denied it. And once again, the Justice Department appealed to the Supreme Court.

Klan leaders were crowing over their apparent immunity from the law. Mississippi's Sheriff Rainey and Deputy Price and Georgia's Sims and Myers became special guests of honor at Klan rallies. They were feted like heroes—utter proof of the invincibility of the Klan. At a South Carolina UKA rally, Imperial Wizard Shelton told a joke: "You know how they finally found them three boys that was buried in that dam near Philadelphia, Mississippi? . . . The mailman found them. He walked by there delivering welfare checks, and the nigger reached up to get his."

Actually, Klansmen were whistling in the dark. Spurred in part by the ugly, unpunished Klan violence, Congress passed the Civil Rights Act, and President Johnson signed it into law on July 2, 1964. Later in the year, the Supreme Court struck down laws in nineteen border and Southern states against "cohabitation" between blacks and whites. A number of Southern governors had had enough of the Klan. When North Carolina Klansmen threatened businessmen for sponsoring integrated Christmas parades, Governor Terry Sanford sent out a warning: "I would urge all members of the KKK to read the Christmas story and the message of goodwill to all men contained in the Bible. In the meantime, I am instructing the State Highway Patrol to provide all aid necessary. . . . If there are illegal acts on the part of the Ku Klux Klan, they will be prosecuted."

On the other hand, Louisiana seemed to be under a white-robed reign of terror, especially in Bogalusa, which a journalist dubbed "Klantown, USA." In January 1965, when the city fathers invited moderate Arkansas congressman Brooks Hays to speak at a local church, Louisiana's Original Knights distributed over six thousand handbills, claiming that Hays was coming to Bogalusa

> to convince you that you should help integration by sitting in church with the black man, hiring more of them in your businesses, serving and eating with them in your cafes, and allowing your children to sit by filthy, runny-nosed, ragged, ugly little niggers in your public schools.
>
> We will know the names of all who are invited to the Brooks Hays meeting and we will know who did and did not attend this meeting. . . . Those who do attend this meeting will be tagged as integrationists and will be dealt with accordingly by the knights of the Ku Klux Klan.

When the hosting church was threatened with bombing, Hays's

visit was canceled. In a brave editorial published in the Bogalusa *News*, Lou Major wrote: "People of sound mind and principles can find little more in the cross burnings than a message of unprincipled hate for mankind. Unfortunately, the people responsible are living and working in our midst every day, people of obvious low mentality without any scruples. We pray the nightriders may grow up into men of God-fearing conscience, before they are called on to answer for their terror tactics which leave a mark on children, wives and decent law-abiding humanity."

But Klan terrorism didn't stop. If anything, passage of the Civil Rights Act seemed to increase it. On January 17, two rural black churches were destroyed by fire in Jonesboro, Louisiana. On the twenty-third, three explosions demolished a black funeral home in New Bern, North Carolina. In February, two black youths in Mobile were wounded by shotgun blasts from passing cars. And on March 5, a Freedom School and library were burned to the ground in Indianola, Mississippi.

Viola Liuzzo was a forty-year-old Detroit housewife and the mother of five, whose husband was a business agent for Local 247 of the Teamsters Union. Everyone who knew Liuzzo spoke of her boundless energy—a zeal that was occasionally erratic and misdirected, but always warm-hearted and generous. A high-school dropout, she passed her equivalency test and took night classes at the Carnegie Institute to become a lab technician. She earned good grades and the respect of her teachers. A fellow Carnegie student recalled, "She would sometimes keep us up all night, pushing us and pushing us. Without her some of us never would have made it through school."

Liuzzo was also politically active, but her political stands often caused her more harm than what was necessary. In her first job as a lab technician at the Parkview Medical Center, she spoke out against sexist work policies, especially as they affected secretaries, and was soon fired. When she demonstrated her opposition to the Detroit school system's policy of allowing students to drop out at age sixteen (as she had) by keeping her two sons out of school and tutoring them at home for a month, she was brought to court and told that the whole matter would be dropped if the children returned to school. Instead she pleaded guilty and was fined $50 and put on probation.

Liuzzo had grown up in Georgia and rural Tennessee and had recently taken an interest in the civil rights movement. Sarah

Evans, a black maid who had worked for her husband's family, became her close friend. Sarah took her to her first meeting of the NAACP, which Liuzzo joined; and she drove Evans to New York, where they attended a seminar on civil rights sponsored by the Unitarian-Universalist United Nations Office. Her second job as a lab technician was at Detroit's more cosmopolitan Sinai Hospital. There she worked closely with a visiting research scientist from Nigeria who encouraged her to seek even more education. In January 1964, she enrolled at Wayne State University, where she became friends with an Episcopalian chaplain who had participated in civil rights demonstations in the South. "He's made me do a lot of thinking," she confided to her husband Jim.

In March 1965, Viola and Jim watched the televised coverage of the aborted voting rights march in Selma, Alabama, where cameramen had managed to capture the brutal spectacle of Colonel Al Lingo's state troopers and Sheriff Jim Clark's mounted posse using tear gas, clubs, and whips on peaceful demonstrators. On March 9 Reverend James Reeb, a Unitarian minister from Boston, had made a fatal change in itinerary and decided to stay on in Selma. That evening, while walking with two minister friends in front of an all-white watering hole called the Silver Moon Cafe, he was accosted by four men who beat them with clubs and lead pipes. Reeb fell into a coma and died two days later. Marches and demonstrations were taking place in many American cities in protest against police violence in Selma.

Tears streamed down Viola's face as she watched the coverage of Reverend Reeb's memorial service and heard Martin Luther King's call for ministers and all lovers of justice to come to Selma and join a march to Montgomery for the cause of black voting rights in Alabama. In Washington, President Johnson was taking advantage of the moment to send a voting rights bill to Congress. Viola brooded for a week. On the afternoon of March 16, she phoned her husband from Wayne State and told him she was driving immediately to Selma. Sarah would take care of the children and she would return right after the march to the Alabama capital. This was the kind of impulsive decision Jim had learned to expect from his wife. Although Jim begged her to reconsider, he knew her mind was made up. He asked her to promise to phone home every evening, which she faithfully obeyed, and told her he would wire money as soon as he could get to Western Union.

Governor Wallace had already met with President Johnson and refused to provide protection for the demonstrators—people he characterized as "Communist-trained anarchists." Johnson asked him to think it over, but after he had done so, Wallace concluded that it was too much of an expense for the state of Alabama. Accordingly, the President called a press conference and announced that he had federalized nineteen hundred men in the Alabama National Guard and that he was sending an additional two thousand army troops, a hundred FBI agents, and another hundred U.S. marshals. Expecting the inevitable reaction, Johnson added, "It is not a welcome duty for the federal government to ever assume a state government's own responsibility for assuring the protection of citizens in the exercise of their constitutional rights."

With headquarters of the United Klans of America in Tuscaloosa, the Klan took a deep interest in the goings-on in Selma and the intrusion of the federal government. Selma had a real potential for dramatizing the South's need for the Klan, as well as for boosting Klan membership. UKA officers sent out directives for Klansmen to "keep under surveillance" the activities of the marchers from Selma to Montgomery. To the journalists stationed in Selma, the Klan's "surveillance" had climaxed on the afternoon of March 21, when an eighty-car Klan motorcade drove along Highway 80 yelling obscenities at the marchers. But a secret strong-arm team of Klansmen had been sent to the scene by Alabama Great Titan Robert Thomas.

Earlier in the year, Thomas had decided that in dealing with civil rights demonstrations, it was pointless to bring out Klansmen in large numbers, when two or three men throwing grenades from rooftops would be much more effective. Thomas felt this tactic would "considerably lessen the danger of having known Klansmen identified at the scene of racial demonstrations." The team Thomas sent to Selma was a trigger-happy bunch. Collie Leroy Wilkins, Jr., Eugene Thomas, and William O. Eaton were hardhat laborers and members of Bessemer Klavern Number 20. They had recently been implicated in the bombing of the Dickey Clay Manufacturing plant outside Bessemer; and Wilkins, who was only twenty-one, was on probation for illegal possession of a sawed-off shotgun. The trio was joined by Gary T. Rowe, a member of Birmingham's equally rugged Eastview Klavern. On March 25, the four men stopped to check things out in Montgomery and then drove to Selma. In the Silver Moon Cafe they met and talked with one of Reverend Reeb's murderers, who was proud of his work. "God bless you boys," he told them. "You boys do your job. I already did mine." That evening, the Klansmen were heading back to Montgomery. At a traffic light they spotted a green Oldsmobile occupied by a middle-aged white woman and a black teenage boy —a shocking combination in 1965 Alabama.

"Lookie there," Wilkins said with more astonishment than anger. "I'll be damned. Lookie there." The Olds had Michigan license plates.

"Let's get 'em," said Thomas who was driving.

The Olds was being driven by Viola Liuzzo. Her passenger was nineteen-year-old LeRoy Moton, a Selma native. The two had been assigned to shuttle the hundreds of arriving ministers, priests, nuns, rabbis, teachers, students, and journalists from the Montgomery airport to Selma and other points. The march to the capital had already concluded with a televised speech by Dr. King, which Governor Wallace had watched through binoculars from his statehouse windows. Viola was ready to go home. She had phoned Jim that evening and the experienced union man had said, "Vi, be careful, because the most dangerous time is *after* the march."

Now heading toward Montgomery, she realized that she was being followed. "These white people don't have any sense," she calmly told Moton, who was growing more frightened by the minute. For twenty minutes she kept ahead of her pursuers, glancing back and forth between the road and rear-view mirror and quietly humming "We Shall Overcome." She was an excellent driver who wasn't afraid of high speeds, and she seemed confident of staying ahead of the car until she reached the city limits of Montgomery where she expected it to retreat.

The pursuing Klansmen realized this "Yankee bitch" was more than they had bargained for and began arguing over whether or not they should run her car off the road. It was risky, because rumor had it that Alabama was crawling with FBI agents, and the FBI could do anything. "If you hit that automobile at all," Wilkins told Thomas, "we may get caught. If you just get a little bit of paint on it we'll get caught."

The speed of the two cars soon reached 100 miles per hour. Finally, Thomas closed in on the Olds' bumper. "Give it some gas," said Wilkins. As the Klansmen pulled alongside the Olds, Viola Liuzzo turned to her left and stared at her pursuers. Their windows were rolled down.

"All right," yelled Thomas, "shoot the hell out of it!"

Wilkins and Eaton stuck out their arms and emptied their .38 caliber revolvers as Thomas sped away. Gary Rowe quickly looked back. The green Olds still seemed to be moving. "I don't think you hit them," he said.

Wilkins slapped Rowe on the knee. "Baby brother," he chuckled, "don't worry about it. That bitch and that bastard are dead and in hell. I don't miss."

LeRoy Moton survived but Viola was dead—killed instantly from two bullets that had shattered her skull. The next day, as the news filled the nation's front pages, Jim Liuzzo was telephoned and visited by scores of state and federal dignitaries offering their condolences. Jim despaired of justice in his wife's murder, but to his and the nation's surprise, the case was broken in twenty-four hours. It so happened that Klansman Gary Rowe was an FBI informer. He had expected an assault that night, but never a murder.

The Klan's murder of a Northern white woman threw Lyndon Johnson into a rage. White House aides described the President's mood as "sheer wrath." Flanked by J. Edgar Hoover and the new attorney general Nicholas Katzenbach, Johnson went on national television. "We will not be intimidated by the terrorists of the Ku Klux Klan any more than by the terrorists of the Viet Cong," he said. "My father fought [Klansmen] in Texas. I have fought them all my life, because I believe them to threaten the peace of every community where they exist. I shall continue to fight them because I know their loyalty is not to the United States but to a hooded society of bigots. Men and women have stood against the Klan at times and places where to do so required a continuous act of courage. If Klansmen hear my voice today, let it be both an appeal and a warning to get out of the Klan now and return to decent society before it is too late."

Klansmen reacted sarcastically to the President's warning. They professed outrage at his blaming Klansmen for the murder before the case went to court. But Johnson was as confident of defeating the Klan as he was of whipping the Cong. He promised a complete congressional investigation of the Invisible Empire. He promised new legislation directed at these "enemies of justice who for decades have used the rope and the gun and the tar and the feathers." He asked Hoover to increase the FBI's surveillance of Klansmen. Hoover assured the President that the bureau was working night and day on the Klan problem, but he also cautioned the President against making too much of the Liuzzo matter. When Johnson asked why in the hell he shouldn't, Hoover told him some strange things, which have only recently come to light.

In an FBI memo dated a day after the murder, March 26, 1965

(and kept classified for nearly twenty years), Hoover recounted a private talk with Lyndon Johnson:

> I stated [Jim Liuzzo] doesn't have too good a background and the woman [Viola] had indications of needle marks in her arms where she had been taking dope; that she was sitting very, very close to the Negro in the car; that it had the appearance of a necking party.

The sexual content of Hoover's statements needs no comment, but his remark about needle marks contradicts an Alabama coroner's report. It's clear that Hoover was still concerned that the exposures of Klan violence were having a positive effect on the civil rights movement. It is difficult to say which he disliked more, the Klan or civil rights; but his actions suggest that he would have been relieved if both of them disappeared and he could return to fighting Communists and gangsters.

Although Johnson ignored Hoover's innuendoes, FBI field men leaked them to local law enforcement officers and to the press. In less than a month, the national topic changed from the willful murder of Liuzzo to her moral character. Just what was this white Yankee woman doing down there in the first place? With meaningful sidelong glances, Imperial Wizard Shelton said, "If this woman was at home with the children where she belonged, she wouldn't have been in jeopardy." Shelton also claimed to have information about Liuzzo's "police record" (her run-in with the Detroit school system) and her unusually liberated relationship with her husband. Soon the UKA distributed leaflets summarizing these "facts." Klansmen also spread rumors that the Selma march had been a veritable orgy where Liuzzo had presided as principal whore.

In a poll of Northern American housewives commissioned by the *Ladies Home Journal*, only 26 percent supported Liuzzo's decision to go to Selma. Most women agreed with the Imperial Wizard that she should have stayed home with the kids:

> I don't think a mother should go away and leave her children with anyone else no matter what the cause.

Another said:

> She was wrong in leaving her home and going down there and meddling. . . . I feel she should have stayed home and minded her own business.

And another:

> She had no right being down there, whatever her feelings were.

Shortly after his wife was buried, Jim Liuzzo began receiving hate mail from all over the country. His phone rang all night with long-distance obscene and sadistic calls, often from people who were drunk. He and his children suffered the jeers and, once, the gunfire of passing motorists. The cruelest stroke was a clipping from the classified section of the Birmingham *News* sent to him anonymously:

> Do you need a crowd drawer? I have 1963 Oldsmobile 2-dr. that Mrs. Viola Liuzzo was killed in. Bullet holes and everything still intact. Ideal to bring in crowd. $3,500.

And this kind of harassment never seemed to end.

The Klan continued to describe Liuzzo as little more than a prostitute. It raised several thousand dollars toward the legal fees of the three Klansmen responsible for her murder. At the state trial, Robert Shelton sat with the defense. The rumors were made sensational by defense attorney Matthew Hobson Murphy, Jr., Imperial Klonsel (lawyer) of the UKA:

> You know what the nigger [LeRoy Moton] said on the stand. . . . He said he passed out for twenty-five to thirty minutes. . . . What's he doing down there all that time? In that car alone with that woman? . . . And this white woman who got killed: White woman! . . . I thought I'd never see the day when Communists and niggers and white niggers and Jews were flying under the banner of the United Nations flag, not the American flag we fought for. . . . I'm proud to be a white man and I'm proud that I stand up on my feet for white supremacy.

The trial resulted in a hung jury. Klansmen in the crowded courtroom burst into cheers and applause. The three killers became local heroes and were paraded at Klan rallies. The young and handsome Collie Leroy Wilkins, Jr., had the same impact on Klanswomen as a rock-and-roll star.

The second trial was prosecuted by Richmond Flowers, Alabama's new aggressive attorney general, who detested the influence "a few hooded jerks" could exert in his state. During the new trial, Flowers ordered all Klansmen placed in the gallery and instructed his staff to keep their eyes on them whenever his back was turned. In his dramatic summation, Flowers ripped a half-dozen pages out of the book of Alabama statutes. "If you don't render the true verdict of guilty," he said, "you might as well tear the meaning of true verdict out of the book." Again the jury failed to convict. As in the previous two cases of Klan homicide, the Justice Department prepared to indict Wilkins and the others under the Ku-Klux statutes.

A far more important effect was seen on August 6, 1965, when President Johnson signed the Voting Rights Act into law. The act not only guaranteed blacks the right to vote but allowed them to win public office in many places in the South for the first time since Reconstruction. Although this was what a great many Southern whites had feared the most, it did nothing but strengthen the South. Within five years, the South would greatly outshine the North in the amicability of its race relations. Somewhere in all this stands the complex tragedy of Viola Liuzzo—the only victim of Klan violence ever to have been systematically denied her martyrdom. Part of this was Hoover's doing, but the rest came from the censure of the American people. Liuzzo had defied not one but two conventions. First she was a carpetbagger, and survey data on the COFO project shows that more than half of the American people disapproved of carpetbaggers. Secondly, she had defied the boundaries of what society deemed acceptable behavior for women. Liuzzo could be called a feminist ten years ahead of her time, but many present-day feminists find her too "impulsive and unfocused" to be included among the pioneers of sisterhood. A full evaluation of Liuzzo's place in history must wait some time in the future.*

The most immediate effect of the Liuzzo murder was that the President ordered Congress to launch a complete investigation of the Ku Klux Klan. By coincidence, HUAC had been conducting a preliminary inquiry into Klan activities since January 1965.

---

* In the meantime, Liuzzo's children—the children she was accused of abandoning—continue in their efforts to win retribution for their mother. "We were always taught a respect for life," Mary Liuzzo has recently said, "so it was no surprise when she got involved in the struggle for civil rights, human rights." In 1983, a $2 million lawsuit against the FBI filed by the five Liuzzo children was dismissed by U.S. District Judge Charles Joiner. Tony Liuzzo, Viola's oldest son, has vowed to "continue to fight as long as I live."

HUAC's involvement was the work of its newest member, Charles Weltner, a liberal Atlanta congressman, who had joined the committee principally to fight the Klan. In order to get the funds needed for a complete investigation, Weltner had given a magnificent speech before the House. "I believe I speak for a vast majority of southerners in calling for action," he said. "For in doing nothing we will inaugurate a second century for the Ku Klux Klan. . . . The boast of the Klan, 'yesterday, today and tomorrow,' is true in part. For the Klan of yesterday is the Klan of today. The year 1865 witnessed the birth of the Ku Klux Klan. Let the year 1965 witness its final demise."

HUAC's request for money put House liberals in a quandary. As in the 1940s, they certainly wanted the Klan exposed; but they didn't believe HUAC's inquisitors should be investigating anybody, and they had plenty of reasons for mistrusting HUAC's oft-repeated promise of a complete Klan investigation. Representative Ryan of New York was afraid the investigation would be "the opening wedge of a witchhunt into civil-rights organizations," and in fact, some HUAC members were already expressing an interest in investigating the Black Muslims. In 1921, an exuberant Colonel Simmons had proclaimed, "Congress *made* us!" Wasn't HUAC more likely to repeat that blunder than any committee in the House? The editors of *Christian Century* thought that sending HUAC after the Klan was like "sending a goose to chase a fox. . . . We do not expect any good to come from the nation's reliance upon a committee which is vigilant in spirit to curtail a secret society of bigots which is vigilant in fact." At a meeting of the SCLC in Baltimore, Martin Luther King added his voice to the opposition: "The SCLC is opposed to the House Committee on Un-American Activities investigating Klan-like groups." King preferred that the President appoint a special commission, "comparable to the Warren Commission," to tackle the Klan. And in contrast to HUAC's customs, King added that such an investigation "should be concerned with only overt acts and not thought processes."

More objections were raised when the full committee announced the members of the subcommittee assigned to the Klan. Few objected to Weltner, a Southern congressman who had strongly supported the Voting Rights Act of 1965. But Chairman Edwin Willis of Louisiana was an unimaginative Communist-finder. Joe Pool, as a member of the Texas legislature, had once favored a bill that would have barred members of the NAACP from holding public office. John Buchanan's hostility toward the Klan came mostly from the blame he placed on it for spurring passage of the Voting Rights Act through the Liuzzo murder; he also favored a law that would bar Martin Luther King from his home state of Alabama. The fifth member of the subcommittee, John Ashbrook, was its only Yankee—and the only congressman from Ohio who had voted against the Civil Rights Act.

In April, the House appropriated $50,000 for an investigation of the Klan by HUAC. The forty-three voting against the funding were a mixed bag of ultra-liberals, ultra-conservatives, and four of the House's six blacks.

With more national attention on the Klan than on LBJ's escalation of the Vietnam conflict, the editors of *Playboy* magazine conducted one of their popular interviews with the UKA's Imperial Wizard. In spite of being "a God-fearing man" opposed to pornography and perversion, Robert Shelton was unable to resist *Playboy*'s offer. Since the editors left all of Shelton's mispronunciations and malapropisms intact, the interview published in August sent gales of laughter through many Northern college dormitories and cooperatives where it was read aloud.

SHELTON: There is several Klans, you know. That is the trouble of throwing every nut in the same bag and saying it's all the same kind of nuts.

PLAYBOY: That's an aptly chosen metaphor. But all of those arrested for recent racial murders—those of Lemuel Penn, Reverend Reeb, and Mrs. Liuzzo—have been members of your own United Klan. . . .

SHELTON: I'm not saying they were and I'm not saying they're not. It would be a violation of my sacred Klan oath to identify members of the Klan. But speaking of violating oaths, we are finding many cases where the Federal Bureau of Investigation is purging witnesses with attempts to bribe.

PLAYBOY: Don't you mean *suborning* witnesses?

SHELTON: I mean they are offering money to get them to make statements on promises of giving them land, relocating their family, giving them money.

PLAYBOY: Can you cite a case?

SHELTON: I certainly can: that pimp Gary Rowe, the FBI informer in this Luziano case.

PLAYBOY: You mean Liuzzo? . . . On several occasions you have called for a House Un-American Activities Committee investi-

gation of CORE, SNCC, and the NAACP for possible Communist infiltration. Would you be as willing to submit to a congressional investigation of the Klan?
SHELTON: Certainly. Why not? What's good for the goose is good for the gander. . . .*

At this time, Klansmen were still publicly praising HUAC, whose efforts they believed mirrored the Klan's own at cleaning up all that was rotten in America. In a sparse rally north of Birmingham, Shelton repeated his belief that anyone who took the Fifth Amendment before HUAC was probably a Communist. Dr. J. M. Edwards, Grand Dragon of Louisiana, wrote to Chairman Willis and actually urged him "to investigate United Klans and make your findings public as soon as possible. . . . I have great admiration for your committee, and I thank you for your untiring efforts to keep America safe."

When HUAC announced it would be calling its first witness, Robert Shelton, on October 17, the Imperial Wizard told reporters, "I'll be there with boots on." He arrived not only in boots, but in a dark suit with a button on the lapel that said NEVER. Much to the committee's interest, he also sported a large diamond ring. When Chief Investigator Donald Appell began by handing Shelton a copy of the UKA's corporation papers and asking him to identify it, his answer, read haltingly from a slip of paper, sent reporters racing out of the caucus room to telephones:

> Sir, I respectfully decline to answer that question for the reason that I honestly feel my answer might tend to incriminate me in violation of my rights as guaranteed to me under the amendents five, one, four and fourteen of the Constitution of the United States.

Walter Goodman wrote in *The Nation:* "For a Kluxer to take the fifth like an ordinary Commy is poetry; for him to take the fourteenth is epic."

During his questioning, Shelton repeated his formal refusal a total of 158 times. Bored reporters started taking bets on which amendment he would stress. Outside the Cannon Office Building, Shelton was much more talkative—in fact he was fairly voluble to reporters after being unable to speak his mind to congressmen.

---

* Originally appeared in *Playboy* Magazine: Copyright © 1965 by *Playboy*.

Shelton claimed that HUAC's persecution would only make the Klan grow. "I'm trying to find some way to keep it going longer." Asked what his NEVER button meant, Shelton replied that it meant *never* to LBJ, *never* to Martin Luther King—

"And never answer a question?" a reporter suggested.

"No comment," Shelton replied.

All of the UKA Dragons and nearly all of the supoenaed Klansmen refused to answer the committee's questions. Sam Bowers and J. B. Stoner were equally uncooperative. The hearing thus became tedious, drawn-out sessions in which the committee's scholarly-looking chief investigator Donald Appell recited facts he had uncovered and asked the witness to "affirm or deny" them; Klansmen then took the Fifth and Appell would move on to more facts. Having cut his investigative teeth during the Alger Hiss case, Don Appell had done his homework well. Over the past nine months, he had attended Klan rallies and dug up the typical scuttlebutt that the committee relished. For example, he revealed that Shelton had channeled large amounts of Klan dues into a front he called the Alabama Rescue Service and then had withdrawn funds from it to buy himself a Cadillac, as well as less exotic items from the local Piggly Wiggly supermarket. Bob Jones was accused of making substantial profits on the sale of sheets in the Tarheel State. South Carolina Dragon Bob Scoggin was exposed as a convicted drunk driver who had been bilking the Veterans' Administration for greatly exaggerated war injuries. And Reverend Roy Woodle—an ex-Kludd who talked so fast that newsmen dubbed him "Woodle Woodpecker"—testified that Klan leaders used shills at rallies to get the collection plate going.

Those in favor of the committee thought it was doing a good job with the Klan. *Time* magazine gushed that "daylight and logic are as lethal to the hugger-mugger mystique of the 'invisible empire' as Lysol is to microbes"—although both claims are debatable. On the other side, Murray Kempton in the *New Republic* pointed out that HUAC's investigation had been prompted by LBJ's call for "justice against terrorists," but had come all the way from there to "focus where its small nature guides it—to the punishment of petty larceny." Kempton regretted that HUAC had discovered a whole bunch of new un-American activities, including: (1) failing to report one's full income to the IRS; (2) buying the family car with company funds; (3) getting a free room from a hotel in return for awarding it the contract to host your company's annual board of directors meeting; and (4) collecting a $4,000 annual salary from a public contractor for no visible service except your status as a friend of the governor.

Fortunately for the reporters who were dying of boredom at the hearings, the proceedings were not without bursts of entertainment. There were Chairman Willis's popeyed, *Keystone Kop* double takes at recitations of Klan crookedness; Joe Pool's indignation when he barked at a Klansman, "There's no use staring at me! You're not scaring me one bit!" And John Buchanan's attempt at wit in "accidentally" referring to Shelton as the "Inferior Lizard." But the best was an involved exchange between Pool and James Venable, Wizard of the National Knights.

Among Venable's numerous crackpot schemes spun from his Klan work was the "Christian Buyers and Voters League," which had launched a crusade against "the kosher food racket." Venable claimed that, as a Zionist-front organization, Heinz Foods was skimping on the pork in its pork-and-beans. He also informed the nation that kosher canned goods could be identified by a tiny little *k* buried in the information on the label. Venable had made a list of more than a thousand of these products and urged Klansmen to boycott them so as not to support the "Zionist conspiracy." Congressman Pool had a terrible time trying to follow Venable's logic:

POOL: Are you telling me, if I buy a can of fish on Friday, I am supporting the Catholic faith?
VENABLE: No, sir.
POOL: What is the difference?
VENABLE: There's a lot of difference between kosher—
POOL: A little *k*?
VENABLE: *Kosher*, and it has certain ingredients in it.
POOL: I kind of like kosher pickles better than I do regular pickles.
VENABLE: I have eaten them myself, your honor.

When Pool recognized the companies of his own Texas constituents on Venable's boycott list, he nearly lost control. He was especially angry over finding the name of Mrs. Baird's Bakery and was not unmindful of how his words would appear in the newspapers of his district.

POOL: Mrs. Baird began her operation by baking birthday cakes. Little by little, her business increased. Through her baking, she was able to put her four sons through college. The whole family

has contributed much to Dallas and even to the entire State.
. . . It is a disservice to the nation to publish a list like this. I am
pointing out your error with regard to companies I am personally familiar with, and I want the record to show this.

VENABLE: . . . I'm sure you're familiar with the companies.

POOL: I'm sure the same list has the same inaccuracies and as-
sumptions all the way through it. I think the whole thing is
wrong anyhow, to say that something is bad and you shouldn't
buy it just because Jewish people have something to do with it.
I think that is a wrong assumption. I think the Jewish people
have done a lot in this world to make America great, and I want
to be sure that gets in the record, too.

VENABLE: I hold no ill will, Mr. Chairman, against any race, color
or creed. Some of the best friends I got are Jewish people.

Robert Sherrill, correspondent to the *Miami Herald*, said that
these and similar buffooneries "eventually became the high points
in the hearings, even to reporters who fully intended to treat the
investigation as a thing of dignity."

The five volumes of testimony generated by HUAC are a rich
source of Klan history during the 1960s. But HUAC's immediate
effect on the Klan—and the committee hoped for a negative one
—was negligible at best. The committee took credit for a few
things. The frightened Grand Dragons of Alabama and Delaware
resigned from the Empire before testifying. Grand Klaliff Grady
Mars committed suicide shortly after taking the Fifth during his
questioning. Joseph DuBois had hoped his war record would save
him from the committee's detailed probing:

APPELL: Mr. DuBois, what is your educational background, sir?

DUBOIS: May I have a drink of water, please? I haven't been this
nervous since just before going into action on Guadalcanal.

But when the questions kept coming, DuBois resigned from the
Klan on the witness stand. Some Klansmen reported that the information about Klan leaders lining their pockets with Klan funds
—plus the fact that, like Commies, they refused to testify openly
—had a deleterious effect on the Klan's rank and file. That is
refuted, however, by data gathered by the Anti-Defamation
League, which showed, as Shelton hoped, that the hearings
boosted Klan membership, at least for a year or so. The biggest
effect the hearings had on the Klan wasn't realized until the com-

mittee cited Shelton, Bob Jones, and Bob Scoggin for contempt of Congress. Calvin Craig's citation was dropped after he agreed to resign from the Klan. Like liberal victims of HUAC before him, Shelton fought the contempt citations as unlawful. "Ours is a righteous cause," he told his followers, "and all the Legions of Hell cannot prevail against it." But the convictions were upheld after appeal, and the three Klan leaders began serving one-year sentences toward the end of the decade. Not until then was the UKA thrown in disarray. Lesser Klansmen made things worse by jockeying for the leadership. This was especially so in the large North Carolina Realm, which had raised $47,000 of the $100,000 in legal expenses for UKA Klansmen appearing before the committee and which suffered internal division after Bob Jones went to jail.

While HUAC hit the Klan at the top, the rank and file suffered more from the FBI's harassment. Soon after the FBI launched its investigation of Sam Bowers and his henchmen, Shelton and his lieutenants had slipped into Mississippi to suck up the disoriented White Knights into the UKA. Consequently, the bureau had extended its surveillance to include Shelton's organization. Some FBI informers were members of both groups, spying on them simultaneously. After forty-five years of immunity from the FBI, Klansmen suddenly found themselves the object of a bureau vendetta. Praise for the FBI's role in suppressing the Klan of the 1960s lasted a decade. In 1975, however, a special U.S. Senate committee learned that the FBI's effectiveness in dealing with the Klan was owed to a nasty little program called Cointelpro.

Cointelpro was essentially a Hoover-hatched scheme of cheap psychological warfare and dirty tricks. At innocuous levels, the program was simple schoolboy mischief. When Klansmen held large conferences in major cities, agents would phone the hotels where they were booked and cancel their reservations. In order to break the weakest suspect in the Lemuel Penn murder case, the FBI sent him a cake on his thirty-seventh birthday; thirty-six of the candles were white, but one was "blood red," indicating that agents were on his trail and would be closing in soon. While the HUAC hearings were in progress, the FBI bombarded Klansmen with postcards saying their leaders had duped them: "By placing themselves above the law of the land through the invocation of the fifth amendment, these unresponsible Klan leaders have joined hands with Communists who also hide behind the fifth amendment." When revelations from Washington began documenting the amount of dues Dragons were pocketing, Klansmen received more postcards: cartoons of bloated Kluxers in barrooms, with captions asking, *Which Klan leaders are spending your money tonight?*

At more serious levels, agents gave money to Klansmen to form independent Klans, splintering the UKA from within. Agents "leaned on" Klansmen's employers, and a number of Klansmen lost their jobs. Consistent with Hoover's favorite obsession, much of Cointelpro's harassment was of a sexual nature. Informers were requested, whenever possible, to sleep with the wives of other Klansmen in order to learn new information and to alienate the affections of the Klansman's spouse. "My instructions," said informer Gary Rowe to the Senate committee, "were to sleep with as many wives as I could." (From all accounts, Rowe performed his duty like a little soldier.) The FBI also created a form letter to be sent "anonymously" to the wives of Klansmen, telling them that their husbands were having affairs with other women. The letter was crafted to sound like the sincere, conscience-struck confession of an average Klanswoman:

> Yes, Mrs.————, he has been committing adultery. My menfolk say they don't believe this but I think they do. I feel like crying. I saw her with my own eyes. They call her Ruby. . . . I saw her strut around at a rally with her lust-filled eyes and smart aleck figure.

Causing marital discord among Klansmen was an especially effective ploy. Another trick played on Klansmen's paranoia. Kluxers were painfully aware that the Empire had been infiltrated by FBI agents; in fact, about 6 percent of all Klansmen in the late 1960s worked for the FBI. The bureau took advantage of their fears by "leaking" information that noninformers were informers. They sent out new cartoon postcards of a wily Klansman saying, "*I am an informer. Color me fed.* Klansmen began developing morbid, occasionally violent degrees of mistrust for each other. One Klansman said, "Everybody suspects everybody. The FBI has infiltrated to the point where you can't trust your best friend."

At its very worst, Cointelpro may have actually provoked Klan violence in order to arrest its perpetrators. The strongest case for this occurred in Mississippi in 1968. After the bombing of a synagogue, the FBI raised $38,500 from the Anti-Defamation League and Meridian's Jewish community in order to pay two informers to "set up" Thomas Tarrants, a dangerously militant, twenty-one-year-old Klansman and professional bomber. The paid informers talked Tarrants into bombing the home of Meyer Davidson, a Jewish businessman. When Tarrants arrived at the Davidson residence late at night, he stepped out of his car with a bomb in one hand and a gun in the other. The police opened fire. To everyone's surprise, Tarrant's accomplice was pretty Kathy Ainsworth, a sweet young elementary schoolteacher by day and a demolitions expert at night. In the ensuing battle, Ainsworth was killed and Tarrants and several lawmen were injured. The Los Angeles Times later accused the FBI of provoking the bloody incident, but the main perpetrator refutes this. Davidson was "a high priority target," Tarrants said in his memoirs written in prison during a Christian conversion. "So the FBI did not not lure us into doing something we had no intention of doing."

After developing Cointelpro for the Klan, the FBI also used it against the Black Panthers, civil rights leaders, and antiwar demonstrators. The FBI agent Joseph Sullivan, chief Klanbuster in the Mississippi murders, was one of Cointelpro's strongest defenders and called it "a fine program." It was extremely cost effective, and Sullivan argued that disruption, not investigation, was the key to breaking the Klan. "Are you going to spend millions of taxpayer dollars," he asked, "going around ringing doorbells and asking questions of people who know nothing, or are you going to very systematically and very carefully penetrate these organizations like the Ku Klux Klan and the Black Panthers and disrupt them from within at a cost of almost nothing, and that's precisely what we did, we disrupted them."

Hoover abruptly terminated Cointelpro in late 1971. The director told disgruntled agents that "the climate of public opinion" demanded it. There's little doubt that Cointelpro exemplified "police-state tactics," as the Los Angeles Times charged. Unfortunately, it also gave Klansmen the opportunity to assume the posture of victims. In 1976, Attorney General Edward H. Levi was obliged to inform nearly sixty Klansmen that they had been Cointelpro victims, and some of them sued the government. (The UKA's suit for $50 million failed.) But people on both sides do not deny the effectiveness of the program. Former Attorney General Katzenbach said that the FBI's activities were "one of the major factors in bringing to an end the Klan's criminal conspiracy of violence that scourged the South. . . ." Robert Shelton agreed that, in combination with the HUAC hearings, "the FBI's counterintelligence program hit us in membership and weakened us for about ten years."

A third factor in the Klan's deterioration in the late 1960s has received little attention: the Presidential campaigns of George C. Wallace. In spring 1968, Hoover estimated that national Klan membership had shrunk from its peak of forty thousand in 1965 to fourteen thousand. Over the next two years that number would annually diminish by half. It's now clear that Wallace's campaigns as the American Independent Party candidate swallowed a lot of disaffected Klansmen. In fact, Wallace offered them the first really viable alternative to the Klan. The Birmingham *Post-Herald* observed, "Haters don't need to join a Klan when they have George Wallace. If you want something hated, just name it—he'll hate it for you." Wallace warmly welcomed the support of active and former Klansmen. In an interview with journalist Tom Wicker, he said, "At least a Klansman will fight for his country. He don't tear up his draft card."

Wallace's impact was felt at two levels. First of all, his 1968 campaign prevented a slight showing of Klan support in the North from becoming stronger. The racism of the white North had been brought out increasingly in the latter half of the decade. After suffering the curses and rock throwing of angry Chicagoans, Martin Luther King suggested that white Mississippians visit the Windy City "to learn how to hate." Following the passage of the Voting Rights Act of 1965 and race riots in major cities, the North had shown signs of what journalists called "white backlash," and small cloisters of Klansmen began appearing in such states as Pennsylvania, New Jersey, Ohio, and Michigan. The Grand Dragons of Indiana and Michigan, William Chaney and Robert Miles respectively, had headed little more than one-man operations; and whatever support they may have had dried up after the two were sent to jail for bombings. For the most part, Northern Kluxdom rarely got farther than a few neo-Nazi crazies—people like Danny Burros of New York City, who killed himself after the *New York Times* revealed he was actually a Jew suffering from a pathological condition of self-hatred. For more self-respecting Northern racists, Wallace was much more palatable than the Klan.

After helping to abort the infant Klan in the North, the Wallace campaigns successfully skimmed the Southern Klans of their most effective and economically well-off supporters. There was hardly anything left of the Southern Klan but leaderless dregs. Journalist Stewart Alsop visited the once powerful Realm of North Carolina and found "something very sad about the dreary little klaverns with their kitchen tables masquerading as 'altars,' and their coffee cans filled with old cigarette butts and hand-lettered, mispelled signs; and something very sad about the Klan."

Of all factors contributing to the decline of the Klan in the late 1960s, there was only one of merit, only one of justice. Prosecutions at the state level against the murderers of the three COFO workers, Lemuel Penn, and Viola Liuzzo had resulted in either acquittals or hung juries. In both the COFO and Penn cases, federal district judges had ruled that the Reconstruction Ku-Klux statutes could not apply since, under the 1951 *United States v. Williams* decision, the right violated—life—did not fall under the protection of the federal government. The Liuzzo case was a different matter, however. The Selma march was a peaceful assembly for the purpose of petitioning the government for a redress of grievances and, as such, came within the purview of the first amendment. It had also been sanctioned by a federal court order. Arguing these distinctions skillfully before an all-white Alabama jury, the Justice Department won convictions against Collie Leroy Wilkins and his two Klan henchmen on December 3, 1965. Under the remnants of the Ku-Klux statutes, the defendants were sentenced to ten years in federal prison for violating Liuzzo's civil rights.

The Justice Department had already appealed the decisions on the COFO and Penn murders to the U.S. Supreme Court, and the government's case was argued by the new solicitor general Thurgood Marshall, soon to be a distinguished member of the Supreme Court himself. The court reexamined its thinking on the Williams case and, in a historic decision that virtually overturned Williams, ruled that the two cases could be tried under the Reconstruction statutes. In 1966, the Justice Department won convictions from a Georgia jury against Howard Sims and Cecil Myers for the violation of Lemuel Penn's civil rights.*

In October 1967, three years after the COFO murders, Samuel Holloway Bowers, Deputy Cecil Price, and their White Knight conspirators stood trial in a Mississippi federal court. The judge was William Cox, who had previously ruled against the federal government's authority in the case, and civil rights leaders expected the worst. On October 19, the jury came out and reported that it was hopelessly deadlocked. In a remarkable decision that

---

* After serving his time, Sims was murdered in 1981 by a friend with a twelve-gauge shotgun similar to the one he had used to kill Lemuel Penn.

astonished everyone, Judge Cox gave the jury new instructions based on *Allen* v. *United States*—the so-called "dynamite" charge:

> This is an important case. The trial has been expensive both to the prosecution and the defense. If you should fail to agree on a verdict, the case is left open and undecided. Like all cases, it must be disposed of at some time. There appears no reason to believe that another trial would not be equally expensive to both sides. Nor does there appear to be any reason to believe that the case can be tried again better or more exhaustively than it has been, on either side. . . . You may conduct your deliberations as you choose, but I suggest that you retire and carefully re-examine and reconsider all of the evidence bearing on the questions before you.

The next day, the Mississippi jury delivered verdicts of guilty for Bowers, Price, and five other defendants.* It seemed as if crosseyed Ben Butler and his fellow radical Republicans had reached beyond the grave to wreak justice on Kluxers a hundred years after Reconstruction.

Looking at the second Reconstruction in the latter part of the 1960s, C. Vann Woodward pronounced it "a galloping revolution" and claimed it had "already scored up more achievements of durable promise than the First ever did." In comparing the two Reconstructions, two points should be made. In an important respect, the two movements were similar: Instead of hobbling the stride toward freedom, the Klan quickened it. By beating the freedom riders, Klansmen accidentally killed Jim Crow in interstate travel. In the wake of Birmingham, St. Augustine, and the COFO murders in Mississippi came the Civil Rights Act of 1964. In the wake of Selma and Viola Liuzzo's murder came the Voting Rights Act of 1965.

In another respect, the two Reconstructions were very different. The first Reconstruction had been a white-led revolution with few blacks in leadership roles. But the vanguard of the second Reconstruction had been black—such brilliant leaders as Martin Luther King, James Farmer, and Thurgood Marshall, as well as devoted field workers from the NAACP, SCLC, CORE, and SNCC. In his essay on the Klan written in 1924, Ho Chi Minh had predicted

---

* The defendants' appeals lasted two years, and they finally went to prison in 1970. Bowers was released in 1976, becoming an ordained Lutheran minister in the course of his imprisonment.

that blacks would be a formidable force "if united" and that when that day came, they would no longer tolerate the Klan or allow "their kinsmen to be beaten or murdered with impunity." It is merely ironic that, when that day came, the United States was also involved in a war with that seer and his countrymen.

In August 1970, a Gallup Poll revealed that 76 percent of the American people strongly disapproved of the Klan, with the rest showing mild approval or no opinion. More interesting was the fact that Americans rated the Klan worse than the Viet Cong. In 1974, the FBI estimated that the number of Klansmen had shrunk to an all-time low of fifteen hundred. It seemed as if the Klan was dying out completely. Of course, it had also seemed that way in 1930, in 1944, and in 1952.

13

"THE BIBLE IN ONE HAND AND A .38 IN THE OTHER"

A Media-Oriented Revival: 1974–1984

An Imperial Wizard of the KKK with a college degree was an oddity in itself, but a twenty-four-year-old Wizard with a high IQ and the good looks of a soap-opera star was downright confusing. New York talk-show host Stanley Siegel said, "He sat on my program and he said the most outrageous things you ever heard about blacks and Jews. The entire time he had this beguiling smile on his face. It was disconcerting." Tom Snyder, host of the late-night talk show, *Tomorrow*, was just as perplexed. "You are intelligent, articulate, charming," Snyder told the Wizard when he was a guest. "I certainly was prepared to dislike him," said Marlene Roeder of the ACLU, "but there he was—charming, intelligent, and agreeing with me on First Amendment rights."

The new Wizard was David Duke of New Orleans, wunderkind of the Invisible Empire and the man most responsible for the 1974 revival of the Klan—just when it seemed to have completely disappeared. Moved by the example of General Nathan B. Forrest and the Reconstruction Klan legends, Duke was concerned over how low the Klan had sunk. "We've got to get out of the cow pasture and into the hotel meeting rooms," he told disciples during the early months of his mission. Duke did just that. He eliminated much of the Klan's claptrap that had been a staple since Colonel

Simmons's day. He preferred the title "National Director" to "Imperial Wizard" and began calling cross burnings "illuminations." He personally wrote and oversaw the production of commercials for radio and television:

> Thousands of organizations work for the special interests of minorities. . . . Give them a little competition—come to a huge rally of the Ku Klux Klan. . . . Hear David Duke, dynamic young leader of the Ku Klux Klan. . . . Enjoy the great Anthony Brothers Band. . . . See the beautiful cross-lighting ceremony.

He also gave the Klan's racism a slick veneer of logic that tugged at liberal doubts and primed a white conservative backlash that was still latent in the mid-1970s. His was an old argument: As blacks rose in society, whites declined. But he gave it immediacy by harping on reverse discrimination, affirmative action, and forced busing. Whites had given up too many "privileges" during the 1960s, he said. "You must understand," he constantly hammered, "that the white people today are becoming a second-class citizens' group in our own country. . . . We are losing our rights all the way across the board. White people face massive discrimination in employment opportunities, in scholarship opportunities in school, in promotions in industry, in college entrance admittance."

Covering one of Duke's cross-country tours for *Playboy*, Harry Crews had to numb himself with vodka to ease the strain of ideological differences with so pleasant a fellow. "I liked Duke and many of the other members of his organization," Crews said. "When they broke out of their racial monologs and rampant paranoia, they were great guys to travel with or talk with or eat with." Duke had a striking physical presence—six-feet-two, trim, handsome, coifed in a stylish razor-cut, and impeccably dressed. In retrospect, he seems a harbinger of the 1980s, in his clean-living, vitamin-gulping devotion to vigorous exercise; and daily weightlifting and one-arm pushups had added bulk to his upper arms and shoulders that looked nice under a corduroy safari jacket. With the exception of Barbara Walters, female interviewers described him as sexy. Journalist Patsy Sims called him "the Klan's answer to Robert Redford." Candice Bergen did a photo layout of him, calling him "a fascinating, extremely interesting person."

Duke was born in Tulsa, Oklahoma, to affluent, middle-class parents who didn't share his "racialism" (one of the new words he employed to clean up the Klan). His father was an engineer for Shell Oil. His family moved a lot, and his early childhood was cosmopolitan. He attended elementary school in the Netherlands and then a private academy in Georgia. His parents moved to New Orleans in the 1960s, where he graduated from John F. Kennedy High School. He enrolled in Louisiana State University but took a year off to teach English to local officers in Laos under the auspices of the State Department. Returning to LSU, he devoted himself to private studies of white supremacy, anti-Semitism, and Nazi history. Once he donned storm-trooper browns and a swastika armband and marched with a placard reading GAS THE CHICAGO SEVEN* to protest a speech by William Kunstler at Tulane University. That was "guerrilla theater," said Duke, "a stunt . . . it was neat." In 1974 he graduated from LSU with a bachelors' degree in history. A member of Louisiana's independent Knights of the Ku Klux Klan during his student years, he took over the leadership of the moribund order shortly after graduation.

Within a year, the Klan's old guard was forced to pay attention to Duke. Robert Shelton was still Wizard of the UKA, though he was now selling used cars part time to make ends meet. And the UKA still had more members than any Klan, though it had been severely drained of fire and imagination after Shelton's imprisonment and the Cointelpro operation. Remarking on Duke in *The Fiery Cross*, Shelton admitted, "He comes on like a reasonable person, serious, sincere and conservatively dressed. No flaming, wild-eyed nut would go over half so well." But Shelton was suspicious of Duke's courtship of the media—the UKA now shunned publicity and required lie-detector tests of all prospective members. (Shelton also suspected that Duke was responsible for a story that had appeared in *The Mobilizer*, a gay tabloid, claiming that the old Wizard had been altered by a homosexual experience during his incarceration.)

Superficially at least, Duke tried to make his Knights as different as possible from the UKA. He recruited on college campuses and

---

* The Chicago Seven were seven young men, including Abbie Hoffman, Tom Hayden and Jerry Rubin, who were the first to be indicted under the 1968 federal antiriot statute for their involvement in the demonstrations during the Democratic National Convention in August 1968. The Chicago Seven were defended by William Kunstler, and the trial was noted for the dramatic, often shocking confrontations between the defendants and seventy-four-year-old Judge Julius J. Hoffman.

tried to enlist "other intellectuals." His Patriot Bookstore in Metairie, Louisiana, stocked "egghead" books in addition to the usual Klan items, such as records of Odis Cochran and the Three Bigots singing "Ship Those Niggers Back." For the first time, women were accepted in Duke's Klan on equal terms with men—Duke had far too much appeal to women to restrict their membership in any way. Catholics were more than welcome. Duke also had a good mail-order recruiting business in the North and even in Canada. During the 1975 Boston busing crisis, he was well received in South Boston. "They are just as Klan-oriented as the Southern people, maybe more so," he observed. In place of the cracked records of "The Old Rugged Cross" played at UKA rallies, Duke hired live bluegrass and rock bands. He tried to minimize the importance of the Klan uniform. He conceded to wearing a white robe at rallies but never the hood. He was never caught publicly saying "nigger" or "kike." He professed nonviolence. "You can't do yourself, your family or our movement any good whatsoever if you are in jail," he told followers. Instead, politics was the new way for the Klan—"the best way to change things in this country." In 1975 he received one-third of the votes in a race for Louisiana State Senate.

Anyone who carefully followed Duke's TV appearances learned that he repeated entire phrases, sentences, sometimes paragraphs. In short, he had very little to say but always said it well. He appeared polite and sensitive, and never seemed to lose his temper. In one interview, veteran columnist Carl Rowan lost control and began ranting while Duke calmly continued with "yes, sir" and "no, sir." Journalists wryly commented on his "rhinestone racism" and "button-down terror," but they seemed willing to follow him anywhere. At a well publicized alien watch at the California–Mexico border, Klansmen in their trucks equipped with spotlights and CBs were outnumbered five to one by reporters. When no aliens appeared, Duke casually remarked, "I think some Mexicans are afraid to enter the country because of the Klan." And the stunt made *Newsweek*.

Since he was the only Klansman able to capture media attention, Duke drew hundreds into his organization, which reached a peak of thirty-five hundred members, and was able to secure the services of several talented men—as well as the usual borderline cases—to represent his Knights in other states. He appointed Dragons in Florida, Alabama, and Texas—and, more significantly, in Connecticut, New York, and California.

The new Dragon in California was Tom Metzger, a TV repairman, former leader of the White Brotherhood, and a transported Hoosier. Back home in Warsaw, Indiana, people remembered Tom as "a likeable, quiet sort of guy with a love for science and electronics." (Metzger eventually created a computerized enemies list and an elaborate video-camera surveillance system over his home in a San Diego suburb.) They couldn't imagine what had led a nice boy like Tom into the Klan; surely it wasn't his Indiana Klan heritage, for Tom had been raised a Roman Catholic. Others wondered how such a "nerd" could win the attention he received in the press. Metzger called himself "a twenty-first-century Klansman" and always wore a .45 Colt pistol, even around the house. One of his innovations was black uniforms instead of white robes. His special black-uniformed security guards also wore riot helmets and carried clubs, mace, and black-lacquered plywood shields. Escorted by this team, he picketed the arrival of Vietnamese boat people in San Diego and led a protest march to the federal courthouse.

Metzger retained the Hoosier's love of practical politics. "I would even work with the political left if we could just get them to recognize the race issue," he said. And he surprised political experts in 1980 by winning the Democratic nomination for congressman of California's forty-third district. Although he lost the election to the Republican incumbent, his radio spots—"Let me raise a little hell for you"—were a novelty in the midst of so many tired campaign slogans.

Don Black was Duke's choice in Alabama. Like Duke, Black was young, clean-cut, and college educated, but that was the extent of the comparison. Black had started a Klan chapter while a student at the University of Alabama, where he was thrown out of the ROTC for his racist activities. "The Klan is going to save America," he promised. "One day we will take America back from the non-whites who stole it from us." But Black's most publicized venture was his attempt to take a foreign country from its native inhabitants. In early spring 1981, he and nine other Klansmen, including two Canadians, conspired to overthrow the island government of Dominica. The fantastic scheme was allegedly hatched by Texas mercenary Mike Perdue, operating in conjunction with Dominica's deposed prime minister Patrick John. If successful, Klansmen were promised territory on the island for use as an international training base and a hideout for Klansmen on the run from the law. It was the first South American filibuster campaign by a Klan group since the Knights of the Golden Circle mustered at the Rio Grande in the 1850s. Unfortunately for Black and his henchmen, the able-bodied seamen they paid $15,000 to transport them to Dominica were U.S. Treasury Agents in disguise. Charged with violating the U.S. Neutrality Act, Black and his companions were sentenced to three years in federal prison. *Time* magazine called the ill-fated venture the "bayou of pigs."

The new Grand Dragon of Texas, Louis Beam, was a graduate of the University of Houston and an army veteran. Beam projected the popularized image of the crazed Vietnam vet. "I've got news for you, nigger," he ranted at a rally, "I'm not going to be in front of my television set, I'm gonna be hunting you. I don't need any of the three Jewish-owned networks to tell me what I've got to do. I've got the Bible in one hand and a .38 in the other hand and I know what to do." The war never seemed to have ended for Louis Beam, and he constantly talked about killing—either the killing he had done during the war or the killing he would do when the "war between the races" finally broke out. An obsessed survivalist, Beam created a number of military-training bases using army surplus equipment. Many Klansmen from all over the nation and even non-Klan survivalists would bivouac with Beam, who boasted that the training his men got was "at least twice superior to what they get at Fort Hood."

To lead the mother state of Louisiana, Duke recruited Elbert Claude Wilkinson, a native of Galvez, who legally changed his name to Bill. Since Wilkinson had been "a bookworm," he graduated from high school at age sixteen. He immediately joined the navy and served as a cryptographer aboard the nuclear submarine U.S.S. *Simon Bolivar.* "I was not taught racial hatred as a child," he once remarked. "I was not taught to discriminate or make life hard for the Negroes. I strictly had a neutral feeling for them." That attitude apparently changed when he was stationed in California, where he became "nauseated" at the sight of "colored and whites dating." After eight years in the navy, Bill and his wife moved to Denham Springs, Louisiana, where he became impressed with Duke's sophistication and media attention and agreed to serve as Louisiana Grand Dragon.

While Duke loved proselytizing and calling attention to himself, he lacked the ability to shape and direct the grass-roots campaign he had so ably begun. His was a one-man operation—"the David Duke Show," as a disgruntled Klansman called it. There were little practical gains from Duke's heavily publicized London tour in spring 1978. He proved he could captivate gatherings from Oxford to Brighton—just as he had done in the States. But after the BBC granted him an interview, British conservatives became irritated with his racist lectures. A headline on the front page of the conservative *Daily Express* screamed: GET HIM OUT OF HERE! Eventually, the Home Secretary signed an order of deportation, and Duke played cat-and-mouse with Scotland Yard for weeks before finally coming home. It was devilishly clever but did nothing to increase the strength or solidarity of the organization he had built, and state leaders grew increasingly critical of him.

One by one, Dragons began to desert the Knights. Tom Metzger went independent with his California group. The Florida Dragon allied his forces with the UKA. The most important defection had occurred as early as 1975, when Bill Wilkinson split from Duke's organization after only a year. After a bitter quarrel over where the proceeds of a particular rally had gone, Wilkinson severed his Denham Springs organization from Duke's control and filed for a corporate charter for an independent order to be called the Invisible Empire, Knights of the Ku Klux Klan. He started grabbing members from Duke's Knights, and from 1979 to 1984, Wilkinson would preside as the dominant Klan leader in the nation.

Although Wilkinson was more intelligent and capable than most national Klan leaders before him, he was short, stumpy, feral, and homespun; he couldn't hope to equal Duke's blitz of the media through glamour. He nevertheless tried in his own way. Before the November election in 1976, he managed to slip into Democratic candidate Jimmy Carter's Sunday school class at the Plains, Georgia, Baptist Church. Later boasting that he had sat two chairs away from the future President of the United States, Wilkinson emerged after the service and donned his Klan robe in time to be photographed in front of the church by startled reporters. The following summer, he was nearly killed at an "Impeach Andrew Young" Klan rally he staged in Plains when an angry anti-Klan demonstrator drove his Jaguar at full speed into the speaker's platform. Of the nineteen people injured, eighteen were newsmen who had been especially drawn to the Klan rally in the President's back yard. ("I make it a point to understand what reporters think is news," Bill slyly commented.) Afterward, the Wizard was confronted by the President's mother. "Do me a favor, young man," she said. "If you ever come back to Plains, you call me beforehand, because I'm leaving." When photographers asked her to pose for a picture with the Wizard, Miss Lillian roared, "Hell, no!"

By summer 1978, Wilkinson hit on the winning strategy that would catapult him and his Invisible Empire to the front ranks of Klan authority: He began taking a public stance of unbridled violence. "We tried the moderate approach in trying to halt the extravagant gains by blacks," he explained, "but it failed. Now we are resorting to other methods." He began traveling and posing for photographers with a security guard armed with enough guns to start a small war—.30-caliber rifles, .45-caliber submachine guns, and the .223-caliber Ruger Mini-14 which became the official weapon of the Invisible Empire. "These guns aren't for killing rabbits," Wilkinson grinned, "they're to waste people. We're not gonna start anything, but if anyone does, we're ready to defend ourselves." Alluding to Duke's intellectual approach, he added, "You don't fight wars with words and books. You fight them with bullets and bombs." Although Duke's personal charm had captured national attention in the early stage of the game, Wilkinson's militant stance would appeal directly to that level of American men most likely to furnish the numbers and the action.

The Klan's new posture struck an immediate responsive chord in the American armed services. In 1976, a violent confrontation between black and white marines at Camp Pendleton had already exposed a Klan nest containing an unauthorized .357-magnum pistol, knives, clubs, KKK literature, and a membership list. The Klansmen had been transferred to different parts of the country. "We're definitely getting railroaded," complained Exalted Cyclops Corporal Daniel Baily, but "they're only moving the problem around. Those who have been moved have been instructed to start their own Klan dens at the new stations." Wilkinson increased his pitch to servicemen and by 1979, armed forces personnel were confronted with increasing Klan activity. Tom Philpott of the *Army Times* summarized a six hundred-page report by the Department of Defense that said every army command confirmed some kind of Klan activity, and that air force personnel were especially concerned about Klan capers in their units in Germany. "The gross evidence of Klan activity appears to be much stronger than any individual commander might think," Philpott concluded. Wilkinson drew many recruits in the navy, and he had an old friend to thank for it. John A. Walker, Jr., who would later plead guilty to spying for the Soviet Union, had served as fellow cryptographer with Wilkinson aboard the *Bolivar*. Apparently "enchanted by skulduggery," Walker was glad to recruit Klan members among enlisted men for his old buddy. A complete Klan chapter was formed aboard the U.S. *Concord* and on perhaps as many as five other ships. A cross was actually burned on the mess deck of the aircraft carrier *America*. Navy officers disagreed with each other over what should be done. They couldn't even decide whether or not sailors of the U.S. Atlantic fleet could wear Klan insignia and T-shirts.

Wilkinson's promotion of violence also had an immediate impact on bitterly frustrated white veterans of the Vietnam War, many of whom felt that American minorities had made vast strides at home while they had made sacrifices in Vietnam that they felt the nation refused to honor. President Carter's willingness to pardon deserters made them all the more resentful, and for a while, Wilkinson became the major spokesman for the angriest of Vietnam vets. From March 1978 to the end of 1979, Klan membership jumped 25 percent.

Wilkinson's first test of his new militance came in Mississippi. In the Tupelo–Okolona area, black members of the United League staged orderly demonstrations and a legal boycott after a twenty-one-year-old black male was shot to death while in police custody. Two grand juries had refused to indict the policemen. Klansmen promptly challenged the league with a series of cross burnings and evening rallies that looked more like military encampments. Wilkinson was frequently on hand to inspire the Klansmen.

In August 1978, a group of Klansmen shot out the windshield of a car driven by Dr. Howard Gunn, a United League leader in Okolona. Two weeks later, Wilkinson held a rally that received national television coverage. "We hurt some niggers," he announced. "We shot up Gunn's car and we're not ashamed of it." Two Klansmen at the rally ceremoniously removed their robes, revealing sheriff's department uniforms underneath, and Wilkinson bragged they were only a small fraction of the number of Klansmen working in law enforcement.

Outraged at Wilkinson's public acknowledgment of Klan violence and his boast of police collusion, civil rights activists joined the United League in an anti-Klan rally held in Tupelo on Thanksgiving Day. The forty Klansmen decided against confronting the four thousand demonstrators, even though the former was reported as being armed with a bazooka and automatic weapons. After the rally, however, a United League bus, which had been sabotaged during the demonstration, put its forty passengers in peril when its steering failed. And Klansmen began following a caravan of demonstrators who were returning home. After crossing the Alabama border, they shot at one of the cars in the caravan and forced it off the road. A Klansman jumped out and held a shotgun to the driver's head, threatening to blow his brains out if he dared move the car. The other Klansmen dragged the occupants of the car outside and beat them with clubs and chains.

At the same time, an even more violent confrontation occurred in Decatur, Alabama. A profoundly retarded twenty-six-year-old black male had been convicted of raping three white women, despite the fact that his Wechsler-tested mental age of three-years and six-months and his severely impaired motor coordination rendered him incapable of driving the car that figured in the crimes. Decatur blacks began a series of legal protest marches against the young man's conviction, and Wilkinson targeted the city for counterdemonstrations by the Klan. In February 1979, about 150 robed Klansmen drove through the area in a raucous motorcade, waving shotguns and pistols. Upset by the revived Klan, the SCLC held a march to the Morgan County Courthouse on May 26. About a hundred Klansmen were waiting for the marchers four blocks from the courthouse. They were armed with guns, knives, clubs, baseball bats, iron rods, chains, and police dogs. As the marchers approached the Klan blockade, Klansmen began chanting, "White power! White power! (What do we want?) White power!"

A Klansman came forward, yelling, "Nigger, that's as far as you go!"

Reverend. R. B. Cottonreader, field organizer for the SCLC, answered back through a bullhorn: "Please clear the streets. We're not stopping. We're coming through!"

A small group of Decatur police formed a line to move back the Klansmen, who then began fighting the police. As soon as the fight broke out, other Klansmen ran to their cars, pulled out the heavy artillery, and started shooting.

Evelyn Lowery, wife of the president of SCLC, was driving a car behind the marchers: "I couldn't believe it. They fired first at my husband and others in the front line. But they were whisked away by our marshals, unharmed. . . . The Klan immediately rushed back to the right side of my car and fired, apparently directly at me. The first bullet pierced the top front windshield post of my car. I instinctively fell to the seat. The next bullet pierced the front windshield. Glass was falling over me, bullets still being fired. I just knew my end had come. I stayed down for at least ten minutes. I heard them saying, 'Kill them all.' "

Approximately twenty shots had been fired in less than a minute. Although Mrs. Lowery escaped uninjured, three black marchers and two Klansmen had been shot. One of the Klansmen had been hit by police fire. Curtis Robinson shot the other Klansman when he began beating with a club the car containing Robinson's wife and five children. No Klansmen were charged with attempted murder, but Robinson was indicted and convicted of shooting the Klansman. Two days after the melee, Wilkinson held a rally of two hundred heavily armed Klansmen at city hall and burned a seven-foot cross. "We are providing vigilante law for Decatur," he announced. "If they are unable to enforce the law, we will." Two weeks later, two thousand civil rights supporters marched against the Klan in Decatur. The SCLC turned to the Justice Department, since the Decatur case seemed to fall within the purview of the Ku-Klux statutes. There were strong indications of conspiracy. Reporters had intercepted CB messages from Klansmen saying, "Get Lowery, Nettles, Cottonreader" (the SCLC leaders). In a 395-page report, however, the department was unable to find a basis for prosecution.

Six months later, a fatal confrontation with the Klan in North Carolina provided not just the major legal case in the latest Klan manifestation but an important stimulus to Klan growth. The North Carolina Knights of the Ku Klux Klan was an independent faction that had split from the UKA while former Dragon Bob Jones was in prison for contempt of Congress. Unlike Jones, Dragon Virgil Griffin—a high-school dropout and textile-mill worker—showed little talent for directing his small, scattered groups of Klansmen made up of mill workers, truckers and blue-collar laborers.

In complete contrast was the local chapter of the Communist Worker's Party, a Maoist, anti-Soviet group of Vietnam War protestors who had moved further left after the breakup of Students for a Democratic Society (SDS) in 1969. The Greensboro chapter of the CWP had begun as an Asian studies group in the early 1970s and included people of extraordinary talents and qualifications. Dr. Michael Nathan was chief of pediatrics at Lincoln Community Health Center in Durham, North Carolina; Nathan was especially responsive to the needs of black and low-income children. Dr. James Waller had given up medical practice to serve as president of a local textile-workers union. Unionization of the textile mills was a primary goal among Greensboro CWP members. North Carolina ranked forty-ninth in per-capita wages paid to production workers and was the least unionized state as far as nonagricultural workers were concerned. Bill Sampson, who held a master of divinity degree from Harvard, was a union organizer. So was Cesar Cauce, a Cuban emigrant who had graduated magna cum laude from Duke. Sandi Smith, a black civil rights activist, had become interested in the physical suffering of mill workers. After graduating in nursing at Bennett College, she had fought a campaign against the practices of Cone Mills—its use of dangerous chemicals and "decrepit machinery," and the pervasive threat of "brown lung disease" caused by cotton dust. All five would die at the hands of Klansmen on November 3, 1979.

The CWP recognized the Klan as its polar opposite and the embodiment of all that was wrong with "capitalist America." It believed that the Klan's "racist views should be denounced forthrightly and in the presence of those propagating it." On July 8, the party spearheaded the disruption of a Klan rally in China Grove, seventy miles southwest of Greensboro, where Klansmen were showing *The Birth of a Nation*. They burned the Klan's Confederate flags and chanted, "Kill the Klan," while Klansmen waved guns and exchanged insults with them. China Grove police pushed the Klansmen into the building where the film was being shown. In October, the party announced a major anti-Klan rally for the following month and dared Klansmen to attend. In an open letter to the North Carolina Knights, CWP members said, "The KKK is one of the most treacherous scum elements produced by the dying system of capitalism. We challenge you to attend our rally in Greensboro."

On October 19, CWP member Nelson Johnson applied for a parade permit, which the Greensboro police granted under the condition that CWP members carry no weapons "open or concealed." The police also agreed to provide security for the rally. Party members began distributing leaflets for their "Death to the Klan" rally, hoping that Klansmen would show up and provoke some kind of confrontation. At the worst, they imagined that Klansmen and some of their own members would be arrested and jailed.

What CWP members didn't know was that the Greensboro police had a paid informer in the Klan—Edward Dawson, who had joined the Klan in 1964 and had been a member in earnest for over ten years. As a Klan security guard, Dawson had been arrested and served time for the destruction of property in Alamance County and had also been involved in a 1969 Fourth of July fracas in which a black girl had been shot and a police car shot up. After serving nine months in prison, Dawson had become an informer for the FBI and now for the Greensboro police, but it was difficult to tell exactly where his loyalties lay. The Greensboro police nevertheless showed him a copy of the parade permit, which revealed the little-known starting point where demonstrators would assemble. They also informed him that CWP members would be unarmed.

For reasons that are not clear, Dawson began a vigorous campaign to entice scattered Klan groups in the Greensboro area to attend the rally. He made personal contacts and put up posters. One Klansman later told the Greensboro *Daily News*, "We'd never have come to Greensboro if it wasn't for Ed Dawson berating us." On October 31, Dawson informed the police that Klansmen would be coming to the rally heavily armed. On the morning of the rally, November 3, he repeated this information to the police and added that Klansmen had carefully studied the demonstrators' parade route.

Another informer was working behind the scenes. Bernard But-kovich was an undercover agent for the Federal Bureau of Alcohol, Tobacco, and Firearms, who had infiltrated a small group of neo-Nazis in the Winston-Salem area. For some reason, Butkovich had worked to form an alliance between scattered Klan and Nazi groups. This was in marked contrast to FBI Cointelpro tactics, aimed at dividing Klansmen into bickering sects—not toward increasing their unity. Butkovich did even stranger things. He urged members to stockpile weapons and buy equipment that converted semiautomatic rifles into fully automatic weapons. He offered to procure illegal explosives, including hand grenades. Like Dawson, Butkovich attended planning sessions of Klansmen and Nazis prior to the November 3 rally and strongly urged Klansmen to attack the Communists.

At 11:20 A.M. on Saturday morning, November 3, the CWP organizers gathered with about fifty demonstrators at Morningside Homes, a poor black housing project in Greensboro. The plan was to march to the Windsor Community Center a half-mile away, where they would join others already gathered and where the rally would properly begin. The tragedy that followed was captured on videotape by reporters assigned to the event.

As the tape begins, adults and children are singing to guitar accompaniment. The camera pans to the right revealing a caravan of nine, older-model, dented cars. (Ed Dawson is in the lead car, directing the caravan of out-of-town Klansmen and Nazis.) As CWP leaders stare at the caravan, they realize the cars contain the enemy. Verbal insults are exchanged. Demonstrators begin chanting, "Death to the Klan!" A group of demonstrators crowd around the lead cars and pummel them with bare fists and placard sticks. The cars stop. Klansmen and Nazis get out and begin a heated exchange with demonstrators. Some of the men on each side get into stick fights. All the cars in the caravan have stopped now. Klansmen calmly walk to the trunks of the rear cars, open them, and take out and distribute rifles and handguns. A shot rings out, and demonstrators run for cover. Armed Klansmen walk about, carefully select victims, fire and reload. Someone seems to be directing their fire. The gunmen do not bother to take cover or to look behind them. They seem like casual participants at a skeet shoot. One of them methodically pumps bullets into the body of a fallen protestor. Another shoots with a lit cigarette dangling from his mouth. Five protestors lie on the ground dead or dying. Another is shot in the head and will survive, severely paralyzed. Eight others lie injured. The gunmen calmly pack their weapons in the cars and slowly drive off. Signe Waller bends over the body of her dead husband. She stares up for a moment and rises in what appears to be a state of shock. She begins walking away, shouting, "Long live the Communist Party! Long live the working class!" *

"Some say it was a shootout," said cameraman Jim Waters of WFMY, Greensboro, "but to me it was a complete massacre." Another cameraman, Ed Boyd of WTVD, Durham, said, "It wasn't any shootout. It was a military execution. It was like in the cowboy movies when they corner you in a box canyon." Whatever it was, it was all over in eighty-eight seconds. And the murdered were not rank-and-file party members or innocent bystanders. The five dead were CWP and union leaders, all of them shot either in the head or heart. (A Nazi later admitted that photographs of the intended victims had been circulated several weeks before November 3.) When the police finally arrived, rather than pursue the caravan, they instead stood with guns drawn over the dead, dying, wounded, and shock-stricken demonstrators. A natural result of confusion, perhaps, but not when one takes into consideration that an unmarked squad car had followed the caravan into the neighborhood and had watched the confrontation without intervening—even when police headquarters knew that the Klansmen were armed and that demonstrators had been forbidden to carry weapons.

Of the forty Klansmen and Nazis in the caravan, only sixteen

---

* This extract is based on the author's repeated viewings of a private videotape of the Greensboro shootings.

were arrested. Of the sixteen, only four Klansmen and two Nazis were brought to trial. In a private meeting with the judge and the defense, the state prosecutor agreed not to call agents Dawson and Butkovich to testify, although the defense was allowed to interview them. To the distress of the victims' spouses, the prosecution dropped all conspiracy charges, so the trial became a simple matter of who pulled triggers—not who planned, engineered, and orchestrated the deadly encounter. Since the people called for jury duty naturally tended to equate Maoist and Soviet Communism, jury selection took weeks, and over twenty-two hundred prospective jurors were examined. One of them claimed, "The only thing the Klan is guilty of is poor shooting." Another said, "I don't think we are out a lot because those people [the CWP leaders] aren't with us anymore. I think we are better off without them."

Ultimately an all-white, all-Christian jury was selected for what is said to have been the longest trial in North Carolina history. It was the first North Carolina trial to introduce videotape as evidence. The tape and testimony identified five of the six accused as doing some of the shooting, but the lawyers of the accused argued self-defense. According to one defense attorney, if the Klansmen "had taken a machine gun and mowed the crowd down, it would have been justified," for members of the CWP "were attacking the very society that gives them the right to be out on the street." Apparently the jury agreed, for it acquitted all the defendants, and charges against other Klansmen and Nazis were dropped. Juror Robert Williams explained, "From the very beginning it was the Communists who did the attacking. It was the Communists who started beating the cars with sticks. From then on, it was a case of self-defense."

Well before the verdict was reached, Wilkinson milked the Greensboro case for all it was worth. "Vicious Communists" had provoked a confrontation with decent "law-'biding" Klansmen. "We are the ones being attacked," Wilkinson declared, "and primarily by Communists in this country." It drew sympathy for the Klan from unusual quarters, and the final months of 1979 provided a congenial setting for the launching of a major Klan recruiting effort. A faltering economy at home and aggression abroad had made many Americans feel that their country had somehow lost its greatness—that it was under attack by moral and political enemies. The Iranian seizure of American hostages magnified these concerns enormously, and Wilkinson blamed the Iranian situation on integration. When America was a segregated country, he argued, it was great and powerful. "But after fifteen years of integration we've dropped from the greatest to a pathetic also-ran, kicked around by second-rate countries like Iran."

Concurrently with the Greensboro case, a general drift to the political right was given moral fervor and middle-class respectability by a revival of fundamentalism. Christening itself the "Moral Majority," the new evangelicals began lobbying for some of the same legislation the Klan had fought for during the 1920s, including prayer in school and the enforced teaching of "creationism" alongside evolution. During the election of 1980, members of Indiana's Moral Majority repeated the 1924 Klan tactic of putting literature hostile to liberal candidates on cars parked at Protestant churches on the Sunday before the vote. While the Klan persistently identified its goals with those of the Moral Majority, the religious right wanted nothing to do with the Klan and steadfastly denied it the support the fundamentalists had lent in the 1920s. Congressman Mark Siljander of Michigan was deeply embarrassed when Klansmen joined his and the Christian Freedom Council's efforts at banning dirty books from the Niles and Three Rivers public libraries. The Klan, said a Siljander spokesman, "is disgustingly more immoral than any pornographic book or magazine ever could be."

In contrast to the 1920s, the new fundamentalists disagreed with nearly everything the Klan stood for. On the matter of Christian supremacy, however, their rhetoric was remarkably similar. Reverend Jerry Falwell, the recognized leader of the Moral Majority, proclaimed, "The idea that religion and politics don't mix was invented by the Devil to keep Christians from running *their own country.*" Reverend Bailey Smith, president of the Southern Baptist Convention—the largest Protestant denomination in America—announced at the SBC's annual meeting in 1980, "God Almighty does not hear the prayer of a Jew. For how in the world can God hear the prayer of a man who says that Jesus Christ is not the true Messiah? It is blasphemous." By carefully limiting its antiblack rhetoric in certain regions and increasing its anti-Semitism and championship of Christian supremacy, the Klan rode on the Moral Majority's shirttails and made remarkable headway—especially in the North, where it became a major focus of attention for the first time in fifty years.

The opening years of the 1980s decade ushered in a full-fledged Klan revival. Indiana was a good barometer of Kluxdom above the Mason–Dixon line. Within three months in 1980, a guard was suspended at the Indiana State Prison for recruiting members for the Klan, a seventeen-year-old New Albany Klan member threatened his high school with legal action if officials refused to place his copy of *White Power* among the books in the library, and fifty-two fully robed Klansmen reenacted the famous Fourth of July 1923 march through the streets of Kokomo. Elsewhere in the North, crosses were burned in Denver, rallies were held in Connecticut and Pennsylvania, educators were disturbed by Klan recruiting in Baltimore schools, and investigators in Harrisburg, Pennsylvania, looked into charges that on-duty policemen were selling Klan memorabilia.

Wilkinson quickly realized that the Klan had tied into a nationwide attitude. By the end of 1980 he perfected a technique that other Klan leaders belittled as "ambulance chasing." He traveled to any part of the country where he saw exploitable racial tensions or serious blue-collar unemployment, which he blamed on reverse discrimination. In January 1980, he drove to Idabel, Oklahoma, where nerves were raw after a black youth had been shot to death behind a "whites only" nightclub; Wilkinson confidently informed reporters that he would "have a klavern here very shortly—within two weeks." When police killed a pregnant black woman in Jackson, Wilkinson went there and addressed a Klan rally five hundred strong, the largest white-robed gathering in Mississippi since the 1960s. In October, a rally near Uniontown, Pennsylvania, drew a crowd of three hundred, including unemployed white coal miners who were willing to blame blacks for the lack of jobs. "We've recruited more people in Pennsylvania in the last three months than we have in the previous five years," Wilkinson happily announced. While the media fussed over Klan expansion under Wilkinson, Robert Shelton, the veteran Wizard of the UKA, took it in stride. "Wilkinson has traversed the nation seeking racial 'hot spots,'" Shelton laconically observed, "where he can come into a community, collect a large amount of initiation fees, sell a few robes, sell some guns which may or may not be legal, collect his money and be on his way to another 'hot spot.'"

Klan innovations received special attention by the media. In Texas, Grand Dragon Louis Beam was running four paramilitary training camps—another had been closed after the instructor was exposed as a convicted contract killer. According to sworn testimony, participants at Beam's camps had access to such sophisticated weapons as AR-15 semiautomatic rifles, the Atchisson Assault 12, and other assorted carbines, rifles, and shotguns. Many

of Beam's trainees were Vietnam veterans, and film clips proved
their expertise in military tactics. One of the most alarming aspects
of the camps was Beam's willingness to train adolescents. "I would
even like to start them a little younger—maybe at six," he remarked. Not to be outdone by one of David Duke's Dragons, Bill
Wilkinson opened Camp My Lai thirty-five minutes from Cullman, Alabama. One weekend a month, Klansmen at My Lai,
named after the controversial Vietnam village, were allowed to
dress in military fatigues, prowl ravines with M-16s on search-and-
destroy missions, run a 100-yard obstacle course, and receive training in target shooting.

Another innovation was Wilkinson's Klan Youth Corps and
summer camps for children. At summer camps, "Ku Klux Kids"
received training with weapons similar to what their parents were
getting at Camp My Lai. They also got indoctrination in Klan
philosophy, sometimes by the Imperial Wizard himself. "Many
things your teachers tell you in school are not true," Wilkinson
told one class, "they're just lies." Among the lies were revisions of
Reconstruction history and conclusions on what the Klan stood
for. "The Klan stands for segregation," Wilkinson informed the
youths. "It stands for America, and it stands for God Almighty."
Among the promises of a lengthy pledge children were taught to
recite was: "I pledge to practice racial separation in all my social
contacts and keep unforced contacts with other races on a strictly
business basis." Wilkinson's kids recruited other youths through
literature they handed out in shopping malls and in their schools.
A brochure written especially for distribution in schools stated:

> An attempt is being made . . . to undermine young people's respect
> for the values of our nation and race. Black studies glorify mythologi-
> cal achievements of the black race. Christian values have been re-
> placed by Jewish history. . . . Jewish publishing houses have complete
> control over the editing, production and writing of our nation's text-
> books. . . . Little notice is given to the violence against students by
> the black savages who roam the corridors at will. Murder of white
> students by black students is on the increase.

The brochure urged white students to organize into cadres, to "get
tough" with "arrogant" minorities, and to protest the actions of
administrators who "appease" blacks.

Journalists were appalled at Wilkinson's youth programs, but he
welcomed the publicity, no matter how negative. Although an

eighteen-year-old New Jersey Klan member told the *Junior Scho-lastic* that the Klan was trying to "get the kids off the streets and give them something to do," the positive aspects of the Klan Youth Corps lost credibility when Wilkinson's youth director was arrested for participating in a plot to bomb a Jewish synagogue and Jewish-owned businesses in Nashville. The impact of the Youth corps was smaller than Wilkinson wanted everyone to believe, but the effects were very visible. In Decatur, boys and girls in Klan T-shirts threw torches into a gasoline-soaked school bus, specially purchased for the occasion, to demonstrate their opposition to busing. Claiming membership in two Klan youth groups, Oklahoma City high school students attacked the frequenters of a gay bar with baseball bats. Outside Houston, the Boy Scouts of America denied an Ex-plorer post charter application from a group of ten boys, ages thirteen to twenty, whose Klansman sponsor had trained them in firearms and hand-to-hand combat, including how to decapitate their enemies with a machete.

Aside from the innovations of Kluxdom in the 1980s, there was plenty that was familiar, and nowhere was it more familiar than in freelance Klan violence. In July 1980, three Klansmen driving through Chattanooga shot five black women; four of the women were walking home and a fifth was transplanting marigolds in her front lawn. When two of the Klansmen were acquitted and the third convicted only on minor charges, young Chattanooga blacks rioted for three successive nights. In a Detroit suburb, four Klans-men were convicted of trying to kill a black man after he had moved into a predominantly white neighborhood; one of the con-victed had trained with Louis Beam in Texas. In Smithburg, West Virginia, a Methodist minister was kidnapped from his car, terror-ized for six months, and finally driven from his parish by Klansmen after he refused to let them speak from his church pulpit. In Toms River, New Jersey, a Klansman and a neo-Nazi were convicted for shooting into the home of a black family. Klansmen were arrested for plotting the bombing of the Baltimore office of the NAACP. And on March 21, 1981, Michael Donald, a nineteen-year-old Mobile, Alabama, black, was abducted, strangled to death, and hanged from a tree by two young Klansmen. Donald had been chosen entirely at random. "We didn't know him," said one of the murderers. "We just wanted to show Klan strength in Alabama." Tried in a federal court under the Ku-Klux statutes, the ringleader was sentenced in 1984 to death in the electric chair—the first time in history that a Klansman received a capital sentence for killing a black.

Alarmed by the Klan's rapid and strident growth, anti-Klan demonstrators became increasingly violent in the early 1980s. Angered by the Greensboro murders, the most violent anti-Klan demonstrators were left-wing radicals, often members of self-styled Maoist organizations. Klan rallies and counterdemonstrations in Oceanside, California; Scotland and Meriden, Connecticut; Boston; and Washington, D.C., resulted in arrests and hospitalizations. Protesters generally began these affrays by verbally heckling the Klansmen, then by throwing rocks and bottles. In Boston, they added eggs and tomatoes to their artillery, and in Oceanside, someone actually threw a bicycle. Policemen often made up a considerable portion of those injured—it was largely due to the well-disciplined riot tactics of police that no one was killed in the five cities. Carl Rowan was deeply irked by the public martyrdom Klansmen asssumed after violent demonstrations from the opposite side and argued that violent demonstrators, especially black demonstrators, "gave credence" to the antiminority "slanders" of the Klan and hoped that those convicted of assault charges would be thrown in jail.

With Klan activities making weekly headlines, it was hardly surprising that the Invisible Empire became an issue in the 1980 presidential race, pitting Republican Ronald Reagan against the incumbent Democrat Jimmy Carter. It was surprising, however, for the Klan to formally launch the national campaign. It had started earlier when Reagan made a speech on behalf of states' rights at the Neshoba County Fair in Philadelphia, Mississippi. Andrew Young criticized Reagan for his insensitivity in praising states' rights at the site of the most infamous triple murder in Klan history. Wizard Wilkinson quickly endorsed Reagan and announced that "the Republican platform reads as if it were written by a Klansman." He especially liked the GOP's lukewarm position on affirmative action. Reagan, of course, repudiated Wilkinson's endorsement, but Carter's Secretary of Health and Human Services, Patricia Harris, told the press that he had taken too long to do so.

On September 1, both candidates formally opened their campaigns, Reagan at the Michigan State Fair in Detroit, and Carter in Tuscumbia, Alabama. Speaking to the Detroit crowd, Reagan remarked, "I am happy to be here, where you are dealing at first hand with economic policies that have been committed, and he's opening his campaign down in the city that gave birth to and is the parent body of the Ku Klux Klan." Not only was Reagan's attack inept and ill-advised, it was historically incorrect; the Klan had been born in Pulaski, Tennessee, and Tuscumbia could hardly be called "the parent body" of the Klan revival. Jimmy Carter tried to make the most of Reagan's gaffe: "I resent very deeply what Ronald Reagan said about the South and about Alabama and about Tuscumbia when he pointed out erroneously that I opened my campaign in the home of the Ku Klux Klan. . . . I think it was inaccurate, and I think it was something that all southerners will resent." Reagan was forced to apologize. "I have phoned both Mayor Sparks of Tuscumbia and Governor James of Alabama," he announced, "to express my disappointment that the Carter campaign had deliberately distorted the intent of my remarks. I also expressed my regret that anything I may have said was interpreted as reflecting adversely on Alabama, or the city of Tuscumbia—birthplace of Helen Keller—or its people. Alabama is a state whose tradition and people I respect."

Democrats as well as Klansmen were delighted with Reagan's remarks. Wilkinson increased his public endorsements of Reagan. The fact that the Klan had been interjected in the campaign, he argued, proved that "the ideals of the Klan" had risen to high levels. "It's risen to such a high level that the GOP platform parallels our views almost one-hundred percent across the board." When Tom Snyder asked him why he dared throw Klan support to Reagan if he actually wanted Reagan to win, Wilkinson retorted that Snyder underestimated Klan strength. "We're not an issue in this Presidential race because we're insignificant," he countered. While Democrats did their best to keep Reagan draped in a white sheet, the issue soon eased out of the campaign. "The time to drop the Ku Klux Klan from the presidential campaigns is now," editorialized the South Bend *Tribune*. "When we hear of efforts and counter-efforts to tar one party or the other with Klan support, we can only conclude the campaign season has gotten off to an abysmal start."

Two months later, Reagan's dramatic victory over Carter was accompanied by news of the verdict in the Greensboro case in which all six Klansmen and Nazis were acquitted. The defendants were jubilant over the verdict. Grand Dragon Virgil Griffin said, "I don't see any difference between killing Communists in Vietnam and killing them over here." In Raleigh, national Nazi leader Harold Covington called the verdict "fantastic. It shows we can beat the system on their own ground." Another Nazi called the decision "a great victory for white America," even though four of the five killed were white. The acquitted Klansmen handed out autographed photos of themselves and tried to charge journalists $100 per interview. When newsmen declined, they gave interviews free. Grinning with his two front teeth missing from a previous fight, Klansmen Jerry Paul Smith said, "I kind of enjoyed the stick fighting, but it kind of got out of hand when the guns came out. . . . I didn't know there was going to be a fight, but if you smack a man in the face with an egg, you got to expect to get your butt whipped." Another acquitted Klansman Coleman Pridmore claimed, "People have been treating us like heroes." Pridmore called the verdict "a victory for America. Anytime you defeat Communism, it's a victory for America."

Buoyed by their victory, Dragon Griffin announced he would run for governor in 1984. Jerry Paul Smith announced he would run for sheriff of Lincoln County in 1982. Nazi leader Harold Covington had already garnered fifty-four thousand votes in his run for attorney general of North Carolina. The following spring, Smith and Pridmore were feted at a banquet in Marietta, Georgia, hosted by Ed Fields, former colleague of J. B. Stoner (finally under indictment for his 1958 bombing activities) and present Wizard of his "New Order Knights" Klan. Fields called the acquittals "a great victory for white people everywhere" and presented the Klansmen with awards for their "courageous and steadfast defense of our Constitutional rights." Later, at a rally in Lincolnton, North Carolina, a robed and hooded Jerry Smith announced, "What happened in Greensboro is nothing compared to what's to come."

By 1981, Wilkinson had every reason to be pleased. The Greensboro verdict seemed like "a green light" for the spread of the Klan and the violence on which it was thriving. Klan membership had nearly doubled in a year, and the Justice Department calculated that Klan activity had increased by 55 percent. Klansmen looked forward to a regression in civil rights under the Reagan administration. The Moral Majority was winning more and more converts to Christian supremacy, and in order to appeal to their members Wilkinson became an ordained minister from a mail-order church. Most important, Wilkinson had completely bamboozled his former boss and archrival David Duke.

Duke had lost interest in his ailing Knights the previous summer and was unable or unwilling to compete with Wilkinson's successful appeals to violence. In private communications, Duke told Wilkinson that he wanted out of the Klan, that he wanted to form a new organization called the National Association for the Advancement of White People. "It would be a racialist movement," Duke explained, "more of a high-class thing, mainly upper-middle-class people." In other words, it wouldn't cut into Wilkinson's clientele. Duke offered to sell his Klan membership to Wilkinson for $35,000. He said he needed that much, because "the beginning is going to be very, very difficult for me." Not only did Wilkinson refuse to buy Duke's members—he was stealing them easily enough already—but he tape-recorded the conversations and turned the tape over to reporters. Duke immediately quit the Klan and appointed Dominica adventurer Don Black in his place. After Black's three-year stint in federal prison, the Louisiana-based Knights virtually disintegrated.

Although the press played up the fact that Duke had "sold-out" his members, the publicity did Duke less damage than Wilkinson hoped. Duke had little chance at making a go of any Klan-like organization without the sheets and "illuminated" cross. Without the mumbo-jumbo, the lure of the Klan was considerably limited. Five years later, the National Association for the Advancement of White People hadn't got off the ground. Wilkinson nevertheless took full credit for Duke's dissolution. "I wiped him out," he gloated. "Now I've got ninety-five percent of the Klansmen in the country." His exultation would soon end in aggravating frustration. For the same reasons Wilkinson was happy about the Klan, other Americans were worried and some were fighting mad. Anti-Klan forces grew in size and determination over the next two years.

Professional educators announced early in 1981 that they would inaugurate a major effort to stop the Klan from recruiting in public schools. In a boldfaced message to members, the National Education Association warned, "THE KKK WANTS YOUR STUDENTS." In June, the NEA unveiled a new curriculum guide and lesson plans for teachers' use in combating the Klan's false and pernicious doctrines. Entitled *Violence, the Ku Klux Klan, and the Struggle for Equality*, the curriculum encouraged class discussions on broad issues of the Klan, white supremacy, and racism. The American Federation of Teachers generally liked its rival union's presentation of Klan history but objected to the extremes it had gone in depicting American racism. It also disagreed with the NEA's portrayal of the Klan as an innately American institution—something the Klan had been saying for sixty-five years. The AFT preferred to regard the Klan as "an aberration." Surprisingly, both Ronald Reagan and the Anti-Defamation League preferred the AFT's more conservative anti-Klan curriculum called *Flames in the Night.* For one thing, it had a better title. Although the two rival unions continued, as always, to throw brickbats at each other, their agreement on a revision of Reconstruction history was a significant move and helped offset Klan influence on the youngest and most vulnerable level of American society.

The ADL and NAACP stepped up their vigilance and reporting on Klan activity. A new anti-Klan organization was formed, however, that shaped itself especially to deal with the revived, media-wise Klan of the 1980s. In response to the Klan's 1979 attack on its nonviolent marchers in Decatur and the arrest of Curtis Robinson, the SCLC had soon afterward called a conference in Norfolk, Virginia. Thirty organizations had responded and, out of the conference, the National Anti-Klan Network was born. Based in Atlanta, the Network began by matching the ADL's research, monitoring and reporting on Klan/Nazi activity. Under the leadership of its coordinator Lyn Wells, it took a strong stand against the Klan's corruption of children and assisted the NEA in creating its curriculum guide. It took a special interest in victims of Klan violence, brought them into support groups, and assisted them in addressing their grievances to proper authorities. It sponsored national and local conferences on strategies to combat the new Klan and worked with members of the media on how to report on Klansmen without encouraging them.

Critical of Reagan's Justice Department, the Network sent delegations to Washington, urging the Civil Rights Division to prosecute acts of Klan violence that fell within its purview. Unhappy with Assistant Attorney General William Bradford Reynolds's apology that he was unable to intervene in the Chattanooga case in which the five black women were shot, the Network formed a coalition with the NAACP and the Center for Constitutional Rights. Private attorneys from this coalition prosecuted the Chattanooga Klansmen under the Ku-Klux statutes, and a federal jury awarded the five victims a judgment of $535,000 in compensatory and punitive damages. In 1983, the Network and eight victims of Klan violence filed suit in U.S. district court against the Justice Department "for its failure to vigorously prosecute the perpetrators of such crimes under the existing federal statutes." Its spokespeople argued that, historically, lax enforcement of the Ku-Klux statutes had a strong "bearing on Klan growth and violence." Within a year, the Network reported in its newsletter that the Justice Department had begun taking a more responsible stance toward Klan outrages. Perhaps the most useful and creative role of the Anti-Klan Network was that of liaison and adviser to communities baffled and worried over what to do when the Klan came to town. In this role, it helped form local coalitions of religious, labor, and civil rights groups to fight the Klan in a direct but practical and nonviolent way.

Soon after the Network's creation, an even more formidable anti-Klan agency came into being. The Southern Poverty Law Center had been founded in Montgomery in 1971 by attorneys Joe Levin, Jr. and Morris Dees, and by Georgia state senator and long-time civil rights activist Julian Bond. Center attorneys worked to advance the legal rights of the poor and powerless through litigation and education. In some ways, the center was reminiscent of a streamlined and far more effective Freedmen's Bureau. Relying solely on donations and contributions, it charged no fees and specialized in class-action suits "to win the greatest possible benefit for the largest number of people." It was expert in civil rights legislation and attracted interns from the finest law schools in the nation. In late 1980, increased cases of Klan violence concerned the center enough to form the "Klanwatch Project." The special staff of Klanwatch collected every possible bit of current data on Klan activities and Klansmen for use in education, litigation, and prosecutions. Newsletters mailed by Klanwatch provided up-to-the-minute reports of Klan activity all over the nation. Klanwatch took a practical nonpartisan public stance. "Klansmen have the same rights as anyone else to march, protest and speak," center spokesmen said, "no matter how wrong or despicable their beliefs may be. But they must be stopped from harassing, killing and intimidating innocent people." Although less critical of the Reagan Justice Department than the Network, Klanwatch nevertheless observed that the "Reagan administration's policies, rightly or wrongly, are perceived by Klansmen and other racists as signals for escalation of attacks on minorities and for a retreat back to segregation, white supremacy and other evils of the past." Center attorneys made a list of model anti-Klan laws that didn't infringe on civil liberties for the use of every legislature and city council. Klanwatch recruited lawyers across the nation to work on a *pro bono* basis against the Klan with the center's assistance. And its personal undertaking of anti-Klan litigation would make it one of the most persistent and successful Klan fighters of the twentieth century.

Early in 1981, immigrant Vietnamese fishermen in the Galveston Bay area were under attack by Dragon Louis Beam and members of his Texas Klan and paramilitary battalions. Calling the fishermen "little webbed-footed gooks," Klansmen argued that they were crowding the bay and competing unfairly with native-American shrimpers. Beam publicly immolated a small boat as "a lesson to Klansmen on how to properly burn a shrimp boat." The next month, someone burned an actual Vietnamese boat and Klansmen began cruising about the bay in armed patrols. The Vietnamese were terrified and turned to the Southern Poverty Law Center. Klanwatch attorneys filed suit against the Texas Klan on April 16. Since many reasonable Texans were sympathetic to the Klan's claims of Vietnamese usurpation, the center's chief trial counsel Morris Dees provided expert witnesses, including the Texas game warden, who testified that the bay was not overfished by the Vietnamese and that the few immigrants had simply "out-worked many lazy Americans." One of the more bizarre highlights of the case was Dees's questioning of Louis Beam. On the basis of his testimony, Beam seems to have taken the litigation personally:

> Anytime an out-of-state agitator, anti-Christ Jew person is allowed to come into the state [from Alabama to Texas] like yourself, Demon Dees! . . . No anti-Christ Jew should be allowed to ask a Christian anything for a court of law. . . . So the issue is not Louis Beam opposed to the Vietnamese. I'm for the Vietnamese. It's Louis Beam versus Morris Dees, anti-Christ Jew!

When it was pointed out to Dees that Beam appeared to be armed with a shoulder pistol, he stopped the deposition and demanded that further testimony be taken under the guard of federal marshals. He demanded a psychiatric examination for Beam and bought a bulletproof vest for himself. On May 14, Judge Gabrielle McDonald issued an order enjoining Klansmen from so much as even appearing in Klan robes within eyesight of a Vietnamese fisherman.

Concerned about a person as disturbed as Beam running military camps, Klanwatch found an obscure Texas statute forbidding private armies. Its suit against Beam's camps was joined by the attorney general of Texas and, on June 3, 1982, Judge McDonald permanently enjoined Klansmen from carrying on combat or combat-related training or even parading in public with firearms. A furious Beam pulled up stakes and abandoned the Texas Klan. Dees called the decision an important precedent for "putting a halt to other similar Klan paramilitary organizations" across the country. Dees promptly filed a suit against Camp My Lai in Alabama and, later, against similar camps in North Carolina and other states. More suits would follow on the heels of Klanwatch victories.

By late 1982, Wilkinson's Empire was under constant siege. An investigation by the Nashville *Tennessean*, subsequently publicized by the Network, revealed that Wilkinson had been informing against Duke's Knights to the FBI. Wilkinson was quickly denounced by other national Klan leaders, who refused to include him in a "unity conference" held on Stone Mountain on Labor Day, and even his own members grew mistrustful of him. Rather than spend money fighting the Klanwatch suit against Camp My Lai, he instead closed it, for a far greater issue was at stake. In 1980, Klanwatch had begun a suit against Wilkinson and his Alabama leaders for their 1979 violence in Decatur. Reporters had caught CB reports directing Klansmen who to hit—strong evidence of conspiracy. An FBI investigation had failed to find the necessary proof of conspiracy, however, and although the Justice Department decried the Klan's actions, it could find no basis for federal prosecution. Wilkinson had been crowing over the department's conclusion ever since his 1980 interview on ABC News' *Nightline*. In fall 1982, however, Dees produced an ex-Klansman who was willing to reveal Klansmen's conspiracy in the Decatur violence and their subsequent coverup for the police, the FBI, and members of the Justice Department. A federal judge promptly terminated the Klan's legal efforts to throw the case out of court, and the Justice Department reopened its investigation.

In essence, the Klanwatch division of the Southern Poverty Law Center had outinvestigated the FBI and the Justice Department combined. Stunned at the high cost of defending themselves, Klansmen began telling everything to center investigators. A Klansman's attorney offered his client's cooperation in exchange for being dropped from the suit. Two unrepresented Klansmen also cooperated in exchange for immunity. Encouraged by the evidence being produced, Klanwatch investigators took to the Alabama backwoods to find other unrepresented Klan witnesses. Whenever they found one, they served a subpoena, which proved to be a highly effective emetic in making the Klansman spill. "Because they thrive on secrecy," said Klanwatch investigator Bill Stanton, "a Klansman looks at a courthouse the way a vampire sees a crucifix."

Wilkinson was clearly fighting a losing battle. In confidential letters to members, he begged for funds, saying that the Klanwatch suit was costing the Empire between $5,000 and $10,000 per month. Klansmen were unsympathetic to his pleas—especially at having to defend something that had occurred before many of them had joined. Wilkinson began losing members right and left. His Alabama Klaverns defected en masse. Others joined rival Klans or dropped out altogether. In January 1983, Wilkinson found a bookkeeping error that he reported to the IRS and for which the Invisible Empire was assessed $8,650 in back taxes, penalties, and interest. He immediately filed bankruptcy. Some saw it as a gambit to escape the $43 million in damages Klanwatch was demanding in the Decatur suit, especially when Wilkinson glibly remarked, "Everyone should try Chapter Eleven."

By midsummer, Klanwatch was moving in high gear. Center attorneys demanded that Wilkinson turn over documents bearing on conspiracy in the Decatur case, including membership lists. Wilkinson refused, saying the demands were "a ploy to destroy the Klan through litigation . . . to make people fearful that their names will be divulged if they join." U.S. District Judge E. B. Haltom threatened Wilkinson with a contempt of court citation if he refused to turn over the documentation. "At this sitting," Haltom said, "this court is of the opinion that both the national Klan and Mr. Wilkinson, as Imperial Wizard, have committed acts that are in contempt of this court's order." He warned Wilkinson, "If I find contempt, the sanctions I impose will be quite severe."

In the early hours of July 28, Klansmen broke into the Southern Poverty Law Center and firebombed the offices of Klanwatch. "It's one thing for somebody to call us and curse into the telephone," said center legal director John Carroll, "but this was a quantum leap in nastiness." The next day, staff members began moving what was left of the property to temporary quarters in downtown Montgomery. "Everytime we pick up a law book that was not destroyed in the blaze," Dees said, "the soot and darkened bindings remind us that we face an enemy who will stop at nothing to disrupt our work." Fortunately, the most important materials needed in ongoing litigation had been preserved in fireproof storage units, and center spokesmen vowed to reconstruct any evidence that had been destroyed. Investigator Bill Stanton said, "This incident just redoubled our determination to fight the Klan in court and win."

Funds came into the center from all over the nation to help build a new fireproof and bombproof building. And center investigators soon gathered enough evidence to win indictments and convictions for the two twenty-one-year-old Klansmen responsible for the arson. But the crowning glory came in May 1984, when a U.S. District Court grand jury handed down indictments for nine Klan leaders involved in the Decatur case; five of them were also indicted for obstructing the FBI's 1980 investigation. The Justice Department won the indictments just nine days before the statute of limitations was due to expire on the case. Dees was elated. "The significant thing is that so many Klan *leaders* were indicted," he noted. "The Klan has always sent the rank-and-file to the street, like the Mafia, but the men indicted here are not foot soldiers. They are the Dons of the Klan." Among those indicted were the Grand Dragon and Grand Chaplain of Alabama, an Imperial Kla-liff, and an Exalted Cyclops. "No one can remember a larger scale Klan case," said FBI special agent Tom Moore.

Disheartened by the Decatur case and still facing a contempt of court citation, Wilkinson decided to throw in the towel. Six months after the indictments were handed down, he resigned as Imperial Wizard and left his foundering, tattered empire in the hands of an Alabama underling. Simply put, Wilkinson had been legally outmaneuvered and his organization hounded to death by the Klanwatch project of the Southern Poverty Law Center and its friends across the nation.

POSTSCRIPT
1985–1987

The first month of 1985 witnessed a surprising political accord between Klansmen and moderate blacks. The issue was a public referendum in Houston ruling out "sexual orientation" as a basis for job discrimination in the city work force. Klansmen joined the predominantly black Concerned pastors and Ministers of Houston in expressing contempt for a measure that would benefit homosexuals. Mayor Kathy Whitmire pleaded, "It would indeed be a step backward if the black community joined with the Ku Klux Klan in opposing the January 19 referendum. . . . Can we ignore Dr. Martin Luther King's struggle for freedom and justice for all mankind?" Reverend C. Anderson Davis countered, "We resent very much the equating of homosexuals with blacks as a minority." A political cartoon had black ministers presenting the familiar hooded white sheets to their congregations as "the new choir robes." A week before the vote, Texas Klansmen marched through Houston carrying placards reading VOTE NO TO BUTCH WHITMIRE and ROUND UP AND QUARANTINE AIDS CARRIERS. The Concerned Pastors and Ministers demanded to know who was gay in the Houston City Council.

The referendum was ultimately defeated by 80 percent of the vote, but stoic gays remarked that the margin against them would have even been worse if the Klan hadn't marched.

In spring, after the House of Representatives defeated a request by President Reagan for military support for the contra rebels fighting the government of Nicaragua, Klansmen rallied to the President's side. Don Black, leader of the shattered remains of David Duke's Knights, who had just been released from prison after serving three years for his attempted overthrow of Dominica, announced the formation of a 120-man Klan unit called the Nathan Bedford Forrest Brigade to assist the contras. Black said the Forrest Brigade would engage in psychological warfare in Nicaragua to foster antigovernment sentiment and would provide "a civil action unit to promote a stable economy." The Klansmen believed they were acting with the President's sanction because Reagan had said in October that it was "traditional" for American volunteers to join such campaigns.

In May, after nearly six years of litigation, the Greensboro Klan–Nazi–Communist case seemed to be nearing an end. Following the 1980 acquittals of Klansmen and Nazis, the spouses of the murdered victims besieged the Justice Department for a criminal civil-rights prosecution. They were supported by a coalition of groups that became the Greensboro Justice Fund. According to fund spokesmen, the Reagan Justice Department "did everything it could to stall a civil rights suit," but the government finally had agreed to file in early 1983. Since Nazi informer Bernard Butkovich had been a federal agent, Justice fund attorneys argued that the government had a conflict of interests in the case and demanded a special prosecutor. The judge ruled that only the Justice Department could grant the request, but Attorney General William French Smith refused. In the course of the federal trial, an attorney for one of the Nazis argued that being a Nazi wasn't as bad as it used to be. "He is a patriotic citizen, just like the Germans were," the attorney said of his client. "The Germans gambled everything and lost all in opposition to communism. Aren't they a lot more attractive now than they were forty years ago at the end of the war?"

For the spouses of the Greensboro victims, the outcome of the fourteen-week federal trial was as disappointing as the 1980 verdict: The Klansman who had allegedly fired the first shot was sentenced to six months work release and all the others were acquitted. Grand Dragon Griffin exclaimed, "I felt like I died and went to heaven." In round three, the Greensboro Defense Fund filed a civil suit naming all the responsible Klansmen and Nazis, federal agents, and members of the Greensboro Police Department. "For the first time we're in charge of our case," said the wife of slain Michael Nathan. "For the first time we're reaching to the real issues."

While those issues were being reached, a new one was raised of historical significance. On March 24, 1985, U.S. District Judge Robert Merhige of North Carolina refused to throw out a counter-suit by the Greensboro Klansmen based on the Ku-Klux statutes. The Klansmen argued they were the victims of a Communist con-spiracy and had been discriminated against because they were white Christians. The judge's decision to allow Klansmen access to the Reconstruction Ku-Klux statutes left Klan fighters reeling in shock. Judge Merhige was legally compelled to be lenient to the Klansmen because they were self-represented. But in further sup-port of his decision, he added, "It may be that when Congress passed the Civil Rights Act of 1871 [sic] it did not foresee that situations would arise in which violent attacks were directed at Klan members. But this does not mean that Congress intended, as a *per se* matter, to exclude members of the Klan and similar orga-nizations from the protection of the Act. . . ." This isn't quite accurate. The radical Republicans had been specifically warned by the Democratic opposition—especially Senator Allen G. Thur-man of Ohio—that the enforcement statutes could easily backfire, and that they could be used against "Sambo and Pompey" as well as the Ku-Klux. In the wording of the original statutes, the Repub-licans were therefore careful to exclude terrorists from their ben-efit. Unfortunately, during the golden age of Jim Crow in the latter part of the nineteenth century, the Supreme Court stripped the statutes to the bone, and the resulting ambiguity allowed Judge Merhige's controversial decision of 1985.*

In the remaining months of 1985, Klanwatchers paid special attention to what seemed to be an evolutionary change in Klux-dom. The fundamentalist Church of Jesus Christ Christian had been formed by Klan leader Reverend Wesley Swift in 1946 and had become increasingly militant in the 1960s with the help of Connie Lynch. Swift took the movement to California, and upon his death in 1970, leadership was assumed by Reverend Richard G. Butler. Butler moved the organization to a compound in Hay-den Lake, Idaho, under the name Church of Jesus Christ Chris-

---

* The remains of the Ku-Klux statutes, as well as additional Klan-restraining legislation from the 1960s, may be found in Appendix E.

tian-Aryan Nations. The organization's politics were buttressed by a racist theology that claimed that whites are God's true chosen people, that blacks are innately inferior, and that Jews are the veritable spawn of Satan. Members believed that both race war and the overthrow of America's "Zionist Occupational Government" was imminent. "If you believe in the Bible," Reverend Butler said, "you know that there is no peaceful solution."

By 1986, the Aryan Nations was operating as a highly secret, dangerously armed consortium of Klansmen, Nazis, militant survivalists, members of the antitax Posse Comitatus, ex-convicts recruited from prisons, and right-wing religious fanatics. An infiltrator claimed that members represented the entire socioeconomic spectrum from blue-collar workers to doctors of philosophy. Affiliates of the Aryan Nations were uncovered in North Carolina, Alabama, Georgia, Texas, Pennsylvania, Michigan, and California.

A vigilante arm known as the Order was believed to have been set up as an underground adjunct of the Aryan Nations. An extremely violent version of the Klavalier Klubs of the 1940s, the Order financed its operations—and allegedly those of the Aryan Nations—with major robberies. In 1984, a Brinks job netting $3.6 million and an armed robbery of $500,000 resulted in the arrests of six members of the Order and the death of a seventh during a shootout with federal agents. Members of the Order were also suspected in the June 1984 murder of Alan Berg, a Denver talk-show host critical of right-wing vigilantes. On November 25, 1984, thirteen members of the Order signed an eight-page "Declaration of War," vowing to kill all politicans, judges, journalists, bankers, soldiers, police officers, and federal agents who got in their way.

In justifying the militance of the Aryan Nations and the violence of the Order, a spokesman explained, "The current system of government does not fit into God's law. The whole government structure is suspect. Our task is to establish God's law as the law of the land. If it be war . . . so be it." Louis Beam, who left the Texas Klan after the legal victories of the Southern Poverty Law Center, served as "ambassador-at-large" for the Aryan Nations and developed a point system for use when the "real war" began. Classification as an "Aryan Warrior" was the ultimate goal under Beam's system. Fractions of points would be awarded as follows: for assassinating members of Congress, one-fifth of a point; judges, one-sixth; FBI agents and federal marshals, one-tenth; journalists and local politicians, one-twelfth. Anyone could instantly become an

"Aryan Warrior" by winning the goal of a full point for assassinating the President of the United States.

The most striking innovation of the Aryan Nations was a computer bulletin board called the "Liberty Net." Anyone with a home computer and modem could tap into the lower access levels of the Net and read twenty-first-century versions of the Reconstruction Klan's spook shows:

> The older and less active spokesmen for the fold and the faith are being replaced by the young lions. These Dragons of God have no time for pamphlets, for speeches, for gatherings. They know their duty. They are the armed party . . . born out of the inability of the white male youth to be heard . . . the products of this satanic, anti-white federal monstrosity. . . . And now, as we have warned, now comes the icemen! Out of the North, once again the giants gather.

A security clearance was required for accessing levels two to seven. According to Level Seven, enemies of the Aryan Nations "shall suffer the extreme penalty when lawful government is restored upon this continent." One of the major enemies identified was Morris Dees, chief trial counsel of the Southern Poverty Law Center: "According to the word of God, Morris Dees had earned two death sentences." From 1985 to 1987, when the nation was largely concerned with terrorism abroad, the Law Center was spending $12,000 per month on bodyguards and security personnel as protection from the Klan.

A newsbreaking story of 1985 revealed that Bill Wilkinson's Klan recruiter in the U.S. Navy, John A. Walker, Jr., was a spy for the Soviet Union. In what many believed to be the worst spy scandal in American history, Walker was indicted on charges of selling top-secret naval communications to the Soviets over a seventeen-year period. He pleaded guilty in 1986. Admiral Elmo Zumwalt, Jr., claimed that Walker's activities "represent a breach of security as serious as any I can recall." Carl Rowan argued that if the Navy had cracked down on Walker's Klan activities in the 1970s, his espionage might have been exposed earlier. "The Navy was and is derelict in not treating as security threats those who lead and feed hate groups aboard ships," Rowan said.

The Walker case was a strange irony that seemed to bring a phase of the Klan to a close. The third era of the Klan had been launched and nurtured on anti-Communism. From the Depression when the Klan fought unions, to the 1940s and 1950s when it strapped its ailing body to HUAC, to the 1960s when it blamed Communism for the civil rights movement, and on to Greensboro —the Klan always managed to find unity and outside support in anti-Communism. And it was somehow fitting for a conniving Kleagle to sell, according to Navy Secretary John Lehman, "hundreds of millions of dollars worth" of U.S. military secrets to the Soviet Union from whose predations Klansmen had long been swearing they were protecting America.

At the end of the second era of the Klan, Ho Chi Minh had belittled it for having "neither doctrine, nor program, nor vitality, nor discipline." The third era of the Klan showed little improvement in those areas. But at the dawn of the Klan's fourth era, it seemed possible that it could overcome those limitations. The post–Vietnam War Klan, with its emphasis on technology and militarism, showed by 1987 a singlemindedness, sophistication and vigor that had not been seen since Reconstruction. And although the group was extremely small and caused little concern, former history warned that it could be in a nascent, transitory state and could burgeon when the time was right.

During twentieth century cross-burning ceremonies, a eulogy was often recited:

Klansmen salute—
Behold the Fiery Cross still brilliant.
All the troubled history fails to quench its hallowed flame.

All the troubled history has demonstrated the remarkable persistence of the Ku Klux Klan. It has managed to swallow rivals and outlive pretenders. Even with overwhelming opposition and periodic dissolution, the Klan has always been able to revive with its primitive, hugger-mugger mystique intact. It has adapted to each age, seduced members of each generation, and allied itself with anything necessary to sustain or propagate itself. And the ironic explanation for its longevity and persistence is that the Klan is indeed an American institution. No other country could have possibly produced it. In the long course of its bigotry and violence, the Klan has evoked the rebelliousness of the Boston Tea Party, the vigilantism of American pioneers and cowboys, and the haughty religion of the New England Puritans. In its corruption of American ideals, it has capitalized on some of the best-loved aspects of the American tradition.

The Klan has remained an American institution because it is an inversion, or shadow, of American democracy. It couldn't be the unpleasant thing it is were it not for the American ideals it mocks. And it has always stood as a reminder of the degree to which American ideals can be forgotten or reduced to mere jingoism. As long as the concepts so powerfully expressed by Jefferson in the Declaration of Independence are less than fully realized in America, the Klan will be around to turn things backward whenever Americans let it.

ACKNOWLEDGMENTS

My longest acknowledgment over time and in space is owed to someone whose name I have long forgotten. As a child, I adored our Southern relations, who were always so much more witty and uninhibited than us staid Yankees. In 1958, when I was fourteen, I wrangled my parents' consent to return to Little Rock with visiting members of our Southern tribe. Shortly after we arrived in Little Rock, my cousin drove me around Central High School on which so much national attention had recently focused. My young mind boggled at the sight of the school, still wrapped in barbed wire and guarded by what looked like soldiers from World War II movies. Shortly after that, I wasn't particularly surprised at my first sight of robed Klansmen, who were maintaining a mobile surveillance of the school and taking down license numbers of cars driving around, just like the FBI. I assumed the white-robed motorists were conventioneers from some madcap Southern society who dressed as outlandishly as the North's Shriners. I was quickly corrected by my cousin. "That's the Ku Klux Klan, cousin," he informed me. "They're *crazy*. They'd sooner kill a nigger than a cat or a dog." After that shocking information, I found myself drawn into the day-to-day turmoil of the white South's response to integration. I was especially puzzled by the consuming emotionalism of the issue. Nor could I grasp its inconsistency: Why, for example, did Chubby Checker have to give two separate concerts in Little Rock, one for whites and one for blacks? If whites objected so much to blacks, why did they want to see Mr. Checker perform in the first place?

I returned home from Little Rock alone on a Greyhound bus. The only empty seat on the bus was beside a tiny black man who informed me he was a professor of history at a small, Southern Negro college. I timidly brought up the subject of integration and he eloquently discussed it at length. He linked the problem to things in America's past I had never read in books, learned in school, or seen at the movies. He used words I could only understand in context—I believe he was the first adult who ever treated me like an adult—but everything he said made extraordinary sense. In Paducah, Kentucky, where the two of us had different buses to catch, he pointed out we would have to say goodbye, for the station was segregated. I knew that he couldn't join me on the white side but I naïvely assumed I could follow him to the "colored" section, where he could continue to educate me for at least another hour. For the first time that evening he treated me as a child and sternly forbade it. "You have no idea the trouble that could cause," he explained. "Why?" I asked, perplexed and a bit hurt. "Because that's the way it is," he replied. I will never forget his enigmatic smile when he made that parting remark. And he, more than anyone, affected the intent, tone, and scope of this book.

Of the years I spent researching this project, the lion's share was done at the Library of Congress and the National Archives. As a published writer, I was given ready access to H and E stacks, and I soon discovered that even the Library of Congress was a victim to something that was happening all over the nation: rare Klan books and files are being stolen. The problem has been increasing over the past seven years, and the clipping files of local libraries and newspapers are especially vulnerable. (The historic KKK clipping file once held by the Kokomo *Tribune*, for example, is now missing.) I have formally requested the librarian of congress to place all the older and otherwise unavailable Klan items in the LC Rare Book and Special Collections Division. Things are under tighter control at the National Archives, and I am especially grateful to Linda George and to the staff of the Old Army Records office at the Archives. As far as the Klan is concerned, the material in the archives is far from being exhausted. There is still much to be learned from the Freedmen's Bureau Records (RG 105), and a promising line of inquiry may be pursued in the Records of the Justice Department (RG 60)—especially in regard to the FBI's peculiar, often ambivalent relationship with the Klan in this century.

I still find that the special collections divisions of university libraries, historical societies, and private agencies yield the most important finds in the shortest amount of time. The D. W. Griffith chapter was researched largely at the Museum of Modern Art in New York; I'm especially grateful to John Gartenberg in the department of film and to the staff of the MOMA library, Special Collections. I'd also like to thank Archie Motley, curator of manuscripts, Chicago Historical Society; Sue Rizor, collection management department, University of Notre Dame Library; and Michael Plunkett, assistant curator of manuscripts, Alderman Library, University of Virginia. Thanks also to the entire staff of the Schomburg Collection of Negro History, New York Public Library. Martin Schmitt was formerly the curator of Special Collections at the University of Oregon Library. In correspondence, Mr. Schmitt answered numerous questions, based on research through the university archives he personally undertook on my behalf. His letters were combinations of detailed information he had uncovered and delightfully witty comments he made on the facts thereof. After a brief hiatus in our correspondence, my last letter to him was answered by his successor who told me, "Martin knew that he was dying of cancer, and he lived only a few months after your correspondence."

I found myself making repeated visits to the well-rounded Klan holdings in the Special Collections division of the Michigan State University Library in East Lansing. I'm most grateful to its kind director, Jannette Fiore, and to her able assistant, Anne Tracy. Because of my fondness for this collection, I have catalogued all the articles, photocopies, documents, cards and clipping files that have gone into the making of this book and have donated them to the MSU Library, Special Collections, where they are available to future students and scholars of the Klan.

Earlier versions of the Indiana chapter were read before the annual conventions of the American Heritage Roundtable and the Indiana Librarians Association. I benefited a good deal from the many people who came up afterward, supporting some of my points, contesting others, and shyly offering additional anecdotes they had heard from neighbors and relatives. Thanks also to Don Maxwell at the Indiana State Library, Indiana Division, Indianapolis; and to Tim Peterson, Indiana Historical Society, Indianapolis.

I was able to interview a number of elderly ex-Klansmen and Klan haters from the 1920s. Without exception, the Klan haters allowed me to cite their names in the footnotes and the ex-Klansmen did not.

Three learned colleagues served as consultants on many phases of the manuscript. Frederick Rhynhart, associate professor of political science, Northern Kentucky University, Covington, served as my principal political consultant. Dr. Rhynhart remains as brilliantly iconoclastic in his political analyses as he was when we were graduate students together during the 1960s, and at one point Freddy insisted I read Machiavelli before continuing with the project. I still don't know why. Rev. Dr. Patricia Bowen, pastor of the Unitarian-Universalist Area Church in Shelburne, Massachusetts, served as my theological consultant; and whenever Patricia was at a loss for an answer to one of my knotty questions, she found the answer in a book, an article, or from another expert within twenty-four hours. My military consultant was Clay Hartley of South Bend, Indiana, who gave me unlimited access to his rare private collection of materials on the U.S. Seventh Cavalry; and by disagreeing with every one of my clever, innovative interpretations, Clay kept me on my toes.

I owe a singular debt to Stetson Kennedy who took valuable time away from his own work-in-progress (*After Appomattox: How the South Won the War*) to furnish me with numerous recollections that rounded out my account of his remarkable undercover work in the Klan during the 1940s. He was extremely generous with articles, letters, and documents from his private Klan files. And bouncing ideas back and forth with him, not to mention the challenging questions he posed, made me completely rethink Chapter 10 and expand the scope of Book Three. Corresponding with Stetson Kennedy was one of the highlights of my work on this project.

I owe a comparable debt to Randall Williams and Morris Dees of the Southern Poverty Law Center (400 Washington St., Montgomery, AL 36104); and to Janet H. Caldwell and Mark Alfonso of the National Anti-Klan Network (Box 10500, Atlanta, GA 30310). Largely through the labors of these two organizations, this book was able to be brought to a close. The activities of the Klan are being observed, recorded, and reported daily by the Law Center and the Network. Readers interested in keeping abreast of the changing nature of the Klan, or in helping keep it under control, are urged to get in touch with these dynamic organizations.

Bill Reiss offered provocative suggestions and wrote lengthy criticisms of the manuscript that exceeded the obligations of a literary agent. Alice Mayhew and the good people at Simon and Schuster were exceptionally tolerant when the course of this project took twice as long as the contracted time.

I owe as much to the kindness of friends as to the kindness of strangers. This book was shepherded from dream to reality through the sage advice and dedication of my former literary agent Walter Betkowski, and I will always be grateful to him. My dearest friends, scattered about the nation, sent clippings, reviewed chapters, tendered support, and badgered me incessantly. My warmest regards to John and Cathy Goodwin, Hal Landen, Rick Mathews, and Jim and Nancy Eastman.

My deepest debt is owed to my long-suffering family. My brother Kerry arranged several private screenings of *The Birth of a Nation* for me and somehow managed to send strange things (including a KKK jackknife) to pique my interest just when it was waning. My mother Ruth was more understanding and generous than I can ever remember, if that is possible. My son Derek grew from a boy to a man in the course of his father's immersion in this project and may possibly have benefited from my lack of interference in the process. I knew things had changed when Derek became my principal consultant on firearms. When I asked him if he had ever heard of a Ruger Mini-14, he brought out an entire catalogue with pictures and price lists of magazine rounds. "What on earth are you doing with this?" I asked dumbfounded. "It's no big deal, Wyn," he assured me. Derek's comments on portions of the manuscript, from ages ten to fifteen, offered me an unusual perspective. Finally, in spite of her unwavering belief in this book, her wise counsel, and sharp proofreading, Barbara still prohibits me from those "cloying, insipid, demeaning acknowledgments" that writers invariably inscribe to their spouses.

APPENDICES

The documents in the appendices have been reproduced as they originally appeared; errors have not been corrected.

APPENDIX A
The Original Ku-Klux
Prescript of Reconstruction *

PRESCRIPT OF THE
*   *

What may this mean,
That thou, dead corse, again, in complete steel,
Revisit'st thus the glimpses of the moon,
Making night hideous; and we fools of nature,
So horridly to shake our disposition,
With thoughts beyond the reaches of our souls?
An' now auld Cloots, I ken ye're thinkin',
A certain *Ghoul* is rantin', drinkin',
Some luckless night will send him linkin',
    To your black pit;
But, faith! he'll turn a corner jinkin',
    And cheat you yet.

CREED.

We the * * reverently acknowledge the Majesty and Supremacy of the Divine being, and recognize the goodness and Providence of the Same.

PREAMBLE.

We recognize our relations to the United States Government and acknowledge the supremacy of its laws.

APPELLATION.

ARTICLE I. This organization shall be styled and denominated the * *

TITLES.

ART. II. The officers of this * shall consist of a Grand Wizard of the Empire and his ten Genii; a Grand Dragon of the Realm and his eight Hydras; a Grand Titan of the Dominion and his six Furies; a Grand Giant of the Province and his four Goblins; a Grand Cyclops of the Den and his two Night Hawks; a Grand Magi, a Grand Monk, a Grand Exchequer, a Grand Turk, a Grand Scribe, a Grand Sentinel, and a Grand Ensign.

Sec. 2. The body politic of this * shall be designated and known as "Ghouls."

---

* U.S. Congress, *Sheafe* v. *Tillman*. 41 Cong., 1 Sess., House Misc. Doc. No. 53 (1870):315–21.

DIVISIONS.

ART. III. This * shall be divided into five departments, all combined, constituting the Grand * of the Empire. The second department to be called the Grand * of the Realm. The third, the Grand * of the Dominion. The fourth, the Grand * of the Province. The fifth, the * of the Den.

DUTIES OF OFFICERS.

GRAND WIZARD.

ART. IV.Sec.1. It shall be the duty of the Grand Wizard, who is the Supreme Officer of the Empire, to communicate with and receive reports from the Grand Dragons of the Realms, as to the condition, strength, efficiency and progress of the *s within their respective Realms. And he shall communicate from time to time, to all subordinates *s, through the Grand Dragon, the condition, strength, efficiency, and progress of the *s throughout his vast Empire; and such other information as he may deem expedient to impart. And it shall further be his duty to keep by his G Scribe a list of the names (without any caption or explanation whatever) of the Grand Dragons of the different Realms of his Empire, and shall number such Realms with the Arabic numerals 1, 2, 3, &c., *ad finem*. And he shall instruct his Grand Exchequer as to the appropriation and disbursement which he shall make of the revenue of the * that comes to his hands. He shall have the sole power to issue copies of this Prescript, through his Subalterns and Deputies, for the organization and establishment of subordinate *s. And he shall have the further power to appoint his Genii; also, a Grand Scribe and a Grand Exchequer for his Department, and to appoint and ordain Special Deputy Grand Wizards to assist him in the more rapid and effectual dissemination and establishment of the * throughout his Empire. He is further empowered to appoint and instruct Deputies, to organize and control Realms, Dominions, Provinces, and Dens, until the same shall elect a Grand Dragon, a Grand Titan, a Grand Giant, and a Grand Cyclops, in the manner hereinafter provided. And when a question of paramount importance to the interest or prosperity of the * arises, not provided for in this Prescript, he shall have power to determine such question, and his decision shall be final, until the same shall be provided for by amendment as hereinafter provided.

GRAND DRAGON.

Sec. 2. It shall be the duty of the Grand Dragon who is the Chief Officer of the Realm, to report to the Grand Wizard when required by that officer, the condition, strength, efficiency, and progress of the * within his Realm, and to transmit through the Grand Titan to the subordinate *s of his Realm, all information or intelligence conveyed to him by the Grand Wizard for that purpose, and all such other information or instruction as he may think will promote the interests of the *. He shall keep by his G. Scribe a list of the names (without any caption) of the Grand Titans of the different Dominions of his Realm, and shall report the same to the Grand Wizard when required; and shall number the Dominions of his Realm with the Arabic numerals, 1, 2, 3, &c., *ad finem*. He shall instruct his Grand Exchequer as to the appropriation and disbursement of the revenue of the * that comes to his hands. He shall have the power to appoint his Hydras; also, a Grand Scribe and a Grand Exchequer for his Department, and to appoint and ordain Special Deputy Grand Dragons to assist him in the more rapid and effectual dissemination and establishment of the * throughout his Realm. His is further empowered to appoint and instruct Deputies to organize and control Dominions, Provinces, and Dens, until the same shall elect a Grand Titan, a Grand Giant, and Grand Cyclops, in the manner hereinafter provided.

GRAND TITAN.

Sec. 3. It shall be the duty of the Grand Titan who is the Chief Officer of the Dominion, to report to the Grand Dragon when required by that officer, the condition, strength, efficiency, and progress of the * within his Dominion, and to transmit through the Grand Giants to the subordinate *s of his Dominion, all information or intelligence conveyed to him by the Grand Dragon for that purpose, and all such other information or instruction as he may think will enhance the interests of the *. He shall keep, by his G. Scribe, a list of the names (without caption) of the Grand Giants of the different Provinces of his Dominion, and shall report the same to the Grand Dragon when required; and he shall number the Provinces of his Dominion with the Arabic Numerals, 1, 2, 3, &c., *ad finem.* And he shall instruct and direct his Grand Exchequer as to the appropriation and disbursement of the revenue of the * that comes to his hands. He shall have power to appoint his Furies; also to appoint a Grand Scribe and a Grand Exchequer for his department, and appoint and ordain Special Deputy Grand Titans to assist him in the more rapid and effectual dissemination and establishment of the * throughout his Dominion. He shall have further power to appoint and instruct Deputies to organize and control Provinces and Dens, until the same shall elect a Grand Giant and a Grand Cyclops, in the manner hereinafter provided.

Damnant quod non intelligunt.

Amici humani generis.

Magna est veritas, et prevalebit.

Nec scire fas est omnia.

Ne vile fano.

Ars est celare artem.

Nusquanm tuta fides.

Quid faciendum?

GRAND GIANT.

Sec. 4. It shall be the duty of the Grand Giant, who is the Chief Officer of the Province, to supervise and administer general and special instruction in the formation and establishment of *s within his Province, and to report to the Grand Titan, when required by that officer, the condition, strength, progress and efficiency of the * throughout his Province, and to transmit, through the Grand

Cyclops, to the subordinate *s of his Province, all information or intelligence conveyed to him by the Grand Titan for that purpose and such other information and instruction as he may think will advance the interests of the *. He shall keep by his G. Scribe a list of the names (without caption) of the Grand Cyclops of the various Dens of his Province, and shall report the same to the Grand Titan when required; and shall number the Dens of his Province with the Arabic numerals, 1, 2, 3, &c., *ad finem.* And shall determine and limit the number of Dens to be organized in his Province. And he shall instruct and direct his Grand Exchequer as to what appropriation and disbursement he shall make of the revenue of the * that comes to his hands. He shall have power to appoint his Goblins; also, a Grand Scribe and a Grand Exchequer for his department, and to appoint and ordain Special Deputy Grand Giants to assist him in the more rapid and effectual dissemination and establishment of the * throughout his Province. He shall have the further power to appoint and instruct Deputies to organize and control Dens, until the same shall elect a Grand Cyclops in the manner herein-after provided. And in all cases, he shall preside at and conduct the Grand Council of Yahoos.

GRAND CYCLOPS.

Sec. 5. It shall be the duty of the Grand Cyclops to take charge of the * of his Den after his election, under the direction and with the assistance (when practic-able) of the Grand Giant, and in accordance with, and in conformity to the provisions of this Prescript, a copy of which shall in all cases be obtained before the formation of a * begins. It shall further be his duty to appoint all regular meetings of his * and to preside at the same—to appoint irregular meetings when he deems it expedient, to preserve order in his Den, and to impose fines for irregularities or disobedience of orders, and to receive and initiate candidates for admission into the * after the same shall have been pronounced competent and worthy to become members by the Investigating Committee. He shall make a quarterly report to the Grand Giant, of the condition, strength and efficiency of the * of his Den, and shall convey to the Ghouls of his Den, all information or intelligence conveyed to him by the Grand Giant for that purpose, and all other such information or instruction as he may think will conduce to the interests and welfare of the *. He shall preside at and conduct the Grand Council of Centaurs. He shall have power to appoint his Night Hawks, his Grand Scribe, his Grand Turk, his Grand Sentinel, and his Grand Ensign. And he shall instruct and direct the Grand Exchequer of his Den, as to what appropriation and disbursement he shall make to the revenue of the * that comes to his hands. And for any small offense he may punish any member by fine, and may reprimand him for the same: And he may admonish and reprimand the * of his Den for any imprudence, irregularity or transgression, when he is convinced or advised that the interests, welfare and safety of the * demand it.

GRAND MAGI.

Sec. 6. It shall be the duty of the Grand Magi, who is the Second Officer, in authority, of the Den, to assist the Grand Cyclops and to obey all the proper orders of that officer. To preside at all meetings in the Den in the absence of the Grand Cyclops; and to exercise during his absence all the powers and authority conferred upon that officer.

GRAND MONK.

Sec. 7. It shall be the duty of the Grand Monk, who is the third officer, in authority, of the Den, to assist and obey all the proper orders of the Grand Cyclops and the Grand Magi. And in the absence of both of these officers, he shall preside at and conduct the meetings in the Den, and shall exercise all the powers of authority conferred upon the Grand Cyclops.

GRAND EXCHEQUER.

Sec. 8. It shall be the duty of the Grand Exchequers of the different Departments of the * to keep a correct account of all the revenue of the * that shall come to their hands, and shall make no appropriation or disbursement of the same except under the orders and direction of the chief officer of their respective departments. And it shall further be the duty of the Grand Exchequer of Dens to collect the initiation fees, and all fines imposed by the Grand Cyclops.

GRAND TURK.

Sec. 9. It shall be the duty of the Grand Turk, who is the Executive Officer of the Grand Cyclops, to notify the Ghouls of the Den of all informal or irregular meetings appointed by the Grand Cyclops and to obey and execute all the lawful orders of that officer in the control and government of his Den. It shall further be his duty to receive and question at the Out Posts, all candidates for admission into the *, and shall *there* administer the preliminary obligation required, and then to conduct such candidate or candidates to the Grand Cyclops at his Den, and to assist him in the initiation of the same. And it shall further be his duty to act as the executive officer of the Grand Council of Centaurs.

GRAND SCRIBE.

Sec. 10. It shall be the duty of the Grand Scribes of the different departments to conduct the correspondence and write the orders of the chiefs of their departments, when required. And it shall further be the duty of the Grand Scribes of the Den to keep a list of the names (without caption) of the ghouls of the Den— to call the Roll at all regular meetings and to make the quarterly report under the direction of the Grand Cyclops.

GRAND SENTINEL.

Sec. 11. It shall be the duty of the Grand Sentinel to detail, take charge of, post and instruct the Grand Guard under the direction and orders of the Grand Cyclops, and to relieve and dismiss the same when directed by that officer.

GRAND ENSIGN.

Sec. 12. It shall be the duty of the Grand Ensign to take charge of the Grand Banner of the *, to preserve it sacredly, and protect it carefully, and to bear it on all occasions of parade or ceremony, and on such other occasions as the Grand Cyclops may direct it to be flung to the night breeze.

ELECTION OF OFFICERS.

ART. V. Sec. 1. The Grand Cyclops, the Grand Magi, the Grand Monk, and the Grand Exchequer of Dens, shall be elected semi-annually by the ghouls of Dens. And the first election for these officers may take place as soon as seven ghouls have been initiated for that purpose.

Sec. 2. The Grand Wizard of the Empire, the Grand Dragons of Realms, the Grand Titans of Dominions, and the Grand Giants of Provinces, shall be elected biennially, and in the following manner, to wit: The Grand Wizard by a majority vote of the Grand Dragons of his Empire, the Grand Dragons by a like vote of the Grand Titans of his Realm; the Grand Titans by a like vote of the Grand Giants of his Dominion, and the Grand Giant by a like vote of the Grand Cyclops of his Province.

The first election for Grand Dragon may take place as soon as three Dominions have been organized in a Realm, but all subsequent elections shall be by a majority vote of the Grand Titans, throughout the Realm, and biennially as aforesaid.

The first election for Grand Titan may take place as soon as three Provinces have been organized in a Dominion, but all subsequent elections shall be by a majority vote of all the Grand Giants throughout the Dominion and biennially as aforesaid.

The first election for Grand Giant may take place as soon as three Dens have been organized in a Province, but all subsequent elections shall be by a majority vote of all the Grand Cyclops throughout the Province, and biennially as aforesaid.

The Grand Wizard of the Empire is hereby created, to serve three years from the First Monday in May, 1867, after the expiration of which time, biennial elections shall be held for that office as aforesaid. And the incumbent Grand Wizard shall notify the Grand Dragons, at least six months before said election, at what time and place the same will be held.

JUDICIARY.

ART. VI. Sec. 1. The Tribunal of Justice of this * shall consist of a Grand Council of Yahoos, and a Grand Council of Centaurs.

Sec. 2. The Grand Council of Yahoos, shall be the Tribunal for the trial of all elected officers, and shall be composed of officers of equal rank with the accused, and shall be appointed and presided over by an officer of the next rank above, and sworn by him to administer even handed justice. The Tribunal for the trial of the Grand Wizard, shall be composed of all the Grand Dragons of the Empire, and shall be presided over and sworn by the senior Grand Dragon. They shall have power to summon the accused, and witnesses for and against him, and if found guilty they shall prescribe the penalty and execute the same. And they shall have power to appoint an executive officer to attend said Council while in session.

Sec. 3. The Grand Council of Centaurs shall be the Tribunal for the trial of Ghouls and non-elective officers, and shall be composed of six judges appointed by the Grand Cyclops from the Ghouls of his Den, presided over and sworn by him to give the accused a fair and impartial trial. They shall have power to summon the accused, and witnesses for and against him, and if found guilty they shall prescribe the penalty and execute the same. Said Judges shall be selected by the Grand Cyclops with reference to their intelligence, integrity and fair-mindedness, and shall render their verdict without prejudice or partiality.

REVENUE.

ART. VII. Sec. 1. The revenue of this * shall be derived as follows: For every copy of this Prescript issued to the *s of Dens, Ten Dollars will be required. Two dollars of which shall go into the hands of the Grand Exchequer of the Grand Giant; two into the hands of the Grand Exchequer of the Grand Titan; two into the hands of the Grand Exchequer of the Grand Dragon, and the remaining four into the hands of the Grand Exchequer of the Grand Wizard.

Fide non armis.

Fiat Justia.

Hic manent vestigia morientis libertatis.

Curae leves loquntur, ingentes stupent.

Dat Deus his quoque finem.

Cessante causa, cessat effectus.

Droit et avant.

Cave quid dicis, quando, et cui.

Dormitur aliquando jus, moritur nunquam.

Deo adjuvante, non timendum.

Spectemur agendo.

Nemo nos impune lacessit.

Patria cara, carior libertas.

Ad unum omnes.

Sec. 2. A further source of revenue to the Empire shall be ten per cent. of all the revenue of the Realms, and a tax upon Realms, when the Grand Wizard shall deem it necessary and indispensable to levy the same.

Sec. 3. A further source of revenue to Realms shall be ten per cent. of all the revenue of Dominions, and a tax upon Dominions when the Grand Dragon shall deem such tax necessary and indispensable.

Sec. 4. A further source of revenue to Dominions shall be ten per cent. of all the revenue of Provinces, and a tax upon Provinces when the Grand Titan shall deem such tax necessary and indispensable.

Sec. 5 A further source of revenue to Provinces shall be ten per cent. on all the revenue of Dens, and a tax upon the Dens, when the Grand Giant shall deem such tax necessary and indispensable.

Sec. 6. The source of revenue to Dens, shall be the initiation fees, fines, and a *per capita* tax, whenever the Grand Cyclops shall deem such tax indispensable to the interests and purposes of the *.

Sec. 7. All of the revenue obtained in the manner herein aforesaid, shall be for the exclusive benefit of the *. And shall be appropriated to the dissemination of the same, and to the creation of a fund to meet any disbursement that it may become necessary to make to accomplish the objects of the *, and to secure the protection of the same.

OBLIGATION.

ART. VIII. No one shall become a member of this *, unless he shall take the following oath or obligation:

"I, ——— of my own free will and accord, and in the presence of Almighty God, do solemnly swear or affirm that I will never reveal to any one, not a member of the * * by any intimation, sign, symbol, word or act, or in any other manner whatever, any of the secrets, signs, grips, pass words, mysteries or purposes of the * * or that I am a member of the same or that I know any one who *is* a member, and that I will abide by the Prescript and Edicts of the * *. So help me God."

Sec. 2. The preliminary obligation to be administered before the candidate for admission is taken to the Grand Cyclops for examination, shall be as follows:

"I do solemnly swear or affirm that I will never reveal any thing that I may this day (or night) learn concerning the * *. So help me God."

ADMISSION.

ART. IX. Sec. 1. No one shall be presented for admission into this *, until he shall have been recommended by some friend or intimate, who *is* a member, to the Investigating Committee, which shall be composed of the Grand Cyclops, the Grand Magi and the Grand Monk, and who shall investigate his antecedents and his past and present standing and connections, and if after such investigation, they pronounce him competent and worthy to become a member, he may be admitted upon taking the obligation required and passing through the ceremonies of initiation. *Provided,* That no one shall be admitted into this * who shall have not attained the age of eighteen years.

Sec. 2. No one shall become a member of a distant * when there is a * established and in operation in his own immediate vicinity. Nor shall any one become a member of any * after he shall have been rejected by any other *.

ENSIGN.

ART. X. The Grand Banner of this * shall be in the form of an isosceles triangle, five feet long and three feet wide at the staff. The material shall be Yellow, with a Red scalloped border, about three inches in width. There shall be painted upon it, in black, a Dracovolans, or Flying Dragon.† with the following

---

† See Webster's Unabridged Pictorial.

motto inscribed above the Dragon, "QUOD SEMPER, QUOD UBIQUE, QUOD AB OM-
NIBUS." †

AMENDMENTS.

ART. XI. This Prescript or any part or Edicts thereof, shall never be changed
except by a two-thirds vote of the Grand Dragons of the Realms, in Convention
assembled, and at which Convention the Grand Wizard shall preside and be
entitled to a vote. And upon the application of a majority of the Grand Dragons,
for that purpose, the Grand Wizard shall appoint the time and place for said
Convention; which, when assembled, shall proceed to make such modifications
and amendments as it may think will advance the interest, enlarge the utility and
more thoroughly effectuate the purposes of the *.

INTERDICTION.

ART. XII. The origin, designs, mysteries and ritual of this * shall never be
written, but the same shall be communicated orally.

REGISTER.
[Months, days, and hours]

1st—Dismal.	7th—Dreadful.
2nd—Dark.	8th—Terrible.
3rd—Furious.	9th—Horrible.
4th—Portentous.	10th—Melancholy.
5th—Wonderful.	11th—Mournful.
6th—Alarming.	12th—Dying.

II.

I—White.	IV—Black.
II—Green.	V—Yellow.
III—Blue.	VI—Crimson.

VII—Purple.

III.

1—Fearful.	7—Doleful.
2—Startling.	8—Sorrowful.
3—Awful.	9—Hideous.
4—Woeful.	10—Frightful.
5—Horrid.	11—Appalling.
6—Bloody.	12—Last.

EDICTS.

I. The Initiation Fee of this * shall be one dollar, to be paid when the candidate is initiated and received into the *.

II. No member shall be allowed to take any intoxicating spirits to any meeting
of the *. Nor shall any member be allowed to attend a meeting when intoxicated;
and for every appearance at a meeting in such condition, he shall be fined the

---

† "What always, what every where, what by all is held to be true."

sum of not less than one nor more than five dollars, to go into the revenue of the *.

III. Any member may be expelled from the * by a majority vote of the officers and ghouls of the Den to which he belongs, and if after such expulsion such member shall assume any of the duties, regalia or insignia of the * or in any way claim to be a member of the same, he shall be severely punished. His obligation of secrecy shall be as binding upon him after expulsion as before, and for any revelation made by him thereafter, he shall be held accountable in the same manner as if he were then a member.

IV. Every Grand Cyclops shall read or cause to be read, this Prescript and these Edicts to the * of his Den, at least once in every three months—And shall read them to each new member when he is initiated, or present the same to him for personal perusal.

V. Each Den may provide itself with the Grand Banner of the *.

VI. The *s of Dens may make such additional Edicts for their control and government as they shall deem requisite and necessary. *Provided*, No Edict shall be made to conflict with any of the provisions or Edicts of this Prescript.

VII. The strictest and most rigid secrecy, concerning any and everything that relates to the * shall at all times be maintained.

VIII. Any member who shall reveal or betray the secrets or purposes of this * shall suffer the extreme penalty of the Law.

> Hush, thou art not to utter what
> I am. Bethink thee; it was our covenant.
> I said that I would see thee once again.

L'ENVOI.

To the lovers of Law and Order, Peace and Justice, we send greeting; and to the shades of the venerated Dead, we affectionately dedicate the * *

Deo duce, ferro comitante.

Tempora mutantur, et nos mutamur in illis.

O tempora! O mores!

Ad utrumque paratus.

Cavendo tutus.

Astra castra, numen lumen.

Ne quid detrimenti Respublica capiat.

Amici usque ad aras.

Nos ducit amor libertatis.

APPENDIX B

The Kloran *of the 1920s* Klan, *With Other Documents* †

* * * * * *

KLOKARD. Your excellency, the sacred altar of the klan is prepared; the fiery cross illumines the klavern.

E.C. Faithful Klokard, why the fiery cross?

KLOKARD. Sir, it is the emblem of that sincere, unselfish devotedness of all klansmen to the sacred purpose and principles we have espoused.

E.C. My terrors and klansmen, what means the fiery cross?

ALL. We serve and sacrifice for the right.

E.C. Klansmen all: You will gather for our opening devotions.

*   *   *   *   *   *   *

(The stanzas are sung to the tune From Greenland's Icy Mountains and the chorus, Home, Sweet Home.)

I.

We meet with cordial greetings
    In this our sacred cave
To pledge anew our compact
    With hearts sincere and brave;
A band of faithful klansmen,
    Knights of the K.K.K.,
We all will stand together
    Forever and for aye.

CHORUS.

Home, home, country and home,
    Klansmen we'll live and die
For our country and home.

II.

Here honor, love, and justice
    Must actuate us all;
Before our sturdy phalanx
    All hate and strife shall fall.
In unison we'll labor
    Wherever we may roam
To shield a klansman's welfare,
    His country, name, and home.

After singing, the Kludd at the sacred altar leads in the following prayer: (All must stand steady with heads reverently bowed.)

---

† U.S. Congress, *The Ku Klux Klan Hearings.* 67 Cong., 1 Sess., House Committee on Rules (1921): 114–26.

Our Father and our God, we, as klansmen, acknowledge our dependence upon Thee and Thy lovingkindness toward us; may our gratitude be full and constant and inspire us to walk in Thy ways.

Give us to know that each klansman by the process of thought and conduct determines his own destiny, good or bad: May he forsake the bad and choose and strive for the good, remembering always that the living Christ is a klansman's criterion of character.

Keep us in the blissful bonds of fraternal union, of clannish fidelity one toward another and of a devoted loyalty to this, our great institution. Give us to know that the crowning glory of a klansman is to serve. Harmonize our souls with the sacred principles and purposes of our noble order that we may keep our sacred oath inviolate, as Thou art our witness.

Bless those absent from our gathering at this time; Thy peace be in their hearts and homes.

God save our Nation! And help us to be a Nation worthy of existence on the earth. Keep ablaze in each klansman's heart the sacred fire of a devoted patriotism to our country and its Government.

We invoke Thy blessing upon our emperor, the imperial wizard, and his official family in the administrations of the affairs pertaining to the government of the invisible empire. Grant him wisdom and grace; and may each klansman's heart and soul be inclined toward him in loving loyalty and unwavering devotion.

Oh, God! For Thy glory and our good we humbly ask these things in the name of Him who taught us to serve and sacrifice for the right. Amen! (All say "Amen!")

CLOSING CEREMONY, KNIGHTS OF THE KU-KLUX KLAN.

The order of business having been finished, the E.C. will arise, give one rap with his gavel and say:

"My terrors and klansmen, the sacred purpose of the gathering of the klan at this time has been fulfilled; the deliberations of this klonklave have ended."

E.C. Faithful Klaliff: What is the fourfold duty of a klansman?

The klaliff will arise and say:

"To worship God; be patriotic toward our country; be devoted and loyal to our klan and emperor, and to practice clannishness toward his fellow klansfen." (And remains standing.)

E.C. Faithful Kludd: "How speaketh the oracles of our God?"

The kludd will arise and say:

"Thou shalt worship the Lord thy God. Render unto the state the things which are the state's. Love the brotherhood: honor the king. Bear ye one another's burdens, and so fulfill the law of Christ." (And remains standing.)

E.C. Faithful Klokard: "What does a klansman value more than life?"

The klokard will arise and say:

"Honor to a klansman is more than life." (And remains standing.)

*   *   *   *   *   *   *

[Tune, America.]

God of Eternity
Guard, guide our great country,
Our homes and store.
Keep our great state to Thee,

Its people right and free.
In us Thy glory be,
Forevermore.

After the singing all look toward the mounted flag and will gtnh and then stand with bowed heads; the kludd standing at the sacred altar will pronounce the following benediction:

THE BENEDICTION.

May the blessings of our God wait upon thee and the sun of glory shine around thy head; may the gates of plenty, honor, and happiness be always open to thee and thine, so far as they will not rob thee of eternal joys.

May no strife disturb thy days, nor sorrow distress thy nights, and when death shall summons thy departure may the Saviour's blood have washed thee from all impurities, perfected thy initiation, and thus prepared, enter thou into the empire invisible and repose thy soul in perpetual peace.

Amen! (All say, "Amen.")

*   *   *   *   *   *   *

QUALIFYING INTERROGATORIES.

The klokard will first ask each candidate his name and then speak to the candidates in the outer den as follows:

SIRS: The Knights of the Ku-Klux Klan, as a great and essentially a patriotic, fraternal, benevolent order, does not discriminate against a man on account of his religious or political creed, when same does not conflict with or antagonize the sacred rights and privileges guaranteed by our civil government and Christian ideals and institutions.

Therefore, to avoid any misunderstanding and as evidence that we do not seek to impose unjustly the requirements of this order upon anyone who can not, on account of his religious or political scruples, voluntarily meet our requirements and faithfully practice our principles, and as proof that we respect all honest men in their sacred convictions, whether same are agreeable with our requirements or not, we require as an absolute necessity on the part of each of you an affirmative answer to each of the following questions:

Each of the following questions must be answered by (each of) you with an emphatic "Yes."

First. Is the motive prompting your ambition to be a klansman serious and unselfish?

Second. Are you a native-born white, Gentile American citizen?

Third. Are you absolutely opposed to and free of any allegiance of any nature to any cause, Government, people, sect, or ruler that is foreign to the United States of America?

Fourth. Do you believe in the tenets of the Christian religion?

Fifth. Do you esteem the United States of America and its institutions above any other Government, civil, political, or ecclesiastical, in the whole world?

Sixth. Will you, without mental reservation, take a solemn oath to defend, preserve, and enforce same?

Seventh. Do you believe in clannishness and will you faithfully practice same towards klansmen?

Eighth. Do you believe in and will you faithfully strive for the eternal maintenance of white supremacy?

Ninth. Will you faithfully obey our constitution and laws, and conform willingly to all our usages, requirements, and regulations?

Tenth. Can you be always depended on?

*   *   *   *   *   *

KLADD. The distinguishing marks of a klansman are not found in the fiber of his garments or his social or financial standing, but are spiritual: namely, a chivalric head, a compassionate heart, a prudent tongue, and a courageous will. All devoted to our country, our klan, our homes, and each other: these are the distinguishing marks of a klansman, oh faithful klexter! And these men claim the marks.

KLEXTER. What if one of your party should prove himself a traitor?

KLADD. He would be immediately banished in disgrace from the invisible empire without fear or favor, conscience would tenaciously torment him, remorse would repeatedly revile him, and direful things would befall him.

KLEXTER. Do they (or does he) know all this?

KLADD. All this he (or they) now know. He (or they) has (or have) heard, and they must heed.

KLEXTER. Faithful kladd, you speak the truth.

KLADD. Faithful klexter, a klansman speaketh the truth in and from his heart. A lying scoundrel may wrap his disgraceful frame within the sacred folds of a klansman's robe and deceive the very elect, but only a klansman possesses a klansman's heart and a klansman's soul.

KLOKARD:

> God give us men! The invisible empire demands strong
> Minds, great hearts, true faith, and ready hands.
> Men whom the lust of office does not kill;
> Men whom the spoils of office can not buy;
> Men who possess opinions and a will:
> Men who have honor; men who will not lie;
> Men who can stand before a demogogue
> And damn his treacherous flatteries without winking!
> Tall men, sun-crowned, who live above the fog
> In public duty and in private thinking;
> For while the rabble, with their thumb-worn creeds,
> Their large professions and their little deeds,
> Mingle in selfish strife, Lo! freedom weeps,
> Wrong rules the land, and waiting justice sleeps.
> God give us men!
> Men who serve not for selfish booty,
> But real men, courageous, who flinch not at duty;
> Men of dependable character; men of sterling worth;
> Then wrongs will be redressed, and right will rule the earth;
> God give us men!

After a pause, the klarogo faces the candidates and says:

"SIRS: Will you (or each of you) by your daily life as klansmen earnestly endeavor to be an answer to this prayer?"

*   *   *   *   *   *   *

The exalted cyclops will arise and address the candidates as follows:

"Sirs, is the motive prompting your presence here serious and unselfish?

"It is indeed refreshing to meet face to face with men (or a man) like you, who, actuated by manly motives, aspire to all things noble for yourselves and humanity.

"The luster of the holy light of chivalry has lost its former glory and is sadly dimmed by the choking dust of selfish, sordid gain. Pass on:"

The exalted cyclops will resume his seat, and the kladd will face his party toward the nighthawk and advance behind the nighthawk until he hears the signal of allw from the klokard. On hearing the signal from the klokard, the nighthawk stops and stands steady; the kladd will also stop his party immediately in front of the klokard's station and face them to the klokard's station and answer the signal by the same. On receiving the answer, the klokard will arise and address the party as follows:

"Real fraternity, by shameful neglect, has been starved until so weak her voice is lost in the courts of her own castle, and she passes unnoticed by her sworn subjects as she moves along the crowded streets and through the din of the market place. Man's valuation of man is by the standard of wealth and not worth: selfishness is the festive queen among humankind, and multitudes forget honor, justice, love, and God and every religious conviction to do homage to her; and yet, with the cruel heart of Jezebel, she slaughters the souls of thousands of her devotees daily. Pass on!"

The klokard will resume his seat, and the kladd will face his party as before and advance behind the nighthawk until he hears the signal of allw from the klaliff. On hearing the signal of the klaliff the nighthawk stops and stands steady; the kladd will also stop his party immediately in front ot the klaliff's station, facing them to the klaliff, and answer the signal by the same. On receiving the answer, the klaliff will arise and address the party as follows:

"The unsatiated thirst for gain is dethroning reason and judgment in the citadel of the human soul, and men maddened thereby forget their patriotic, domestic, and social obligations and duties and fiendishly fight for a place in the favor of the goddess of glittering gold; they starve their own souls and make sport of spiritual development. Pass on!"

The klaliff will resume his seat, and the kladd will face his party as before and advance behind the nighthawk until he hears the signal of allw from the kludd. On hearing the signal of the kludd, the nighthawk stops and stands steady; the kladd will also stop his party immediately in front of the kludd's station, facing them to the kludd, and then answers the signal by the same. On receiving the answer, the kludd will arise and address the party as follows:

"Men speak of love and live in hate,
　　Men talk of faith and trust to fate,
Oh, might men do the things they teach!
　　Oh, might men live the life they preach!
Then the throne of avarice would fall, and the clangor
　　Of grim Selfishness o'er the earth would cease;
Love would tread out the baleful fire of anger,
　　And in its ashes plant the lily of peace.
　　　　Pass on!"

The kludd will resume his seat, and the kladd will face his party as before and advance behind the nighthawk until he hears the signal of allw from the exalted cyclops. On hearing the signal of the exalted cyclops, the nighthawk stops and goes to and takes position at the sacred altar; the kladd will also stop his party immediately in front of the exalted cyclops's station, facing them to the exalted cyclops, and then answer the signal with the same. On receiving the answer, the exalted cyclops will arise and address the party as follows:

"Sirs, we congratulate you on your manly decision to forsake the world of selfishness and fraternal alienation and emigrate to the delectable bounds of the invisible empire and become loyal citizens of the same. The prime purpose of this great order is to develop character, practice clannishness, to protect the home and the chastity of womanhood, and to exemplify a pure patriotism toward our glorious country.

"You as citizens of the invisible empire must be actively patriotic, toward our country and constantly clannish toward klansmen socially, physically, morally, and vocationally; will you assume this obligation of citizenship?

"You must unflinchingly conform to our requirements, regulations, and usages in every detail and prove yourselves worthy to have and to hold the honors we bestow; do you freely and faithfully assume to do this?

"Sirs, if you have any doubt as to your ability to qualify, either in body or character, as citizens of the invisible empire, you now have an opportunity to retire from this place with the good will of the klan to attend you; for I warn you now if you falter or fail at this time or in the future as a klansman, in klonklave or in life, you will be banished from citizenship in the invisible empire without fear or favor.

"This is a serious undertaking; we are not here to make sport of you nor indulge in the silly frivolity of circus clowns. Be you well assured that 'he that putteth his hands to the plow and looketh back is not fit for the kingdom of heaven' or worthy of the high honor of citizenship in the invisible empire, or the fervent fellowship of klansmen. Don't deceive yourselves; you can not deceive us, and we will not be mocked. Do you wish to retire?"

E. C. Faithful kladd, you will direct the way for these worthy aliens to the sacred altar of the empire of chivalry, honor, industry, and love, in order that they may make further progress toward attaining citizenship in the invisible empire, Knights of the Ku-Klux Klan.

*　　　*　　　*　　　*　　　*　　　*　　　*

DEDICATION.

The E. C. addresses the candidates as follows:
"Sirs, have (each of) you assumed without mental reservation your oath of allegiance to the invisible empire? Mortal man can not assume a more binding oath; character and courage alone will enable you to keep it. Always remember that to keep this oath means to you honor, happiness, and life; but to violate it means disgrace, dishonor, and death. May honor, happiness, and life be yours."

*　　　*　　　*　　　*　　　*　　　*　　　*

(Then he folds up the vessel from the sacred altar, containing the dedication fluid, and addresses the candidates as follows:)
"With this transparent, life-giving, powerful, God-given fluid, more precious and far more significant than all the sacred oils of the ancients, I set you (or each of you) apart from the men of your daily association to the great and honorable

task you have voluntarily allotted yourselves as citizens of the invisible empire, Knights of the Ku-Klux Klan.

"As a klansman may your character be as transparent, your life purpose as powerful, your motive in all things as magnanimous and as pure, and your clannishness as real and as faithful as the manifold drops herein, and you a vital being as useful to humanity as is pure water to mankind.

"You will kneel upon your right knee."

Just here the following stanza must be sung in a low, soft, but distinct tone, preferably by a quartet:

[Tune, Just As I Am Without One Plea.]

To Thee, oh God! I call to Thee—
True to my oath, oh, help me be!
I've pledged my love, my blood, my all;
Oh, give me grace that I not fall.

　　*　　　　*　　　　*　　　　*　　　　*　　　　*　　　　*

E.C. Sirs, 'Neath the uplifted fiery cross which by its holy light looks down upon you to bless with its sacred traditions of the past I dedicate you in body, in mind, in spirit, and in life to the holy service of our country, our klan, our homes, each other, and humanity.

　　*　　　　*　　　　*　　　　*　　　　*　　　　*　　　　*

DEDICATORY PRAYER.

God of all, author of all good, Thou who didst create man and so proposed that man should fill a distinct place and perform a specific work in the economy of Thy good government. Thou has revealed Thyself and Thy purpose to man, and by this revelation we have learned our place and our work. Therefore we have solemnly dedicated ourselves as klansmen to that sublime work harmonic with Thy will and purpose in our creation.

Now, oh, God, we, through Thy goodness, have here dedicated with Thine own divinely distilled fluid these manly men at the altar kneeling, who have been moved by worthy motives and impelled by noble impulses to turn from selfishness and fraternal alienation and to espouse with body, mind, spirit, and life the holy service of our country, our klan, our home, and each other. We beseech Thee to dedicate them with the fulness of Thy spirit, keep him (or each of them) true to his (or their) sacred, solemn oath to our noble cause, to the glory of Thy great name. Amen. (All say "amen.")

　　*　　　　*　　　　*　　　　*　　　　*　　　　*　　　　*

THE KLONVERSATION.

　　*　　　　*　　●　*　　　　*　　　　*　　　　*　　　　*

After the instructions have been given the klokard will say:

"The kladd will now conduct you to the exalted cyclops, where you will receive from him the CS and PW, the sacred symbol and imperial instructions, to which give earnest heed."

The kladd conducts the party to the station of the E.C. and says:

"Your excellency, these klansmen (or this klansman), having been instructed in the way of the klavern, now awaits to receive from you the CS and PW, the sacred symbol of the klan and imperial instructions."

E.C. will arise and say:

"My fellow klansman (or klansmen) the insignia or mark of a klansman is honor. All secrets and secret information of the invisible empire is committed to you on your honor. A klansman values honor more than life itself. Be true to honor, then to all the world you will be true. Always remember that an honorable secret committed is a thing sacred.

"I am about to commit to you three vital secrets of the invisible empire—the CS and PW and the sacred symbol, the mioak. Do you swear to forever hold them in sacred, secret reverence, even unto death?

"The CS and PW enables you to meet with and enjoy the fellowship of klansmen in klonklave assembled.

"For the present and until changed the CS is ——— and the PW is ———.

"The mioak, the sacred symbol of the klan is that (he explains what it is) by which klansmen recognize each other without word, sound, or sign.

"I now present you with the material insignia of a klansmen, the sacred symbol of the plan, by name the mioak. Be faithful in its wearing. It must be morn on your person where it may be readily seen. Tell no person in the whole world what it is, its meaning and significance, even by hint or insinuation, as it is a positive secret of the plan. Don't fail to recognize it by whomsoever it is worthily worn; always appreciate its sacred significance and be true to same. As a test of your honor I invest you with this symbol and commit to you its sacred secret."

He pins on the breast of the new klansman the insignia and explains its symbolic meaning.

"You will now receive imperial instructions. Carefully preserve and seriously study this document and give earnest heed to same, for on the practice of its teachings in your daily life depends your future advancement."

"You (or each of you) now are instructed klansmen, possessing all the rights, privileges, and protection as such will take your place with klansmen in the sacred fellowship of the invisible empire."

The E.C. will then give two raps with his gavel, take his seat and proceed with the other business.

*   *   *   *   *   *   *

THE IMPERIAL PROCLAMATION.

*   *   *   *   *   *   *

To all nations, people, tribes, and tongues, and to the lovers of law and order, peace and justice, of the whole earth, greeting:

I, and the citizens of the invisible empire through me, proclaim to you as follows:

We, the members of this order, desiring to promote real patriotism toward our civil Government; honorable peace among men and nations; protection for and happiness in the homes of our people; love, real brotherhood, mirth, and manhood among ourselves, and liberty, justice, and fraternity among all mankind; and believing we can best accomplish these noble purposes through the channel of a high-class mystic, social, patriotic, benevolent association, having a perfected lodge system with an exalted, ritualistic form of work and an effective form of government, not for selfish profit but for the mutual betterment, benefit, and protection of all our oath-bound associates, their welfare, physically, socially, morally, and vocationally, and their loved ones, do proclaim to the whole world that we are dedicated to the sublime and pleasant duty of providing generous aid, tender sympathy, and fraternal assistance in the effulgence of the light of life and amid the sable shadows of death, amid fortune and misfortune, and to the exalted privilege of demonstrating the practical utility of the great, yet most-neglected, doctrine of the fatherhood of God and the brotherhood of man as a vital force in the lives and affairs of men.

In this we invite all men who can qualify to become citizens of the invisible empire to approach the portal of our beneficent domain and join us in our noble work of extending its boundaries; in disseminating the gospel of "klankraft," thereby encouraging, conserving, protecting, and making vital the fraternal human relationship in the practice of a wholesome clanishness; to share with us the glory of performing the secred duty of protecting womanhood; to maintain forever white supremacy in all things; to commemorate the holy and chivalric achievements of our fathers; to safeguard the sacred rights, exalted privileges, and distinctive institutions of our civil Government; to bless mankind, and to keep eternally ablaze the secred fire of a fervent devotion to a pure Americanism.

The invisible empire is founded on sterling character and immutable principles based upon a most sacred sentiment and cemented by noble purposes; it is promoted by a sincere, unselfish devotion of the souls of manly men, and is managed and governed by the consecrated intelligence of thoughtful brains. It is the soul of chivalry and virtue's impenetrable shield—the devout impulse of an unconquered race.

Done in the aulic of his majesty, the imperial wizard and emperor of the invisible empire, Knights of the Ku-Klux Klan, in the imperial palace, in the imperial city of Atlanta, Commonwealth of Georgia, United States of America, this the 4th day of July, A.D. 1916 Anno Klan L.

Signed by his majesty,

[SEAL.]   WILLIAM JOSEPH SIMMONS
                                                  Imperial Wizard.

*   *   *   *   *   *   *

A SACRED DUTY—A PRECIOUS PRIVILEGE.

A true American can not give a higher and more sincere expression of appreciation of and gratitude for what was accomplished by our fathers in the defense of home and the sacred rights of our people than by becoming a "citizen of the invisible empire, Knights of the Ku-Klux Klan." He can not align himself with any institution that will mean so much for himself, his home, and his country as this great order.

It stands for America first—first in thought, first in affections, and first in the galaxy of nations. The Stars and Stripes forever above all other and every kind of government in the whole world.

Benevolence—in thought, word, and deed based upon justice and practically applied to all. To right the wrong; to succor the weak and unfortunate; to help the worthy and to relieve the distressed.

Clannishness—real fraternity practically applied—standing by and sticking to each other in all things honorable. Encouraging, protecting, cultivating, and exemplifying the real "fraternal human relationship" to shield and enhance each other's happiness and welfare. A devoted, unfailing loyalty to the principles, mission, and purposes of the order in promoting the highest and best interest of the community, State and Nation.

What it is: It is a standard fraternal order enforcing fraternal conduct, and not merely a "social association." It is a duly incorporated, legally recognized institution, honest in purpose, noble in sentiment and practical in results that commands the hearty respect of all respectable people throughout the Nation. It is not encouraging nor condoning any propaganda of religious intolerance nor racial prejudice. It is an association of real men who believe in being something, in doing things worth while, and who are in all things 100 per cent pure American. Yet it is vastly more than merely a social fraternal order.

Its initial purpose: An enduring monument to the valor and patriotic achievements of the Ku-Klux Klan. That this monument be not embodied in cold, emotionless stone, but in living, pulsating human hearts and active human brains, and find a useful expression in the nobility of the character of real manly men; this is the only memorial that will adequately befit the memory of the valiant Ku-Klux Klan.

Its lineage: The most sublime lineage in history, commemorating and perpetuating, as it does the most dauntless organization known to man.

Its secret: Sacred guardianship to the most sacred cause.

Its courage: The soul of chivalry and virtue's impenetrable shield. The impulse of an unconquered race.

Its teachings: To inculcate the sacred principles and noble ideals of the world's greatest order of chivalry; and direct the way of the initiate through the veil of mystic philosophy into the empire invisible.

Its character: The noblest concepts of manhood idealized in thought and materialized in practice in all the relationships of life—mystery and action mastery and achievement.

Its ritualism is vastly different from anything in the whole universe of fraternal ritualism. It is altogether original, weird, mystical, and of a high class, leading up through four degrees. Dignity and decency are its marked features. It unfolds a spiritual philosophy that has to do with the very fundamentals of life and living, here and hereafter. He who explores the dismal depths of the mystic cave and from thence attains the lofty heights of superior knighthood may sit among the gods in the empire invisible.

Its patriotism: An uncompromising standard of pure Americanism untrammeled by alien influences and free from the entanglements of foreign alliances. Proclaiming the brotherhood of nations but wedding none, thereby unyielding in the dignity of our own independence and forever faultless in our freedom.

Its mission: Duty—without fault, without fail, without fear, and without reproach.

Its society: The practical fraternal fellowship of men whose standard is worth not wealth; character, not cash, courageous manhood based upon honor untarnished by the touch of hypocrisy or the veneering of society's selfish social valuations.

Its place: In the heart of every "true American," alongside of every other fraternal order, and in its original casting, unique mannerism, sacred sentiment, noble purpose, and peculiar mysticism it is separate and apart from any and all and peerless in its distinctive peculiarities.

Its fraternity: Not merely reciting in ceremony pretty, time-worn platitudes on brotherly love, but to enforce a fraternal practice of clanishness, thereby making devotion to its standard worth while. "The glory of a klansman is to serve."

Its origin: This great institution, as a patriotic, ritualistic fraternal order, is no hastily "jumped-up" affair. It has been in the making for the past 20 years. It is a product of deliberate thought. The one man (William Joseph Simmons) who is responsible for it conceived the idea 20 years ago. For 14 years he thought, studied, and worked to prepare himself for its launching. He had dedicated his life to this noble cause. He kept his own counsel during these years and in the silent recesses of his soul he thought out the great plan. During the early days of October, 1915, he mentioned his ambition to some friends, among whom were three men who were bona fide members of the original klan when it disbanded. They most heartily cooperated with him. Having met with such encouragement, he invited several of his friends to a meeting on the night of October 26, 1915, at which time he unfolded his plans, and as a result all present, 34 in number, signed a petition for a charter. The petition was accepted and on Thanksgiving night, 1915, when were seen emerging from the shadows and gathering around the spring at the base of Stone Mountain (the world's greatest rock, near Atlanta, Ga.) and from thence repaired to the mountain top and there, under a blazing fiery cross, they took the oath of allegiance to the invisible empire, Knights of the Ku-Klux Klan. The charter was issued by the State of Georgia, December 4, 1915, and signed by Hon. Philip Cook, secretary of state. In the development of the order a petition was made to the superior court, Fulton County Ga., for a special charter, and said charter was issued July 1, 1916. The imperial wizard issued his imperial proclamation July 4, 1916.

And thus on the mountain top that night at the midnight hour while men braved the surging blasts of wild wintry mountain winds and endured a temperature far below freezing, bathed in the sacred glow of the fiery cross, the invisible empire was called from its slumber of half a century to take up a new task and fulfill a new mission for humanity's good and to call back to mortal habitation the good angel of practical fraternity among men.

PREREQUISITES TO CITIZENSHIP IN THE INVISIBLE EMPIRE.

This order is founded upon dependable character. It is not an ultra-exclusive institution, but its membership is composed of "picked" men.

No man is wanted in this order who hasn't manhood enough to assume a real oath with serious purpose to keep the same inviolate.

No man is wanted in this order who will not or can not swear an unqualified allegiance to the Government of the United States of America, its flag, and its Constitution.

No man is wanted in this order who does not esteem the Government of the United States of America above any other government, civil, political, or ecclesiastical, in the whole world.

No man is wanted in this order who can not practice real fraternity toward each and every one of his oath-bound associates.

Only native born American citizens who believe in the tenets of the Christian religion and owe no allegiance of any degree or nature to any foreign Government, nation, political institution, sect, people, or person, are eligible.

DEGREE FEES.

Membership in this order can not be bought; it is given as a reward for service unselfishly rendered. If you really believe in the order, and will practice its principles, and conform to its regulations and usages and contribute the sum of $10 toward its propagation and can otherwise qualify then membership is awarded you upon this service rendered and pledged of future fidelity to the institution. This is not a selfish, mercenary, commercialized proposition, but the direct opposite.

THE KU-KLUX KREED.

We, the order of the Knights of the Ku-Klux Klan, reverentially acknowledge the majesty and supremacy of the Divine Being, and recognize the goodness and providence of the same.

We recognize our relation to the Government of the United States of America, the supremacy of its Constitution, the Union of States thereunder, and the constitutional laws thereof, and we shall be ever devoted to the sublime principles of a pure Americanism and valiant in the defense of its ideals and institutions.

We avow the distinction between the races of mankind as same has been decreed by the Creator, and we shall ever be true to the faithful maintenance of White Supremacy and will strenuously oppose any compromise thereof in any and all things.

We appreciate the intrinsic value of a real practical fraternal relationship among men of kindred thought, purpose, and ideals and the infinite benefits accruable therefrom, and we shall faithfully devote ourselves to the practice of an honorable clannishness that the life and living of each may be a constant blessing to others.

"Non silba sed anthar."—Original creed revised.

* * * * * * *

OBJECTS AND PURPOSE.

ARTICLE II.

SECTION 1. The objects of this order shall be to unite only white male persons, native-born gentile citizens of the United States of America, who owe no allegiance of any nature or degree to any foreign Government, nation, institution, sect, ruler, person, or people; whose morals are good; whose reputations and vocations are respectable; whose habits are exemplary; who are of sound minds and at or above the age of 18 years, under a common oath into a common brotherhood of strict regulations for the purpose of cultivating and promoting real patriotism toward our civil Government; to practice an honorable clanishness toward each other; to exemplify a practical benevolence; to shield the sanctity of the home and the chastity of womanhood; to forever maintain white supremacy; to teach and faithfully inculcate a high spiritual philosophy through an exalted ritualism, and by a practical devotedness to conserve, protect, and maintain the distinctive institutions, rights, privileges, principles, traditions, and ideals of a pure Americanism.

* * * * * * *

SEC. 3. This order is an institution of chivalry, humanity, justice, and patriotism; embodying in its genius and principles all that is chivalric in conduct, noble in sentiment, generous in manhood, and patriotic in purpose; its peculiar objects being: First, to protect the weak, the innocent, and the defenseless from the indignities, wrongs, and outrages of the lawless, the violent, and the brutal; to relieve the injured and the oppressed; to succor the suffering and unfortunate, especially widows and orphans. Second, to protect and defend the Constitution of the United States of America and all laws passed in conformity thereto, and to protect the States and the people thereof from all invasion of their rights thereunder from any source whatsoever. Third, to aid and assist in the execution of all constitutional laws, and to preserve the honor and dignity of the State by opposing tyranny in any and every form or degree attempted from any and every source whatsoever by a fearless and faithful administration of justice, and to promptly and properly meet every behest of duty without fear and without reproach.

TERRITORIAL JURISDICTIONS, ASSEMBLIES, ETC.

ARTICLE III.

SEC. 1. *The invisible empire.*—The phrase "invisible empire" in a material sense denotes the universal geographical jurisdiction of this order and it shall embrace the whole world. The convention of the invisible empire shall be known as the imperial klonvokation. The phrase "invisible empire" in a spiritual sense denotes or applies to all the secrets and secret knowledge and information, secret work and working and things of this order, and to all that has been, to all that now is, and to all that is to be, the past, the present, and the future, yesterday, to-day, and forever; the dead of yesterday, the living of to-day, and the contemplated of to-morrow of the life that now is and of that which is to come.

*　　　*　　　*　　　*　　　*　　　*　　　*

MEMBERSHIP.

ARTICLE IV.

SECTION 1. The qualification for membership in this order shall be as follows: An applicant must be white male gentile person, a native-born citizen of the United States of America, who owes no allegiance of any nature or degree whatsoever to any foreign Government, nation, institution, sect, ruler, prince, potentate, people, or person; he must be at or above the age of 18 years, of sound mind, good character, of commendable reputation, and respectable vocation, a believer in the tenets of the Christian religion, and whose allegiance, loyalty, and devotion to the Government of the United States of America in all things is unquestionable.

*　　　*　　　*　　　*　　　*　　　*　　　*

KLANS.

ARTICLE XVII.

*　　　*　　　*　　　*　　　*　　　*　　　*

SEC. 25. A klan, or a member of this order, must not use the official costume or any part of same of the order on any occasion, or for any purpose other than in ceremony of this order, or in an official klavalkade (parade) under penalty of forfeiture of charter of the klan or expulsion from this order of the member.

SEC. 26. No klan and no member of this order shall use the name of this order or any part thereof for any purpose that contravenes in any manner the laws of the land, or in any manner that will in any way reflect, or probably reflect, upon the reputation and good name of this order, or compromise or injure this order or any member of this order in any way.

*   *   *   *   *   *   *

OFFENSES AND PENALTIES.

ARTICLE XIX.

SECTION 1. Offenses against this order deserving penalties shall be: Treason against the United States of America: violating the oath of allegiance or any supplementary oaths or obligations thereto of this order; criminal act or acts proven; disregard of public decency; disrespect for virtuous womanhood; betraying or violating a sacred trust of a klansman; a purposely violation of this constitution and the laws of this order, or the by-laws of a klan of this order; excessive drunkenness in public places, drunkenness or drinking intoxicating liquors during a klonklave or on the premises thereof, or entering a klonklave in an intoxicated condition; the frequent use of profane language or vulgarity during a klonklave, or in an assembly of klansmen just prior thereto; conspiring against the interest and prosperity of this order or any klansman in any way, or being a party thereto, or being a party to any move, conspiracy, or organization whose existence or purpose is antagonistic or injurious to or is an imitation or counterfeit of this order, or whose name, style, or title is a colarable imitation of the name of this order; swearing allegiance to or otherwise becoming a citizen or subject of any nation, government, or institution of any nature or classification, or any ruler, potentate, prince, or person, or any cause whatsoever that is foreign to or is inimical to the Government of the United States of America and its established institution, or aiding or abetting such a government, nation, institution, ruler, potentate, prince, or person against the interest, well being, or dignity of the United States of America or the distinctive institutions of its Government.

*   *   *   *   *   *   *

THE PRACTICE OF KLANISHNESS.

*   *   *   *   *   *   *

(1) *Patriotic klanishness.*—An unswerving allegiance to the principles of a pure Americanism as represented by the flag of our great Nation, namely, liberty, justice, and truth. Real, true Americanism unadulterated; a dogged devotedness to our country, its government, its ideals, and its institutions. To keep our Government forever free from the alien touch of foreign alliances and influences that liberty's effulgent torch be not dimmed. By your vote as a citizen select only men of pure patriotic impulses to serve in positions of public trust. Vote not politics but patriotism. Exercise your rights and prerogatives as a civil citizen for the best interest of your state and community and for the general public weal; the making of just and equitable laws and the righteous enforcement of same; bitterly oppose tyranny in any and every form and degree, and displace the corrupt politicians with dependable patriotic statesmen: "He who saves his country saves all things and all things saved bless him; but he who lets his country die lets all things die and all things dying curse him."

*   *   *   *   *   *   *

THE KU-KLUX KLAN YESTERDAY, TODAY, AND FOREVER.

The purpose of the modern Ku-Klux Klan is to inculcate the sacred principles and noble ideals of chivalry, the development of character, the protection of the home and the chastity of womanhood, the exemplification of a pure and practical patriotism toward our glorious country, the preservation of American ideals and institutions and the maintenance of white supremacy.

*   *   *   *   *   *   *

While membership in the Ku-Klux Klan is open only to white American citizens, the organization wages war on no individual or organization, regardless of race, color, or creed. It takes no part as an organization in any political or religious controversy, and it concedes the right of every man to think, vote, and worship God as he pleases.

Among the principles for which this organization stands, in addition to those already enumerated, are: Suppression of graft by public officeholders; preventing the causes of mob violence and lynchings; preventing unwarranted strikes by foreign agitators; sensible and patriotic immigration laws; sovereignty of State rights under the Constitution; separation of church and state; and freedom of speech and press, a freedom of such that does not strike at or imperil our Government or the cherished institutions of our people.

If there be any white American citizen who owes allegiance to no flag but the Star Spangled Banner and who can not subscribe to and support these principles let him forever hold his peace, for he is basely unworthy of the great flag and its Government that guarantees to him life, liberty, and the pursuit of happiness. That person who actively opposes these great principles is a dangerous ingredient in the body politic of our country and an enemy to the weal of our National Commonwealth.

*   *   *   *   *   *   *

The Anglo-Saxon race, the only race that has ever proved its ability and supremacy and demonstrated its determination to progress under any and all conditions and handicaps, owes its high place in the world to-day to the fact that this spirit has been kept alive from the foundation of the world and has never lagged in any land or clime.

And if the Anglo-Saxon race is to maintain its prestige, if it is to continue as the leader in the affairs of the world and to fulfill its sacred mission it must maintain and jealously guard its purity, its power, and its dignity; and while it should aid and encourage to the limit of its ability all men of whatever race or creed, it must forever maintain its own peculiar identity as the Anglo-Saxon race and preserve the integrity of its civilization, for the shores of time hold the shipwreck of all the mongrel civilization of the past which is evidence that in keeping with the laws of creative justice nature has decreed that mixed civilizations, together with governments of mixed races, are doomed to destruction and oblivion.

From the past the voice of the great Lincoln must be heard:

"There are physical differences between the races which would forever forbid them living together on terms of political and social equality."

The imperative call of higher justice to the real patriots of our Nation is:

"In the name of our valiant and venerated dead and in due respect to their stainless memory and in the interest of peace and security of all peoples now living and for the sake of all those yet to be, keep Anglo-Saxon American civilization, institutions, politics, and society pure, and thereby, since we have received this sacred heritage, transmit it with clean hands and pure hearts to generations yet unborn, thereby keeping faith with the mind, soul, and purpose of our valiant sires and transmit our name into the future without dishonor and without disgrace.

"Let the solemn behest of higher duty be promptly and properly met in all the relationships of life and living without fault, without fail, without fear, and without reproach, now and forevermore."

The Ku Klux may be antagonized and forced to fight many battles, but perish? Never! To destroy it is an impossibility, for it belongs in essence to the realms spiritual. It is unshaken by unjust criticisms, no power can thwart it in its onward conquest of right; it courts not the plaudits of the populace, nor is it swerved from its course by the libel of its foes. Attuned with Deity, functioning only for all humanity's good, misjudged by ignorance, misunderstood by many, slandered by prejudice, sweeping on under the divine leadership of Deity, it never falters and will never fall.

The spirit of the Ku-Klux Klan still lives, and should live, a priceless heritage to be sacredly treasured by all those who love our country, regardless of section, and are proud of its sacred traditions. That this spirit may live always to warm the hearts of manly men, unify them by the force of a holy clannishness, to assuage the billowing tide of a fraternal alienation that surges in human breasts, and inspire them to achieve the highest and noblest in the defense of our country, our homes, humanity, and each other is the paramount ideal of the Knights of the Ku-Klux Klan.

APPENDIX C-1

Sam Bowers's Imperial Executive Order, May 3, 1964 *

To: All Officers and Members.
From: Forthcoming Enemy attack and countermeasures to be used in meeting same.

THIS ORDER WILL BE READ TO OR BY AND UNDERSTOOD BY EVERY MEMBER OF THIS ORGANIZATION

It is absolutely necessary that each and every member of this organization stand fast and remain calm at this time; while he is working deliberately to prepare himself and his unit for effective combat against the enemy.

The military and political situation as regards the enemy has now reached the crisis stage. Our best students of enemy strategy and technique are in almost complete agreement that the events which will occur in Mississippi this summer may well determine the fate of Christian Civilization for centuries to come.

This organization is the physical Spear upon which the enemy will either

---

* U.S. Congress, *Report: The Present-Day Ku Klux Klan Movement.* 90 Cong., 1 Sess., House Committee on Un-American Activities (1967): 169–71

impale himself and perish, or sweep aside, then to proceed almost unhindered in his evil work of destroying civilization. The manner in which we conduct ourselves and use our strength this summer will determine which of these fates our Nation will follow.

This is indeed an awesome and critically responsible position in which we now find ourselves. Every member must Soberly and PRAYERFULLY face this Responsibility, and draw his strength from the Spiritual Source which tells us, deep in our hearts, that our Cause is truly Just.

It must be emphasized that our Cause is far from hopeless. The enemy, it is true, appears to have victory within his grasp, but he is vacillating at this very moment when he should be closing it. His leadership is not as united as it should be, and there is conflict and dissention [sic] in his ranks. His naked and brutal methods are coming into more complete exposure every day and he is losing public support. He must achieve his victory soon or lose the initiative to our side. If this should happen, he is doomed, and his leaders know this. Our task now is to delay and frustrate him at the very brink of his triumph.

This summer, within a very few days, the enemy will launch his final push for victory here in Mississippi. This offensive will consist of two basic salients, which have been designed to envelope [sic] and destroy our small forces in a pincer movement of Agitation, Force by Federal Troops, and Communist Propaganda.

The two basic salients are as follows, listed in ONE-TWO order, as they will be used:

1. Massive street demonstrations and agitation by Blacks in many areas at once, designed to provoce White militants into counter-demonstrations and open, pitched street battles, resulting in civil chaos and anarchy to privide [sic] an "EXCUSE" for:

2. A *decree* from the Communist authorities in charge of the National Government, which *will* declare the State of Mississippi to be a Stae [sic] of open revolt, with a complete breakdown of Law and Order, and declaring Martial Law, followed by a massive occupation of the State by Federal Troops, with all known Patriotic Whites placed under Military Arrest. If this Martial Law is imposed, our homes and our lives and our aims will pass under the complete control of the enemy, and he will have won his victory. We will, of course, resist to the very end, but our chance of Victory will undoubtedly end with the imposition of Martial law in Mississippi by the Communist Masters in Washington.

Our situation calls for the highest degree of combined intelligence and courage, combined with a sincere, Christian Devotion, which Christian Soldiers have ever been called upon to demonstrate. We can not permit ourselves even one mistake in combating the enemy this summer. All of our actions must be disciplined, precise, courageous and intelligent. There is no margin for error.

When the first waves of Blacks hit our streets this summer, we must avoid, open daylight conflict with them, if at all possible, as private citizens, or as members of this organization. We should join with and support local police and duly constituted law-enforcement agencies with Volunteer, LEGALLY DEPUTIZED men from our own ranks. We must absolutely avoid the appearance of a mob going into the streets to fight the Blacks. Our first contact with the troops of the enemy in the streets should be as LEGALLY-DEPUTIZED Law enforcement officers. It must ALSO be understood at this point that there are many different local police situations. Where we find corrupt and cowardly—and Police, obviously, our members cannot submit to their control, but we should still try to work with them at arms length in every reasonable way possible to avoid being labelled as outlaws.

IN ALL CASES, however, there must be a SECONDARY group of our members, standing back away from the main area of conflict, armed and ready to move on very short notice who are not under the control of anyone but our own, Christian officers. This secondary group must not be used except in clear cases where local law enforcement and our own Deputized, Auxillary [sic] First Groups are at the point of being overwhelmed by the Blacks. Only if it appears reasonably certain that control of the streets is being lost by the Established forces of Law can the Secondary Group be committed. Once committed, this Secondary Group must move swiftly and vigorously to attack the Local headquarters of the enemy, destroy and disrupt his leadership and communications (both local and Washington) and any news communication equipment or agents in the area. The action of this Secondary group must be very swift and very forceful with no holds barred. The attack on the Enemy headquarters will relieve the pressere [sic] on the First group in the streets and as soon as this has been done, the Second group must prepare to withdraw out of the area. They will be replaced by another Secondary group standing at Ready. It must be understood that the Secondary group is an extremely swift and extremely violent Hit and Run group. They should rarely be in action for over one-half hour, and under no circumstances for over one hour. Within two hours of their commitment they should be many miles from the scene of action. The local law enforcement agencies and the first group should then find it fairly simple to restore local order and control the local situation. The enemy should be completely confused when he loses his headquarters and his leadership.

This Secondary group must be used only under the EMERGENCY conditions herin [sic] stated. We must cooperate with our Law enforcement officials, but we must never place ourselves entirely at that disposal, nor under their complete control. We must always remember that while Law enforcement officials have a "JOB" to do, we, as Christians, have a Responsibility, and have taken an OATH to preserve the Christian Civilization. May Almighty God grant that their "JOB" and our OATH never come into conflict; but should they ever, it must be clearly understood that we can never yield our principles to anyone, regardless of his position. RESPECT FOR CHRISTIAN IDEALS CANNOT YIELD TO RESPECT FOR PERSONS NOR STATUTES AND PROCEDURE WHICH HAVE BEEN TWISTED BY MAN AWAY FROM ITS ORIGINAL DIVINE ORIGIN. Remember what the Master said regardin [sic] the rightuseness [sic] of the Scribes and the Pharisees and be guided accordingly. We must all throughly [sic] understand this Important Principle and keep it clearly in mind when we are dealing with officialdom.

When the Black waves hit our communities we must remain calm and think in terms of our INDIVIDUAL enemies rather than our MASS ENEMY. We must roll with the MASS punch which they will deliver in the streets during the day, and we must counterattack the INDIVIDUAL leaders at night. In our night work any harassment which we direct against the MASS of the Enemy should be of a minor nature and should be primarilly [sic] against his equipment (transportation and communication) rather than the PERSONS of the MASS enemy. Any Personal attacks on the enemy should be carefully planned to include *only* the leaders and prime white collaborators of the enemy forces. These attacks against these selected, individual targets should, of course, be as severe as circumstances and conditions will permit. No severe attacks should be directed against the general mass of the enemy because of the danger of hurting some actually innocent person. The leaders, of course, are not innocent, and they should be our prime targets, but the innocent must be protected.

A great deal of attention should be given toward detecting those enemy agents who bomb, burn and kill their own homes, churches and people in order to provide a sympathetic base for their National Propaganda Machine. These bombings and killings are always blamed on our side, but it is the Insane Communist agitators themselves who are doing it. If we could catch them at it we could score a nice victory. Stay alert.

We must use all of the time which is left to us in these next few days preparing to meet this attack. Weapons and ammunition must be accumulated and stored; squads must drill; Propaganda equipment must be set up ready to roll; counter-attack maps, plans and information must be studied and learned; radios and communications must be established; and a Solemn, determined Spirit of Christian Reverence must be stimulated in all members.

May Almighty God grant that our arms be guided to success in this, our greatest trial.

VERITAS et ARMIS

APPENDIX C-2

The Klan Ledger, Sam Bowers and the White Knights of
the Ku Klux Klan of Mississippi*

An Official Publication of the WHITE KNIGHTS of
THE KU KLUX KLAN of Mississippi

DEDICATED TO THE PRESERVATION OF
CHRISTIAN CIVILIZATION

July 4, 1964

We are now in the midst of the "long, hot summer" of agitation which was promised to the Innocent People of Mississippi by the savage blacks and their communist masters. On this Famous Date, the Anniversary of the founding of the American Republic, under the auspices and blessing of Almighty God, we ask that each Mississippian, each American, get down upon his knees and offer up thanks to our Creator, Savior and Inspiration for his manifold grace and blessings.

THIS THEN IS OUR PRAYER

OUR FATHER, GOD OF LIFE AND LIBERTY, WE HUMBLY THANK THEE FOR THE STRENGTH, COURAGE AND INTELLIGENCE WHICH

---

* U.S. Congress, *Hearings on Ku Klux Klan Organizations.* 89 Cong., 1 Sess., House Committee on Un-American Activities (1965): 2756-58.

THOU HAST GIVEN TO OUR PERSECUTED PEOPLE. WE THANK THEE THAT OUR SATANIC ENEMIES, THE DOMESTIC COMMUNISTS WHO OCCUPY THE SEATS OF POWER IN OUR GOVERNMENT HAVE FAILED TO PROVOKE THE VIOLENCE IN OUR GREAT STATE WHICH WOULD BRING DOWN MARTIAL LAW AND COMPLETE DICTATOR-SHIP. THANK YOU O LORD, FOR OPENING THE EYES OF ALL THE GOOD PEOPLE OF OUR GREAT NATION TO THE EVIL WHICH HAS BEEN FORCED UPON US. HELP US TO OVERCOME OUR ENEMIES, KEEP OUR FEET ALWAYS UPON THE PATH OF RIGHTEOUSNESS, AND PURGE OUR HEARTS FROM MALICE AND VENGEANCE, GIVE OUR ARMS THE STRENGTH, OUR HEARTS THE COURAGE, AND OUR MINDS THE WILL TO DESTROY THESE AGENTS OF SATAN. WE THANK THEE FOR THE RAINS WHICH HAS NOURISHED OUR CROPS AND THY SPIRIT WHICH MAKES THEM GROW. BLESS AND KEEP ALL OF US, THY CHILDREN, AND MAKE US WORTHY OF THY INFINITE BLESSINGS. WE ASK, IN THE NAME OF THY SON, CHRIST JESUS, WHO TAUGHT US HOW TO LIVE AND DIE FOR THY KINGDOM HERE ON EARTH. AMEN.

The recent events in Neshoba County and Statewide call for a message to the general public and the citizens of the great State of Mississippi. The arch-traitor and long-time betrayer of patriots the world over, Dulles, has used his lying tongue to try and convince the American Public that this organization was involved in the so-called "disappearance."

We were *NOT* involved, and there was *NO DISAPPEARANCE.* Anyone who is so simple that he cannot recognize a communist hoax which is as plain as the one they pulled on Kennedy in Dallas (and which Earl Warren is working so hard to cover-up), had better do a little reading in J. Edgar Hoover's primer on communism; *"MASTERS OF DECEIT".*

We refuse to be concerned or upset about this fraud. What we are concerned about is the welfare of the citizens of the State of Mississippi. . . .

We are going to serve notice that we are not going to recognize the authority of any bi-racial group, *NOR THE AUTHORITY OF ANY PUBLIC OFFICIAL WHO ENTERS INTO ANY AGREEMENT WITH ANY SUCH SOVIET OR-GANIZATION.* We Knights are working day and night to perserve Law and Order ·here in Mississippi, in the only way that it can be preserved: by strict segretation of the races, and the control of the social structure in the hands of the Christian, Anglo-Saxon White men, the only race on earth that can build and maintain just and stable governments. We are deadly serious about this business. We have taken no action as yet against the enemies of our State, our Nation and our Civilization, but we are not going to sit back and permit our rights and the rights of our posterity to be negotiated away by a group composed of athestic priests, brainwashed black savages, and mongrelized money-worshippers, meeting with some stupid or cowardly politician. Take heed, atheists and mongrels, we will not travel your path to a Leninist Hell, but we will buy *YOU* a ticket to the Eternal if you insist. Take your choice, *SEGRETATION, TRANQUILITY AND JUSTICE,* or, *BI-RACISM, CHAOS AND DEATH.* . . .

*HISTORY SHOWS THAT THERE IS BUT ONE WAY TO DEAL WITH DIC-
TATORS.* We must take the Constitution of the United States of America as our
guide in dealing with all gangsters. That is why we have it. That is why James
Madison, Ben Franklin, George Washington, Patrick Henry and the others la-
bored so hard to build it. *THEIR CONSTITUTION WAS AN UNQUALIFIED
SUCCESS.* Its purpose was and is to make it impossible to set up a Dictatorship
in America *WITHOUT VIOLATING ITS CLEAR SPIRIT, PRINCIPLES AND
LANGUAGE. THE CONSTITUTION BELONGS TO THE PEOPLE.* It is not
the property of any Court, Congress or Executive Officer. That is why it was
written in CLEAR, SIMPLE LANGUAGE and given wide distribution, so that
the honest individual citizen would have a yardstick to measure the thugs and
scoundrels whom the founders of our constitution knew were BOUND TO GET
INTO PUBLIC OFFICE. The Constitution is the Basic Power of all governmental authority in America. It is the Supreme Law of the Land. It establishes the
principle that this is a government of Laws and not of men. The Supreme Court
gets all of its power from the Constitution. The Congress gets all of its power
from the Constitution. The President gets all of his power from the Constitution.
If those who sit on the bench of the Supreme Court depart from the Constitution
then they are NOT the Supreme COURT. If the cravens who sit in the seats of
Congress depart from the Constitution—then they are NOT the Congress. If the
man who sits in the White House departs from the Constitution—then he is
NOT the President. THIS principle is the Spirit of American Liberty. It is what
government by LAW and not by men MEANS. Any officer of governmental
standing who departs from the CLEAR Principles of the Constitution automatically thereby cuts off the course of his lawful power and becomes nothing more
than an armed thug, regardless of how many marshalls or troops he may command. If in any such unconstitutional situation, any marshalls or troops engage
in any violence against a citizen of this State while attempting to force him to
comply with some unlawful order, he will be committing a FELONY against the
Peace and Dignity of Mississippi and America. . . .

APPENDIX C-3

*Questionnaire for Prospective Members: White Knights of the
Ku Klux Klan of Mississippi* *

STANDARD EXAMINATION FORM

To be used by all Christian American Patriots as an aid in properly identifying
all unknown Persons who may be seeking information. At least one other Christian American Patriot should be present when giving this EXAMINATION.
Persons who refuse to take this EXAMINATION or who fail to answer the
questions in a forthright and satisfactory manner should be regarded as ENE-
MIES of the Constitutional Republic of the United States of America and should
be considered as Emissaries of the anti-Christ, Satan.

---

* U.S. Congress, *Hearings on Ku Klux Klan Organizations.* 89 Cong., 1 Sess., House
Committee on Un-American Activities (1965): 2923-24

1. Do you believe in Almighty God, the ONE Supreme Creator, Ruler and Judge of the Universe?

2. Do you believe in the Redeeming Spirit of the Christ, Jesus, Son of the Living God and the SOLE Intecessor for the Sins of Mankind, by Whom NONE cometh unto the Kingdom of the Father, except by HIM?

3. Do you believe that the Holy Scriptures are the Greatest tangible asset which is possessed by man on this earth, and that the WORD contained therein must be the Prime Guide by which man must conduct himself here on earth?

4. Do you acknowledge the King James Version of the Holy Writ as the Prime Writ for Americans and recognize the attempts to "revise" and "standardize" and "merge" this version with other texts as nothing but a deliberate attempt to degrade and profane the "Word" into just another collection of religious writings?

5. Do you believe that any mortal man here on earth has the power to pardon or to redeem the sins of another, or that any mortal man can accumulate the power or ability whereby he could become an Advocate in the Court of Almighty God to intercede for the remission of the sins of another?

6. Do you believe that the Mercy and Advocacy of Christ is available to all those who humbly and honestly seek Him?

7. Do you believe that any Human Being has the power to cut another Human Being off from, and deny the Salvation of Christ to another?

8. Do you believe that the most any True Christian can do for a fellow Human Being is to help his fellow to see the Path to the Living Christ and try to gently lead him Up that Path, but that no one may or can be FORCED to accept Christ, and each individual must accept or reject Christ according to his individual will?

9. Do you believe that a powerful, supernatural Force of Evil, called Anti-Christ or Satan does exist in the world?

10. Do you recognize the Fact that all men are continually being torn between the Force of Christ and the Anti-Christ Forces of Satan?

11. Do you recognize the Fact that man is absolutely helpless before Satan until he truly and humbly Accepts the Living Christ as his own Personal Savior; and that all of man's intelligence, and his material gifts; his education, his prestige, his property, his money, his good intentions and his works are worthless against Satan, UNLESS there is an Absolute, Primary Foundation of an undying Belief in, Acceptance of and Reliance upon The Living Christ at the root-center of each man's Being?

12. Do you accept the Living Christ, Jesus as your Personal Savior and your ONLY Hope against Satan?

13. Do you recognize that all good intentions and works which are not founded in Christ are either meaningless or Evil?

14. Do you believe that Satan impels some men to rule and control the earthly life and destiny of other men, and gives them power to do so?

15. Do you believe that Almighty God so ordained man that he should live free of the control of the will of other men, and that no man has the right to initiate Trespass against another, or initiate by any means whatsoever anything to bring another man under the control of his will?

16. Do you recognize that a True Christian American Patriot will turn the other cheek to those who wrong him, but will destroy those who attempt to destroy him, and will seek to destroy those who seek to destroy him, because anything less would be suicide?

17. Do you believe that Christianity requires that a True Christian should not resist having his earthly life taken by a killer?

18. Do you recognize the fact that the United States of America is the only Governmental System ever built in the world with the announced intention and recognized purpose of protecting the Life, Liberty, and the RIGHT to pursue Happiness of each and every one of the Law-Abiding, responsible citizens under its jurisdiction, after FIRST recognizing the FACT that these Rights were God-given in the FIRST place and were therefore not within the province of any man, group of men, or government either to GRANT or to DENY?

19. Do you understand that this one point covered in Question #18 is the Basic and Fundamental point which makes the United States of America unique in the world and therefore absolutely different from, and therefore properly in opposition to every other governmental system in the world?

20. Do you recognize that the fundamental, founding purpose and Spirit of all True Law in the USA is to implement the Will of God which obviously decrees: That man shall live free from the control of the will of his neighbor, and not trespass against his neighbor?

21. Do you believe that the preceeding principle is the True Spirit of American Law, which is of Divine Origin?

22. Do you recognize the fact that statutes and decisions must conform to this Spirit in order to be ranked as True American Law?

23. Do you recognize the fact that men under the influence of Satan are able to twist laws, enact laws and enforce laws under the material power of Governmental Authority which are contrary to the Spirit of American Law, and which, therefore, do not rank as True American Law?

24. If the letter of the Law conflicts with the Spirit of the Law, WHICH will you adhere to, obey and enforce?

25. Do you acknowledge that those persons who cause or permit the Letter of the Law to conflict with the Spirit of the Law in America are the Prime Enemies of the Republic of the United States of America and of every innocent citizen and person under its jurisdiction?

26. Do you believe that your personal, physical survival is tied to the maintenance of a governmental administration in America which will continuously implement the Constitutional Spirit of American Law?

27. Do you regard an Enemy of the Republic of the United States of America and the Spiritual Ideals which are protected by its Constitution as YOUR personal enemy?

28. Do you differentiate between the Government of the United States of America and the PERSONS who hold offices and positions under its Constitution?

29. If the minions of material governmental authority threaten, attempt to, or use physical force and violence to enforce compliance with some letter of law which is in clear conflict with the Constitution and the Spirit of American Law, do you believe that the Private Citizens of America have a right to oppose them with physical force, using the Constitution and the Supremacy of the Will of Almighty God as their Authority?

30. Do you believe in Democracy?

31. Do you believe in Plebescite Cannabilism?

32. How can demagogues be controlled in a Democracy?

33. Are man-made laws more useful when they are aimed at doing "good," or when they are aimed at shackeling Satan?

34. What is your definition of "communism"?

35. What is the motivating force behind "communism"?

36. Do you believe that the Spirit of American Law will be helped or be injured by becoming entangled in Foreign Affairs?

37. Do you believe that the International Bankers have anything worthwhile to offer America?

APPENDIX D
Poster: Invisible Empire, Knights of the Ku Klux Klan, 1982 *

KU KLUX KLAN
RALLY

LAGRANGE, GEORGIA
SATURDAY MAY 15, 1982
RALLY SITE OPENS AT 3:00 P.M. -
SPEAKING STARTS AT 7:00 P.M.

Go South on Highway 27 approx. 2½ miles. Turn left on lower Big Springs Road, go about 2½ miles and it's just past I-185 on right.

---

* Courtesy of the National Anti-Klan Network

RAIN OR SHINE
WHITE PUBLIC WELCOME - BRING THE WHOLE FAMILY
TRADITIONAL CROSS LIGHTING CEREMONY

NO DRUGS OR ALCOHOL ALLOWED

REFRESMENTS AND KLAN SOUVENIRS

GUEST SPEAKERS WILL BE WORLD KNOWN IMPERIAL WIZARD BILL WILKINSON AND GREAT TITAN CRAMER ROGERS ALSO GREAT TITAN CLYDE ROYALS.

WORLD KNOWN SPEAKER BILL WILKINSON WHO HAS ORGANIZED THE KLAN NATIONWIDE AND IN MANY FOREIGN COUNTRIES, INCLUDING ENGLAND.

We are on the move TO SEND THE GOVERNMENT IN WASHINGTON A MESSAGE. The message is simply that the white majority is fed up with federal controls over jobs, schools and virtually every facet of our lives.

We want to run our own cities and states! We denounce the hypocracy of affirmative action and demand an immediate end to this treacherous program before it destroys our nation.

The Bible teaches that a man with 5 talents shall receive 5 talents worth of goods, and that a man with only 1 talent shall receive 1 talent worth of goods. This is what we want . . . each man to advance according to his ability and initiative, not by government decree.

There are thousands of organizations working for the interests of Blacks. How many groups stand up for the cultural values and ideals of the White Majority? Not many, as a result we are faced with reverse discrimination in jobs, promotions, and scholarships—busing for forced integration—high taxes for minority welfare—a high rate of brutal crime—gun-control—anti-White movies and TV programs—in short, a society oriented to the wishes of minorities. We of the Ku Klux Klan are unapologetically committed to the interests, ideas, and cultural values of the White Majority. We are determined to maintain and enrich our cultural and racial heritage.

We are growing fast and strong because we have never compromised the truth. Interested in finding out more? We'll send you a copy of the KLANSMAN newspaper and more information FREE. Write:
NATIONAL OFFICE.

COME OUT AND JOIN THE PEOPLE WHO WILL BE AT THE RALLY AND WE SHALL SEND OUR MESSAGE TO WASHINGTON.

APPENDIX E
Federal Legislation to Protect U.S. Citizens from the Ku Klux Klan *

18 U.S.C.

241. CONSPIRACY AGAINST RIGHTS OF CITIZENS †

If two or more persons conspire to injure, oppress, threaten, or intimidate any citizen in the free exercise or enjoyment of any right or privilege secured to him by the Constitution or laws of the United States, or becasue of his having so exercised the same; or

If two or more persons go in disguise on the highway, or on the premises of another, with intent to prevent or hinder his free exercise or enjoyment of any right or privilege so secured

—They shall be fined not more than $10,000 or imprisoned not more than ten years, or both; and if death results, they shall be subject to imprisonment for any term of years or for life.

As amended Apr. 11, 1968, Pub.L. 90-284, Title I, 103(a), 82 Stat. 75.

242. DEPRIVATION OF RIGHTS UNDER COLOR OF LAW

Whoever, under color of any law, statute, ordinance, regulation, or custom, willfully subjects any inhabitant of any State, Territory, or District to the deprivation of any rights, privileges, or immunities secured or protected by the Constitution or laws of the United States, or to different punishments, pains, or penalties, on account of such inhabitant being an alien, or by reason of his color, or race, than are prescribed for the punishment of citizens, shall be fined not more than $1,000 or imprisoned not more than one year, or both; and if death results shall be subject to imprisonment for any term of years or for life.

As amended Apr. 11, 1968, Pub.L. 90-284, Title I, 103(b), 82 Stat. 75.

245. FEDERALLY PROTECTED ACTIVITIES ‡

(a)(1) Nothing in this section shall be construed as indicating an intent on the part of Congress to prevent any State, any possession or Commonwealth of the United States, or the District of Columbia, from exercising jurisdiction over any offense over which it would have jurisdiction in the absence of this section, nor shall anything in this section be construed as depriving State and local law enforcement authorities of responsibility for prosecuting acts that may be violations of this section and that are violations of State and local law. No prosecution of any offense described in this section shall be undertaken by the United States except upon the certification in writing of the Attorney General or the Deputy Attorney General that in his judgement a prosecution by the United States is in the public interest and necessary to secure substantial justice, which function of certification may not be delegated.

(2) Nothing in this subsection shall be construed to limit the authority of Federal officers, or a Federal grand jury, to investigate possible violations of this section.

(b) Whoever, whether or not acting under color of law, by force or threat of force willfully injure, intimidates or interferes with, or attempts to injure, intimidate or interfere with—

---

* Courtesy of the National Anti-Klan Network
† Reconstruction Ku-Klux Statutes
‡ Civil rights legislation of the 1960s

(1) any person because he is or has been, or in order to intimidate such person or any other person or any class of persons from—

(A) voting or qualifying to vote, qualifying as a candidate for elective office, or qualifying or acting as a poll watcher, or any legally authorized election official, in any primary, special, or general election;

(B) participating in or enjoying any benefit, service, privilege, program, facility, or activity provided or administered by the United States;

(C) applying for or enjoying employment, or any prerequisite thereof, by any agency of the United States;

(D) serving, or attending upon any court in connection with possible service, as a grand or petit juror in any court of the United States;

(E) participating in or enjoying the benefits of any program or activity receiving Federal financial assistance; or

(2) any person because of his race, color, religion or national origin and because he is or has been—

(A) enrolling in or attending any public school or public college;

(B) participating in or enjoying any benefit, service, privilege, program, facility or activity provided or administered by any State or subdivision thereof;

(C) applying for or enjoying employment, or any perquisite thereof, by any private employer or any agency of any State or subdivision thereof, or joining or using the services or advantages of any labor organization, hiring hall, or employment agency;

(D) serving, or attending upon any court of any State in connection with possible service, as a grand or petit juror;

(E) traveling in or using any facility of interstate commerce or using any vehicle, terminal, or facility of any common carrier by motor, rail, water, or air;

(F) enjoying the goods, services, facilities, privileges, advantages, or accommodations of any inn, hotel, motel, or other establishment which provides lodging to transient guests, or of any restaurant, cafeteria, lunchroom, lunch counter, soda fountain, or other facility which serves the public and which is principally engaged in selling food or beverages for consumption on the premises, or of any gasoline station, of any motion picture house, theater, concert hall, sports arena, stadium, or any other place of exhibition or entertainment which serves the public, or of any other establishment which serves the public and (i) which is located within the premises of any of the aforesaid establishments or within the premises of which is physically located any of the aforesaid establishments, and (ii) which holds itself out as serving patrons of such establishments; or

(3) during or incident to a riot or civil disorder, any person engaged in a business in commerce or affecting commerce, including, but not limited to, any person engaged in a business which sells or offers for sale to interstate travelers a substantial portion of the articles, commodities, or services which it sells or where a substantial portion of the articles or commodities which it sells or offers for sale have moved in commerce; or

(4) any person because he is or has been, or in order to intimidate such person or any other person or any class of persons from—

(A) participating without discrimination on account of race, color, religion or national origin, in any of the benefits or activities described in subparagraphs (1) (A) through (1) (E) or subparagraphs (2) (A) through (2) (F); or

(B) affording another person or class of persons opportunity or protection to so participate; or

(5) any citizen because he is or has been, or in order to intimidate such citizen or any other citizen from lawfully aiding or encouraging other persons to participate, without discrimination on account of race, color, religion or national origin, in any of the benefits or activities described in subparagraphs (1) (A) through (1) (E) or subparagraphs (2) (A) through (2) (F), or participating lawfully in speech or peaceful assembly opposing any denial of the opportunity to so participate—

shall be fined not more than $1,000, or imprisoned not more than one year, or both; and if bodily injury results shall be fined not more than $10,000, or imprisoned not more than ten years, or both; and if death results shall be subject to imprisonment for any term of years or for life. As used in this section, the term "participating lawfully in speech or peaceful assembly" shall not mean the aiding, abetting, or inciting of other persons to riot or to commit any act of physical violence upon any individual or against any real or personal property in furtherance of a riot. Nothing in subparagraph (2) (F) or (4) (A) of this subsection shall apply to the proprietor of any establishment which provides lodging to transient guests, or to any employee acting on behalf of such proprietor, with the respect to the enjoyment of the goods, services, facilities, privileges, advantages, or accomodations of such establishment if such establishment is located within a building which contains not more than five rooms for rent or hire and which is actually occupied by the proprietor as his resident.

(c) Nothing in this section shall be construed so as to deter any law enforcement officer from lawfully carrying out the duties of his office; and no law enforcement officer shall be considered to be in violation of this section for lawfully carrying out the duties of his office or lawfully enforcing ordinances and laws of the United States, the District of Columbia, any of the several States, or any political subdivision of a State. For purposes of the preceding sentence, the term "law enforcement officer" means any officer of the United States, the District of Columbia, a State, or political subdivision of a State, who is empowered by law to conduct investigation of, or make arrests because of, offenses against the United States, the District of Columbia, a State, or a political subdivision of a State.

Added Pub.L. 90-284,Title I, 101(a), Apr. 11, 1968, 82 Stat. 73.

NOTES

Notes are keyed to the text by page number and by person, subject, or quotation. The repositories of rare books, pamphlets, and other unusual material are identified after the date of the material.

BOOK ONE: 1865–1915
Prologue. "Beware the People Weeping"

10 MOONLIGHT-AND-MAGNOLIA SCHOOL OF HISTORY: A review and analysis of the problem is offered in Melton McLauren, "Images of Negroes in Deep South Public School State History Texts," *Phylon* 32 (Fall 1971): 237–46.

10 "I WOULD HIT HER ALL IN THE FACE . . .": Anonymous former slave in George P. Rawick, ed., *The American Slave: A Composite Autobiography*, (Slave Narratives Collected by Fisk University) (Westport, CT: Greenwood, 1972), XVIII:134.

10 SOUTHERN JUSTIFICATIONS OF SLAVERY: John McCardell, *The Idea of a Southern Nation: Southern Nationalists and Southern Nationalism, 1830–1860* (New York: Norton, 1979), pp. 50, 90; William S. Jenkins, *Pro-Slavery Thought in the Old South* (Chapel Hill: Univ. North Carolina Press, 1935), passim.

10 "ANY PAMPHLET, NEWSPAPER, HANDBILL . . .": Hinton R. Helper, *The Impending Crisis of the South* (New York: A. B. Burdick, 1860), pp. 360–61.

11 *DRAPETOMANIA* AND *DYSAETHESIA:* Jenkins, *Pro-Slavery Thought*, p. 260.

11 "SO ENGRAFTED . . . HAPPINESS, TRANQUILITY . . .": Quoted in Winthrop Jordan, *The White Man's Burden: Historical Origins of Racism in the United States* (New York: Oxford Univ. Press, 1974), p. 208.

11 "THE LOWER RACE OF HUMAN BEINGS . . .": Dunbar Rowland, ed., *Jefferson Davis, Constitutionalist: His Letters, Papers, and Speeches*, 10 vols. (New York: Little & Ives, 1923), IV: 49.

11 PSYCHOLOGICAL EFFECTS OF EMANCIPATION ON WHITES: Alexis de Tocqueville, as prescient as ever, said, "If I were called upon to predict the future, I should say that the abolition of slavery in the South will, in the common course of things, increase the repugnance of the white population to the blacks," in *Democracy in America*, trans. George Lawrence (New York: Anchor-Doubleday, 1969), p. 367. In his tour of the South in 1865, Carl Schurz observed, "It frequently struck me that persons who conversed about every other subject calmly and sensibly would lose their temper as soon as the negro question was touched," in U.S. Congress, *Report of Carl Schurz on the Condition of the South*, 39 Cong., 1 Sess, Senate Exec. Doc. No. 2 (1865): 17. About this same time, a journalist recorded the feelings of a South Carolina planter: "We can't feel towards [blacks] as you do; I suppose we ought to, but it isn't possible for us. They've always been our owned servants, and we've been used to having them mind us without a word of objection, and we can't bear anything else from them now. If that's wrong, we're to be pitied sooner than blamed, for it's something we can't help," in J. T. Trowbridge, *A Picture of the Desolated States and the Work of Restoration* (Hartford, CT: Stebbins, 1868), p. 291.

11 "THE NEGRO WILL ALWAYS NEED . . .": *The Nation*, 27 July 1865.

11 "THAT CHILD IS ALREADY BORN . . .": Natchez *Democrat*, 8 January 1866.

11 "NEVER BE ANOTHER CROP . . .": In Theodore B. Wilson, *The Black Codes of the South* (University, AL: Univ. Alabama Press, 1965), p. 44. Visitors to the defeated South often reported being told, "You Northern people are utterly mistaken in supposing anything can be done with these negroes in a free condition. They can't be governed except with the whip," in Sidney Andrews, *The South Since the War* (Boston: 1866; Library of Congress Microfiche), p. 25.

11 "I TELL YOU, THE NIGGER IS A NO-ACCOUNT . . .": In John W. DeForest, *A Union Officer in the Reconstruction* (1869; reprint New Haven: Yale Univ. Press, 1948), p. 101.

11 "THE NIGGER IS GOING TO BE MADE A SERF . . .": In Trowbridge, *Desolated States*, p. 427.

12 DEFECTION OF HOUSEHOLD SLAVES: Joel Williamson, *After Slavery: The Negro in South Carolina During Reconstruction, 1861–1877* (New York: Norton, 1975), pp. 34–35.

12 THE FREEDMEN'S BUREAU: U.S. Congress, *Report of the Commissioner of the Bureau of Refugees, Freedmen, and Abandoned Lands*, 39 Cong., 1 Sess., House Exec. Doc. No. 11 (1865): 1–58; Martin Abbott, *The Freedmen's Bureau in South Carolina, 1865–1872* (Chapel Hill: Univ. North Carolina Press, 1967). See also W. E. Burghardt DuBois, "The Freedmen's Bureau," *Atlantic Monthly* 87 (March 1901): 354–65; John and LaWanda Cox, "General O. O. Howard and the 'Misrepresented Bureau,'" *Journal of Southern History* 19 (November 1953): 427–56.

12 CARPETBAGGERS: For a revised analysis of carpetbaggers, their motives and behavior, see Richard N. Current, "Carpetbaggers Reconsidered," in *A Festschrift for Frederick B. Artz*, eds. David H. Pinkney and Theodore Ropp (Durham, NC: Duke Univ. Press, 1964), pp. 139–57; William C. Harris, "The Creed of the Carpetbaggers: The Case of Mississippi," *Journal of Southern History* 40 (May 1974): 199–224; Jack B. Scroggs, "Carpetbagger Constitutional Reform in the South Atlantic States, 1867–1868," ibid. 27 (November 1961): 475–93. Still

of interest is Louis F. Post, "A 'Carpetbagger' in South Carolina," *Journal of Negro History* 10 (January 1925): 10–79.

12 "ENCOURAGED LAZINESS, FOSTERED THE HOPE . . .": Abbott, *Freedmen's Bureau*, pp. 120–21.

12 MORE WHITES BENEFITED FROM CHARITY: The fact is also sustained in U.S. Congress, *Report of the Secretary of War*, 40 Cong., 2 Sess. (1867–1868), I: 667; Paul D. Phillips, "White Reaction to the Freedmen's Bureau in Tennessee," *Tennessee Historical Quarterly* 25 (1966): 52; William S. McFeely, *Yankee Stepfather: General O. O. Howard and the Freedmen* (New Haven: Yale Univ. Press, 1969), p. 209; W. A. Poillon to Carl Schurz, 9 September 1865, *Report of Carl Schurz*, p. 73.

13 "THE PEOPLE, THE WHITE RACE . . .": O. O. Howard in U.S. Congress, *Operations of the Bureau of Refugees, Freedmen, and Abandoned Lands*, 39 Cong., 1 Sess., House Exec. Doc. No. 123 (1866): 4.

13 WORK OF THE FREEDMEN'S BUREAU: DeForest, *Union Officer*, pp. 73–75; John Hope Franklin, *From Slavery to Freedom: A History of Negro Americans* (New York: Knopf, 1974), p. 248; *American Missionary* 12 (June 1868): 135.

13 BLACKS' REFUSAL TO WORK FOR FORMER MASTERS: "Freedmen frequently show great disinclination to make contracts with their former masters. They are afraid lest in signing a paper they sign away their freedom, and in this respect they are distrustful of most southern men," in *Report of Carl Schurz*, p. 30. After slavery, "not a freedman would hire out to work on plantations where [his previous overseers] were known to be employed," in Trowbridge, *Desolated States*, p. 367. See also Thomas W. Higginson, *Army Life in a Black Regiment* (Boston: Fields, Osgood, 1870; Library of Congress Microcard), p. 249.

13 SUPPORT OF MULATTO CHILDREN: Trowbridge, *Desolated States*, p. 339.

13 "THE FEELING OF THE PEOPLE . . .": S. Melcher to J. T. Alden, 17 January 1866, File 440: "Selected Records of the Tennessee Field Office," Record Group 105: Bureau of Refugees, Freedmen, and Abandoned Lands, National Archives and Records Service, Washington, D.C. (hereafter cited RG 105: BRFAL, NARS).

13 "LEARNING WILL SPOIL . . . RUIN OF THE SOUTH": *Report of Carl Schurz*, p. 25.

13 "SETTLED DETERMINATION . . . MUST NOT BE EDUCATED": In Abbott, *Freedmen's Bureau*, p. 93.

13 "WHITE CRAVATTED GENTLEMEN . . .": Richmond *Times*, 16 January 1866, quoted in Henry L. Swint, *The Northern Teacher in the South, 1862–1870* (Nashville: Vanderbilt Univ. Press, 1941), p. 106.

14 "A WHOLE RACE TRYING . . .": Booker T. Washington, *Up From Slavery* in *Three Negro Classics*, ed. John Hope Franklin (New York: Avon, 1965), p. 44.

14 "THE CHILDREN OF THESE SCHOOLS . . .": In Trowbridge, *Desolated States*, p. 466.

14 "THERE ARE FEW MORE AFFECTING SIGHTS . . .": Ibid., p. 338.

14 MISS STANLEY'S CATECHISM: *American Missionary* 10 (June 1866): 139; see also Swint, *Northern Teacher*, pp. 88–90. Southerners complained that these radical ideas of Northern teachers "attacked those usages and traditions which gave to Southern life a charm and distinction not elsewhere found in America"

—which is certainly a creative way of viewing white supremacy—in William Garrott Brown, "The Ku Klux Movement," *Atlantic Monthly* 87 (1901): 642.

14 "THE POLITE SALUTATION . . .": *American Missionary* 10 (March 1866): 50.

15 "I'M A-GOIN' FOR TO TELL YOU . . .": Andrew Johnson in Ralph Korngold, *Thaddeus Stevens: A Being Darkly Wise and Rudely Great* (New York: Harcourt, Brace, 1955), p. 252.

16 "A VERY DELICATE QUESTION . . .": Thaddeus Stevens to Andrew Johnson, 16 May 1865, Andrew Johnson Papers, Manuscript Division, Library of Congress.

16 "FOUR-FIFTHS OF OUR ENEMIES . . .": *Proceedings of the Convention of the Colored People of Virginia, Held in the City of Alexandria*, 1865, reprinted in *Reconstruction: 1865–1877* ed. Richard N. Current (Englewood Cliffs: Prentice-Hall, 1965), pp. 19–20.

16 "I FOUGHT THREE YEARS AND WAS DISCHARGED . . .": Samuel Harris to Zachariah Chandler, 5 November 1866, Zachariah Chandler Papers, Manuscript Division, Library of Congress.

17 "A FOUL FIEND . . . CRIMES SO RICHLY DESERVE": J. L. Mack to Benjamin Wade, 22 July 1865, Benjamin Franklin Wade Papers, Manuscript Division, Library of Congress.

17 "I AM SURE YOU WILL PARDON ME . . .": Thaddeus Stevens to Andrew Johnson, 6 July 1865, Johnson Papers.

17 "TROUBLE, CONTROVERSY AND EXPENSE . . .": Charles Sumner to Benjamin Wade, 12 June 1865, Wade Papers; see also Sumner to Wade, 9 June 1865.

17 "IF WE ARE TO GO ON . . .": Benjamin Butler to Benjamin Wade, 26 July 1865, ibid.

17 OUTRAGES IN THE SOUTH: *Report of Carl Schurz*, pp. 17, 18, 19, 69, 70–71, 73–74. "Several cases of outrages have come to my knowledge, perpetrated by men in disguise, and in the night," in Wager Swayne to O. O. Howard, 26 December 1865, in U.S. Congress, *Report of the Commissioner of Refugees, Freedmen, and Abandoned Lands*, 39 Cong., 1 Sess., Senate Exec. Doc. No. 27 (1866): 66. The dating of Swayne's report is critical since it describes Klanlike activity well before the Klan was conceived and long before Radical Reconstruction gave it "justification."

18 "PATTEROLLERS": Willie Lee Rose, ed., *A Documentary History of Slavery in North America* (New York: Oxford Univ. Press, 1976), pp. 179–180. See also Williamson, *After Slavery*, p. 97. A complete account of black attitudes toward the slave patrols survives in the slave narratives recorded by unemployed writers for the WPA in the 1930s: "Slave Narratives, a Folk History of Slavery in the United States from Interviews with Former Slaves. Typewritten Records Prepared by the Federal Writers' Project, 1936–38, assembled by the Library of Congress project, Work Projects Administration, for the District of Columbia," 1941; Library of Congress microfilm (hereafter cited "Slave Narratives"). See, for example, Emmaline Heard, vol. 4, pt. 2, p. 152; Samuel Boulware, vol. 14, pt. 1, pp. 68–69; Charlie Davis, vol. 14, pt. 1, p. 252. The WPA writers recorded these narratives in black dialect with so much inconsistency that they are more fulsome than picturesque. I have therefore taken the liberty of disregarding their phonetic spellings in my quotations from the narratives.

19 BLACK INSOLENCE: "A negro is called insolent whenever his conduct varies

in any manner from what a southern man was accustomed to when slavery existed," in *Report of Carl Schurz*, p. 31. For the antebellum slave codes, see Rose, *Slavery in North America*, pp. 177, 181–82; Wilson, *Black Codes*, pp. 26, 30. Examples of "insolence" in text are from Williamson, *After Slavery*, p. 47; *New York Times*, 4 April 1865, 2 July 1865; Joseph G. de Roulhac Hamilton, ed., *The Papers of Randolph Abbot Shotwell* (Raleigh: North Carolina Historical Commission, 1936), III: 351; James E. Sefton, *The United States Army and Reconstruction, 1865–1877* (Baton Rouge: Louisiana State Univ. Press, 1967), p. 51; Trowbridge, *Desolated States*, p. 576; *Report of Carl Schurz*, p. 17; Francis B. Simkins, "The Ku Klux Klan in South Carolina, 1868–1871," *Journal of Negro History* 12 (1927): 633; DeForest, *Union Officer*, pp. 35–36; Gladys-Marie Fry, *Night Riders in Black Folk History* (Knoxville: Univ. Tennessee Press, 1975), p. 114–15; Post, "A 'Carpetbagger' in South Carolina," p. 67.

20 "OH NO, SIR . . .": Gordon in U.S. Congress, *Report of the Joint Select Committee to Inquire into the Condition of Affairs in the Late Insurrectionary States* (hereafter cited *KKK Testimony*), 42 Cong., 2 Sess., Senate Rpt. No. 41 (1872), VI: 338.

20 "THE GREATEST MAJORITY WERE BASED . . .": Laurence A. Baughman, *Southern Rape Complex: Hundred Year Psychosis* (Atlanta: Pendulum, 1966), p. 135. See also ibid., 91–92; Jordan, *White Man's Burden*, p. 80; Otto Olsen, "The Ku Klux Klan: A Study in Reconstruction Politics and Propaganda," *North Carolina Historical Review* 39 (1962): 344.

20 SOUTHERN RAPE COMPLEX: Clanton in *Documentary History of Reconstruction*, ed. Walter L. Fleming (1906; reprint Gloucester, MA: Smith, 1960), 2: 331. The definitive work on this subject is Baughman, *Rape Complex*. W. J. Cash's early analysis is still worthwhile and all the more remarkable for its date of publication: *The Mind of the South* (1941; reprint New York: Vintage, 1969), pp. 117–20; see also Ronald G. Walters, "The Erotic South: Civilization and Sexuality in American Abolitionism," *American Quarterly* 25 (May 1973): 177–201. The role of the Southern white female in this "complex" is analyzed by Jordan, *White Man's Burden*, pp. 77, 80–82; see also Arnold Madison, *Vigilantism in America* (New York: Seabury, 1973), pp. 57–58.

21 JOHNSON'S SOUTHERN GOVERNMENTS: Williamson, *After Slavery*, p. 73; Kenneth M. Stampp, *The Era of Reconstruction, 1865–1877* (New York: Vintage, 1965), pp. 67–69; Robert Cruden, *The Negro in Reconstruction* (Englewood Cliffs: Prentice-Hall, 1969), pp. 19–20.

21 SCALAWAGS: For a revised analysis of scalawags, their motives and behavior, see Otto H. Olsen, "Reconsidering the Scalawags," *Civil War History* 12 (1966): 304–20; Allen Trelease; "Who Were the Scalawags?" *Journal of Southern History* 29 (November 1963): 445–68; Warren A. Ellem, "Who Were the Mississippi Scalawags?" ibid. 38 (May 1972): 217–40.

21 THE BLACK CODES: U.S. Congress, *Reports of Assistant Commissioners of Freedmen and Synopsis of Laws Respecting Persons of Color in the Late Slave States*, 39 Cong., 2 Sess., Senate Exec. Doc. No. 6 (1866): 170–230; see also Wilson, *Black Codes*, passim. Wilson feels that, given the South's prejudices and the precedents of the antebellum codes, the Black Codes "were surprisingly mild" (p. 147). Peter Camejo comes closer to the truth in calling the codes "an attempt to establish a peonage system," in *Racism, Revolution, Reaction, 1861–1877* (New York: Monad, 1976), p. 145. The Northern press generally took a dim view of the codes, and Republicans reviled the new stat-

utes for weeks. Senator Henry Wilson complained that the Mississippi Code "will not allow a black man to lease lands or buy lands outside of the cities. Where in God's name is he to go? Into the public highway? Then he is a vagrant [and] under the vagrancy laws sold into bondage," in U.S. Congress, Senate, *Congressional Globe*, 39 Cong., 1 Sess., pt. 1 (1865): 111; for further debate, see ibid., pp. 109–14.

22 BARTON'S TESTIMONY: U.S. Congress, *Report of the Joint Committee on Reconstruction*, 39 Cong., 1 Sess., House Rpt. No. 30, pt. 3 (1866): 102–107.

23 CUSTER'S TESTIMONY: Ibid., pt. 4: 72–78. Custer had complained about the anti-Union behavior of Texans well before his appearance before the Joint Committee. On 8 January 1866, he wrote to Senator Zachariah Chandler, saying that white Southerners "are as much secessionists *today* in their beliefs and sentiments as they were one year ago. . . . I dread the day when the States not lately but *still* in rebellion are permitted to send their representatives and occupy seats in the National Congress": Chandler Papers.

23 INCREASING INCIDENTS OF SOUTHERN VIOLENCE: John Seague to Zachariah Chandler, 16 May 1866, Chandler Papers; General Terry's report of 27 January 1866 is reprinted in U.S. Congress, *Use of the Army in Certain of the Southern States*, 44 Cong., 2 Sess., House Exec. Doc. No. 30 (1876): 64; General Sickles's report of 19 January 1866 is in U.S. Congress, *Report of the Secretary of War*, 39 Cong., 2 Sess. (1866): 63. Of particular interest to the present study are the monthly reports of outrages in File 444: "Tennessee Field Office, Affidavits Relating to Outrages, 1866–1868," RG 105: BRFAL, NARS.

24 CIVIL RIGHTS ACT: *Statutes at Large*, XIV: 27; James D. Richardson, ed., *A Compilation of the Messages and Papers of the Presidents*, (Washington: Government Printing Office, 1896–1899), VI: 413.

24 MEMPHIS RIOT: U.S. Congress, *The Riot at Memphis*, 39 Cong., 1 Sess., House Exec. Doc. No. 122 (1866): 1–3. Lieutenant General Grant's report of 9 July 1866 is reprinted in *Use of the Army*, p. 65. See also Phillips, "White Reaction to the Freedmen's Bureau," p. 58.

25 FOURTEENTH AMENDMENT: Dwight L. Dumond, "The Fourteenth Amendment Trilogy in Historical Perspective," *Journal of Negro History* 43 (July 1958): 177–85; John Hope Franklin, *Reconstruction after the Civil War* (Chicago: Univ. Chicago Press, 1961), pp. 62–68.

25 "THE UNION HAS NO VALUE IN ITSELF . . .": Henry W. Bellows, *Public Life in Washington or the Moral Aspects of the National Capital*, Address read on Sunday evening, May 7, 1866, to his own congregation (New York: 1866; Library of Congress Microcard), p. 18.

26 ORGANIZED PERPETRATORS OF VIOLENCE: *Reports of Assistant Commissioners . . . and Synopsis*, pp. 96, 113, 55. See also John A. Carpenter, "Atrocities in the Reconstruction Period," *Journal of Negro History* 47 (October 1962): 234–47.

26 ELLIS HARPER'S BAND: *Reports of Assistant Commissioners . . . and Synopsis*, p. 129; U.S. Congress, *Report of the Secretary of War*, 40 Cong., 2 Sess. (1867–1868), I: 202; affidavit of Hudson Groves regarding Hudson Perdue, 22 November 1866, File 444, RG 105: BRFAL, NARS.

27 "TOTALLY INADEQUATE TO MEET THE DEMANDS": *Reports of Assistant Commissioners . . . and Synopsis*, pp. 112–13.

27 "I WISH I COULD SEE YOU . . .": Quoted in Stampp, *Reconstruction*, p. 115.

27 RADICAL RECONSTRUCTION: U.S. Congress, *Correspondence Relative to Reconstruction*, 40 Cong., 1 Sess., Senate Exec. Doc. No. 14 (1867): 3–12.

28 "LIKE THE SIBYL . . .": Georges Clemenceau, *American Reconstruction, 1865–1870*, trans. Margaret MacVeagh (New York: Dial, 1928), pp. 292–93.

1. *"The Shrouded Brotherhood"*

31 "GENERIC NAME OF KU KLUX . . .": G. P. L. Reid to Walter Fleming, n.d., Walter Fleming Papers, Archives and Manuscript Division, New York Public Library, New York.

31 KLAN AROSE BEFORE RADICAL RECONSTRUCTION: U.S. Congress, *Report of the Joint Select Committee to Inquire into the Condition of Affairs in the Late Insurrectionary States* (hereafter cited *KKK Testimony*), 13 vols. 42 Cong., 2 Sess., Senate Rpt. No. 41 (1872): I: 82–83; Albion Tourgée, *The Invisible Empire* (1883; reprint Ridgewood, NJ: Gregg, 1968), p. 117. James Crowe recalled the Klan being born as early as winter 1865–66 in S. E. F. Rose, *The Ku Klux Klan or Invisible Empire* (New Orleans: Graham, 1914), p. 20; John Lester recalled its birth later in May 1866 in J. C. Lester and D. L. Wilson, *Ku Klux Klan: Its Origin, Growth, and Disbandment, with an Introduction and Notes by Walter L. Fleming* (1905; reprint New York: DaCapo Press, 1973), p. 53; historian Allen Trelease, however, has found no evidence for the Klan's existence before June 1866: *White Terror: The Ku Klux Klan Conspiracy and Southern Reconstruction* (New York: Harper & Row, 1971), p. 3.

31 TENNESSEE BEFORE AND DURING THE WAR: William Gillette, "Anatomy of a Failure: Federal Enforcement of the Right to Vote in the Border States During Reconstruction" in *Radicalism, Racism, and Party Realignment: The Border States During Reconstruction*, ed. Richard O. Curry (Baltimore: Johns Hopkins Press, 1969), pp. 268–69; Paul D. Phillips, "White Reaction to the Freedmen's Bureau in Tennessee," *Tennessee Historical Quarterly*, 25 (1966): 58.

32 PULASKI: Mr. and Mrs. William B. Romine, *A Story of the Original Klan* (Pulaski: Pulaski Citizen, 1924), pp. 3–8. On the Scottish roots of this region, see Lester and Wilson, *Ku Klux Klan*, p. 23; William Garrott Brown, *The Lower South in American History* (1902; reprint New York: Greenwood, 1969), p. 8; William W. Henry, "The Scotch-Irish of the South" in *The Scotch-Irish in America: Proceedings of the Scotch-Irish Congress at Columbia, Tennessee* (Nashville: Publishing House of the Methodist–Episcopal Church, South, 1893), pp. 110–31.

32 REPEATED DEPREDATIONS IN PULASKI: See the monthly reports sent by George Judd to F. G. Palmer in File 440: "Selected Records of the Tennessee Field Office, 1865–1872," Record Group 105: Bureau of Refugees, Freedmen, and Abandoned Lands, National Archives and Records Service, Washington, D.C. (hereafter cited RG 105: BRFAL, NARS). There was a noticeable increase in floggings, shootings, and other acts of cruelty committed on blacks from June to August, just as the Klan was getting started.

32 FOUNDERS OF THE KLAN: Susan L. Davis, *Authentic History: Ku Klux Klan, 1865–1877* (New York: American Library Service, 1924), pp. 16–21. Inspired by *The Birth of a Nation*'s success, Davis's book is an almost unreadable jumble

of half-truths, errors, and bizarre digressions; nevertheless she was able to interview a number of important Tennessee Klansmen still living in the 1920s, and her work contains information available nowhere else.

33 "THE REACTION WHICH FOLLOWED . . .": Lester and Wilson, *Ku Klux Klan*, p. 52.

33 FOUNDING AND NAMING THE KLAN: Ibid., 21–22, 54, 56–57; Davis, *Authentic History*, pp. 7–10. Despite the simple combination of Greek and Scotch for the Klan's name, people later offered widely divergent interpretations of it. The Romines suggest the Pulaski Six were influenced by "Cukulcan," a figure in Mexican mythology in *Original Klan*, p. 7; in a similar vein, Gladys-Marie Fry stresses the influence of an Indian chieftain in Georgia folklore called "Clocletz" in *Night Riders in Black Folk History* (Knoxville: Univ. Tennessee Press, 1975), p. 119; Tourgée repeats the widespread belief that the Klan's name was derived from the vocal "clucks which were used by them as a signal" during raids in *Invisible Empire*, p. 13. J. P. Green claimed that "Ku Klux Klan" was onomatopoeic for the cocking and firing of a rifle in *Recollections of the Inhabitants, Localities, Superstitions and Ku-Klux Outrages of the Carolinas* (Cleveland: n.p., 1880), p. 136. This version was later read by Arthur Conan Doyle and used in his Sherlock Holmes story, "The Five Orange Pips." See also Allen Ward, "A Note on the Origin of the Ku Klux Klan," *Tennessee Historical Quarterly* 23 (June 1964): 182.

33 "AS NATURALLY AS 'DUMPTY' . . .": Brown, *Lower South*, p. 200.

33 ELABORATE COSTUMES: Lester and Wilson, *Ku Klux Klan*, p. 58; Ryland Randolph to Walter Fleming, 21 August 1901, Fleming Papers. An early Tennessee Klan costume is described as consisting of a "false face" attached to "a tall peaked hat with red and white spots . . . white pants with a red stripe, and . . . a long white robe, trimmed in red" in U.S. Congress, *Sheafe* v. *Tillman*. 41 Cong., 2 Sess., House Misc. Doc. No. 53 (1870): 263.

34 "HAVE FUN, MAKE MISCHIEF . . .": Walter L. Fleming, "Prescript of the Ku Klux Klan," *Publications of the Southern History Association* 7 (September 1903): 327.

34 "RATHER A PRETTY AND SHOWY . . .": *KKK Testimony*, IX: 660.

34 KLAN INITIATIONS: Lester and Wilson, *Ku Klux Klan*, pp. 60–61, 63–64. "No person could be initiated as the member of any camp until his name had been submitted to the camp and the application unanimously agreed to by the members of the camp": James E. Boyd to Walter Fleming, n.d., Fleming Papers.

35 INITIAL EXPANSION OF THE KLAN: Lester and Wilson, *Ku Klux Klan*, pp. 69–70.

35 "IMPRESSION SOUGHT TO BE MADE . . .": Randolph to Fleming, 21 August 1901, Fleming Papers.

35 "THERE IS MUCH EXCITEMENT . . .": Reprinted in Walter Fleming, ed., *Documentary History of Reconstruction*, (1906; reprint Gloucester, MA: Peter Smith, 1960), II: 365.

36 "THE AWFULEST BOOGERS": Alice Duke in "Slave Narratives, a Folk History of Slavery in the United States from Interviews with Former Slaves. Typewritten records prepared by the Federal Writers' Project, 1936–38, assembled by the Library of Congress project, Work Projects Administration, for the District of Columbia," 1941, Library of Congress microfilm (hereafter cited "Slave Narratives"), vol. 14, pt. 1, p. 336.

36 BLACKS NOT TAKEN IN BY KLAN'S RUSE AS GHOSTS: *Sheafe* v. *Tillman*, 159; *KKK Testimony*, III: 403, VI: 10, 14, IX: 813; Fry, *Night Riders*, p. 168; Grady H. McWhiney and Francis B. Simkins, "The Ghostly Legend of the Ku Klux Klan," *Negro History Bulletin* 14 (February 1951): 109–12. Jack White, an Alabama black who was "kluxed" by his disguised neighbor John Hardy, escaped a beating by recognizing Hardy's voice. White said to him, "Mr. Hardy, I know you, sir. I have never done you any harm, and you should not take my pistols from me." Caught offguard, Hardy whipped White's roommate but left White alone (deposition of Jack White, 2 September 1869, File 2146: "Papers Relating to Crimes Committed by the Ku-Klux Klan in Alabama, 1869–70," Record Group 94: Adjutant General's Office, NARS).

37 FROM BURLESQUE TO "PATTEROLLERS": "The condition of affairs generally in the country districts of Tennessee was most deplorable in the first part of the year, murders, robberies, and outrages of all kinds being committed without any effort on the part of the civil authorities to arrest the offenders": Gen. George H. Thomas in U.S. Congress, *Report of the Secretary of War*. 40 Cong., 2 Sess. (1867–1868), I: 182.

37 "READY FOR ANYTHING DESPERATE . . .": Quoted in Thomas B. Alexander, "Ku-kluxism in Tennessee, 1865–1869," *Tennessee Historical Quarterly* 8 (1949): 198.

37 "THERE WAS NO DIFFERENCE BETWEEN THE PATROLS . . .": J. T. Tims, "Slave Narratives," vol. 2, pt. 6, p. 340.

37 NASHVILLE MEETING: Lester and Wilson, *Ku Klux Klan*, p. 37.

38 "TO REORGANIZE THE KLAN . . .": Stanley Horn, *Invisible Empire: The Story of the Ku Klux Klan*, 1866–1871 (1939; reprint Montclair, NJ: Patterson Smith, 1969), pp. 32–33.

38 GEORGE GORDON: See Enoch L. Mitchell, "The Role of General George Washington Gordon in the Ku-Klux Klan," *Western Tennessee Historical Society Papers* No. 1 (1947): 73–80.

39 KNOW-NOTHINGS AND KNIGHTS OF THE GOLDEN CIRCLE: The most lively account of the Know-Nothings is Carleton Beals, *Brass-Knuckle Crusade: The Great Know-Nothing Conspiracy, 1820–1860* (New York: Hastings House, 1960). See also Thomas J. Curran, *Xenophobia and Immigration, 1820–1930* (Boston: Twayne, 1975); Ira M. Leonard and Robert D. Parmet, *American Nativism, 1830–1860* (New York: Van Nostrand Reinhold Co., 1971); Agnes McGann, "Nativism in Kentucky to 1860" (Ph.D. diss., Catholic University, 1944). On the Knights of the Golden Circle, see Ollinger Crenshaw, "The Knights of the Golden Circle: The Career of George Bickley," *American Historical Review* 47 (1941): 23–50; C. A. Bridges, "The Knights of the Golden Circle: a Filibustering Fantasy," *Southern Historical Quarterly* 44 (1941): 287–302; Jimmie Hicks, "Some Letters Concerning the Knights of the Golden Circle in Texas, 1860–1861," *Southwestern Historical Quarterly* 65 (1961): 80–86; J. W. Pomfrey, *A True Disclosure and Exposition of the Knights of the Golden Circle* (Cincinnati: privately printed, 1861; Library of Congress microfilm).

40 SELECTION OF FORREST AS WIZARD: Accounts of how Forrest came to be Wizard of the Klan are conflicting: Davis, *Authentic History*, pp. 81, 86–87; James Dinkins quoted in Henry C. Warmoth, *War, Politics and Reconstruction: Stormy Days in Louisiana* (New York: Macmillan, 1930), pp. 70–71; Andrew Lytle, *Bedford Forrest and his Critter Company* (New York: McDowell,

Obolensky, 1960), pp. 382–83. In all accounts, however, the role of John W. Morton is critical. Forrest had been nicknamed "The Wizard of the Saddle" during his Civil War service, and it is conceivable that the Memphis clique created the Klan's highest office with Forrest in mind, even before offering it to him.

41 "A BEGGAR . . . ENTIRELY DEPENDENT": *KKK Testimony*, XIII: 24.

41 "FORREST COMMANDED MORE BRAVE MEN . . .": Unidentified Klansman's handwritten answers to questions typed and submitted to him by Walter Fleming, n.d., Fleming Papers.

41 "SIX FEET ONE . . .": Cincinnati *Commercial*, 1 September 1868.

41 KLAN PARADES: Davis, *Authentic History*, p. 89; *Report of Evidence Taken Before the Military Committee in Relation to Outrages Committed by the Ku-Klux Klan in Middle and West Tennessee* (Nashville: S. C. Mercer, 1868; pamphlet in Library of Congress), p. 40; J. K. Nelson to W. P. Carlin, 18 May 1868, File 440, RG 105. BRFAL, NARS.

41 "THE GRAND TURK OF THE KUKLUX . . .": Quoted in Trelease, *White Terror*, p. 22.

42 "WHEN THE BLACK CAT . . .": U.S. Congress, House, *Congressional Globe*, 42 Cong., 1 Sess., pt. 2, Appendix (1871): 287.

42 "SHROUDED BROTHERHOOD . . .": Tuscaloosa *Independent Monitor*, April 1868, reprinted in Fleming, *Documentary History*, 2: 366. Thirty-three years later, when Randolph was asked if these notices had any meaning, he replied, "Well, they had this much meaning: the very night of the day on which these notices made their appearances, three notably offensive negro men were dragged out of their beds, escorted to the old bone yard (¾ mile from Tuscaloosa), and thrashed in the regular *ante bellum* style until their unnatural nigger pride had a tumble, and humbleness to the white man reigned supreme," in Randolph to Fleming, 21 August 1901, Fleming Papers.

43 "IN CAVES IN THE BOWELS . . .": James M. Beard, *K.K.K. Sketches* (Philadelphia: Claxton, Remsen & Haffelfinger, 1877), pp. 72–73.

43 SCOTTISH WITCH CULT: Ronald Seth, *In the Name of the Devil* (New York: Tower, 1969), pp. 7–35; Walter Scott, *Demonology and Witchcraft: Letters Addressed to J. G. Lockhart* (1830; reprint New York: Bell, 1970), pp. 274–332.

44 "THE IRISH PEOPLE . . . OF THE CITY": Forrest to Thomas, 15 July 1867, *Report of the Secretary of War* (1867–1868), I: 234.

44 UNION LEAGUE: Phillips, "Freedmen's Bureau in Tennessee," p. 58; *KKK Testimony*, VI: 321.

45 "[YOU] DERIDED THE IDEA . . .": *American Missionary* 12 (October 1868): 219–20.

45 "A SOCIETY WHICH TEACHES THE NEGRO . . .": Nashville *Union and Dispatch*, 24 April 1868.

45 "IS VERY NUMEROUS AND SEEMS . . .": Report of July 1867, File 440, RG 105: BRFAL, NARS.

46 JUNE TO OCTOBER: *Report of the Secretary of War* (1867–1868), I: 688.

46 "AN ORGANIZATION WELL MATURED . . .": Michael Walsh to W. P. Carlin, 11 January 1868, File 440, RG 105: BRFAL, NARS.

46 "GREATLY EXERCISED BY THE PRESENCE . . .": W. Bosson to Gen. George H. Thomas, 5 March 1868, Andrew Johnson Papers, Manuscript Division, Library of Congress, Washington, D.C.

46 "LAWLESS AND DIABOLICAL": U.S. Congress, *Report of the Secretary of War,* 40 Cong., 3 Sess. (1868–1869), I: 144.

46 "THIS RESISTANCE TO THE LAW . . .": General Thomas to the Adjutant General, 9 March 1868, Johnson Papers.

46 DEMOCRATIC NEWSPAPERS: Nashville *Union and Dispatch,* 1 February 1868; Richmond *Examiner* quoted in New York *Tribune,* 6 April 1868.

47 "THERE ARE TRUE AND TRIED MEMBERS . . .": Notice sent by "Province No. 1" to the Columbia (TN) *Herald,* 20 June 1868, reprinted in *Report of the Secretary of War* (1868–1869), I: 177. Klansman G. P. L. Reid claimed that nearly a thousand Klansmen could be mobilized at four hours notice: Reid to Fleming, Fleming Papers.

47 "THE KKK APPEAR TO BE ON THE 'WAR PATH' . . .": *Sheafe v. Tillman,* p. 292.

47 "THE KU-KLUX HAVE COMMITTED SO MANY . . .": Ibid., p. 293.

47 "HAVE COMPELLED A MORE COMPLETE . . .": Ibid., p. 301.

48 "I BELIEVE THE OBJECT OF THE KLAN . . .": *Report of Evidence . . . Tennessee,* p. 40.

48 "IN KU-KLUX COUNCIL . . .": Ibid., p. 39.

48 "HIDDEN RECESS, UNTERRIFIED'S RETREAT . . .": *Sheafe v. Tillman,* pp. 304–305.

48 "EXHIBITS ITSELF IN THE MOST INFERNAL . . .": *Report of the Secretary of War* (1868–1869), I: 173.

48 KLAN OUTRAGES IN TENNESSEE: *Sheafe v. Tillman,* pp. 240, 261–63, 293, 295, 297, 299, 302. See also Phillips, "Freedmen's Bureau in Tennessee," pp. 56–60; *Report of Evidence . . . Tennessee,* passim.

49 "THERE IS *NO INTENTION* . . .": *Report of the Secretary of War* (1868–1869), I: 181.

49 "UNLESS SOMETHING IS DONE . . .": *Sheafe v. Tillman,* p. 303.

49 "EX-REBEL . . . IN EVERY RESPECT": Message to the Legislature, 28 July 1868, in *Messages of the Governors of Tennessee, 1857–1869,* ed. Robert H. White (Nashville: Tennessee Historical Commission, 1959), V: 609–10.

50 "SOME OF, AND I MIGHT SAY . . .": *Report of Evidence . . . Tennessee,* pp. 66–67.

50 FORREST INTERVIEW: Cincinnati *Commercial,* 1 September 1868, reprinted in *KKK Testimony,* XIII: 32–34. See also Forrest's disclaimer, ibid., p. 35. The Grand Wizard's interview appeared right before the 1868 election, and he probably hoped its implicit threat would intimidate Republican voters. His remark that the Klan had now turned to "political matters and interests" is substantiated by the fact that Imperial Headquarters in Memphis had issued a revised Prescript with a few interesting additions: New Klansmen had to disavow the principles of the Republican party, the Union League, and equal rights for blacks.

51 PROPAGATING THE KLAN: Forrest's recruiting activities in the South are documented in Alan Conway, *The Reconstruction of Georgia* (Minneapolis: Univ. Minnesota Press, 1966), p. 171; Herbert Shapiro, "The Ku Klux Klan During Reconstruction: The South Carolina Episode," *Journal of Negro History* 49 (January 1964): 35; Tourgée, *Invisible Empire,* pp. 13–14. See also *KKK Testimony,* VI: 432–33.

51 "CONTAGION OF RAPINE AND BLOODSHED . . .": Robert Cypert to Andrew Johnson, 18 August 1868, Johnson Papers.

52 "COULD VERY WELL AVOID . . .": Georges Clemenceau, *American Reconstruction, 1865–1870*, trans. Margaret MacVeagh (New York: Dial, 1928), p. 247.

52 SOUTHERN CONSERVATIVE PRESS: See Gillette, "Anatomy of a Failure," p. 277; Otto Olsen, "The Ku Klux Klan: A Study in Reconstruction Politics and Propaganda," *North Carolina Historical Review* 39 (1962): 343.

52 *THE MASKED LADY OF THE WHITE HOUSE; OR, THE KU-KLUX KLAN: A MOST STARTLING EXPOSURE* (Philadelphia: C. W. Alexander, 1868, copy in Library of Congress: Rare Book and Special Collections Division).

52 *THE TERRIBLE MYSTERIES OF THE KU-KLUX KLAN* by Scalpel, M.D. (Edward H. Dixon) (New York: n.p., 1868).

52 KU-KLUX FEVER: Horn, *Invisible Empire*, pp. 326–341; Hubert C. Skinner and Amos Eno, *U.S. Cancellations: 1845–1869* (New Orleans: American Philatelic State College Press and Louisiana Heritage Press, 1980), p. 309; Post, " 'Carpetbagger' in South Carolina," p. 40; E. C. Buell, *Ku-Klux Klan Songster* (New York: Dick and Fitzgerald, 1868; copy in Library of Congress: Rare Book and Special Collections Division), pp. 9–11.

53 "THE NATION HELD ITS SIDES . . .": Tourgée, *Invisible Empire*, p. 13.

2. *"We Are the Law Itself"*

54 ESSIC HARRIS OUTRAGE: U.S. Congress, *Report of the Joint Select Committee to Inquire into the Condition of Affairs in the Late Insurrectionary States* (hereafter cited *KKK Testimony*), 13 vols. 42 Cong., 2 Sess., Senate Rpt. No. 41 (1872), II: 86–102.

57 NO SAFETY FOR BLACKS, CARPETBAGGERS, SCALAWAGS, 1868–1871: It has been estimated that, during this period, the Klan committed at least twenty thousand murders and tens of thousands of other acts of violence. See Dorothy Sterling, ed., *The Trouble They Seen: Black People Tell the Story of Reconstruction* (Garden City: Doubleday, 1976), p. 393.

57 GEOGRAPHIC SPREAD OF THE KLAN: *KKK Testimony*, VII: 611; William Gillette, "Anatomy of a Failure: Federal Enforcement of the Right to Vote in the Border States during Reconstruction" in *Radicalism, Racism, and Party Realignment: The Border States During Reconstruction*, ed. Richard O. Curry (Baltimore: Johns Hopkins Press, 1969), p. 274; Otto Olsen, "The Ku Klux Klan: A Study in Reconstruction Politics and Propaganda," *North Carolina Historical Review* 39 (1962): 354; Everette Swinney, "Enforcing the Fifteenth Amendment, 1870–1877," *Journal of Southern History* 28 (May 1962): 217. J.C.A. Stagg argues that, in South Carolina at least, the distribution of Klan violence makes no sense geographically and the concentration of sharecroppers offers a better explanation. His argument is flawed by his reliance on Democratic newspapers and demographic data later than 1875. See "The Problem of Klan Violence: The South Carolina Up-Country, 1868–1871," *Journal of American Studies* 8 (December 1974): 309.

57 "NEARLY ALL" THE DEMOCRATS: *KKK Testimony*, IV:1260.

57 "WERE ALL THE KU-KLUX ARRESTED . . .": Cincinnati *Gazette* quoted in U.S. Congress, House, *Congressional Globe*, 42 Cong., 1 Sess., pt. 2, Appendix (1871): 286.

57 COMPOSITION OF KLAN MEMBERSHIP: *KKK Testimony*, IV: 984; V: 1602–1603, 1613; VI: 321. Of the seventy-nine Klansmen convicted in Randolph

Shotwell's den, 67 percent were between the ages of twenty and thirty, with an average age of twenty-eight; see Joseph G. de Roulhac Hamilton, ed., *The Papers of Randolph Shotwell*, 3 vols. (Raleigh: North Carolina Historical Commission, 1936), III: Appendix. See also Francis B. Simkins, "The Ku Klux Klan in South Carolina, 1868–1871," *Journal of Negro History* 12 (1927): 619–20.

58 "LOW-DOWNERS": John W. DeForest, *A Union Officer in the Reconstruction* (1869; reprint New Haven: Yale Univ. Press, 1948), p. 153.

58 COERCION IN JOINING THE KLAN: Deposition of William R. Albright, 1 August 1870, File 60: "Statements, Depositions, and other Records Submitted by Governor William W. Holden, Relating to Crimes of the Ku-Klux Klan against Citizens of North Carolina, 1869–1871," Record Group 94: Adjutant General's Office, National Archives and Records Service, Washington, D.C. (hereafter cited RG94: AGO, NARS); Joel Asheworth to William W. Holden, 28 October 1871, ibid.; *KKK Testimony*, II: 394, 535. See also deposition of W. S. Bradshaw, 30 July 1870, File 60, RG 94: AGO, NARS; *KKK Testimony*, IV: 1260; V: 1863.

58 KLAN LEADERS: Stanley Horn, *Invisible Empire: The Story of the Ku Klux Klan, 1866–1871* (1939; reprint Montclair, NJ: Patterson Smith, 1969), pp. 170, 194, 245; Susan Davis, *Authentic History: Ku Klux Klan, 1865–1877* (New York: American Library Service, 1924), pp. 45, 217, 228, 236, 254, 276.

58 "SO-CALLED 'CHIEF'-SHIP . . .": In Hamilton, *Shotwell Papers*, III: 46. "As a rule, clans acted independently of any central authority": Ryland Randolph to Walter Fleming, 15 October 1901, Walter Fleming Papers, Archives and Manuscript Division, New York Public Library, New York.

59 "WHEREAS, THE ORDER OF THE K.K.K. . . .": Davis, *Authentic History*, pp. 125–128. Davis claims to have received a copy of this order from Forrest's former Grand Scribe.

59 KLAN COSTUMES: *KKK Testimony*, II: 471; III: 407; VI: 15; VII: 849; VIII: 528–29; IX: 723, 813–14, 919; XI: 273–74, 278; Elizabeth Howe, "A Ku Klux Uniform," pamphlet reprinted from *Buffalo Historical Society Publications* 25 (1921, copy in New York Public Library): 3. See also Albion Tourgée, *The Invisible Empire* (1883; reprint Ridgewood, NJ: Gregg Press, 1968), p. 131; Gladys-Marie Fry, *Night Riders in Black Folk History* (Knoxville: Univ. Tennessee Press, 1975), pp. 122–25.

60 IMPROMPTU DISGUISES: Ibid., pp. 128–31; *KKK Testimony*, XI: 327.

60 WOMEN'S DRESSES: Ibid., II: 87, 473; VI: 519, 567; XI: 510.

60 "TO MAKE THEM LOOK BIG . . .": Ibid., III: 521.

60 "I DO SOLEMNLY SWEAR . . .": Ibid., V: 1419.

61 KLAN GRIPS AND PASSWORDS: James E. Boyd to Walter Fleming, n.d., Fleming Papers; *KKK Testimony*, II: 530; V: 1862; "Ku Klux Mysteries," *American Historical Magazine* 6 (January 1901): 46–47; *The Nation's Peril, Twelve Years Experience in the South, Then and Now; the Ku-Klux Klan: A Complete Exposition of the Order* (New York: Friends of the Compiler, 1872, copy in the New York Public Library), pp. 25–31; Lewis Merrill to the Adjutant General, 9 June 1871, File 2586: "Report of Major Lewis Merrill, Commanding at Yorkville, South Carolina, and Correspondence Relating to the Operation at Yorkville, South Carolina, and Correspondence Relating to the Operation of the Ku-Klux Klan in South Carolina, 1871–1872," RG 94: AGO, NARS.

61 "TO ALARM THE VICTIMS . . .": Randolph to Fleming, 21 August 1901, Fleming Papers.

61 DEN OPERATIONS: Ibid., Boyd to Fleming, Fleming Papers; *KKK Testimony*, II: 533; IV: 1256–60; VI: 3.

61 KLANSMEN DISGUISING THEIR VOICES: "He does not speak in his natural tone of voice and uses a mystical style of language," in U.S. Congress, *Report of the Select Committee of the Senate to Investigate Alleged Outrages in the Southern States*. 42 Cong., 1 Sess., Senate Rpt. No. 1 (1871): 2; Boyd to Fleming, Fleming Papers; *KKK Testimony*, V: 1595; correspondent to the New York *Post* quoted in "Broadside Found Among the Papers of Zachariah Chandler," Rare Book and Special Collections Division, Library of Congress, Washington D.C. Several blacks who testified before the Joint Select Committee described the disguised voices as "outlandish" and "unnatural" (*KKK Testimony*, III: 586; V: 1406).

62 COOPERATION BETWEEN DENS: Ibid., I: 68; II: 537; Tourgée, *Invisible Empire*, pp. 39–40.

62 "BY FORCE AND TERROR . . .": Message to the House of Representatives, 19 April 1872, Ulysses S. Grant Papers, Manuscript Division, Library of Congress.

62 "PUNISHING IMPUDENT NEGROES . . .": Randolph to Fleming, 21 August 1901, Fleming Papers.

62 "THE CIVIL OR POLITICAL PROMOTION . . .": Boyd to Fleming, ibid.

62 "KILLING AND WHIPPING AND CROWDING . . .": *KKK Testimony*, V: 1863.

63 THE KLAN AND CARPETBAG TEACHERS: see O. O. Howard, *Autobiography of Oliver Otis Howard*, 2 vols. (New York: Baker & Taylor, 1907), II: 374–89; Henry L Swint, *The Northern Teacher in the South, 1862–1870* (Nashville: Vanderbilt Univ. Press, 1941), pp. 107–31.

63 "THE WORST WORK THE KU KLUX . . .": William Garrott Brown, "The Ku Klux Movement," *Atlantic Monthly* 87 (1901): 642.

63 "CARPETBAGGERS LIVED IN CONSTANT DREAD . . .": Quoted in William Garrott Brown, *The Lower South in American History* (1902; reprint New York: Greenwood, 1969), p. 213.

63 KLAN ATTACKS ON MALE TEACHERS: U.S. Congress, *Sheafe v. Tillman*. 41 Cong., 2 Sess., House Misc. Doc. No. 53 (1870): 261–63; Howard, *Autobiography*, II: 378, 386–87; deposition of E. Mulligan, 30 July 1869, File 2146: "Papers Relating to Crimes Committed by the Ku-Klux Klan in Alabama, 1869–1870," RG 94: AGO, NARS; *KKK Testimony*, XI: 325–28.

64 "ERE THE NEXT QUARTER . . .": Reprinted in *American Missionary* 12 (August 1868): 183; see also ibid. 14 (December 1870): 283.

64 "THEY TREATED ME GENTLEMANLY . . .": *KKK Testimony*, XII: 779.

64 "WE CAN INFORM YOU . . .": O. O. Howard to the Secretary of War, 1 May 1871, File 1688: "Correspondence Relating to the Charge by R. W. Flournoy of Pontotoc, Mississippi," RG 94: AGO, NARS.

64 "I AM NO ALARMIST . . .": R. J. Donaldson to A. Pleasonton, 5 May 1871, File 1723: "Copies of Letters from Revenue Officers in the Seventh District of North Carolina, the Second District of Missouri, and the First District of South Carolina Reporting Threats Made to Them by the Ku-Klux Klan," RG 94: AGO, NARS. The Klan sent a note to Donaldson saying, "You are hereby notified that 15 days will be allowed you to wind up your affairs and leave this country for good; if you do not take heed, you must abide the consequences."

65 "THE SPIRIT OF DEFIANCE . . .": C. C. Vest to Pinkney Rollins, 10 April 1871, ibid. In this same file, see also W. H. Deaver to Pinkney Rollins, 3 March

1871; C. H. Morgan to the Adjutant General-Department of the East, 9 June 1871.

65 A. P. HUGGINS OUTRAGE: This is one of the few cases where documentation exists both from the victim and one of the assailants: *KKK Testimony*, XI: 265–76; R. C. Beckett, "Some Effects of Military Reconstruction in Monroe County, Mississippi," *Publications of the Mississippi Historical Society* 8 (1904): 177–86.

67 "PARTICEPS CRIMINIS": Tourgée, *Invisible Empire*, p. 92.

68 "WE GAVE HIM TWENTY-FIVE LASHES . . .": Aberdeen (MS) *Tri-Weekly Examiner*, 15 March 1871, quoted in U. S. Congress, House, *Congressional Globe*, 42 Cong., 1 Sess. (1871): 446. For newspaper accounts of the Huggins outrage, see New York *Tribune*, 24 March 1871; *New York Times*, 28 March 1871.

68 "DID NOT UNDERSTAND THE NEGROES . . .": Beckett, "Some Effects of Military Reconstruction," p. 178. Klansmen were reported as saying that "they might put up with the men who come from the North being Republicans, but those at home who are Republicans are traitors to the South," in *KKK Testimony*, XI: 331.

69 KLAN ATTACKS ON SCALAWAGS: Ibid., III: 41, 571, 574; V: 1864–65; VI: 363–68, 545–60, 567–70; Olsen, "The Ku Klux Klan," pp. 357–58; Frank J. Wetta, "Bulldozing the Scalawags," *Louisiana History* 21 (Winter 1980): 43–58.

69 WILLIAM CHAMPION AND THE BOWDENS OUTRAGE: *KKK Testimony*, III: 365–71, 379–83.

71 "I WRITE THIS TO YOU . . .": John Hamilton to "Lieutenant-Sir" (probably James Miller), circa August 1869, File 2146, RG 94: AGO, NARS. For Klan retaliation on blacks who reported them, see *KKK Testimony*, VI: 375; VII: 1172. Regarding the prosecution of a case of Klan violence, Maj. Charles Morgan noted, "It is doubtful whether any conviction will follow, the young men being able to share an *alibi*. It is claimed that this defense is supported by testimony of some of the K.K.K. in every case where one of their number is arrested"; see Morgan to the Adjutant General-Department of the East, 11 May 1871, File 1612: "Reports by Major Charles H. Morgan, Commanding the Post at Raleigh, Relating to Activities of the Ku-Klux Klan in North Carolina," RG 94: AGO, NARS. See also *KKK Testimony*, VII: 618–19.

72 KLAN ATTACKS ON BLACK REPUBLICANS: Ibid., III: 327, 369, 386–91, 521; IV: 1244, 1256–57; VI: 10–11, VII: 610, 668–69; Tom Rosboro in "Slave Narratives: A Folk History of Slavery in the United States from Interviews with Former Slaves. Typewritten records prepared by the Federal Writers' Project, 1936–1938, and assembled by the Library of Congress project, Work Projects Administration, for the District of Columbia," 1941; Library of Congress Microfilm (hereafter cited "Slave Narratives"), vol 14, pt. 4, p. 43.

72 "ANTHONY THURSTER, THE NEGRO PREACHER . . .": Ogelthorpe (GA) *Echo* quoted in J. P. Green, *Recollections of the Inhabitants, Localities, Superstitions and Kuklux Outrages of the Carolinas* (Cleveland: n.p., 1880), p. 144. See also *KKK Testimony*, VI: 12.

73 "THE WAY THINGS ARE, WE CANNOT VOTE . . .": Ibid. II: 95.

73 KLAN ATTACKS ON BLACK LEADERS: Ibid., IV: 1256; VI: 516–17, 520–21; XI: 280; deposition of Mary Campbell, 4 August 1869, File 2146, RG 94: AGO, NARS. See also Dinah Cunningham, "Slave Narratives," vol. 14, pt. 1, p. 236.

73 KLAN ATTACKS ON BLACK POLITICIANS: U.S. Congress, *Hoge* v. *Reed.* 41 Cong., 1 Sess., House Misc. Doc. No. 18 (1869): 35, 42; *KKK Testimony,* VII: 607–08, 696–97, 735–37; IX: 998–99.

73 ELIAS HILL OUTRAGE: Ibid., V: 1406–15, 1477.

75 KLAN ATTACKS RE: LEGAL AND LABOR ISSUES: Ibid, III: 402–405, 585–90; VI: 8, 560–67; VII: 653; XI: 277.

75 KLAN ATTACKS RE: LAND USE: Ibid, VI: 387; XI: 336.

76 "AS SOON AS THEIR CROPS ARE MADE . . .": Ibid., VII: 701. For further incidents of Klan raids on sharecroppers, see ibid., VI: 9, 12–13, 420, 545–46; VII: 727; deposition of Walter Scott, *Report of Evidence Taken Before the Military Committee in Relation to Outrages Committed by the Ku Klux Klan in Middle and West Tennessee* (Nashville: S. C. Mercer, 1868; pamphlet in Library of Congress), p. 36; deposition of Pink Harris, 27 July 1868, File 444: "Tennessee Field Office, Affidavits Relating to Outrages, 1866–1868," RG 105: Bureau of Refugees, Freedmen and Abandoned Lands, NARS. See also Stagg, "Problem of Klan Violence," pp. 303–18; Sterling, *The Trouble They Seen,* pp. 51–52.

76 KLAN RAPES: Deposition of John Hamilton re: Reaner Berry, File 2146, RG 94: AGO, NARS: Charles Morgan to the Adjutant General-Department of the East, 4 May 1871, File 1612, ibid., *KKK Testimony,* VI: 377, 387. See also Simkins, "The KKK in South Carolina," p. 633; Walter Wilson, "The Meridian Massacre of 1871," *Crisis* 81 (February 1974): 52.

77 "OTHER GOOD INDUSTRIOUS FREEDMEN . . .": O. O. Howard to Secretary of War, File 1688, RG 94: AGO, NARS.

77 KLAN ATTACKS ON PROSPEROUS BLACKS: *KKK Testimony,* V: 1591–93; VI: 1–3; VII: 618–19; see also ibid., 732.

77 HENRY LOWTHER OUTRAGE: Ibid., VI: 357–63.

78 LOWTHER'S FEAR OF BEING IN JAIL: Frequently, when a black was imprisoned, Klansmen "would just go there and demand the keys from the jailer, and take him out and kill him" (ibid., VII: 609); see also Wilson, "Meridian Massacre," pp. 49–52.

78 LOWTHER'S CASTRATION: For further incidents of Klan castrations, see *KKK Testimony,* IV: 1184.

79 "GREAT IS CHIVALRY . . .": Reprinted in *American Missionary* 13 (February 1869): 40.

79 REPUBLICANS, LAW OFFICERS EQUALLY HELPLESS: *KKK Testimony,* I: 19–41; William Gillette, *Retreat from Reconstruction: 1869–1879* (Baton Rouge: Louisiana St. Univ. Press, 1979), p. 17; *American Missionary* 14 (January 1870): 17–19.

79 BLACKS SLEEPING IN THE WOODS: *KKK Testimony,* I: 34–35. "Mother heard the horses trotting and she rushed us out of our beds and took us and buried us in the fodder out in our barn and told us to be as quiet as possible. Both my parents went and hid at the edge of the woods": W. M. Green, "Slave Narratives," vol. 14, pt. 2, p. 200.

79 "THERE IS NOTHING IN THIS COUNTRY . . .": Charles Snyder to Elihu Washburne, 1 February 1868, Elihu Washburne Papers, Manuscript Division, Library of Congress.

79 "BANDS OF KU-KLUX . . .": Quoted in *American Missionary* 14 (June 1870), p. 139.

3. *"Let Us Have Peace"*

80 GRANT'S FIRST INAUGURATION: *New York Times,* 5 March 1869; New York *World,* 5 March 1869; Ben Perley Poore, *Perley's Reminiscences of Sixty Years in the National Metropolis,* 2 vols. (Philadelphia: Hubbard, 1886), II: 251.

82 "SOONER ACHIEVED IN MISSISSIPPI . . .": *Independent,* 18 April 1867.

82 "THE MOST IMPORTANT EVENT . . .": James D. Richardson, ed., *A Compilation of the Messages and Papers of the Presidents,* 10 vols. (1896–99), VII: 56.

83 "UNLESS CONGRESS INTERFERES . . .": *American Missionary* 14 (January 1870): 12.

83 "GHOSTS, HOBGOBLINS . . .": Columbia (SC) *Daily Phoenix,* 1 March 1870, quoted in U.S. Congress, *Report of the Joint Select Committee to Inquire into the Condition of Affairs in the Late Insurrectionary States* (hereafter cited *KKK Testimony*), 42 Cong., 2 Sess., Senate Rpt. No. 41 (1872), IV: 929.

83 "THE REPUBLICAN LEADERS NEED . . .": New York *World,* 23 March 1870.

83 THE BLOODY SHIRT: "The bloody shirt of the martyr was exposed in the mosch of Damascus" in *Decline and Fall,* Milman edition, V: 161. The expression is found as early as 1590 in Sir Philip Sidney's *Arcadia:* "That all the men there shoulde dress themselves like the poorest sorte of the people in Arcadia, having no banners, but bloudie shirtes hanged upon long staves . . ." (Book One, Chapter Six). In 1939, Stanley Horn concocted the fantastic story that, on the floor of Congress, Ben Butler literally waved the bloody shirt in which Allen Huggins had been beaten by the Klan: "It was from this that the 'bloody shirt' expression originated; and thus the humble nightdress of that forgotten carpetbagger has become immortalized in the vernacular of the nation," in *The Invisible Empire, the Story of the Ku Klux Klan, 1866–1871* (Boston: Houghton Mifflin, 1939), p. 151. A number of Butler's biographers and several historians of the Klan have taken Horn's tale seriously, but there is no truth in it.

83 FIRST ENFORCEMENT ACT: *U.S. Statutes at Large,* XVI: 140–46.

83 "THE CIVIL AUTHORITIES ARE INSUFFICIENT . . .": Lewis M. Douglas to General (name undecipherable) Crawford, 7 July 1869, File 2146: "Papers Relating to Crimes Committed by the Ku-Klux Klan in Alabama, 1869–70," Record Group 94: Adjutant General's Office, National Archives and Records Service, Washington, D.C. (hereafter cited RG 94: AGO, NARS).

84 "THE CIVIL OFFICERS ARE PARALYZED . . .": Charles Harkins to Lt. P. H. Flood, 5 March 1870, ibid. Regarding the Klan's activities, Harkins said, "for cold-blooded premeditated assassinations, they stand unparalleled in the annals of crime."

84 "THE COMMISSIONER'S OFFICE IS MADE . . .": Charles Morgan to Adjutant General, Department of the South, 18 June 1871, File 1612: "Reports by Major Charles H. Morgan, Commanding the Post at Raleigh, Relating to Activities of the Ku-Klux Klan in North Carolina," ibid. In this same letter, Morgan remarks, "I feel satisfied that the [Klan] has its strongest supporters among the women of the country, who are notoriously bitter beyond description in their feelings toward northern people and southern Republicans. It can hardly be doubted that these women manufacture the disguises worn by the Klan, which are in some instances quite fancifully trimmed."

84 "WE ARE DRIVEN TO THE WALL . . .": U.S. Congress, *Outrages Committed by Lawless Bands in Tennessee*. 41 Cong., 3 Sess., Senate Exec Doc. No. 22 (1871): 1–2.

84 "FEW REPUBLICANS DARE SLEEP . . .": R. K. Scott to General Alfred Terry, 17 January 1871, in U.S. Congress, *Outrages in the South*. 41 Cong., 3 Sess., Senate Exec. Doc. No. 28 (1871): 1.

84 "SOME OF THESE VICTIMS . . . FLAGRANT VIOLATIONS OF LAW": U.S. Congress, Senate, *Congressional Globe*, 41 Cong., 3 Sess. (1871): 579.

85 "THIS ORGANIZED CONSPIRACY IS IN EXISTENCE . . .": W. W. Holden to U. S. Grant, 1 January 1871, File 60: "Statements, Depositions, and Other Records Submitted by Gov. William W. Holden, Relating to Crimes of the Ku-Klux Klan Against Citizens of North Carolina, 1869–1871," RG 94: AGO, NARS.

85 SECOND ENFORCEMENT ACT: *U.S. Statutes at Large*, XVI: 433–40.

85 SENATE DEBATE OVER AN INVESTIGATION IN NORTH CAROLINA: U.S. Congress, Senate, *Congressional Globe*, 41 Cong., 3 Sess. (1871): 571, 573, 577.

86 JAMES E. BOYD'S TESTIMONY: U.S. Congress, *Report of the Select Committee of the Senate to Investigate Outrages in the Southern States*. 42 Cong., 1 Sess., Senate Rpt. No. 1 (1871): 17–27, 142–44.

86 BENJAMIN FRANKLIN BUTLER: Richard S. West, Jr., *Lincoln's Scapegoat General: A Life of Benjamin F. Butler* (New York: Houghton Mifflin, 1965), pp. 139–40, 206, 231; David Macrae, *The American at Home* (New York: Dutton, 1952), p. 170; see also Hans L. Trefousse, *Ben Butler, the South Called Him Beast!* (New York: Twayne, 1957).

87 BUTLER PUSHES GRANT FOR A NEW ATTORNEY GENERAL: Jacob Dolson Cox, "How Judge Hoar Ceased to be Attorney General," *Atlantic Monthly* 76 (August 1895): 162–73; William S. McFeely, *Grant: A Biography* (New York: Norton, 1981), pp. 364, 367–68.

87 AMOS T. AKERMAN: A biography of this important attorney general has yet to be undertaken. The best portrait of Akerman is found in the two letter books of his private correspondence, available on microfilm from the Alderman Library, University of Virginia, Charlottesville, Virginia.

88 MERIDIAN RIOT: U.S. Congress, House, *Congressional Globe*, 42 Cong., 1 Sess. (1871): 445–46; Walter Wilson, "The Meridian Massacre of 1871," *Crisis* 81 (February 1974): 49–52.

88 "I AM DRIVEN FROM HOME . . .": J. A. Moore to Adelbert Ames, March 1871, quoted in U.S. Congress, House, *Congressional Globe*, 42 Cong., 1 Sess. (1871): 446.

89 "WE BELIEVE YOU ARE NOT FAMILIAR . . . *WILL PROTECT US*": Petition from Kentucky Negroes to Congress, 25 March 1871, in *A Documentary History of the Negro People in the United States*, ed. Herbert Aptheker (New York: Citadel, 1951), pp. 594–95, my italics.

89 "A CONDITION OF AFFAIRS NOW EXISTS . . .": U.S. Congress, *Message from the President, Relative to the Condition of Affairs in the South*. 42 Cong., 1 Sess., House Exec. Doc. No. 14 (1871): n.p.

90 RESPONSE TO THE PRESIDENT'S MESSAGE: *New York Times*, 24 March 1871; Davenport *Daily Gazette*, 25 March 1871; Richmond *Dispatch*, 25 March 1871.

90 "WE ARE TRYING TO LEGISLATE . . .": James A. Garfield to W. C. Howell, 30 March 1871, James A. Garfield Papers, Manuscript Division, Library of Congress, Washington, D.C.

90 "I HAVE NEVER SUFFERED MORE . . .": Garfield to Burke A. Hinsdale, 30 March 1871, ibid.

90 KU-KLUX BILL: *U.S. Statutes at Large,* XVII: 13–15, my italics.

90 REACTION TO THE KU-KLUX BILL: *American Missionary* 15 (April 1871): 85; New York *Standard,* 5 May 1871; *Journal of Commerce,* 8 April 1871; New York *Evening Post,* 29 March 1871; Savannah *Republican,* quoted in *New York Times,* 28 March 1871; Jackson *Clarion,* quoted in ibid.

90 "A MERE MILITARY CHIEFTAIN . . .": U.S. Congress, House, *Congressional Globe,* 42 Cong., 1 Sess. (1871): 409.

91 ROBERT B. ELLIOTT: *New York Times,* 23 January 1868; New York *Tribune,* 3 April 1871; Peggy Lamson, *The Glorious Failure: Black Congressman Robert Brown Elliott and the Reconstruction in South Carolina* (New York: Norton, 1973), passim.

92 ELLIOTT'S SPEECH TO CONGRESS: Ibid., pp. 128–30; U.S. Congress, House, *Congressional Globe,* 42 Cong., 1 Sess. (1871): 389–92.

92 BUTLER'S SPEECH TO CONGRESS: Ibid., pp. 441–51; *New York Times,* 5 April 1871.

93 SEVENTH U.S. CAVALRY: U.S. Congress, *Report of the Secretary of War.* 42 Cong., 2 Sess. (1871–72): 61; Melbourne C. Chandler, *Of Garry Owen in Glory* (Annandale, VA: Turnpike Press, 1960), pp. 35–38.

94 GRANT'S PROCLAMATION: *Harper's Monthly* 43 (June 1871): 150.

94 "DON QUIXOTE'S ATTACK . . .": Detroit *Free Press,* 6 May 1871.

94 "WHEN YOU GET TO SOUTH CAROLINA . . .": *KKK Testimony,* V: 1482.

94 LEWIS W. MERRILL: Clay Hartley to W.C.W., 17 January 1980; Kenneth Hammer, *Biographies of the Seventh Cavalry* (Fort Collins, CO: Old Army Press, 1972), p. 7; Barry C. Johnson, "Custer, Reno, Merrill and the Lauffer Case," limited edition monograph reprinted from the English Westerners' *Brand Book* (London), vols. 12–13 (July–October 1970): 1–2; New York *Tribune,* 13 November 1871, 16 November 1871.

95 SEVENTH CAVALRY IN YORKVILLE: Lewis Merrill to Adjutant General, Dept. South, 23 September 1872, in U.S. Congress, *Report of the Secretary of War.* 42 Cong., 3 Sess. (1872–73), I: 86–87.

95 "NOT ONLY A VERY LARGE ONE . . .": *KKK Testimony,* V: 1482.

95 "I NEVER CONCEIVED OF SUCH A STATE . . .": Ibid.

96 "THE KU-KLUX ACT COMPREHENDS ALL PERSONS . . .": Yorkville *Enquirer,* 18 May 1871, quoted in ibid., pp. 1498–99.

96 MERRILL GATHERS INFORMATION ON THE KLAN: Lewis Merrill to Adjutant General, Dept. South, 4 May 1871, 17 May 1871, 9 June 1871, 14 September 1871, File 2586: "Reports of Major Lewis Merrill, Commanding at Yorkville, and Correspondence Relating to the Operations of the Ku-Klux Klan in South Carolina," RG 94: AGO, NARS.

96 MERRILL'S LENGTHY REPORT TO TERRY: Merrill to Adjutant General, Dept. South, 9 June 1871, ibid.

97 "AN OFFICER OF GREAT INTELLIGENCE . . .": General Alfred Terry to Assistant Adjutant General, 11 June 1871, "Letters Received, Adjutant General's Office," ibid.

98 TERRY'S RECOMMENDATION ON THE KLAN: Ibid,; see also James E. Sefton, *The United States Army and Reconstruction, 1865–1877* (Baton Rouge: Louisiana State Univ. Press, 1967), p. 222.

98 JOINT SELECT COMMITTEE GOES TO SOUTH CAROLINA: *Journal of the Joint Select Committee,* in *KKK Testimony,* I: 588–93.

98 "FRIGHTENED THE ORDER HERE THAT I ANTICIPATE . . .": Merrill to Adjutant General, Dept. South, 16 (?) July 1871, File 2586, RG 94: AGO, NARS.

98 MERRILL BEFORE THE SUBCOMMITTEE: KKK Testimony, V: 1465–86.

99 GRANT CONSIDERS SUSPENDING HABEAS CORPUS: New York Tribune, 1 September 1871; McFeely, Grant, p. 370.

99 MERRILL VERSUS THE COURT OF SESSIONS: Merrill to Adjutant General, Dept. South, 17 January 1872, File 2586, RG 94: AGO, NARS.

100 "ORGANIZED AND ARMED. THEY EFFECT . . .": A. T. Akerman to U.S. Grant, 16 October 1871, in U.S. Congress, Condition of Affairs in the Southern States. 42 Cong., 2 Sess., House Exec. Doc. No. 268 (1872): 1–2.

100 SEVENTH CAVALRY ROUTS THE KLAN: Merrill to Adjutant General, Dept. South, 17 January 1872, File 2586, RG 94: AGO, NARS; Report of the Secretary of War, (1872–73), I: 91–92; Louis F. Post, "A 'Carpetbagger' in South Carolina," Journal of Negro History 10 (January 1925): 44.

101 LOUIS POST: Post was born in Hackettstown, New Jersey, in 1849. After his "apprenticeship" in civil rights in South Carolina, he became editor of Chicago's The Public (1898–1913) in which he championed progressivism and denounced the lynching of blacks in the South. He was a member of the organizational meeting of the NAACP in 1909. As Woodrow Wilson's assistant secretary of labor, he condemned the deportation of immigrants during the Red Scare and refused to cooperate with Attorney General A. Mitchell Palmer. See Dominic Candeloro, "Louis Post as a Carpetbagger in South Carolina: Reconstruction as a Forerunner of the Progressive Movement," American Journal of Economics and Sociology 34 (October 1975): 423–32.

101 BITTER DENUNCIATIONS BY SOUTH CAROLINA NEWSPAPERS: Columbia Phoenix, 9 November 1871; Yorkville Enquirer, 9 November 1871; Spartanburg Spartan, 9 November 1871, all quoted in New York World, 14 November 1871.

101 MERRILL AND THE BIG "PUKER": Post, " 'Carpetbagger' in South Carolina," pp. 45–46.

102 TRIALS OF KLANSMEN: The complete transcript of the first trials is in The Great Ku Klux Trials, Official Report of the Proceedings Before U.S. Circuit Court . . . November Term, 1871 (Columbia, SC: The Columbia Union, 1872; copy in Schomburg Collection of Negro History, New York Public Library, New York).

102 "AS LITTLE APPARENT HORROR . . .": Francis B. Simkins, "The Ku Klux Klan in South Carolina, 1868–1871," Journal of Negro History 12 (1927): 619.

102 "I HAVE LISTENED WITH UNMIXED HORROR . . .": Great Ku Klux Trials, p. 129.

102 "TO RISE UP, AND . . . SHOW . . .": Augusta Constitutionalist, quoted in Savannah News, 9 November 1871, quoted in KKK Testimony, VII: 1217.

102 SWAMPING THE COURTS IN SOUTH CAROLINA: Condition of Affairs in the Southern States, pp. 5–12; A. T. Akerman to B. D. Silliman, 9 November 1871, Akerman Letterbooks; Everette Swinney, "Enforcing the Fifteenth Amendment, 1870–1877," Journal of Southern History 28 (May 1962): 211–13.

103 "IF IT BE TRUE THAT BLACK MEN . . .": Nation, 23 March 1871.

103 "WE MUST DO THE BEST . . .": Akerman to Robert A. Hill, 27 July 1871, Akerman Letterbooks.

103 "IF IT TAKES A COURT OVER ONE MONTH . . .": Swinney, "Fifteenth Amendment," p. 213.

103 AKERMAN RECOMMENDS COMPROMISES: Homer Cummings and Carl

McFarland, *Federal Justice: Chapters in the History of Justice and the Federal Executive* (New York: Macmillan, 1937), p. 239.

103 DISTRICT ATTORNEY CORBIN COMPLAINS: D. T. Corbin to George H. Williams, 20 February 1872, in *Condition of Affairs in the Southern States*, p. 19; Cummings and McFarland, *Federal Justice*, p. 240.

104 *"IN VIEW OF THE LARGE NUMBER OF INDICTMENTS . . ."*: KKK Testimony, I: 99–100, my italics.

104 JOINT SELECT COMMITTEE'S MAJORITY REPORT: Ibid., pp. 82–100, 231–33, 271.

105 "HAVING THE RIGHTS OF A CITIZEN . . .": Ibid., p. 99.

106 JOINT SELECT COMMITTEE'S MINORITY REPORT: Ibid., pp. 442, 475–97, 509–14, 522–24, 539. Van Trump's arguments against black suffrage harken back to antebellum rhetoric: "Pseudo philanthropists may talk ever so loud and eloquently about an 'equality before the law,' where equality is not found in the great natural law of race ordained by the Creator. That cannot be changed by statute which has been irrevocably fixed by the fiat of the Almighty" (p. 526). Van Trump had been editor of the Lancaster (OH) *Gazette and Enquirer* and an unsucessful Know-Nothing candidate for governor of Ohio in 1856; see *Biographical Directory of the American Congress, 1774–1971* (1971), p. 1853.

107 "IT IS AN AXIOMATIC TRUTH . . .": *KKK Testimony*, I: 515.

107 GRANT'S SECOND INAUGURATION: *The Nation*, 13 March 1873; *New York Times*, 5 March 1873; New York *World*, 5 March 1873; Mary Logan, *Reminiscences of the Civil War and Reconstruction*, George W. Adams, ed. (Carbondale: Southern Illinois Univ. Press, 1970), pp. 241–44; Poore, *Perley's Reminiscences*, pp. 294–99.

109 "MY INTENTION IS TO SUSPEND . . .": Cummings and McFarland, *Federal Justice*, p. 238.

110 GRANT'S POLICY OF INTERVENING IN THE SOUTH: For an unfavorable assessment of Grant, see William Gillette, *Retreat from Reconstruction, 1869–1879* (Baton Rouge: Louisiana State Univ. Press, 1979), pp. 166–85; for a favorable one, see Richard N. Current, "President Grant and the Continuing Civil War," in *Ulysses S. Grant: Essays and Documents*, ed. David L. Wilson and John Y. Simon (Carbondale: Southern Illinois Univ. Press, 1981), pp. 1–8.

110 THE END OF RECONSTRUCTION: See Gillette, *Retreat from Reconstruction*; Stanley P. Hirshson, *Farewell to the Bloody Shirt: Northern Republicans and the Southern Negro, 1877–1893* (Bloomington: Indiana Univ. Press, 1962); Keith Ian Polakoff, *The Politics of Inertia: The Election of 1876 and the End of Reconstruction* (Baton Rouge: Louisiana State Univ. Press, 1973): Edwin C. Rozwenc, ed., *Reconstruction in the South* (Lexington, MA: D. C. Heath, 1972), pp. 245–305.

111 *"BUT THIS IS NOT TRUE PEACE . . ."*: Stephen B. Oates, *Let the Trumpet Sound: The Life of Martin Luther King, Jr.* (New York: Harper and Row, Literary Guild ed., 1982, p. 81, my italics.

Postscript

112 FLAGGING IDEALISM OF THE NORTH: For examples of this, see the editorials by Horace Greeley in the New York *Tribune*, 7 April 1877; and by E. L. Godkin in the *Nation* 20 (11 February 1875): 91.

113 "THE MOMENT ANY PARTY . . .": New York *Evening Post*, 11 March 1874.

113 REPUBLICAN ABANDONMENT OF SOUTHERN BLACKS: The definitive work on the subject is Stanley P. Hirshson, *Farewell to the Bloody Shirt: North Republicans and the Southern Negro, 1877–1893* (Chicago: Quadrangle, 1968).

113 "THE JUDGMENT THIS DAY . . .": Gilbert Osofsky, ed., *The Burden of Race* (New York: Harper Torchbooks, 1968), p. 239.

113 DISFRANCHISEMENT OF BLACKS: Ibid., pp. 164–76; Mary Frances Berry and John W. Blassingame, *Long Memory: The Black Experience in America* (New York: Oxford Univ. Press, 1982), pp. 160–69; Stetson Kennedy, *Jim Crow Guide to the U.S.A.* (London: Lawrence & Wishart, 1959), pp. 150–64.

114 AMERICAN PROTECTIVE ASSOCIATION: Donald L. Kinzer, *An Episode of Anti-Catholicism: The American Protective Association* (Seattle: Univ. Washington Press, 1964); Humphrey J. Desmond, *The A.P.A. Movement* (Washington: New Century, 1912); Thomas J. Curran, *Xenophobia and Immigration* (Boston: Twayne, 1975), pp. 97–103; John Higham, *Strangers in the Land* (New Brunswick: Rutgers Univ. Press, 1955), p. 81; Gustavus Myers, *A History of Bigotry* (New York: Capricorn, 1960), pp. 163–91. The APA and the revived Ku Klux Klan are compared in Robert L. Duffus, "Ancestry and End of the Ku Klux Klan," *World's Work* 46 (September 1923): 532–33.

114 WHITECAPS: Madeleine E. Nobel, "The Whitecaps of Harrison and Crawford County Indiana" (Ph.D. diss., University of Michigan, 1973); William F. Homes, "Whitecapping: Agrarian Violence in Mississippi, 1902–1906," *Journal of Southern History* 35 (May 1969): 165–85; Richard M. Brown, "Historical Patterns of Violence in America" in *The History of Violence in America*, ed. Hugh D. Graham and Ted R. Gurr (New York: Bantam, 1966), pp. 70–71. Brown suggests that the Whitecaps served as "an important link between the first and second Ku Klux Klans." A comprehensive monograph on the Whitecap movement would be quite useful.

115 COMPOSITE SKETCH OF RECONSTRUCTION: James Ford Rhodes, *History of the United States* (1906; reprint New York: Macmillan, 1920), VI: 125; Woodrow Wilson, *A History of the American People* (New York: Harper Brothers, 1902), V: 50; Rhodes, *History*, p. 191; Wilson, *History*, p. 46; Rhodes, *History*, p. 202; ibid., p. 191; Wilson, *History*, p. 49; Rhodes, *History*, p. 435; John S. Reynolds, *Reconstruction in South Carolina* (Columbia, SC: The State Co., 1905), pp. 182–83; Walter Lynwood Fleming, *Civil War and Reconstruction in Alabama* (1905; reprint New York: Peter Smith, 1949), p. 654; Wilson, *History*, p. 58; William Archibald Dunning, *Reconstruction, Political and Economic, 1865–1877* (New York: Harper Brothers, 1907), p. 189; Wilson, *History*, p. 62; Walter Lynwood Fleming, Introduction to J. C. Lester and D. L. Wilson, *The Ku Klux Klan: Its Origin, Growth and Disbandment* (1905; reprint New York: DaCapo Press, 1973), p. 19; idem, *Reconstruction in Alabama*, p. 689.

BOOK TWO: 1915–1930
4. "*Writing History with Lightning*"

119 JOSEPH CARL BREIL: For the score of *The Birth of a Nation*, Breil selected from existing folk tunes and light classics, including "Coming Through the Rye," "Dixie," "Peer Gynt," and "Light Cavalry Overture"; see Seymour Stern, "Griffith: I—'The Birth of a Nation,'" *Film Culture*, no. 36 (Spring–Summer 1965): 108–13. Breil later turned to writing original scores for silent films. His

opera *The Legend* was produced at the Metropolitan Opera House, New York, in 1919 and deserves its obscurity. Griffith had always shown a keen interest in the music accompanying films; prior to *The Birth*, he had provided *Judith of Bethulia* with a cue sheet suggesting music for various scenes; see Clarence E. Sinn, "Music for Pictures," *Moving Picture World* 20 (4 April 1914); 50.

119 LOS ANGELES PREMIERE: Karl Brown, *Adventures with D. W. Griffith* (New York: Farrar, Straus, & Giroux, 1973), pp. 87–88; Los Angeles *Times*, 9 February 1915.

120 TITLE CHANGED TO *THE BIRTH OF A NATION*: There is little doubt that Tom Dixon prompted the title change: "When I saw the finished film I immediately suggested to Griffith the changing of the title. I did this not because the book was in any sense inaccurate but because its argument was more narrow and militant and stood for less than the film drama" (Dixon interviewed in the New York *Sun*, 12 April 1915); this is confirmed by Griffith in an interview published in the New York *American*, 28 February 1915; see also Russell Merritt, "Dixon, Griffith, and the Southern Legend," *Cinema Journal* 12 (1972): 39, fn. 32. The title itself comes from Woodrow Wilson's description of the excitement of Congress over passing the Thirteenth Amendment abolishing slavery: "Men dreamed . . . they had that day seen a new nation born, a new era ushered in," in Woodrow Wilson, *A History of the American People* (New York: Harper Brothers, 1902), V: 7.

120 "I DUNNO . . . HOW SHOULD *I* KNOW?": New York *Mail*, 13 March 1915.

120 LONG-RANGE EFFECTS OF *BIRTH OF A NATION*: See Everett Carter, "Cultural History Written with Lightning: The Significance of *The Birth of a Nation*," *American Quarterly* 12 (Fall 1960): 347–57; Richard Griffith and Arthur Mayer, *The Movies* (New York: Simon & Schuster, 1970), p. 37; *New York Times*, 6 June 1916; Maxim Simcovitch, "The Impact of Griffith's *Birth of a Nation* on the Modern Ku Klux Klan," *Journal of Popular Film* 1 (Winter 1972): 45–54; *Variety*, 9 February 1949; Edward Wagenknecht and Anthony Slide, *The Films of D. W. Griffith* (New York: Crown, 1975), pp. 58–61.

120 GRIFFITH'S EARLY LIFE: Iris Barry and Eileen Bowser, *D. W. Griffith: American Film Master* (New York: Museum of Modern Art, 1965), pp. 6–9; D. W. Griffith, Autobiographical Manuscript, D. W. Griffith Papers, Museum of Modern Art, New York; Henry Stephen Gordon, "The Story of David Wark Griffith," *Photoplay* 10 (June 1916): 35, 37; D. W. Griffith, "Are Motion Pictures Destructive of Good Taste?" *Arts and Decoration* (December 1923): 12–13.

121 "WE ARE JUST GRINDING OUT . . .": Bitzer wrote two versions of ths soliloquy, which are here combined. Bitzer in Barry and Bowser, *D. W. Griffith*, p. 17; Billy Bitzer, *Billy Bitzer: His Story* (New York: Farrar, Straus & Giroux, 1973), p. 89.

122 WOODS AND DIXON: Linda Arvidson, *When the Movies Were Young* (New York: Dutton, 1925), p. 251.

122 THOMAS DIXON: Raymond Allen Cook, *From the Flint: the Amazing Careers of Thomas Dixon* (Winston-Salem, NC: John Blair, 1968). See also idem, *Thomas Dixon* (New York: Twayne, 1974); Michael Davis, *The Image of Lincoln in the South* (Knoxville, KY: Univ. Kentucky Press, 1971), pp. 46, 149; Merritt, "Dixon, Griffith," pp. 26–44.

123 "ONION-LADEN BREATH . . .": Thomas Dixon, *The Clansman* (New York: Grosset & Dunlap, 1905), p. 155.

123 "FOR A RUSSIAN . . . FROM BARBARISM.": Ibid., pp. 290–92.

123 "THE WORLD HAD NOT SEEN . . .": Ibid., p. 316.

123 WOODROW WILSON AND SEGREGATION: See George C. Osborn, "The Problem of the Negro in Government, 1913," *The Historian* 23 (May 1961): 330–47; Kathleen Wolgemuth, "Wilson and Federal Segregation," *Journal of Negro History* 44 (April 1959): 158–73; idem, "Woodrow Wilson's Appointment Policy and the Negro," *Journal of Southern History* 24 (November 1958): 457–71.

124 FAILURE OF *THE CLANSMAN* AS A PLAY: John Hammond Moore, "South Carolina's Reaction to the Photoplay, *The Birth of a Nation*," *Proceedings of the South Carolina Historical Association* (1963): 32–35.

124 "I WAS FROM YANKEE COUNTRY . . .": Bitzer, *His Story*, p. 106.

124 "AS BITTER A HYMN OF HATE . . .": Brown, *Adventures with D. W. Griffith*, p. 32.

124 GRIFFITH'S DIRECTION OF *BIRTH OF A NATION*: Bitzer, *His Story*, p. 106; Brown, *Adventures with D. W. Griffith*, pp. 29–30; Lillian Gish, *The Movies, Mr. Griffith, and Me* (Englewood Cliffs, NJ: Prentice-Hall, 1969), pp. 131–47; Anita Loos, *A Girl Like I* (New York: Viking, 1966), p. 79.

124 GRIFFITH AND BILL CLUNE: Milton MacKaye, " 'The Birth of a Nation,' " *Scribners Magazine* 102 (November 1937): 44.

125 NAACP OPPOSITION: W.E.B. DuBois, "Fighting Race Calumny," *The Crisis* 10 (May 1915): 40; Thomas R. Cripps, "The Reaction of the Negro to the Motion Picture *Birth of a Nation*," *The Historian* 25 (May 1963): 347.

125 DIXON'S MEETING WITH WILSON: Dixon to Joseph P. Tumulty, 27 January 1915, Woodrow Wilson Papers, Manuscript Division, Library of Congress, Washington, D.C.; Cook, *Fire from the Flint*, pp. 168–70; Dixon to Tumulty, 1 May 1915, Wilson Papers.

126 "IT IS LIKE WRITING HISTORY . . .": Wilson's famous response to the film has often been quoted and has been erroneously called "apocryphal." The first mention of it seems to have been from Griffith himself (New York *American*, 28 February 1915); it was later given much publicity by the New York *Post*, 4 March 1915. Given Griffith's great respect for Wilson, it is unlikely that he would have made up the remark. That Griffith was present at the White House when Wilson made the statement is documented in his "bread-and-butter" note to the President (Griffith to Wilson, 2 March 1915, Wilson Papers): "If we carry out the proposed series of motion pictures dealing with matters historical and political, *of which I spoke to you*, I should be most happy to have someone representing your views to pass upon our ideas before beginning the initial work" (my italics). See also Dixon to Wilson, 20 February 1915, Wilson Papers.

126 DIXON AND JUSTICE WHITE: Cook, *Fire from the Flint*, pp. 171–72; Cripps, "Reaction of the Negro," p. 349.

127 PRIVATE WASHINGTON SHOWING: Washington *Herald*, 20 February 1915.

127 ADVERTISING THE NEW YORK PREMIERE: *New York Times*, 14 February 1915; New York *Dramatic News*, 6 March 1915; Stern, "Griffith: I," p. 67.

127 NAACP TAKES ACTION: DuBois, "Calumny," p. 40; Cook, *Fire from the Flint*, p. 173.

128 LIBERTY THEATER, MARCH 3: *Variety*, 5 March 1915; unidentified, undated clippings, D. W. Griffith Pressbooks, vols. 1 and 2, Special Collections, Museum of Modern Art Library, New York.

128 *BIRTH OF A NATION,* DESCRIPTION OF THE NEW YORK PREMIERE: This

has been reconstructed from my notes after seeing the Museum of Modern Art's copy of the film and from subsequent repeated viewings of an abbreviated print. Details of the music are from Stern, "Griffith: I," pp. 108–13; the audience reaction comes from newpaper clippings in the Griffith Pressbooks, Museum of Modern Art.

129 THE INTERMISSION: *New York Times,* undated clipping, Case File 2247, Wilson Papers; New York *Herald,* 4 March 1915.

129 BLACK MILITIAMEN: Half of the black extras and all of the black principals in the film are played by white actors in blackface. There has been much criticism of this, and Griffith's defenders have offered the excuse that there were too few black players in Los Angeles in 1915 (Stern, "Griffith: I," p. 14; Gish, *The Movies,* p. 134). The excuse has been contested by Peter Noble, *The Negro in Films* (New York: Arno Press and the New York Times, 1970), pp. 179–80, and is contradicted by Griffith's own explanation: "That matter [using black actors] was given consideration, and on careful weighing of every detail concerned, the decision was to have no black blood among the principals; it was only in the legislative scene that Negroes were used, and then only as 'extra people' "; see Griffith in Henry Stephen Gordon, "The Story of David Wark Griffith," *Photoplay* 10 (October 1916): 93.

130 "A BLACK PENIS PUSHING . . .": The description is by Seymour Stern ("Griffith: I," p. 118) and is fairly typical of his scholarship and prose.

131 RIDE OF THE KLANSMEN: This spectacle provoked unprecedented excitement in a film audience. See *Moving Picture World,* 13 March 1915; New York *Press,* 4 March 1915; New York *Evening Telegram,* 4 March 1915. Jay Leyda has noted, "The ride of the Klan . . . [set] the pattern for the cheapest and most hollow film sensations, the ornament of every film that hoped to stamp out all intellectual stimulus with a brutal physical impact on its audience," in "The Art and Death of D. W. Griffith," *Sewanee Review* 57 (1949): 350–56. It certainly established the standard denouement of American "westerns."

131 "BASED UPON TRUTH . . .": D. W. Griffith in a letter to the New York *Globe,* 9 April 1915.

131 "I WILL TAKE THIS OCCASION . . .": D. W. Griffith in a letter dated 12 February 1947 to the editor of *Sight and Sound,* reprinted in Noble, "Negro in Films," p. 275.

132 *BIRTH OF A NATION* CONSISTENT WITH HISTORY: Along with the major sources of Reconstruction history, Griffith's film was also consistent with nearly every secondary source available in 1915. The more important of these may be cited: Myrtal L. Avary, *Dixie After the War* (New York: Doubleday, 1906); William G. Brown, *The Lower South in American History* (New York: Macmillan, 1902); Walter H. Cook, *Secret Political Societies in the South during the Period of Reconstruction* (Cleveland: Evangelical Publishing House, 1914); Eyre Damer, *When the Ku Klux Rode* (1912; reprint Westport, CT: Negro Universities Press, 1970): T. W. Gregory, "Reconstruction and the Ku Klux Klan, A Paper Read Before the Arkansas and Texas Bar Associations," 22-page pamphlet; copy in the Walter Lynwood Fleming Papers, Manuscript Division, New York Public Library, New York; William T. Richardson, *Historic Pulaski: Birthplace of the Ku Klux Klan* (Nashville: Methodist Publishing House, 1913); S. E. F. Rose, *The Ku Klux Klan or Invisible Empire* (New Orleans: L. Graham, 1914); W. D. Wood, "The Ku Klux Klan," *Quarterly of the Texas State Historical Association* 9 (April 1906): 262–68.

132 EFFECT OF *BIRTH OF A NATION* ON HISTORY: Historian John Hope Franklin contends that the film's influence on twentieth-century histories of Reconstruction "has been greater than any single force," in " 'The Birth of a Nation'
—Propaganda as History," *Massachusetts Review* 30 (1979): 433.

132 NEW YORK REVIEWS: New York *Globe and Commercial Advertiser*, 5 March
1915; New York *Dramatic Mirror*, 10 March 1915; New York *Morning Telegraph*, 4 March 1915; New York *Tribune*, 4 March 1915; *New York Times*,
undated clipping, Case File 2247, Wilson Papers; New York *World*, 4 March
1915.

132 THE FILM'S VERSION OF RECONSTRUCTION: Dorothy Dix in an unidentified, undated clipping, Case File 2247, Wilson Papers; New York *American*, 4
March 1915; Thomas B. Gregory in the New York *American*, 5 March 1915.
See also the endorsement of the film's version of history by Booth Tarkington
and other notables in the Boston *Globe*, 9 April 1915.

133 ELDERLY KLANSMEN: John A Wyeth in the New York *Sun*, 14 April 1915;
other recollections by Reconstruction Klansmen appear in several clippings in
the Griffith Pressbooks, Museum of Modern Art.

133 DIXON TO WILSON: 4 March 1915; 5 March 1915, Wilson Papers.

133 OSWALD VILLARD: New York *Evening Post*, 6 March 1915; DuBois, "Calumny," p. 41. For a chronical of the antagonism between Villard and Wilson,
see Villard to Wilson, 21 July 1913; Wilson to Villard, 23 July 1913; Villard to
Wilson, 24 August 1913, Wilson to Villard, 29 August 1913, Wilson Papers.

133 "THE GROUND OF MY PROTEST . . .": Frederic C. Howe in an unidentified, undated clipping, Griffith Pressbooks.

133 JANE ADDAMS'S CHALLENGE: Jane Addams in New York *Evening Post*, 13
March 1915.

134 CRITICISM FROM HIGH CIRCLES: Upton Sinclair in an undated clipping
from the New York *Call*; Jacques Loeb, Samuel Crothers, and Albert B. Hart
in unidentified, undated clippings, Griffith Pressbooks. See also Francis Hack-
ett, "Brotherly Love," *New Republic* 2 (20 March 1915): 185.

134 TOM DIXON'S PEPPERY DEFENSE: New York *Sun*, 12 April 1915.

134 PACE OF THE CONTROVERSY QUICKENED: DuBois, "Calumny," p. 41; New
York *World*, 24 March 1915.

134 MAYOR MITCHELL: DuBois, "Calumny," pp. 41–42.

135 "BREACH OF THE PEACE": Numerous clippings of the egg incident, from
newspapers coast to coast, may be found in the Griffith Pressbooks, Museum
of Modern Art. By March 9, the film was bringing in $2,000 a day at the Liberty
(Dixon to Tumulty, 9 March 1915, Wilson Papers). See also W.E.B. DuBois,
"The Slanderous Film," *The Crisis* 10 (December 1915): 76–77.

135 MAYOR CURLEY HEARINGS: W.E.B. DuBois, "Fighting Race Calumny,"
The Crisis 10 (June 1915): 87; Cripps, "Reaction of the Negro," pp. 354–55;
Boston *Post*, undated clipping, Griffith Pressbooks.

135 COBLEIGH AND DIXON: Rolfe Cobleigh in an affidavit, dated 26 May 1915,
Boston, reprinted in NAACP, *Fighting a Vicious Film: Protest Against The
Birth of a Nation"* (Boston: Boston Branch of the National Association for the
Advancement of Colored People, 1915), p. 26, Museum of Modern Art Li-
brary.

136 BOSTON RIOT: Boston *Evening Transcript*, 19 April 1915; Boston *Globe*, 19
April 1915; Boston *Post*, 19 April 1915; Boston *Sunday Globe*, 18 April 1915;
Christian Science Monitor, 19 April 1915.

136 JUSTICE WHITE: White to Tumulty, 5 April 1915, Wilson Papers.

136 WILSON'S ANNOYANCE: Alexander Walters (President of the National Colored Democratic League) to Wilson, 30 April 1915; Thomas. C. Thatcher to Wilson, 17 April 1915; Tumulty to Wilson, Memo dated 24 April 1915, Wilson Papers.

137 "DEAR TUMULTY . . . UNSPEAKABLE FELLOW TUCKER.": Wilson to Tumulty, undated memo, Case File 2247, Wilson Papers. Monroe Trotter headed a delegation that had called on Wilson in the White House in November 1914, to complain about his segregation policy. When Wilson appeared unmoved, Trotter had told him that a continuation of the policy would cost him the black vote. Calling Trotter's threat "blackmail," Wilson had angrily dismissed the delegation; see *New York Times* 13 November 1915.

137 "DEAR TUMULTY . . . AN OLD ACQUAINTANCE.": Wilson to Tumulty, 28 (?) April 1915, Wilson Papers.

137 "THERE IS NO POSSIBILITY . . .": Cambridge *Chronicle*, 15 May 1915.

138 "I HAD A GOOD LAUGH . . .": Dixon to Tumulty, 1 May 1915, Wilson Papers.

138 "THIS PLAY IS TRANSFORMING . . .": Dixon to Wilson, 7 September 1915, ibid.

138 NORTHERN REACTION: *Moving Picture World*, 1 May 1915; Trenton *Times*, 24 August 1915; Philadelphia *Public Ledger*, 14 August 1915; Pittsburgh *Press*, 25 August 1915; Chicago *Examiner*, 24 August 1915; Milwaukee *Free Press*, 11 March 1915; Spokane *Review*, 20 July 1915; Portland *Oregonian*, 21 August 1915; see also Edward Wagenknecht, *The Movies in the Age of Innocence* (Norman, OK: Univ. Oklahoma Press, 1962), p. 109.

138 SOUTHERN REACTION: Bosley Crowther, "The Birth of 'The Birth of a Nation,' " *New York Times Magazine* 116 (7 February 1965): 85; Moore, "South Carolina's Reaction," pp. 37–40.

139 "SOCIAL GROUPS AND SOCIETIES . . .": Chicago *Examiner*, 29 October 1915.

5. *"Here Yesterday, Here Today, Here Forever"*

140 "THE NUMBER OF PEOPLE ON THE BORDERLINE . . .": Clarence Darrow, *The Story of My Life* (New York: Scribners, 1960), p. 279.

140 SIMMONS'S EARLY LIFE: William G. Shepherd, "How I Put Over the Klan," *Colliers* 82 (14 July 1928): 7, 32; Charles O. Jackson, "William J. Simmons: A Career in Ku Kluxism," *Georgia Historical Quarterly* 50 (1966): 351–53; William J. Simmons, *America's Menace or the Enemy Within* (Atlanta: Patriotic Books, 1926), pp. 60–65; Winfield Jones, *Knights of the Ku Klux Klan* (New York: Tocsin, 1941), pp. 74–80; Marion Monteval, *The Klan Inside Out* (Chicago: n.p., 1924), pp. 7–8; New York *World*, 26 September 1921.

141 "ONCE WE HAD A NEIGHBORHOOD . . .": *New Republic* 35 (15 August 1923): 328.

142 "THEIR WEIGHT WAS . . . FOURTH AT POKER.": Ralph McGill, *The South and the Southerner* (Boston: Little, Brown, 1963). p. 131.

142 "IT WAS RATHER DIFFICULT . . .": Shepherd, "How I Put Over," p. 32.

143 "ITS RITUALISM IS VASTLY . . .": *The ABC of the Knights of the Ku Klux Klan*, Exhibit G in U.S. Congress, *The Ku Klux Klan Hearings*. 67 Cong., 1

Sess., House Committee on Rules (1921): 121 (hereafter cited as *KKK Hearings*).

143 "WHAT DO YOU THINK OF IT, WALTER? . . .": Ward Greene, "Notes for a History of the Klan," *American Mercury* 5 (June 1925): 240.

143 LEO FRANK CASE: Harry Golden, *A Little Girl Is Dead* (New York: World, 1965); Leonard Dinnerstein, *The Leo Frank Case* (New York: Columbia Univ. Press, 1968); Clement C. Moseley, "The Case of Leo M. Frank, 1913–1915," *Georgia Historical Quarterly* 51 (March 1967): 42–62; *New York Times*, 8 March, 12 March 1982. On March 11, 1986, the Georgia Board of Pardons and Paroles gave Frank a posthumous pardon.

143 THOMAS E. WATSON: Golden, *A Little Girl*, pp. 214, 220, 283; Gustavus Myers, *A History of Bigotry* (New York: Capricorn, 1960), pp. 192–210; C. Vann Woodward, *Tom Watson: Agrarian Rebel* (New York: Oxford Univ. Press, 1963), pp. 435–46. Woodward maintains "if any mortal man may be credited . . . with releasing the forces of human malice and ignorance and prejudice, which the Klan merely mobilized, that man was Thomas E. Watson" (p. 450). "Jimmy Cheezy," by the way, refers to Giacomo della Chiesa who became Pope Benedict XV (1914–1922).

144 KNIGHTS OF MARY PHAGAN: Golden, *A Little Girl*, pp. 288–89.

144 CHARTERING THE KKK: Jones, *Knights of the KKK*, p. 82; *KKK Hearings*, Exhibit A, pp. 101–102.

145 "JESUS, DOC . . .": McGill, *South and Southerner*, p. 132.

145 "IT WAS PITCH DARK . . . FOR HUMANITY'S GOOD . . .": In his lifetime, Simmons told several versions of this story which are herewith combined: Shepherd, "How I Put Over," pp. 32–34; *Dawn*, 9 December 1922; *KKK Hearings*, Exhibit G, p. 122.

146 AMERICAN ORDER OF KLANSMEN: *Fraternal Monitor* 30 (November 1916): 23.

146 BIRTH OF A NATION AND REVIVED KLAN: Crowther, "Birth of 'The Birth,' " p. 85; Maxim Simcovitch, "The Impact of Griffith's *Birth of a Nation* on the Modern Ku Klux Klan," *Journal of Popular Film* 1 (1972): 45–48.

147 "NEVER BEFORE, PERHAPS . . .": Atlanta *Constitution*, 7 December 1915.

147 "ONLY NATIVE BORN AMERICANS . . .": Jones, *Knights of the KKK*, p. 113; *KKK Hearings*, Exhibit G, p. 122. Contrast this with the innocuous goals stated in an early Klan pamphlet by the Wizard: W. J. Simmons, *Imperial Proclamation of the Imperial Wizard* (Atlanta: KKK, 1917; copy in Rare Book and Special Collections, Library of Congress, Washington, D.C.).

148 RISING NATIVISM: Madison Grant, *The Passing of the Great Race* (New York: Scribners, 1916), p. 263, and see also Charles C. Alexander, "Prophet of American Racism: Madison Grant and the Nordic Myth," *Phylon* 23 (1962): 73–90; William McDougall, *Is America Safe for Democracy?* (1921; reprint New York: Arno, 1977); Prescot F. Hall, "Aristocracy and Politics," *Journal of Heredity* 10 (1919): 166; see also Seymour M. Lipset, "An Anatomy of the Klan," *Commentary* 40 (October 1965): 78.

148 "ANY MAN WHO CARRIES . . .": *Selected Literary and Political Papers and Addresses of Woodrow Wilson*, ed. Ray Stannard Baker and William E. Dodd (New York: Grosset & Dunlap, 1926–1927), II: 370.

149 WAR-TIME SUPPRESSION: H. Peterson and G. Fite, *Opponents of War, 1917–1918* (Madison: Univ. Wisconsin Press, 1957); Robert H. Wiebe, *The Search for Order: 1877–1920* (New York: Hill & Wang, 1967), pp. 286–302; Guy

B. Johnson, "A Sociological Interpretation of the New Ku Klux Movement," *Social Forces* 1 (May 1923): 441; Norman F. Weaver, "The Knights of the Ku Klux Klan in Wisconsin, Indiana, Ohio, and Michigan" (Ph.D. diss., University of Wisconsin, 1954), pp. 30–35.

149 "CONSCRIPTED PUBLIC OPINION . . .": *New Republic* 21 (31 December 1919): 144.

149 KLAN AND WILSON'S DOMESTIC PROGRAM: William Shepherd, "Ku Klux Koin," *Colliers* 82 (21 July 1928): 8–9; *New York Times*, 1 September 1918.

150 "YOUR FRIENDS STATE YOU ARE . . .": Form letter in Presidential Papers of Calvin Coolidge, Case File 28, Manuscript Division, Library of Congress.

150 "THERE WERE TIMES . . .": Shepherd, "How I Put Over," p. 35.

151 RACE RIOTS AND LYNCHINGS: Mary Frances Berry and John W. Blassingame, *Long Memory: The Black Experience in America* (New York: Oxford Univ. Press, 1982), pp. 317–18; Richard Hofstadter and Michael Wallace, eds., *American Violence: a Documentary History* (New York: Vintage, 1971), pp. 245–49.

151 "UNDER SIMILAR CIRCUMSTANCES . . .": *Crisis* 17 (May 1919): 13–14.

151 "BEFORE PROHIBITION IS EFFECTIVE . . .": *New York Times*, 22 January 1919.

152 RED SCARE: Stanley Coben, "A Study in Nativism: the American Red Scare of 1919–1920," *Political Science Quarterly* 79 (March 1964): 52–75; Robert K. Murray, *Red Scare: A Study in National Hysteria, 1919–1920* (Minneapolis: Univ. Minnesota Press, 1955); Louis F. Post, *The Deportations Delirium of Nineteen-Twenty* (Chicago: Kerr, 1923); John Higham, *Strangers in the Land* (New York: Atheneum, 1963), pp. 194–233.

152 "I CONSIDER IT AN HONOR . . .": *Literary Digest* 64 (3 January 1920): 15.

152 LOUIS F. POST: Post, *Deportations Delirium, passim*; Dominic Candeloro, "Louis Post as a Carpetbagger in South Carolina: Reconstruction as a Forerunner of the Progressive Movement," *American Journal of Economics and Sociology* 34 (October 1975): 423–32.

153 "IN THE LIGHT . . .": *Christian Science Monitor*, 25 June 1920.

153 "WE HAD IMAGINED OURSELVES . . .": Charles Ferguson quoted in Robert Coughlan, "Klonklave in Kokomo" in *The Aspirin Age*, ed. Isabel Leighton (New York: Simon & Schuster, 1949), p. 111; see also Paul L. Murphy, "Sources and Nature of Intolerance in the 1920s," *Journal of American History* 51 (June 1964): 60–76.

153 CLARKE AND TYLER: *Literary Digest* 70 (24 September 1921): 34–40; Robert L. Duffus, "How the Ku Klux Klan Sells Hate," *World's Work* 46 (June 1923): 174–83; Greene, "Notes," p. 241; Edgar I. Fuller, *The Visible of the Invisible Empire: "The Maelstrom,"* ed. George LaDura (Denver: Maelstrom, 1925), p. 18; Ezra A. Cook, *Ku Klux Secrets Exposed* (Chicago: Cook, 1922), p. 27; McGill, *South and Southerner*, pp. 133–34; Jones, *Knights of the KKK*, p. 109; New York *World*, 26 September 1921.

154 "CAME INTO CONTACT . . . FROM PUBLICITY": *Literary Digest* 70 (24 September 1921): 34–40.

154 "MR. SIMMONS . . . IT'LL COST SOMETHING": *KKK Hearings*, p. 87.

154 CLARKE'S PROMOTION PROGRAM: Charles C. Alexander, "Kleagles and Cash: the Ku Klux Klan as a Business Organization, 1915–1930," *Business History Review* 39 (1965): 351–53; Jones, *Knights of the KKK*, pp. 112–13; Henry P. Fry, The *Modern Ku Klux Klan* (Boston: Small & Maynard, 1922),

pp. 47–49; New York *World*, 26 September 1921; *KKK Hearings*, pp. 86–88, 151–52.

155 KLEAGLES' ACTIVITIES: Duffus, "How the Klan Sells Hate," pp. 178–79; Simcovitch, "Birth of a Nation," pp. 48–51; Stanley Frost, "When the Klan Rules," *Outlook* 136 (23 January 1924): 145; New York *World*, 9 September 1921; Samuel T. Moore, "How the Kleagles Collected the Cash," *Independent* 113 (December 1924): 517–19.

155 "WANTED: FRATERNAL ORGANIZERS . . .": Robert A. Goldberg, "The Ku Klux Klan in Madison, 1922–1929," *Wisconsin Magazine of History* 58 (1974): 33. The Klan also found Masonic support in Oregon, especially among Scottish Rite Masons; see William Toll, "Progress and Piety: The Ku Klux Klan and Social Change in Tillamook, Oregon," *Pacific Northwest Quarterly* 69 (April 1978): 76. One Klansman of the 1920s recalled the Klan as "the fun-making social side of the Masons," in M. L. Dillon, "Captain Jason W. James—Frontier Anti-Democrat," *New Mexico Historical Review* 31 (April 1956): 99.

156 "NEVER BEFORE HAD A SINGLE SOCIETY . . .": Higham, *Strangers*, p. 289; see also Weaver, "Knights of the KKK," pp. 300–301.

156 "THE DECLARATION OF INDEPENDENCE . . .": Flyer in the Edwin Banta Papers, Box 1, "K" File, Manuscripts and Archives Division, New York Public Library, New York, New York.

157 IMPACT OF CLARKE'S PROGRAM: Alexander, "Kleagles and Cash," p. 353; *KKK Hearings*, p. 87; *New York Times*, 23 September 1937.

157 EARNINGS OF CLARKE, TYLER, SIMMONS: *KKK Hearings*, p. 154.

157 SIMMONS AS FIGUREHEAD: Frank Bohn, "The Ku Klux Klan Interpreted," *American Journal of Sociology* 30 (January 1925): 391–92; Walter F. White, "Reviving the Ku Klux Klan," *Forum* 65 (April 1921): 429–30; *New Republic* 28 (21 September 1921): 88–89.

159 "THE KLAN IS ORGANIZED . . .": Quoted in Mark Sullivan, *Our Times*, (New York: Scribners, 1936), VI: 545–46; for the effect of this article on Klan growth, see *KKK Hearings*, p. 24.

159 KLAN CONTINUED TO PROSPER: Monteval, *Klan Inside Out*, pp. 41–42; Fry, *Modern Klan*, pp. 42–43; *Imperial Night-Hawk*, 4 April 1923; *KKK Hearings*, p. 133.

159 "THERE WAS SO MUCH MONEY . . .": Shepherd, "Ku Klux Koin," p. 38.

159 "THE KKK HAS NOT YET STARTED . . .": New York *World*, 13 September 1921.

159 NATHAN BEDFORD FORREST III: Stanley Frost, *The Challenge of the Klan* (Indianapolis: Bobbs-Merrill, 1924), p. 31. Forrest later became Grand Dragon of Georgia.

160 KLAN VIOLENCE: New York *World*, 19 September 1921; Albert de Silver, "The Ku Klux Klan, Soul of Chivalry," *Nation* 113 (14 September 1921): 285; Higham, *Strangers*, p. 290.

160 NEW YORK *WORLD*: New York *World*, 6–26 September 1921; see also Silas Bent, *Newspaper Crusaders: a Neglected Story* (New York: Whittlesey, 1939), pp. 139–40; John Hohenberg, *The Pulitzer Prize Story* (New York: Columbia Univ. Press, 1959), pp. 70–76.

161 "THE PICAYUNISH COWARDICE . . .": New York *World*, 19 September 1921.

161 "THE FORMER METHODIST EXHORTER . . .": Ibid., 13 September 1921; H. L. Mencken, *A Carnival of Buncombe*, ed. Malcolm Moos (Baltimore: Johns Hopkins Press, 1956), p. 47.

161 "I DROPPED INTO A CLAM CHOWDER . . .": New York *World*, 15 September 1921.

162 "THE PUBLICITY GIVEN US . . .": Ibid., 11 September 1921.

162 "WEEK-KNEED AND WON'T STAND . . .": Ibid., 26 September 1921.

162 "WE DEMUR TO THE WORDING . . .": *KKK Hearings*, Exhibit H, p. 127.

162 SIMMONS IN WASHINGTON: Atlanta *Constitution*, 11–12 October 1921.

163 "I AM A SICK MAN . . .": *KKK Hearings*, p. 68.

163 SIMMONS'S MONOLOGUE: Ibid., pp. 71–74, 87–89, 96, 130–31, passim.

163 SIMMONS'S DEATHBED SPEECH: Ibid., pp. 138, 142; Atlanta *Constitution*, 14 October 1921.

165 "EXALTED TO A POSITION OF HONOR . . .": Reuben H. Sawyer, *The Truth about the Invisible Empire* (Portland, OR: Pacific Northwest Domain No. 5, 1922; copy in New York Public Library), n.p.

165 "NOT A SINGLE SOLITARY SOUND REASON . . .": Article from the *Smart Set* reprinted in *Dawn*, 17 March 1923.

165 HARDING'S INITIATION: The matter was a major issue in letters sent to Coolidge during the 1924 election (see Case File 28, Calvin Coolidge Papers, Manuscript Division, Library of Congress). The description here is from the recollections of former Imperial Klokard Alton Young, who had been a member of the Presidential Induction Team. Stetson Kennedy and Elizabeth Gardner tape-recorded Young's recollections in the late 1940s, while Young was on his death bed in a New Jersey hospital (Stetson Kennedy to W.C.W., 5 June 1985).

165 EFFECT AT IMPERIAL HEADQUARTERS: E. Y. Clarke, 1 January 1922, quoted in Jones, *Knights of the KKK*, p. 111; *Nation* 115 (5 July 1922): 8–10.

166 "IT WASN'T UNTIL NEWSPAPERS . . .": Shepherd, "Ku Klux Koin," p. 38. Regarding the *World*'s exposé, Klansmen later argued with justification: "They had made the Klan appear in the light of a martyr in the eyes of an American public which in every battle or contest demands fair play" (*Papers Read at the Meeting of the Grand Dragons—Knights of the Ku Klux Klan—at their first Annual Meeting Held at Asheville, North Carolina, July 1923*, p. 95).

6. "I Found Christ through the Ku Klux Klan"

167 "SHALL THE FUNDAMENTALISTS WIN?": *Christian Century*, 8 June 1922; though Fosdick identified fundamentalists principally with the Baptist and Presbyterian denominations, Methodists must also be included.

167 SOCIAL GOSPEL: Paul A. Carter, *The Decline and Revival of the Social Gospel* (Ithaca: Cornell Univ. Press, 1954); Henry F. May, *The End of American Innocence* (New York: Knopf, 1959). For the relationship between the *Titanic* disaster and the decline of the social gospel, see Wyn C. Wade, *The Titanic: End of a Dream* (New York: Rawson, 1979), pp. 63–66, 296.

168 FUNDAMENTALISM: The best history of fundamentalism to date is George M. Marsden, *Fundamentalism and American Culture* (New York: Oxford Univ. Press, 1980); see also Paul A. Carter, "The Fundamentalist Defense of the Faith" in *Change and Continuity in Twentieth-Century America: the 1920s*, ed. John Braeman, Robert H. Brenner, and David Brody (Columbus: Ohio State Univ. Press, 1968), pp. 179–214; Norman Furniss, *The Fundamentalist Controversy, 1918–1931* (New Haven: Yale Univ. Press, 1954).

168 "IT MUST BE REMEMBERED THAT . . .": *The Presbyterian* 90 (8 January

1920): 3, my italics. A contemporary corrective to Kennedy's remarks about the founding fathers may be found in William Seagle, "A Christian Country," *American Mercury* 6 (1925): 226–233.

169 "HEAVE AN EGG . . .": In Edward D. Jervey, "Henry L. Mencken and American Methodism," *Journal of Popular Culture* 12 (1978): 80.

169 "I DON'T KNOW ANY MORE . . .": William G. McLoughlin, Jr., *Billy Sunday Was His Real Name* (Chicago: Univ. Chicago Press, 1955), p. 123.

169 FUNDAMENTALISM AND THE KLAN: "Though not all Fundamentalists were Klansmen, virtually all Klansmen—aside from the obvious charlatans—were Fundamentalists": Robert M. Miller, "The Ku Klux Klan" in *Change and Continuity*, p. 223. Journalist Stanley Frost, who interviewed hundreds of Klansmen in the 1920s, reported, "Every Klansman I have met, save one, is a Fundamentalist . . ." in *The Challenge of the Klan* (Indianapolis: Bobbs-Merrill, 1924), p. 174.

169 "STIMULATE A RENEWED INTEREST . . .": Quoted in Frank Bohn, "The Ku Klux Klan Interpreted," *American Journal of Sociology* 30 (January 1925): 398.

169 "ORTHODOX TENETS OF EVANGELICALISM . . .": John Moffatt Mecklin, *The Ku Klux Klan: a Study of the American Mind* (New York: Harcourt, Brace, 1924), p. 19.

170 CLARKE'S RELIGIOUS INTERESTS: Edgar I. Fuller, *The Visible of the Invisible Empire: "The Maelstrom,"* ed. George La Dura (Denver: Maelstrom, 1925), pp. 26–27.

170 KLEAGLES AND CLERGYMEN: F. Dean Lueking, "Roots of the Radical Right," *Lutheran Quarterly* 18 (1966): 197–204; Miller, "Ku Klux Klan," pp. 222–23; Ezra A. Cook, *Ku Klux Klan Secrets Exposed* (Chicago: Cook, 1922), p. 29; William M. Likens, *Patriotism Capitalized or Religion Turned into Gold* (Uniontown, PA: Watchman, 1925; copy in Library of Congress); Gerald W. Johnson, "The Ku-Kluxer," *American Mercury* 1 (February 1924): 211. Norman Weaver claims that when ministers refused to join the Klan, pressure was put on them by the Klan members of their congregations, in "The Knights of the Ku Klux Klan in Wisconsin, Indiana, Ohio, and Michigan" (Ph.D. diss., University of Wisconsin, 1954), p. 13.

170 "I BELIEVE IN GOD . . .": "A Klansman's Creed," Klan pamphlet in Ku Klux Klan Collection, Special Collections, Michigan State University Library, East Lansing, MI (hereafter cited KKK Collection, MSU.)

170 "WE MAGNIFY THE BIBLE . . .": William J. Mahoney, *Some Ideals of the Ku Klux Klan* (Atlanta: KKK, n.d.), n.p.; for nearly identical tracts see George S. Clason, *Catholic, Jew, Ku Klux Klan* (Chicago: Nutshell, 1924), p. 10; Walter C. Wright, *Religious and Patriotic Ideals of the Ku Klux Klan* (Waco: Wright, 1926), p. 15.

171 "IF THEY HAD BROUGHT THEIR PLEDGE . . .": Dixon Merritt, "Klan and Anti-Klan in Indiana," *Outlook* 144 (8 December 1926): 465.

171 MINISTERS IN THE KLAN: Passim in David M. Chalmers, *Hooded Americanism* (New York: Doubleday, 1965); Charles C. Alexander, *The Ku Klux Klan in the Southwest* (Lexington: Univ. Kentucky Press, 1966); Kenneth T. Jackson, *The Ku Klux Klan in the City: 1915–1930* (New York: Oxford Univ. Press, 1967); Michael Williams, *The Shadow of the Pope* (New York: McGraw-Hill, 1932).

171 POSTWAR LOSS OF POWER AND STATUS: Guy B. Johnson, "A Sociological

Interpretation of the New Ku Klux Movement," *Social Forces* 1 (May 1923): 442–43; H. L. Mencken in *A Carnival of Buncombe*, ed. Malcolm Moos (Baltimore: Johns Hopkins Press, 1956), pp. 165–66.

172 "FIFTY YEARS AGO . . .": E. F. Stanton, *Christ and Other Klansmen or Lives of Love* (Kansas City: Stanton & Harper, 1924; copy in Library of Congress), p. 35.

172 "THE RETURN OF THE PURITANS . . .": Chalmers, *Hooded Americanism*, p. 218.

172 "MILITANCE" AND "VIRILTY": Bernard A. Weisberger, *They Gathered at the River* (Boston: Little, Brown, 1958), pp. 241, 247; *Dawn*, 2 December 1922, 24 March 1923; *Kourier*, January 1925, July 1925, December 1925; see also Robert A. Goldberg, "The Ku Klux Klan in Madison, 1922–1929," *Wisconsin Magazine of History* 58 (1974): 34; William D. Jenkins, "The Ku Klux Klan in Youngstown, Ohio: Moral Reform in the Twenties," *Historian* 41 (1978): 80–87. Klansmen likewise criticized "modernist" ministers as "pulpit dilettantes" and "sweet-scented sentimentalists" (*Papers Read at the Meeting of Grand Dragons —Knights of the Ku Klux Klan—at their first Annual Meeting Held at Asheville, North Carolina, July 1923*, p. 133).

173 "A FEW YEARS BEFORE . . .": William E. Wilson, *The Wabash* (New York: Farrar & Rinehart, 1940), p. 294.

173 "PILGRIM FATHERS ARRIVED . . .": *Our Sunday Visitor*, 5 August 1923; see also Lem A. Dever, *Confessions of an Imperial Klansman* (Portland, OR: Dever, 1924; copy in Library of Congress), p. 12.

173 KLAN OPPOSED BY HIGHER CHURCH AUTHORITIES: Robert M. Miller has reviewed the official publications of Protestant sects during the twenties and concluded that the Klan was "not an instrument of Protestantism," in "A Note on the Relationship Between the Protestant Churches and the Revived Ku Klux Klan," *Journal of Southern History* 22 (August 1956): 355–68. This is looking at Protestantism only from the top, however. For a different conclusion, see Robert A. Goldberg, *Hooded Empire: the Ku Klux Klan in Colorado* (Urbana: Univ. of Illinois Press, 1981), p. 188. It had long been thought that Mormons had stayed away from the Klan; that assumption is overturned in Larry R. Gerlach, *Blazing Crosses in Zion: the Ku Klux Klan in Utah* (Logan: Utah State Univ. Press, 1982), pp. 107–108.

173 "SECRET ASSOCIATIONS ARE NO . . .": The lines quoted are pieced together from two excerpts of Marvin's sermon printed in *Dawn*, 12 May 1923, and *Imperial Night-Hawk*, 6 June 1923.

173 MCGHEE VS. MCMURRAY: Kansas City *Journal*, 3 September 1923; for more on this subject see Frost, *Challenge of the Klan*, p. 175; Mencken, *Buncombe*, p. 195; *New York Times*, 24 February 1924.

174 ANGER OVER THE HELPLESSNESS OF GOVERNMENT: Sue W. Abbey, "The Ku Klux Klan in Arizona, 1921–1925," *Journal of Arizona History* 14 (1973): 13; *Dawn*, 23 December 1922; *Searchlight*, 4 March 1922; Jenkins, "The Klan in Youngstown," p. 83; see also Goldberg, "The Klan in Madison," p. 37.

174 "FIGHTING BOB" SHULER: Duncan Aikman, "Savonarola in Los Angeles," *American Mercury* 21 (December 1930): 423–30; *Literary Digest* 114 (29 October 1932): 20; Ralph L. Roy, *Apostles of Discord* (Boston: Beacon, 1953), pp. 329–32; Edmund Wilson, "The City of Our Lady the Queen of the Angels: II," *New Republic* 69 (9 December 1931): 89–93. For Shuler's defense of the Klan, see *Literary Digest* 76 (20 January 1923): 18–19; for his attack on Aimee Mc-

Pherson, see Robert P. Shuler, A *Study of Healing Cults and Modern Day "Tongue" Movements* (Los Angeles: Shuler, 1924). Shuler's broadcasts on his own radio station were noted for their anti-Catholicism and anti-Semitism. In 1932, he frightened both Democrats and Republicans by running for the U.S. Senate in California on the Prohibition ticket. In the 1950s, he suggested that all Methodist ministers take a loyalty oath against Communism. He supported MacArthur for the Presidency in 1952, endorsed Franco's Spain, and retired from his Trinity pulpit in 1953.

175 KLAN STEPS UP THE RELIGIOUS CAMPAIGN: *New York Times,* 18 November 1923; *Imperial Night-Hawk,* 18 April 1923, 2 May 1923, 6 June 1923; Alexander, *The Klan in the Southwest,* p. 87. For the issue of the Bible in public schools, see Philip N. Racine, "The Ku Klux Klan, Anti-Catholicism, and Atlanta's Board of Education, 1916–1927," *Georgia Historical Quarterly* 57 (1973): 63–75; *Dawn,* 28 July 1923, 11 August 1923; *Kourier,* May 1925.

175 "THE KU KLUX KLAN IS SWEEPING . . .": In Bohn, "Klan Interpreted," pp. 400–401.

176 "EVIDENCE THEIR DEVOTION TO . . .": G. E. Carr to All Exalted Cyclops. 10 December 1926, KKK Collection, MSU.

176 CHURCH VISITATION: Robert L. Duffus, "How the Ku Klux Klan Sells Hate," *World's Work* 46 (June 1923): 180; Alexander, *The Klan in the Southwest,* pp. 87–88; Weaver, "Knights of the KKK," p. 159.

176 "DEAR MR. JEETER . . .": Abbey, "The Klan in Arizona," p. 13.

176 "IN THE EARLY DAYS OF CHRISTIANITY . . .": Indianapolis *Times,* 2 April 1923.

176 BILLY SUNDAY, BOB JONES, AND THE KLAN: McLoughlin, *Billy Sunday,* pp. 274–76; Indianapolis *News,* 15 May 1922; William R. Snell, "Fiery Crosses in the Roaring Twenties: Activities of the Revised Klan in Alabama, 1915–1930," *Alabama Review* 23 (1970): 268.

177 "I AM A SEARCHLIGHT . . .": In *American Mercury* 1 (April 1924): 432.

177 "AND GIVE $50 TO A . . .": *New York Times,* 17 December 1922.

177 "GOOD MEN, CHRISTIAN MEN . . .": Leroy Percy, "The Modern Ku Klux Klan," *Atlantic Monthly* 130 (July 1922): 126–28.

178 "PUTTING CHRISTIANITY TO A USE . . .": Glenn Frank, "Christianity and Racialism," *Century* 109 (December 1924): 279. For more arguments in this vein, see Frank R. Kent, "The Ku Klux Klan in America," *Spectator* 130 (17 February 1923): 279–80; Lloyd C. Douglas, "The Patriotism of Hatred," *Christian Century* 40 (25 October 1923): 1371–74.

178 "WOULD HUNDREDS OF PROTESTANT MINISTERS . . .": *Imperial Night-Hawk,* 16 May 1923.

178 A UNIFYING FORCE FOR DISPARATE PROTESTANT SECTS: Wright, *Religious and Patriotic Ideals,* p. 16; Klan flyer, KKK Collection, MSU; *Dawn,* 16 December 1922; *Imperial Night-Hawk,* 14 February 1924.

178 CHRISTIAN PERSECUTIONS: Norman Cohn, *The Pursuit of the Millennium* (New York: Oxford Univ. Press, 1970); Ezra H. Byington, *The Puritan in England and New England* (Boston: Roberts, 1896).

179 THE KLAN'S ANTI-SEMITISM: Cook, *Klan Secrets Exposed,* p. 45; Alma White, *The Ku Klux Klan in Prophecy* (Zarephath, NJ: Good Citizen, 1925), p. 27; *Principles and Purposes of the Knights of the Ku Klux Klan are Outlined by an Exalted Cyclops of the Order* (Portland, ME: n.p., n.d.; copy in Calvin Coolidge Papers, Manuscript Division, Library of Congress). See also Samuel

H. Campbell, *The Jewish Problem in the United States* (Atlanta: KKK, 1923; copy in Rare Book and Special Collections, Library of Congress; Hiram W. Evans, *The Attitude of the Knights of the Ku Klux Klan Toward the Jew* (Atlanta: KKK, 1923; copy in Rare Book and Special Collections, Library of Congress); Stanton, *Christ and Other Klansmen*, p. 15.

179 "CHRISTIANITY IN AN ITALIAN DRESS . . .": Charles E. Jefferson, *Roman Catholicism and the Ku Klux Klan* (New York: Revell, 1924; copy in New York Public Library), pp. 146, 151.

179 "DO YOU KNOW . . .": In Everett R. Clinchy, *All in the Name of God* (New York: John Day, 1934), p. 107.

179 "I WOULD RATHER BE A KLANSMAN . . .": Election placard, KKK Collection, MSU.

180 "PATRIOTS, VIEW THE HELLISH . . .": In Clinchy, *In the Name of God*, p. 108. See also *Fellowship Forum*, 1 November 1924; J. S. Fleming, *What Is Ku-Kluxism?* (Goodwater, AL: Fleming, 1923); Williams, *Shadow of the Pope*, passim.

180 HELEN JACKSON: *Dawn*, 2 June 1923; *Our Sunday Visitor*, 27 May 1923. Jackson's maiden name was Helen Barnowska. Her sister committed her to a Catholic reformatory in 1895. Other "escaped nuns" like Jackson were Mabel McClish and Mary Slattery.

180 "FIVE STATES NOW . . . ROMAN CATHOLICS": "Roman Catholic Statistics," flyer, KKK Collection, MSU; *Dawn*, 26 May 1923.

181 "NEARLY ALL THE BAWDYHOUSES . . .": In Jackson, *The Klan in the City*, p. 189.

181 "THE KLAN SHOULD BE DEFENDED . . .": Ibid., p. 176.

181 ALMA BRIDWELL WHITE: Quotations are from Alma White, *The Klan in Prophecy*, pp. 130, 112–13; idem, *Heroes of the Fiery Cross* (Zarephath, NJ: Good Citizen, 1928), pp. 17, 149. For White's career, see *American Magazine* 123 (May 1937): 101; *Literary Digest* 122 (5 September 1936): 30–31; *National Cyclopedia of American Biography*, 35: 151–52; *New York Times*, 27 June 1946; *Our Sunday Visitor*, 2 September 1923; *Time* 34 (18 December 1939): 40; ibid. 48 (8 July 1946): 73–74. Bishop White's Klan books and tracts are excluded from her official bibliography in the *National Cyclopedia* article. She definitely deserves a complete monograph, preferably by a feminist scholar in theology or American history.

182 STAR-SPANGLED BANNER: *Dawn*, 28 July 1923.

182 KLAN DENOUNCED THE BOY SCOUTS: James E. West (president of the Boy Scouts of America) to C. B. Slemp, 18 October 1924, Coolidge Papers.

182 HAROLD THE KLANSMAN: George Alfred Brown, *Harold the Klansman* (Kansas City: Western Baptist Publishing Company, 1923; copy in Special Collections, MSU Library), pp. 25, 300.

183 THE KLAN AS CHURCH: California *Voice*, 24 July 1924; Emerson H. Loucks, *The Ku Klux Klan in Pennsylvania: A Study in Nativism* (Harrisburg: Telegraph Press, 1936), p. 120.

183 MEMPHIS CITY CLUB: *Our Sunday Visitor*, 3 July 1923.

183 "A WHITE ROBE OF LIGHTWEIGHT COTTON . . .": *Constitution and Laws of the Knights of the Ku Klux Klan* (Atlanta: KKK, 1921), Article XIV, Section 2. For those interested, a Klan robe from the 1920s is available for detailed inspection in the Costume Collection of the Chicago Historical Society.

183 "A HOLY EXPERIENCE": Private information, 8 April 1981. The author re-

grets this citation, but none of the Klansmen and women survivors from the 1920s, who were interviewed for this book, permitted the use of their names or descriptions of their backgrounds.

183 KLANKRAFT AND CATHOLICISM: For further comparison, see Richard Hofstadter, *The Paranoid Style in American Politics and Other Essays* (New York: Knopf, 1966), p. 32.

184 "I AM A MEMBER OF THE KLAN . . .": In Robert S. Lynd and Helen M. Lynd, *Middletown: A Study in Contemporary American Culture* (New York: Harcourt, 1929), p. 483.

184 "THIS IS A ONE-HUNDRED PERCENT . . .": *Fellowship Forum*, 1 November 1924.

184 KLAN WEDDINGS: Ibid., 5 December 1925; Craig Swallow, "The Ku Klux Klan in Nevada During the 1920's," *Nevada Historical Quarterly* 24 (1981): 209; see also *New York Times*, 27 April 1925.

185 "I WANT TO JOIN THE CHURCH . . .": *California Voice*, 24 July 1924.

185 "NO PERSON OR PERSONS . . .": In Stanley L. Swart, "A Memo on Cross Burning—and Its Implications," *Northwest Ohio Quarterly* 43 (1971): 70.

185 CROSS-BURNING CEREMONIES: Private information, 20 November 1981, 16 January 1982; *Fiery Cross*, 23 March 1923; Swart, "Memo on Cross Burning," p. 70; Loucks, *The Klan in Pennsylvania* p. 35; for another instance of dynamite accompaniment, in a Long Island ceremony, see *New York Times*, 19 March 1924. Robert M. Miller remarks, "The obscene spectacle of men of God gathered about a cross ignited by their hands is perhaps tempered only by a sense of pity for Christians possessed of such anxiety," in "Ku Klux Klan," p. 225.

7. *"Practical Patriotism"*

186 CLARKE'S REAL-ESTATE VENTURES: Charles C. Alexander, "Kleagles and Cash," *Business History Review* 39 (1965): 355; Winfield Jones, *Knights of the Ku Klux Klan* (New York: Tocsin, 1941), p. 142; Thomas G. Dyer, "The Klan on Campus: C. Lewis Fowler and Lanier University," *South Atlantic Quarterly* 77 (1978): 453–69.

186 Z. R. UPCHURCH: Alexander, "Kleagles and Cash," p. 356. Among the Kleagles who quit the Klan at this time were two who wrote informative anti-Klan books: Henry Peck Fry, *The Modern Ku Klux Klan* (Boston: Small, Maynard, 1922); Edgar I. Fuller, *The Visible of the Invisible Empire: "The Maelstrom,"* ed. George La Dura (Denver, Maelstrom, 1925).

187 DR. HIRAM WESLEY EVANS: Charles O. Jackson, "William J. Simmons: A Career in Ku Kluxism," *Georgia Historical Quarterly* 50 (December 1966): 360; Alexander, "Kleagles and Cash," p. 357; idem, *The Ku Klux Klan in the Southwest* (Lexington: Univ. Kentucky Press, 1966), pp. 79, 109–10; William M. Likens, *Patriotism Capitalized or Religion Turned Into Gold* (Uniontown, PA: Watchman, 1925; copy in Library of Congress), pp. 196–99; W. P. Beazell, "The Rise of the Ku Klux Klan," *World Tomorrow* 7 (March 1924): 71–73; Hugh Emmons Testimony, South Bend *Tribune*, undated clipping, Ku Klux Klan File, South Bend Public Library, South Bend, Indiana; Fuller, *Visible of the Invisible*, p. 93.

187 EVANS AND STEPHENSON: Private information, 16 July 1981.

188 "DOUBTLESS THE ANGELS THEMSELVES . . .": William G. Shepherd, "The Fiery Double-Cross," *Colliers* 82 (28 July 1928): 9.

188 "TOMORROW MORNING COMES THE ELECTION . . .": Ibid.

189 "COLONEL SIMMONS . . . ALL VISITORS": Ibid., p. 47.

189 "ARTICLE I, SECTION 2 . . .": *Constitution and Laws of the Knights of the Ku Klux Klan, Inc.* (Atlanta: KKK, 1921, Revised 1926).

190 SOUTHERN PUBLICITY ASSOCIATION OUSTED: *Dawn*, 17 March 1923; *Imperial Night-Hawk*, 28 March 1923.

190 ATLANTA KLAVERN NUMBER 1: Ibid., 18 July 1923; *The Whole Truth about the Effort to Destroy the Klan* (Atlanta: KKK, 1923; copy in Rare Book and Special Collections, Library of Congress), p. 5. Evans eventually suspended the charter of the Atlanta Klavern.

190 SIMMONS GOES TO COURT: *New York Times*, 4–8 April 1923, May 8, May 25, 1923; Shepherd, "Double-Cross," p. 48.

190 IMPERIAL KLONCILIUM: *Minutes of the Imperial Kloncilium, Meeting of May 1 and May 2, 1923 which Ratified W. J. Simmons' Agreement with the Knights of the Ku Klux Klan, Together with Certified Copies of all Litigation instituted by W. J. Simmons against the Imperial Wizard and the Knights of the Ku Klux Klan* (Atlanta: KKK, 1923; copy in Library of Congress); *Whole Truth*, pp. 9, 28; *Dawn*, 21 April 1923.

190 A HOPELESS TRUCE: Alexander, "Kleagles and Cash," p. 358; *Whole Truth*, pp. 14–16, 22–23; William J. Simmons, *America's Menace or the Enemy Within* (Atlanta: Patriotic Books, 1926), pp. 78–115; *Fiery Cross*, 16 March 1923; Shepherd, "Double-Cross," p. 48.

191 "BECAUSE EVANS AND HIS ASSOCIATES . . .": *New York Times*, 12 January 1924.

191 "A CHEAP POLITICAL . . . WHITE MAN OF AMERICA": Clarke to Calvin Coolidge, 27 December 1923, Presidential Papers of Calvin Coolidge, Case File 28, Manuscript Division, Library of Congress. After his complete banishment from the Klan, Clarke launched in 1926 a rival fraternity with a strong fundamentalist emphasis. Called "The Supreme Kingdom," its goals included banning the teaching of evolution in public schools and the reinstatement of "Christianity throughout the nation." The movement collapsed in 1929. See Stewart G. Cole, *The History of Fundamentalism* (Hamden, CT: Archon, 1963), pp. 275–79; Norman Furniss, *The Fundamentalist Controversy* (New Haven: Yale Univ. Press, 1954), pp. 62–66.

191 "LIKE GENERAL LEE . . .": Simmons, *America's Menace*, p. 102.

191 "THE SETTLEMENT MEANS . . .": *New York Times*, 13 February 1924.

191 "IN NO OTHER SOCIETY . . .": Ibid., 14 February 1924.

191 "THE COUNTRY IS NOW GETTING . . .": In *Literary Digest* 80 (8 March 1924): 38.

192 "THE REASON I RESIGNED . . .": Ibid.

192 SIMMONS'S LATER LIFE: *New York Times*, 22 February 1925, 23 September 1937; Jackson, "William J. Simmons," pp. 363–64; private information, 16 July 1981.

192 EVANS'S LEADERSHIP: Evans did put the Klan on a responsible fiscal base; between July 1923 and July 1924, the Klan reported a total income of $8 million (Alexander, "Kleagles and Cash," p. 364). *Articles on the Klan and Elementary Klankraft* (Atlanta: KKK, 1924–1925; included with the deposition of Orion Norcross, *State of Indiana* v. *The Knights of the Ku Klux Klan*, November

1928, Number 41769 in the Marion Circuit Court of Marion County, Indiana; microfilm in the Indiana State Library, Indianapolis) (hereafter cited *Indiana v. KKK*); *Klan Building: An Outline of Proven Klan Methods for Successfully Applying the Art of Klankraft in Building and Operating Local Klans* (Atlanta: KKK, 1923; copy in Rare Book and Special Collections, Library of Congress), pp. 9–10.

193 "THE KLAN IS AN ORGANIZATION . . .": Stanley Frost, "When the Klan Rules," *Outlook* 136 (9 January 1924): 64.

193 "EVERY TRUE KLANSMAN . . .": *Imperial Night-Hawk*, 18 April 1923.

193 ALFRED FULLER: Ibid., 28 March 1923, 9 May 1923.

193 CAMPBELL SOUP: Ibid., 19 September 1923.

193 KU-KLUX *KULTUR*: See brochure on Klan paraphernalia published by the Klan Manufacturing company, Dayton Ohio, in Ku Klux Klan Collection, Special Collections, Michigan State University Library (hereafter cited KKK Collection, MSU).

193 KLAN RECORDS AND PLAYER-PIANO ROLLS: "American Music for the American Home," brochure published by Lutz Music Company, York, Pennsylvania, in KKK Collection, MSU.

193 CONVENTION OF GRAND DRAGONS: *Papers Read at the Meeting of Grand Dragons—Knights of the Ku Klux Klan—at their first Annual Meeting Held at Asheville, North Carolina, July 1923*, pp. 6–13, 97–98, 100–104.

194 MER ROUGE: Alexander, *The Klan in the Southwest*, pp. 68–75; Leonard L. Cline, "In Darkest Louisiana," *Nation* 116 (15 March 1923): 292–93.

194 RIOT IN LORENA, TEXAS: Leon Jaworski, "Masks and the Law: A Natural and Unavoidable Conflict" in *The Ku Klux Klan: A History of Racism and Violence*, ed. Randall Williams (Montgomery, AL: Southern Poverty Law Center, 1982), pp. 67–68. In the Klan's official version of this riot, Sheriff Buchanan was "drunk"; see U.S. Congress, *The Ku Klux Klan Hearings*. 67 Cong., 1 Sess., House Committee on Rules (1921): 131–32.

194 KLAN VIOLENCE IN THE NORTH: William M. Likens, *The Trail of the Serpent* (n.p., 1928), pp. 48, 54–56; Robert A. Goldberg, *Hooded Empire: The Ku Klux Klan in Colorado* (Urbana: Univ. Illinois Press, 1981), pp. 31–32.

195 "ROBES AND HELMETS MUST NOT . . .": *Klan Building*, p. 14.

195 "IN SOME INSTANCES OFFICERS OF THE LAW . . .": Ibid., p. 15, my italics.

195 THE KLAN AND THE 1924 IMMIGRATION ACT: *Kourier*, February 1925; Stetson Kennedy, *I Rode with the Ku Klux Klan* (London: Arco, 1954), p. 262. Kennedy recounts that a Kludd told him the Klan had spent over $1 million to get this act passed.

195 "IT IS A GOOD POLICY . . .": *Klan Building*, p. 10.

195 "SUGGESTIONS FOR KLAN SPEAKERS": Stanley L. Swart, "A Memo on Cross Burning—and Its Implications," *Northwest Ohio Quarterly* 43 (1971): 73.

196 "OPEN MEETINGS ALWAYS STRESSED . . .": Deposition of Harry E. A. MacNeel, *Indiana v. KKK*.

196 HARRY S. TRUMAN: Alfred Steinberg, *The Man from Missouri* (New York: Putnam, 1962), p. 64.

196 KLANSMEN WON ELECTIONS: David Chalmers, "The Ku Klux Klan in Politics in the 1920s," *Mississippi Quarterly* 18 (1965): 235–36, passim; Arnold Rice, *The Ku Klux Klan in American Politics* (Washington, D.C.: Public Affairs, 1962), pp. 58–80, passim.

197 HUGO BLACK: William E. Leuchtenberg, "A Klansman Joins the Court: The

Appointment of Hugo L. Black," *University of Chicago Law Review* 41 (1973): 1–31; Virginia Van Der Veer, "Hugo Black and the K.K.K.," *American Heritage* 19 (1968): 60–64, 108–11.

197 THE KLAN AND THE DEMOCRATIC CONVENTION: David B. Burner, "The Democratic Party and the Election of 1924," *Mid-America* 46 (1964): 92–113; Herbert Eaton, *Presidential Timber* (New York: Free Press, 1964), pp. 290–312; Lee N. Allen, "The McAdoo Campaign for the Presidential Nomination in 1924," *Journal of Southern History* 29 (May 1963): 211–28.

197 "A NATIONAL MENACE . . .": William R. Snell, "Fiery Crosses in the Roaring Twenties: Activities of the Revised Klan in Alabama, 1915–1930," *Alabama Review* 23 (October 1970): 265; see also *New York Times*, 4 November 1923.

198 "WHEN NORTH CAROLINA ANNOUNCED . . .": Will Rogers, *Convention Articles of Will Rogers*, ed. Joseph A. Stout (Stillwater, OK: Oklahoma State Univ. Press, 1976), pp. 63–64.

198 "THE DEADLOCK THAT DEVELOPED . . .": Frank R. Kent paraphrased in Burner, "Election of 1924," p. 101.

198 "GENTLEMEN, WE ARE FACED . . .": In Eaton, *Presidential Timber*, p. 305.

199 "THE BATTLE THAT WENT ON . . .": H. L. Mencken, *A Carnival of Buncombe*, ed. Malcolm Moos (Baltimore: Johns Hopkins Press, 1956), p. 81.

199 "HEARTY COOPERATION IN KEEPING . . .": Rogers, *Convention Articles*, p. 48.

199 MARCUS GARVEY: Edmund D. Cronon, *Black Moses: The Story of Marcus Garvey and the Universal Negro Improvement Association* (Madison: Univ. Wisconsin Press, 1955); Robert L. Allen, *Black Awakening in Capitalist America* (New York: Anchor, 1970), pp. 100–101.

199 "GARVEY'S MOTIVES WERE CLEAR . . .": W.E.B. DuBois, "Back to Africa," *Century* 83 (February 1923): 547.

200 "WE ASK YOU TO TELL US . . .": 27 (?) October 1924, Coolidge Papers. In the same file, see the letters from Henry J. Arnold, 6 September 1924, and James Weldon Johnson, 29 May, 15 September 1924. Johnson, who was president of the NAACP at the time, was so upset by Coolidge's refusal to answer him, he advised fellow blacks to abandon the party of Lincoln and vote Democratic.

200 "THE FULL SYMPATHY OF 4 MILLION . . .": Garvey to C. B. Slemp, 27 October 1924, Coolidge Papers.

200 "MAY I ADVISE, WITHOUT OFFENDING . . .": Edwin Banta to C. B. Slemp, 26 August 1924, ibid. Advice to the same effect was sent to Coolidge by T. C. Cochran, Roswell Davis, Elmer Henderson, and Joseph Himmaugh—all on 23 August 1924.

200 "DOES VIOLENCE TO THE SPIRIT . . .": In *Outlook* 138 (3 September 1924): 5.

200 "WHEN COTTON GROWS ON THE FIG TREE . . .": 1924 election placard, KKK Collection, MSU.

200 "MORE RESPECT FOR THE FRANCHISE . . .": "Some of the Accomplishments of the Knights of the Ku Klux Klan," flyer, ibid.

201 ANTI-KLAN ORGANIZATIONS: Dallas County Citizens League, "The Ku Klux Klan" (Denver: American Publishing Society, n.d.; pamphlet in ibid.), p. 1; Chicago *New World*, 31 August 1923; St. Louis *Globe-Democrat*, 30 Novem-

ber 1923; New York *World*, 18 August 1923; *New York Times*, 7 September 1923; St. Louis *Post-Dispatch*, 31 July 1923; *New York Times*, 22 March 1924.

201 NATIONAL VIGILANCE ASSOCIATION: *Fellowship Forum*, 24 November 1923; *Christian Science Monitor*, 12 November 1923.

201 ANTI-MASK LAWS: Jack Swertfeger, Jr., "Anti-Mask and Anti-Klan Laws," *Journal of Public Law* 1 (1952): 195–96.

201 "THE HONORED EXAMPLE OF PRESIDENT GRANT . . .": Nicholas Carroll to Calvin Coolidge, 4 September 1923, Coolidge Papers.

202 "BY THEIR EXAMPLE, THE HOODED . . .": *Our Sunday Visitor*, 18 February 1923.

202 INDIANAPOLIS *TIMES*: George E. Stevens, "Winning the Pulitzer Prize: The Indianapolis *Times* Battles Political Corruption," *Journalism History* 2 (1975): 80–83.

202 MEMPHIS *COMMERCIAL APPEAL*: Gary R. Blankenship, "The *Commercial Appeal's* Attack on the Ku Klux Klan, 1921–1925," *West Tennessee Historical Society Papers* 31 (1977): 44–58.

202 JULIAN HARRIS AND THE *ENQUIRER-SUN*: Clement C. Moseley, "The Political Influence of the Ku Klux Klan in Georgia, 1915–1925," *Georgia Historical Quarterly* 57 (1973): 245–46; Arnold Shankman, "Julian Harris and the Ku Klux Klan," *Mississippi Quarterly* 28 (1975): 147–69; William F. Mugleston, "Julian Harris, the Georgia Press, and the Ku Klux Klan," *Georgia Historical Quarterly* 59 (1975): 284–95.

202 NGUYEN SINH CUNG: Charles Fenn, *Ho Chi Minh* (New York: Scribners, 1973), p. 26; Jean Lacouture, *Ho Chi Minh* (New York: Random House, 1968), pp. 17–18.

203 CUNG ON LYNCHING: "Lynching: A Little Known Aspect of American Civilization," *La Correspondance Internationale* No. 59, 1924, reprinted in Ho Chi Minh, *Selected Works*, (Hanoi: Foreign Languages Publishing House, 1960), I: 99–105. Cung's account is completely objective. Such details as saving teeth and bits of the rope as souvenirs, as well as hanging the burned corpse, were typical of lynching at the turn of the century; see Ida B. Wells-Barnett, *On Lynchings* (New York: Arno, 1969).

204 CUNG ON THE KLAN: "The Ku Klux Klan," *La Correspondance Internationale* No. 74, 1924, reprinted in *Selected Works*, I: 127–32, my italics.

8. "Ain't God Good to Indiana?"

I am indebted to the pioneer efforts of four scholars whose work blazed the trail for my research on this chapter: Norman F. Weaver, "The Knights of the Ku Klux Klan in Wisconsin, Indiana, Ohio, and Michigan" (Ph.D. diss., University of Wisconsin, 1954); John A. Davis, "The Ku Klux Klan in Indiana, 1920–1930: An Historical Study" (Ph.D. diss., Northwestern University, 1966); Frank M. Cates, "The Ku Klux Klan in Indiana Politics: 1920–1925" (Ph.D. diss., Indiana University, 1971); Jill S. Nevel, "Fiery Crosses and Tempers: The Ku Klux Klan in South Bend, Indiana, 1923–1926" (senior thesis, Princeton University, 1977).

215 KLONKLAVE IN KOKOMO: Kokomo *Tribune*, 22, 29 June, 2, 5 July 1923; *Imperial Night-Hawk*, 27 June, 11 July 1923; *Fiery Cross*, 6, 13 July 1923;

Morton Harrison, "Gentlemen from Indiana," *Atlantic Monthly* 141 (May 1928): 676–77; Dixon Merritt, "Klan and Anti-Klan in Indiana," *Outlook* 144 (8 December 1926): 465; Robert Coughlan, "Klonklave in Kokomo" in *The Aspirin Age, 1919–1941,* ed. Isabel Leighton (New York: Simon & Schuster, 1949), pp. 107–10; private information, 6 December 1981.

216 "KLANKRAFT IN INDIANA . . .": *Imperial Night-Hawk,* 11 July 1923.

216 "ONLY WHEN IT BECAME 'IMPOSSIBLE' . . .": Clarence Darrow, *The Story of My Life* (New York: Scribner's, 1960), p. 289.

217 "WE'D CIRCLE AROUND . . .": In William G. Shepherd, "Indiana's Mystery Man," *Colliers* 79 (8 January 1927): 9.

217 "MY WORTHY SUBJECTS . . .": Harrison, "Gentlemen," pp. 676–77.

218 KLAN PARADES IN INDIANA: Ibid., p. 680; for other examples, see *Dawn,* 7, 14 April, 26 May, 16 June 1923.

218 INDIANA—THE STRONGEST KLAN STATE: Hoosier Klan membership at its peak in 1924 has been variously estimated between 200,000 and 500,000. The best estimate seems to be 350,000, which is a reasonable figure based on the *Indiana* v. *KKK* information and Indiana's 1925 adult WASP population.

218 "MY GOD . . . OLD-TIME ZEST": Duncan Aikman, "The Home-Town Mind," *Harpers* 151 (November 1925): 668.

219 "THERE WAS NOT THE SAME . . .": Robert Hull, "The Klan Aftermath in Indiana," *America* 38 (15 October 1927): 8.

219 "SHARE OF BITTER REGRETS . . .": Lowell Mellett, "Klan and Church," *Atlantic Monthly* 132 (November 1923): 592.

219 "FOUL, STRANGE, UNNATURAL . . .": Meredith Nicholson, "Hoosier Letters and the Ku Klux," *Bookman* 67 (March 1928): 7.

219 INDIANA BEFORE THE CIVIL WAR: Howard H. Peckham, *Indiana: A Bicentennial History* (New York: Norton, 1978), pp. 20–133; J. Russell Smith, *North America* (New York: Harcourt, Brace, 1942), pp. 367–69; Harlow Lindley, *Indiana as Seen by Early Travelers* (Indianapolis: Indiana Historical Commission, 1916), p. 482; Elmer Davis, "Have Faith in Indiana," *Harpers* 153 (October 1926): 616; Meredith Nicholson, *The Hoosiers* (New York: Macmillan, 1915), pp. 7–8, 32–34.

219 INDIANA DURING AND AFTER THE WAR: Emma Lou Thornbrough, *Indiana in the Civil War Era, 1850–1880* (Indianapolis: Indiana Historical Bureau and Indiana Historical Society, 1965), pp. 180–225; Peckham, *Indiana,* pp. 130–60; George F. Milton, *Abraham Lincoln and the Fifth Column* (New York: Vanguard, 1942), p. 199.

220 HOOSIERS AND POLITICS: Merritt ("Klan and Anti-Klan," p. 469) remarked in 1926 that "in Indiana, politics is never adjourned." In 1978, Peckham determined that the proportion of Hoosiers who turn out to vote still exceeds the national average (*Indiana,* p. 138). Indiana is one of the few states, if not the only one, to celebrate Dyngus Day—an obscure Polish holiday falling on the Monday after Easter—when local Democrats and Republicans woo prospective voters to their headquarters with unlimited supplies of free sausage and beer. By ten P.M., hardly a street is safe from drivers under the influence of alcohol and political revelry. It is easy to see today how a politically oriented Klan could have done so well in Indiana.

220 INDIANA'S GOLDEN AGE: Clifton J. Phillips, *Indiana in Transition: The Emergence of an Industrial Commonwealth, 1880–1920* (Indianapolis: Indiana Historical Bureau and Indiana Historical Society, 1968), pp. 181–224; John B.

Martin, *Indiana: An Interpretation* (New York: Knopf, 1947), p. 90; Peckham, *Indiana*, p. 112.

220 HOOSIER WRITERS: Minnie O. Williams, *Indiana Authors* (Indianapolis: Bobbs-Merrill, 1916), foreword, n.p.; Nicholson, *Hoosiers*, pp. 214–71; Phillips, *Indiana in Transition*, pp. 503–43; Peckham, *Indiana*, pp. 156–57. Kin Hubbard, the "Hoosier Rochefoucauld," remarked: "Everyone in the state is either a politician or a writer. Of course there's a fair sprinkling of tradesmen an' farmers, but only enough t' supply the wants of the writers and politicians," in, Irving Leibowitz, *My Indiana* (Englewood Cliffs: Prentice-Hall, 1964), p. 252. Hubbard's quip epitomizes the strange syzygy of moronic simplicity and arrogance that laid Indiana wide open to the Klan.

220 "*FOLKS, A FELLER NEVER KNOWS . . .*": In Ralph D. Gray, ed., *The Hoosier State* (Grand Rapids: Eerdmans, 1980), I: 14–15. Herschel's doggerel, written in 1919, is engraved on a plaque in the rotunda of the Indiana State Capitol.

221 STEPHENSON'S EARLY LIFE: Shepherd, "Mystery Man," p. 8; Edgar A. Booth, *The Mad Mullah of America* (Columbus, OH: Ellison, 1927), pp. 6–12; Louis F. Budenz, "There's Mud on Indiana's White Robes," *Nation* 125 (27 July 1927): 81; Samuel T. Moore, "How the Kleagles Collected the Cash," *Independent* 113 (13 December 1924): 517; Coughlan, "Klonklave in Kokomo," p. 124; private information, 27 October 1981.

222 STEVE'S EARLY WORK IN THE KLAN: Deposition of D. C. Stephenson, *Knights of the Ku Klux Klan* v. *Reverend John F. Strayer, et al*, April 1928, Number 1897 in Equity District Court of the U.S. for the Western District of Pennsylvania, pp. 3–21; deposition of Orion Norcross, *State of Indiana* v. *The Knights of the Ku Klux Klan*, November 1928, Number 41769 in the Marion Circuit Court of Marion County, Indiana; microfilm in the Indiana State Library, Indianapolis (hereafter cited *Indiana* v. *KKK*); Budenz, "Mud on Indiana's Robes," pp. 81–82; Weaver, "Knights of the KKK," pp. 146–50; Booth, *Mad Mullah*, pp. 45, 313.

223 "I DID NOT SELL THE KLAN . . .": Moore, "How the Kleagles," p. 517.

223 "NOW WE'RE GOING TO SIGN . . .": Shepherd, "Mystery Man," p. 48. For more on the relationship between the fundamentalist clergy and the Indiana Klan, see deposition of Hugh Emmons, *Indiana* v. *KKK*; Nevel, "Fiery Crosses," p. 35; Joseph P. O'Mahony, "The Ku Klux Klan in Indiana," *America* 30 (15 December 1923): 202; Indianapolis *Times*, 27 March, 12 June 1922, 2 April 1923; Hull, "Klan Aftermath," p. 8; Harrison, "Gentlemen," pp. 679, 684.

223 "YOU DO NOT MEET WITH THREE . . .": John Gunther, *Inside USA* (New York: Harpers, 1947), p. 386. See also Samuel T. Moore, "Consequences of the Klan," *Independent* 113 (20 December 1924): 535–36; Merritt, "Klan and Anti-Klan," p. 465; Martin, *Indiana*, p. 96; Budenz, "Mud on Indiana's Robes," p. 81.

224 KLAN'S ALL-DAY OUTINGS: Weaver, "Knights of the KKK," p. 155; Nevel, "Fiery Crosses," p. 36; *Dawn*, 5, 12, 19, 26 May 1923; Shepherd, "Mystery Man," p. 9. Steve liked the format of all-day outings because it saved the Klan the expense of renting an auditorium and because cross burnings always "gave a thrill" to prospective members, in Moore, "How the Kleagles," p. 519.

225 HORSETHIEF DETECTIVES ASSOCIATION: Max Bentley, "The Ku Klux Klan in Indiana," *McClure's Magazine* 56 (May 1924): 23–25; Peckham, *Indiana*, p.

90; depositions of Hugh Emmons and Thomas W. Swift, *Indiana* v. *KKK*; Davis, "Have Faith," pp. 618–20; Harrison, "Gentlemen," pp. 678, 680.

225 "WOMEN ARE PROVING . . .": *Dawn*, 21 April 1923.

225 STEVE REMITTED $641,475: Charles C. Alexander, "Kleagles and Cash," *Business History Review* 39 (1965): 359.

226 "OUT IN INDIANA, EVERYONE . . .": *New York Times* quoted in Thomas M. Conroy, "The Ku Klux Klan and the American Clergy," *Ecclesiastical Review* 70 (1924): 49. See also Moore, "Consequences," pp. 534–35; Robert L. Duffus, "The Ku Klux Klan in the Middle West," *World's Work* 46 (August 1923): 363–72; Harrison, "Gentlemen," p. 680; Indianapolis *Times*, 20 January 1923; South Bend *Tribune*, 1 February 1923.

226 *THE FIERY CROSS*: At its peak the *Fiery Cross* had a circulation of 400,000, in addition to the many copies its newsboys sold on the street: Neil Betten, "Nativism and the Klan in Town and City: Valparaiso and Gary, Indiana," *Studies in History and Society* 4 (1973): 3. Among the resolutions at the 1923 convention of the American Order of Scottish Clans was one directing its executives to take legal action against the Indiana Klan for infringing on the name "The Fiery Cross," which was the name of its own organ (*Fraternal Monitor*, November 1923).

226 INDIANA KLAN'S ANTI-CATHOLICISM: Hull, "Klan Aftermath," pp. 8–10; Harrison, "Gentlemen," p. 678; Nevel, "Fiery Crosses," p. 71; Coughlan, "Klonklave in Kokomo," p. 114; Mellett, "Klan and Church," pp. 587–88; William E. Wilson, "That Long, Hot Summer in Indiana," *American Heritage* 16 (August 1965): 56–64.

226 "SEE, ALL THOSE FINGERS . . .": In Robert S. Lynd and Helen M. Lynd, *Middletown; A Study in Contemporary American Culture* (New York: Harcourt, 1929), p. 482. Associated with the New York Institute of Social and Religious Research, the Lynds chose Muncie out of 143 cities as the most representative "possible of contemporary American life."

227 "JUST WHY, OUT OF ALL . . .": Davis, "Have Faith," p. 617.

227 NORTH MANCHESTER AMBUSHES "THE POPE": Conroy, "Klan and American Clergy," p. 55; Harrison, "Gentlemen," p. 679. The incident is one of the most repeated stories in Indiana, though many North Manchesterians belittle it as apocryphal.

227 "READY, AT THE BEHEST . . .": Hull, "Klan Aftermath," p. 8.

227 SOME CATHOLICS FOUGHT BACK: *Our Sunday Visitor* offered $1,000 to anyone who could prove any Catholic "atrocity" alleged by the Klan: "The most deplorable aspect of it all is that hundreds of Protestant ministers and many sectarian periodicals are helping along this anti-American and anti-Catholic propaganda—presumably in good faith," in *Visitor*, 27 May 1923; Merle Blue to W.C.W., 12 November 1981; Indianapolis *News*, 17 August 1922; South Bend *Tribune*, 29 January 1923.

228 "REVEREND CLERGY, YOU ARE SIX . . .": Quoted in Arthur J. Hope, *Notre Dame: One Hundred Years* (South Bend: Icarus, 1978), pp. 372–73.

228 STEVE WAS QUITE A SUCCESS: Shepherd, "Mystery Man," pp. 8, 47; Moore, "How the Kleagles," p. 517; Merritt, "Klan and Anti-Klan," pp. 465–66; Harrison, "Gentlemen," p. 684; Booth, *Mad Mullah*, pp. 132, 155, 299; private information, 28 October 1981.

229 "POWERFUL PERSONALITY . . .": Stanley Frost, "The Klan Shows Its Hand in Indiana," *Outlook* 137 (4 June 1924): 188.

229 "DECISIVE AND ENERGETIC . . .": Moore, "How the Kleagles," p. 517; see also Martin, *Indiana*, pp. 185, 192–93.

230 "PERMIT NO SELECTION . . .": Indianapolis *Times*, 13 April 1923. Steve signed this telegram "the Old Man."

230 THE STEPHENSON MACHINE: Booth, *Mad Mullah*, pp. 45–46; Harrison, "Gentlemen," p. 684; Hull, "Klan Aftermath," p. 8; depositions of D. C. Stephenson, Samuel Bemenderfer, and Hugh Emmons, *Indiana* v. *KKK*.

230 "GOD HELP THE MAN . . .": In Martin, *Indiana*, p. 194.

230 "FAILURE ON THE PART . . .": D. C. Stephenson, "Field Regulations No. 3" included with deposition of Orion Norcross, *Indiana* v. *KKK*.

231 "IT WAS THE ENTHUSIASTIC SINCERITY . . .": Ibid.

231 KLAVERNS EARNED INCREASED RESPECT: Noting the growing tendency of non-Klansmen to look favorably upon the Klan, the South Bend *Tribune* editorialized: "Klanism is a state of mind. A man does not have to belong, wear the regalia and subscribe to the formal teachings if he has in him the suspicion and hostility emanating from religious and racial bigotry" (9 June 1923).

232 KLAVERNS GOT CANDIDATES ELECTED: Deposition of Hugh Emmons, *Indiana* v. *KKK*.

232 "IT MATTERS NOT WHETHER . . .": Indianapolis *Times*, 15 April 1924.

232 "REMEMBER—EVERY CRIMINAL . . .": Frost, "Klan Shows Its Hand," p. 188. Although this placard was later used by Klansmen all over the country, it first appeared in the 1924 Indiana primary and is clearly Steve's handiwork.

232 "IN INDIANA, [THE KLAN] HAS SHOWN . . .": Ibid., p. 190, my italics. On May 29, 1924, James Weldon Johnson of the NAACP asked Coolidge, as head of the Republican Party, to denounce the Klan "in view of the situation in Indiana where the Republican nominee for governor was given and publicly accepted the endorsement and the votes of the Klan forces . . ." (Johnson to Calvin Coolidge, Presidential Papers of Calvin Coolidge, Case File 28, Manuscript Division, Library of Congress). Johnson and other black leaders were apparently successful in turning Hoosier blacks away from the 1924 Klan-dominated GOP ticket in Indiana. See *New York Times*, 16 October 1924; Emma L. Thornbrough, "Segregation in Indiana during the Klan Era of the 1920s," *Mississippi Valley Historical Review* 47 (March 1961): 612–13.

233 THE KLAN AND VALPARAISO UNIVERSITY: *Dawn*, 2 June, 18 August, 15 September 1923; *New York Times*, 28 July, 16 August, 6 September 1923; *New Republic*, 36 (5 September 1923): 35–36; *Literary Digest* 78 (5 September 1923): 42–46; Betten, "Nativism and the Klan," pp. 9–10.

234 "BECAUSE I CANNOT WITH ANY ELEMENT . . .": In Edgar I. Fuller, *The Visible of the Invisible Empire: "The Maelstrom,"* ed. George La Dura (Denver: Maelstrom, 1925), pp. 88–89. See also deposition of Orion Norcross, *Indiana* v. *KKK*; *Fiery Cross*, 12 October 1923; *Dawn*, 13 October 1923.

234 "A FEW BEATINGS AND SOME TAR . . .": Deposition of Hugh Emmons, *Indiana* v. *KKK*.

234 "DONATED $100,000 TO ERECT . . .": Indianapolis *News*, 10 May 1924.

235 "YELLOW-LIVERED SOUTHERNERS . . .": Shepherd, "Mystery Man," p. 47.

235 "AN IGNORANT, UNEDUCATED UNCOUTH . . .": Moore, "How the Kleagles," pp. 517–18.

235 "WE'RE GOING OUT TO KLUX . . .": Martin, *Indiana*, p. 194. See also Indianapolis *Times*, 12 May 1924; *New York Times*, 12 May 1924.

235 ST. JOSEPH VALLEY KLAVERN: South Bend *Tribune*, 13 March 1924; Davis, "Have Faith," p. 624; deposition of Hugh Emmons, *Indiana* v. *KKK*.

235 "THE KLAN HAS NO QUARREL . . .": In Cates, "Klan in Indiana Politics," p. 139 fn.

236 NOTRE DAME RIOT: South Bend *Tribune*, 18, 20 May 1924, 17 October 1973, 7 July 1975; Nevel, "Fiery Crosses," pp. 68–94; Hope, *Notre Dame*, pp. 374–75; Fred Rosebeck to W.C.W., 28 November 1981.

237 STEVE PUT THE KLAN INTO HIGH GEAR: Budenz, "Mud on Indiana's Robes," pp. 81–82; M. Chomel, "The Klan Issue in Indiana," *America* 32 (25 October 1924): 31–32; *New York Times*, 25 September, 28 October 1924.

237 RELIGIOUS ANGLE GREW MORE PRONOUNCED: Deposition of Hugh Emmons, *Indiana* v. *KKK*.

238 THE KLAN SPLIT AND THE GENERAL ASSEMBLY: South Bend *Tribune*, 10 November 1924; Indianapolis *Times*, 2 January 1925; Indianapolis *News*, 27 February 1925.

238 KLAN'S LEGISLATIVE FAILURES: Ibid., 21 January, 17 February, 25 February, 9 March, 28 July, 1925; Harrison, "Gentlemen," p. 682.

238 STEVE AND THE GENERAL ASSEMBLY: Indianapolis *Times*, 14 January 1925; Merritt, "Klan and Anti-Klan," p. 466.

239 MADGE OBERHOLTZER: South Bend *Tribune*, 14, 16 April 1925.

239 ABDUCTION AND RAPE OF MADGE OBERHOLTZER: The account is based on Madge's premortem affidavit and other depositions in *Reports of Cases Decided in the Supreme Court of the State of Indiana* (16 May 1933–22 December 1933), 205: 166–82; and on testimony from the trial reported in the South Bend *Tribune*, Indianapolis *Times*, and *New York Times*, 13 October–17 November 1925. See also Francis X. Busch, "The D. C. Stephenson Case" in *Guilty or Not Guilty?* (Indianapolis: Bobbs-Merrill, 1952), pp. 77–124.

244 HOOSIER KLANSMEN ABANDON THE KLAN: *New Republic* 42 (15 April 1925): 224; *New York Times*, 9 January 1926; South Bend *Tribune*, 12 September 1926; Booth, *Mad Mullah*, pp. 283–84; Betten, "Nativism and the Klan," p. 13; private information, 28 October 1981.

245 "THE JURY WAS FIXED . . .": Shepherd, "Mystery Man," p. 48.

245 "I AM ASKING YOU . . .": South Bend *Tribune*, 13 November 1925.

245 STEVE OPENS HIS "BLACK BOXES": *New York Times*, 7–31 July, 11 November, 2 October, 15 December 1926. One of Steve's "boxes" was never opened. This he gave in the form of a brown valise to a friend, an executive at the Bendix Corporation. The daughter of the executive later burned it without ever opening it (private information, 27 October 1981).

246 "IN RETURN FOR THE POLITICAL SUPPORT . . .": Indianapolis *News*, 7 October 1926.

246 EXPOSURES OF CORRUPTION: Alva W. Taylor, "What the Klan Did in Indiana," *New Republic* 52 (16 November 1927): 330–32; Harrison, "Gentlemen," p. 682; Budenz, "Mud on Indiana's Robes," pp. 81–82; Merritt, "Klan and Anti-Klan," p. 467; George E. Stevens, "Winning the Pulitzer Prize: the Indianapolis *Times* Battles Political Corruption," *Journalism History* 2 (1975): 80–83.

246 "BY AS CHEAP A LOT . . .": Nicholson, "Hoosier Letters," p. 10.

247 "THIS IS A HIGH PRICE TO PAY . . .": Idem, quoted in Davis, "The KKK in Indiana," p. 111.

247 "WE WILL REDEEM OURSELVES . . .": Jeannette C. Nolan, *Hoosier City* (New York: Messner, 1943), p. 287.

247 "LET'S CHANGE THE SUBJECT": Dale Burgess, *Just Us Hoosiers and How We Got That Way* (Indianapolis: Unified College Press, 1966), pp. 128–31.

247 "HE JUST CHEWED . . . WITH THAT GIRL!": Sarah Dishon to W.C.W., 10 November 1981; Fred Rosebeck to W.C.W., 28 November 1981.

247 STEVE REMAINS A FITTING METAPHOR: Steve's life sentence was unusually severe for second-degree murder, and he maintained to the end that he had been "framed" by Klan executives and was "a political prisoner." A long incarceration did nothing to disturb this conviction, and a fellow inmate remembered him as "the most arrogant asshole I've ever met in my life." After serving twenty-five years, Steve was paroled in March 1950. To a group of hostile reporters who visited him in prison before he left, he said: "I am leaving Indiana for good and cogent reasons. . . . With utmost good will I am going to a section of the country where members of my political party (Republican) are as scarce as hen's teeth. This means that I have no intention of participating in politics. I must return to a greatly changed social order stripped of property, position and all but my inner strength. With this single asset I shall be secure. I ask nothing of my fellow man except an opportunity to walk in peace with God."

Steve was paroled to the custody of his daughter who lived in Oklahoma and with whom he had first become acquainted while he was incarcerated. This arrangement proved unsatisfactory, however, and he bolted from parole five months later. "He still lived back in 1924 when he was a man of wealth and power," said his daughter. "He suffered from delusions and seemed to think he was persecuted," she added. After the FBI joined the search, Steve was found working as a printer in Minneapolis. There was a year of legal tussling (Steve had acquired a formidable legal education in prison) before the sixty-year-old former Dragon was returned to the state prison at Michigan City.

He served three more years and was paroled for the second time in December 1954. For a while, he lived in Seymour, Indiana. He married for the third time in 1958 and, as was his custom, soon abandoned his wife and disappeared. He surfaced in the news in 1961 when he was arrested in Independence, Missouri, for assaulting a sixteen-year-old girl. Details of the misadventure were equivocal, and charges were dropped so long as Steve left Missouri.

For a while, he drifted about, working as an itinerant printer and cleaning type in newspaper offices with a device and process he had invented in prison. He then moved to Jonesboro, Tennessee, and worked full-time for the Jonesboro *Herald and Tribune*. In 1964, he married for the fourth and last time. This marriage appears to have been quite successful. After he died in the arms of his loving wife on June 28, 1966, newsmen flocked to Jonesboro, and his widow was shocked to learn of her model husband's past notoriety (private information, 22 March 1982; South Bend *Tribune*, clippings 1941–1978, Ku Klux Klan File, South Bend Public Library).

Postscript

248 "WE WILL TAKE UP THE TORCH . . .": *New York Times*, 23 August 1925.

248 MEETING OF GRAND DRAGONS: Cleveland *Plain Dealer*, 22 August 1925.

249 MARCH ON WASHINGTON: *Washington Post*, 7–9 August 1925; Everett R. Clinchy, *All in the Name of God* (New York: John Day, 1934), p. 105.

251 "THE MILITARY FOR . . .": *Klansman's Manual* (Atlanta: Knights of the Ku Klux Klan, 1924), pp. 11–12.

251 "NOTHING BUT A GESTURE . . .": Deposition of D. C. Stephenson, *Knights of the Ku Klux Klan v. Reverend John F. Strayer, et al.*, April 1928, Number 1897 in Equity, District Court of the U.S. for the Western District of Pennsylvania, pp. 8–10.

251 "[THE KLAN] HAS BECOME A TRAVESTY . . .": *Independent* 116 (16 January 1926): 58–59.

252 "IT'S GREAT TO BE A GEORGIAN . . .": Columbus *Enquirer-Sun*, 12 September 1926.

252 "WE ARE A MOVEMENT OF THE PLAIN . . .": Hiram W. Evans, "The Klan's Fight for Americanism," *North American Review* 223 (March 1926): 49.

252 "I AM BOURGEOIS . . .": *Kourier*, January 1926.

252 "DOCTOR HIRAM EVANS . . .": Emporia *Gazette*, 15 May 1926, quoted in Charles W. Sloan, "Kansas Battles the Invisible Empire," *Kansas Historical Quarterly* 40 (Autumn 1974): 405.

253 "WOMEN FOUGHT WOMEN . . .": *New York Times*, 31 May 1927.

253 "THE KU KLUX KLAN HOLDS THAT . . .": "The Ku Klux Klan Makes an Observation on the Presidency," Realm of Michigan, n.d. (brochure in Special Collections in Michigan State University Library).

253 AL'S LETTER FROM THE "POPE": Sin Seer (pseudonym), "Al and His Pals," n.p., n.d. (Special Collections, MSU Library.)

253 "ONCE THE WORLD'S . . .": *Washington Post*, 2 November 1930.

254 "CREATING FALSE ISSUES . . .": John M. Mecklin, *The Ku Klux Klan* (New York: Harcourt, Brace, 1924), p. 240.

BOOK THREE: 1930–1987

9. *"The Klan Is an American Institution"*

257 "IT IS NOT NECESSARY . . .": *New York Times*, 22 December 1930.

257 "TODAY IT CARRIES . . .": *Outlook* 157 (7 January 1931): 32.

257 "NOT MANY PERSONS . . .": In *Literary Digest* 118 (21 July 1934): 19.

258 "WE HAVE REACHED THE END . . .": *Kourier*, March 1930.

258 COMMUNISM IN THE SOUTH IN THE 1930S: John H. Moore, "Communists and Fascists in a Southern City: Atlanta, 1930," *South Atlantic Quarterly* 67 (Summer 1968): 437–54; Arnold Rice, *The Ku Klux Klan in American Politics* (Washington, D.C.: Public Affairs Press, 1962), pp. 101–102; *Kourier*, December 1930, February 1935.

258 DENNIS HUBERT CASE: Moore, "Communists and Fascists," p. 444.

259 "DON'T BE FOOLED . . .": *Kourier*, November 1932.

259 "PUBLIC-SPIRITED PEOPLE . . .": *Literary Digest* 118 (21 July 1934): 19.

260 "YOU MAY NOT BE MAKING A LOT . . .": John R. Salter, Jr., "Reflections on the Klan and Poor People" in *The Ku Klux Klan: A History of Racism and Violence*, ed. Randall Williams (Montgomery: Southern Poverty Law Center Special Report, 1982), p. 63.

260 INTERNATIONAL LABOR DEFENSE COMMITTEE: Letter from Louis Colman, *The Nation* 139 (4 July 1934): 20.

260 JOSEPH SHOEMAKER CASE: Jack Jameson, *Night Riders in Sunny Florida* (New York: Workers Library Publishers, 1936); *Tampa—Tar and Terror* (New

York: Norman Thomas and the National Committee for the Defense of Civil Rights in Tampa, n.d. (Special Collections, MSU Library); *New York Times*, 17 December 1935; Robert Ingalls, "The Murder of Joseph Shoemaker," *Southern Exposure* 8 (Summer 1980): 16–20.

262 THE BLACK LEGION: Concurrently with the movie, a vigilante group calling itself the Black Legion sprang up in the Midwest, heavily concentrated in the Detroit area. Composed of ex-Klansmen, the group lasted about five years. Members took a Klan-like oath, but with revolvers pointed at their heads, and swore they'd be "torn limb from limb and scattered to the carrion" if they ever betrayed the Legion's secrets (Stetson Kennedy, "Who Goes There—Kooks or Klux?," unpublished manuscript, n.d., courtesy of the author).

262 "THE CIO IS INFESTED . . .": *New York Times*, 12 July 1937.

262 THE KKK VS. LABOR: W. J. Cash, *The Mind of the South* (1941; reprint New York: Vintage, 1969), pp. 401–405; Stetson Kennedy, *Southern Exposure* (Garden City: Doubleday, 1946), pp. 167–69; idem to W.C.W., 14 May 1985; Rice, *Klan in American Politics*, p. 104. Regarding the Klan as paid unionbusters, Stetson Kennedy adds, "The Exalted Cyclops invariably pocketed whatever 'honorarium' might be paid for union-busting, while the rank-and-file Ghouls who were called upon to do the actual dirty work got nothing more than assurances that they were acting in a good cause. . . . From the point of view of those with an economic stake in union-busting, the KKK—with its ideology, anonymity, secrecy, and discipline—was bound to be regarded as a made-to-order answer to the union-buster's prayers. Besides, the dumb Klux on the whole would work for nothing, whereas goon squads organized by the Pinkerton Agency commanded a high price" (Kennedy to W.C.W., 5 June 1985).

263 "IN A VERY REAL SENSE . . .": Idem, "Labor and the Klan: Growing Confrontation," undated, unidentified clipping, courtesy of the author.

263 ATLANTA FLOGGINGS: Atlanta *Constitution*, 5–7 February 1939, 9–14 March 1940, 16–19 April 1940; Grady Kent, *Flogged by the Ku Klux Klan* (Cleveland, TN: White Wing, 1942; copy in Library of Congress); Richard H. Rovere, "The Klan Rides Again," *The Nation* 150 (6 April 1940): 445–46.

264 "THAT PROVES TO ME . . .": *Life* 11 (8 December 1941): 41. Recalling Eugene Talmadge as governor, Stetson Kennedy writes, "Speaking before the Georgia Bankers Association at the Atlanta Biltmore . . . he arrived in tie-and-tails, but with a long-eared coonhound in tow, which he tied in the lobby with a piece of robe around its neck. Upon occupying the Governor's Mansion, he brought Ole Bessie up from his farm on Sugar Creek and staked her out on the front lawn, avowing that he just couldn't fulfill his gubernatorial duties without the benefit of Ole Bessie's milk. Also during one of his incumbencies, he ordered the planting of cotton in the divides along Peachtree Street, 'So these city folks can see what it looks like' " (Kennedy to W.C.W., 5 June 1985).

264 "PROTESTANTS! WHY DID . . .": *Kourier*, September 1936.

265 "I FRANKLY CONFESS . . .": Atlanta *Constitution*, 19 January 1939.

265 "YOU WERE HARD ON ME . . .": Ralph McGill, *The South and the Southerner* (Boston: Little, Brown, 1963), p. 137.

265 EVANS AND ASPHALT: Ellis Gibbs Arnall, *The Shore Dimly Seen* (New York: Lippincott, 1946), p. 43.

265 JAMES COLESCOTT: *New York Times*, 11 June 1939; Heywood Broun, "Up Pops the Wizard," *New Republic* 99 (21 June 1939): 186–87; Rovere, "Klan Rides Again," p. 446; Winfield Jones, *Knights of the Ku Klux Klan* (New York: Tocsin, 1941), pp. 153–56; private information, 28 October 1981.

265 "MOPPING UP THE CESSPOOLS . . .": U.S. Congress, *Report: The Present-Day Ku Klux Klan Movement.* 90 Cong., 1 Sess., House Committee on Un-American Activities (1967): 8.

266 "I AM AGAINST FLOGGINGS . . .": Atlanta *Constitution,* 11 July 1939.

266 "THE FIERY CROSS . . .": Brown, "Up Pops," p. 186.

266 "PAPERS ALL STATE HITLER . . .": Will Rogers, *Autobiography of Will Rogers,* ed. Donald Day (Boston: Houghton-Mifflin, 1949), p. 314.

266 "THE IDEAS AND METHODS . . ." New York *Herald Tribune,* 16 July 1933.

266 GERMAN ORDER OF THE FIERY CROSS: *New York Times,* 10–11 September 1925; *Living Age* 327 (17 October 1925): 128.

267 "THE AIM OF SECRET . . . SUCH ORGANIZATIONS": Adolf Hitler, *Mein Kampf,* trans. Ralph Manheim (Boston: Houghton-Mifflin, 1943), pp. 543, 546.

267 "MAY THESE AMERICAN REPORTS . . .": In *Kourier,* February 1925.

268 "WHILE THE KU KLUX KLAN HAS BEEN WAGING . . .": Ibid., March 1934.

268 "HITLER HAS APPRECIATED . . .": *New York Times,* 9 September 1934.

268 "WHEN HITLER HAS KILLED . . .": Stetson Kennedy, *I Rode with the Ku Klux Klan* (London: Arco, 1954), p. 221.

268 FRITZ KUHN AND THE GERMAN-AMERICAN BUND: Harold Lavine, *Fifth Column in America* (New York: Doubleday, Doran, 1940), pp. 158–67; Leland V. Bell, *In Hitler's Shadow: The Anatomy of American Nazism* (Port Washington, NY: Kennikat Press, 1973), pp. 9–90; Sander A Diamond, *The Nazi Movement in the United States, 1924–1941* (Ithaca: Cornell Univ. Press, 1974), pp. 318–19.

270 BUND AND AMERICAN INDIAN: *New Republic* 95 (17 May 1939): 31; Bell, *Hitler's Shadow,* p. 90.

270 "THE SOUTHERN KLANS . . .": McGill, *South and Southerner,* p. 143.

271 KLAN–BUND RALLY: *New York Times,* 19 August 1940; Boston *Globe,* 19 August 1940; John Roy Carlson, *Under Cover* (New York: Dutton, 1943), pp. 152–53.

271 "UNDER CLOSE AND CONSTANT . . .": *New York Times,* 20 August 1940.

271 "TO ADHERE TO THE PRINCIPLES . . . BUND AND THE KLAN": Ibid., 23–24 August 1940; Atlanta *Constitution,* 23 August 1940.

272 DIES COMMITTEE: St. Louis *Post-Dispatch,* 26 October 1939; William Gellerman, *Martin Dies* (New York: John Day, 1944); August R. Ogden, *The Dies Committee* (Washington, D.C.: Catholic Univ. of America Press, 1945); Lewis H. Carlson, "J. Parnell Thomas and the House Committee on Un-American Activities, 1938–1948" (Ph.D. diss., Michigan State University, 1967).

272 DIES COMMITTEE HEARINGS ON THE KLAN–BUND: Ogden, *Dies Committee,* pp. 216–17; *New York Times,* 3 October 1940.

273 HENRY FORD AND THE KLAN: U.S. Congress, House, *Congressional Record,* 77 Cong., 2 Sess. (1942): A1084.

273 DIES COMMITTEE HEARINGS ON COLESCOTT: U.S. Congress, *Executive Hearings.* 77 Cong., 2 Sess., House Special Committee to Investigate Un-American Activities and Propaganda in the United States (1942), VI: 2920–45.

274 "ESTEEMED KLANSMEN . . .": U.S. Congress, House, *Congressional Record,* 77 Cong., 2 Sess. (1942): A1085.

274 "JUST AS LOGICAL . . .": *The Nation* 162 (8 June 1946): 678.

274 "THE KLAN IS A DANGEROUS . . .": *New York Times,* 22 March 1942.

274 "AFTER ALL, THE KU KLUX KLAN . . .": In Cedric Belfrage, *The American Inquisition, 1945–1960* (Indianapolis: Bobbs-Merrill, 1973), p. 56.

275 "I WAS SITTING THERE . . .": Kennedy, *I Rode,* p. 87.

275 "THE KLAN IS DEAD . . .": Idem, "My Evening with the Wizard," August 1944, Stetson Kennedy Papers, Schomburg Collection of Negro History, New York Public Library.
275 "I AM STILL IMPERIAL WIZARD . . .": *New York Times*, 5 June 1944.
275 "IT WAS THAT NIGGER-LOVER . . .": Kennedy, *I Rode*, p. 87.

10. *"Divisible Invisible Empire"*

276 "THERE IS A REAL POSSIBILITY . . .": *New York Times*, 10 November 1944.
276 "JUST TO LET THE NIGGERS . . .": Stetson Kennedy, *Southern Exposure* (Garden City: Doubleday, 1946), p. 213.
277 "WE ARE REVIVED": *Time* 47 (20 May 1946): 20.
277 "SOME FOLKS PLAY GOLF . . .": Stetson Kennedy, "Green of the White Sheet," *Readers Scope* (November 1946): 85.
277 "THERE AIN'T A NIGGER . . .": Roi Ottley, "I Met the Grand Dragon," *The Nation* 169 (2 July 1949): 10–11.
277 "THE TIME MAY SOON . . .": Kennedy, "Green of the White," p. 87.
277 "IF ANYONE WANTS TO EAT . . .": Lester Velie, "The Klan Rides the South Again," *Colliers* 122 (9 October 1948): 14.
278 "THE HISTORIC ESTEEM . . . FOR THEM": New York *Star*, 3 September 1948.
278 "NO CIO OR AFL . . .": Harry T. Brundidge, "The Klan Rides Again," *Cosmopolitan* 121 (August 1946): 27.
278 "THIS COUNTRY . . . FAST ENOUGH": John Hope Franklin, "Civil Rights and the Truman Administration" in *Conference of Scholars on the Truman Administration and Civil Rights* (Independence, MO: Harry S. Truman Library Institute, 1968), p. 137. In vetoing a bill for segregated schools on federal property, Truman told Congress, "We have assumed a role of world leadership in seeking to unite people of great cultural and racial diversity for the purpose of resisting aggression, protecting their mutual security and advancing their own economic and political development. We should not impair our moral position by enacting a law that requires discrimination based on race. Step by step we are discarding old discriminations; we must not adopt new ones," ibid., p. 144.
278 AGK'S FEAR OF FEDERAL GOVERNMENT: Stetson Kennedy, "Facts About the Klan," n.d., Stetson Kennedy Papers, Schomburg Collection of Negro History, New York Public Library.
279 "THIS WILL TEACH . . .": *Newsweek* 32 (19 July 1948): 20.
279 "WE WELCOME THE KU KLUX KLAN . . .": Quoted in Alva W. Taylor, "Klan Seen Trying for a Comeback," *Christian Century* 67 (1 February 1950): 150.
279 "THERE'S SUCH AN ENORMOUS . . .": Velie, "Klan Rides the South," p. 15.
279 KLAN IN THE NORTH: *Time* 47 (3 June 1946): 25.
280 *"DE JURE* and *DE FACTO* . . .": Stetson Kennedy, "The Ku Klux Klan—What to Do About it," *New Republic* 113 (1 July 1946): 929.
280 "QUIETLY OUTRAGEOUS": Joe Klein, *Woody Guthrie* (New York; Knopf, 1980), p. 365.
280 KENNEDY'S EARLY CAREER: Barbara Harte and Carolyn Riley, eds., *Con-*

temporary Authors, (Detroit: Gale Research, 1969), V–VIII: 634; Laura Kavesh, "Freedom Fighter," Orlando (FL) *Sentinel Star*, 5 July 1981; Stetson Kennedy to W.C.W., 17 April, 14 May 1985; Ann Banks, "First-Person Florida," Miami *Herald*, 1 March 1981; Stetson Kennedy, unpublished biographical notes, 3 January 1985, Stetson Kennedy Private Files, hereafter cited SKPF.

281 "WHOSE HABITUÉS . . .": Idem, *I Rode with the Ku Klux Klan* (London: Arco, 1954), p. 24. Unless otherwise identified, all other quotations in this section are from this same source—the principal source of Kennedy's undercover activities in the Klan.

282 KENNEDY'S VALUABLE ACCOUNTS OF KLANSMEN are, for the most part, housed in a collection in his name at the Schomburg Collection of Negro History, New York Public Library, hereafter cited SCNH; see also *PM*, 24 March, 4 August 1947; New York *Star*, 5 September 1948.

282 J. B. STONER: Atlanta *Constitution*, 5 July 1946. Kennedy adds, "When I asked J. B. about the war he replied, 'I supported the U.S. war effort because I resented Hitler's efforts to get rid of our Jews for us. Every nation has a right to get rid of its own Jews' " (Kennedy to W.C.W., 5 June 1985).

283 "THAT WILL SAVE . . . JEWS": Idem, "Birthday Party for Dr. Samuel Green," 18 January 1946, SCNH.

283 KLAN AND LAW ENFORCEMENT: Idem to W.C.W., 14 May 1985.

283 DREW PEARSON: Kennedy's first contact with Pearson occurred during the war, when he sent him evidence that the Nazis were using the Franco Regime to spread anti-American propaganda in Latin America. For each of Kennedy's KKK dispatches, Pearson paid him $5 to $10; ibid., 17 April 1985.

284 REWARD OF $1,000; Kavesh, "Freedom Fighter."

284 "SO BITTER IN THEIR": Harold H. Martin, "The Truth about the Klan Today," *Saturday Evening Post* 222 (22 October 1949): 122.

284 GREEN BARS THE DOOR: Kennedy to W.C.W., 14 May 1985.

285 "ALWAYS PAINFULLY . . . BRAINS OUT": Ibid., 17 April 1985.

285 "ANTI-DEMOCRATIC FORCES": Stetson Kennedy, *Southern Exposure*, jacket cover. Kennedy dedicated this landmark book "To all—who strive for a new South—for all"; it remains the definitive source for the KKK's antiunion activities during the 1930s and 1940s.

285 AGK'S LOSS OF CHARTER: *New York Times*, 14 June 1947; Atlanta *Constitution*, 5 April 1965.

286 LEGAL PROSECUTION: New York *Sun*, 3 February 1948; New York *Post*, 4, 22 February 1948.

286 "AS SOON AS AN UNDERSTANDING . . .": Unidentified, undated clipping, SKPF.

286 "TO COMBAT . . . ORGANIC LAW": Application for Articles of Incorporation under the General Not for Profit Corporation Act, State of Illinois, Stetson Kennedy et al., n.d., SKPF.

286 "ONLY A PERVERT . . .": Horace Glass, "Stetson Kennedy: Humanity's Advocate," Mandarin (FL) *Weekly Advertiser*, 2 March 1981.

287 "IN A VIEW OF . . . STATE. . . .": Edward J. Barrett to Stetson Kennedy, 24 July 1947, SKPF.

287 KENNEDY VERSUS HUAC: Kennedy, *I Rode*, pp. 191–97; idem to W.C.W. 14 May 1985.

287 "EXPENDING A CONSIDERABLE . . . COURTS": J. Edgar Hoover to Thomas Clark, 24 September 1946, quoted in "Justice," *Report of the Commission on*

Civil Rights, Book 5, 1961 (Theodore Hesburgh Civil Rights Collection, University of Notre Dame Library, Notre Dame, Indiana), pp. 213–14.

288 "IN EACH CASE . . .'": Clark to Hoover in ibid., pp. 214–15.

288 "BURDENSOME . . . IN THERE": Ibid.

288 KENNEDY VERSUS FBI: Stetson Kennedy, "Does the FBI Actually Ask Aid of KKK in Dixie?" *Afro-American*, 24 September 1949; idem to W.C.W., 14 May 1985.

288 FBI VERSUS KENNEDY: Ibid.; "KW" to the Director, 16 September 1952; A. H. Belmont to D. M. Ladd, 10 November 1952; FBI Form No. 1, 4 June 1953; all the above in FBI Case File No. 100-348615, SKPF. Hoover was infuriated by a letter from an Australian writer who had read Kennedy's books: "Mr. Stetson Kennedy . . . says your organisation refuses to attack the KKK. Is it to be presumed your government and the President's [Eisenhower's] golf games in Georgia may be upset by such an attack? American justice is very strange" ([Deleted] to J. Edgar Hoover, 5 August 1957, in ibid.).

289 "NUMBER-ONE KLANBUSTER": Kennedy's later career is summarized in Chapter eleven. There is clearly a need for a first-rate biography of this unique American. In addition to the KKK material he deposited at the Schomburg Library, a large collection of Kennedy papers may be found in the Southern Labor Archives, Georgia State University, Atlanta. See also Glass, "Stetson Kennedy"; Kavesh, "Freedom Fighter"; Thomas Ralph Peters, Jr., "Stetson Kennedy: The 'Naturalist' Conservatism of a Southern Radical" (M.A. thesis, Georgia State University, 1983). At the present writing, Peters plans to expand his thesis into a doctoral dissertation at Emory University.

289 MAKING "HUMMON" GOVERNOR: Stetson Kennedy, "Report to the Georgia Bureau of Investigation," 18, 29 April 1946, 24 March 1947, SCNH; New York *Star*, 3, 7 September 1948; *New Republic* 119 (6 September 1948): 10; *New South* 4 (March 1949): 3–5.

289 "THEY'RE BOLSHEVIK KLANS . . .": *Newsweek* 32 (19 July 1949): 20; see also Velie, "Klan Rides the South," p. 15.

289 "THE KLAN DON'T HATE . . .": Stetson Kennedy, "Interview with Dr. E. P. Pruitt," 16 August 1946, SCNH.

290 MRS. MCDANAL: *Time* 54 (7 November 1949): 24.

290 "DO YOU WANT SOME . . . HOLY AND INCORRUPTIBLE": John Powell, "The Klan Un-Klandestine," *The Nation* 173 (29 September 1951): 255.

290 HAMILTON'S ARREST: *Time* 59 (25 February 1952): 28, (11 August 1952): 21; *Newsweek* 39 (26 May 1952): 31.

291 LYCURGUS SPINKS: Taylor, "Trying for a Comeback," p. 148; Martin, "Truth about the Klan," p. 122.

291 SPINKS MEETS THE PRESS: "The Imperial Emperor of the KKK Meets the Press," *American Mercury* 69 (November 1949): 529–38.

294 "EVERY DAMN TOMTIT . . .": Martin, "Truth about the Klan," p. 122.

294 "GOD STAMPED UGLINESS . . .": Nathan Perlmutter, "Bombing in Miami: Anti-Semitism and the Segregationalists," *Commentary* 25 (June 1958): 502.

295 FLORIDA BOMBINGS: Robert J. Murphy, "The South Fights Bombing," *Look* 23 (6 January 1959): 13–17.

295 HARRY T. MOORE CASE: *New York Times*, 27 December 1951; Joseph North, *Behind the Florida Bombings* (New York: New Century, 1952; copy in Special Collections, MSU Library); Stetson Kennedy, "Who Cares Who Killed Harry T. Moore?," *The Crisis* 89 (May 1982): 18–21; idem to W.C.W., 14 May 1985;

Harry T. Moore to F. A. Dunn, 28 September, 23 October 1950, typescript copies, SKPF. On Sheriff Willis V. McCall, see Stetson Kennedy, "Murder Without Indictment," *The Nation* 173 (24 November 1951): 444–46.

296 MAMIE CLAY CASE: *New York Times*, 4 April, 1–2 December 1949, 10 18, 19 March 1950; *Time* 55 (20 March 1950): 20.

297 U.S. VERSUS WILLIAMS: *New York Times*, 4 December 1965; Robert Sherrill, "Expose of Tedium, Terror and Fiscal Tricks at HUAC," *New South* 21 (Winter 1966): 63.

297 ANTI-KLAN LEGISLATION: Idem, "A Look Inside the Invisible Empire," *New South* 23 (Spring 1968): 6; Irving Bierman, "Alabama Rips Off the Hood," *Christian Science Monitor*, 2 July 1949, p. 3; *Newsweek* 35 (17 April 1950): 67; *New Republic* 126 (26 May 1952): 6.

297 "THE PHILOSOPHY THAT ALL MEN . . .": R. Carter Pittman, "The 'Blessing of Liberty' vs. the 'Blight of Equality,' " *North Carolina Law Review* 42 (December 1963): 88.

297 "THEY'VE GONE IN . . .": *New York Times*, 24 September 1957. See also Daisy Bates, *The Long Shadow of Little Rock* (New York: David McKay, 1962); Numan V. Bartley, "Looking Back at Little Rock," *Arkansas Historical Quarterly* 25 (1966): 101–106.

298 "SOMEHOW, SOME TIME . . .": Arkansas *Gazette*, 9 September 1957.

298 "WE CAN HOPE THAT WE . . .": Ibid., 24 September 1957.

298 "I AM PLEADING WITH YOU . . .": Robert F. Burk, *The Eisenhower Administration and Black Civil Rights* (Knoxville: Univ. Tennessee Press, 1984), p. 175.

298 "CIVIL RIGHTS IN THE EISENHOWER . . .": Ibid., p. 263.

299 "A FLESH-AND-BLOOD MATERIALIZATION . . .": C. Vann Woodward, "From the First Reconstruction to the Second," *Harpers* 230 (April 1965): 129.

299 "DON'T LET THIS HAPPEN . . .": Hodding Carter III, *The South Strikes Back* (Garden City: Doubleday, 1959), p. 83.

299 WHITE CITIZENS COUNCILS: Neil R. McMillen, *The Citizens' Council* (Urbana: Univ. Illinois Press, 1971); Carter III, *South Strikes; New Republic* 137 (23 September 1957): 6; James W. Vander Zanden, "The Citizens' Councils," *Alpha Kappa Deltan* 29 (Spring 1959): 3–10.

299 "WE WANT THE PEOPLE ASSURED . . .": Carter III, *South Strikes*, p. 39.

299 "KEEP AND PITCH OUR BATTLE . . .": McMillen, *Citizens' Council*, pp. 22–23.

299 "THE NEGRO PROPOSES . . .": In Benjamin Muse, *Ten Years of Prelude* (New York: Viking, 1964), p. 42.

299 "LITTLE WHITE GIRLS . . .": McMillen, *Citizens' Council*, pp. 186–87.

300 "THE MANICURED KLUXISM . . .": In Dan Wakefield, *Revolt in the South* (New York: Grove, 1960), p. 53.

300 A COLLECTION OF UNEDUCATED MISFITS: James W. Vander Zanden, "The Klan Revival," *American Journal of Sociology* 65 (March 1960): 456–62. See also Ralph McGill, *The South and the Southerner* (Boston: Little, Brown, 1963), p. 143; New York *Herald Tribune*, 16 April 1957.

300 "WE FEEL AN OBLIGATION . . .": *New South* 14 (July–August 1959): 11.

300 ROBERT WILLIAMS IN MONROE: Robert Williams, "The Swimming Pool Showdown," *Southern Exposure* 8 (Summer 1980): 22–24. Williams later authored *Negroes With Guns*, considered a revolutionary handbook by black

militants in the late 1960s; see Robert L. Allen, *Black Awakening in Capitalist America* (Garden City: Anchor, 1970), pp. 28–30.

301 "THERE COMES A TIME . . .": Harris Wofford, *Of Kennedys and Kings* (New York: Farrar, Straus & Giroux, 1980), p. 114.

302 "A LOT OF PEOPLE FIGURED . . .": Wakefield, *Revolt*, p. 50.

302 "THE OLD COUNTERSIGNS . . . ": In Vander Zanden, "Klan Revival," p. 460.

302 "A CONGLOMERATION OF DIFFERENT . . .": U.S. Congress, *Report: The Present-Day Ku Klux Klan Movement*. 90 Cong., 1 Sess., House Committee on Un-American Activities (1967): 12 (hereafter cited *HUAC Report*).

302 "WHEN THEY BOMB . . .": Stephen B. Oates, *Let the Trumpet Sound: The Life of Martin Luther King, Jr.* (New York: Harper & Row, Literary Guild ed. 1982), p. 105.

302 J. B. STONER: U.S. Congress, *Hearings on Ku Klux Klan Organizations*. 89 Cong., 1 Sess., House Committee on Un-American Activities (1965): 3809–10 (hereafter cited *HUAC Hearings*). On Stoner's trial and conviction for the 1958 Bethel Baptist bombing, see *New York Times*, 15 May 1980, 3 June 1983; *National Anti-Klan Network Newsletter* (Winter 1983): 7.

303 ASA "ACE" CARTER: New York *Herald Tribune*, 16, 24 April 1957; *Commentary* 29 (January 1960): 45–51.

303 EDWARD AARON MUTILATION: *HUAC Report*, p. 15; William B. Huie, *Three Lives for Mississippi* (New York: WCC Books, 1965), pp. 18–34.

303 JAMES "CATFISH" COLE: Raleigh *News and Observer*, 21 January 1958; New York *Herald Tribune*, 23 April 1957; *HUAC Hearings*, p. 1905.

304 KKK AND LUMBEE INDIANS: Charles Craven, "The Robeson County Indian Uprising Against the KKK," *South Atlantic Quarterly* 57 (Autumn 1958): 433–42; Brewton Berry, "The Myth of the Vanishing Indian," *Phylon* 21 (Spring 1960): 51–57; *HUAC Hearings*, p. 1906.

304 ELDON LEE EDWARDS: *New York Times*, 25 October 1955, 30 September, 1 October 1956; New York *Herald Tribune*, 23 April 1957; Fletcher Knebel and Clark Mollenhoff, "Eight Klans Bring New Terror to the South," *Look* 21 (30 April 1957): 59–69.

305 "WE HAVE BEEN ACCUSED . . .": "Special Report," CBS TV, 22 July 1957.

305 "THE WAVE OF CROSS-BURNINGS . . .": *U.S. News & World Report* 48 (18 April 1960): 54.

306 "IF LEGAL BARRIERS . . .": Ibid., p. 52.

306 "NOT SINCE RECONSTRUCTION . . .": Wakefield, *Revolt*, p. 23.

306 "I KNEW I WAS NOT WANTED . . .": John Steinbeck, *Travels with Charley* (1962; reprint New York: Penguin, 1984), p. 245. Supporting Steinbeck's observation, though from a different point of view, is a remark by the Charleston *Evening Post* (10 April 1958): "No, the South does not like the Klan—and neither does it like outside meddlers who have given the Klan its shot in the arm."

306 "IT IS THE AMERICAN TRADITION . . .": Wofford, *Kennedy and Kings*, p. 62.

11. *"The Roaring Sixties"*

307 "ABOUT ONE-HALF . . .": Harris Wofford, *Of Kennedy and Kings* (New York: Farrar, Straus & Giroux, 1980), p. 62.

308 KENNEDY'S CATHOLICISM: The Klan's position on the matter is surveyed in Arnold Rice, *The Ku Klux Klan in American Politics* (Washington, D.C.: Public Affairs Press, 1962), pp. 124–29. For the opposition of clergymen, see *New York Times*, 14 November 1958, 25 June 1959, 11 February 1960. Two doctoral dissertations have compared the Catholic issue in the campaigns of 1928 and 1960. Although both acknowledge that anti-Catholicism was less potent politically in 1960, they agree that Kennedy handled it with far greater eloquence and skill than Alfred E. Smith. See William D. Smith, "Alfred E. Smith and John F. Kennedy: the Religious Issue during the Presidential Campaigns of 1928 and 1960" (Ph.D. diss., Southern Illinois University, 1964); Elias Macropoulos, "The Treatment, With Respect to the Roman Catholic Issue, of the Democratic Candidates in the Presidential Elections of 1928 and 1960" (Ph.D. diss., New York University, 1966).

308 "ANYBODY THAT'LL VOTE . . .": Donald E. Williams, "Protest Under the Cross," *Southern Speech Journal* 27 (Fall 1961): 51.

308 "DID IT EVER OCCUR . . .": Paul J. Gillette, "Part-Time Wizard" in *The Ku Klux Klan: the Invisible Empire* (New York: Natlus Publications, 1964; copy in Library of Congress), p. 54.

308 "HAS GOT NEGROES ALL OVER . . .": Williams, "Protest Under the Cross," p. 50.

308 "WELL, MR. GRIFFIN, I BELIEVE . . .": *New York Times*, 14 October 1960.

309 "EVERY TIME HUMAN BEINGS . . .": In Williams, "Protest Under the Cross," p. 50.

309 JFK AND THE GROWTH OF THE KKK: ADL officials estimated that from March 1960 to January 1961, Klan membership grew from 8,500 to between 35,000 and 50,000; see Arnold Forster and Benjamin R. Epstein, *Report on the Ku Klux Klan* (New York: ADL, 1966), p. 20. This seems unreasonably high, but I accept that the numbers at least doubled.

309 "IT IS A REAL CONSTITUTIONAL . . .": C. Vann Woodward, "The 'New Reconstruction' in the South," *Commentary* 21 (June 1956): 501–508.

310 FREEDOM RIDERS: New York *Post*, 16 May 1961; Carl M. Brauer, *John F. Kennedy and the Second Reconstruction* (New York: Columbia Univ. Press, 1977), pp. 98–109. For the freedom riders' suits against the FBI, see *National Anti-Klan Network Newsletter* (Summer–Fall 1982): 11, (Winter 1983): 14, (Spring–Summer 1983): 3.

311 "AS WE ENTERED . . . GET HIM GOOD": Kate Stacy, "FBI Helped Klan," *Workers' Power*, 12 December 1975; New York *Post*, 16 May 1961.

311 KLAN, POLICE AND FBI IN BIRMINGHAM: U.S. Congress, Senate, *Hearings Before the Select Committee to Study Governmental Operations with Respect to Intelligence Activities*. 94 Cong., 1 Sess. (1975), VI: 110–18 (hereafter cited *Hearings on Intelligence Activities*); Nancy Cole, "Informer Reveals FBI's Role in Ku Klux Klan Attacks," *Intercontinental Press* 13 (15 December 1975): 1758–59.

312 "JOHN, JOHN, WHAT DO . . .": Arthur M. Schlesinger, Jr., *A Thousand Days* (New York: Fawcett, 1965), p. 855.

312 "SOUTHERN AFFILIATES WERE . . .": *National Anti-Klan Network Newsletter* (Winter 1983): 14.

312 "WHETHER WE AGREE . . .": JFK press conference, 19 July 1961, transcribed from private audiotape.

312 "BLESS GOD! WE NOW . . .": Brauer, *Second Reconstruction*, p. 103.

312 EVOLUTION OF THE UKA: U.S. Congress, *Report: The Present-Day Ku Klux*

Klan Movement. 90 Cong., 1 Sess., House Committee on Un-American Activities (1967): 16–21 (hereafter cited *HUAC Report*); U.S. Congress, *Hearings on Ku Klux Klan Organizations.* 89 Cong., 1 Sess., House Committee on Un-American Activities (1965): 2107–08, 2182 (hereafter cited *HUAC Hearings*).

312 ROBERT SHELTON: Gillette, "Part-Time Wizard" in *Ku Klux Klan,* pp. 53–56; Margaret Long, "The Imperial Wizard Explains the Klan," *New York Times Magazine* (5 July 1964): 8, 25–26; Kirk Loggins and Susan Thomas, "The 'New' Klan: White Racism in the 1980s," Nashville *Tennessean,* special tabloid, February 1980, p. 26; *HUAC Report,* p. 93; Robert Shelton interview, WKAR FM audiotape, circa 1971; copy in Voice Library, Michigan State University Library, East Lansing.

314 CALVIN CRAIG: *Life* 58 (23 April 1965): 33; Warren Pritchard, "Interview with a Former Grand Dragon," *New South* 24 (Summer 1969): 62–79.

315 BOB JONES: Pete Young, "A Few Soft Words for the Ku Klux Klan," *Esquire* 72 (July 1969): 104, 135–37; Frye Gaillard, *Race, Rock and Religion* (Charlotte, NC: East Woods Press, 1982), pp. 127–37.

315 "IT HAS BEEN BROUGHT . . . OUR COUNTRY": *HUAC Hearings,* p. 1713.

316 JAMES VENABLE: *Life* 58 (23 April 1965): 33; *HUAC Hearings,* pp. 3483–4029; *New York Times,* 25 February 1965.

316 "HERE'S MY PROBLEM, GOVERNOR . . .": Kennedy's taped phone conversations with Barnett were first made available to the public in late 1983; unable to transcribe them with sufficient speed, I have bolstered the excerpt here with Schlesinger, Jr., *Thousand Days,* pp. 862, 864.

317 "LITTLE BROTHER [RFK] . . .": Walter Lord, *The Past That Would Not Die* (New York: Harper & Row, 1965), p. 149.

317 "ON A STAND-BY ALERT . . .": Ibid., p. 184.

317 "PRETTY ROUGH . . . THOSE GUYS": Schlesinger, Jr., *Thousand Days,* pp. 865–66.

317 "THIS COUNTRY, OF COURSE . . . ": JFK press conference, 24 January 1963.

318 "PRESIDENT KENNEDY COULD HAVE . . .": *Time* 80 (12 October 1962): 19–22.

318 JFK'S EARLY BELIEFS ABOUT RECONSTRUCTION: John F. Kennedy, *Profiles in Courage* (1955; reprint New York; Perennial, 1964), pp. 112, 115–16, 134.

318 "THESE AND OTHER SIMILAR . . .": Brauer, *Second Reconstruction,* p. 204.

318 "IF SOUTHERN WHITES . . .": Quoted in Stephen B. Oates, *Let the Trumpet Sound* (New York: Harper & Row, Literary Guild ed. 1982), p. 203 fn.

318 "I'M COMING TO BELIEVE . . .": Schlesinger, Jr., *Thousand Days,* p. 882. Kennedy made this remark to Schlesinger after extending his condolences to the family of Medgar Evers at the White House. Byron de la Beckwith, who had connections with the Mississippi Klan, was tried but acquitted for Evers's murder. Afterward, he remarked to a Klansman, "Killing that nigger gave me no more inner discomfort than our wives endure when they give birth to our children. We ask them to do that for us. We should do just as much," in Willian H. McIlhany III, *Klandestine: The Untold Story of Delmar Dennis and His Role in the FBI's War Against the Ku Klux Klan* (New Rochelle, NY: Arlington, 1975), p. 38.

319 "LET'S BE READY": Theodore Sorensen, *Kennedy* (New York: Harper & Row, 1965), p. 491.

319 "THERE WASN'T ANY INTEREST . . .": In Oates, *Let the Trumpet Sound*, p. 210.

320 "A SNARLING POLICE DOG . . .": In Ralph G. Martin, *A Hero for Our Time* (New York: Macmillan, Literary Guild ed., 1983), p. 452.

320 "AND IT SEEMS TO ME . . .": JFK press conference, 8 May 1963.

320 KLAN RALLY IN BIRMINGHAM: WRVR FM audiotape, 11 May 1963, Voice Library, MSU.

321 UKA BOMB TRAINING: *HUAC Hearings*, pp. 2158–60; Harold H. Martin and Kenneth Fairly, "We Got Nothing to Hide," *Saturday Evening Post* 238 (30 January 1965): 31.

321 "IN THE NAME OF THE GREATEST . . .": Brauer, *Second Reconstruction*, p. 253.

322 THE KKK AND THE INTEGRATION OF U OF A: *Hearings on Intelligence Activities*, p. 130; Brauer, *Second Reconstruction*, pp. 253–57; *HUAC Hearings*, p. 3087.

322 CIVIL RIGHTS BILL: The Civil Rights Act of 1875 guaranteed blacks equal rights in inns, conveyances and theaters and forbade their exclusion from jury duty. It was struck down by the Supreme Court during the Arthur administration in 1883; see Stanley P. Hirshson, *Farewell to the Bloody Shirt* (Chicago: Quadrangle, 1968), pp. 103–105. The first sentence of Kennedy's bill said, "Discrimination by reason of race, color religion, or national origin is incompatible with the concepts of liberty and equality to which the Government of the United States is dedicated"; see Joan Martin Burke, *Civil Rights* (New York: Bowker, 1974), p. 167 passim.

323 "LET'S BE NON-VIOLENT . . .": *Newsweek* 62 (26 August 1963): 32; see also Claude Sitton, "Once More—The KKK," *New York Times Magazine* (11 August 1963): 8–9 plus.

323 "IT'S A SIT-IN": Henry Fairlie, "An Englishman Goes to a Klan Meeting," *New York Times Magazine* (23 May 1965): 28.

323 "WE DON'T WANT PEOPLE . . .": Long, "Imperial Wizard," p. 25.

323 "UNTIL KLAN MEMBERSHIP . . .": Article by Daniel Duke, *Atlanta Journal*, undated clipping, courtesy of Stetson Kennedy.

323 "MANY WELL-MEANING NIGRAS . . .": Long, "Imperial Wizard," p. 25.

323 "I THINK IT IS A CONVENIENT . . .": JFK press conference, 17 July 1963.

324 "I DIDN'T COME OUT . . .": *Newsweek* 62 (26 August 1963): 33.

324 SHELTON'S PLANE CRASH: Greenville (SC) *News*, 28 August 1963; *HUAC Hearings*, pp. 2116–17.

324 SIXTEENTH STREET BAPTIST BOMBING: Ibid., pp. 3232–33; Bill Cornwell, "The Birmingham Bombers, 1963–1976," *The Nation* 223 (4 September 1976): 165–67; *New York Times*, 17–18 February 1980.

325 J. B. STONER AND BOMBS: *HUAC Hearings*, pp. 3810–11.

325 CONNIE LYNCH: Trevor Armbrister, "Portrait of an Extremist," *Saturday Evening Post* 237 (22 August 1964): 80–83; Gillette, "The Extreme Extremist" in *Ku Klux Klan*, pp. 57–58.

326 "FOR THE LAST THIRTY YEARS . . . UNDER THE GROUND": Ibid., pp. 58–59. This singular speech has often been reprinted with minor variations. The excerpt here is from the eyewitness account of Irvin Cheney, who also recounts the mobbing of Dr. Hayling and his friends.

328 "IN A RIGHT-THINKING COMMUNITY . . .": David M. Chalmers, *Hooded Americanism* (1965; reprint Chicago: Quadrangle, 1968), p. 377.

328 "WE NEED TO DO A LOT . . .": Martin and Fairly, "Nothing to Hide," p. 33.

328 VIOLENT AND INTIMIDATING ACTS: Arnold Forster, *Report on the Ku Klux Klan* (New York: Anti-Defamation League of B'nai B'rith, 1965), pp. 33–34.

330 "THUS, WHEN THE TIME . . . CHILDREN'S CRUSADE": Stetson Kennedy to W.C.W., 28 May 1985.

330 "WHEN YOU HAVE ONE MAN . . .": Larry Goodwyn, "Anarchy in St. Augustine," *Harpers* 230 (January 1965): 78.

330 "THE MANAGEMENT COOPERATED . . .": Stetson Kennedy to W.C.W., 28 May 1985.

331 "WE ARE CARVING OUT . . .": Elizabeth B. Drew, "The Politics of Cloture," *The Reporter* 31 (16 July 1964): 20.

331 "I KNOW WHAT YOU FACED . . .": Oates, *Let the Trumpet Sound*, pp. 289–90.

331 "MARTIN LUCIFER COON . . .": Armbrister, "Extremist," p. 80; see also *New York Times*, 20 June 1964.

332 "I JUST DON'T SEE HOW . . .": George McMillan, "The Klan Scourges Old St. Augustine," *Life* 56 (26 June 1964): 21.

12. *"His Hot and Awful Light"*

333 "PAINT HIM BLACK . . .": Stetson Kennedy, *Jim Crow Guide to the U.S.A.* (London: Lawrence & Wishart, 1959), p. 229.

333 SAM BOWERS: U.S. Congress, *Hearings on the Ku Klux Klan Organizations.* 89 Cong., 1 Sess., House Committee on Un-American Activities (1965): 2908–41 (hereafter cited *HUAC Hearings*); Jack Nelson, "Terror in Mississippi," *New South* 23 (fall 1968): 48–57.

334 "THE TYPICAL MISSISSIPPI RED-NECK . . .": In William H. McIlhany III, *Klansdestine* (New Rochelle, Arlington, 1975), p. 31.

334 "AS CHRISTIANS, WE ARE DISPOSED . . .": *Newsweek* 67 (11 April 1966): 39.

335 "IT SHOULD BE DONE IN SILENCE . . .": *HUAC Hearings*, p. 2941.

335 MICHAEL SCHWERNER AND COFO: Richard Woodley, "A Recollection of Michael Schwerner," *The Reporter* 31 (16 July 1964): 23–24; Rita Schwerner affidavit in *Mississippi Black Paper* (New York: Random House, 1965), pp. 59–63.

336 "THEY MADE US AWARE . . .": Florence Mars, *Witness in Philadelphia* (Baton Rouge: Louisiana State Univ. Press, 1977), p. 113.

336 COFO ORIENTATION: Len Holt, *The Summer That Didn't End* (New York: Morrow, 1965), pp. 51–85; Robert Woodley, "It Will Be a Hot Summer in Mississippi," *The Reporter* 30 (21 May 1964): 21–24.

337 "*SEE HOW HEAVEN* . . .": Andrew Goodman, "Corollary to a Poem by A. E. Housman," *Massachusetts Review* 6 (Autumn–Winter 1964–65): 12.

337 "SIGNS POINT TOWARD . . .": *U.S. News & World Report* 56 (15 June 1964): 46–48; see also *Newsweek* 63 (88 June 1964): 45–46.

337 "OUTSIDERS WHO COME . . .": *Neshoba Democrat*, 9 April 1964.

337 "IT IS ABSOLUTELY NECESSARY . . .": U.S. Congress, *Report: The Present-Day Ku Klux Klan Movement.* 90 Cong., 1 Sess., House Committee on Un-American Activities (1967): 169; see Appendix C.

338 "THIS IS AS GOOD A TIME . . .": Don Whitehead, *Attack on Terror* (New York: Funk & Wagnalls, 1970), p. 48.

338 SCHWERNER, CHANEY, GOODMAN CASE: John Doar and Dorothy Landsberg, "The Performance of the FBI in Investigating Violations of Federal Laws Protecting the Right to Vote, 1960–1967" in U.S. Congress, Senate, *Hearings Before the Select Committee to Study Governmental Operations with Respect to Intelligence Activities.* 94 Cong., 1 Sess. (1975), VI: 933–39 (hereafter cited *Hearings on Intelligence Activities*). This case is the most infamous in Klan history, and my account is largely based on the extensive secondary literature. The best works are William B. Huie, *Three Lives for Mississippi* (New York: WCC Books, 1965); Mars, *Witness in Philadelphia*; Whitehead, *Attack on Terror*. Also useful are Holt, *Summer That Didn't End*; William McCord, *Mississippi: The Long Hot Summer* (New York: Norton, 1965); Jack Mendelsohn, *The Martyrs: Sixteen Who Gave Their Lives for Racial Justice* (New York: Harper & Row, 1966), pp. 109–32. William McIlhany's *Klandestine* contains much original information but is marred and annoyingly interrupted by the author's paeans to the John Birch Society.

340 "WE THROW TWO OR THREE . . .": McCord, *Long Hot Summer*, p. 81.

340 "WE ARE NOW IN THE MIDST . . .": *The Klan Ledger*, 4 July 1964 in *HUAC Hearings*, pp. 2756–57; see Appendix C.

340 "THE FBI AGENTS . . .": Meridian *Star*, 8 November 1964; *HUAC Hearings*, p. 2777.

341 "WET NURSING . . . THE SOUTH": *Washington Post*, 19 November 1964.

341 FBI IN MISSISSIPPI: Doar and Landsberg, "Performance of the FBI," pp. 933–39; *Newsweek* 67 (11 April 1966): 38–39; Neil J. Welch and David W. Marston, *Inside Hoover's FBI* (Garden City: Doubleday, 1984), pp. 92–108; Victor S. Navasky, *Kennedy Justice* (New York: Atheneum, 1971), pp. 437–38.

342 "WHAT MAKES THIS LYNCHING . . .": William B. Huie, "The Untold Story of the Mississippi Murders," *Saturday Evening Post* 237 (5 September 1964): 14.

342 "WE WERE INVADED . . .": In Whitehead, *Attack on Terror*, pp. 202–203.

342 "DESPITE WHAT YOU THINK . . .": W.C.W. to John Goodwin, 19 September 1964.

343 "SCHWERNER, CHANEY, AND GOODMAN . . .": Mars, *Witness in Philadelphia*, p. 108.

343 BOWERS'S KLAN ACTIVITIES AFTER THE MURDERS: *Newsweek* 64 (21 December 1964): 22–24, 66 (1 November 1965): 34; *HUAC Hearings*, pp. 2936–37.

344 "THE RIGHT OF EVERY PERSON . . .": Whitehead, *Attack on Terror*, p. 219.

344 LEMUEL PENN CASE: The definitive account is Bill Shipp, *Murder at Broad River Bridge* (Atlanta: Peachtree, 1981). See also "Criminal Law: Conspiracy— Georgia," *Race Relations Law Reporter* 12 (Summer 1967): 634–43; *Newsweek* 64 (17 August 1964): 29–30; William B. Huie, "Murder: The Klan on Trial," *Saturday Evening Post* 238 (19 June 1965): 86–89.

345 "IF THEY GET AWAY . . .": John Barron, "The FBI's Secret War Against the Ku Klux Klan," *Readers Digest* 88 (January 1966): 91.

345 "YOU'LL NEVER BE ABLE . . .": Ibid., p. 92.

346 "YOU KNOW HOW THEY . . .": Harold H. Martin and Kenneth Fairly, "We Got Nothing to Hide," *Saturday Evening Post* 238 (30 January 1965): 28.

346 "I WOULD URGE ALL MEMBERS . . .": *Newsweek* 64 (21 December 1964): 23.

346 "TO CONVINCE YOU THAT . . .": Paul Good, "Klantown, USA," *The Nation* 200 (1 February 1965): 110.

347 "PEOPLE OF SOUND MIND . . .": In Ibid., pp. 112–13.

347 VIOLA LIUZZO CASE: Mendelsohn, *The Martyrs*, pp. 176–95; Detroit *Free Press*, 26–29 March 1965; Johnny Greene, "Did the FBI Kill Viola Liuzzo?," *Playboy* 27 (October 1980): 100–108 plus; *HUAC Hearings*, p. 3259; *Newsweek* 66 (1 November 1965): 36.

349 "IT IS NOT A WELCOME DUTY . . .": Charles E. Fager, *Selma 1965* (New York: Scribner's, 1974), pp. 148–49.

349 WILKINS, THOMAS, AND EATON: *HUAC Hearings*, p. 3062; *Hearings on Intelligence Activities*, pp. 110–119.

350 "VI, BE CAREFUL . . .": Greene, "Viola Liuzzo," p. 102.

350 "IF YOU HIT THAT . . . I DON'T MISS": The dialogue here is synthesized from two separately published segments: Mendelsohn, *The Martyrs*, p. 191; *Newsweek* 66 (1 November 1965): 36.

351 GARY ROWE, FBI INFORMER: *Hearings on Intelligence Activities*, pp. 110–19; Gary Rowe interview, *Today Show*, NBC Television, 6 July 1976. Ten years after Mrs. Liuzzo's death, and shortly after Wilkins and Thomas were released from prison after serving time for her murder, they charged Rowe with being the principal trigger man in the case. The state of Alabama served Rowe with an indictment but it was overturned in federal court in 1980. Rowe's attorney argued, "The only way to force the Government to reveal Rowe's new identity was to get him indicted, and the Ku Klux Klan would not hesitate to employ perjury and political influence in its quest for revenge. . . . The Klan's strategy failed in that Rowe was never incarcerated or extradited to Alabama for trial. Still, the Klan proved that it can penetrate the Federal witness-protection program, that it can use the Alabama legal system to carry out its terrorist plots, and that it never forgets its enemies." There has been considerable speculation that Rowe was more involved in the shooting than he cared to admit. Though an erratic and inconsistent person, Rowe has steadfastly denied culpability in the Liuzzo case, and all known facts support him. After being forced to break cover during the indictment, Rowe has returned to safety with a new FBI-furnished identity; see *Playboy* 28 (February 1981): 56, 59; *Newsweek* 92 (24 July 1978): 41.

351 "WE WILL NOT BE INTIMIDATED . . .": Detroit *Free press*, 27 March 1965.

352 "I STATED [JIM LIUZZO] . . .": Greene, "Viola Liuzzo," p. 174.

352 "IF THIS WOMAN . . .": Detroit *Free Press*, 27 March 1965. For the Klan's smear campaign against Mrs. Liuzzo, see *HUAC Hearings*, pp. 3328–31.

353 "I DON'T THINK . . . HER FEELINGS WERE": Lyn Tornabene, "Murder in Alabama," *Ladies Home Journal* 82 (July 1965): 42–44. Tornabene concluded her review of the survey, in which 55.2 percent of the women were against Mrs. Liuzzo, by asking, "Can women really manage to make their homes tight little, safe little islands in these days and the days to come?"

353 "DO YOU NEED A CROWD . . .": Greene, "Viola Liuzzo," p. 108.

353 "YOU KNOW WHAT THE NIGGER . . .": Mendelsohn, *The Martyrs*, p. 192.

354 "IF YOU DON'T RENDER . . .": *Newsweek* 66 (1 November 1965): 36; see also Richmond Flowers, "Southern Plain Talk About the Ku Klux Klan," *Look* 30 (3 May 1966): 36–44.

354 THE LIUZZO CHILDREN: *National Anti-Klan Network Newsletter* (Spring–Summer 1983): 3, (Fall 1983): 5.

355 "I BELIEVE I SPEAK . . .": Atlanta *Constitution*, 5 April 1965.

355 "SENDING A GOOSE . . . VIGILANT IN FACT": *Christian Century* 82 (14 April 1965): 453.

355 "THE SCLC IS OPPOSED . . .": Ibid. (2 September 1965): 1149; see also *The Nation* 200 (19 April 1965): 406–407.

355 HUAC SUBCOMMITTEE COMPOSITION: Robert Sherrill, "Exposé of Tedium, Terror and Fiscal Tricks at HUAC," *New South* 21 (Winter 1966): 57–58; *HUAC Hearings*, p. 3065.

356 "SHELTON: THERE IS SEVERAL KLANS . . .": *Playboy* 12 (August 1965): 45–46 plus. This interesting interview was very capably conducted by Bern Keating (Marcia Terrones to W.C.W., 5 June 1985).

357 "TO INVESTIGATE . . . AMERICA SAFE": *HUAC Hearings*, pp. 2650–51.

357 "I'LL BE THERE WITH . . .": *Newsweek* 66 (1 November 1965): 34.

357 "SIR, I RESPECTFULLY . . .": *HUAC Hearings*, p. 1604.

357 "FOR A KLUXER . . .": Walter Goodman, "The Klan Discovers HUAC," *The Nation* 201 (8 November 1965): 329; see also idem, "The H.U.A.C. Meets the K.K.K.," *New York Times Magazine* (5 December 1965): 48–49.

358 "I'M TRYING TO FIND . . .": *Christian Century* 82 (24 November 1965): 1435–36.

358 "AND NEVER ANSWER . . .": Murray Kempton, "The Klan Clams up," *New Republic* 153 (30 October 1965): 12.

358 "DAYLIGHT AND LOGIC . . .": *Time* 86 (29 October 1965): 29.

358 "FOCUS WHERE IT'S SMALL . . .": Kempton, "Klan Clams Up," pp. 11–13.

359 "POOL: ARE YOU TELLING ME . . .": *HUAC Hearings*, pp. 3586–87.

359 "POOL: MRS. BAIRD . . .": Ibid., p. 3596.

360 "EVENTUALLY BECAME THE HIGH . . .": Sherrill, "Exposé of Tedium," p. 60.

360 "APPELL: MR. DUBOIS . . .": *HUAC Hearings*, p. 1829.

360 HUAC'S EFFECT ON THE KKK: Richard T. Schaefer, "The Ku Klux Klan: Continuity and Change," *Phylon* 32 (Summer 1971): 152–53: *HUAC Hearings*, p. 3258; Justin Finger, "The Exploiters," *ADL Bulletin* (November 1966): 3.

361 OURS IS A RIGHTEOUS . . .": *The Fiery Cross* reprinted in *HUAC Hearings*, p. 2900.

361 COINTELPRO: *Hearings on Intelligence Activities*, pp. 400–405, 992–95; *Newsweek* 86 (25 August 1975): 75; Ovid Demaris, *The Director: An Oral Biography of J. Edgar Hoover* (New York: *Harper's* magazine, 1975), pp. 324–27.

362 "MY INSTRUCTIONS WERE TO SLEEP . . .": *Hearings on Intelligence Activities*, p. 130.

362 "YES, MRS.———— . . .": Ibid., p. 404.

362 EVERYBODY SUSPECTS EVERYBODY . . .": Phoenix *Arizona Republic*, 3 April 1967.

362 FBI MERIDIAN SCAM: Los Angeles *Times*, 13 February 1970; Frye Gaillard, *Race, Rock, and Religion* (Charlotte: East Woods, 1982), pp. 132–33. After Kathy Ainsworth was killed, Sam Bowers wrote to the police, complaining they had murdered "a Christian, American patriot . . . doing her best to preserve Christian civilization by helping to destroy the body of an animal of Satan's synagogue" (Nelson, "Terror in Mississippi," p. 48).

363 "SO THE FBI DID NOT LURE . . .": Thomas A. Tarrants III, *The Conversion of a Klansman* (Garden City: Doubleday, 1979), p. 126.

363 "ARE YOU GOING TO SPEND . . .": Demaris, *The Director*, pp. 324–25.

363 "ONE OF THE MAJOR FACTORS . . .": *Hearings on Intelligence Activities*, p. 213.

363 "THE FBI'S COUNTERINTELLIGENCE . . .": *The Fiery Cross*, No. 13, 1978.

364 "HATERS DON'T NEED . . .": In Robert Sherrill, "A Look Inside the Invisible Empire," *New South* 23 (spring 1968): 8.

364 "AT LEAST A KLANSMAN . . .": Tom Wicker, "George Wallace: A Gross and Simple Heart," *Harpers* 234 (April 1967): 41–49.

364 THE KLAN IN THE NORTH: For a typical account, see William C. Tremblay, "Reporter Joins KKK, Finds Tame 'Yes Men,' " *Editor and Publisher* 100 (20 May 1967): 15. The investigative reporter remarked that Michigan Klansmen "don't do much of anything—except collect dues."

364 DANNY BURROS: *Time* 86 (12 November 1965): 54.

364 "SOMETHING VERY SAD . . .": Stewart Alsop, "Portrait of a Klansman," *Saturday Evening Post* 239 (9 April 1966): 25.

365 SUPREME COURT RULINGS ON APPLICABILITY OF KU-KLUX STATUTES: In the Penn case, the Court stated that "Section 241 [see Appendix E] must be read as it is written" and that its "language includes rights and privileges protected by the Fourteenth Amendment"—including interstate commerce. Since Penn was engaged in interstate travel at the time he was killed, the Court ruled that his murder fell within the purview of Section 241. In the Mississippi case, the Court ruled that Section 242 applied: "the State [Neshoba County Sheriff's Office], without the assemblance of due process of law, as required by the Fourteenth Amendment, used its sovereign power and office to release the victims from jail so that they were not charged and tried by law, but instead could be intercepted and killed," *Hearings on Intelligence Activities*, p. 951; see also Sherrill, "Exposé of Tedium," pp. 62–63.

366 "THIS IS AN IMPORTANT CASE . . .": In Whitehead, *Attack on Terror*, p. 281.

366 "A GALLOPING REVOLUTION . . . EVER DID": C. Vann Woodward, "From the First Reconstruction to the Second," *Harpers* 230 (April 1965): 128, 133.

367 1970 GALLUP POLL: "The Public's Rating of Controversial Organizations," *Gallup Opinion Index* 62 (August 1970): 11, 69.

13. "A Bible in One Hand and a .38 in the Other"

368 "HE SAT ON MY PROGRAM . . .": Kirk Loggins and Susan Thomas, "The 'New' Klan," Nashville *Tennessean*, special tabloid, February 1980, p. 17.

368 "I CERTAINLY WAS PREPARED . . .": *Newsweek* 90 (14 November 1977): 45.

368 "WE'VE GOT TO GET . . .": Ibid. 87 (12 January 1976): 34.

369 "THOUSANDS OF ORGANIZATIONS . . .": Wayne King, "The Violent Rebirth of the Klan," *New York Times Magazine* (7 December 1980): 158; see also Ted Stewart, "The KKK Takes to TV Plugs," *Sepia* 25 (March 1976): 82.

369 "YOU MUST UNDERSTAND . . .": "An Interview with David Duke," *Easyriders* 9 (July 1980): 25. In the course of this interview for bikers, Duke remarked, "I am the best leader the Klan has got today. I know the facts about integration and busing and I know the history of the Klan very well. I have been very successful in bringing forth the ideas of the organization to the American public," p. 83.

369 "I LIKED DUKE . . .": Harry Crews, "The Button-down Terror of David Duke," *Playboy* 27 (February 1980): 104.

369 DAVID DUKE: Ibid., pp. 102–104 plus; David Duke interview, *Donahue Show*, ABC TV, 21 July 1978; Loggins and Thomas, " 'New' Klan," pp. 17–21; Patsy Sims, *The Klan* (New York: Stein & Day, 1978), pp. 178–82.

370 "HE COMES ON LIKE . . .": *The Fiery Cross*, No, 13, 1978.

371 "THEY ARE JUST AS KLAN-ORIENTED . . .": *Newsweek* 84 (16 December 1974): 16A.

371 "YOU CAN'T DO YOURSELF . . .": In Jerry Thompson, "My Life with the Klan," Nashville *Tennessean*, special tabloid, December 1980, p. 13.

371 "I THINK SOME MEXICANS . . .": *Newsweek* 90 (14 November 1977): 45.

372 TOM METZGER: Loggins and Thomas, " 'New' Klan," pp. 28–30; Pittsburgh *Press*, 1 June 1980; South Bend *Tribune*, 5, 17 June 1980; private information, 17 June 1985.

372 DON BLACK AND DOMINICA: Randall Williams, ed., *The Ku Klux Klan: A History of Racism and Violence* (Montgomery: Klanwatch Special Report, 1982), pp. 60, 64; *The Nation* 232 (30 May 1981): 656; *Klanwatch Intelligence Report* (November–December 1981): 1.

373 LOUIS BEAM: Williams, *Racism and Violence*, p. 60; *Klanwatch Intelligence Report* (March 1981): 1; Loggins and Thomas, " 'New' Klan," p. 43.

373 BILL WILKINSON: Ibid., pp. 4–5, 11; King, "Violent Rebirth," pp. 150–60; *Life* 4 (June 1981): 32–40.

373 DUKE'S BRITISH TOUR: *Newsweek* 91 (20 March 1978): 45.

374 WILKINSON IN PLAINS: King, "Violent Rebirth," p. 158; *The Economist* 264 (9 July 1977): 36.

374 "DO ME A FAVOR . . .": Loggins and Thomas, " 'New' Klan," p. 12.

375 WILKINSON'S STANCE OF VIOLENCE: Williams, *Racism and Violence*, pp. 49, 61; King, "Violent Rebirth," p. 159; Loggins and Thomas, " 'New' Klan," p. 12.

375 KLAN IN THE MILITARY: *Newsweek* 88 (13 December 1976): 37; "Black Marines Battle Ku Klux Klan at Camp Pendleton Base," *Black Scholar* 8 (April 1977): 46–49; *Klanwatch Intelligence Report* (April 1981): 3.

375 JOHN A. WALKER, JR. AND THE NAVY KLAN: *Time* 125 (3 June 1985): 23; C. R. Gibbs, "The Klan Is Not Back—It Never Went Anywhere," *Bilalian News*, 13 June 1980, p. 5.

376 VIOLENCE IN MISSISSIPPI: Ken Lawrence, "The Ku Klux Klan Revival in Mississippi," research report prepared by the Anti-Repression Resource Team for the conference of the National Anti-Klan Network, 1981, 7 pp.; "Violence, Vigilantism and the Invisible Empire," *Klanwatch Intelligence Report* (March 1981): 6–7; Andrew Marx and Tom Tuthill, "Resisting the Klan: Mississippi Organizes," *Southern Exposure* 8 (Summer 1980): 25–28.

377 VIOLENCE IN DECATUR: King, "Violent Rebirth," p. 159; Rick Dunn, "Decatur March Marks New Movement Era," reprinted from *SCLC National Magazine* by the National Anti-Klan Network, n.d., 5 pp.; *National Anti-Klan Network Newsletter* (hereafter cited *NAKN Newsletter*) (Winter 1983): 13.

377 "I COULDN'T BELIEVE IT . . .": "Victims of Racist Violence Tell Their Stories," flyer published by the National Anti-Klan Network, n.d.

378 THE GREENSBORO CASE: Terry Eastland, "The Communists and the Klan," *Commentary* 69 (May 1980): 65–67; Michael Parenti and Carolyn Kazdin, "The Untold Story of the Greensboro Massacre," *Monthly Review* 33 (November 1981): 42–50; "The Greensboro Civil Rights Suit: The Struggle Against Racist Violence," flyer published by the Greensboro Justice Fund, n.d.; Philip Zwerling and Martha Nathan to W.C.W. (form letter), 21 March 1983; "The Case

of the 80s," flyer published by the Greensboro Justice Fund, n.d.; *Washington Post*, 22 June 1980; E. Lansing *State News*, 18 November 1980; *NAKN Newsletter* (Fall 1984): 2; Vanessa Gallman, "Klan Confrontations: Offensive, Defensive Tactics," *Southern Exposure* 8 (Summer 1980): 29; Milo Hunter to W.C.W. (telephone), 13 May 1985. In response to the public outcry against Greensboro, Robert Shelton wrote that the UKA was "in no way involved in this unwise and unnecessary incident that has caused the Klan Movement in America a loss of credibility and a colossal black eye": *The Fiery Cross*, No. 23, 1980.

380 "ADULTS AND CHILDREN ARE SINGING . . .": Based on videotape shown on *Frontline,* NET TV, 31 January 1983.

381 "SOME SAY IT WAS A SHOOTOUT . . .": Greensboro *Record*, 20 April 1982.

382 "THE ONLY THING THE KLAN . . .": Pittsburgh *Press*, 27 July 1980.

382 "I DON'T THINK WE ARE OUT . . .": Ibid.

382 "HAD TAKEN A MACHINE GUN . . .": Parenti and Kazdin, "Greensboro Massacre," p. 48.

382 "FROM THE VERY BEGINNING . . .": South Bend *Tribune*, 18 November 1980.

382 "WE ARE THE ONES BEING ATTACKED . . .": Bill Wilkinson interview, *Nightline*, ABC TV, 13 November 1980.

383 "BUT AFTER FIFTEEN YEARS OF INTEGRATION . . .": Pittsburgh *Post-Gazette*, 27 October 1980.

383 "IS DISGUSTINGLY MORE IMMORAL . . .": South Bend *Tribune*, 16 January 1983.

383 "THE IDEA THAT RELIGION . . .": In Norman Lear, People for the American Way form letter, 24 August 1984.

383 "GOD ALMIGHTY DOES NOT HEAR . . .": *Time* 116 (29 September 1980): 85. On the revival of fundamentalism in the 1980s see Flo Conway and Jim Siegelman, *Holy Terror* (Garden City: Doubleday, 1982).

384 "HAVE A KLAVERN HERE VERY SHORTLY . . .": South Bend *Tribune*, 27 January 1980.

384 "WE'VE RECRUITED MORE PEOPLE . . .": Pittsburgh *Post-Gazette*, 24 October 1980.

384 "WILKINSON HAS TRAVERSED . . .": *The Fiery Cross*, No. 24, 1981.

385 "I WOULD EVEN LIKE . . .": Robert Keating, "The Ku Klux Kids," *Rolling Stone* (11 June 1981): 62.

385 CAMP MY LAI: *New York Times*, 28 September 1980; *Newsweek* 96 (6 October 1980): 52; Chicago *Tribune*, 26 October 1980.

385 "MANY THINGS YOUR TEACHERS . . . GOD ALMIGHTY": *Thirty Minutes*, CBS TV, 20 September 1980.

385 "AN ATTEMPT IS BEING MADE . . .": In "Klan Youth Corps: 'Hand-Me-Down' Racism," *Klanwatch Intelligence Report* (April 1981): 6–7.

386 ACTIVITIES OF KKK YOUTH CORPS: Keating, "Ku Klux Kids," pp. 22–23 plus; *Thirty Minutes*, CBS TV, 20 September 1980; Guy Martin, "Ain't Nothin' You Can Do But Join the Klan," *Esquire* 93 (March 1980): 35–38; *New York Times*, 24 November 1980; "We're the Future Klan," flyer reprinted from the *NEA Reporter* by the National Anti-Klan Network, June 1981.

386 FREELANCE KLAN VIOLENCE: *Klanwatch Intelligence Report* (March–April 1982): 12; South Bend *Tribune*, 1 January 1981; Williams, *Racism and Violence*, p. 46; Pittsburgh *Post-Gazette*, 1 January 1981; *Unitarian: Universalist World*, 1 April 1981; *Washington Post*, 22 May 1981.

386 CHATTANOOGA CASE: Chattanooga *Times*, 12 September 1981, 27 February 1982; Harry Jaffe, "Women vs. the KKK," *Family Circle* (4 October 1983): 46–50; Chicago *Tribune*, 26 October 1980. One of the Klansmen involved in the attack was later jailed for raping a seven-year-old girl; see *NAKN Newsletter* (Winter–Spring 1984): 7.

386 MICHAEL DONALD CASE: Ibid. (Fall 1983): 6; *Newsweek* 103 (13 February 1984): 30.

386 "WE DIDN'T KNOW HIM . . .": Morris Dees to W.C.W. (form letter), 16 January 1984.

387 VIOLENT ANTI-KLAN DEMONSTRATIONS: Pittsburgh *Post-Gazette*, 17 March 1980; Pittsburgh *Press*, 14 September 1980; *Washington Post*, 22 March 1981; Washington *Star*, 22 March 1981; Boston *Globe*, 17 October 1982; Detroit *Free Press*, 2 December 1982; Carl T. Rowan, "Punish Rioters Who Help the Klan," AP release, 4 December 1982.

387 KLAN AND THE 1980 CAMPAIGN: South Bend *Tribune*, 2 September 1980; Pittsburgh *Post-Gazette*, 3 September 1980; *U.S. News & World Report* 89 (29 September 1980): 7; see also Thompson, "My Life With the Klan," pp. 18–20.

388 "IT'S RISEN TO SUCH A HIGH . . .": Bill Wilkinson interview, *Tomorrow* show, NBC TV, 23 September 1980.

388 "THE TIME TO DROP . . .": South Bend *Tribune*, 4 September 1980.

388 "I DON'T SEE ANY DIFFERENCE . . .": Loggins and Thomas, " 'New' Klan," p. 43.

388 "FANTASTIC. IT SHOWS . . .": South Bend *Tribune*, 18 November 1980.

389 "I KIND OF ENJOYED THE STICK . . .": Pittsburgh *Press*, 23 November 1980.

389 "PEOPLE HAVE BEEN TREATING . . .": Ibid.

389 "A GREAT VICTORY FOR WHITE PEOPLE . . .": *Klanwatch Intelligence Report* (April 1981): 1.

389 "WHAT HAPPENED IN GREENSBORO . . .": King, "Violent Rebirth," p. 160.

389 "IT WOULD BE A RACIALIST . . .": Ibid.: see also Chicago *Tribune*, 26 October 1980.

390 NAAWP: David Duke interview, *Crossfire*, CNN TV, 27 July 1984. In this interview, Duke, as leader of the NAAWP, said the exact same things he had been saying for years as Wizard of the KKK.

390 "I WIPED HIM OUT . . .": King, "Violent Rebirth," p. 160.

390 NEA VERSUS NFT: *New York Times*, 31 October 1981; "An Open Letter to the Anti-Defamation League," flyer published by the National Anti-Klan Network, n.d.

391 NATIONAL ANTI-KLAN NETWORK: Mark Alfonso to W.C.W., 18 August 1982; Janet H. Caldwell to W.C.W., 4 April 1985; ibid. (telephone), 3 June 1985; *NAKN Newsletter* (Fall 1983): 1, (Winter–Spring 1984): 7. The NAKN's approach to specific problems is described in Jaffe, "Women vs. the KKK," pp. 46–50.

391 REPORTING ON KLANSMEN WITHOUT ENCOURAGING THEM: This became a major issue with Klan-fighters of the 1980s. See Dean Calbreath, "Kovering the Klan," *Columbia Journalism Review* (March–April 1981): 42–45; "How the Media Helps the Klan," *Klanwatch Intelligence Report* (March–April 1982): 14.

392 SOUTHERN POVERTY LAW CENTER: Morris Dees to W.C.W., 21 November 1980; Randall Williams to W.C.W. (telephone), 4 June 1985; Randall Williams interview, *Late Night America*, NET TV, 2 October 1984.

392 "KLANSMEN HAVE THE SAME RIGHTS . . .": "New Tools to Fight the Ku Klux Klan," brochure published by the Southern Poverty Law Center, n.d.

392 "REAGAN ADMINISTRATION'S POLICIES . . .": *Klanwatch Intelligence Report* (May–June 1982): 11.

392 LOUIS BEAM AND THE VIETNAMESE: Julian Bond to W.C.W. (form letter), 7 July 1981; Morris Dees to W.C.W. (form letter), 15 September 1981; *Klanwatch Intelligence Report* (June 1981): 1. A similar problem had occurred in Cullman, Alabama, in 1979 when Klansmen objected to Vietnamese refugees working at a local textile mill; see Loggins and Thomas, " 'New' Klan," p. 41.

393 "ANYTIME AN OUT-OF-STATE . . .": David A Baylinson to W.C.W. (form letter), 14 June 1985.

393 BAN ON TEXAS PARAMILITARY CAMPS: Houston *Chronicle*, 4 June 1982; *Poverty Law Report* (September–October 1982): 2, 10; *NAKN Newsletter* (Summer–Fall 1982): 7.

394 KLAN UNITY CONFERENCE: Ibid., p. 5; *Klanwatch Intelligence Report* (September–October 1982): 11; Julian Bond to W.C.W. (form letter), 10 January 1983. The principal leaders at this conference were Glenn Miller (NC), Robert Miles (MI), Don Black (AL), Edward Fields (GA), David Duke (LA), and Sam Bowers (MS). They elected Don Black to head the organization, but Black soon afterward began serving a three-year term in prison for the Dominica fiasco. Julian Bond remarked, "One of the most disturbing things about this Klan unity effort is that for the first time no attempt is being made to hide the Klan–Nazi connection."

394 KLANWATCH'S DECATUR SUIT: *New York Times*, 5 November 1980; Morris Dees to W.C.W. (form letter), 15 September 1981; Julian bond to W.C.W. (form letter), 15 December 1982.

394 "BECAUSE THEY THRIVE . . .": *Newsweek* 103 (28 May 1984); 69.

395 "EVERYONE SHOULD TRY . . .": *Time* 121 (7 February 1983): 20.

395 "A PLOY TO DESTROY . . .": *NAKN Newsletter* (Fall 1983): 15.

395 "AT THIS SITTING . . .": Ibid.; see also *Poverty Law Report* (Fall 1983): 4.

395 "IT'S ONE THING FOR SOMEBODY . . .": *New York Times*, 31 July 1983.

395 "EVERYTIME WE PICK UP . . .": Morris Dees to W.C.W. (form letter), 23 September 1983.

395 "THIS INCIDENT JUST REDOUBLED . . .": *NAKN Newsletter* (Fall 1983); 15; for the convictions of the Klansmen arsonists, see Montgomery *Advertiser*, 13 December 1984.

396 INDICTMENTS IN DECATUR CASE: *Newsweek* 103 (28 May 1984): 69.

396 "THE SIGNIFICANT THING . . .": Morris Dees to W.C.W. (form letter), 1 June 1984.

396 "NO ONE CAN REMEMBER . . .": Ibid.

Postscript

397 HOUSTON REFERENDUM: Houston *Chronicle*, 15–20 January 1985; Houston *Post*, 15–20 January 1985; Harold H. Best III to W.C.W., 16 May 1985.

398 "A CIVIL ACTION UNIT . . .": *NAKN Newsletter* (Winter 1985): 5.

398 "DID EVERYTHING IT COULD . . .": William K. Tabb and Martha Nathan, "Civil Rights, the Klan and Reagan Justice," *The Nation* 235 (21–28 August 1982): 139–41.

398 "HE IS A PATRIOTIC CITIZEN . . .": *NAKN Newsletter* (Winter–Spring 1984): 15.

398 "I FELT LIKE I DIED . . .": Ibid., p. 1.

398 "FOR THE FIRST TIME WE'RE . . .": *Newsweek* 105 (8 April 1985): 87.

399 "IT MAY BE THAT WHEN CONGRESS . . .": *Waller* v. *Butkovich*, Memorandum: Civil Action No. 80-605-G, U.S. District Court for the Middle District of North Carolina, Greensboro Division, 24 March 1985, p. 16.

399 DEBATE ON KU-KLUX STATUTES DURING RECONSTRUCTION: U.S. Congress, Senate, *Congressional Globe*, 42 Cong., 1 Sess. (1871): A218–20.

400 THE ARYAN NATIONS: *Poverty Law Report* (Winter 1984): 3; *Newsweek* 106 (4 March 1985): 23–26; Morris Dees to W.C.W. (form letter), 8 March 1985; Peter Lake interview, *Late Night America*, NET TV, 29 March 1985; Atlanta *Constitution*, 17 March 1985; Randall Williams to W.C.W. (telephone), 4 June 1985. The bible of the Aryan Nations is a bizarre novel by Virginia publisher William Pierce. Titled *The Turner Diaries*, it foretells the violent overthrow of the U.S. government by right-wing militants determined to create a pure-white Christian society; see Flint (MI) *Journal*, 18 June 1980.

400 "THE CURRENT SYSTEM OF GOVERNMENT . . .": *NAKN Newsletter* (Winter–Spring 1984): 10.

401 LIBERTY NET: *Washington Post*, 15 December 1984; *Newsweek* 104 (24 December 1984): 84.

401 "THE OLDER AND LESS ACTIVE SPOKESMEN . . .": *NAKN Newsletter* (Winter 1985): 1.

401 "ACCORDING TO THE WORD OF GOD . . .": David A. Baylinson to W.C.W. (form letter), 14 June 1985; *Village Voice*, 9 April 1985.

401 "REPRESENT A BREACH OF SECURITY . . .": *Time* 125 (3 June 1985): 23.

401 "THE NAVY WAS AND IS . . .": Carl T. Rowan, "What Soviet Espionage Means," AP release, 18 June 1985.

Index

514